2-23-23

★ ★ ★ ★ ★ ★ ★ ★ ★ ★ ★ ★ ★ ★ ★

FIRST
CALL

★ ★ ★ ★ ★ ★ ★ ★ ★ ★ ★ ★ ★ ★ ★

Also by Thomas D. Boettcher

VIETNAM: *The Valor and the Sorrow*

THOMAS D. BOETTCHER

★ ★ ★ ★ ★ ★ ★ ★ ★ ★ ★ ★ ★ ★

FIRST CALL

★ ★ ★ ★ ★ ★ ★ ★ ★ ★ ★ ★ ★ ★

THE MAKING OF THE MODERN U.S. MILITARY, 1945–1953

LITTLE, BROWN AND COMPANY

BOSTON   TORONTO   LONDON

Excerpts from *The Forgotten War: America in Korea, 1950–1953,* by
Clay Blair, Jr. Copyright © 1987 by Clay Blair. Reprinted by
permission of Times Books, a division of Random House, Inc. and
of the Scott Meredith Literary Agency.

Excerpts from *Eisenhower: The President* by Stephen Ambrose.
Copyright © 1984 by Stephen E. Ambrose. Reprinted by
permission of Simon & Schuster and John Ware Literary Agency.

Excerpts from *Memoirs: 1925–1950* by George F. Kennan. Copyright
© 1967 by George F. Kennan. Reprinted by permission of Little,
Brown and Company.

Excerpts from *Conflict and Crisis: The Presidency of Harry S.
Truman, 1945–1948* by Robert J. Donovan. Copyright © 1977 by
Robert J. Donovan. Reprinted by permission of W. W. Norton and
Company, Inc. and Sterling Lord Literistic, Inc.

Excerpts from *Tumultuous Years: The Presidency of Harry S.
Truman, 1949–1953* by Robert J. Donovan. Copyright © 1982 by
Robert J. Donovan. Reprinted by permission of W. W. Norton and
Company, Inc. and Sterling Lord Literistic, Inc.

Library of Congress Cataloging-in-Publication Data

Boettcher, Thomas D., 1944–
    First call : the making of the modern U.S. military, 1945–1953
by Thomas D. Boettcher. — 1st ed.
        p.   cm.
    Includes bibliographical references and index.
    ISBN 0-316-10092-7
    1. United States — Armed Forces — History.   I. Title.
UA23.B5637   1992
355'.00973'09045 — dc20   91-31983

10 9 8 7 6 5 4 3 2 1

RRD VA

*Published simultaneously in Canada
by Little, Brown & Company (Canada) Limited*

Printed in the United States of America

*For Pam
and our daughters
Evelyn and Lily*

In memoriam

FREDRICK CHARLES BOETTCHER
my dad
1906–1991

and

ANNIE LOUISE HOWELL
Evelyn's first best friend
1987–1991

CONTENTS

ACKNOWLEDGMENTS

T HIS BOOK began in 1986 as another project, a history of the United States military from the end of World War II to the present day. But this was too long a period for the kind of story development I planned, so not long thereafter I focused my research and writing on the 1945–1953 period, during which the organizational and philosophical foundations of the modern American military were laid. For my change of plans I acknowledge the influence of a number of extraordinary people who, in various important ways, had a part in these early Cold War years. My interviews with them led to my decision and thus, this book. They are Bryce Harlow, who, under Congressman Carl Vinson's chairmanship, was the first general counsel of the House Armed Services Committee during the military reorganization fights, and subsequently Chief of Congressional Liaison for President Dwight Eisenhower; Clark Clifford, Special Counsel to President Harry Truman; Admiral Arleigh Burke, the legendary destroyer captain who played a central role in advancing in Washington the Navy's case during the reorganization struggle, and who became Chief of Naval Operations; General Curtis LeMay, the finest leader the Air Force has produced, who created Strategic Air Command, essentially, and became Air Force Chief of Staff; Lieutenant General James Doolittle, the fearless commander whom President Truman appointed to examine the treatment of those in the enlisted ranks by the officer corps; Lieutenant General Victor Krulak, who as a top assistant to the senior Marine Corps officer in the Pacific, rubbed elbows with General Douglas MacArthur and observed firsthand some of the early military decisions of the Korean War being formulated, such as to land forces behind enemy lines at Inchon; Brigadier General Edwin Simmons, the director of Marine Corps History and Museums, whose tenure there was enriched by his having served in Korea as a young combat officer; General Lyman Lemnitzer, an important commander and staff officer for three decades, who under Presidents Eisenhower and John Kennedy served as Chairman of the Joint Chiefs of Staff; and Lieutenant General James Gavin, the famous paratrooper, who was a major figure in reshaping Army doctrine to reflect the development of atomic weaponry.

The contributions of these men notwithstanding, I am indebted to Debra Roth of Little, Brown more than anyone, except my wife. Debbie and I began working together on this project shortly after it was under way. She is a young editor of the old school with a bright future. She is very exacting in a most unselfish way. She pored over the manuscripts of each of my drafts, line by line. Her effort could not have been greater had her name been planned for the cover, instead of mine. Nor did she ever fail me as an advocate. I'll always be grateful for her enthusiastic support from start to finish.

I would also like to thank my first editor for this book, Chris Coffin, who convinced the powers-that-be at Little, Brown that they should commission this work; copyeditors Mike Mattil and Michael Brandon, for the care with which they processed it through its final publishing stages; my agent Don Cleary, for his faithful efforts and encouragement; my friend Catherine Lyon, for reading parts of the manuscript at a couple of stages and making many useful comments; and my typist Robin Patterson, not only for her diligent work but also for her always acting like this book was the most interesting typing job she ever had.

Finally, I want to thank my wife, Pam. Anything worth doing requires sacrifice, but this book required more of her than either of us could have imagined. She hung in there faithfully, day after day, week after week, as I disappeared into my study to type.

PRINCIPAL OFFICERS

President of the United States

Franklin D. Roosevelt,
   March 4, 1933–April 12, 1945
Harry S. Truman,
   April 12, 1945–January 20, 1953
Dwight D. Eisenhower,
   January 20, 1953–January 20, 1961

DEPARTMENT OF STATE

Secretary of State

Edward R. Stettinius,
   November 1944–June 1945
James F. Byrnes,
   July 1945–January 1947
George C. Marshall,
   January 1947–January 1949
Dean G. Acheson,
   January 1949–January 1953
John Foster Dulles,
   January 1953–April 1959

Under Secretary of State

Joseph C. Grew,
   December 1944–August 1945
Dean G. Acheson,
   August 1945–June 1947
Robert A. Lovett,
   July 1947–January 1949
James E. Webb,
   January 1949–February 1952
David K. E. Bruce,
   February 1952–January 1953

Walter B. Smith,
   February 1953–October 1954

WAR DEPARTMENT

Secretary of War

Henry L. Stimson,
   January 1940–September 1945
Robert P. Patterson,
   September 1945–July 1947

Under Secretary of War

Robert P. Patterson,
   December 1940–September 1945
Kenneth C. Royall,
   November 1945–July 1947

Assistant Secretary of War

John J. McCloy,
   April 1941–November 1945
Howard C. Petersen,
   December 1945–July 1947

Assistant Secretary of War for Air

Robert A. Lovett,
   April 1941–December 1945
Stuart A. Symington,
   January 1946–July 1947

Chief of Staff

General George C. Marshall,
   September 1939–November 1945

General Dwight D. Eisenhower,
 November 1945–February 1948

NAVY DEPARTMENT

Secretary of the Navy

James Forrestal,
 May 1944–July 1947

Under Secretary of the Navy

H. Struve Hensel,
 January 1945–March 1946
W. John Kenney,
 March 1946–July 1947

Assistant Secretary of the Navy for Air

Artemus L. Gates,
 September 1941–July 1945
John L. Sullivan,
 July 1945–July 1946

Chief of Naval Operations

Admiral Ernest J. King,
 March 1942–December 1945
Admiral Chester W. Nimitz,
 December 1945–December 1947

Commandant of the Marine Corps

General Alexander A. Vandegrift,
 January 1944–December 1947

DEPARTMENT OF DEFENSE
(established July 1947)

Secretary of Defense

James Forrestal,
 September 1947–March 1949
Louis A. Johnson,
 March 1949–September 1950
George C. Marshall,
 September 1950–September 1951
Robert A. Lovett,
 September 1951–January 1953
Charles E. Wilson,
 January 1953–October 1957

Deputy Secretary of Defense

Robert A. Lovett,
 September 1950–September 1951

William C. Foster,
 September 1951–January 1953
Roger M. Kyse,
 February 1953–May 1954

DEPARTMENT OF THE ARMY

Secretary of the Army

Kenneth C. Royall,
 September 1947–April 1949
Gordon Gray,
 June 1949–April 1950
Frank Pace, Jr.,
 April 1950–January 1953
Robert T. Stevens,
 February 1953–July 1955

DEPARTMENT OF THE NAVY

Secretary of the Navy

John L. Sullivan,
 September 1947–May 1949
Francis P. Matthews,
 May 1949–July 1951
Dan A. Kimball,
 July 1951–January 1953
Robert B. Anderson,
 January 1953–May 1954

DEPARTMENT OF THE AIR FORCE

Secretary of the Air Force

W. Stuart Symington,
 September 1947–April 1950
Thomas K. Finletter,
 April 1950–January 1953
Harold E. Talbott,
 February 1953–August 1955

CHIEFS OF STAFF

Chief of Staff to the Commander in Chief

Admiral William D. Leahy,
 July 1942–March 1949

Chairman of the Joint Chiefs

General Omar N. Bradley,
  August 1949–August 1953
Admiral Arthur M. Radford,
  August 1953–August 1957

Chief of Staff of the Army

General Dwight D. Eisenhower,
  November 1945–February 1948
General Omar N. Bradley,
  February 1948–August 1949
General J. Lawton Collins,
  August 1949–August 1953
General Matthew B. Ridgway,
  August 1953–June 1955

Chief of Naval Operations

Admiral Chester W. Nimitz,
  December 1945–December 1947
Admiral Louis E. Denfeld,
  December 1947–November 1949
Admiral Forrest P. Sherman,
  November 1949–July 1951
Admiral William M. Fechteler,
  August 1951–August 1953
Admiral Robert B. Carney,
  August 1953–August 1955

Chief of Staff of the Air Force

General Carl A. Spaatz,
  September 1947–April 1948
General Hoyt S. Vandenberg,
  April 1948–June 1953
General Nathan F. Twining,
  June 1953–June 1957

Commandant of the Marine Corps

General Alexander A. Vandegrift,
  January 1944–December 1947
General Clifton B. Cates,
  January 1948–December 1951
General Lemuel C. Shepherd, Jr.,
  January 1952–December 1955

CENTRAL INTELLIGENCE AGENCY

Director

General Hoyt S. Vandenberg,
  June 1946–April 1947
Rear Admiral Roscoe H. Hillenkoetter,
  May 1947–October 1950
General Walter Bedell Smith,
  October 1950–February 1953
Allen W. Dulles,
  February 1953–November 1961

BUREAU OF THE BUDGET

Director

Harold D. Smith,
  April 1939–June 1946
James E. Webb,
  July 1946–January 1949
Frank Pace,
  January 1949–April 1950
Frederick J. Lawton,
  April 1950–January 1953
Joseph M. Dodge,
  January 1953–April 1954

★ ★ ★ ★ ★ ★ ★ ★ ★ ★ ★ ★ ★ ★ ★ ★

FIRST
CALL

★ ★ ★ ★ ★ ★ ★ ★ ★ ★ ★ ★ ★ ★ ★ ★

CHAPTER 1

★ ★ ★ ★ ★ ★ ★ ★ ★ ★ ★ ★ ★ ★

PASSING IN REVIEW

"**T**HIS IS the happiest day of my life," said Harry Truman. It was an extraordinary statement for him to make, especially since his wife, Bess, was standing right beside him. Always before he had told her that that day had something to do with her. The date was October 27, 1945. No President since has had a better day as Commander in Chief.

Four million people jammed the docks and New York shoreline of the Hudson River and overflowed onto the terraces of the nearby motorways of Manhattan. Thousands more looked down on the river from towering apartment and office buildings. On the opposite bank, another million crowded the slopes and heights of the New Jersey hills and the Palisades. Even the George Washington Bridge, which spanned the river, was loaded with people. Others in masses of small craft were kept huddled against the water's edge by roving Coast Guard picketboats. People had come to watch Truman review part of the panoply of fleets that had helped win the recent world war and coincidentally made him — a parochial politician, raised a farmer, who had become an unelected President — the most important leader in the world.

The forty-seven warships awaiting him on the Hudson were impressive, but they were actually only a small fraction of the total number the United States had put to sea. At the end, the United States had more than twice that many aircraft carriers on line — ninety-nine. The whole fleet numbered 1,166 large warships. America's combined land, sea, and air forces were the mightiest the world had ever seen. On paper, at least, these enormous inventories and a monopoly on atomic bombs had made the nation more dominant militarily than any country had ever been.

The ships that day were anchored in a line seven miles long. The battleship *Missouri*, on whose deck the Japanese had officially surrendered, was there with its 2,700-man crew — the very symbol of victory. So were the battleship *New York;* the 968-foot carrier *Midway*, the Navy's biggest ship; and the carrier *Enterprise*, whose planes and guns had sunk 185 enemy ships and shot down 911 enemy planes. Ten submarines in the review line had scuttled collectively a million tons of Japanese shipping.

Sailors in blue uniforms and white caps lined the perimeter of each vessel. Battle streamers loaded lines above the decks, each multicolored pennant representing a place such as Midway Island, the Philippine Sea, or Leyte Gulf, where fleets of ships and planes collided, fought to destroy one another, and thousands of men died. These vessels had made it back from such places, and there was something palpable about the aura they had earned. Though not parade-fresh clean, most having been out of combat less than three months, they sat proudly in the waters of the Hudson, dirty in the noble way of workingmen. Some still bore the scars of battle.

People were in a festive mood, but they had spent their spontaneous, riotous joy during earlier celebrations honoring war heroes Dwight Eisenhower, Jonathan Wainwright, and Chester Nimitz.

The weather had been overcast and gray until the destroyer *Renshaw*, with Truman standing on its bridge, turned about to begin passage upriver to review the powerful assemblage. Then, in dramatic fashion, strong winds opened up large patches of bright blue sky, sweeping the scud into towering thunderclouds beyond the shores, as if the Almighty were having a look. Powerful sunbeams shot through the openings and bathed the ships, turning a nice occasion into a glorious one.

Three destroyers loaded with attachés and admirals from twenty-two countries and news reporters from the world over trailed the *Renshaw*, which steadied at ten knots as it passed the heavy cruiser *Macon*, the first ship in line. The sailors on the *Macon*'s deck snapped to attention and saluted their Commander in Chief as he passed by, while others, unseen behind enormous, thick slabs of armor, began firing twenty-one-gun salutes from five-inch cannons. Flames flashed and thick, white smoke from special powder billowed with each concussion that flattened against the buildings and cliffs and came back in rolling echoes. The bedlam continued for about an hour, rippling rapid-fire from one gun to another, then from one ship to another, as Truman passed each and circled back to review the opposite side. Three hundred merchant ships anchored at dockside added to the din, their captains having tied open their steam whistles in a continuous, shrieking salute.

The ships were only part of the show. As Truman initially passed the *Macon*, planes began appearing in the southern sky — at first a few, then a dozen, finally an enormous swarm stretching overhead and beyond, horizon to horizon. It was the largest air armada ever assembled during peacetime. There were twelve hundred Navy planes in all — Hellcats, Corsairs,

Avengers, and Helldivers. They had taken off from twenty-three bases, some traveling from as far as South Carolina and Ohio before rendezvousing over Long Branch, New Jersey, and sweeping in over the fleet, crossing the line of ships at an angle. Wave after wave flew by at altitudes ranging from twenty-five hundred to four thousand feet. Eleven minutes elapsed before all roared past a single point. At the far horizon they turned in formation and made a second pass over the fleet. They did this twice. The deep drone of their big piston engines, the whistle screams, and the cacophony of cannon shots were deafening. The Americans who witnessed this elaborate military spectacle could not help but feel proud and secure.

Yet not all was right with the world these days. The war had left enormous vacuums of power where defeated nations once held sway. All manner of people and nations were now rushing to fill these voids, including the United States and the Soviet Union — natural enemies since the Communists had seized control of the Russian Revolution, but not so directly contentious until now. American and Soviet divisions were deployed uneasily opposite each other throughout Central Europe, in the Middle East in Iran, and even on the Asian continent, along the thirty-eighth parallel in the Korean Peninsula. Furthermore, Communist parties challenged for power throughout Western Europe, especially in France and Italy. In many smaller countries and colonies, from Greece to Indochina, Communist revolutionaries fought for control. The world was as volatile and dangerous as it had been in 1939, though this perception had not yet emerged, even among Truman and his highest-ranking military men. They had little inkling that epochal forces were already in motion that would virtually destroy Truman's presidency, haunt the Democratic party for decades, and remake the American military.

Americans were generally aware of trouble with the Russians but were not alarmed. Though uneasy, they wanted to believe that differences could be worked out. They found reassurance in the nation's vaunted military, a show of which they had come to witness this day; however, this same public was by and large behind the enormous political pressure to disarm that was mounting daily. Some top people in the military establishment were warning against doing so too rapidly. James Forrestal, the Secretary of the Navy, was one. General George C. Marshall, the Army Chief of Staff, was another.

Earlier in the day, Truman himself had tried to explain to a million people gathered on the Sheep Meadow in Central Park and to a nationwide radio audience why the United States needed to maintain a relatively large armed force, by prewar standards, and how it should be done. According to a survey by E. C. Hooper, Inc., 94.6 percent of all radios in use in the New

York City area were tuned in to the broadcast of this address over the Columbia Broadcasting System. In a very vague warning to the Soviet Union, the President told his audience: "We shall not relent in our efforts to bring the golden rule into the international affairs of the world." Like most of his listeners, Truman wanted in general to ameliorate differences with the Russians and thought he could. His thinking about them, which he later explained to his friend John Nance Garner, the former Vice President, was this: "We are not going to have any shooting trouble with them but they are tough bargainers and always ask for the whole earth, expecting maybe to get an acre."

Truman's basic idea for national defense, he told his audience, was universal military training, which was a fancy name for the old minuteman idea. Recently he had proposed his version to Congress. His proposition was to put all young men through basic training during peacetime so that in the event of war the military establishment could more quickly assign them to units. Another purpose was to give each man some exposure to military fundamentals and discipline. Future soldiers, sailors, and airmen would all train together.

Just about everyone in the audience politely applauded when he raised the subject, even the young men whom he wanted to send off to boot camp. The idea was so typically American. There was a strong feeling in the United States against a large standing army, yet most Americans believed they themselves should be kept in reserve in case duty called. The traditional belief was that a large standing army was a threat to democracy. And that the United States, between two oceans, was safe. Exclusive possession of the bomb was making Americans feel even more secure.

Truth be known, Marshall, too, since the armistice, had been less concerned about external threats than about getting on with peacetime activities. Having served as commander of all Army field forces during the war, he now gave top priority to getting those forces home in good order, without undercutting occupation duties. He had had some experience with such matters after the Great War, but the task this time, owing to sheer numbers, was much more daunting — and excluding Truman himself, Marshall now had the ultimate responsibility for this massive logistical operation. In all, about 10,400,000 men and women had served under him in the Army, including the Army Air Forces, during the recent war. Had he somehow formed them up to pass in review, the parade would have lasted more than a couple of months, nonstop. Ninety-six percent of them had served overseas. Transporting home those still there when the fighting stopped was taking time and very close management.

The prospect of military reorganization also diverted Marshall's attention from external threats. For all concerned, including Marshall, the thought of what it was going to take to reorganize was dreadful. The Army and the Navy had never been part of the same military command structure. Making them so was going to be a painful process. Over many decades they had developed entirely different management systems, as two duchies might. They had become different cultures, as distinct as the uniforms they wore. Periodically over the years, various leaders had proposed reform, but only the national disaster at Pearl Harbor was impetus enough to force change. This horrific event was blamed on incredibly poor coordination and communication between the Army and the Navy, which together had shared defense responsibility for the Hawaiian Islands.

In 1943 Marshall had proposed to the Joint Chiefs of Staff that a single, vertical command structure be established that would put at the top a military man called the Chief of Staff to the President; this Chief of Staff would be in charge of separate ground, sea, and air components, as well as a supply service. This organizational concept was like the Army's own vertical command structure. Marshall was essentially proposing that the Army's way of doing things be imposed on the Navy, which had a flat, decentralized organizational structure. This initiative of his had caused heartburn in some wardrooms, but even admirals Ernest King and Chester Nimitz were not too worried, because Franklin Roosevelt, a Navy man, was in the White House then. Nonetheless, they and other astute admirals and generals realized early on in the war that some sort of postwar reorganization was inevitable. Modern warfare was forcing a closer integration of land, sea, and air operations.

Contributing impetus to this inexorable movement toward organizational change were Army aviators, who believed that during the war they had proved their bombing doctrines and that they could win the next war without soldiers and ships. In organizational terms, they believed that the Army Air Forces had earned equal status with the ground Army and the Navy. They, therefore, strongly endorsed postwar reorganization because they were certain it would entail creating an Air Force independent of the Army. Some of them, such as General Carl Spaatz, who had been Eisenhower's top air officer in Europe, were even saying that the new Air Force should absorb Navy air. Such talk did not bode well for a friendly reorganization tussle. Navy aviators, which included Marine Corps pilots, deemed this an absurd proposition. At Midway, the nation's first major victory of the war, they felt they had firmly established airpower as a central, inextricable element of seapower. It was not for mere ceremony that as Truman was reviewing the warships lined up on the Hudson, the vast air armada had appeared overhead. To associate airpower with seapower dramatically, Navy brass had put every plane they could muster into the flyby. They wanted to impress this connection on newspeople, the public, and the President.

Marshall's 1943 proposal had constituted the first step in the postwar military reorganization process. Later he had submitted a more formal proposal to the Committee on Post-War Military Policy, a special body formed by the House of Representatives. And a few days before Truman celebrated victory with the Navy in New York harbor, Marshall had ordered the Army's public-affairs officer, Lieutenant General J. Lawton Collins, up to Capitol Hill to testify about an even more fully developed Army reorganization plan. It came to be known as the Collins Plan, which served Marshall's purposes. Although he had done most of the basic thinking on this proposal also, he wanted younger officers to reorganize the military and formulate postwar national-defense policy since they would have to make both work.

Furthermore, Marshall was tired. For some time, he had been thinking about retiring. He had been in the Army more than forty years and had led it the last six. Since the first of the year, his wife, Katherine, had been after him to step down. He, of course, had waited until the war was won before writing Truman a letter asking for permission to do so. The President, who was not eager to lose a man he relied on so heavily, had kept the request on his desk for more than three weeks. About the time of the Navy celebration, he finally relented, telling Marshall he would relieve him of duty the following month, which would allow time for General Eisenhower to make the transition out of his responsibilities as head of the American Occupation Zone in Germany, take some leave, and get to Washington. For the time being, however, Truman would not agree to retire Marshall; he wanted him available for recall.

The change-of-command ceremony was set for November 20. In the meantime, the Marshalls plotted their carefree days just ahead like two children with permission to plan the family vacation. They settled into a routine of evenings spent examining brochures and maps in excited anticipation. Very quickly they had it all figured out. They would first drive out to their home in Leesburg, Virginia, and prepare to close it up for winter. This done, they would drive to Pinehurst, North Carolina, before the end of the fall hunting season. They would then follow the warm weather south, spending January and February fishing in the Gulf of Mexico. In early springtime they would return to Pinehurst. A month or so after that they would drive back to Leesburg and open up their gardens. They discussed and reaffirmed this plan many times.

The change-of-command ceremony went off as planned. Six days later, on November 26, Truman conducted a noontime ceremony honoring Marshall in the courtyard of the Pentagon and delivered a speech of glowing praise about him. "In a war unparalleled in magnitude and in horror," said Truman, "millions of Americans gave their country outstanding service. General of the Army George C. Marshall gave it victory. . . . He takes his place at the head of the great commanders of history."

The next day, after a leisurely morning, the Marshalls set their personal plans in motion. He dismissed his driver, took the wheel of their car, and steered a course onto Route 7 for Leesburg. Normally he picked up hitchhikers, but this time, to speed their thirty-five-mile journey, he did not. An hour or so later, as he turned into their driveway, the refrain of a popular old song that was blaring from a jukebox at a nearby service station matched their sentiments exactly. It was the single word "Hallelujah!" repeated over and over.

Earlier than most, Katherine Marshall was awakened to the fact that Americans were now living in a world much different from the one they had known before and during the war. Upon arriving home, she headed upstairs for a nap before dinnertime. She heard the phone ring while climbing the stairs but thought nothing of it. An hour later, she learned it had been Truman calling. She was opening the front door to join her husband, who was on the front porch resting on a chaise lounge and listening to a radio, when an announcer reading the three-o'clock news said that the President had made General Marshall his special ambassador to China and was sending him off as soon as possible. The news hit her like an electric shock. She could not move. And she was so angry she could not speak. Marshall stood up and walked over to her, putting his arms around her. "That phone call as we came in was from the President," he said. "I could not bear to tell you until you had had your rest." They had been out of Washington a total of about three hours. He was as disappointed as she was.

What had dashed their plans was the resignation of a fellow named Patrick Hurley, at 12:30 that day, from the job Marshall had now been assigned. Without notifying Truman beforehand, Hurley, who was back in the United States to confer and get some rest, delivered this news at the National Press Club. Explaining his decision, he made sensational charges, among them that "a considerable section of our State Department is endeavoring to support Communism generally as well as specifically in China." He accused these officials of undermining his efforts.

Hurley, a wildly flamboyant and self-confident oil business attorney from Tulsa, Oklahoma (a "fast traveler," as Henry Stimson, the Secretary of War during the war, described him), had been Herbert Hoover's Secretary of War. Franklin Roosevelt had appointed a number of Republicans, Stimson and Hurley among them, to various positions while trying to forge a bipartisan foreign policy during the conflict. Resigning as he did, Hurley started the transformation of China policy into a highly partisan political issue. His accusations were a harbinger. Though Democrats and Republicans working together would create some extraordinarily enlightened and durable foreign-policy achievements within the next couple of years, the harmony that made them possible would quickly disintegrate shortly thereafter. The China issue was sensitive from the outset because if the Communists controlled China, they threatened Japan, which had become the responsibility of the United States and key to all American policy in the Pacific.

Marshall departed Washington, bound for Chungking, on December 15. Time had not eased his wife's anger. She had not reconciled herself to what was happening. Out on the tarmac, she kept these feelings bound up inside, but several days later, after shedding some private tears, no doubt, she unburdened herself of her feelings in a letter to Colonel Frank McCarthy. McCarthy, Marshall's personal secretary early in the war and Secretary of the General Staff later, was one of a coterie of military people, including an aide, a driver, a cook, and an orderly, who had become an extended family. He had sent Katherine some yellow roses, and although she was aware that her correspondent was recovering from a near mental and physical breakdown brought on by years of long days and nights working for Marshall during the war, she could not contain herself. "When I saw his plane take off without anyone to be close to him whom he had known and depended on," she wrote,

> I could not stand it. . . . I give a sickly smile when people say how the country loves and admires my husband. That last week testifying from nine to five every day [at congressional hearings on Pearl Harbor], with the luncheon hours spent with the President and Secretary [of State James] Byrnes, trying to get some idea of what might be done on this mission, then dumped into his lap to write the whole policy after he got home at night. I shall never forget that week and I shall never forget how this country showed its love and admiration. This sounds bitter. Well, I am bitter. The President should never have asked this of him and in such a way that he could not refuse.

After so much dislocation and death, the whole world was virtually obsessed with thoughts of hearth and home. For millions of Americans, the war had separated families and put personal plans on hold for about four years. Getting home was what preoccupied the two senior men Marshall sat down with a few hours after reaching Shanghai, his first stop in China. Lieutenant General Albert Wedemeyer, who had succeeded Joseph Stilwell as senior US general there, wanted some leave to go to the bedside of his dying mother. Walter Robertson, a courtly investment banker who had ended up running the lend-lease mission in Australia and was now counselor of economic affairs at the China embassy, just wanted to get back to normal, which included reunion with his wife and children in Richmond, Virginia. Not a career man, he forthrightly told Marshall he wanted to go home. "And he looked at me," recalled Robertson, "and said, 'I want to go home too.'" The Virginian ended up staying another year without complaint.

Such patience was exceptional. In Berlin and Seoul, GIs staged public protests about not getting home more quickly. All they were interested in, said one chaplain, was brandy to drink, women to sleep with, and the next boat home. To make a political point of the mounting impatience at home, their wives were organizing a campaign to mail Eisenhower thousands of pairs of baby shoes.

About the only American serviceman in Asia not clamoring to get home for at least a short stay, it seems, was General Douglas MacArthur, who had not returned stateside in more than eight years. Taking up gardening had most certainly not entered his mind. This was one old soldier determined not to fade away.

Truman and Marshall had tried to get him back for a parade like that lavished on other war heroes, but to their irritation, he always found an excuse not to return. His official reason, which he cabled to Marshall, was that "the delicate and difficult situation which prevails here . . . would make it unwise to leave." He told a member of his staff: "If I returned for only a few weeks, word would spread through the Pacific that the United States is abandoning the Orient." Such was his ego. However, as was usually the case with MacArthur, there were reasons publicly stated and the real reason. Though nearly sixty-six, eleven months older than Marshall, he still had the towering ambition of his youth, and this made him somewhat paranoid. He believed that Truman would retire him if and when he returned. He had been a general for an incredible twenty-eight years; Marshall, by contrast, only nine. For MacArthur, adjusting to anything else was not going to be easy — except, perhaps, becoming the Commander in Chief himself.

There was talk about that. Inevitably, there would be. Despite the pain, the war had been the most positive political experience in American history. Being associated with the war effort in even a small way would have its political benefits. During the course of the war, the next eight US Presidents were in uniform. In the fall of 1945, the men mentioned most often in this context were MacArthur and Eisenhower. Marshall was mentioned some, too, but he would not give the idea credence by commenting; he would "never say a word on the subject," observed Stimson.

This sort of conversation interested Truman, who had as well developed a political sensitivity as anyone who has held the office. He did not trust MacArthur, though the two had not met. His predecessor had had the same misgivings. "Douglas, I think you are our best general, but I believe you would be our worst politician," Roosevelt told him face-to-face. FDR imagined that even the White House was too small to contain MacArthur's ego. And he believed MacArthur had a general's touch when it came to politics — hands of stone.

During the years 1943 and 1944, MacArthur did not help himself with the Democrats by surreptitiously encouraging conservatives to help make him the Republican nominee for President. Some of his staff officers acted as liaison with Washington operatives, including Senator Arthur Vandenberg of Michigan and Congresswoman Clare Boothe Luce of Connecticut, who was less known in power circles as a legislator than as the wife of Henry Luce, the cofounder of Time Inc. and publisher of its powerful magazines. Vandenberg led the MacArthur boomlet. His plan was to establish MacArthur as the leading compromise candidate, the one whom Republican delegates would draft if their convention deadlocked on a choice between Robert Taft and Thomas Dewey.

On June 2, 1943, Lieutenant General Robert Eichelberger, one of MacArthur's corps commanders, wrote in his diary that he had discussed the Republican nomination for the next year with MacArthur. "I can see that he expects to get it," he observed, "and I sort of think so, too." Former President Herbert Hoover had also acknowledged MacArthur's appeal as a candidate, but, ever the practical politician, he believed Taft would win the nomination. With this scenario in mind, Hoover in March 1944 told MacArthur's chief of staff, Major General Richard Sutherland, that MacArthur's people should work to get him nominated as "vice-president . . . in control of the entire war." Sutherland "thought MacArthur would be pleased to undertake such an appointment."

But, alas, Vandenberg's plan, and consequently Hoover's, went awry. As Vandenberg had feared, some "MacArthur for President Clubs" in the Midwest entered the general in several primaries, including that of his home state of Wisconsin. Without a formal organization even there, without MacArthur actively campaigning, and caught in the middle of a local power struggle, his candidacy garnered only half as many electoral votes as Dewey's did, and so it was finished off there. His supporters did not know the word *quit*, though. Indicative of their zealous admiration was a series of letters Republican congressman Albert Miller of Nebraska exchanged with Mac-

Arthur and made public in 1944. In them, Miller denounced "left wingers and New Dealism" and told MacArthur that "you owe it to civilization and the children yet unborn to be our next president." MacArthur replied that he agreed "unreservedly." People like Miller would cause Truman inestimable trouble in the years ahead.

Truman was not eager to improve MacArthur's chances in 1948 by bestowing on him the title of Supreme Commander of Allied Powers (SCAP) and placing him in charge of occupation forces in Japan so he could keep his name in the news and demonstrate that he could not only defend a country but also run it. But he sensed that he had no choice. MacArthur was one of the great figures of American military history and was the obvious selection. Truman, after all, had designated MacArthur to accept Japan's surrender aboard the *Missouri*.

Furthermore, even Roosevelt had helped boost MacArthur as a figure of mythic proportions. When the nation was in need of something to cheer about, he awarded MacArthur a Congressional Medal of Honor after having him brought out of the Philippines by PT boat and submarine. Later, Roosevelt made good MacArthur's promise to return, intervening when most of his war planners, including Marshall, thought Japan could be defeated more quickly if the Philippines were bypassed.

So denying MacArthur the SCAP appointment would have made a "martyr out of him and a candidate for president," Secretary of the Interior Harold Ickes, a MacArthur hater if there ever was one, noted in his diary on August 18, 1945. Ickes had confided this judgment to Truman and eight days later recorded the President's assessment. "MacArthur would probably be a candidate anyway," Truman said. This was what some of MacArthur's staff members were telling various reporters off the record. The 1948 contest would be "the last election he can enter or influence," one of them told reporter Mark Gayn. "We all think he will make a try."

Actually, his job as the occupation chief in Japan was better preparation for his becoming king. This had been true from the start. As he rode into Tokyo, thirty thousand Japanese soldiers lined his route. And in a deferential act previously reserved for their emperor, they turned their backs to him, as if unworthy of his sight. He would rule seventy million people. By decree he would redistribute land, free political prisoners, liberate the press, enfranchise women, destroy monopolies, and create unions, all to decentralize power and introduce representative government. Almost entirely this agenda had been carefully worked out beforehand by the State Department, with some help from the Joint Chiefs, but few would deny MacArthur's masterful execution of the plan, and most Americans and all Japanese would credit it in full to him.

MacArthur had never had the opportunity to articulate what he would do as President, but this made no difference to those who supported his candidacy; they were drawn to his personality, or rather, presence, not his programs. Most were zealous men and women whose political convictions were a blend of religious faith and patriotism in equal measures. MacArthur spoke their language. He said that unless Christianity filled Japan's "spiritual vacuum," communism would. He wrote the president of the Southern Baptist Convention to say that the postwar situation was "an opportunity without counterpart since the birth of Christ for the spread of Christianity among the peoples of the Far East." In response, evangelist Bob Jones assured him by letter that he and his congregation were "learning how to load the Gospel Gun and how to shoot it."

The fundamental doctrine of such people, who universally loved MacArthur, was this: at home, self-reliance and hard work; abroad, hating Communists as evil incarnate and opposing them as if fulfilling a covenant with God. Their foreign-policy creed was essentially the gospel according to newspaperman John O'Sullivan, who in the mid-1800s had popularized the conviction that the nation had a manifest destiny to exert its influence throughout the world as an act of benevolence. Almost all were conservative Republicans and, in that tradition (up to that time), many were isolationists. But to them, isolationism generally applied only to the nation's staying out of Europe. An anomaly about these isolationists' views was that, for a complex combination of reasons, they viewed the Pacific and Asia as legitimate spheres of American influence. This was especially true of China, about which the *New York Times*'s military editor, Hanson Baldwin, had warned in a 1943 article published in *Reader's Digest*, "Missionaries, war relief drives, able ambassadors and the movies have oversold us." It helped Generalissimo Chiang Kai-shek, the leader of Nationalist China, that he was a Christian convert. This affirmed in Americans' minds that he was a force for good and that they were, too, in supporting him. This is how Theodore White, *Time*'s correspondent in China at the time, assessed his publisher's view of the situation; White concluded that Henry Luce was determined to "cement China and the United States together with Christianity."

Born in China of missionary parents, Luce was more sensitive than the President was to Americans' sentiments about China, sentiments that would develop into a powerful political force. In the fall of 1945 the President sincerely believed that his best option was to cut off aid to Chiang, whose forces were fighting Mao's Communists. And he would. But to make amends for this political blunder, he would end up going to war on his own in Korea.

Truman's troubles with MacArthur people started soon after he appointed the general SCAP in mid-August 1945. Robert Wood and Philip LaFollette, two key backers of the 1944 MacArthur candidacy, prompted their man to make a preemptive move against the Democratic administration. Truman had recently asked Congress for an extension of the draft. Wood wrote MacArthur that this was a "very clever ruse on the part of politicians" who planned to put "the burden of blame on MacArthur." LaFollette warned of plans to "shift onto your shoulders responsibility in the public mind for retaining men in service." What they were talking about were the repatriation problems Marshall had grappled with before setting off for Leesburg. Wood advised MacArthur to announce that his troop level needs were minimal so that Democrats' attempts to "pillor[y] him in the eyes of the public" would fail. This is what MacArthur did. On September 7, 1945, he issued a statement in which he forecast a "drastic cut" in the number of soldiers he needed to fulfill occupation duties; tens of thousands would be affected. He attributed this good fortune to his clever management of the job and to Japanese cooperation. He said he was ready to send everybody he did not need home as "rapidly as ships can be made available." Truman would regret having made MacArthur the occupation chief in Japan when he had the chance to retire him, for this annoying behavior by the general was a foreboding signal of serious trouble with him ahead.

Republicans would keep the repatriation issue alive well into 1946. The irony of their accusations was that in the near future Truman and his fellow Democrats would supplant Republicans as those most identified with demobilization and disarmament. To the American people, Truman would come to represent a determined policy to cut the military to bare bones. And Republicans would represent support for a strong military, especially as it pertained to the Navy.

By January 12, 1946, when the Army got around to honoring itself for its role in the recent war, it was rather obvious just how much Truman was in step with the people. Formally called the Victory Parade, the march in midtown Manhattan was dedicated "to all the guys who walked through the mud," said Major General James Gavin before he led it. His 82d Airborne Division, led most of the war by Major General Matthew Ridgway, had an unmatched combat record, so it was named the featured unit and placed up front. Elements of the 13th, 17th, and 101st Airborne Divisions, the latter with Major General Maxwell Taylor in the lead, followed. On this day Gavin and Taylor were two of the brightest stars in an army full of them.

At precisely one o'clock, Gavin raised his pistol and fired a shot that set the proceedings in motion. A band struck up "The All American Soldier" and in company-size units of about one hundred men, they stepped out smartly in tight formation, nine abreast.

That morning a light rain had cleansed the air, and by noon the sun was smiling through partly cloudy skies and the temperature had climbed into the forties. Polished combat boots and helmets shone. Glittering bayonets attached to carbines slung over each man's right shoulder lined up diagonally and in rows and columns with engineering precision.

The uniform of the day included olive green shirts with black ties, Eisenhower jackets, and khaki trousers. Colorful combat ribbons were arranged in rows on each soldier's chest.

The look of the day was grim; smiles from marchers were rare. Chin straps and jaws were tight. They wanted to be seen and remembered as combat veterans. Two-and-a-half hours elapsed before all of them passed the reviewing stand.

Midway through the march, another air armada, more interesting than impressive, and much smaller than that in the Navy's show, appeared off to the west. Forty Douglas C-47s of the Army Air Forces, flying at about two thousand feet over the Hudson, lumbered along pulling troop gliders, the kind in which thousands of GIs had landed at Normandy. A few fighter escorts idled in formations alongside. Over Yonkers this five-mile sky train turned and retraced its route. In formations like this one, the Eighty-second had flown into combat at Sicily beachhead, Salerno, Anzio, Normandy, Cherbourg, Nijmegen, the Bulge, and the Rhine.

Long lines of machines followed the marching formations of men. Most were ugly, foreboding, a little frightening. Some had names such as "Angel of Death" painted on them. They included armored cars, tank destroyers, Sherman tanks weighing thirty-six tons each, and dozens of smaller medium tanks with their eight-inch howitzers raised in salute at exactly the same angle. The ground reverberated beneath viewers' feet as these pachyderms rumbled along, their heavy steel treads gouging the pavement. Onlookers fell silent.

In fact, the crowd was relatively quiet all day long; unresponsive, even. The cascading ticker tape did not hide the lack of enthusiasm. The marching soldiers sensed it.

"The war's over, you people," one yelled. "Get off your hands! Come on and give out!"

He won a brief cheer for his unit.

Some practical reasons were partially to blame for the muted response, the obvious one being that people cannot keep cheering and clapping for several hours. Another was that there were only three bands in the entire line of march. As a consequence, the rhythmic clump of combat boots firmly hitting the pavement was about all one could hear during long periods. The sound was ominous, foreign, un-American. This display was also much more personal and tangible than the Navy one. The reality of it all — people killing people — was as comprehensible and crude as the bayonet points. People's senses were not overwhelmed as they had been by warships of enormous size and might. But they intended no disrespect to the young men marching by, whom they honored by standing there in the cold.

Still, the bottom-line truth of the matter was that the time for parades and gaudy exhibitions of military force had passed. Even as Gavin led the parade up Fifth Avenue, such shows were dated, perceived even as a little inappropriate by the American people.

The public's mood had changed dramatically in the seventy-seven days since the Navy's review. Like the GIs clamoring to get home and out of uniform, civilians had refocused their attention. Now they worried about housing, jobs, strikes, inflation, and another economic depression, not war. A million of them who had attended the Navy ceremony did not show up this time. One of these was Truman himself. The Commander in Chief stayed home.

Deserving though they were, Truman and the American people were not going to get the respite they wanted or a chance to turn inward. Underscoring this was the fact that both Marshall and MacArthur were kept on active duty past retirement to serve the nation overseas. Matters military did not recede into the background, as Truman hoped and anticipated they would. In desperate political battles, he grappled with military-related difficulties his next seven years as President.

Truman's military fights ended up remaking the US armed forces organizationally and philosophically. The first of these disputes arose internally. His decisions to create an Air Force independent of the Army and to unify command and control of those two service branches and the Navy sparked a revolt so strong that he almost lost control of these forces. Essentially, it was a bitter debate about strategy — how the United States should bring all its land, sea, and air components together to wage war. Decades-old rivalries and different ways of doing things intensified the reaction. So did Truman's tight-fisted military budgets. Largely because of him, Democrats to this day suffer the consequences of the American people's deeming them weak on defense. Actually, Truman's antimilitary feelings and his opposition to a large standing army were charter tenets of American tradition. But not until World War II did the United States become the leader of the great democracies, which together came to be known variously as the West and the free world. Truman was the first American President to have to contend with the peacetime responsibilities this leadership entailed. One of these was the nation's having to spend enormous sums to support huge military forces, war or not.

Truman's second military fight — unlike the first, which was played out in Washington — involved real combat. The war in Korea was the direct result of Communist forces led by Mao Tse-tung winning control of China, a victory Truman was blamed for; the active support of Mao's China and Stalin's Soviet Union enabled Communist North Korea to invade US-backed South Korea. The latter was outside the sphere of American strategic interests, but Truman felt compelled to intervene, so as to contain communism in Asia as well as in Europe. By 1946, the Republicans were successfully exploiting the charge that Truman and other Democrats were soft on communism. This nearly caused him to lose control of the military yet again, as he tried to limit the scope of the war by limiting the nation's war objectives. The stakes were much greater than during the earlier reorganization fight: this time his whole presidency was put at risk. The challenge was led by MacArthur, but Marshall stood with Truman and saved him.

All told, the story of how the thirty-third President survived his mistakes and one of the most turbulent periods of American history is one of conviction and courage. A New Deal Democrat, Truman wanted to resume Roosevelt's domestic work, but enemies conspired against him. To his own chagrin and surprise, this provincial man has as his legacy ground-breaking work as Commander in Chief and head of state. His military and foreign-affairs policies — which his successor, Dwight Eisenhower, affirmed — endured for more than forty years.

CHAPTER 2

★ ★ ★ ★ ★ ★ ★ ★ ★ ★ ★ ★ ★ ★ ★

TAKING UP POSITIONS

I
N THE LIFE of a nation, the end of a war marks a new beginning.
So, too, does the death of a great leader. Consequently, when in mid-1945
Franklin Roosevelt died and the United States won two great wars, one in
Europe and one in Asia, Americans should have realized that the nation was
heading off sharply in a new direction. Politicians knew this instinctively,
which is why seven of ten cabinet members resigned during this four-month
period. (Within another six months, a big turnover in military leadership
would follow. By then, General Marshall, Admiral Ernest King, and General Henry ["Hap"] Arnold, who was Commanding General of the Army
Air Forces, would all have stepped down.) Though these people leaving
government would offer various reasons for doing so, and even though
Truman wanted some of them to go, their attitudes were generally about the
same as Marshall's: they believed that others should organize the peace —
younger people who would have to make work what was decided. A re-
vamping of basic US policy was going to be necessary, and military-policy
questions were going to be at the top of the agenda.

Earlier generations of American leaders had not been very good at carefully coordinating military and foreign-affairs policies, but this one was
going to have to be. Complicating the task of this new group would be the
atomic-bomb explosions on Hiroshima and Nagasaki, which had future
implications even more profound than the victory they assured. One ram-
ification was the need to rethink military strategy. This incredibly destructive weapon, which bespoke the emergence of airpower as a major force,
made some sort of reorganization within the military inevitable. This meant
that subtle compromises would have to be negotiated by admirals and generals whose nature was not to concede anything. Terrible external pressures
were going to make their work even more difficult.

The new generation that took charge of the military establishment was on average only about ten years younger than the old one. In terms of military experience, what generally distinguished the two was the older group's having had much-higher-level job responsibilities during World War I. Roosevelt had been Assistant Secretary of the Navy, while Truman had been only a captain in the field artillery. The venerable Henry Stimson, who had served every President since Theodore Roosevelt in some important capacity, had actually been Secretary of War his first time six years *before* the United States entered World War I; during the conflict itself, he was an Army colonel. His successor as Secretary of War in 1945, Robert Patterson, had served as a junior infantry officer and had been wounded in action. Marshall, a senior member of General John Pershing's staff, had made a key contribution to the planning and execution of the huge Saint-Mihiel and Meuse-Argonne offensives. Eisenhower, his successor, had run a training camp in Pennsylvania.

Only two World War II leaders of a military-service branch would remain on duty afterward to help formulate postwar policy. One was James Forrestal, who stayed on as Secretary of the Navy; the other was Marine Corps Commandant Alexander Vandegrift, a Congressional Medal of Honor winner who was the first Marine four-star general. However, both men were actually of the younger generation, having risen to the top ahead of their peers. During World War I, Forrestal had served as a lieutenant junior grade in Washington; Vandegrift, a career officer, had been a captain assigned to a constabulary force in Haiti. It so happened that both men were particularly adamant about involving themselves aggressively in postwar military policy-making, and that Forrestal, as a cabinet member, was also intent on shaping foreign policy because it dictated the Navy's mission, military forces being instruments used to achieve political goals. Navy people tend to be very sensitive to the peacetime relationship of foreign policy and military power because warships are so well suited for power diplomacy. A single ship flying the flag can frequently make a telling political point, without the complications that sending ground and air units entails.

Forrestal, a deliberate man, laid out his thinking in a diary he started keeping shortly before becoming Secretary of the Navy. Frequently he dictated his thoughts to a stenographer, who typed them; he then inserted these pages into black spiral binders that he also used to save important magazine and newspaper articles. Some of his dictated material was sensitive, so he kept the binders in his office. He actively referred to them, the clippings especially.

Forrestal was determined not to let the turbulence of the times direct him. He was set on controlling the Navy's course through this epochal transition period. In a diary entry he made in the spring of 1945, he described one danger he foresaw: "I am more impressed than ever as things develop in the world today that policy may be frequently shaped by events unless someone has a strong and clear mental grasp of events; strong enough and clear enough so that he is able to shape policy rather than letting it be developed by accidents." Forrestal thereupon decided that he himself would be that "someone," and before many months had passed, he, in fact, would be more active than any top leader in developing a coherent rationale to buttress military and foreign policy. And many in the Truman administration would resent him for it.

Franklin Roosevelt's death had sparked Forrestal to act on reorganization, which would be the top postwar military-policy question, far and away. The late President had been a Navy man long before his days as the Navy's assistant secretary. The best measure of FDR's love for the sea and the Navy — a fondness that deepened throughout his life — was his art collection. His personal belongings, which movers carted out of the White House after he died, included more than five thousand prints, oil paintings, and watercolors of US Navy ships in the age of fighting sail. He quit collecting in 1939, he said, because there was no space on the walls of the White House for more. Perhaps only his cousin Theodore had been a better friend of the Navy establishment while President. During the war FDR had personally monitored whether Navy officers were getting their fair share of promotions. Whenever Marshall brought him the general officers' promotion list for approval, Roosevelt never failed to ask him about the Navy's promotion list for flag officers. It was a good thing, because even with this presidential interest Navy promotions lagged behind those of the Army and the Army Air Forces. All things considered, lots of senior sailors and Marines were especially upset when Roosevelt died; doubly so because reorganization was imminent.

Because of Marshall, and his being so politically astute, the Army was way ahead of the Navy in selling its reorganization plan in Washington. Opposed to any kind of reorganization plan, Navy leaders had procrastinated. By contrast, Marshall's memories of how the Army was dismantled and virtually destroyed during the years between the world wars had spurred him to act. (During the twenties, a regiment that was transferred from Philadelphia to Saint Louis had to walk because there was no money for train tickets.) So had his Army Air Forces officers, who wanted their own independent service. But Forrestal acted quickly to catch up. He broached the subject of reorganization and the size of the peacetime Navy in a meeting with Truman only six days after Roosevelt died. He said his department had prepared a briefing that he hoped the President would be interested in when he had time, and he recommended to Truman that he read a study on military reorganization called the Morrow Board Report, which was done for President Calvin Coolidge in 1925. Forrestal was being cautious with the new President, unaware of where he himself and the Navy stood with him. Having been the number-two man on the Democratic ticket during the 1944 campaign, Truman had deferred to Roosevelt. And rigorous press scrutiny had focused on the candidates for the presidency. Furthermore, Truman had been installed as chief executive so recently that his position on many issues was undefined.

But there were a couple of strong clues about what to expect. For the August 26, 1944, issue of *Collier's,* Truman, as a vice presidential candidate, had written an article explaining why he was in favor of merging the services. His presentation mostly cited perceived efficiencies to be gained. He also decried the rivalries between the services, suggesting that they had to be minimized, beginning with West Point and Annapolis. He proposed that at some time during their "final period of instruction," the cadets should be transferred to the Naval Academy and the midshipmen to the Military Academy.

Another clue about what to expect from Truman as Commander in Chief was his having served in the Army. Navy and Marine Corps officers had always felt that Presidents who were former Army officers victimized them. In Truman's case, he would compound their worries with his distaste for elitism, which he believed career Navy officers, Annapolis and West Point graduates, and the Marine Corps, in general, represented to the nth degree. This attitude was evident in the tone of some indiscreet remarks made by the President's old Missouri National Guard buddy Harry Vaughan, whom he had appointed his military aide and would eventually promote to major general. Within days of Truman's succeeding Roosevelt, Vaughan told a neighborhood audience back in Missouri: "During the Roosevelt Administration the White House was a Navy wardroom; we're going to fix that."

Such indiscretions by Vaughan would become so commonplace during Truman's presidency that whenever something cockeyed happened at the White House, staffers in-the-know would roll their eyes and say, "Cherchez le Vaughan." But Truman's reaction was always one of reassurance. He would tell Vaughan that political enemies were actually attacking the President by attacking his old friend. Loyalty was Truman's byword, and in Vaughan's case it was reinforced by the important role Vaughan had played in Truman's 1940 Senate reelection campaign, a campaign that profoundly impressed Roosevelt, who had thought Truman was finished. Tom Pendergast, Truman's political patron early on, had been convicted of income tax fraud shortly before the election campaign commenced, tainting Truman's candidacy. Through intermediaries, Roosevelt offered Truman a face-saving position on the Interstate Commerce Commission as enticement not to seek reelection and encouraged Missouri's Democratic governor, Lloyd Stark, the millionaire owner of Stark Nurseries, to run in Truman's place. Truman refused to step aside and defeated Stark in the primary before going on to win the general election. Vaughan had been Truman's campaign treasurer and had come up with a direct-mail scheme that overnight raised six hundred one-dollar contributions to pay for ads to answer Stark's last-minute charge that Pendergast was funding Truman's reelection. For a campaign that had spent only about $21,000, this was a princely sum.

Truman was also fond of Vaughan because Vaughan could make him laugh. Theirs was the classic big guy–little guy routine that moviemakers exploit by making the latter the much smarter of the two. Though only an inch taller, Vaughan was about forty pounds heavier than Truman, who was five-feet-ten and averaged 180 pounds. Vaughan relished talking about how the President, holding a losing poker hand, would bluff him into folding. He loved Harry Truman till the day he died.

After meeting with Truman in April 1945, Forrestal's next step in trying to thwart Army reorganization plans was to focus on making Marshall — still in his capacity as Army Chief of Staff at the time — more conciliatory. He began by inviting him, King, and Harry Hopkins, who had been Roosevelt's chief domestic-policy adviser and was advising Truman on an interim basis, to lunch at his home, which was one of the most prominent in Georgetown. The stately, three-story Federalist structure with Georgian accents was built around 1790 on a bluff high above the Potomac River, at a point near the Francis Scott Key Bridge. Forrestal could see the Pentagon several miles away, across the river in Virginia, from an octagonal watchtower built by a previous owner who owned trading ships and enjoyed watching them plow the Potomac; Georgetown was once a port for such seafaring ships.

Washington being the way it is, Forrestal's owning this distinguished Georgetown residence and having a skilled household staff to run it made him a formidable player in the capital, where parlor patter in homes of the wealthy can be more important than what is said on the floors of the House and the Senate. Forrestal had the money needed to compete in this league, having made a fortune on Wall Street as an investment banker.

Unfortunately for him and the Navy, Marshall was one military man not impressed by the accoutrements of wealth and privilege. Marshall seemed not to care that the only material possessions he had accumulated in life were the government's promise of a small pension and some pieces of furniture he and his first wife, Lily, had acquired before she died. Had not Katherine Marshall, his second wife, had money of her own, they could not have purchased the place in Leesburg they called home.

Such people can be hard to deal with, even when they do not have five stars on their shoulders. They are not persuaded by what normally moves people and are stubborn about changing their minds. This was the reaction Forrestal got from Marshall. The Navy Secretary recorded in his diary that at the luncheon the general "said he was unshakably committed to the thesis of a single civilian Secretary with a single military Chief of Staff."

While presenting his case, Marshall had actually been passionate, and such displays of emotion were rare for him. It was obvious to Forrestal, King, and Hopkins that unification stirred Marshall deeply and personally. While he was Chief of Staff, the postwar Army was not going to go begging again while the Navy fared relatively well. The Army's steep decline after World War I had lasted about twenty years. Given this experience, Marshall had decided that this time around the Army would be better off if funds were appropriated to a unified military department and then divvied up. "At considerable length he described the condition which prevailed at the end of the last war," Forrestal recalled. Regard for the Army had gotten so low then that President Warren G. Harding had had no compunction about ignoring Pershing's advice and even putting a Naval Academy graduate in charge of the Army. He made John W. Weeks, USNA class of 1881, Secretary of War. Marshall told Forrestal that Weeks would not allow Pershing to talk to Harding. And, according to Forrestal, "Marshall continued to express his fear of the starvation of the Army in another period of peace."

So the battle lines were drawn. Forrestal told Marshall that the "Navy could not concur in the conception of a single department. The Navy would only assent to some sort of system of cooperation and coordination." These were key words — *cooperation* and *coordination* — in the struggle about to ensue. They encapsulated the essence of the Navy's whole management approach and were diametrically different from the word *control*, which was the essence of the Army's approach. Coordination versus control; that was what the difference boiled down to. The Navy wanted to retain its decentralized management approach; the Army wanted to impose on the Navy its centralized approach. Compromise did not seem possible.

At this point, Forrestal, who was capable of being as shrewd as Marshall, decided that the Navy had to develop its own reorganization plan. As he explained the situation in a May 27, 1945, letter to Senator David I. Walsh, a Massachusetts Democrat who was chairman of the Senate Naval Affairs Committee, "the Navy Department cannot be in a position of merely taking the negative in this discussion, but must come up with positive and constructive recommendations." To this end, Forrestal appointed Ferdinand Eberstadt, his closest friend, to study the problem and develop a Navy reorganization plan. The two had met at Princeton when Eberstadt was chairman of the board of the school paper and Forrestal was a younger staffer. Eberstadt, like Forrestal, had become an investment banker.

In his planning, Forrestal reasonably anticipated that Walsh and Congressman Carl Vinson of Georgia, the chairman of the Naval Affairs Committee of the House, would support the Navy's plan. The Army could not be so sure of the chairmen on the Military Affairs committees, Senator Elbert Thomas and Congressman Andrew May. This was because the Army's plan would require reorganization within Congress itself. To conform with the merger of the services into a single military department, the Military Affairs and Naval Affairs committees for each legislative body would have to be merged into a single panel. Walsh and Vinson would be the chairmen because of seniority.

Unable to get Marshall to see things the Navy's way, Forrestal refocused his top-level lobbying back on Truman, in hopes of winning him over. This was not going to be easy; Truman had appointed close Missouri friends, men who reinforced some of his parochial tendencies, to both of his top uniformed-aide positions. Normally, people who hold these positions are not very important in the scheme of things unless by unusual circumstance they have the President's ear — which both did in this instance. Vaughan was the first staff person to see him each morning. Vaughan's counterpart on the Navy side was Commodore James K. Vardaman, Jr., whom Truman had met at Fort Riley, Kansas, during summer Reserve training. At these two-week encampments during the years 1935 to 1940, Truman led one artillery regiment, Vaughan another, and John Snyder, whom he would appoint Secretary of the Treasury, a third. Vardaman later transferred into the Naval Reserve and became an intelligence officer. Vaughan and Vardaman were just cronies of Truman; nothing much more than being the President's close friends qualified them for their jobs.

Very quickly Forrestal learned that access to Truman was going to be a problem. He was not included in the entourage that Truman took with him to Potsdam, Germany, on July 7, 1945, for extended negotiations with Churchill and Stalin focusing on what to do with a defeated Germany and the newly liberated nations of Europe, Poland in particular. Stimson was not invited either, and since people associated both men with Wall Street and the Republican party, their exclusion had a faint outline of partisan politics about it. Forrestal especially was becoming an alarmist about the Russians. The image slowly emerging was of Republicans' being more worried about dealing with Communists than Truman and other Democrats were. Patrick Hurley had helped focus this perception by the partisan way he resigned as Truman's special envoy to China.

That Truman and most of the American delegation bound for Potsdam traveled to and from Europe aboard a Navy ship, the heavy cruiser *Augusta*, needled Forrestal. What also would have disturbed him, had he known it, was that Vardaman brought in another Naval Reserve officer like himself to "guard" his office in the White House from the Regular Navy while he was away with Truman. That was the word Clark Clifford, the Reserve officer summoned, later used to describe his assignment upon being ordered to Washington from San Francisco as a thirty-nine-year-old Navy lieutenant on temporary wartime duty. Before the war, he had been the attorney for a shoe manufacturing company Vardaman owned in Saint Louis. Vardaman's instructions to Clifford reflected the distrust he, Vaughan, and Truman had for Regular officers, whom Forrestal, while Navy Secretary, had come to represent.

Forrestal's basic problem with Truman was personal. The President, who was one of the boys, so to speak, had already decided that Forrestal was not his kind of guy. They had become acquainted when Truman was in the Senate. Their relationship was businesslike and amicable, but because the two were very different people, it did not improve beyond this starting point, which ruled out Forrestal's ever being admitted to Truman's inner circle of advisers. Forrestal tried to soften up his image with Truman by joining a number of the small-stakes poker games hosted by the President. Clifford eventually became responsible for putting these together, an informal duty he was pleased to continue even after he left the White House to practice law. At them, all Forrestal did was lose money. He did not mind this, but he never could countenance the boredom he felt. Even as a young man he had not idled away time in such a manner. The company was usually good, but he always felt uncomfortable being there, anyway. Cursing and crude behavior had not offended him; there was none of that at Truman's poker sessions, recalled the United Press's Merriman Smith, an occasional player. It was just that playing games was out of character for Forrestal.

Different though they were, Forrestal had started out in life not far above the low station from which Truman emerged. He was born and raised in a little burg on the upper Hudson called Matteawan, which in later years merged with another village under the name Beacon. One of his grandmothers had emigrated from Ireland to the United States as a young widow and, after getting a job as a domestic servant, sent for Forrestal's father, then only nine. He became a successful proprietor of a construction-and-carpentry company and married a teacher who was the daughter of a farmer. This woman was a devout Catholic who tried to persuade James, the youngest of her three sons, to become a priest. The first mass in the area had been said in her father's home.

James instead became a reporter when he was graduated from high school at age sixteen, and he went to work covering such stories as twenty-eight-year-old Franklin Roosevelt's campaign for the New York State Senate. After three years of this, during which time he worked for three different papers in the area, he advanced to the city editor position of the *Poughkeepsie News Press*. However, the region was too provincial to hold his interest, so without consulting his parents, he applied to Dartmouth College and was accepted. He studied there one year and then got himself transferred to Princeton, which he knew was populated by the sons of some of the nation's richest and most powerful families; already he had great ambition, though as yet it was unfocused. Forrestal was the type of young man who knew instinctively that the contacts he would make at Princeton would be as important as the education there, and so he cultivated them assiduously. Princeton was probably the most celebrated college in the country the fall he enrolled because Woodrow Wilson, its former, innovative president, was running for President of the United States.

Forrestal's father helped him with expenses, but the young man had a reputation among his classmates for always being short of money. Even though he wore expensive clothing, friends thought he had come from a poor family — a perception that was accurate only in a relative sense. He mixed with such scions as Allen Dulles, the future Central Intelligence Agency director whose uncle Robert Lansing would be Secretary of State under Woodrow Wilson, and James McGraw, the future president and chairman of the board of McGraw-Hill Publications, a company his father cofounded. Forrestal gained the acceptance of such young men to the point of being invited to join what at the time was the school's most exclusive "eating" fraternity, the Cottage Club.

Forrestal was an average student. His crowning achievement at Princeton was being named chairman of the board of the *Daily Princetonian* his senior year, as Eberstadt before him had been. As such, he was also the publisher of the class annual, the *Nassau Herald*. Given his talent for administration and mastery of detail, he probably was the one responsible for shipping a copy off to the Library of Congress. That institution had not received copies previously, and has not since. Indicative of Forrestal's headstrong nature and self-confidence was his dropping out of school six weeks before graduation over a dispute with an English professor about class attendance. He did not return to complete his work for a diploma.

During the next year, in quick succession, Forrestal accepted and then quit three jobs as he searched for what he wanted, his ambition still unfocused. The last of these three jobs was reporting for the *New York World*, a position that familiarized him with Wall Street and piqued his interest in it. He applied for work with the investment banking firm of William A. Read and Company and was hired to sell bonds by a Princeton alumnus who was impressed by his high position on the staff of the school paper.

Forrestal also rose to the top at Read, and very fast. Within seven years he was a partner and within ten years a vice president. In 1928, at the age of thirty-six, he earned on the Street the nickname "boy wonder" when he played a key role in the merger of Dodge and Chrysler. Ten years later he was named president of Dillon, Read and Company, which was the product of a merger of Read with another investment banking firm.

Roosevelt brought Forrestal into government in May 1940, three days after announcing the appointment of Henry Stimson as War Secretary and Frank Knox as Navy Secretary. Forrestal was to be one of the heralded "Secret Six," highly successful businessmen whom the President said would serve with a "passion for anonymity" as White House administrative assistants. Up to this time, Forrestal had been apolitical, though his father had been active in the Democratic party and as a reward for his political work had been appointed a postmaster by President Grover Cleveland.

Most people thought Forrestal was a Republican because of his association with Wall Street. As it happened, this actually worked in his favor, since Roosevelt, as noted, at the time was forming a coalition government of sorts to meet the expected war emergency. Furthermore, Harry Hopkins, who had interviewed Forrestal for the White House job, liked what he had heard. Forrestal had been derisive about many of his Wall Street colleagues, and this pleased Hopkins, since most of them hated Roosevelt. Forrestal told Hopkins that all one needed to succeed on Wall Street was average intelligence and a willingness to work, commodities in short supply there.

Forrestal had one black mark to overcome — trouble with the Internal Revenue Service. He had devised a scheme to avoid paying taxes on the huge commission he made on the Dodge-Chrysler merger. The tax dodge involved trading shares between two dummy companies he set up in Canada and the United States. What he did was not illegal at the time, but he embarrassed himself. Owing to the prominence of the merger, he ended up having to testify about it before the Senate Banking and Currency Committee. His filing of an amended tax return and his endorsement of the Securities and Exchange Act seemed to settle all accounts. The vast majority of his colleagues opposed the bill.

About the same percentage were shocked that Forrestal quit his prestigious and well-paying Dillon, Read presidency to go to work for Roosevelt in such an undefined, low-profile capacity. His explanation was that he wanted to give something back to the country in the form of public service.

No doubt he also wanted and needed new challenges. He could not go any higher where he was and he had earned all the money he wanted.

For someone as organized as Forrestal, working for Roosevelt had to have been exasperating initially. According to Stimson, Roosevelt was the worst administrator he, Stimson, had ever experienced, and keeping up with his train of thought was "very much like chasing a vagrant beam of sunshine around a vacant room." One of his aggravating techniques was to assign the same task to several people so that they would all end up competing with one another.

Fortunately, FDR compensated in other ways for his deficient management skills. He was an inspiring leader with an innovative mind and, unlike Truman, was an uncanny judge of talent. He had formed an extraordinary cadre of people to lead the military during the war. Marshall was the first he appointed with the war in mind; Roosevelt made him Army Chief of Staff in September of 1939. Forrestal was soon made Under Secretary of the Navy. When Knox died of a heart attack on April 28, 1944, Roosevelt named Forrestal his successor.

Forrestal had gotten himself appointed Navy Under Secretary after warning Hopkins that he was being underutilized at the White House and would resign at the end of 1940 unless challenged by something better. He had in mind the newly created Navy Under Secretary post, and the ploy worked. Knox assigned him an assortment of responsibilities involving contracts, taxes, legal matters, and liaison activities with certain government agencies. It was a prosaic job description, which Forrestal transformed. His position became a major power center in Washington. He controlled the Navy's vast wartime programs for procurement and ship construction. He essentially bought the US Navy that fought the war. This included not only the 1,166 big warships still riding the waves at war's end, but also 67,770 other ships and boats in the inventory then, such as transports, minesweepers, and landing craft, and the 41,272 aircraft still flying for the Navy.

Forrestal was intelligent, but the dominant trait that distinguished him from virtually everyone was his capacity for long, hard work. Even his recreation was intense. During his younger days, he frequently boxed, and he had gotten his nose permanently flattened as a result; a professional he was sparring with broke it in retaliation for a well-placed punch. Forrestal was a driven man. During his early years on Wall Street, he frequently worked until one or two in the morning and through the weekend. "He thought he could work beyond anyone else's limit," recalled a friend. "He was driving for superiority." He delayed marriage until he was thirty-four; to save time for work, he had the ceremony conducted at New York's Municipal Building during lunch hour and afterward returned to the office. Even the two children that the union produced did not distract him much; nannies tended them far more often than their parents did and later they were sent off to boarding schools.

Truman appreciated a hard worker, having grown up on a farm, but there was so much about Forrestal that was countervailing — his Wall Street and Republican connections; his being married to a divorcée, a former *Vogue* editor; his sending his children away to school, as British aristocrats do; his fancy addresses; his having been carted around by chauffeurs for as long as Forrestal himself could remember. Many of the same attributes would apply to men Truman would become close to — such as Averell Harriman, then ambassador to the Soviet Union, who had inherited a hundred million dollars from his father — but Truman would for other reasons become comfortable with them, which made all the difference. Perhaps Harriman was more at ease with his money than Forrestal was. Harriman was also more of a politician, as his later winning the New York governorship would indicate, and Truman liked being around politicians.

Truman's tendency to keep at arm's length, even professionally, people he did not personally get along with would land him in trouble. So would taking at face value the assurances of those with whom he did. He relied too much on a firm handshake and good eye contact. Back in Independence, where a man had to live down a broken promise, these intangibles probably had value. But in the more complex world at large, they had little. Indeed, Truman seems not to have been a good judge of character, if his confidence in Vaughan and Vardaman is a measure. Vaughan would repeatedly embarrass him, and Vardaman, whose ego was such that he was easily manipulated by Truman's enemies, would compromise him. Later, when Vardaman had the security of a six-year appointment to the Federal Reserve Board, courtesy of his old friend Harry, he would regale others at dinner parties with farcical stories about Truman's presidency. Truman was lucky to have become President at a time when the heat of war had distilled a small pool of highly capable leaders from the vast reservoir of possibilities; he could not have found them otherwise. Even so, his temperament was such that he sometimes allowed personal considerations to subvert his judgment about someone of proved talent, such as Forrestal.

Truman's hang-up with Forrestal was literally of the latter's making, however. The Navy Secretary had transformed himself in about thirty years' time and was not entirely comfortable in his new suit of skin. There was something about him that put many people on edge. Truman had picked up on this immediately; few people in public life are as capable of being as relaxed as Truman was. He was pleased with himself, in fact; a few years earlier he had complimented himself in his diary for having all his vices under control. Unlike Forrestal, Truman had always built upon the past, even perpetuated it by bringing his old friends along with him as he climbed the ladder of success. Forrestal tried to erase all traces of his past. He had rejected his parent's religion, having quit attending mass while at Princeton. And years had passed since he had been to Matteawan. His sons, who were teenagers in 1945, had never met their cousins who lived there.

On the other hand, Forrestal was disdainful of the world he had conquered, as the disparaging remarks about Wall Street he made to Hopkins indicated. And he refused to be part of the café high society in which his wife had become very prominent. Forrestal willingly stayed home while she attended these affairs, escorted by other men. In this regard, a longtime Wall Street associate identified "a socialistic streak in him right from the start. He was always a little contemptuous of wealth, and yet he would always strive for it." All things considered, Truman would have been much more comfortable with Forrestal's brother Henry, who had stayed in Matteawan to run their father's business.

Uninvited, Forrestal landed at Gatow Airport outside Berlin en route to Potsdam on July 28; the conference had only four days to run. That evening Truman received his interloping Secretary of the Navy with good grace, dining with him at what reporters were calling the Little White House, a three-story, yellow-stucco villa that had once been the home of a movie producer. This residence was located in Babelsberg, a resort town on a lake twelve miles from Berlin and contiguous to Potsdam.

Picking up his conversation with the President where they had left off April 18, Forrestal cautiously began drawing Truman out, hoping at the same time to win his goodwill. They talked mostly about foreign affairs. Truman's salient remark that evening, as Forrestal recorded it, was that "he was being very realistic with the Russians and found Stalin not difficult to do business with." The statement was not consistent with recent problems. Perhaps Truman did not want to reinforce the hard-liner views of Forrestal. On the other hand, Stalin and Truman seemed to be getting along personally. No doubt the reason was the raw US power that abounded. As long as US forces remained in strength, Truman's positive assessment about doing business with Stalin had promise. These Soviet Communists had retained the czars' respect for military power. It so happened that when Forrestal and his entourage were driven in to see Berlin the next day, they encountered some dramatic evidence of American muscle. Pulled up alongside the road and arrayed track-to-track for about thirty miles were the tanks and light armored vehicles of a US armored division. Not a bolt was missing and the equipment was the latest. Commodore Henry A. Schade reported to Forrestal that some Russians with them were "much impressed."

Two days after having dinner with Truman at the Little White House, Forrestal met him for breakfast there, and their dialogue resumed. Joining them were Eisenhower, accompanied by his son John in an unofficial capacity; Lieutenant General Lucius Clay, who was the American deputy military governor in Germany; Vaughan; Vardaman; and some others. This time the conversation focused on what presently bothered Forrestal even more than potential trouble with the Russians: postwar military plans and policies. Forrestal gingerly broached the subject. Truman explained what he was going to do and, just as important, revealed the thinking that motivated him.

What was rather startling was how his policy was mostly going to be a function of social equations. The numbers would come later, evidently; how many divisions, ships, and planes the United States needed concerned him less than what he perceived as social inequities within the services. In a few months he would appoint Lieutenant General James Doolittle, a Reserve officer, to lead a commission in studying whether such military customs and courtesies as enlisted men's saluting officers should be continued. He did not forewarn Forrestal about this as they talked that morning, though everyone seated at the breakfast table got the impression Truman was going to enjoy making admirals and generals howl. In his diary, Forrestal reiterated Truman's philosophical bent.

> [The President] is in favor of a single Department of Defense, but I gather that his interest in it is not so much from the belief that it will provide greater efficiency in . . . [the individual services'] operations or procurement, but because of its relation to education and universal military training. His purpose is to wrap the entire question up into one package and present it to Congress. He talked a good deal of what he called the citizen sources of officers in both Services and of the destruction of "political cliques that run the Army and Navy." This seems to be a fixation with him, although he admitted he hadn't had so much experience with the Navy. . . .
>
> His views on [military] education in general I gather to be these: He would have a common basic and beginning education for all officers, Army, Navy and Air Force, on the general thesis that modern war is a composite and not separate business. He is particularly anxious to have all men who become officers spend at least a year in the ranks before doing so, so that they get an understanding of the attitude and problems of the ordinary soldier or bluejacket. . . . So far as West Point and Annapolis are concerned, he said he regarded them more or less as finishing schools . . . for . . . specialist training.

Forrestal could not believe what he had heard. Truman seemed to be acting out of spite, as if he, the President of the US, and not Admiral Karl Doenitz, the last acting authority of the Reich, had recently surrendered. According to Forrestal, the President told the group that he had talked to Marshall about all this and that he was in "complete agreement." Forrestal inserted an exclamation point after this comment in his dictation. Eisenhower's reaction was not recorded. He was an extremely prominent member of the West Point clique Truman was describing. But it was obvious that the President had not been thinking of Eisenhower in these terms; Truman had the bad habit of dismissing as exceptions those examples that disproved his case. At the time, he liked Ike very much and admired him.

This is not to say that Truman offered his arguments without foundation. "It was clear," Forrestal observed, "that most of his thinking was predicated upon his experience in the Army during the last war and in the National Guard [actually the Army Reserve] since then. He remarked that he had gone every year to a refresher training course and had read and thought a great deal about military problems."

Indeed he had.

Truman's direct involvement in military affairs started in 1905, when at the age of twenty-one he joined the National Guard, the year it was organized in Kansas City, Missouri, where he was working as a bookkeeper in a bank. He was living with his sister Mary Jane and Grandmother Young on the latter's farm, which he and his sister ran. He held the rank of private, the lowest, and was assigned to Battery B, working as number-two man on an old three-inch gun. Once a week, he and about sixty others paid twenty-five cents to drill; the collected funds were used to rent and maintain the armory. At the time, the Spanish-American War was still a fresh, positive memory in the national conscience and Theodore Roosevelt, one of its heroes, was just beginning his second term as President. During high school Truman had thought about going to either West Point or Annapolis, as a way to get an education free, but his poor eyesight had voided these options.

Guard membership was a good way to meet other community-minded young men and socialize; the experience then was similar to Jaycee membership today in many midwestern communities. Almost all the Kansas City guardsmen worked in banks and stores. The Guard gave most of them, including Truman, the first identity as adults that they could visualize lasting well into the future. Relatively few got to go to college in those days, so, unless a young man ran his own farm, years ordinarily passed before he worked at a given job long enough to be identified with it and deem it his profession. Truman was trying to escape the farm, and worked successively as a railroad clerk, a bank bookkeeper, a postmaster, an oil-lease entrepreneur, a merchant, and a salesman.

This is why the Guard was so important to nearly everybody who belonged. Each member could see some progression, even if only a stripe or two, and the experience elevated all their lives above the humdrum. The Guard channeled and sustained Truman's ambition long before he had any other outlet for its fulfillment. There was a certain nobility associated with the exercise, as if each participant was taking up arms for his country, though the thought of fighting in Europe probably never occurred to anyone in the Kansas City unit.

Truman was trying to strike it rich in the oil business when the National Guard of Missouri was called to arms for World War I. The oil venture had been the first big risk he had taken in life, his mother having cosigned five notes so he could become a one-third partner in some leases in Kansas and Oklahoma. Though oil exploration was booming in the region, Truman's company drilled nothing but dry holes before liquidating its interests for lack of manpower. Too many hands were leaving the oil fields to go fight instead.

Truman helped form Missouri recruits into additional batteries, which, when combined, constituted a regiment. With that done, the men who were assigned to each battery elected their officers. Those in what was eventually designated Battery F of the 129th Field Artillery of the 35th Division elected Truman first lieutenant. Each battery had two officers; Truman was the junior in his, but was more than pleased. Making sergeant had been his goal.

All the Missouri artillerymen were first shipped off to Fort Sill, Oklahoma, for six months of training. Truman got extra duty there as the regimental canteen officer, and with the help of Eddie Jacobson, an enlisted man with some merchandising experience, the quasi-commercial operation was a rousing success. Truman earned good efficiency reports — so good, in fact, that a senior officer bucked one of them back. "No man can be that good," he said.

Truman arrived in wartime France about three months before any American unit was sent into battle. Pershing was putting all soldiers in the American Expeditionary Force through a rigorous training program upon arrival. During this period a letter from home informed Truman that oil had been discovered on one of the leases his partnership had been forced to sell. It developed into the Teter Oil Pool, one of the largest ever found in Kansas. Fortune was not to be his fame.

Otherwise, he was doing well. In quick succession he was appointed regimental adjutant (which was an administrative-support job), made officer in charge of Battery D, and promoted to captain. But for the time being, at least, these rewards probably did little to ease his anguish about fate's cruel tease; he still had not accumulated enough money to get married, or so he thought. In matters of money and the heart, he was a very deliberate man. By daughter Margaret's account, he and Bess had, by this time, been "paired" for about three years.

Truman trained about four months in France before he and his 100-man unit fired their first salvos at the enemy. The Germans returned the greeting, killing six horses and, in Truman's words, scattering all but five or six of his men "like partridges." None was killed, however.

Truman fought in both the Saint-Mihiel and Meuse-Argonne offensives, almost getting killed at the start of the latter. He had gone to sleep along the edge of a forest the night before the attack and, fortunately, had awakened very early; during the morning darkness his battery was scheduled to fire the first of three thousand rounds in an opening fusillade. Minutes after he quit his repose, German artillery fire obliterated the tree line where he had been.

The next morning he had another close call, but of a different kind. Advancing on horseback in darkness behind the moving front, he was smacked in the face by a low tree limb that swept off his pince-nez spectacles. Terror gripped him; he was virtually blind without his glasses. Pulling his mount up short, he wheeled about, hoping to spot them. Miraculously, they lay on his horse's back, a few inches behind the saddle.

Sixty-six days after Truman first experienced combat, the war ended. He was no hero, but had served honorably. He had learned that he was courageous, calm in the face of fire, and that he could lead. A confident self-esteem began to emerge — a sense that, given the chance, he was as good as any man. It was clear that he was determined to seize any opportunity that came his way: Vaughan remembered that "after a couple of weeks in the trenches without any chance to take a bath or to change clothes, the rest of us would look like bums with mud sticking all over us and he always looked immaculate." This characterized him later in life. By his personal appearance and deportment, he demanded respect, as if to say it were his due. While in Congress, Truman wore tailor-made suits and one year was named to a fashion arbiter's list of the ten best-dressed senators.

Truman's only war-related injury was damage to his eardrums. A French battery positioned on a ridge had fired a 155-millimeter cannon as Truman passed by below on a road. True to character, Truman took the time to tell the officer what he thought about things. For the rest of his life, Truman experienced disorientation amid loud noises.

Truman's life would not remotely have been the same had he not joined the Guard. Most of his closest friends in life were Missouri Guard members with whom he served in France, and reservists. His performance there and, especially, his having become an officer enhanced his status among them and the rest of the community. Being ordered off to war also spurred him to ask Bess Wallace to marry him. Guard membership indirectly led to Truman's greatest personal tragedy — a failure in a business at age thirty-eight — and ultimately to his greatest achievement, the presidency.

Military service remained an active part of his life after the war. He joined the Reserve and in 1921 took the lead in establishing an organization of men from the Kansas City area who had served in the Army, the Navy, or the Marine Corps. Their purpose, said Truman, was to speak out "in the interest of national defense," which was much in the news, primarily because of Brigadier General Billy Mitchell, whose pilots during tests that year proved that airplanes loaded with bombs could sink a battleship. They sent to the bottom of Chesapeake Bay the *Ostfriesland,* which had been confiscated from Germany.

The Kansas City reservists elected Truman their first president. Pershing subsequently endorsed the idea of having this military/fraternal organization, causing it to go nationwide. As a result, Truman and a few other reservists who concurrently organized similar chapters in other cities are recognized as cofounders of the Reserve Officers Association of the United States. Truman also became the first statewide president of ROA in Missouri.

Truman's business failure was a clothing store, which was the idea of Jacobson, who was inspired by the success of the Fort Sill canteen. They prospered the first year, meeting their obligations and having two good incomes left over. Jacobson was chief buyer; Truman was chief salesman. Vets frequently congregated at the business, embellishing war stories under the flags of the Allies that hung from the ceiling at the back. Truman made the most of slack periods by reading history.

When things turned sour, Truman laid the blame on the coming to power of President Harding and his Republican administration. They had tightened credit by raising interest rates, which Andrew Mellon, the new Secretary of the Treasury, said was part of a salutary "wringing-out process." Farm prices plummeted and the economies of the Midwest contracted. Suddenly, Truman had lots more time to read history. Customers were few and far between. Many businesses failed, including his clothing store. Truman avoided bankruptcy, but it took him twelve years to retire the last of his debt obligations. His brother Vivian helped him along the way by purchasing at a discount one of his notes at a public sale.

By then Truman had begun his political career. The year he closed down his clothing store he was elected judge of the Eastern District of Jackson County, a job called county commissioner or county executive in most states. His military service had created the opportunity. When Tom Pendergast's political machine was looking for a candidate to endorse, Truman's name popped up. Truman had served in France with James Pendergast, Tom's nephew. Young Jim recommended Truman for the job, describing him to his elders as a captain "whose men didn't want to shoot him."

Endorsement by Pendergast was not tantamount to election, but it certainly helped, and Truman won. He lost reelection to a harness maker, but after selling American Automobile Association memberships for two years was elected presiding judge of all Jackson County. He held the office eight years, established a reputation for honesty and effectiveness, and in 1934 won election to the US Senate. Key to victory was a statewide network of guardsmen, reservists, veterans, county officials, and Masons. Truman was active in lodge work, too.

As Forrestal was discovering, Truman was not the sort of person to run for high office without a clear self-perception and a firm grasp on what he believed. He strongly supported Roosevelt and was a self-proclaimed Jeffersonian Democrat — a liberal whose political hero and role model was Andrew Jackson. Jefferson and Jackson had laid the foundation for the Democratic party's liberal traditions. And especially pertinent in its shaping effect on Truman's views — as military historian Samuel Huntington has pointed out — is the fact that Jackson first defined military policy for American liberals.

Even when Truman was a young man, Jackson was his hero, perhaps because Jackson County was named after him. His respect for Old Hickory never waned. Jacobson specifically remembered that Jackson was the subject of many of the books and articles Truman read in their store. When Truman, while presiding judge, had some funds left over after constructing new courthouses in Kansas City and Independence, he commissioned a statue to honor Jackson; casts of it were placed in front of each building. Truman retained a replica of the statue and years later displayed it in the Oval Office. While President, Truman caused the name of the Democrats' most important annual rite to be changed from Jefferson Day to Jefferson-Jackson Day.

The influence of Jackson on Truman as Commander in Chief is striking and not surprising, given that Truman deemed history as functional as a road map. "My debt to history is one which cannot be calculated," he wrote in his memoirs. While President he frequently examined how his predecessors handled similar problems and himself tried to apply lessons learned. The first situation so addressed was the matter of his succeeding a President who died in office. Sensing the possibility, Truman had hit the books beforehand. "I learned of the unique problems of Andrew Johnson, whose destiny it was to be thrust suddenly into the presidency to fill the shoes of one of history's great leaders," he later observed. "When the same thing happened to me, I knew just how Johnson had coped with his problems, and I did not make the mistakes he made."

Andrew Jackson's story was, by contrast, one of success — an inspiration to Truman, not a warning, as Johnson's had been. Jackson had been propelled into national prominence as the hero of the Battle of New Orleans during the war of 1812 and, as a consequence, is remembered as having been an Army general. But, significantly, he was not a career military officer. Before he was a general, Jackson had a long and varied career as a lawyer, judge, planter, and politician. These successful pursuits led to high standing in the Tennessee militia, and this in turn facilitated his being commissioned a general in the US Army at the outbreak of fighting. After the war he served only seven years on active duty.

Jackson believed that military service was as basic an obligation as voting and that all able-bodied males should receive military training. His thinking was that citizen-soldiers, because they lived among the population, would be inspired by the idea of liberty and democracy as no professional soldier who was isolated from the general community could be. Jackson also believed that the citizen-soldier would fight better and in all aspects serve the country better.

Jackson despised privilege and believed that a person should progress only on merit. This was the root of his idea of selecting officers from men in the ranks, as Truman was recommending decades later. When possible, officers should be elected by those they lead, Jackson thought. He did not think that an effective military leader had to progress slowly up through the rank order, as was the lot of the professional soldier. As he saw it, such a procedure deprived the country of leaders who during peacetime were more gainfully employed in civilian professions. In Jackson's day, warfare was not very technical. Well-led, courageous men of conviction could do the job with little additional training. And Jackson's experience was that men were born with leadership qualities, or not, and that a lifetime in uniform could not improve upon what was God-given.

The corollary of what Jackson believed was that large military forces were a threat to democracy, its autocratic system being antithetical. He and his followers viewed the professional officer corps as a closed society, an "aristocratic caste," incapable of leading freeborn Americans. Jacksonians resented West Pointers because their school represented the notion that its young graduates should, in effect, have the top military positions reserved for themselves years ahead of time. So Military Academy graduates, and professional officers generally, did not fare well during Jackson's presidency. (The Naval Academy had not yet been founded.)

Sylvanus Thayer, West Point's superintendent, became so disgusted with the derision heaped upon the school, the attempts to undermine it, and the intrusion of what he perceived as the spoils system, that he resigned in disgust. Of course, what to Thayer was spoils was to Jackson an attempt to break up the "West Point clique" by appointing men from outside the professional military to important positions. For example, when Jackson's War Department formed four new regiments of dragoons, West Point graduates were appointed to only four of the thirty officer positions thus created. The other officers were appointed directly from civilian life. Furthermore, during Jackson's eight-year presidency, no West Point graduates held the Army's highest command positions.

The assault on West Point by Jacksonians reached its peak the year Jackson left office. Opposition to the professional military establishment the school engendered was so intense that a congressional committee investigating the institution recommended that it be abolished. The proposal failed, but Jackson and his followers did leave a lasting imprint on the nation's military academies: they established the basic selection process by which young men and women gain admission. Before Jackson's time, career military officers made all appointments to West Point; however, as a means of assuaging Jacksonian hostility, military leaders began seeking recommendations from congressmen and then affirming their nominations. This procedure had political advantages for all concerned and became popular. As a consequence, Congress formalized the procedure. Since then, the standard means of gaining an appointment to one of the academies has been through members of Congress.

Also important in shaping Truman's views about postwar military policy was his experience in the US Senate. While serving as a legislator, he developed a detailed understanding of how the nation armed itself; put another way, he came to understand the military establishment as a business enterprise. This knowledge was the product of his experience as chairman, from 1941 to mid-1944, of the US Senate's Special Committee to Investigate the National Defense Program, which became widely known as the Truman Committee. It prepared him, probably as none of his presidential predecessors had been, for appreciating Congress's important role in providing for the nation's defense. And what his committee uncovered formed the basis of his thinking about military spending during most of his presidency.

Setting up the special committee had been Truman's idea. Not long after he was sworn in for his second Senate term, angry constituents began writing to complain about waste at two Army installations in Missouri, Fort Leonard Wood and Camp Crowder. The nation had not entered the war yet, but the military buildup had started. Harry Vaughan, who at the time was Truman's newly hired administrative assistant, accumulated about a hundred of the letters before preparing a uniform response and going to Truman for approval. Instead of sending it out, Truman decided to investiage the allegations personally before responding. A four-day recess was coming up, and he decided to put the time to good use. "If they're wasting money out at Camp Crowder and Fort Leonard Wood, they're wasting it down at Fort Lee and over at Fort Meade," he told Vaughan. So during the break Truman got into his car and drove to the two installations near the capital, which he entered unannounced and investigated unescorted. He came back with a number of stories that were almost as amusing as disturbing. At one of the posts, he watched two men taking turns driving nails with the same hammer.

What he saw convinced him that a congressional oversight committee would help keep costs down by exposing abuses. Sending people to jail afterward would serve no useful purpose, he decided. "Let's keep them from being crooks," he told Vaughan. Initially, Democratic leaders in the Senate and Roosevelt himself were wary of Truman's proposal, but "I explained that I was not going to do any witch-hunting," he later wrote.

During 1941 alone, the Truman Committee conducted about seventy hearings and heard 252 witnesses. The first hearing was about construction of military training camps, and thereafter they focused on everything from the management of important commodities such as aluminum, copper, lead, zinc, and steel to such military-related topics as the automobile industry, small business, labor, the aviation industry, plant financing, lobbying, shipbuilding, military housing, ordnance plants, and government administration of the war production program. Under Truman's leadership, the committee never strayed from its charter; it never delved into war strategy, only into the arming of the nation. It conducted hearings throughout the war and is credited with saving $15 billion and many lives by exposing abuses and sometimes outright fraud.

A notable example of the committee's work involved malfunctioning aircraft engines manufactured by Wright Aeronautical Corporation that were killing student pilots. The Army Air Forces, preoccupied with getting large numbers of aircraft, fast, actually defended the company until some of the committee members traveled to Lockland, Ohio, where the Curtis-Wright engines were made, and heard testimony from scores of witnesses. The Air Force then reevaluated the engines and imposed modifications.

Another example involved the Martin B-26 bomber, which also was crashing with unexplained frequency during training missions. Truman ordered an engineering study of the plane and found that the wingspan was too short and was causing instability. Glenn Martin, the company's chief executive officer, initially told the committee that it was too late to make a design change, but when Truman warned that committee members would make certain that the Army Air Forces did not purchase the B-26, Martin quickly changed his mind. "Well, if that's the way you feel about it, we'll change it," he said.

The committee caught Carnegie-Illinois Steel, the principal subsidiary of United States Steel, cheating the Navy on deliveries of sheet steel. Company supervisors had ordered its inspectors to fake tests certifying the tensile strength of finished steel plate. On another Navy matter, investigation of shipping losses, the committee learned that the Germans had sunk twelve million tons' worth of American ships during 1942, a million more tons than US shipyards had produced that year. Frank Knox, the Secretary of the Navy then, publicly denied the findings when the committee released them to the media, but when called before the committee to testify during executive session, he confirmed the report. Exposure of the acute problem led to a greatly intensified anti-submarine campaign — beginning with increased appropriations from Congress — that was eventually won.

The committee also uncovered many instances of the services' competing with each other for the same precious commodities. At one point a plant working on a critical Army order was threatened with shutdown for lack of copper, though virgin copper was piled to the rafters in a nearby Navy warehouse, awaiting future use in ships. In this instance, Under Secretary Forrestal seems to have been doing his job too well.

While Truman was at the Potsdam Conference, the pace of events that would end the war had quickened. On July 16, 1945, the atomic bomb was tested at a site near Alamogordo, New Mexico, code-named Trinity, an allusion to the fact that at the time there were only three of the devices. No one had known what to expect exactly, not even the scientists who were certain that atomic fission was possible. In fact, some scientists believed the weapon would not work. Fleet Admiral William D. Leahy, the Chief of Staff to the Commander in Chief of the Army and Navy, was one of the military men who sided with the doubters.

The Manhattan Project, as the atomic-bomb development program was called, would end up costing $2 billion. From the start, when it was only an idea that Albert Einstein had passed along to Franklin Roosevelt, it had been the War Department's responsibility. Administering the whole thing devolved on Stimson, who established an advisory group composed of Marshall, Dr. Vannevar Bush, president of the Carnegie Institution of

Washington and director of the Office of Scientific Research and Development, and Dr. James B. Conant, president of Harvard University and chairman of the National Defense Research Committee. Major General Leslie Groves was appointed the operations officer in charge of the project, and J. Robert Oppenheimer, a physicist from the University of California, was designated its chief scientist, a position that carried the title of director of the Los Alamos Scientific Laboratory. Truman later credited Oppenheimer "more than any other man" with creating the atomic bomb. The result of his effort and that of everyone else involved exceeded expectations — a point Groves later confirmed in his official report with this description: "For a brief period there was a lighting effect within a radius of 20 miles equal to several suns in midday; a huge ball mushroomed and rose to a height of over ten thousand feet before it dimmed."

At the time that the explosion ripped the silence of the desert, Truman was preparing for a drive into Berlin to view the destruction that had been wrought there by conventional weaponry. He got word of the successful test after returning that evening to Babelsberg. Stimson, who had preceded Forrestal in inviting himself to the conference venue, delivered it personally.

The President decided to keep the news a closely guarded secret. Churchill was notified immediately because Great Britain had been involved in the Manhattan Project from the outset. The President did not tell Stalin for another eight days, by which time the Russian leader probably already knew. He had a spy named Klaus Emil Fuchs, a German refugee who was an atomic physicist, standing a few feet from Groves and Oppenheimer during the test.

Truman's first step after the successful test was to call Secretary of State Byrnes, Marshall, Chief of Naval Operations King, and Army Air Forces commander Arnold to the Little White House to reassess war strategy. They recommended that plans for the invasion of Japan continue on schedule and that atomic bombs be used on real, not demonstration, targets. Marshall thought the invasion and ensuing fight might cost 500,000 American lives. There had been some talk about first warning the Japanese about the atomic bomb and then demonstrating its power, but Marshall and an advisory group headed by Stimson decided this plan would not shock Japanese leaders sufficiently to make them surrender. There was also a chance that the aerial detonation of the atomic bomb would not work; the test had been a static detonation. A failure during a demonstration would have awful repercussions. Furthermore, there were only two weapons left. More would not be available until the end of the year.

When Truman finally told Stalin that he had a weapon of unusual destructive force, the latter replied that he was glad to hear it and hoped the United States would make "good use of it against the Japanese." Truman wrote in his memoirs that he never had any doubts about using the bomb as a military weapon; and the same day he told Stalin about it, he had orders passed down through the chain of command to do so. General Carl Spaatz's orders on July 24 from General Thomas T. Handy, the Army's deputy chief of staff, informed him as chief of the AAF's Strategic Forces that the 509th Composite Group, commanded by Colonel Paul W. Tibbets, Jr., was to drop the "first special bomb as soon as weather will permit visual bombing after about 3 August 1945 on one of the targets: Hiroshima, Kokura, Niigata and Nagasaki."

A warning to Japan to surrender, which became known as the Potsdam Declaration, was issued upon Truman's instructions by the Office of War Information on the evening of July 26, 1945, the day Churchill returned to London for his unfavorable election news. Truman had come to Potsdam with a draft of the warning. In final form it carried his name and that of Churchill and Chiang. Hurley, Truman's special envoy, had coordinated approval of the message with the Chinese leader, whom he had located in a mountain hideaway across the Yangtze River from Chungking. The President himself had fully apprised Stalin beforehand. The Russian was not a signatory because his country was not at war with Japan at the time.

The Japanese did not formally respond to the Potsdam Declaration, but two days after its issuance announcers on Radio Tokyo called it "unworthy of consideration," "absurd," and "presumptuous," and voiced Japan's determination to fight on.

The conference ended at four o'clock in the morning, local time, on August 1, 1945, and the US delegation headed home. Truman was in his fourth day at sea, following a brief stopover in Great Britain for lunch with King George VI, when Captain Frank Graham, the White House Map Room officer, handed him a message from Stimson, who had flown back to Washington, informing him that the "Big bomb" had been dropped on Hiroshima at 7:15 PM, August 5, Washington time, and that first reports indicated complete success "even more conspicuous than earlier test." Understandably elated, Truman, the next day at lunch in the wardroom, could not hold back telling the *Augusta*'s officers that the Pacific war might be over soon. "This is the greatest thing in history," he told some sailors. "It's time for us to get home." On August 7, the ship sailed into Chesapeake Bay.

In the few days before the Hiroshima explosion, the Soviets had begun raising new demands for Chinese concessions before they would declare war on Japan. But when the atomic bomb burst over Hiroshima, Stalin shut down all this dilatory talk and went back to war as fast as he could. On

August 8 at 5:00 PM, Soviet foreign minister Vyacheslav Molotov called in to the Kremlin the Japanese ambassador, Takao Saito, and told him that the following day the Soviet Union would consider itself at war with Japan. Averell Harriman, the American ambassador, had been summoned earlier the same day by Molotov and given the news, which came only a day late of fulfilling Stalin's promise to enter the Pacific war three months after the defeat of Germany.

The next day, as announced, Soviet army units launched attacks into Manchuria against Japanese occupation forces there. Resistance was not heavy and evidently some vanguard units at the three main attack points had advanced about twelve kilometers when the third atomic bomb was dropped, on Nagasaki, later in the day.

The following day, August 10, the Japanese government indicated for the first time its willingness to surrender. Radio Tokyo made an announcement that read in part: "The Japanese government is ready to accept the terms enumerated in the joint declaration which was issued at Potsdam, July 26, 1945, by the Heads of Government of the United States, Great Britain, and China, and later subscribed to by the Soviet Government."

The atomic bombs had had their intended stunning effect. And it so happened that almost all American planners were as surprised as the enemy. Within the United States, knowledge of the Manhattan Project had been so restricted that Roosevelt had not told Truman about it. Consequently, virtually all planners were laboring under the assumption that the war would last until late 1946, at least, which was what Marshall projected, thinking in terms of winning the war on the ground with air and naval support.

CHAPTER 3

★ ★ ★ ★ ★ ★ ★ ★ ★ ★ ★ ★ ★

CHOOSING UP SIDES

WITHIN the US government, responsibility for developing many of the postwar politico-military plans of action had fallen on a new administrative body composed of three civilians called the State-War-Navy Coordinating Committee (SWNCC). Their purpose was to bring foreign policy into military decision-making. As the war in Europe had drawn to a close, the Allies had set up the European Advisory Commission to weigh such considerations, and this step, in turn, had led to the creation of the SWNCC to support the American delegation. Asia, as well as Europe, then became a focus of interest for the SWNCC, as the war there came to an end. SWNCC members effectively functioned much like the National Security Council later would.

In a sense, these officials were charged with reconciling idealism with reality; fundamentally, this meant reconciling Truman's declaration that the United States wanted no reparations or territory with the need to keep the Soviets from filling the huge power vacuums in Europe and Asia. A stipulation the committee had to deal with was Stimson's formulation that the United States was unwilling to fight the Soviet army on the Asian mainland to thwart Soviet ambitions there. This was the view of most military planners, who had not needed Stimson to influence their thinking that war on the Asian continent was anathema. As a consequence, the Korean Peninsula was a region of special focus for the committee. Because, at its closest point, the peninsula was only 108 miles across the Korea Strait from Japan, and because it was nearly surrounded by coastal waters, the United States was in a favorable position to affect events there by a show of sea- and airpower. By contrast, Manchuria was not so favorably situated; it was beyond US help because of its more northern latitude, its being landlocked, and its long border with the Soviet Union.

The War Department's representative on the SWNCC was Assistant

Secretary John J. McCloy, whose staff backup was provided by the Strategic Policy Section of the Operations Division. The section was staffed chiefly with four bright, young colonels, three of whom had been Rhodes scholars. One was Dean Rusk, whose assignment had been arranged by Marshall. Rusk had been deputy chief of staff for Joseph Stilwell, and in that capacity had drafted most of Stilwell's messages to the War Department. Impressed by them, Marshall had inquired about who was writing them, and subsequently had had Rusk ordered to Washington.

After the Hiroshima blast, the key to establishing dominion over the Japanese-held territories was getting forces into position to accept the surrender of Japanese units there. This was basic to establishing a claim, though the long-term situation might change. McCloy's stand, consistent with Stimson's, was that the United States should not risk any sort of fight on the Asian mainland and that the future of the continent was mostly up to China and the Soviet Union. Accordingly, his position was that the United States should not concern itself with surrender ceremonies there. On this issue the State Department was more aggressive than the War Department.

The matter was resolved in an all-night meeting of the SWNCC in the waning hours of the war on September 2, 1945. Staff people were also present and actively participated in the discussion. Rusk, though in uniform, was inclined to support the State Department view. He argued that the United States should establish a "toehold" on the Asian continent in the Korean Peninsula because doing so would help check Soviet expansionism and would directly support Chiang's Nationalist Chinese government, which at this point was being pressed increasingly hard by the Soviets about concessions. His argument had unstated reverse implications, too, which were that American troops in Korea would pose a threat to Mao's control of China should the Communists depose the Nationalists. Rusk, more than anyone else at this session, knew this was more than a remote possibility; Stilwell, his former boss, deemed it a probability. Indeed, because Rusk had served in China with Stilwell, the SWNCC accorded unusual weight to what he had to say. Consequently, he was instrumental in carrying the argument that US troops should be dispatched to Korea to disarm Japanese.

When tired committee members finally agreed to this proposition, they instructed Rusk and another of the Strategic Policy Section's Rhodes scholars, Colonel Charles Bonesteel, who was its chief, to go into an adjoining room to decide what part of the Korean Peninsula they proposed the United States occupy. Pursuant to orders, the two young men excused themselves and began examining with care a National Geographic Society map of the peninsula. The region was as familiar to them as, say, Vermont might be to a Georgian, which Rusk was. Their task was to recommend a northernmost line across the peninsula. They looked for a natural demarcation, such as a river or a mountain range, but did not find any to accommodate this purpose. No appropriate river flowed across the peninsula, and the Taebeck Mountains ran down the peninsula like a spine, not across it. As a result, Rusk recommended to Bonesteel that the thirty-eighth parallel be the line south of which American troops would disarm Japanese soldiers in Korea. It was far enough north to put Seoul, the traditional seat of government, south of it. Bonesteel had no better idea and so he concurred. The SWNCC also affirmed Rusk's recommendation. The State Department proposed to the Soviet Foreign Ministry that Soviet troops accept the surrender of Japanese units north of the thirty-eighth parallel and that American troops do the same with those south of it. In the same message, the State Department, at the behest of the SWNCC, recommended to the Soviet Union that its troops accept the surrender of all Japanese soldiers in Manchuria.

Rusk was personally surprised when the Soviet government agreed to his proposal. It so happened, however, that his studied though uninformed choice had historical significance. In 1896 the Russian and Japanese governments had signed an agreement that divided the Korean Peninsula at the thirty-eighth parallel into two spheres of influence. And during recent years when Japan had controlled the entire peninsula, its army had used the thirty-eighth parallel to divide the region into two administrative zones.

The basic order to effectuate the surrender of Japanese army troops in Korea and throughout the rest of Asia was issued by Hirohito. His "General Order No. 1," as it was entitled, was written by the SWNCC staff support people, including Rusk, and was imposed on the emperor by the President through MacArthur. Other provisions of the order specified that in China, Formosa, and in that part of Indochina north of the sixteenth parallel and from Burma to the Solomons, the Japanese would surrender either to British or to Australian commanders. In Japan itself, the Philippines, and the rest of the Pacific's vast expanse, Japanese units were to surrender to American commanders. Getting Allied troops in place would take considerable time, so September 2, 1945, was designated as the date.

On this great day the main surrender ceremony aboard the *Missouri* lasted 26½ minutes, as scheduled, and was transmitted live by radio throughout the world. It was over by 10:57 PM, September 1, 1945, Eastern War Time, and for the first time in a long time, the United States was at peace. But it was a fitful peace. Before the end of the year, Truman would be telling an audience of Washington reporters at the annual Gridiron Dinner: "Sherman was wrong! I'm telling you *peace* is hell." He was making a joke; he did not realize that already he was contending with the mounting pressures of what would be recognized as another war, though of a different kind.

True to form, Forrestal had begun noting some of the bad omens in his diary. On September 7, 1945, he made this entry:

[Foreign Service Officer Burton Y.] Berry's dispatches from Bucharest and Harriman's from Moscow indicate that the Russians have no idea of going through with the Allied Nations' statement of policy about Rumania, namely to permit the establishment of free and democratic institutions in Rumania. . . . [Ambassador Laurence A.] Steinhardt makes strong recommendations from Czechoslovakia against the complete withdrawal of American forces. He says this will be an open invitation to the Communists in the country and to Russian influence from without to take over.

None of these warnings seemed to have had much impact on military-policy formulations in Washington, though. On October 16, 1945, Forrestal wrote that the nation was "going back to bed at a frightening rate, which is the best way I know to be sure of the coming of World War III." He was deeply disturbed about how Truman, encouraged by Congress and the public, was dismantling the armed forces. He started passing out to friends copies of Rudyard Kipling's poem about a peacetime soldier, "Tommy Atkins," which included these lines:

> *For it's Tommy this, an' Tommy that, an' "Chuck 'im out, the brute!"*
> *But it's "Savior of 'is country" when the guns begin to shoot.*

In thanking him for the poem, Bernard Baruch, who had been advising Presidents since World War I and was another former financier, wrote him: "This is my second round trip into war, peace and the aftermath, and I can tell you that already I see nothing but a repetition of what took place after the war."

Neither man would find assurance in Truman's long-term military policies, which by year's end the President had had time to formulate. Forrestal, in particular, was upset because, in the first of these, Truman supported the Army's reorganization plan as set forth on Capitol Hill by J. Lawton Collins in October 1945. In December of 1945, Truman sent Senator Elbert Thomas, an ally and the Utah Democrat who was chairman of the Senate Military Affairs Committee, his administration's formal proposal for unification and asked him to hold hearings and to prepare legislation to conform with it as much as possible.

Truman's second long-term military-policy recommendation had to do with spending. In January 1946, a few days after the Army's victory parade, he delivered his budget message to Congress. The rationale behind its very stringent numbers for the military was this: they would get no more than one-third of what was left after the government paid all its fixed expenses. The President had set forth this thinking during a cabinet meeting in December. His formula presumed that world affairs did not impose their imperative independent of other considerations. It had nothing to do with reality in the world and almost everything to do with his own deep-seated philosophies. He was banking on Stalin's conduct not becoming too outrageous. He hoped that he could keep the Soviet leader in line through personal dealings and by having a monopoly on atomic bombs.

Most Americans seemed to think the bomb was a panacea. This was the attitude of the budget director, Harold D. Smith, a holdover from Roosevelt's administration. Truman actually was developing some misgivings on this point, his plans for dealing with Stalin notwithstanding. He managed to suppress them because he was convinced that the military had to be cut way back, all things considered. Smith tried to reassure him. During a budget-planning conference, he said, "Mr. President, you have an atomic bomb up your sleeve." To which Truman replied, "Yes, but I am not sure it can ever be used."

Disagreements about China policy are what led to the great rift that, as the public perceived it, generally divided Democrats and Republicans throughout the long cold war to come. The split had to do with how to fight the spread of communism, or at least with how hard to fight its spread. By the time Truman sent Marshall off to Chungking as his personal emissary in December 1945, his administration's official position was that Chiang, in some way, had to share power with Mao. This was based on the assessment that the Nationalists were not strong enough militarily to gain control of all of China. At the time, the Communists were administering a region in which 90 million of the 450 million Chinese lived. Marshall was ordered to mediate some sort of compromise agreement between the two sides. It was hoped that his personal prestige and that of the United States would be enough to get this done. When this proved not to be the case, Marshall was ordered to use US financial and military aid as leverage to make Chiang compromise. As a result, when Mao's forces defeated Chiang's about four years later, Republicans blamed Democrats for having lost China to the Communists. The accusation, which left an indelible impression, was that the Truman administration had so undercut Chiang that he had no chance of winning. The monumental power shift in China also split the US military, putting Marshall on one side and MacArthur on the other, with the former, as Truman's emissary, associated with the Democrats.

For many Americans, it made no difference that Truman, with Marshall's substantial help, later formulated the basic, ultimately bipartisan politico-military policies and plans that the nation used to fight and win the cold war; what mattered was that the Democrats had lost China — a sin for which they could never redeem themselves. The Democratic party was perceived as soft on communism no matter how hard its mainstream members tried to prove otherwise. Subsequent events served only to reinforce that perception.

Within the US government, the split about how to support Chiang began during World War II. A measure of Roosevelt's early optimism was his seeing to it that Chiang was invited to the Cairo Conference in 1943 to sit as an equal, supposedly, with himself and Churchill. The American President was determined to have Chiang emerge from the war a powerful leader of a unified China that would stabilize all of Asia. Roosevelt was also optimistic about Chiang's tapping China's enormous manpower potential to create a huge army to fight the Japanese.

From the outset, Roosevelt's hope that Chiang's Nationalist army would become a mighty force to turn against the Japanese was frustrated by the Chinese leader's preoccupation with Mao. A civil war had raged since 1927, and during its course the Nationalists and the Communists had become implacable enemies. They had been forced to ease off one another following Japan's conquest of Manchuria in 1931, but nothing fundamental had changed about their relationship. Chiang was determined to husband his forces for resumption of full-scale civil war. Establishing the pattern that would be followed later, the Roosevelt administration then began using US lend-lease aid as both carrot and stick to prod the Nationalist leader. Stilwell, who as the senior US general in China was the agent of this policy, failed to make Chiang's army aggressive and effective; but it was not for lack of trying. Chiang would not be moved.

Lack of success with the Nationalist leader eventually caused American war planners, led by Marshall, to modify their objectives in China. Hopes that Chiang could defeat the Japanese there dissipated; the modified aim became that of keeping China in the war, tying down about twenty Japanese divisions. To this end, Stilwell was ordered to use US military aid for a different purpose: to entice Chiang into working out some sort of accommodation with Mao so that together their forces would fight the Japanese invaders full-time. Stilwell was, as before, unsuccessful; to help him, Roosevelt sent Hurley over. But by then Stilwell and his top advisers had concluded that the United States was backing the sure loser in China, a leader who could probably survive the war against the Japanese but would eventually be driven from power by the Communists.

From the outset of the world war, the US military was divided over China; some American airpower advocates allied themselves with Chiang and undermined Stilwell. Their staunch advocacy was a portent of trouble to come, in the immediate and the long terms. Hurley eventually allied himself with them. Chief among them was Brigadier General Claire Chennault, a

Chiang favorite who had formed the Flying Tiger units and was the number-two-ranking Army aviator in China under Brigadier General Clayton Bissell. The Chennault claque, which did not include Bissell, helped Chiang eventually get Stilwell relieved.

Chennault was motivated by ambitions for himself and for the Army Air Forces. In the summer of 1942 he wrote Stilwell that all he needed to neutralize Japanese activity in Burma and India and to inspire Chiang's troops to victory in China was five hundred combat planes, one hundred transports, and "complete authority in this theater." Chennault later recognized this to be a ridiculously low number and modified his request accordingly, but he never lost faith that airplanes could win with little or no help from the Army, the Navy, or Chiang.

He predicated his thesis mostly on the planes' being able to destroy Japanese shipping in the South China Sea, a notion that Stilwell derided. Who will hold the airfields when the Japanese attack them? he asked. The idea of winning a war without soldiers was ludicrous, he thought. Marshall agreed with Stilwell completely, but Roosevelt was enticed by airpower concepts, as Truman would be; it seemed such a relatively inexpensive way to bring American military power and technology to bear and at the same time risk relatively few American lives. (Chennault got his ideas into the Oval Office through Harry Hopkins, Roosevelt's principal adviser, using young Joseph Alsop — who had formerly been Chennault's special aide — as an intermediary. The well-connected Alsop was a distant cousin of Eleanor Roosevelt and had access. President Roosevelt liked to exploit such informal sources for information.)

When China was central to American war plans in the Pacific, the idea was to build air bases there from which bombing raids on Japan could be launched. To do this, regions of China within range were going to have to be retaken. But, subsequently, the B-29 was developed — it had the unheard-of range of 1,500 miles — and then the Navy and the Marine Corps achieved great success advancing through the Central Pacific to the Gilbert and the Marshall islands. The northernmost of these was about 2,500 miles from Japan, but the Marianas, the next grouping of islands north, was within the B-29's range; the island of Saipan was 1,450 miles from Tokyo. So, given this alternative and the difficulties in China, Marshall and other strategists concentrated the war effort up through the islands. Chennault's proposal for exclusive use of airpower in China was thus ignored. One consequence was that his thinking retained the allure of an idea untested. Ultimately, it would wed politically the more ardent airpower advocates with those who wanted to use unlimited force to stop aggression by Asian Communists.

Even before Hurley resigned, the dilemma for those formulating long-range US policy in China was this: the only alternative was to support Chiang, and yet, as Stilwell explained to Stimson, "nothing can be done in China until we get rid of" him. If Mao's Communists won out, China would move toward the Soviets, but Stilwell deemed getting out of China the best of the bad choices facing the United States, lest the Chinese people be forever alienated and a Communist China move even closer to the Soviets. "Unless we stand clear," Stilwell warned, "we will be classed with France, England, Holland, and Chungking." He suspected that most Chinese associated Chiang's rule with the old order, which was tied to colonial exploitation. In contrast, Hurley's black-and-white judgment was that the United States should help Chiang all it could, despite his shortcomings, because he was fighting Communists.

Postwar, within the State-War-Navy Coordinating Committee, the State Department view prevailed in regard to China. The committee recommended sending the Marines into north China to accept the surrender of Japanese commanders there and to disarm enemy soldiers. Their mission and the environment in which they operated proved to be even more complicated than that of the US Army soldiers in Korea. In China, both the Communist and the non-Communist factions were well organized and poised to rush into the territories the Japanese had controlled. Among the concerns was that both sides in this civil war would press into service Japanese soldiers who surrendered to them unless Americans were present. There were about a million Japanese soldiers in China.

Among the specific objectives assigned the Marines was occupying various ports and airfields that could be used to transport Chiang's troops north to assume control once the Japanese there were repatriated. This amounted to significant involvement in the civil war, but the Joint Chiefs preferred to view it in terms of facilitating the restoration of control by the properly constituted Chinese authorities. Confusion and disagreement inevitably developed. General Albert Wedemeyer, Stilwell's successor as the senior American general in China, thought the Marines' presence constituted a decision within the Truman administration to be more actively involved in the civil war. He thought that the Marines were there to facilitate the Nationalists' taking control of all Chinese territory south of the Great Wall. The difference in interpretation was profound, though in execution, subtle; in either case, the longer the Marines remained in China, the greater the pressure to see things as Wedemeyer did.

By November 1945, pressure had built up to the point that the Joint Chiefs were aggressively seeking answers to whether and when the Marines should be withdrawn. In this regard, a JCS paper about what to do precipitated a meeting of the Secretaries of State, War, and Navy on November 27, 1945. Under Secretary of State Dean Acheson, who participated in these discussions, summarized for the group the conclusions reached at this high-level parley. These conclusions were at cross-purposes — or as Acheson later put it, they created a "duality of policy," although, he added, "it was not so clear to us at the time." Byrnes, Patterson, and Forrestal decided that the Marines must be kept in China for the time being so as to help move Nationalist units north and support them; they also decided that concurrently the United States should seek to arrange a truce between the Nationalists and the Communists, if they began fighting over areas held by the Japanese, and, more fundamentally, that the United States should "support the efforts" of these two main factions to bring about a "political settlement under Chiang Kai-shek." How any US emissary could win the trust of the Communists, for the purpose of mediation, while aiding the Nationalists militarily was not properly thought out. According to Acheson, the "conclusions seemed to emerge inevitably from the facts."

The same day these formulations were made (and the day Marshall left Washington for Leesburg), Hurley conducted the dramatic press conference during which he resigned as the President's special emissary to China. At the time, as noted, he was in Washington for consultations and a rest. He must have perceived the direction administration policy was taking and decided that he, as a prominent Republican, was being set up for blame, although the reason he gave reporters for resigning was that he was being undercut by Communist sympathizers in the State Department. He evidently had in mind John Carter Vincent, director of the Office of Far Eastern Affairs, who had worked for Stilwell. And probably also Acheson. Acheson had had Vincent develop State Department thinking for the November 27 meeting of the secretaries. (In another five years, by which time millions of Americans would be almost hysterical about communism, Republican conservatives would trace "losing" China to the policy-making of this period. For Acheson's role in these deliberations, Republican conservatives would call him a "fellow traveler" of Communists and *Life* would editorialize that he, Secretary of State by then, should be fired for believing that "coexistence" with Communists was possible.)

The conclusions reached by the secretaries on November 27 became the basis for the instructions (in the form of a letter from Truman) that Marshall carried with him to Chungking in December, though considerably more wrangling ensued before he left. Marshall's primary goal, as written in the letter dated December 15, 1945, was "the unification of China by peaceful, democratic methods . . . as soon as possible." To achieve this,

Marshall was "authorized to . . . state, in connection with the Chinese desire for credits, technical assistance in the economic field, and military assistance . . . , that a China disunited and torn by civil strife could not be considered realistically as a proper place for American assistance along the lines enumerated." This leverage and the authority to control the support of the Marines, which the President delegated to him, were the chips Marshall took with him to encourage Chiang to make concessions. In the overall scheme of things, they did not amount to much, but Marshall had even less ability to force reconciliation on the Communists. And so, later, Chiang would seem to be a victim for having been singled out, as if he were the only party pressed to compromise his position. What became more obvious daily to top policymakers in the Truman administration, as these instructions indicate, was that the United States had virtually no ability to control events in China, short of inserting US Army soldiers and Marines into the fighting; Republican conservatives disputed this, though.

Marshall's endeavors in China had a hopeful beginning. Within a month, he achieved a cease-fire in northern China, excluding Manchuria. He also fostered political discussions about the makeup of a coalition government. By late February 1946, he even got Nationalist and Communist representatives to sign an agreement entitled the "Basis for Military Reorganization and for the Integration of the Communist Forces into the National Army."

Nonetheless, these positive steps did not fundamentally alter the situation, because both sides remained determined to win absolute control of all of China. Marshall had stepped into the middle of a winner-takes-all struggle between two enemies bent on destroying each other. The Soviets, who had occupied Manchuria so as to disarm the Japanese, complicated matters for Marshall by facilitating a transfer of power there to Mao's forces.

American disengagement from the civil war followed in stages. First to stop was US military aid to the Nationalists, which Marshall recommended halting as part of a plan to foster a unified Chinese army. Next came cessation of Marine support; this followed Marshall's conclusion that Chiang had forgone even the pretense of a peaceful resolution and had adopted a policy of force. By the end of 1946, Truman, on Marshall's recommendation, had ordered the Marines out of China, fearful that they would be drawn into the fighting otherwise. A portent of the disputes that later exploded because of these policy decisions was Forrestal's dalliance in having the Navy ship the Marines out. Marshall complained about the delay to Truman, who, in turn, ordered the Navy Secretary to get the job done forthwith. Marshall himself left China shortly thereafter, his failed mission having lasted almost exactly a year.

CHAPTER 4

★ ★ ★ ★ ★ ★ ★ ★ ★ ★ ★ ★ ★ ★

STEPPING OUT OF THE PAST

TWO DAYS before sending his message on military reorganization to Senator Thomas's Military Affairs Committee, on December 18, 1945, Truman invited discussion of the subject during a cabinet luncheon. Forrestal told him that on a couple of different levels he did not like what the President was doing. He said that Truman's plan incorporated only Army thinking and that Thomas's committee was "a highly prejudiced body which had reached a conclusion in advance." He said that the Navy had not fully presented its case and that he was worried it would never get the chance.

Truman's response surprised all in attendance. He said he did not plan to muzzle anyone in the military establishment, uniformed or civilian, and that each could speak his mind on the subject. There would be only one proviso, which Clark Clifford informed Forrestal about the next day by phone. Before giving contrary views during congressional testimony, an officer was to state that he understood that the announced policy of the administration was to favor such a proposal.

Forrestal, who preferred a low profile for himself, added his own restriction for Navy Department personnel. Thinking it unseemly for officers to engage in public debate with the President, he issued a directive that ordered all in the Navy and the Marine Corps to refrain from stating opinions on unification unless testifying before Congress. He later rescinded it, but the practical result was that the Navy would be slow to catch up with the Army and the Army Air Forces in presenting its case directly to the public via the media.

Alexander Vandegrift, Commandant of the Marine Corps, thought that Forrestal's approach was much too gentlemanly and that the Navy Department was not being nearly as aggressive as it should be. "As I tried to impress them the other day at a conference," Vandegrift wrote Marine Lieutenant General Holland Smith, "we have got to forget methods that we have used before because as much as we hate to realize it, this is not the day of when knighthood was in flower and it's more like a street brawl than a tilting joust." Vandegrift was also dismayed that so many admirals did not comprehend the dangers ahead. His letter to Smith also addressed this point. "I feel that our Navy friends rested too long on their laurels and the belief that no harm could come to them," he said. "It is just within the last few weeks that they seem to realize the fact that Mr. Roosevelt is dead. Things are not particularly encouraging on the question of the merger. Everyone is now working very hard on testimony, etc., and we still hope we can beat it, if not in the Senate then in the House."

Vandegrift was convinced that nothing less than the Corps's survival was at stake, and he had had the whole war to stew about the notion. Ironically, he had been tipped off about what to expect right after the great Marine victory at Guadalcanal. There, with US fortunes at low ebb, the First Marine Division under Vandegrift had been put ashore and then virtually abandoned after a Japanese fleet surprised the US-Australian covering force and in a few short hours sank five cruisers and one destroyer while damaging other ships. Vandegrift and his men saw bright flashes on the horizon and heard distant explosions, but they did not know the outcome until morning, when the bodies of American sailors began floating ashore, black from burns and oil, and ships such as the cruiser *Chicago*, its bow shot away, limped past off the Marines' beachhead. The battle of Savo Island, as this brutal contest at sea came to be called, was the worst naval disaster in American history, and many had consigned Vandegrift's Marines to a similar fate, predicting another Bataan or Wake Island.

Vandegrift himself took the precaution of having Lieutenant Colonel Merrill Twining, his operations-and-training officer, draw up plans for dispersing and fighting on in the jungle should the Marines' enclave be overrun. But even with the Japanese totally controlling the air for a time, the Marines fought off strong enemy units and eventually broke out of their enclave. They were relieved by the Army's Twenty-fifth Infantry Division after more than four months of daily combat, by which time three-fourths of them had contracted malaria. Almost seven hundred died on Guadalcanal, but they and the survivors made US control of this vital island a foregone conclusion and thus were key to stopping Japan's advance in the South Pacific. Furthermore, the Marines' victory at Guadalcanal was the first US land victory of World War II.

Yet shortly thereafter, indirectly, Vandegrift got word about what the Army wanted to do with the Corps from the Twenty-fifth's commander, none other than Major General J. Lawton Collins, whose name would be applied to the Army's reorganization plan after the war. Both were at

Nouméa, New Caledonia, at the same time for a couple of days — Vandegrift on his way to Australia to rest and refit his division, Collins on his way to Guadalcanal to pick up where Vandegrift had left off. Nouméa had become a focal point for the initial American buildup in the Pacific. The roster of officers serving there or passing through read like a *Who's Who* of present and future American leaders. Lieutenant Junior Grade Richard M. Nixon worked there as a Navy air transport officer. Lieutenant Commander Arleigh Burke was there the same time as ambassador's son John F. Kennedy, another lieutenant junior grade, under whom he would later serve while Chief of Naval Operations.

The occasion that prompted Collins, himself a future Army Chief of Staff, to remark about the Corps's future was an informal gathering at the Army's senior officers' billet at Nouméa. Present by chance was Merrill Twining, who had been invited by his brother Nathan, an Army brigadier general and future Air Force Chief of Staff. Merrill Twining would attain three-star rank, but not become Commandant. During a social hour, these officers and other generals enjoyed a wide-ranging, spirited discussion that included the subject of postwar reorganization of the military. Evidently, Collins was not aware of a Marine's being present or had forgotten about him; being a reserved southern gentleman and rather intellectual, he was not given to gratuitous insult. Collins told the group that the Corps should be eliminated and its duties absorbed by the Army. The objection was that the Marines were trying to become a second army. The others present seemed to affirm this view, but Collins's assertions were particularly upsetting to Twining since Collins was acknowledged to be one of Marshall's favorites and probably espoused his views.

Collins's remarks deflated Twining, who was puffed with pride about what the Marines had done at Guadalcanal. First thing the next day, he reported all to Vandegrift. (He would have done so the evening before, but the general was having dinner with Admiral William Halsey.) The upshot was that when Vandegrift became Commandant about a year later, he brought Merrill Twining with him to Washington and ordered him to form a "Marine Corps Board" to study amphibious concepts and postwar planning. Concurrently, he made Twining his principal strategist for the upcoming reorganization battle.

The American public was confused and even appalled by the vitriol that otherwise even-tempered military men began spewing on the eve of the first postwar congressional hearings on unification. Their confusion was natural, since they had little sense of how the services differed and how rivalries between them had grown over the years. The services had slowly developed different ways of doing things, different ways of fighting wars, different strategic concepts. And postwar strategy-making, which is a complicated business, was what the reorganization struggle was most fundamentally about. Service pride or esprit de corps was secondary. The interservice rivalries that the combination of strategic differences and service pride had engendered greatly complicated Truman's plan to reorganize the US military.

The oldest rivalry was that between the Army and the Navy, though until World War II it had been kept in check. To casual observers, it amounted to little more than contests between students at associated academies; however, a stoic countenance masked the resentment of many Army officers, who believed that during the years between the world wars Congress had gutted the Army to favor the Navy with appropriations.

Earlier in the nation's history, Army and Navy differences were of little consequence because each was so small. Nor during the early days did their personnel have much contact with one another. Some Army and Navy intellectuals traded ideas back and forth, but generally each service dealt with the other only superficially. Each liked it that way. Since the Revolutionary War, each planned and executed its own operations, virtually independent of the other.

Then, during the 1940s, in the war against Japan, leaders of the two services were forced to work closely together. The strategy in that vast region was a compromise between what MacArthur wanted and what Nimitz wanted. Making the relationship work was difficult, and the Army-Navy disputes that arose were a harbinger of troubles to come. Victory brought with it new global responsibilities for the United States; Army and Navy leaders could address them only if they carefully integrated their strategies. Much more rapidly changing weapons technology and very lean postwar military budgets intensified this need. So did the emergence of airpower as an equivalent force. The era of multiservice warfare had arrived.

Of the two groups, Navy officers had the better understanding of the other's operations, and probably still do. As Edward Beach pointed out in *The United States Navy*, it is axiomatic "of naval warfare that the entire purpose of navies and sea power is to influence the land" — which is not to say that the Navy merely supports the Army, a notion that many Army officers tend to believe. The Navy's role is far more extensive than ferrying troops across the sea and supplying them.

Of considerable consequence, given the fight against reorganization that Forrestal was about to lead, was the fact that the two services' different ways of doing things was largely a function of their vastly different organizational structures. As noted, the Army had developed a centralized, or vertical, command structure; the Navy had developed a horizontal command structure, one that dispersed command and control. Each service had rigidly locked on to these organizational concepts during the years between the Civil War and World War I.

For armies, the consummate organizational form conceptualized during this period was the German general-staff model. This system had been evolving for decades, but the world took notice when in 1870/71 Prussia vanquished France in six short months by completely immobilizing the French army and forcing Paris, under siege and without food or hope, to surrender. No one doubted at that point that Germany had the strongest army in the world and that its general staff was largely responsible. Soon afterward, the armies of such countries as Turkey, Italy, Russia, and Japan set up versions of the German general staff and copied the associated schools and methods.

In the United States, the Army ordered a change in uniform for West Point cadets. Suddenly, the spiked German helmet replaced the kepi of Napoléon's great armies as the dominant feature of what they wore. The Marine Corps adopted the spiked helmet as well. But the Army wanted to go well beyond this visible manifestation of German influence. The German general-staff model became its ideal. General William Tecumseh Sherman called the German system of military organization — the key feature of which was a vertical command structure — "simply perfect."

Sherman, of Civil War fame, was Commanding General of the Army from 1869 to 1884 and during that period was key to a US Army renaissance. He had been a college president at the outbreak of the Civil War, so the Germans' emphasis on the scholarly study of warfare and on promotion based on merit, rather than solely through political patronage or seniority, appealed to him. The whole idea of their orderly processes did. At West Point he encouraged the postbellum trend toward a broader study of the military sciences, and greatly bolstered professionalism by enhancing the careers of those who were graduated from advanced schools, such as those for artillery and engineering and a third, which he founded, the forerunner of the Command and General Staff College. However, one counterproductive aspect of Sherman's emphasis on professionalism was that the Army's thinking became more insulated from outside influences, such as Navy thinking. As the Army became more professional, it became more parochial.

The key exception to such parochial tendencies was the Army's attitude toward German military thinking, so it was not surprising that Karl von Clausewitz's book *On War* got a rousing reception in the United States when first translated into English in 1873. *On War* had an enormous impact because a top Prussian officer had written it and because it presented a cogent philosophy of warfare as well as a sound rationale for the military profession. There had never been anything quite like it before. The book became mandatory reading for every US Army officer and remains so to this day.

Predictably, Emory Upton, a key adviser to Sherman, formally recommended adoption of the German general-staff model upon returning from a two-year, around-the-world fact-finding trip undertaken after Sherman ordered him to prepare an evaluation of the world's best armies. Sherman endorsed Upton's proposal, making it the Army's official position; nonetheless, it stalled. Primarily because of different cultural and governmental traditions in this country, Congress, which controlled setting up the military's command structure, would not allow military leaders to duplicate the German general-staff system here — except in name.

Nevertheless, Americans who wanted to reorganize in the German way were given a boost in 1895 by the publication of Spenser Wilkinson's analysis *The Brain of the Army*, an explanation of how the United States might incorporate some aspects of the German system. Wilkinson saw particularly great value in the vertical command structure that the German approach entailed. His book impressed the right people — the most important being Elihu Root, who in 1899 became William McKinley's Secretary of War. (Given later history, it is significant that young Henry Stimson was then serving under Root, his mentor.)

Root's major contribution was to push organizational reforms through Congress that were loosely patterned after the German example. The General Staff Act of 1903, passed during the administration of Theodore Roosevelt, was the culmination of his work. It established for the first time a vertical command structure in the Army. All the various Army departments, whether combat arms or support bureaus, were subordinated to the supervision of a Chief of Staff, who, in turn, reported to the Secretary of War, who was accountable to the President, the constitutional Commander in Chief. This was an important, fundamental change.

The old system had been a form of the horizontal-type command structure in that it had more than one line of authority. One emanated from the Commanding General, who was the top battle commander and controlled what were essentially military matters. A second emanated from the Quartermaster General, who controlled support activities, such as supply and engineering. The Quartermaster General reported directly to the Secretary of War, whereas the Commanding General reported directly to the President. This arrangement created confusion and made rivals of the Commanding General and the Quartermaster General.

Army officers quickly developed a liking for the new vertical command structure because a single military figure, the Chief of Staff, finally controlled all the Army. No longer did two top officers vie for power and have to coordinate to get things done.

Coordination was, of course, the Navy way, and Forrestal was determined to keep it so. As in the Army's case, the period between the Civil War and World War I had a profound impact on the Navy. The Navy stopped being a semisocial organization during this time; professionalism prevailed for it, too. The Navy seemed to find its soul, its reason for being. And some reorganizational reforms were involved, as well.

Rear Admiral Stephen Luce was the chief figure to set this evolutionary process in motion. He eventually became a person of great influence in the Navy, far beyond that normally associated with even the two-star rank he attained. It is said of Luce that he taught the Navy how to think. In 1873 he founded the Naval Institute, a private society, to foster scholarship in all aspects of the Navy — tactics, strategy, history, and so forth. Located on the Naval Academy grounds, the organization began publishing books and a monthly magazine called *The Proceedings of the United States Naval Institute*, or *Proceedings*, as it is commonly known. In 1884 Luce caused the Naval War College to be founded at Newport, Rhode Island, by congressional authority. One year later he enticed to the school its most famous instructor and the US Navy's first and still foremost theorist, Alfred Thayer Mahan.

At the time he was recruited to teach, Mahan was a minor figure in command of a small ship in the Pacific. Luce had read some articles Mahan had written, but was probably more intrigued by his potential because of who his father was. Dennis Hart Mahan had taught at West Point for forty years and was a leader in military education for decades. He placed great emphasis on the need for military men to study history; this was probably his most enduring contribution. When the academy forced him to retire, he stepped off a boat into the Hudson River and drowned — by suicide, some say.

His son, who chose Annapolis instead of West Point for his schooling, did not disappoint Luce. The younger Mahan's lectures were published in 1890 as the volume *The Influence of Sea Power upon History, 1660–1783*. It was a much broader study than Clausewitz's, whose book was a philosophy of warfare. Mahan's was a philosophy of history. He espoused a sort of social Darwinism and talked about the inevitability of war, while glorifying national expansion. Focusing on the British example, he explained the central role of a navy as a nation's source of international power. The book was precisely what all good Englishmen believed but no one, not even one of their own, had expressed so clearly before.

The tepid response the book initially received in the United States warmed considerably once word spread about the very enthusiastic reaction of the British, who had the largest navy in the world.

Some of the older US officers resented Mahan's success at the Naval War College, though, and unfortunately one of them was responsible for all officer assignments. The chief of the Bureau of Navigation, who had no understanding of the power of ideas, perhaps because he had never acted on one of his own, ordered Mahan out of the classroom and back to a ship, where he finished his active-duty service career. "It is not the business of a naval officer to write books," the bureau chief said.

Theodore Roosevelt, when he became President, signaled to the rest of the world that the United States was taking its place in the front rank of nations and that its instrument of power would be its Navy. He concurrently was reshaping the Army, with Root as his chief mover in that realm. As Bradley A. Fiske, a prominent Navy intellectual and reformer who was aide for operations for several years during Woodrow Wilson's presidency, once observed, no President since George Washington had taken his responsibilities as Commander in Chief so seriously as Theodore Roosevelt. And though his popular military image is that of an Army officer leading a charge up San Juan Hill, his most significant and enduring military contributions were to the Navy, which, because of them, celebrates his birthday, October 27, as Navy Day.

It was Roosevelt who caused the nation to build a two-ocean Navy, the Spanish-American War having demonstrated to him the need. The newly acquired colonial possessions made it necessary. He caused the Panama Canal to be built, too; the primary catalyst for it was not commerce, but Navy needs. He had in mind the Mahan dictum that a nation must concentrate its battle fleet against an adversary. The canal facilitated this; because of it, the Atlantic and Pacific fleets would not have to sail around the tip of South America in order to rendezvous. During the Spanish-American War, the battleship *Oregon*, under full steam, had needed sixty-seven days to sail from San Francisco all the way down around Cape Horn and then all the way up the east coast of South America to the Caribbean Sea.

Roosevelt's signal to other nations about the new US leadership role was his ordering the "Great White Fleet" of battleships to circumnavigate the globe. And because he had had the judgment and daring to pluck from the ranks a brilliant young officer named William Sims, that fleet was more than nicely painted the color that gave it its name. Though its ships were obsolescent, the US Navy was by then recognized as having the best gun crews in the world. Sims, a genius of sorts in practical application, had made it so, first as Inspector of Target Practice and then as Roosevelt's Naval aide. A few years earlier, the US Navy had had some of the worst.

Of more lasting consequence was Roosevelt's lack of success in effecting the organizational changes within the Navy that he wanted. Thus, years later, the Navy, even more set in its ways, would fight change much more adamantly. Roosevelt's objective was to reorganize the Navy along the same lines that Root, his War Secretary, was reorganizing the Army; this amounted to centralizing authority by instituting a vertical chain of command, with a Chief of Naval Operations (CNO) at the top. Roosevelt's intent was to make the CNO responsible for the Navy's military operations and all its so-called bureaus, such as Yard and Docks, Ordnance, and Navigation, whose ranking officers currently reported to him. But he was blocked primarily by Senator Eugene Hale, a Republican from Maine who chaired the Senate Naval Affairs Committee. Hale, who had built up thirty years' seniority by the time he retired in 1911, more than anyone then serving in the Senate, had a long history of association with the powers that be within the Navy. About twenty years earlier, before his election to the Senate, he had declined President Rutherford Hayes's invitation to become Secretary of the Navy. He insisted that the Navy's command structure be left alone.

Also undermining Roosevelt's campaign to reorganize the Navy was a split among his chief reformers. Although Sims and Fiske supported him, Luce and Mahan did not. The latter two preferred improving the existing structure by incorporating changes that fostered conformance with the structure of the British navy. US Navy organization had remained unchanged since the administration of Martin Van Buren, and, as with the Army's old organizational scheme, its supporting rationale was that the Navy's strictly military operations, such as war planning and management of combat operations, required no special expertise. Supposedly, only its civil operations did — such activities as legal affairs, supply, management of the navy yards, and engineering. The premise of this scheme was that the Secretary of the Navy was competent to manage the fleet during wartime, so no career officer in overall command of combat forces reported to him. But this arrangement had proved impractical during the Civil War and by the late nineteenth century was so outmoded by the pace of technological change and world events that it had become dangerous for the United States.

Fiske continued touting Roosevelt's reorganizational reforms after the latter's presidency ended. And six years later, when Woodrow Wilson was in office, Fiske finally succeeded, though only to the degree that Luce and Mahan supported. This limited change came about no thanks to the new Secretary of the Navy, Josephus Daniels, who, true to his liberal Democratic roots, preferred the status quo, which he described as a "calculated policy of dispersion." Such was his inherent distrust of the career military.

In a fashion, Fiske justified Daniels's wariness of career officers. Circumventing Daniels, the admiral persuaded allies in Congress to attach to the Navy appropriations bill a rider that prescribed reorganizing the Navy. It specified that a CNO would be "responsible for the readiness of the Navy for war and be charged with its general direction." This amounted to the vertical command structure of the German army.

Daniels vigorously resisted this change. And because — through word association — it smacked of the general-staff idea, many in the Navy were convinced that Army generals would somehow be in charge of the fleet. The Navy Secretary succeeded in getting Fiske's proposed rider altered, though he could not block change altogether. The war in Europe had created a sense of urgency in Congress and was enhancing the influence of career military men like Fiske. Contrary to Daniels's wishes, the new law, which passed in 1915, established the CNO position, although with less authority than Fiske had tried to have legislated. The new law specified that the CNO "shall, under the direction of the Secretary of the Navy, be charged with the operations of the fleet, and with the preparation and readiness of plans for its use in war." This was still a big change, but the CNO would not be allowed to control the separate bureau chiefs, as Fiske had wanted. They remained independent of the CNO and reported directly to the Navy Secretary. To a large extent, therefore, the Navy's dispersed system of authority stayed in place. Coordination remained a Navy byword. The idea of Army-style centralized control from the top did not seriously impinge on Navy thinking again until after World War II, when simultaneous deep spending cuts made a bitter rivalry out of the two services' differences. The intensity of the Navy reaction was presaged by short-lived hearings on the subject conducted in the spring of 1944 by Congressman Clifton Woodrum's Committee on Post-War Military Policy. They quickly became so rancorous that Roosevelt, through back channels, had them abruptly canceled because he wanted the services fighting the nation's enemies, not one another.

The three other interservice rivalries started developing during the World War I years. The most openly intense was that between Army aviators and the Navy. A second involved the same Army aviators and Army ground officers. The third was that which preoccupied Vandegrift, the rivalry between the Army and his Marine Corps.

The first two were the product of a debate about the future of airpower in military affairs — the extent of it and who should control it. From the outset, Army aviators perceived themselves as misunderstood by Army ground officers and the Navy and felt stifled because they were caught in between. The result was that they started agitating for an independent service all their own. The man who first led this effort was Brigadier General William ("Billy") Mitchell, who emerged from World War I the highest-ranking Army aviator. At Saint-Mihiel, he had marshaled a force of 1,481 aircraft, the largest air armada the world had ever seen. In his view, this exhibition was only a small measure of airpower's grand future.

Two men greatly influenced Mitchell's thinking — Major General Hugh Trenchard of England and General Giulio Douhet of Italy. The three were contemporaries, Mitchell being the youngest. Douhet was the first to write down some coherent principles for applying airpower to warfare. For many years, his book *The Command of the Air,* first published in Italy in 1921, was to air forces what Clausewitz's work *On War* was to armies and Mahan's *Influence of Sea Power upon History* was to navies.

Mitchell's basic proposition was that an air force should supplant the Navy as the country's strategic force in being — a shocking idea at the time, since all but a few aviation zealots deemed planes incapable of sinking a warship. There was no proof it had ever been done, even during World War I. Furthermore, since planes did not yet have the range to fly across oceans, the idea that an air force could project US military power far beyond American shores was considered ludicrous. In fact, the attitude prevailing within the Navy was that so-called airpower would never amount to much. According to naval historian Elting Morison, "the [Navy] General Board scarcely recognized the existence of the plane in 1919, and in 1920 it admitted only that the plane was the adjunct of the capital ship, which was the backbone of the Fleet." The most important of these capital ships were battleships, which, by definition, were the most heavily armored, slowest, and largest warships, whose main batteries had the biggest guns of the fleet.

The nation had been a sea power ever since it became a world power at the turn of the century. The Navy was not exactly the senior service, as in Great Britain, but it was first among equals, or so the American admirals believed. The Secretary of War was more senior than the Secretary of the Navy in the presidential order of succession, but that did not affect the general perception among the nation's leaders. From the earliest days of the Republic, they looked to the Navy to project power, if only occasionally, and to keep foreign intruders away. It was the obvious strategic concept to follow because of oceans on two sides. Having a comparable natural advantage, Britain had become a sea power. Without this natural advantage and pro-tection, Germany and Russia, for example, had been forced to develop their armies; they were basically land powers. So the US Navy was deemed the country's force in being, even though, like the Army, it had suffered through periods of neglect. If war broke out, the basic war plan had always been to have the Navy, virtually alone, protect the nation and its interests while the

Army raised and trained its forces. No one questioned this strategy until Mitchell after World War I; his pronouncements then were given widespread attention partly because he was a hero and a high-ranking officer with many official and social connections in Washington. That he was an aviator also helped focus attention on himself and his ideas. During the twenties, the decade of "early morning horizons," as Anne Morrow Lindbergh described it, airplanes and aviators were subjects of intense public fascination. Eventually, all the publicity Mitchell generated hit a nerve.

Mitchell was born into a Wisconsin family of wealth and influence. Both his grandfather Alexander Mitchell and his father, John Lendrum Mitchell, were Democratic congressmen, and he was very much a product of the state's reformist political traditions. A friend during his youth was Douglas MacArthur, the same age, who along with his mother lived in Milwaukee while his father, Arthur, an Army lieutenant colonel, was posted to the Department of the Dakotas in Saint Paul, Minnesota. The senior Mitchell and the senior MacArthur were close friends, having served together in Wisconsin's Twenty-fourth Regiment during the Civil War.

Billy Mitchell's military career began auspiciously. At age eighteen he was the youngest US Army officer to serve in the Spanish-American War, an appointment no doubt facilitated by his father, who was then in the Senate. And at age thirty-two he became the youngest officer ever to have been appointed to the Army General Staff.

Mitchell's Army branch initially was the Signal Corps, which in 1907 got the first military aircraft because they were deemed ideal communications and observation vehicles, though not considered to be of much more use than that. The mechanically inclined and adventuresome Mitchell was attracted to them, became a pilot, and ended up flying combat during World War I. He expected to be named chief of the Army Air Service after that conflict; but there were few good command positions in the peacetime Army then and a surplus of generals, so a more senior ground officer got the position instead. Mitchell was appointed his deputy.

Not being in charge did not lower Mitchell's profile, though. Virtually all the pilots, the media, and most of Congress seemed to perceive him as the chief anyway. He became a one-man lobby for the advancement of military aviation. Accustomed to money and having been around politics all his life, he moved easily through Washington's power circles. He had a home in Washington and another, Rosemere, in Virginia's hunt country near Middleburg. He entertained lavishly to advance his views, and his widowed mother supplemented his income for that purpose. His independently wealthy wife, Caroline, also contributed, though she felt his lobbying was extravagant.

That he got away with being so independent for so long is remarkable, since he was still in uniform; mostly it was due to his popularity with the general public. Mitchell had his enemies, of course, and jealousy was sometimes a factor. He was resented by some men in the military, where social standing, as a rule, is normally a function only of rank. Furthermore, some of them had a sense that Mitchell's high profile was not appropriate for a military man. For Navy aviators, who to a man disliked him intensely, personality was not so much a factor, though. They correctly surmised, even before Mitchell said so publicly, that he wanted all military aviation controlled by an Army air arm, or by an independent air force. Almost everyone else in the Navy hated him because of his pronouncements about airpower making seapower obsolete.

Mitchell directed his first public salvo at high-ranking Navy officers in February 1920. Testifying before members of the House Military Affairs Committee, he charged: "They look with abhorrence — all navies do — on a system of attack against their vessels by airplanes, because it will mean eventually the diminution or entire elimination of their strength on water, and many think, therefore, that helping aviation will diminish naval strength."

Soon thereafter, Mitchell and the Navy were joined in battle. Sensibilities were easily offended in those days. Within hours, Navy Secretary Daniels was bitterly protesting what he called Mitchell's intrusion into naval affairs. The response of Secretary of War Newton Baker was to give Mitchell a tongue-lashing and order him to keep quiet about the Navy.

Mitchell was not cowed, but for a time he did become more cautious. He began making his charges more general, not so obviously directed at the Navy. A *New York Times* headline about one of his speeches reflected his new tactic and the theme he would develop: "Declares America Helpless in Air War." The *New York Herald* later reported one such speech that read like H. G. Wells's fantasy *The War of the Worlds*. In it Mitchell described the aftermath of an air raid on Manhattan.

> The sun rose today on a city whose tallest tower lay scattered in crumbled bits of stone. . . . Bridges did not exist. . . .
>
> The sun saw, when its light penetrated the ruins, hordes of people on foot, working their way very slowly and painfully up the island. A few started with automobiles but the masses of stone buildings barricading the avenues soon halted their vehicles. Rich and poor alike, welded together in a real democracy of misery, headed northward. They carried babies, jewel cases, bits of furniture, bags, joints of meat and canned goods made into rough packs.
>
> Always they looked fearfully upward at the sky. . . . Bodies lay like revelers overcome in grotesque attitudes. . . . The majority had died swiftly of poison gas.

The speech was his imagined description of destruction wrought by strategic bombers, which, even at this early date, were becoming the basis of American airmen's military doctrine. Mitchell, as well as Douhet and Trenchard, believed that nations' leaders would surrender rather than subject their populations to such punishment. It followed that nations without air forces to counter in kind were helpless. This strategic-bombing doctrine, with which General Curtis LeMay came to be so closely associated during World War II (and the Vietnam War), would be central to the reorganization struggle. Strategic bombing was a way airmen could wage war and conceivably win it without involving soldiers and sailors; therefore, it boosted their proposal for an independent air force.

When Mitchell started moving public opinion his way, Navy leaders reacted aggressively. Hoping to preempt him, they announced that the Navy itself would conduct tests to see if planes could sink ships. The man they put in charge of these tests was Chester Nimitz, then a thirty-five-year-old captain. Mitchell deserves virtually all the credit for the Navy decision to conduct tests, though some aviation proponents within the Navy moved matters along — men such as Fiske and Rear Admiral William Moffett, who detested Mitchell and would soon head the Bureau of Naval Aeronautics.

The Navy's target for the tests was the *Indiana*, a battleship of Spanish-American War vintage. The proceedings were secret. Why this was so later became a matter of great controversy in Congress. Prodded by Mitchell, some members were to accuse the Navy of trying to mislead them.

The explosives used were static charges tied to the deck of the ship. The planes dropped only dummy bombs, ostensibly to measure more effectively how well bombs penetrated decks. William Leahy, then forty-five and the director of naval gunnery, wrote the final report. "The entire experiment points to the improbability of a modern battleship being either destroyed or completely put out of action by aerial bombs," he asserted.

On the basis of this conclusion, which was released to the media, congressmen got the impression that Mitchell's challenge had been given a fair test. They also believed that damage to the *Indiana* had been minimal. Then, somehow, an ill-gotten photograph of the damage landed in the hands of the editors of the *London Illustrated News*, who published it. Damage appeared extensive.

Mitchell denied providing the photograph, though when irate members of the House Military Affairs Committee called him to testify, he showed up with a raft of drawings, charts, and more photographs from the *Indiana* test that Captain C. M. H. Roberts, an armament specialist with the Army Ordnance Corps, had obtained. Roberts had managed to get the Navy's permission to observe the tests.

The session was one of those hearings that a committee chairman and his allies use principally to attack established policy — in this instance, Navy policy. These committee members had a natural bias favoring the Army over the Navy (which was the reason why twenty years later Truman sent his military reorganization plans to a Military Affairs committee). Mitchell probably coordinated his testimony ahead of time with various members, who orchestrated the famous aviator through it, allowing him to expound at length. They sensed that the Navy had backed itself into a corner, that it could no longer avoid a very direct and very public challenge of planes versus a battleship, a challenge involving Mitchell's Air Service. And their intent, given the leading questions they posed to Mitchell, was formally to set in motion the challenge, which was done eventually by committee member Bascom Slemp, a Virginia Republican who later became President Calvin Coolidge's secretary, or chief of staff. "It seems to me," he said, "that the principal problem is to demonstrate the certainty of your conclusions." To which Mitchell replied, with great satisfaction, "Give us the warships to attack and come and watch it." Within two days resolutions passed in both houses of Congress that endorsed a plan to have airplanes try to sink a warship.

A resolution does not have the authority of law, however, so the test was still not a sure thing. Navy allies then went to work in earnest. The Naval Affairs committees in the House and the Senate, the Navy's power bases, convened hearings. In these settings airpower advocates within the Navy were called as witnesses. And so, too, unavoidably, was Mitchell.

The newest and most notable Navy air advocate to appear was none other than Rear Admiral William Sims, sixty-three by this time and nearing the end of his remarkable career. Though his reputation was strongly associated with battleships, he had that rare intellectual discipline that allowed him to detach himself emotionally from his own beliefs and past, and keep his mind open to new ideas. "The Navy should have solved this problem long ago," he testified.

Prompted by the *Indiana* tests, Sims had given airpower careful thought and decided to conduct some theoretical tests of his own. He wrote Fiske, his friend, explaining his plans for what he called a "money game" — "that is, give each side at the War College a certain amount of money; one side to build [with the money it had] sixteen battleships, six airplane carriers, and six battle cruisers; the other, to build twenty-two aircraft carriers." Each side was to have the same supporting vessels. Several weeks later, Sims reported to Fiske in a personal letter the outcome and its impact on those involved. The side composed only of aircraft carriers had won decisively, sinking most of the battleship fleet in the mock battle.

From that point on, Sims, who had been skeptical of airplanes' potential use to the Navy, became an unwavering advocate, though he steadfastly opposed creation of a separate air force. "If I had my way," he told Fiske, "I would arrest the building of great battleships and put money into the development of the new devices and not wait to see what other countries are doing."

Sims was so certain that aviation would have a great impact on the Navy that after the hearings he invited Mitchell to speak at the Naval War College. "Can it be that the Navy is reluctant to give up the big ships to live in?" he asked Mitchell rhetorically during a private conversation. He knew, of course, that for many in the Navy the answer was yes.

Service on battleships had become the standard route to the top ranks, so it was former battleship captains who so adamantly resisted Mitchell's challenges. Allied with powerful congressmen on the Naval Affairs committees, these men presented the rest of Congress and Mitchell with the prospect of endless hearings on airpower. Various subcommittees were going to duplicate the efforts of others interminably, it seemed. Then Senator William Borah, an Idaho Republican, forced decisive action. He introduced a resolution that called for the Navy to halt all ship construction until Congress could determine what constituted a "modern navy."

Quickly, Navy leaders reacted before matters were taken completely out of their hands. They announced plans for bombing tests off the Virginia capes on Chesapeake Bay; aircraft of the Navy, the Marine Corps, and the Army Air Service would attempt to sink four captured German vessels at anchor — a submarine, a destroyer, a cruiser, and the battleship *Ostfriesland*, which had fought at Jutland. The planes would try to locate and hit a second battleship, the *Iowa*, which would be under way by remote control. In the same announcement the Navy also pledged to provide later a third battleship to the Air Service for tests of its own.

By involving their pilots and planes in the first tests, wherein the *Ostfriesland* bombing was the center-ring show, Navy leaders narrowly averted a winner-takes-all contest, one in which they conceivably could have lost control of their air arm to Mitchell's Army Air Service. The participants, the press, and the public did, in fact, see the tests in an adversarial context. And Mitchell would be the clear winner. The "monster" 2,000-pound bombs Mitchell's pilots dropped on the *Ostfriesland* sank the great battleship. However, since the admirals could claim at least some credit because of Navy and Marine participation, their allies in Congress forcefully used the sinking to shake loose funds for a carrier. In a matter of days after that event, Congress appropriated funds for the Navy's first carrier, the *Langley*.

Mitchell expected even better days for himself to follow. During the presidential election campaign the previous fall, Republican Warren Harding, induced by the British example, had endorsed reorganizing the nation's military establishment by setting up a Ministry of Defense with coequal Army, Navy, and Air Force departments. Thinking along these lines, various congressmen had introduced bills to combine under one command the air forces of the Army, the Navy, and the Marine Corps — the same idea Mitchell had proposed.

Then, just when Mitchell was tantalizingly close to realizing these dreams, they began slipping away. Reorganization bills could not get out of committee and onto the floor, where Mitchell, at least, believed they would pass. Reorganization of the military required, as noted, concomitant reorganization within Congress, and members of Naval and Military Affairs committees were not willing to risk the seniority and power they had accumulated. Only a very compelling need would drive reform through such resistance. And the ineffectual Harding was not willing to risk the political capital to try. He had been in office only three months when the *Ostfriesland* was sunk but already had moved military reorganization way down on his priority list of campaign promises.

Still atop his list was restoring comity between the Army and the Navy. To facilitate this, Harding stunned the military by putting in charge of the Army John Weeks, the Naval Academy graduate who blocked Chief of Staff Pershing from even meeting with the President. But Pershing was pleased that Weeks's first order of business was to stamp out in Army ranks the "Bolshevik bug," the name the general used to describe a contemporary strain of insubordination that, in Pershing's mind, Mitchell suffered from badly (the Russian Revolution was not yet four years old). Mitchell's air theories did not grate on Pershing so much as his attitude that the Air Service should receive carte blanche appropriations, even though the Army as a whole was being virtually disbanded.

Pershing's response to Mitchell was to appoint as the latter's superior Major General Mason Patrick — a West Point classmate of Pershing's who was also a ground officer. Being passed over a second time as chief of the Air Service was almost more than Mitchell could abide. When in protest he offered to resign, his hand was called immediately. He was escorted into the office of Major General James Harbord, the Army deputy chief of staff, who told him to submit his letter of resignation that afternoon if he was so displeased. Mitchell backed down and was never quite as confident.

Ironically, what most made Mitchell a figure of historical importance was his demise. He was crushed by the powers that be in the Navy and the ground Army because he was such an influential advocate for airpower. That is how Army aviators perceived it, anyway, and their witnessing firsthand what happened to Mitchell caused them to set as their goal establishing their own independent service and not settling for anything less.

Mitchell's end followed a series of warnings issued to him about making his criticism so public. President Calvin Coolidge did not reappoint him assistant chief of the Air Service because Army Secretary Weeks and the Navy Secretary threatened to resign if he did.

There followed for Mitchell an exile of sorts at Fort Sam Houston, Texas. This entailed a demotion to colonel, since his brigadier general rank was tied to his former high position. He was also given a written warning to desist.

Mitchell kept his emotions in check for about six months, all the while becoming more frustrated than ever. He confided in future Army Air Forces Commanding General Hap Arnold — a good friend, though much lower in rank at the time and seven years younger — that "air power doesn't seem to be getting anywhere at all." A Navy air disaster caused him to speak out, finally. The dirigible *Shenandoah*, en route to the Iowa State Fair, where it was billed as a "battleship of the skies," broke apart at six thousand feet as it crossed a squall line. Thirteen crewmen were killed.

For a response, reporters turned to Mitchell, who decided to use this tragedy and another Navy air crash the day before to spur a national debate on aviation policy — or at least this was the appraisal of Ira Eaker, who had been Mitchell's executive officer and later became deputy chief of staff of the Army Air Forces under Arnold. According to S. L. A. Marshall, the city editor of the *El Paso Herald* (for whom the ensuing Mitchell story was his first big break professionally), Mitchell confided in Marshall that he wanted to invite court-martial.

Three days after the *Shenandoah* went down, Mitchell issued an inflammatory statement more than six thousand words long. Introducing this document, he told reporters: "These accidents are the result of the incompetency, the criminal negligence, and the almost treasonable negligence of our national defense by the Navy and War Departments." The written portion contained all kinds of incendiary charges — among them, that nonaviators were risking the lives of crewmen, forcing them to fly "flaming coffins"; and that "a battleship today is a useless element in the national defensive armament of the United States."

Reaction was swift. Weeks immediately relieved Mitchell of his duties. Then, in order to seize the initiative from the aviator and his allies in Congress, Coolidge announced the appointment of Dwight Morrow, a Morgan Guaranty banker (and the future father-in-law of Charles Lindbergh), to head a blue-ribbon panel to study the country's aviation policy. His report, the one Forrestal later recommended to Truman for reading, would propose the creation of an Army Air Corps that would be larger and somewhat more influential than the Army Air Service was. And within a month, Coolidge approved Weeks's recommendation to court-martial Mitchell for insubordination and conduct prejudicial to the service.

A month following notice, proceedings commenced in Washington. The trial lasted about two months; the deliberations, less than thirty minutes. Mitchell was found guilty on the first secret ballot by at least two-thirds of the members of the court-martial board, all of whom were Army generals. MacArthur, whose public criticism of his superiors decades later would yield similar travail, was one of them. Mitchell's punishment was relief of command, rank, and duty for five years and forfeiture of all pay during the period. Coolidge later modified the order by half, but Mitchell chose to resign his commission and leave military service.

When after World War II an inexorable movement toward reorganizing the US military developed, all that had happened to Mitchell and his associates was still a fresh memory. Arnold, Eaker, Spaatz, and many other wartime leaders had been close to him and largely blamed the Navy for his fall. And because the Army Air Forces had emerged from World War II perceived as the service of the future, there was hell to pay for the Navy.

The years had not ameliorated feelings. During Mitchell's trial, Arnold had been caught leaking anti-Navy and anti-Army General Staff documents to friends in the media and in Congress and was himself banished. His exile was to Fort Riley, Kansas, which he described as "the worst facility in the entire Air Service." Initially, Arnold was offered even less desirable options: resignation from the service or court-martial. The top military leaders were trying to extinguish the Mitchell cult. After talking it over with his wife, Eleanor, Arnold decided to fight back; he told them to court-martial him. Wary of more bad publicity, the Army backed down and sent him off to Fort Riley instead.

Arnold's document suppliers, whose names he kept secret, had been Eaker and Major Millard Harmon (who, like his cohorts, later became an Army Air Forces general). At a farewell party for Mitchell at Bolling Field on the eve of his departure for Texas, Arnold, his two accomplices, and about twenty other aviators informed him that they planned to resign their commissions en masse to protest his not being reappointed assistant air chief. Mitchell reproached them sternly. "Not a one of you will resign," he said. "Not a one. And that's an order." Somberly, he asked, "Who will carry on . . . when I'm gone?"

The names of all in attendance are not known, but few, if any, did resign. Had Mitchell instead encouraged their protest, the top Army Air Force command structure during World War II would have been remarkably different. So, too, would have been the tone of the military reorganization debate after the war. That debate was driven by Army Air Forces officers more than any other group in uniform, and their leadership cadre was formed by the two dozen men at this gathering. Virtually all of them became generals. One of them, preferring anonymity, commented years later to Mitchell biographer Burke Davis: "We obeyed him the rest of our lives. And long after he was dead." Their feelings about the Navy never lost the personal edge sharpened during the twenties and thirties. Indeed, events reinforced old prejudices.

The degree to which this resentment devolved and turned into hate was evident in another battleship bombing test, in 1937, involving Curtis LeMay. The incident was an indication of how worried the Navy was about Army Air winning control of Navy land-based missions. At noon on August 12, the *Utah*, playing the part of an enemy ship intent on attacking a coastal city, was to enter a huge, 100,000-square-mile quadrant off the California coast. The *Utah* was supposed to remain within this sector until noon the following day, during which time Navy land-based reconnaissance planes were to find it for the Air Corps, whose planes would try to intercept and bomb it. Lieutenant Colonel Robert Olds, a senior officer who had served under Mitchell during the *Ostfriesland* test, was in charge of the Army air crews; thirty-one-year-old Captain LeMay was with him in the lead plane, a B-17, as chief navigator.

On two occasions during the test the Navy's planes radioed the *Utah*'s location to the bomber fleet. The first time, by chance, the bombers were loitering nearby. Within minutes they arrived over the target area, only to find an empty sea. Olds lodged a complaint that evening and the Navy apologized, saying that the reading had been miscalculated by one degree. Given the distances involved, one degree moved a sighting sixty miles.

The next morning the reconnaissance planes and the bombers headed out to sea again in search of the *Utah*. The Air Corps crews were almost desperate. As in Mitchell's day, great significance was given to the test, at least by the Army Air Corps, even though no notoriety was associated with it this time. Major General Frank Andrews, who was in charge of all combat units in the Air Corps, had even flown out from his headquarters to ride along as an observer with Olds and LeMay. Andrews was a contemporary of Arnold; he was a year older, and both were West Point graduates.

Upon receiving word of the second sighting, LeMay quickly plotted his locations and determined that the bombers could not reach the target before the noon deadline. He and his companions cursed the Navy for another subterfuge.

Olds saw only one thing to do. He ordered his crews down under the fog bank below for a last-resort reconnaissance of their own.

Ten minutes before the deadline, Olds and his copilot let out a war whoop. A big battleship lay directly ahead. Blind luck had led them to it. It was one degree latitude off the reported Navy sighting — again, sixty miles.

Olds ordered his men to attack the battleship and drop their loads of fifty-pound dummy bombs — made of wood and corrugated metal, and filled with water — despite the fact that hundreds of sailors were lounging on the decks. Obviously, they had been told the exercise was over; they should have been below. When they spotted the planes streaking toward them, they ran for their lives. Some bombs hit the ship, spraying wood splinters and metal shards. No doubt some sailors were injured, maybe even killed, by debris. Casualties, if any, are unknown; Navy records about the exercise have disappeared.

That night Olds and Navy officers had long, contentious phone conversations. As LeMay remembered it, the issues they argued were not why Air Corps bomber crews bore down on American sailors or what the sailors were doing on deck in the first place. They fought over what the day's events had proved. In the end, neither side was convinced of anything new. The battleship Navy sailed off for a few more years of bliss, not to be disturbed by upstart aviators. And another generation of Air Corps officers went away talking about how much they hated the Navy.

Another example of events reinforcing old prejudices — though a different set of old prejudices — occurred later in 1937 when Army Chief of Staff Malin Craig fired General Andrews. This event was rooted in the estrangement between Army ground officers and Army pilots. Andrews's offense was his endorsement of the Air Corps Reorganization Bill during testimony before the House Military Affairs Committee. The legislation would have granted the Air Corps its own budget and control over its promotion list. In a replay of what happened to Mitchell before his court-martial, Andrews lost his job, was reduced in rank from major general to colonel, and was exiled to Fort Sam Houston. His key staff members were fired, too. Colonel Hugh Knerr lost one rank and was eventually forced to retire. Lieutenant colonels George H. Kenney and Joseph T. McNarney would, in the long term, be luckier; both became top Air Force generals. But Kenney's prospects, especially, looked grim at the time. Craig made Kenney — who became a ranking bomber commander during World War II and the Strategic Air Command's first commander — an infantry instructor at Fort Benning, Georgia.

After Marshall succeeded Craig, the situation improved for Army aviators. Most notably, in June 1941 legislation was enacted that created the larger and more autonomous Army Air Forces out of the Army Air Corps. The latter had been the transformed version of the Army Air Service effected by Congress during the twenties, about six months after the Morrow Board's recommendations were published. The main reason for American aviators' improved status under Marshall involved the fighting already under way overseas: with great success, Germany had made airpower central to its war plans. Another reason was that Marshall and Arnold had been good friends for decades. In 1914 during Army maneuvers in the Philippines, Lieutenant Arnold was so impressed by Lieutenant Marshall that he wrote his wife, Eleanor, to say, "That man will one day be the Army Chief of Staff." These two men's personal relationship notwithstanding, most Army aviators deemed other Army officers narrow ground-pounders who would never see planes as anything more than flying artillery.

Their animosity toward Navy officers was much more personal. Their distaste for them had class overtones — as if air officers were poor boys struggling against an entrenched, narrow-minded aristocracy. Arnold alluded to this feeling in his autobiography. Referring to early attempts by air officers to establish their own service, he wrote: "The Navy raised hell like a country gentleman finding poachers on his property."

Not surprisingly, the next generation of Army aviators picked up on this attitude. LeMay, who was commissioned a second lieutenant in 1929 out of Ohio State University, carried it with him into retirement. More than forty years after Forrestal's Navy began maneuvering to block Truman's plan to reorganize the military, he said of admirals, "When it comes down to what's good for the country and what's good for the Navy, they pick the Navy every time; to hell with the country."

The Army–Marine Corps rivalry, which had come to haunt Alexander Vandegrift, started at a place in France called Belleau Wood. There, during World War I, Marines fought a battle that forever changed the role and image of the Corps. Marines had always been looked upon as the Navy's soldiers, but after Belleau Wood, the Corps, to the chagrin of the Army, began developing an identity independent of the Navy.

In the days of sailing ships, when crews of frigates latched on to adversaries' ships with grappling hooks and tried to board, Marines were the men who carried the fight in hand-to-hand combat. The age of steam ended this kind of warfare, so the Corps's mission for a time was limited to more prosaic work, such as guarding the Navy's ships, brigs, and bases. Gradually, the Marines also became a sort of colonial police force; although such duty was sometimes difficult and dangerous, it was not, as most Marines saw it, the stuff of dreams and glory. During the entire 142-year history of the

Corps up to the time of Belleau Wood, Marines had at most fought only small-unit skirmishes, usually against poorly trained, native populations in such places as Haiti, the Philippines, the Dominican Republic, Nicaragua, and the area around Peking. The pretext for this work was usually the protection of American lives and property. The duty of securing advanced sea bases for the Navy's ships prominently involved the Corps during World War II. But none of these traditional roles justified Marines' being a few hundred feet south of Belleau Wood during World War I when a lead division for the kaiser's armies began probing Allied lines as prelude to a final drive on the capital of France. Belleau Wood is northeast of Paris, far from the sea, and that is why many Army officers became quite exercised about having Marines there in the first place.

The Corps's chief recruiter when the United States declared war on Germany and the Central Powers was Major A. S. McLemore. His recruiting slogan "First in the Fight" was no more than a wish, really, and was not based on any precedent. Yet it hit a responsive chord among the patriotic young men of the day, who had an intensely romanticized view of war and were eager to get into combat. They queued up in long lines at Marine recruiting stations that rapidly met their quotas. The Corps got to pick and choose rather carefully who was going to join. Many were turned away. The ranks included a number of students from Ivy League colleges, as the Corps started developing during this period a certain cachet it has nurtured ever since. McLemore's slogan was so successful, and so captured the image Marine leaders wanted the Corps to project, that its slightly modified form, "First to Fight," is still a standard. Response to it also led to creation of another, "A Few Good Men," which trumpets Corps exclusivity. Better still, McLemore's slogan became self-fulfilling.

In spite of obstruction by Pershing and the War Department, a Marine regiment of 3,600 men was on the first troop convoy to France. Woodrow Wilson had overruled the Army's objections, concluding that any unit that wanted to fight ought to be allowed to do so. Old academy ties had also been instrumental. The War Department had informed Major General George Barnett, the Commandant and an Annapolis graduate, USNA class of 1881, that the only troop ships then available were filled with Army soldiers. But Admiral William Benson, the Chief of Naval Operations, USNA class of 1877, had, unbeknownst to the Army, held three other transports in reserve for the Marines. At the last instant, he produced them for their convenience and off they went to war with the Army.

Once the Marines arrived in France, the Army employed other dilatory tactics, but gradually they impressed Pershing with their spit and polish, and, after some months, pressing events worked in their favor. General

Erich Ludendorff, the German commander, launched a huge offensive that he hoped would end the war before US forces were built up to sufficient size to have an impact. Pershing had been keeping American units out of battle, insisting on more training. He had also been holding out for an all-US sector along the front; he was under orders to avoid assigning American units piecemeal to serve under British and French commanders.

Ludendorff's offensive forced Pershing to modify his plans. The Germans broke through French lines in the Chemin des Dames region of the northeast and drove thirty miles in seventy-two hours, an astounding advance, given that hideous trench warfare had deadlocked the front for three years. At one point, the Germans were less than fifty miles from Paris. The French government had begun moving its offices from the capital when Pershing ordered five American divisions into the breach. One of them was the newly formed Second Division. One of its two brigades was composed entirely of 9,444 Marines. Another Marine regiment and a Marine machine-gun battalion had arrived in France and joined up with the first regiment shipped over.

Pershing put an Army officer in charge of the Marine brigade — his personal chief of staff, Brigadier General James Harbord, the same fellow who later, as the Army's deputy chief of staff, reined in Billy Mitchell.

The scene Harbord and his Marine brigade marched into as they and thousands of US Army troops advanced up the Paris-Metz Road toward their fateful rendezvous with the enemy was made for movies. Thousands of beaten French soldiers fleeing the Teuton charge jammed the highway with at least a hundredfold more civilians. A few edged along in vehicles, others in wagons or on horseback. But most walked, struggling with bundles of possessions as they did. Some pulled livestock in tow. The Americans, advancing in the opposite direction, initially rode in trucks. Ironically, given later history, the drivers taking them into the nation's first war of this century were Vietnamese soldiers of the French colonial forces.

The object of the American divisions' advancing up the road was, roughly, to block the German advance as far back as possible. Congestion was such that, before long, American commanders decided that it would be faster to walk than ride, so they had their men off-load and begin marching east toward Château-Thierry. The Marines got as far as some wheat fields near the forested hunting reserve of Belleau Wood, which was north of the road and about a square mile in size. Attacking from the north, the Germans had reached Château-Thierry, where they wheeled west toward Paris. Instead of advancing directly along the road, the 461st Imperial Infantry, acting on directions from the kaiser's son, an army group commander, filtered down into Belleau Wood.

By this time both sides were alerted to the other's presence, though the fact that the Marine brigade lay directly in front of the Germans was entirely by chance. The brigade was only one of many American units, all the rest Army, stretched out for miles along the road, ahead and behind them. The Germans had dug into the small forest behind boulders and trees, setting up dozens of machine-gun positions with an interlocking fire. They intended to use Belleau Wood as a stronghold from which to stage another thrust of their advance. When the Germans' initial probing attacks began, the Marines, who were directly below the woods, in hastily dug positions, repelled them. Harbord's quick response was to order the Marines to attack.

German machine-gun bullets cut the wheat stalks like a scythe, and Marines fell right and left, but others kept advancing. "Come on, you sons-of-bitches. Do you want to live forever?" screamed Gunnery Sergeant Daniel Daly at one critical point, exhorting his men forward. Allied artillery support was minimal; there had not been time. And there were no tanks behind which to advance. The Marines resorted to rifle fire and bayonets. They paid a very heavy price; 1,497 were casualties the first day — and the battle lasted twenty. Both sides courageously fought hand-to-hand in a deadly miasma of smoke and dust; splintered trees and broken bodies lay all around. High superiors far from the scene spurred both sides. German leaders wanted the first major battle with a US unit to be an object lesson. But at the end, it was an American, Major Maurice Shearer, who was able to report, "Woods now U.S. Marine Corps entirely."

Had it not been for Floyd Gibbons of the *Chicago Tribune*, the battle would not have had the impact it did. Americans would not have known until after the war that Marines had done the fighting. By then their feat of arms would have been overwhelmed by the enormous scope of Army operations and achievements. Without Gibbons, Belleau Wood certainly would not have caused an Army–Marine Corps rift.

Gibbons was with the Marines when the battle began; at the time he was probably the best-known American war correspondent. He had achieved fame during passage to France before the United States entered the war. Germany was waging a campaign of unrestricted submarine warfare, so Gibbons deliberately purchased a ticket on Cunard's 18,000-ton *Laconia*, thinking it was a likely target. His choice was a good one; the *Laconia* was indeed torpedoed and it sank. Gibbons was one of the survivors in a lifeboat that was approached afterward by the surfaced submarine.

"What ship was dat?" the captain shouted from the conning tower, curious about his victim. There followed a bizarre interrogation at sea, which Gibbons dutifully recorded and later filed as part of an absorbing narrative that caused a sensation back home and was noted throughout the world.

Lawmakers read the article aloud in both houses of Congress, entering it into the *Congressional Record*. That the Germans did not care a whit what they were sinking and whom they were killing had been revealed in strikingly personal terms by the submarine captain's questions.

And so it was that when the Marines advanced across the wheat fields toward the blazing guns of the 461st, they were observed by a reporter of international renown. "I am up front and entering Belleau Wood with the U.S. Marines," Gibbons wrote for the first sentence of a skeleton dispatch. After sending if off by runner, Gibbons was struck down by three bullets, one of which ripped out his left eye, and an inaccurate report began circulating that he had been killed.

This sad news reached the American censors in Paris, where the one assigned to review Gibbons's report was a friend of his. As a tribute, he allowed the first line to stand as written. Ordinarily, on orders from Pershing, all references to unit number and branch of service were excised from news dispatches. Security precautions were very exacting during World War I.

Because of Gibbons's account in the *Tribune*, editors throughout the country knew exactly which American soldiers were carrying the fight at Belleau Wood. And since that information had been published by the *Tribune*, they did not feel constrained about doing so themselves. Furthermore, from their standpoint, Gibbons's presence and his injuries had enhanced the battle's importance; they ordered to Belleau Wood their reporters, who began producing great quantities of copy to satisfy the public's insatiable appetite for news from the front. Word that American boys were taking all the kaiser could give and tossing it back in full measure electrified the country. It was what people had yearned for months to read. Marines became national heroes during the extended battle. Their victory was an occasion for national joy.

Almost immediately the victory became legend. Premier Georges Clemenceau of France was so moved he announced that the Marines had "saved Paris." This was an exaggeration, although, in fact, the Germans never again got closer to Paris than Belleau Wood. Clemenceau's perspective was distorted by exhilaration that Americans in large numbers were finally entering the war and by a sense that the tide had turned in the Allies' favor. However, it is no exaggeration to say that some Americans came to believe that the Marines had won the war. Franklin Roosevelt, then the Assistant Secretary of the Navy, visited the scene and on the spot ordered a change in Marine uniform regulations to honor permanently the men who won the battle. Henceforth, all enlisted men throughout the Corps were to wear the Marine insignia of eagle, globe, and anchors on their collars; previously only officers had worn it.

After the war, Wilson asked the Belleau Wood Marines to pass in review in front of the White House. And in 1926 the battle was the subject of a hit movie, the biggest money-maker Metro-Goldwyn-Mayer had ever produced and one that became an enduring classic of the silent cinema. *The Big Parade* starred John Gilbert and was cowritten by Laurence Stallings, a former *Atlanta Journal* reporter who had quit that paper to join the Marines at the outbreak of war. He had become an officer and fought at Belleau Wood, where he lost his right kneecap in the fighting. Later, his whole right leg was amputated. By contemporary standards, *The Big Parade* was a fairly realistic movie in showing the horrors of war. Writers and journalists such as Stallings and Gibbons continued telling and embellishing the Belleau Wood story. Because of one long-forgotten reporter, a new word entered the war correspondent's lexicon. Seeing the Marines, who had no shovels, using knives and mess kits to scrape shallow depressions into the ground for protection, he called the hollows "foxholes," a description so apt it stuck.

Army men who fought during World War I never reconciled themselves to the acclaim Marines won for the Corps at Belleau Wood. Even the lowly doughboy knew that they had not been the first in the fight; the first fights had involved Army troops at Seicheprey, Catigny, and then Château-Thierry. And such matters being as they are, these soldiers would argue among themselves about which encounter constituted the first US victory of the war.

"We did it first at Seicheprey!" claimed soldiers of the First Division's Eighteenth Infantry Regiment.

"The hell you say! We did it first at Catigny!" answered those of the First's Twenty-eighth Regiment. They would commence this vocal arrangement whenever in formation together. It was that kind of war for Americans, and they were that kind of generation. The Marines' position on the issue was that at Belleau Wood they had won the first *major* US victory.

What also rankled Army men was how small the Belleau Wood operation was. The Army had as many men in France cooking biscuits as the Corps had fighting there. Three months after Belleau Wood, 665,000 US Army soldiers, accompanied by a relative handful of Marines, slammed against the Germans at Saint-Mihiel, creating a gigantic battlefront. And two weeks after that, 820,000 attacked at Meuse-Argonne. Furthermore, some Army doughboys had helped out at Belleau Wood.

But beyond such jealousy, the real reason Army leaders were upset about Belleau Wood was that it made a second army out of the Corps. This fact caused the ensuing rivalry. The Army thought it should be the country's only one. Waging war was difficult enough without the added complication of having two similar ground forces, Army generals believed fervently.

There were three times as many Marines at Belleau Wood as had been in the whole Corps during the Spanish-American War. It was the largest unit of Marines ever assembled. And their performance, the associated publicity, and the political power that came from their popularity broke the Marines out of the mold of the past. Belleau Wood was so primal a happening for the Corps that four veterans of it eventually served as Commandant: Wendell Neville, Thomas Holcomb, Clifton Cates, and Lemuel Shepherd, Jr. Cates often observed that Belleau Wood and Guadalcanal, the most important battles in the Corps's history, had a special quality that set them apart — as if to say that what Marines did in both places was so ennobling that no army could ever humble the proud Corps. Or so it seemed, at the end of World War II. But the US Army would try.

Upon receiving Truman's proposals for reorganizing the military, Senator Elbert Thomas appointed a working group that included himself and two other members of his Military Affairs Committee, Republican Warren Austin of Vermont and Democrat Lister Hill of Alabama, to write the ideas into formal legislation. The effect was to energize the debate, for and against. Notwithstanding his earlier statements to the contrary, the President had difficulty accepting criticism of his strongly held ideas from his military subordinates. Reacting to word that Chester Nimitz, while at some fete at the British embassy, had voiced opposition not only to unification but also to his cherished universal-military-training proposal, Truman told Budget Director Harold Smith, "Nimitz does not know that I know he said it, but I think it is pretty bad business for an admiral in his position."

Forrestal and his Navy officers, including Nimitz, were every bit as defensive as the President, however. Arleigh Burke recalled that there was a sense that the rest of the military had ganged up against them, the deal being, in his words, that "the Army would not oppose the Air Force attempts to get control of all air in exchange for Air Force support of the general staff system."

Air Force officers were, by contrast, full of confidence about their future. Some of them even flaunted a bold machismo, believing that they had won the war with the atomic bomb and that they would have won it with conventional ones if left alone. "We could have won the war in Europe without an invasion," LeMay maintained decades later. Airpower's potential seemed unlimited; the idea that armies and navies would soon be obsolete was gaining wide acceptance.

A wide-eyed admiral who attended a dinner given by the Aviation Writers Association on the evening of March 14, 1946, recorded Carl Spaatz's perception of this future. Spaatz, the new Commanding General of the

Army Air Forces, delivered a fifteen-minute speech that for press purposes was off the record. In a memo to Forrestal the next day, the admiral detailed what Spaatz supposedly said.

> The United States knows as a result of the recent war that it must have an air force. The air force that the nation must have, if it is to be properly protected, is the Army Air Force. It would be a waste of the taxpayers' money to have two. . . .
>
> Why should we have a Navy at all? The Russians have little or no Navy; the Japanese Navy has been sunk, the navies of the rest of this world are negligible; the Germans never did have much of a Navy. The point I am getting at is who is the big Navy being planned to fight. There are no enemies for it to fight, except apparently the Army Air Force. In this day and age to talk of fighting the next war on oceans is a ridiculous assumption. It will be fought in the air by an air force with the weapons necessary to fight the next [war]. The B-29 is that weapon and the Army Air Force perfected it so that we would be ready to meet all comers in the air. . . . The only reason for us to have a Navy is just because someone else has a Navy and we certainly don't need to waste money that way. . . .
>
> There is only one airplane that can carry the atomic bomb and that is the B-29. If they insist on a carrier, the only carrier that could do the job would be of a size so great that it would have a flight deck six thousand feet long. It takes that to land and take off a B-29.

Dwight Eisenhower, who was the new Army Chief of Staff, was considerably more discreet and conventional in advancing his service's interests against those of the Marine Corps than Spaatz was in advancing the Army Air Forces' against the Navy. Ike put his thoughts about what to do with the Corps into a memorandum that he submitted for consideration to the other JCS members, which during these years did not include the Commandant. In it Eisenhower only conceded the need for small Marine units to guard Navy ships and installations and to conduct limited amphibious operations. His contention, expressed in the memo, was that "once Marine units attain such a size as to require the combining of arms [infantry, artillery, armor, and air], they are assuming and duplicating the functions of the Army and we have in effect two land armies." Pursuant to this conclusion, he recommended that the Corps be "limited to some 50,000 or 60,000 men." During World War II, it had totaled nearly 500,000 when at peak strength.

As had been the case back at Nouméa, a close associate of Vandegrift's was in a position to warn him. This time the officer was Brigadier General Merritt Edson, who, like Merrill Twining, had served under the future Commandant at Guadalcanal. Edson had won the Congressional Medal of Honor for his brave service there as a raider battalion commander. While at Guadalcanal he became a regimental commander, and after the war was named the Marine Corps's liaison to the Chief of Naval Operations. Alert for anything affecting the Corps, Edson discovered the Eisenhower memo and secretly delivered a copy to Vandegrift. A clever man, Vandegrift kept knowledge of it to himself and ordered Edson to do the same. Later it became clear that Vandegrift's acute sense of timing had dictated this decision, made at about the time Spaatz was unburdening himself before the Aviation Writers Association.

In an obtuse way, though, Spaatz's impassioned speeches were as carefully calculated as Vandegrift's keeping quiet about the Eisenhower memo. The aviator was trying to sway public opinion to the Army Air Forces side and thus pressure indirectly members of Congress. Upset by this, Forrestal asked Truman to "call a halt to the propaganda," though the Navy was promoting itself, too, albeit in a more low-key fashion than Army Air Forces interests were; the Navy was circulating among editors, publishers, and reporters a brochure about its own reorganization scheme, the Eberstadt Plan. In any event, Spaatz was not so blatantly public about all his moves. Like Eisenhower, he also put some of his ideas in writing and submitted them to the other Joint Chiefs for consideration.

In the midst of all this maneuvering, public and private, Truman, on the Army's recommendation, signed an executive order that abolished the horse cavalry. Given how overdue this action was, Truman should have realized how tenaciously the military holds on to the past and honors it. Within a month, other events would establish this point more clearly for him. Commenting to his cabinet about ordering the last of the cavalrymen to hang up their lances, he said, "I don't know just what bearing this has on unification."

Six days later, on April 9, 1946, a much more profound change was advanced a tentative step. Thomas's working group completed drafting its military reorganization legislation, which came to be called the Thomas bill, and released it to the press. It constituted virtually all that Truman, the Army, and the Army Air Forces wanted. It proposed merging all the armed services under the authority of a civilian Secretary of Common Defense and a military Chief of Staff, who together represented a new system of centralized control. It created an independent Air Force of coequal status with the Army and the Navy. However, it demoted the service secretaries, who no longer would have cabinet rank. To help the Secretary of Common Defense administer his huge enterprise, it created slots for four new assistant secretaries of Common Defense. It also proposed establishing a Council of Common Defense, or Security Council; a National Security Resources Board; and a Central Intelligence Agency. It proposed keeping the Chiefs of Staff in being, but, as with the service secretaries, diminished their status, making them subservient to the military officer who held the new Chief of Staff position.

All this centralization discomfited Navy officials, but no more so than what the bill left unsettled — the future of the Marine Corps and of naval land-based aviation. The bill did not abolish the Corps nor did it prohibit the use of land-based planes by the Navy, but one section of it provided the President with sweeping executive authority to do just that. So the mutterings in Navy corridors of the Pentagon suddenly became a roar, to which Truman reacted, though it was much too early for him to single anyone out for punishment. Increasingly sensitive to criticism of his reorganization ideas, he, during a press conference, "gave warning to the Navy Department to fall in line behind him as Commander in Chief or prepare itself for a possible shake-up," reported the *New York Times*.

Had military policy been the exclusive purview of the President, the Navy and the Marine Corps would have been in trouble. Fortunately for them, the Constitution conferred upon Congress a countervailing responsibility when it enumerated for the legislative branch the "Power To lay and collect Taxes . . . [to] provide for the common Defence" of the United States. And so it was that a member of Congress was able to come to the rescue. Senate Naval Affairs Committee chairman David Walsh had his committee hold public hearings on the Thomas bill. Presented this opportunity, the opposition brought its objections to bear.

The first witness, on May 1, 1946, was Forrestal, who in very measured words acknowledged that the proposed legislation — "the Army proposal," as he repeatedly referred to it — was an improvement on earlier versions. But it was so simplistic that it rested on the premise of "merge now and organize later," he said.

Forrestal's testimony broke as sensational news. A cabinet officer was deriding a major piece of legislation concerning his department that was strongly endorsed by the President. In the context of all the discussions about unification that Truman, Forrestal, and other key figures had been conducting privately for months, it was not surprising. Forrestal had followed Truman's ground rules; though he seemed peevish, the President even defended him the next day. But the press and the public had not been privy to most of the cabinet-level discussions and had been privy to none of Truman and Forrestal's private exchanges. The *New York Herald Tribune*'s report said that the Navy Secretary had "served notice today that the Navy will use every means in its power to defeat a pending merger bill which is backed by the Army and has received a tentative nod of approval from President Truman."

Two days later, Nimitz testified. The crux of what he had to say was an explanation of why during World War II he had changed his mind about unification. Early on he had been an advocate. But wartime experience had taught him, he said, that a single military authority in Washington should only "coordinate" efforts of the services and not try to "control" them. He said that in some instances Army officers had not shown an "adequate appreciation" of the capabilities and limitations of naval forces. What seemed to worry him most was the airpower issue. In the Pacific theater of operations, strategic bombers of the Army Air Forces had been controlled from the nation's capital, and he and MacArthur, the senior commanders in the Pacific, had had no authority to tell Army Air Forces generals where to bomb to support land and sea operations; he and MacArthur had first had to prove to Army Air Forces headquarters back in Washington that they needed strategic-bomber support.

During his testimony, Nimitz left unsaid his feeling that the Army Air Forces were going to be even more independent as a separate service and that the Navy would have a terrible time justifying the air support it needed. This made the Navy all the more protective of its air arm, which was, as Nimitz pointed out, "a thoroughly integrated" part of the whole. If a task force admiral "needed air support for his amphibious or other units he ordered his carrier task force to provide it; he did not have to barter for nor justify his need for support."

Two days later, it was Vandegrift's turn. He was impassioned, blunt, even bitter, and his testimony marked an important juncture in the unification debate. He was not a flamboyant man, but Billy Mitchell could not have worked himself onto center stage at that instant with better lines.

"For some time," Vandegrift told the committee,

> I have been aware that the very existence of the Marine Corps stood as a continuing affront to the War Department General Staff, but had hoped that this attitude would end with the recent war. . . . But following a careful study of circumstances as they have developed in the past six months, I am convinced that my hopes were groundless, that the War Department's intentions regarding the Marines are quite unchanged, and that even in advance of this proposed legislation it is seeking to reduce the sphere of the Marine Corps to ceremonial functions and to the provision of small, ineffective, combat formations and labor troops for service on the landing beaches.

Having kept Eisenhower's memo secret up to this time, he now, by making it public, used it to reinforce dramatically his contention that the proud Marine Corps was about to be done in by deal makers who were controlling events from back rooms. This perception would soon be reinforced when reporters found out that Spaatz had seconded Eisenhower's memo about the Marine Corps and that Eisenhower had seconded a Spaatz memo about a new Air Force's taking over the missions now being fulfilled by the Navy's land-based air units.

Heretofore, public discussion about unification led by commentators and politicians had focused on organizational aspects, a favorite topic being whether a Chief of Staff with all the military under him might become a dangerous "man-on-horseback" figure who could threaten the nation's democratic institutions. There had also been a lot of discussion about the relative importance of the Army, the Navy, and the Army Air Forces. Many experts had testified about that, almost all of them sounding very reasonable, such that listeners' dulled senses were the cumulative effect of their conflicting views. There had been relatively little public attention paid to the future of the Marine Corps and of Navy land-based air, even though in military circles these were the hot topics. With his dramatic testimony, Vandegrift changed all that and woke up somnolent Marine Corps allies with a clarion call.

"In placing its case in your hands the Marine Corps remembers that it was this same Congress which, in 1798, called it into a long and useful service to the nation," he said.

> The Marine Corps feels that the question of its continued existence is likewise a matter for determination by the Congress and not one to be resolved by departmental legerdemain or a quasi-legislative process endorsed by the War Department General Staff.
>
> The Marine Corps, then, believes that it has earned this right: To have its future decided by the legislative body that created it, nothing more. Sentiment is not a valid consideration in determining questions of national security. We have pride in ourselves and in our past but we do not rest our case on any presumed ground of gratitude owing [*sic*] us from the nation. The bended knee is not a tradition of our Corps. If the Marine as a fighting man has not made a case for himself after one hundred-seventy years of service, he must go. But I think you will agree with me that he has earned the right to depart with dignity and honor, not by subjugation to the status of uselessness and servility planned for him by the War Department.

His presentation concluded, Vandegrift folded his papers and straightened his back. After a second of total silence, shouts and applause burst forth. Sustained bedlam rocked the room, Marines all around, shaking hands and wearing big smiles. He had stopped Army plans cold. This version of the Thomas bill was finished, and within a week Truman would reconcile himself to this fact and call together all his top military leaders for a kind of peace conference.

Vandegrift himself later observed: "Widespread publicity achieved all I hoped for this testimony and more." This was an understatement. During the next few days, the public, mostly by a spontaneous show of support, established the point that the Marine Corps had become a powerful political force. Members of Congress were swamped by phone calls, letters, and telegrams. For these angry constituents, eliminating the Corps was like taking "In God We Trust" off the dollar bill. The Marines raising the flag atop Mount Suribachi on Iwo Jima was an icon image for them. Eliminate the Marine Corps? God forbid!

CHAPTER 5

★ ★ ★ ★ ★ ★ ★ ★ ★ ★ ★ ★ ★ ★

FIGHTING FOR AIR

THE WORLD was not waiting for Washington to work things out. The Soviets were moving confidently, while the United States traipsed along without rhythm or rhyme. When the foreign ministers of Great Britain, France, the Soviet Union, and the United States met in Moscow back in December 1945, forty-two-year-old George Kennan saw this firsthand. The loose approach of US Secretary of State James Byrnes belied the import of the agenda. The four emissaries had gathered to reach a consensus on how to control atomic energy, map the Balkans, pacify China, occupy Japan, and make peace with all their vanquished European enemies except Germany. Collectively, they had the power to impose the decisions they might make. Ambassador to the USSR Averell Harriman invited Kennan to join the American delegation as an observer for the afternoon session on the nineteenth. Kennan, a Foreign Service officer who for eighteen years had been a Russian specialist, was the chargé d'affaires at the embassy. He recorded what he saw in his diary.

> Molotov, conducting the meeting, sat leaning forward over the table, a Russian cigarette dangling from his mouth, his eyes flashing with satisfaction and confidence as he glanced from one to the other of the other foreign ministers, obviously keenly aware of their mutual differences and their common uncertainty in the face of the keen, ruthless, and incisive Russian diplomacy. . . .
>
> I sat just behind Byrnes and could not see him well. He plays his negotiations by ear, going into them with no clear or fixed plan, with no definite set objectives or limitations. He relies entirely on his own agility and presence of mind and hopes to take advantage of tactical openings. In the present conference his weakness in dealing with the Russians is that his main purpose is to achieve some sort of an agreement, he doesn't much care what. The realities behind this agreement, since they concern only such people as

Koreans, Rumanians, and Iranians, about whom he knows nothing, do not concern him.

Why the Russians were being so uncooperative was still unclear to almost all Washington officialdom. Truman and his Secretary of State still thought that the wartime alliance could work during peacetime and that, as the President himself had stated, they could "do business with" Stalin. Only later would it become obvious that Stalin was stalling in negotiations while the democracies disarmed and, as he envisioned it, their economies slipped back into a depression and their societies into chaos.

By early 1946 Stalin was evidently certain this was coming to pass and that he would soon hold sway from Berlin to Seoul, for in a speech to the Supreme Soviet on February 9, he said in effect that peaceful coexistence with the United States was impossible because of its capitalist economy. Concurrently, he announced a five-year program that called for a huge expansion of armament and industry so that the Soviet Union would be ready for "any eventuality."

Supreme Court Justice William O. Douglas told a reporter he thought Stalin's speech was "the declaration of World War III." The jurist was still somewhat the political figure, his name having been mentioned prominently as a potential running mate for Franklin Roosevelt before Truman was selected. Democratic-party liberals still looked upon him as one of their leaders, so his views were elicited. Unlike most prominent liberals, Douglas was worried about Soviet intentions, and his friend Jim Forrestal had been urging him to speak out. This, of course, meant that the Secretary of the Navy was putting himself at odds with the President in yet another realm. Truman's foreign policy — like his military policy — was that of a liberal. The liberals' approach to dealing with the Russians presumed — as had Roosevelt's at Yalta — that the United States and the Soviet Union had a community of aims. Boorish Soviet behavior, as noted, had begun changing FDR's perception in the couple of months after Yalta before he died, but he had not had time to reorient the huge bureaucracy under him. So his earlier optimism about the Communist ally had survived him in the form of post-war policies emanating from the various departments.

Those Americans forced to conduct business with the Soviet Communists on a daily basis had a much different opinion of them, though. Best known among these was Ambassador Harriman, who was being influenced not only by his direct dealings with the Russians but also by Kennan. Like Forrestal, Harriman seemed to distrust the Soviets instinctively. No doubt this had a lot to do with their Wall Street backgrounds. Their roots also help explain why there were so few people in the administration equally as wary of

Communists; Harry Truman was not in the habit of appointing investment bankers to high office. Forrestal's view might also have been slightly influenced by his oldest son, Michael, a nineteen-year-old Princeton student, who was attached to Harriman's staff in Moscow at the time.

By the time of Stalin's anti-American diatribe to the Supreme Soviet, Kennan had been on station eighteen months, during which time, he later wrote, "I had experienced unhappiness not only about the naivete of our underlying ideas as to what it was we were hoping to achieve in our relations with the Soviet government but also about the methods and devices with which we went about achieving it." It was in this context that he had worked up a set of guidelines for dealing with the *Stalin* regime (the emphasis was his). It included this warning: "Don't assume a community of aims with them which does not really exist." Kennan tried in all manner of ways to effect a change of attitude within the bureaucracies back in Washington, including buttonholing almost every American visitor, but had made no progress. "So far as official Washington was concerned, it had been to all intents and purposes like talking to stone," he recalled. Those manning the Russian Desk back at the State Department had understood what was going on but had been ignored, too. Then, in mid-February 1946, there arose from the Department of the Treasury what Kennan described as an "anguished cry of bewilderment" about Soviet unwillingness to adhere to the charters of the World Bank and the International Monetary Fund. Nowhere in American government had Roosevelt's hope of postwar cooperation with the Russians been more fervently embraced than it had at Treasury, whose staff by this time was utterly confounded by events. One of these individuals had asked the State Department to clear up the confusion for them and, according to Kennan, the Russian Desk people had transmitted "in tones of bland innocence" his inquiries: What lay behind the behavior of the Soviet government? How did one explain it?

Kennan was bedridden, fighting off a severe cold when this cable was delivered to him among a stack of others. Harriman was back in Washington preparing to leave his post for good, so Kennan was in charge. Despite the distractions of work and illness, made temporarily worse by the aftereffects of a strong dose of sulfa drugs, Kennan jumped at the opportunity thus presented. "Now, suddenly, my opinion was being asked," he recalled. "Here was a case where nothing but the whole truth would do. They had asked for it. Now, by God, they would have it." So he summoned his secretary, Dorothy Hessman, and went to work dictating his thoughts to her.

The final product of their effort was a document remarkable for its length as well as its content. Concerned that someone monitoring the telegraph lines might force him to condense what he had to say, he broke it into four self-contained parts: "the basic features of the Soviet post-war outlook; the background of that outlook; its projection on the level of official policy, i.e., policy implemented through 'front' organizations and stooges of all sorts; the implications of all this for American policy."

Fortunately, this little ruse did not cause Kennan's telegram to escape the detection of the US Navy's attaché assigned to the Moscow embassy, Rear Admiral Houston L. Maples, who decided to read what was tying up other embassy traffic on George Washington's Birthday, 1946. What he discovered was "Kennan's long telegram," as it has been known in the years since. Maples was impressed; the tone of the cable matched an American military man's natural wariness of Communists, and he knew that his superiors would want to see it. That the Secretary of the Navy was preoccupied with developing some sort of vision of the postwar world that he could relate to military requirements was well known. It so happened that Kennan in his telegram articulated for Forrestal precisely the same impressions that had begun forming in his mind. Among them were these:

> At the bottom of the Kremlin's neurotic view of world affairs is the traditional and instinctive Russian sense of insecurity. . . .
>
> . . . Russian rulers have invariably sensed that their rule was . . . fragile . . . [and] unable to stand comparison or contact with political systems of Western countries. . . .
>
> [Russian rulers] have learned to seek security only in [a] patient but deadly struggle for total destruction [of] rival power, never in compacts and compromises with it. . . .
>
> [Marxism] is a fig leaf of [Russian leaders'] moral and intellectual respectability.
>
> The very disrespect of Russians for objective truth — indeed, their disbelief in its existence — leads them to view all stated facts as instruments for furtherance of one ulterior purpose or another. . . .
>
> While many of the persons who compose . . . [the inner central core of Communist parties in other countries] may also appear and act in unrelated public capacities, they are in reality working closely together as an underground operating directorate of world communism, a concealed Comintern tightly coordinated and directed by Moscow. . . .
>
> Wherever it is considered timely and promising, efforts will be made to advance official limits of Soviet power. For the moment, these efforts are restricted to certain neighboring points . . . such as northern Iran [and] Turkey. . . .
>
> On an unofficial plane, particularly violent efforts will be made to weaken power and influence of Western powers over colonial, backward, or dependent peoples. On this level, no holds will be barred. Mistakes and weaknesses

of Western colonial administration will be mercilessly exposed and exploited. . . .

Soviet power, unlike that of Hitlerite Germany, is neither schematic nor adventuristic. It does not work by fixed plans. It does not take unnecessary risks. [It is] impervious to logic of force. For this reason it can easily withdraw — and usually does — when strong resistance is encountered at any point. Thus, if the adversary has sufficient force and makes clear his readiness to use it, he rarely has to do so. If situations are properly handled, there need be no prestige-engaging showdowns.

Forrestal had many printings made of this telegram and distributed hundreds if not thousands of copies throughout official Washington, transforming in the process the obscure Kennan into a prominent figure. Finally someone had provided a rationale for what the Russians were up to. Coming from Forrestal, the telegram became in effect required reading in many circles. This was true for all admirals and generals in the Pentagon. The President reportedly read it, too.

Forrestal's being so engaged with global politics was natural for a Navy Secretary, though the intensity of his interest was unusual. Fleets — even a single ship — are, as mentioned, very conducive for use as a strategic force. The seas usually lead to the shores of every major nation, and did so in 1946. Navies can affect events thousands of miles from their home ports; by merely flying the flag in troubled waters, warships can, as noted, firmly make a political point, with much more ease and much less risk than troop units can. They can easily be removed, as well. Conversely, they have the staying power that aircraft do not have.

Such thinking is axiomatic to experienced Navy officers, and it so happened that about this time one of them, Rear Admiral Forrest P. Sherman, a very bright fellow whose best days in the service of the Navy and the nation were yet to come, conceived of just such a highly effective use of a warship. This was in late February, when Kennan's long telegram was the talk of the Pentagon. Perhaps one good idea begat another. Turkey's ambassador to the United States had died in Washington during the war, and because of the fighting his body had not been shipped home but was instead temporarily interred at Arlington National Cemetery. Sherman's idea was to return it to Turkey on a bier befitting an ally's emissary — a warship. The political purpose would be to please the Turks and, more important, give warning to the Russians, who were pressing the leaders of Turkey for various concessions, such as internationalizing the Bosporus and the Dardanelles. These important waterways, legs of a Russian route from the Black Sea to open waters, belonged to the Turks, historically Russia's enemies.

Forrestal, who for some weeks had been thinking about urging

Truman to approve redeployment of a Mediterranean task force, given the instability in Europe, enthusiastically endorsed the proposal. Another Navy officer's suggestion that the *Missouri* be used sealed the deal with the Commander in Chief. Secretary of State Byrnes endorsed the idea, though he successfully opposed as undue provocation Forrestal's plan to send along a task force escort. Even alone, the impact of the battleship when it sailed into port on April 5, 1946, was so positive that the President decided to approve Forrestal's idea of sending US warships to visit a variety of Mediterranean ports later in the year. Hundreds of thousands of Turks watched from the steep banks of the Bosporus when the great warship glided into port at Istanbul.

Truman's ordering the *Missouri* to Turkey was one of the very first American gambits in the developing cold war and constituted just the sort of correlation of military power and national policy that Forrestal was delving into; however, at this point, the Truman administration was far from having formulated a strategic-political doctrine, so it was an isolated military action that did not fit into a general policy context. Winston Churchill deemed it a splendid idea, this kind of power gesture having been the sort of thing the British were good at when Britannia had ruled the waves. However, he posed to Forrestal one caveat, which was "that a gesture of power not fully implemented was almost less effective than no gesture at all." Churchill believed that the task force escort should have been sent along, as the Navy Secretary had recommended.

The former prime minister passed along this judgment in person. At the time he was in the United States to deliver a speech at Westminster College in tiny Fulton, Missouri, on March 5, 1946. Harry Vaughan, a Westminster alumnus, had played a key role in convincing Churchill to do so. (It was probably the most important thing he did as Truman's military aide.) Because of Vaughan's intercession, Truman personally endorsed the letter of invitation written by Westminster's president. In his own hand Truman wrote: "This is a wonderful school in my home state. Hope you can do it. I'll introduce you." And he did.

The presentation that Churchill delivered became one of his most famous, but his discerning audience, which packed a gymnasium, did not applaud eagerly all he had to say. Passages that dealt with US responsibility for seeing that another world war be avoided were greeted with "marked applause." His proposal for a "fraternal association," his euphemism for a postwar Anglo-American alliance, brought only moderate hand-clapping. Accustomed to being ahead of his time, Churchill was unperturbed. He conveyed his ideas with the clarity and style for which he was famous.

From Stettin in the Baltic to Trieste in the Adriatic, an iron curtain has descended across the Continent. Behind the line lie all the capitals of ancient states of central and eastern Europe. Warsaw, Berlin, Prague, Vienna, Budapest, Belgrade, Bucharest, and Sofia, all these famous cities and the populations around them lie in what I might call the Soviet sphere, and all are subject, in one form or another, not only to Soviet influence but to a very high and in some cases increasing measure of control from Moscow.

With this speech Churchill inserted himself into the same US policy dialogue that Kennan had so recently and prominently involved himself in. It was the former prime minister's answer to a question that was often heard in conversations those days in Washington. Senator Arthur Vandenberg had repeated it on the Senate floor only a few days earlier. " 'What is Russia up to now?' It is, of course, the supreme conundrum of our time," he had said. Such was the uncertainty of American leaders in early 1946. No one wanted to believe that the great wartime ally had already decided to be an enemy in the postwar world.

With the nation not having a foreign policy worthy of the name, a coordinated plan of action for the military services, which would be a function of it, was a long way off. In the meantime, military leaders would have to get together on reorganization. Otherwise, when handed their political objectives, they would be unable to act on them. Unfortunately, military reorganization was also a long way off.

In early 1946 the closest the military could come to developing future plans was imagining what the next war would be like; each branch had already assigned people to devise theories and test them. They all started with three common presumptions, each of them rather remarkable. The first was that the next conflict involving the United States would be another world war. The second was that airpower was of primary importance to each branch. The third was that atomic bombs would be used.

That Army Air Forces leaders would think in these terms was not surprising. Spaatz, for example, believed fervently that what Mitchell, Trenchard, and Douhet had predicted — the overwhelming dominance of airpower — was now at hand. The atomic bomb seemed to validate this conclusion because it had forced Japan to capitulate so quickly. The grisly scene Mitchell once described of dazed New Yorkers struggling over the rubble of fallen Manhattan skyscrapers seemed a grim possibility in this new age. The premise was that sometime in the midfifties the Russians would develop the atomic bomb and be capable of delivering it. Spaatz and his top generals accordingly wanted the nation to put its defense dollars into a strategic bomber force of such overwhelming might that the enemy would never seriously contemplate any sort of attack against the United States. Presently their best bomber was the B-29, and they had others in various stages of development. Their next one would be the B-50, followed soon thereafter by the B-36, which with its projected 3,500-mile range would become the world's first intercontinental aircraft. Its first test flight would be on August 8, 1946.

As for Navy doings, airpower during World War II had impressed every doubting admiral. This was officially acknowledged with the creation of a new position, deputy chief of naval operations for air. The first man appointed to the job was Vice Admiral Marc Mitscher; the second was another prominent aviator, Vice Admiral Arthur W. Radford. The Navy had put to sea an incredible ninety-eight carriers during the war and this had opened up things for Navy aviators. Indeed, air officers were in the process of replacing battleship officers as the dominant leadership group. What they envisioned as the main instrument of naval power in the years ahead was a giant aircraft carrier, which they referred to as the Supercarrier. Mitscher had first suggested it two months after Hiroshima. The idea was to construct a ship big enough for long-range bombers to take off from its deck. To accommodate the big wings of these aircraft, it would have no superstructure.

Launching Army Air Forces–type bombers from carriers would not be entirely new to the Navy. During the war, Commander Francis Low, a Navy officer on Admiral King's staff, had conceived the idea for the so-called Doolittle Raid. In this operation, which took place about four months after Pearl Harbor, when the whole nation needed a morale boost, some sixteen Army Air Forces B-25 Mitchell bombers took off from the deck of the *Hornet* and succeeded in bombing Tokyo. Though these medium-range bombers were small, even in comparison to the B-29, they were too large to land on the *Hornet*'s decks; in fact, they did not have the range to return to ship. The lucky ones made planned crash landings in regions of China controlled by Chiang's Nationalists. The Navy planned to make the Supercarrier large enough to retrieve even bigger bombers. To Army Air Forces officers, this indicated that the Navy was trying to elbow in on their strategic air role — an accusation vehemently denied. The Navy did concede wanting the capability to drop atomic bombs, and it used the need for that capability to justify the Supercarrier. In 1946 nuclear weapons were very large and heavy; planes carrying them had to be big. Navy officials said they planned to use these bombs in the normal course of naval warfare.

As for the ground Army and its future, the war — beginning with the German blitzkrieg offensives — had demonstrated how decisive airpower was to the success of its units, too. Major General James Gavin, after the victory parade, had been ordered down to Fort Bragg, North Carolina, to test various concepts. According to him, airpower was "the most significant entity of our [Army] war power in World War II. Without it we never could have established ourselves on the Normandy Peninsula, and we might not have established ourselves in southern Europe." However, by airpower, Army leaders, especially paratroopers like Gavin, meant air transports and fighter planes used for close air support of combat troops, not bombers. Gavin was one of many ground officers who were dubious about the effectiveness of the Army Air Forces' vaunted strategic bombing campaigns during the war. It followed that he was one Army general who supported closer integration of the Army Air Forces with the ground Army; he opposed its being reconstituted as a separate service.

As for the atomic bomb, Gavin said it had already prompted Army leaders to "throw the books out the window." Doctrine would have to be rewritten. The presumptions were that the bomb would be used on the next war's battlefields as a tactical weapon, that the enemy would have it, and that ground units would have to be more mobile and dispersed to avoid destruction. This last premise he would test at Fort Bragg; "our earliest thinking in the Army was in terms of how to defend against use of the atomic bomb on us, and how to team up with nuclear bombers in the offensive," Gavin recalled. The obvious best targets for atomic bombs would be staging areas where troops, weapons, and supplies would be concentrated and isolated. No one had worked out theoretically how to use the bomb on enemy units locked in battle with US troops without killing equally as many Americans.

A principal reason Army officers were so negative about the Marine Corps's future was their belief that atomic weapons could easily wipe out highly concentrated amphibious assault forces. Marines did not see it this way, the success of a landing always having been somewhat dependent upon the element of surprise. The Army presumed that the Marines would be hit during the staging portion of their landings when they would be most vulnerable. A similar supposition made many believe that fleets of ships were a thing of the past. A test was being planned for midyear at Bikini Atoll in the Pacific to see what an atomic bomb would do to a concentration of ships.

The perceived need for mobility also meant there was a lot of interest in short-takeoff-and-landing aircraft. This type plane was to be used intratheater, for shuttling loads to forward bases near the fighting front. A good one was already far along. Michael Stroukoff of the Chase Aircraft Company had developed the C-122; capable of flying onto and off of plowed fields with little difficulty, it satisfied requirements far beyond expectations. This design evolved into the C-123. Other Army mobility tests involved helicopters. Thirteen of them manufactured by Bell Aircraft were delivered to the Eighty-second Airborne at Fort Bragg for Gavin to test. At first he deployed them as communications vehicles used mostly for observation, thus duplicating the initial reaction of Army officers to airplanes thirty-seven years earlier. The Marine Corps, which also had some helicopters to work with, did a better job of recognizing and developing their potential.

Gavin called World War II "the last great war of the machine age," and the Army's long-range planning in early 1946 reflected this thinking. He and others had decided that the future would be shaped by rapidly changing technologies that would make future wars even more dangerous than the one just ending. A long-term Navy project just beginning in early 1946 involved using atomic energy to power ships. In April the Monsanto Chemical Company, which operated part of the huge Oak Ridge facilities of the Manhattan District, sent a secret letter to the Navy and to the Army Air Forces, inviting military officers to participate in the construction of the world's first atomic reactor. Company executives figured that the military might one day want to build a ship or airplane powered by such a nuclear generator. The Navy sent a delegation of eight headed by a forty-six-year-old captain named Hyman G. Rickover.

Since aviation was the most technologically driven of the various forces of war (indeed, the drive to improve existing technology is fundamental to aviation culture), it followed that the Army Air Forces were best prepared in early 1946 to adapt to long-term technological change. However, General Hap Arnold deserves considerable credit for this having been the case. The fact that the Germans had produced an operational jet fighter was frightening to Arnold. So during the war he institutionalized the personal relationship of scientists with the AAF's highest ranking officers so as to facilitate innovation. He wanted them to tell Army Air Forces generals what future needs would be, rather than vice versa, on the premise that a scientist had the education and inclination to keep up with technological change better than a military officer normally would. To this end, in late 1945 Arnold caused Project RAND to be funded under the auspices of the Douglas Aircraft Company. He, much more than Spaatz, his successor, had high hopes for RAND; Spaatz, an operations man through and through, was not as comfortable with "long-haired scientists," as he referred to them. RAND's first study, published on May 2, 1946, was titled "Preliminary Design of an Experimental World-Circling Spaceship" — something theorists conceived as having all sorts of military applications. Its most obvious use would be as a platform for reconnaissance and weapons delivery. The authors of this RAND study concluded that

> the achievement [of sending a craft into space] would probably inflame the imagination of mankind, and would probably produce repercussions in the world comparable to the explosion of the atomic bomb. . . . Since mastery of

the elements is a reliable index of material progress, the nation which first makes significant achievements in space travel will be acknowledged as the world leader in both military and scientific techniques. To visualize the impact on the world, one can imagine the consternation and admiration that would be felt here if the U.S. were to discover suddenly that some other nation had already put up a successful satellite.

Some of this planning was introducing another discordant note into the interservice relationships. The planning had to do with missiles, another long-range project. In early 1946, the Navy, the Army Air Forces, and the ground Army each had some sort of missile program. Six days after the RAND authors submitted their satellite study, the services jointly conducted the first successful firing in the United States of a German V-2 rocket. The rub building up was the Army Air Forces' wanting a single missile program for the nation's military and wanting to control it. According to the *New York Times*'s Hanson Baldwin, who covered the launch at White Sands Proving Ground, New Mexico, Army Air Forces leaders were developing a "fear psychosis" about it, much like that which the Navy was accused of displaying over unification of the military. This reaction could be traced to an observation Arnold once made about World War II being the last war of the pilots, by which he meant, as Baldwin explained it, "that in any future 'push button' conflict, long-range rockets, and guided pilotless missiles would replace them." Without piloted aircraft, an independent air force would have no reason for being — unless it controlled the missile program. This explained Army Air Forces leaders' fear. Major General Curtis E. LeMay, the deputy chief of the air staff for research and development, was asking for funds in the range of $200 million to $300 million for the giant Army Air Forces missile development center. Baldwin did not think this center would be built anytime soon. He gave this as the view of the Navy and the ground Army: "The missile program, particularly the long-range missile program, is still in its infancy, and with a whole new world in science and in the art of war still to be opened, it would be a profound mistake, it is held, to attempt at this time to sharply define the limitations under which each service should develop missiles."

AAF leaders' singular anxiety about the missile program notwithstanding, behind all these advance plans was the sense that airpower and its awful weaponry would dominate the next war. This had become a generally accepted presumption, one that would lead to disastrous consequences. It accounted for most of the intense anxiety that virtually all Navy officers and many Army ground officers had about unification. They feared that organizationally their particular service branch, by losing control of its air support, would become useless, obsolete. And though admirals could not imagine war without ships, and ground generals a war without soldiers, the notion began to take hold in the country at large that the likes of Spaatz and LeMay were going to deliver on Billy Mitchell's premise by winning the next war by themselves.

So uncertainty was the reason innovative ideas were such hot property in early 1946. The war had wrought great change, and no one knew where it all would lead. This was true across the board. That the Democrats were in power when the war was won had not assured them of anything but being held responsible for everything that went wrong afterward. Indeed, because the United States had recently won two great wars, Americans in 1946 believed that their leaders should be able to control events, so Truman and the Democratic majorities in Congress were soon blamed for everything from inflation to troubles in Europe and Asia. Before very long the Republicans would have a theme for the congressional elections in November. "Had enough?" they would ask the voters.

Significantly, American leaders in 1946 shared the public's belief that the United States could control events just about anywhere. This accounted for the administration's high level of frustration with Chiang and over the problems in China. (What was truly remarkable was the degree to which the nation really could control events.) Solving problems at home and abroad seemed mostly a function of figuring out how to bring the country's assets to bear.

As was typical of him, Forrestal was taking the lead in figuring out how to control events with the nation's military assets, which were diminishing rapidly. While struggling with the issues of military reorganization, he, as noted, took up trying to correlate the nation's economic and military means with political objectives — a task that was complicated business. Correlating these means and ends amounted to creating a strategic-political doctrine. This would have been trying enough as only an academic exercise, but as he saw it, the Soviet Union was posing an immediate as well as an ominous threat to the nation's security.

With characteristic initiative and attention to organization, Forrestal decided that the military establishment should create some sort of forum wherein its leaders could learn about the complexities of world politics so that their thinking and recommendations about the use of military power would be more relevant and useful. Pursuant to this objective, he had been the principal mover behind the old Army and Navy Staff College's being transformed during the spring of 1946 into the National War College, the military's first school for strategic-political doctrine. He then became involved in assembling a first-rate staff, faculty, and student body. It was decided that the latter would be composed mostly of one hundred military officers ranging in rank from lieutenant colonel to brigadier general, or the equivalent. The Navy, the Army, the Army Air Forces, and the Marine Corps would all be represented. To broaden the base of discussion and to encourage a knowledgeable exchange of ideas, ten Foreign Service officers of equivalent rank were to be students, too.

As fate would have it, Forrestal was in the process of thinking about a faculty when George Kennan sent his long telegram to Washington. Upon reading it Forrestal knew immediately he wanted him at the school. Rarely do a writer's efforts pay the handsome and quick dividends they did in this case. Virtually overnight (within ninety days, actually) Kennan's cogitation transported him, his wife, Annelise, and their children from a small Moscow apartment to quarters at Fort McNair normally reserved for generals and their families. At this new residence their back door opened up to a broad lawn of green grass that bordered the Washington Channel and gave them an unobstructed view of the Potomac River beyond. Eisenhower reportedly had intervened to get Kennan his general's quarters. And because of Forrestal, Kennan was made one of three commandants at the college, his responsibility being, in his words, the "more strictly political portions of the combined military-political course of instruction."

Understandably, Kennan was inspired by the opportunities presented and the recognition. It can be said without exaggeration that at no time since those days has official Washington so candidly admitted a lack of understanding of what was happening in the world and so eagerly searched for answers. Intellectuals such as Kennan were held in high esteem; "officers of Cabinet rank, generals, and Senators sat at our feet as we lectured," he recalled. "The college came to provide a sort of academic seminar for the higher echelons of governmental Washington generally." Professors Sherman Kent and Bernard Brodie of Yale and Hardy Dillard of the University of Virginia comprised Kennan's department. Forrestal attended many of their lectures.

The first session of the War College in the fall of 1946 focused on how military and nonmilitary means could be used to advance the nation's interests — in other words, the strategic-political doctrine, which the United States had never had. "It was a mark of the weakness of all previous American thinking about international affairs," Kennan recalled, "that there was almost nothing in American political literature of the past one hundred years on the subject of the relationship of war to politics." Indeed, the National War College amounted to the first time the US government prescribed this area of inquiry in a formal academic setting for such an aggregate body of its officers. "American thinking about foreign policy," said Kennan, "had been primarily addressed to the problems of peace. . . . Thinking about war, confined for the most part to military staffs and institutions of military training, had been directed almost exclusively to the technical problems of military strategy and tactics."

Alfred Thayer Mahan had addressed the political-military relationships, of course, but Kennan concluded during his comprehensive research that Mahan's works focused on seapower too much and were dated. And Kennan found that no other American's thinking measured up to that of Mahan. For Kennan, Billy Mitchell's writings were not a factor.

Looking elsewhere, Kennan and his colleagues focused on European thinkers' works — including those by Machiavelli, Clausewitz, Gallieni, and even Lawrence of Arabia. "But it was obvious," Kennan wrote,

> that in no instance was the thinking of those earlier figures fully relevant or remotely adequate to the needs of a great American democracy in the atomic age. All this, clearly, was going to have to be rethought. A strategic-political doctrine would have to be devised for this country which gave promise not simply of expanding the material and military power of a single nation but of making the strength of that nation a force for peace and stability in international affairs and helping, in particular, to avoid the catastrophe of atomic war.

Two fundamental conclusions emerged in Kennan's mind during his year at the War College. One, which put him entirely at odds with current thinking in military circles, was that atomic weapons had made total war an outmoded concept, the experience of the nineteenth and the first half of the twentieth centuries notwithstanding — and, for that matter, the whole American experience notwithstanding. The Mexican War, the Civil War, the Indian Wars, the Spanish-American War, and World Wars I and II had conditioned most Americans, especially its military officers, to believe that wars of the United States were all-out contests that concluded only after the unconditional surrender of its foes.

To the contrary, Kennan decided that if war should come, American policymakers must limit its scope and avert World War III. An adversary the size of the Soviet Union would be impossible to occupy anyway, he decided. Along with other astute observers of the power vacuums in Europe and Asia and the resulting political turmoil, Kennan was rapidly coming to the conclusion that total war created as many problems as it solved. His research convinced him that the eighteenth century evidenced pertinent lessons to be applied during the new era at hand. A dictum of the French statesman Talleyrand distilled the thinking that Kennan believed was newly relevant: "Nations ought to do one another in peace the most good, in war — the least possible evil." Impressed by this rationale, Kennan, while at the college, became a proponent of limited warfare. His second conclusion, which for him was fundamental, was that the United States should only use its atomic weapons to retaliate for an attack in kind. The United States at the time had a monopoly on these bombs, but it was a situation that everyone knew would not last forever.

From his two fundamental observations, Kennan derived some corollaries: that the country would need "small mobile forces" ready for rapid deployment; that the nation's first line of defense could be trouble spots thousands of miles away; and that atomic bombs could never be used as forward weapons on the battlefield. In this regard, he envisioned an important role for the Marine Corps, saw the necessity of keeping much of the nation's military force at a high level of readiness, and recognized the need for close interservice collaboration.

Not all of this came to Kennan while at the college; some of his thinking developed later. Nor were all his views original; for example, he never specifically voiced the no-first-strike idea because it was so generally accepted in those days.

Kennan's signature containment idea did begin to germinate while he was at the school, though. After he had done most of his research for the start of the school's first fall term, he was invited to address a large meeting of State Department personnel, and it was there that he, evidently before anyone else in government, articulated the crux of the strategic-political doctrine the United States would implement vis-à-vis the Soviet Union. The preponderance of world opinion was with the United States, he told his audience, and that "should enable us, if our policies are wise and nonprovocative, to contain [the USSR] both militarily and politically for a long time to come." His thinking became more precise as the school year progressed. Before long he was discussing the concept of deterrence with audiences. He told the National Defense Committee of the United States Chamber of Commerce that "the greatest value of our forces lies in their quality as a deterrent." And he would warn them, "If we do not maintain such forces, there will always be an incentive to unruly people elsewhere to seize isolated and limited objectives on the theory that we would be able to do nothing about it at the moment and that they could count on making the seizures with impunity and talking about it afterward."

Had Kennan built on this propitious start and remained at the National War College for many years, he probably would have developed for himself a reputation somewhat along the lines of that which Dennis Hart Mahan developed for himself at West Point — that of a highly regarded man of ideas who helped shape the thinking of people who later rose to positions of great power and influence. But as remarkable as Kennan's rise to prominence had already been, it had just begun. His having Forrestal as a patron would bring him to the attention of George Marshall, who, having been reluctantly drawn out of retirement and into the field of diplomacy, would soon make an indelible mark there, too, using Kennan as his instrument.

Kennan was not the only man in Washington with a lot on his mind. For almost the entire month of May, Truman struggled to settle nationwide strikes of railroad workers and coal miners. Coal was then the nation's principal fuel source, and the ripple effect throughout the economy was about to overwhelm the country. At one point during the month, 960,000 workers were idled by the two strikes. The steel and auto industries had begun layoffs and were close to shutting down.

Truman was beside himself. One drastic action he took was to ask Congress to draft railroad workers into the Army so that he could order them all back to work. Evidently, this idea was his own, though Eleanor Roosevelt, reading it differently, wrote him to say, "I have seen my husband receive much advice from his military advisers and succumb to it every now and then, but the people as a whole do not like it."

Both strikes were settled toward the end of the month (though the agreement with John L. Lewis's miners soon came undone). Wages were the main dispute. The nation was having a difficult time converting back to a peacetime economy. The lifting of wage and price controls was igniting inflation, which in turn incited workers to demand more pay.

That Truman, in a speech to Congress that he discarded, called one labor leader a Communist shows that the world situation was on his mind, even during these high-stakes labor negotiations in which he directly involved himself. Perhaps because of the current international instability, he tried in the middle of this awful month to get military reorganization going again. The meeting of his top military advisers that he convened to restart momentum following Alexander Vandegrift's testimony was held May 13, 1946, during these domestic travails. Present that afternoon were Attorney General Thomas Clark; Navy Secretary James Forrestal; War Secretary Robert Patterson; William Leahy, the chief of staff of the Commander in Chief of the Army and the Navy; military aide Harry Vaughan; Chief of Naval Operations Chester Nimitz; Commanding General of the Army Air Forces Carl Spaatz; Lieutenant General Thomas T. Handy, the Army's deputy chief of staff; and Captain Frank C. Nash, Forrestal's special assistant. Army Chief of Staff Dwight Eisenhower was away in Tokyo.

The reaction in Congress following Vandegrift's testimony had been considerable. The House Appropriations Committee, in reporting out the Navy budget for the next fiscal year, "went out of its way to praise the Corps highly" while giving it the full amount requested, reported the *New York Times*'s Baldwin. Even more significant, Congressman Carl Vinson and Senator David Walsh, the respective chairmen of the House and Senate Naval Affairs committees, on May 19, 1946, sent Forrestal a letter advising him not to "trade" with Truman or the Army on reorganization. They voiced confidence that Congress would not pass the Army reorganization plan backed by the President. Their assurances put Forrestal in a very strong position; they were telling him, in effect, that Truman would have to make concessions to the Navy and the Marine Corps. Indeed, even before this letter was sent, the President had opened his May 13 meeting by doing just that. Leahy acted as his agent. After some preliminary remarks, the President called on the old admiral, who had stayed aloof from the whole reorganization debate thus far. Leahy said that his experience during World War II had convinced him that having a single uniformed officer in charge of all the armed forces would be dangerous. It was too easy and tempting for a fellow with that kind of power to usurp that of the President and threaten the nation's democratic institutions, he explained. Leahy suggested that during the war he himself could have arrogated a great deal of power not his.

Truman responded by saying that all along he, too, had had reservations about having a military man in charge of all the services. This was not surprising, his being the thoughtful liberal that he was. What was surprising was that he had not voiced worries about "the man on horseback" earlier. Perhaps he had not done so because of the special admiration he felt for both Marshall and Eisenhower; drawing on personal experience, the President tended to generalize, sometimes without due thought. Without much reflection, he might have assumed that future Chiefs of Staff would have Marshall's and Eisenhower's basic qualities. Truman told the group that he was going to excise from his reorganization proposal the part about having a single Chief of Staff. This, of course, was one of the Army's key ideas and was symbolic of a unified military. That Truman would discard it was a major concession to the Navy.

With that out of the way, Leahy broached another concern: naval aviation, a much more highly charged issue. The Navy's position was that its land-based planes were absolutely essential for protecting the fleet and that a different service branch could not perform this function properly. Leahy suggested that some sort of agreement could be reached that would reassure the Navy and satisfy Army Air Forces leaders. His statement seemed to confirm indirectly that Truman had decided he could not win legislative support for his proposed arrangement of the various roles and missions; they could only be worked out through a sort of peace treaty, with the Secretary of the Navy and the Secretary of War as signatories. As for the Marine Corps, Leahy said he endorsed Eisenhower's statement, made the day before from Tokyo, that although he did not want the Corps to become a second army, he would be the last to endorse its abolition. Eisenhower, too, had responded to Vandegrift's testimony.

Having put these concessions and assurances on the table for discussion, Truman invited Patterson's comments. The Secretary of War then fell in line. According to Forrestal's diary notes, Patterson said he was not prepared to "jump into the ditch and die for the idea" of a single Chief of Staff. He also said that he was prepared to sit down with Forrestal once again to work things out. Forrestal assented to this, as did Nimitz and Handy, and Truman assigned them a deadline of May 31 for submitting a report on those aspects of reorganization on which they could agree.

The very next day, Forrestal, Patterson, Nimitz, and Ferdinand Eberstadt, the architect of the Navy's reorganization plan, went to work on the project. They met in Forrestal's office and afterward the Navy Secretary had lunch served there for himself and Patterson. What surprised them was how little was left unsettled organizationally, given Truman's concessions to the Navy; roles and missions were another matter, but the two planners treated them separately from organizational issues. Both agreed to keeping the existing collective leadership structure of the Joint Chiefs of Staff. They also agreed to establishing the Departments of the Navy, the Army, and the Air Force, and concurred that each was to be headed by a civilian of cabinet-level rank and a military officer who would also be a member of the Joint Chiefs.

What they could not agree on was the extent of the power of the Director of Defense, the civilian who would oversee the three military departments. According to Eberstadt's notes, Patterson wanted to give this official "full power and responsibility for the administration of the three military Departments." Forrestal and Nimitz opposed this. They thought that his powers "should not extend to administration," which, in effect, would mean control. In his diary Forrestal later recounted his comments to Patterson: "I said I could not agree to anything which would involve the destruction of the integrity of the Navy. By that I meant its ceasing to have the status of a separate entity rather than merely a branch, its own Secretary having a seat in the Cabinet and access to the President." In this regard, Forrestal wanted the Director of Defense's duties clearly enumerated; he sensed that to do otherwise was tantamount to a decision to "merge now and organize later." In contrast, Patterson wanted the Defense Director to have "the broadest kind of direct control over the three subsidiary Departments." Forrestal firmly reiterated his position: "I said we would never agree to administrative control over the Navy. That we might consider the word 'supervise' but that was as far as we would go."

The two men were unable to resolve their difference of opinions about the power of the Director of Defense before submitting their joint report to Truman on May 31. Patterson even hardened his position. The War Secretary insisted on reducing the status of the Army and the Navy departments, making them "branches"; the same would apply to the new Air Force he was advocating. This meant that the civilian leaders of these services would no longer have cabinet status; Patterson's Director of Defense would, and that would greatly enhance the latter's power over the other three.

Agreements noted in their report included those about creating a Council of Common Defense, which would be composed of various foreign-affairs and military officers; a National Security Resources Board; a more all-encompassing Central Intelligence Agency than the present makeshift one; and a Military Munitions Board. These were Navy ideas, all part of the Eberstadt Plan. The Navy, for its part, assented to the creation of a Department of Air, but Forrestal noted that Navy leaders' preference was for the Army to integrate its air components, as the Navy had. As for roles and missions, the Army endorsed granting the new Air Force full responsibility for "the military air resources of the United States," except those planes borne by ships and certain minor service aircraft. The Navy would not agree to this, Forrestal said, maintaining that its land-based planes used for reconnaissance, antisubmarine warfare, and the protection of shipping were indispensable. Furthermore, in the report Patterson said that the Army wanted to impose stringent limitations on the Marine Corps to keep it an amphibious force.

Four days after the two service secretaries submitted their report, the President called them, Eisenhower, and Nimitz to the Oval Office for a meeting. His main purpose was not to invite discussion but to set the stage for issuing a new package of recommendations to Congress. Writing in his diary, Forrestal was cynical about what he observed.

> Both Patterson and Eisenhower went to great pains to emphasize that no matter what the President's decision was to be, they would accept it cheerfully and loyally and do their best to support it. . . . I realized that [their] . . . remarks flowed from the realization that the President was already pretty much on the Army's side of the case and they had nothing to risk in volunteering such a statement. I was considerably entertained by Patterson's saying at the end that he greatly regretted the impression that this merger was something the Army was trying to "put over." I refrained from observing that it would be quite difficult to have any other impression inasmuch as it had been the Army's promotion from the outset.

Eleven days later, on June 15, Truman affirmed Forrestal's suspicions. By letter he answered the secretaries' joint communication of May 31; he mailed four other letters to the chairmen of the Naval and Military Affairs committees of the House and Senate. He then released all of these documents to the press. Even though Forrestal was disappointed with the overall content, the impact of his persistence and his and Eberstadt's thoughtful work was readily apparent. The President had endorsed having a Council of Common Defense, a National Security Resources Board, and a revamped CIA, and, true to his word, had eliminated his previous proposal for a single military Chief of Staff in charge of all the military. However, Truman had endorsed giving the new Secretary of National Defense, or Director of Defense, as Patterson and Forrestal had informally entitled him, centralized control of all the services, which disturbed Forrestal as much as a recommendation for a single Chief of Staff. The National Defense Secretary would be in charge of the Secretaries of the Army, the Navy, and the new Air Force, and would be the only one of the four who would be a member of the cabinet.

The President had no choice but to keep hands off the Marine Corps, the idea of diminishing its role having proved to be "political dynamite," in Baldwin's words. Truman affirmed in writing the Corps's existing status. But it seems he tried to effect a trade-off. He evidently hoped that his accepting the Marine Corps's present mission status would prompt the Navy to accept the Army Air Forces' view about the Navy's land-based aircraft. He proposed that the new Air Force take over the reconnaissance, antisubmarine, and ship protection roles that the Navy's land-based planes were fulfilling. If, at this point, he really believed that the Navy establishment, already aroused by the threat to the Marine Corps, would readily compromise on this, such that he could get military reorganization through Congress in the few days left in the legislative session, he must not have been paying much attention in recent weeks.

It so happened that before retiring the previous evening, Forrestal had read an account of the Battle of Savo Island. That Japanese victory and American disaster was attributed to land-based reconnaissance. A lone Japanese reconnaissance plane, land-based, had spotted the US fleet, whose commander had been unaware that a Japanese fleet was even in the area; he had had no land-based aircraft. The Japanese had controlled all the airfields in the area. Vandegrift's men on Guadalcanal had witnessed firsthand the result — dead American sailors washing ashore and shot-up US ships limping by. The Marine division itself might have been lost had they not been so superbly trained and led.

The lesson of Savo Island fresh on his mind, Forrestal met with Truman privately a few days later. By this time, Senator Thomas's subcommittee was already hard at work drafting another version of what was still an Army plan essentially; Thomas, upon being asked to comment on the President's most recent initiative, had told reporters it was "splendid confirmation" of his subcommittee's earlier work. Forrestal noted in his diary what he said to Truman during their meeting. Tactfully, he warned the President that "the Navy felt so strongly as to be fanatic about" the issue of land-based aircraft and that it "*must* have the means" to carry out its mission.

> I told the President that my general view of Cabinet members' responsibilities in supporting and securing orderly government was this: That he supports policies of his President up to the point where he encounters sincere and *major* disagreement. That he should then ask to withdraw from the Cabinet. I remarked parenthetically that I didn't take myself over-seriously in this whole matter and that I had no illusions that my resignation, if it occurred, would have any earth-shaking consequences.

Forrestal's opposition would not come to this, though. Members of Congress were eager to adjourn — they did so on August 3, 1946 — so they could get home and campaign. Truman and Forrestal were both fortunate that the President's new recommendations came during the last days of the congressional session. Since reorganization would not be an election issue, it being a rather arcane subject to the public, and would not be addressed until the Eightieth Congress convened in January 1947, there was time to work things out peacefully.

Though a military reorganization bill had not gotten very far in the Seventy-ninth Congress, the House and the Senate had done some internal reorganizing that would greatly facilitate it during the next session. Members decided in effect to unify the Naval Affairs and the Military Affairs committees, forming in their place a single Armed Services Committee for each body. This was part of an overall internal reorganization that Congress put itself through. Pressures for change were catching up with this American institution also. The conclusion of the recent world war, more than anything else, was the cause. The many new, younger members represented a need to update the way Congress operated, though individually they had little influence. And the tenor of the times was such that consolidation or "streamlining" was considered improvement, especially in regard to the armed forces. The sentiment was that the Navy and Military Affairs committees had to be merged so as to reflect modern warfare's close integration of forces. Another consideration was military expenditures being a much greater percentage of the overall budget, even during peacetime. World War II had ushered in a new era, a vastly more costly one, and for a time the Army, the Army Air Forces, and the Navy had gotten everything they wanted. But now, during postwar austerity, for Congress to decide to buy some bombers meant that it could not buy some ships. This sort of decision-making involved balancing interests, and most members thought this could best be done by a single committee. The necessary legislation was authored by Congressmen A. S. ("Mike") Monroney of Oklahoma, a Democrat, and Charles M. LaFollette of Indiana, a Republican. The reorganization would go into effect when the Eightieth Congress convened. This military merger within Congress was a strong signal that most members wanted something like it done for the military itself. At this point, it was really only a matter of what form it would take.

With Congress out of town, Truman and his staff had time to look farther down the road. Thinking that he should take better measure of the Soviets, the President called Clark Clifford in and told him to prepare a list of their violations of agreements with the United States. A few weeks earlier Truman had announced he was appointing Clifford to Judge Samuel I. Rosenman's old position of special counsel to the President. As such Clifford had become, among other things, Truman's national security adviser. President Franklin Roosevelt had created the post for Rosenman, and when the latter retired on February 1, 1946, Truman said he considered the slot a wartime position and thus would not fill it. But Clifford, while naval aide, so impressed him with his advice and quiet confidence during the railroad strike, Truman reactivated the post for the thirty-nine-year-old fellow Missourian.

Clifford, in turn, had his assistant George Elsey, an intense twenty-eight-year-old historian educated at Harvard and Princeton, initiate the project of compiling the list of Soviet agreement violations. Elsey was another former Reserve officer and had been Truman's assistant naval aide when Clifford was the chief. On his own initiative and with Clifford's and Truman's approval, Elsey developed the assignment into a much larger project — a broad review of "American Relations with the Soviet Union," as the finished report was entitled. It was long overdue. Postwar conferences, pressing day-to-day problems, and the transition from a wartime to a peacetime economy had kept the small White House staff totally preoccupied. Now, with Washington rife with talk about the menacing moves of Stalin's Soviet Russia and with military reorganization in limbo, it was the obvious and necessary next step.

The year had started out with Stalin's very belligerent speech of February 9, 1946 — his "declaration of World War III," as Justice Douglas had described it. The dictator had then reinforced the perception that he was moving toward war by bringing pressure on certain sensitive points in the Balkans and the Middle East. By late summer, this activity had intensified.

On August 7, 1946, the Soviet Union issued its demand that Turkey "share in the defense of" the Dardanelles and the Bosporus — which, translated, meant "share control of." On August 9, Yugoslav fighter planes forced down an unarmed US Army transport plane. This incident pertained to a dispute over title to the far northeastern province of Venezia Giulia, whose principal city was Trieste, which was Italian before the war. The line of occupation ran through the center of the province — Anglo-American forces on one side of it and Soviet-backed Yugoslav troops of Marshal Tito, a Communist, on the other. The Yugoslavs wanted the province, which would give them control of the whole eastern coast of the Adriatic. On August 19, the Yugoslavs actually shot down an unarmed Army transport; the crash killed all the American crewmen aboard. Concurrent with these happenings, the Soviet Union was backing border pressure by Yugoslavia and Bulgaria to force Greece to cede its northern provinces. And at the United Nations, the Soviets were loudly supporting the installation of a Communist government in Athens. Meanwhile, in the Iranian province of Azerbaijan, the Soviets were arming a separatist movement. These were the Soviet moves that shaped the perceptions of Clifford, Elsey, and others as they contributed to the report Truman had ordered prepared. Dean Acheson later observed: "The Russians themselves greatly helped our education. In picking the Straits and Iran as points of pressure, they followed the route of invasion by barbarians against classical Greece and Rome and later of the czars to warm water."

Elsey and Clifford began by examining all kinds of documents, including Kennan's long telegram. Then, with Truman's full backing, which was made known, they sent questionnaires to top officials in the foreign-policy and military-affairs establishments, asking them to comment. They followed these up with interviews. Respondents included Byrnes, Patterson, Forrestal, Leahy, Spaatz, Eisenhower, Nimitz, Attorney General Tom Clark, Lieutenant General Hoyt Vandenberg, who was then the CIA director, and a few others "with special knowledge in this field."

"These gentlemen have prepared careful estimates of current and future Soviet policies, extensive reports on recent Soviet activities affecting the security of the United States, and recommendations concerning American policy with respect to the Soviet Union," Clifford informed the President in his cover letter to the top-secret memorandum. The report ended up being more than a hundred thousand words long. That seven of the nine respondents listed were military people indicates not only the postwar prominence of the military but also what US–Soviet relations were coming to. One line in particular summarized the worry of those who had had input: "Although the Soviet Union at the present moment is precluded from military aggression beyond the land mass of Eurasia, the acquisition of a strategic air force, naval forces and atomic bombs in quantity would give the U.S.S.R. the capability of striking anywhere on the globe. Ability to wage aggressive warfare in any area of the world is the ultimate goal of Soviet military policy."

Elsey wrote the first draft, to which Clifford made changes. Their basic determination, based on the advice received, was that the United States had to keep Western Europe, the Middle East, China, and Japan out of the Soviet sphere of influence. Kennan was asked to critique the second draft; passages from his long telegram were actually included in the copy. "I think the general tone is excellent and I have no fault to find with it," he remarked. In several months, he would produce a study of his own. Forrestal liked the memorandum, too. Clifford would later say that the Secretary of the Navy had by this time become his closest friend in government; the comment reflects not only their compatibility of views but also the discerning Forrestal's recognition that Clifford would become very influential with Truman.

Clifford and Elsey's memorandum became one of fundamental importance to the Truman administration. Aid to Greece and Turkey, the Truman Doctrine, the Marshall Plan, even intervention in Korea, were foreshadowed by it. So were the concepts of nuclear deterrence and containment, though the latter word, which Kennan within a year's time would popularize, was not used in the narrative. Among the observations and recommendations made were these:

> The Soviet Union will never be easy to "get along with" . . . [and this is] a fact to be faced objectively and courageously. If we find it impossible to enlist Soviet cooperation in the solution of world problems, we should be prepared to join with the British and other Western countries in an attempt to build up a world of our own. . . .
>
> . . . this government must, as a first step toward world stabilization, seek to prevent additional Soviet aggression. The greater the area controlled by the Soviet Union, the greater the military requirements of this country will be. Our present military plans are based on the assumption that, for the next few years at least, Western Europe, the Middle East, China and Japan will remain outside the Soviet sphere. If the Soviet Union acquires control of one or more of these areas, the military forces required to hold in check those of the U.S.S.R. and prevent still further acquisitions will be substantially enlarged. That will also be true if any of the naval and air bases in the Atlantic and Pacific, upon which our present plans rest, are given up. . . .
>
> The language of military power is the only language which disciples of power politics understand. The United States must use that language in order that Soviet leaders will realize that our government is determined to uphold the interests of its citizens and the rights of small nations. . . .

> The Soviet Union's vulnerability is limited due to the vast area over which its key industries and natural resources are widely dispersed, but it is vulnerable to atomic weapons, biological warfare and long-range air power. Therefore, in order to maintain our strength at a level which will be effective in restraining the Soviet Union, the United States must be prepared to wage atomic and biological warfare. . . . A war with the U.S.S.R. would be "total" in a more horrible sense than any previous war and there must be constant research for both offensive and defensive weapons.

Clifford had had the Government Printing Office typeset the memorandum, and he personally delivered it to Truman in the late afternoon on September 21, 1946. The President thanked him and said he would read it that evening.

At about seven the next morning, Clifford's home phone rang. Truman was on the line.

"How many copies of that memorandum do you have?" he asked.

"I have ten," said Clifford.

"I want all of them," Truman said. "I think you'd better come down now, Clark, and go to your office and get them out of the safe and I want them all delivered to me. If this got out it would blow the roof off the Kremlin. We'd have the most serious situation on our hands that has yet occurred in my administration."

Following instructions, Clifford dressed quickly and drove to the White House, retrieved the ten copies, and delivered them to the President. Though Truman's concern about Soviet reaction was warranted, he worried as much or more about the reaction from the liberal wing of his own party. The fall election campaign for Democrats had gotten off to a disastrous start because of an internal split brought on by this very subject. The effort had come a cropper only two days before, when Truman fired Henry Wallace, his Secretary of Commerce, who had been the Vice President during Roosevelt's third term.

Wallace, enamored of the thought that this was "the century of the common man," as he put it, preached a foreign-policy gospel about the brotherhood of man. By most indications, he trusted the Soviets more than he did the leaders of the US military, who were going to start World War III, he was convinced. In a memorandum dated July 23, 1946, he had warned Truman that "there is a school of military thinking that advocates a 'preventive war,' an attack on Russia *now* before Russia has atomic bombs." He implored Truman for "a shift in some of our thinking about international affairs," and recommended that the United States consider giving the Soviets the atomic bomb to balance things out. Wallace thought US policy vis-à-vis the Soviets was too tough already. He thought that the Bikini Atoll test and talk about military bases and long-range bombers were sending the wrong signals.

Evidently, someone on Wallace's staff slipped a copy of this private memorandum to C. B. Baldwin, the chief organizer of a September Madison Square Garden rally of liberal groups organizing to combat the reelection of New York's Republican governor Thomas E. Dewey. Upon reading it, Baldwin asked Wallace to share these thoughts in a speech at the rally. This he did; his presentation on September 12, 1946, included such lines as "The tougher we get, the tougher the Russians will get," and "We must not let our Russian policy be guided or influenced by those inside or outside the United States who want war with Russia." And, Wallace stated, the United States should recognize "that we have no more business in the *political* affairs of Eastern Europe than Russia has in the *political* affairs of Latin America, Western Europe, and the United States. . . . Whether we like it or not the Russians will try to socialize their sphere of influence just as we try to democratize our sphere of influence." It had developed recently that a key feature of US foreign policy involved keeping Eastern Europe from being dominated by the Soviet Union; Byrnes was just then negotiating the details in Paris at a conference of foreign ministers. Wallace had inveigled Truman into approving the speech, having summarized its contents when they discussed it for about five minutes. He therefore included this statement in his narrative: "And just two days ago, when President Truman read these words, he said they represented the policy of his administration."

The stakes were big; an uproar ensued. "We can only co-operate with one Secretary of State at a time," Senator Arthur Vandenberg told reporters. Byrnes had no reaction until Wallace's July 23 memorandum was made public, at which point he cabled Truman, warning him that the Secretary of Commerce's public criticism of the administration's foreign policy had to stop; otherwise, he said, "I must ask you to accept my resignation immediately." The next day, in one of his infamous poison-pen letters, Truman ordered Wallace to submit his resignation; this was seven days after Wallace had delivered his speech.

The Wallace episode was very significant. At the moment that Truman was about to lead his administration through a thorough reevaluation of US foreign policy, the liberal wing of his party alienated itself from him. He was a liberal himself, though not the dogmatic kind Wallace was, so liberals might have exerted considerable influence on his decision-making. Instead, because of Wallace, their leading exponent, they locked themselves out of the discussions.

Wallace was not the only prominent liberal speaking out. At the same rally at which Wallace spoke, Senator Claude Pepper, a Florida Democrat, delivered this assessment of the Truman administration's emerging foreign policy: "What do you expect in a foreign policy which really meets the approval of Senator Vandenberg and John Foster Dulles [the GOP's top foreign policy expert]?" The President revealed in a diary entry his alienation from liberals such as Pepper and Wallace. Referring to the latter, he wrote, "I am not so sure he is as fundamentally sound intellectually as I had thought. . . . [He is] a pacifist 100 per cent." Elaborating, Truman wrote:

> I do not understand a "dreamer" like that. . . . The Reds, phonies and "parlor pinks" seem to be banded together and are becoming a national danger. . . . They can see no wrong in Russia's four and one-half million armed forces, in Russia's loot of Poland, Austria, Hungary, Rumania, Manchuria. They can see no wrong in Russia's living off the occupied countries to support the military occupation. But when we help our friends in China who fought on our side it is terrible.

The Clifford-Elsey memorandum would remain a secret until the Vietnam War, when Clifford, by then Secretary of Defense, stunned Arthur Krock of the *New York Times* by handing him a copy of it during an interview about how the nation had come to get involved in that conflict. Nonetheless, the memo's impact in 1946 was important. By ordering Clifford to involve all the administration's senior foreign-policy and military-affairs people, Truman had begun the process of forming a consensus within the government that the Soviet Union was the nation's chief enemy and that the two great powers were locked in a life-or-death struggle worldwide. This perception would last about forty years.

After Truman's break with the liberal wing of his party over foreign affairs, it was inevitable that he would move to the right on these issues, especially since the results of the fall elections had the Republicans picking up 56 seats in the House of Representatives and 12 in the Senate, enough to take control of both bodies, by 246 to 188 and 51 to 45, respectively. (An American Labor Party candidate won a House seat.) Truman was too adroit a politician not to try to capture some of the issues with which the Republicans had won. Economic issues had been the primary ones of the campaigns.

Americans were tired of strikes and shortages of consumer goods and housing, and were becoming as upset about inflation as they had been about wage and price controls. They were also concerned about trouble with the Soviet Union, maybe even war. Stalin and Molotov, his foreign minister, had fueled their fears by so openly vilifying the United States. And talk of Communist spies stealing state secrets had added to the public's unease.

Early in the year a spy network operating out of the Soviet embassy in Ottawa had been exposed, as had its primary purpose: to obtain American atomic-bomb secrets. Then, a short time later, a British scientist, Dr. Alan Nunn May, had been arrested on charges of giving secret information and samples of uranium 235 to a Soviet agent. May was later convicted. Such sensational news incited worrisome reactions, such as Congressman John E. Rankin's announcing that the House Un-American Activities Committee was "trailing" spies operating in the United States. All in all, these goings-on had made communism an issue in 1946. Across the country, Republican candidates had won by developing the aforementioned theme that it was time for a change — to wit, that the government had to intervene to stop all the disruption and shortages caused by strikes, that government spending had to be cut so as to bring inflation under control, and that communism, both internal and external, had to be recognized as a threat to the nation that needed to be addressed (though the latter had not yet become the highly charged issue it would).

One long-term consequence of the election was its having fielded Republican victors who would be instrumental in reshaping the image of the GOP and who within a few years would be key to developing as a *predominant* issue the charge that Democrats were soft on communism. Among them were thirty-eight-year-old Joseph McCarthy, who won a Wisconsin Senate seat, and thirty-three-year-old Richard Nixon, who won a California congressional seat. At the time, the Republican party was split between a liberal wing led by Thomas Dewey and a conservative wing led by Robert Taft. Franklin Roosevelt's successes had caused the GOP to broaden its base by moving left, though Taft had not budged. It was in the middle political ground between Wallace on the left and Taft on the right that Truman and Dewey would battle in 1948.

Taft was chairman of the Republican Policy Committee, a position he would use as his platform from which to manage the Republican majorities in the House as well as the Senate; his prestige and power within his party were extraordinary. He had declined the position of Senate minority leader in 1944 (when Charles L. McNary of Oregon died) on the grounds that the position had too many time-consuming bureaucratic duties. For the same reason, he would decide not to become majority leader. Though his influence was substantial, domestic affairs was Taft's area of expertise and interest, so on foreign affairs he generally deferred to his friend Arthur Vandenberg after World War II, for a time.

Taft stood for the bedrock Republican values of individualism and free enterprise. And in foreign affairs, he stood for isolationism. Translated, this meant staying out of European affairs; Pacific involvement indeed was generally accepted by Republicans, who deemed that part of the world as natural an American sphere of influence as the Americas.

World War I had brought Democrats out of their isolationist shell; Wilson's fight for US participation in the League of Nations was symbolic of their transformation. The young Republicans elected to Congress in 1946 would, in a fashion, remake their party's image in regard to involvement in international affairs. They would make interventionism acceptable, even to most right-wing conservatives, by tying such involvement to the fight against communism. They would be for stopping communism wherever it threatened. Their concession to isolationists would be their emphasis on the minimal use of American troops overseas; instead, they would stress the use of airpower, including atomic bombs. Because these "New Nationalists," as some historians refer to them, would prove to be as conservative as Taft about other basic Republican tenets, they would secure a pivotal and powerful central position within their party.

In the short term, the Republican election victories of 1946 had considerable impact on military reorganization. Taft signaled this to be so. During lunch with Forrestal not long after the elections, he broached the subject and was sympathetic to the Navy Secretary's complaining that the Army was making "easy assumptions" about control of the seas. That Taft's son Lloyd was then serving in the Navy helped Forrestal advance his arguments. In fact, most Republicans favored Navy proposals over those of the Army. There were a couple of reasons for this. For one, conservatives like Taft were wary of the vertical, more centralized command structure that was basic to the Army plan. To him and other conservatives, it was another manifestation of Democrat-inspired big government. Second, since the Truman administration had from the outset of the military reorganization struggle pushed Army ideas, it followed that the loyal opposition would tend to take up the cause of the Navy.

Truman had assigned Clifford the job of writing the administration's new reorganization bill, but not much had been done, the Thomas bill being deemed as not much more than relevant notes, given the Navy's reaction to it. Clifford had been preoccupied with other projects, such as his and Elsey's memo on US-Soviet relations. Forrestal got things moving on November 12, 1946, seven days after the election, by hosting a meeting at his home. Present were some military officers who were keen theoreticians — Forrest Sherman; Arthur Radford, the new deputy chief of naval operations for air; and Major General Lauris Norstad, the director of plans and operations for the War Department's General Staff. Radford was just now establishing himself as a key figure in the unification debate, as was a civilian present, Stuart Symington, the assistant secretary of war for air.

Clearly, Forrestal had momentum moving in his direction owing to the election results, and by taking the initiative he planned to keep it that way. According to Sherman, who took notes, Symington seemed to accede to whatever the Navy Secretary insisted on. That the Secretary of Defense would be a coordinator rather than an administrator was becoming more settled. In this regard, Forrestal would not assent to Symington's suggestion that the Defense Secretary have authority to remove service secretaries. Interestingly, some newspapers, such as the *New York Times*, had reported that Truman might make Symington the first Defense Secretary.

On another matter, the dinner guests were also quite accommodating to one another: predictably, they agreed to leave the Marine Corps as it was. A surprise, however, according to Sherman's account, was Symington's agreeing "unmistakably to the continuance of Navy land-based squadrons for anti-submarine warfare." There was some question whether this represented official AAF views. All present must have been affected by the pleasant environs of Forrestal's home and perhaps a few drinks, because they were even agreeable about strategic airpower. In Sherman's words, "Mr. Symington explained that the Army Air Forces actually feared that the Navy might set up a strategic air force of its own and threaten their existence. He was told by Radford and me that there was no such danger." Such assurances suggest there was a certain unreality about the conversation — as if, given the agreeable circumstances, they were trying first and foremost to enjoy themselves this particular evening. The Supercarrier was not even mentioned.

More meetings followed this good start, and what characterized them was the parties' drifting apart again. At this juncture, all were being forced to think more deeply than ever before about their interrelationships. Implications emerged that had not been perceived initially. And the longer an agreement hung in the balance, the more nervous the parties became about assurances; lingering distrust and bad feelings, the product of many years of rivalry, began dictating the dialogue. Thus, a December 4 luncheon meeting of the same people who had met at Forrestal's home became unpleasant, though only twenty-two days had elapsed.

The exchanges were sharp. Radford asked Symington and Norstad what reason they had to think that there was even a place for a strategic air force in wars of the future. Kennan's writings on the need to limit warfare might have prompted the question, which was perceived as rude. Radford, whose blunt honesty would make him famous, added that he did not even think that bombers could reach their intended targets because they needed the protection of fighters, which would not have the range to stay with them. Among the evidence he cited were the enormous losses of Army Air Forces planes and crews during the raids on Schweinfurt and Regensburg during 1943, casualties that were blamed on lack of fighter cover. Norstad's reply was that the B-29 could bomb from 40,000 feet, whereas the most advanced fighters could only reach 38,000 feet — to which Radford countered that bombing from such a high altitude was very inaccurate.

The Navy stance was hardening. Another example of this occurred the next day, when Forrestal met with two senior offices, Marc Mitscher, who had become Eighth Fleet commander, and Vice Admiral Louis E. Denfeld, who was deputy chief of naval operations for personnel. According to Forrestal's diary comments, Mitscher affirmed Radford's statements made the day before and

> said that for twenty-five years Naval Air had been trying to protect itself both within the Navy and outside the Navy. . . . They had to resist the attempt in 1925, shortly after Mitchell's attack [on the *Ostfriesland*], of the Army Air Forces taking them over. He said this was always the object of Army Air — complete control of all the air forces in the country . . . and cited what had happened in England. . . . After the RAF took over, the Royal Navy had no freedom either in [plane] design or procurement, [and] they had given up reconnaissance and antisubmarine work [to the RAF].

In terms of personnel management, Mitscher noted, the result in Great Britain of putting the RAF in charge of Navy Air was Navy pilots becoming outcasts within their own service. To this diary entry Forrestal added his own comment. "In this connection," he wrote, "I had a report later in the day that a lieutenant commander, one of our best pilots with a splendid war record in the Pacific, had been approached by the Army Air Forces with an offer to make him a lieutenant colonel in that organization if he would transfer"; and he also noted that at the new Air University at Maxwell Field, Alabama, officers "openly proclaim their ultimate objective to be complete domination of all military air activities in the United States."

All this talk further sensitized Forrestal to the dangers in shallows ahead, so he reopened his investigation into what the Army *really* wanted to do to the Marine Corps and started meeting with potential allies in Congress, such as Republican senators Wallace White of Maine, the new majority leader, and C. Wayland Brooks of Illinois, both of whom assured him that fellow Republican Chandler Gurney of South Dakota, who would probably head the Senate's new Armed Services Committee, would be a reasonable person with whom to work.

Though not as adept at the game as Forrestal, Army Air Forces leaders were also actively lobbying their interests. Particularly active was General George C. Kenney, who back in 1937 had been fired and sent off to be an infantry instructor because his boss had endorsed the Air Corps Reorganization Bill. During the war he got back on track and rose to the top ranks of the Army Air Forces. Now he was commander of the new Strategic Air Command, and with the zeal of a man with some scores to settle, he was talking to anyone of influence who would listen to him. Word was out that Kenney had set up an appointment to visit Colonel Robert R. McCormick, the publisher of the *Chicago Tribune*, who thus far had been pro-Marine and anti-unification.

By the end of the year, Patterson had become alarmed about the recharging acrimony. A recent book by a Japanese author named Katō, who attributed the World War II defeat of Japan in large part to the alienated relationship of its army and navy, had made a deep impression on Patterson. So, after a cabinet meeting on January 3, 1947, Patterson invited himself to ride with Forrestal back to the Navy Department. During the discussion that ensued, he told Forrestal that the continuing estrangement was going to damage the services and undermine the nation's defense unless brought to a halt. He said that those in Army and Navy uniforms "must have the attitude that they're all truly brothers in arms." He was willing to be flexible about roles and missions, he said. Writing in his diary, Forrestal commented, "The whole conversation was in an entirely different key and tenor than any talk I've ever had before with Patterson."

Pursuant to the two secretaries' determination to iron things out, their subordinates resumed deliberations. On January 16, 1947, Symington, Norstad, and Sherman agreed on the final draft of a letter reconciling the views of all branches of the services about reorganization. It amounted to a considerable victory for Forrestal. The Eberstadt Plan had become the agreed-to form. The services would be integrated more than they would be merged or unified. The new entity's official name would accurately imply its loose structure; it would be called the National Military Establishment, not the Department of National Defense. The byword would be coordination, not control. Patterson had decided the Navy's plan was better than nothing. Actually, what he had decided was that it was a start. Following its enactment, the Army planned to keep on lobbying for a more centrally controlled organization. This was not evident at the time, however; Forrestal and the Navy tended to think that the reorganization dispute was about to be settled once and for all.

Forrestal called Clark Clifford to give him the news. Clifford, who more and more was demonstrating an instinctive feel for political timing, wanted to release the agreement to reporters immediately. Forrestal demurred; he wanted first to inform the Navy's principal supporters in the House and the Senate, both as a courtesy to them and as a "way of enlisting their sympathetic cooperation in the future," as he put it. After giving Forrestal time to do this, Clifford announced the good news at six o'clock that evening.

Washington was a Babel in January 1947, especially Congress. It had been this way since the massive leadership turnover in mid-1945, and the situation had gotten worse ever since. American politics was in transition. The recent Republican victories in the congressional elections had confirmed this fact. No consensus had emerged on much of anything of substance, even within the parties themselves. Leaders were speaking different languages. For example, some of the key proponents of deep cuts in military spending were Republicans, such as Congressman John Taber of New York, yet their party was trying to develop the theme that it was tougher on communism.

But in the realm of foreign-affairs policy, this confusion was about to dissipate suddenly. It had nothing to do with the fact that the new Congress, which convened on January 3, 1947, was Republican-controlled, or that George Marshall became Truman's new Secretary of State on January 8. It had everything to do with the course of events elsewhere in the world. These developments were announced simply enough. On February 20, 1947, Prime Minister Clement Attlee reported during a speech in the House of Commons that Great Britain would be ending British rule in India; the British had been there 250 years. And the very next day, the British embassy in Washington privately informed the State Department that Great Britain would be pulling out of Greece and Turkey; the Treaty of Versailles after World War I had established those nations as part of the British protectorate. American diplomats had been closely monitoring these situations and were not surprised. Still, it was like the death of a friend who had been a long time dying; it would take some getting used to.

The twenty-first was a Friday, and late that afternoon, the secretary to Lord Inverchapel, the British ambassador, called Marshall's office to say that his embassy wanted to deliver "a blue piece of paper," which in diplomatic parlance means an important document. The Secretary of State had left work early to drive to Leesburg with his wife, Katherine, for the weekend, so Under Secretary Acheson, after learning the subject of the communication, arranged to have it delivered to Loy W. Henderson, the director of the Office of Near Eastern and African Affairs. A short time later Herbert M. Sichel, the British embassy's First Secretary, handed it to Henderson.

That delivery and their shaking hands was as close as the ailing old empire got to a proper transfer of its global leadership role to its former colony. A de facto transfer had occurred during the war, but given what it meant to both nations and to the world, a more formal event was in order — perhaps some solemn ceremony in which the king handed the President his scepter and the two made their marks in wax. Two senior bureaucrats shaking hands and one handing the other some paperwork would have to do, though. Great Britain was in the same position as the proud old proprietor who after years running his business is forced to sign it over because he can't meet his payroll. So there was something sad about the way the transfer was handled, with John Bull having to slip out the back door red-faced, embarrassed as much as he was desperate.

The paperwork Sichel handed Henderson contained two messages. One read, in part: "His Majesty's Government have already strained their resources to the utmost to help Greece and have granted . . . assistance up to 31st March, 1947. . . . The United States Government will readily understand that His Majesty's Government, in view of their own situation, find it impossible to grant further financial assistance to Greece." The other message had the same import: "In existing financial situation His Majesty's Government could not, as the United States will readily appreciate, contemplate themselves making any further credits available to Turkey."

Great Britain was going broke. It could not afford to keep its troops in Greece, even though they were about all that was keeping Communist insurgents from taking control there. Turkey's problem was different. Its leaders did not seem to have the confidence to withstand pressure from the Soviets unless Turkish forces were modernized and better equipped. Great Britain had been trying to help out. The credit crunch had come as all of Europe was enduring the worst winter in memory, an unfortunate quirk of nature that had caused record snowfalls, paralyzed business, and made economic recovery from the war's devastation all the more difficult. The British were demoralized.

Marshall remained in Leesburg for the weekend, pondering the impending crisis, whose implications Acheson had described in a prescient memorandum handed him Friday morning, a half-day before Sichel came calling. State Department economists could read balance sheets and cash flow charts. His memo read, in part: "Unless urgent and immediate support is given to Greece, it seems probable that the Greek Government will be overthrown and a totalitarian regime of the extreme left will come into power." Acheson's conclusion was that the situation "might eventually result in the loss of the whole Near and Middle East and northern Africa" to Soviet domination. To take up Great Britain's burden was going to require an open-ended commitment and about $250 million the first year. Convincing Congress that the United States had to do so would not be easy; Taber and the new Speaker, Congressman Joseph Martin of Massachusetts, had already pushed through the House a resolution calling for a $6-billion cut in Truman's budget. Clever politicians were going to have to give the matter careful thought to get majorities in Congress to accept the short-term and long-term commitments. For his part, Marshall decided the situation could wait until Monday and that the nation would be better off if in the meantime he worked in his garden with his wife.

That Truman would want to help Greece and Turkey was a good probability. As Clifford and Elsey's book-length memo indicated, a consensus was developing among the administration's leaders around the conclusion that the United States had to take drastic action against the Soviets. Truman had actually made some preliminary moves: ordering the *Missouri* to Turkey and Greece and other ships to various Mediterranean ports, arranging economic aid for South Korea, and warning Stalin in no uncertain terms about encroachments against Iran. Also indicative of his hardening attitude was his firing of Wallace.

The crisis was discussed without resolution during the cabinet meeting of Monday, February 24, but two days later Marshall delivered to Truman a memorandum that he, Patterson, and Forrestal had prepared about what to do. They wrote that "we should take immediate steps to extend all possible aid to Greece and, on a lesser scale, to Turkey." Truman was in general agreement, his attitude being that Stalin had to be shown "we mean business," recalled John Steelman, a staff member. The next day Truman called congressional leaders to the White House to ask for their support.

His designated chief advocate that day was Marshall, who, as planned, took the floor and in deliberate manner advanced the administration's arguments, which included the warning that unless the United States stepped in, "Soviet domination might thus extend over the entire Middle East to the borders of India. . . . The effect of this upon Hungary, Austria, Italy and France cannot be overestimated. It is not alarmist to say that we are faced with the first crisis of a series which might extend Soviet domination to Europe, the Middle East and Asia." By the time Acheson finished his follow-up, an impassioned argument steeped in historical context, the small audience was thinking in terms of Carthage and Rome. The under secretary maintained that nothing less than the nation's survival was at risk should the Soviets extend their domain over two-thirds of the earth's surface and three-quarters of its population.

Of all the listeners, the one person whom Truman and his advocates absolutely had to sway was Senator Vandenberg. For years he had been an ardent isolationist of the Republican old guard, but on January 10, 1945, after almost eighteen years in the Senate, he delivered to his colleagues a remarkable speech in which he renounced isolationism and endorsed his nation's taking up a worldwide leadership responsibility. The war's devastation and loss of life had traumatized him, whereupon he decided that the

United States should help prevent such catastrophes by involving itself in international affairs. He had been so obdurate about his old views that his change of heart had an immediate impact; Roosevelt took fifty copies of Vandenberg's speech to Yalta to convince doubters during negotiations that he had bipartisan support. The long-term consequences of the speech were even more significant. The speech led Vandenberg to be in the pivotal position in the debate over aid to Greece and Turkey. His support for it and other initiatives that soon followed helped Truman establish a foreign policy that the nation adhered to for decades.

When Acheson finished talking, Vandenberg, looking grave, rose and said, "Mr. President, if you will say that to the Congress and the country, I will support you and I believe that most of its members will do the same." The senator also advised Truman to emphasize the importance of stopping communism. This, he thought, would be the only way to overcome the strong sentiment in Congress to cut spending. Aid to Britain itself had been approved only after six long months of debate.

The State Department was assigned the dual task of writing the proposed policy and Truman's speech. Because Marshall was to depart Washington for a meeting of foreign ministers in Moscow, he put Acheson in charge of both projects. Acheson wanted to come up with something bold and dramatic, and he saw to it that both documents met his specifications. Kennan, because of his newfound prominence in the field, was asked to comment on the speech. His judgment was that it went too far; he thought the President would be pledging the United States to an unlimited commitment. Marshall's criticism was in a different vein. According to Charles Bohlen, who was with him, he felt that the speech was very stridently anti-Communist; but Marshall did not intercede.

By this time, the White House already had a copy of the speech, and Clifford had begun molding it to suit Truman's personal style. Elsey, Clifford's assistant, was troubled by the speech for a combination of the reasons Kennan and Marshall were. In a March 7 memorandum to Clifford he wrote: "There has been no overt action in the immediate past by the U.S.S.R. which serves as an adequate pretext for 'All-out' speech."

Clifford's focus was different, however. He was thinking about Truman's reelection campaign. Foremost in his mind was Vandenberg's advice. The whole rationale for providing the aid was to stop communism. That had to be emphasized — further dramatized, even. By presenting the aid request this way, the President could wrest away from the Republicans an issue with which they were gaining popularity. Truman and Clifford were just beginning to be on a roll politically, one that would continue through election night in 1948.

Clifford had convinced Truman to take on John L. Lewis in the courts when he ordered his United Mine Workers out on strike in 1946; the work stoppage jeopardized the successful conversion of the economy to peacetime conditions. Americans generally disliked Lewis, mostly for ordering strikes even during wartime, so Truman's popularity soared when the labor leader, faced with huge fines, backed down. One White House staff member said the successful confrontation with Lewis gave the President such an infusion of confidence "you could hear his balls clank." Truman had seized from Republicans an issue with which they had won the fall elections. Now, with this business of aiding Greece and Turkey, he moved confidently to grab another.

Elsey later recalled that Clifford's view of the aid speech was that it was to be "the opening gun in a campaign to bring people up to [the] realization that the war isn't over by any means." It would foist on penurious, anti-Communist Republicans a Hobson's choice — a vote for more foreign aid or a vote against helping two struggling societies fight off communism. Clifford, whose standing with Truman had surged after the showdown with Lewis, reinforced Truman's natural disposition to take a stand and come out fighting.

Truman eventually delivered the speech on March 12, 1947, to a joint session of Congress. He requested $400 million in economic and military aid for Greece and Turkey and asked for authority to send military advisers to help. They would be the first American military advisers sent outside the Western Hemisphere. Unlike his preliminary moves against the Soviets, such as his ordering the *Missouri* to Turkey, the President gave these recommendations a policy context, which came to be known as the Truman Doctrine. As stated by him that evening, it was this: "It must be the policy of the United States to support free peoples who are resisting attempted subjugation by armed minorities or by outside pressures." As Kennan had observed in his critique, this was a remarkably expansive commitment. Millions of young Americans would soon be astonished to learn where it would take them. Harold Callender of the *New York Times* reported from Paris that prominent diplomats there read the speech with "amazement since they expected nothing so stern and forthright." It seemed to them that what Truman was saying constituted "a new and broadened Monroe Doctrine that seems certain to compel a showdown between the Soviet Union and the Western World."

Hearings on Truman's proposals to aid Greece and Turkey militarily and economically were set up quickly. With Marshall in Moscow, Acheson was the chief administration official who testified. Politicians on opposite ends of the spectrum had similar reactions to his recommendations. Senator

Alexander Wiley, a conservative Wisconsin Republican, said that "the people of America are mightily concerned about whether this is the opening wedge to our taking over the job that Britain has done so well in the last one hundred-fifty years around the globe." Liberal Democrat Claude Pepper, a member of the Senate Foreign Relations Committee, told Acheson: "My America is stepping out into a new field, reaching out and, yes, without mincing words, assuming the function of the British Empire." That Truman wanted to send military advisers worried Vandenberg. "It scares me to death," he said. Senator Alexander Smith, a New Jersey Republican, saw no end to such a precedent. Pointing to "Communist infiltration in South America," he asked, "Are we going to be called on to finance resistance to Communism in other countries like that?" These men talked as if they actually had a choice but to try to save Greece and Turkey from the Communists. They did not, really, Truman having put the debate in that context. The President had aggressively exploited Americans' fear of communism. He had seen how Republican candidates successfully developed the issue to win control of Congress, and fearful that Congressman J. Parnell Thomas, the zealous new chairman of the House Un-American Activities Committee, would make matters worse for the Democrats, he ginned up his own counterpart, the Temporary Commission on Employee Loyalty. In doing so he decreed that anyone applying for a job in the federal government would be subjected to a loyalty check. He specified, too, that all heads of agencies and departments would be responsible for weeding out anyone disloyal who was already on the job. This led to the creation of Loyalty Review Boards, whose proceedings were as effective in exposing Communists as the trials of old Salem were in rooting out witches. Truman also had an "Attorney General's List" of subversive organizations compiled and published. Tom Clark's guiding thought in putting it together must have been "better safe than sorry," for he included such institutions as the National Negro Congress and the Ohio School of Social Sciences. Within a couple of years, the young Republicans in Congress, the New Nationalists, aided by events, would recapture this issue for their party by developing the public fear to hysterical proportions, and they would foist on Truman the same no-choice option in Korea as now lay before Congress.

In the present situation, one concession to reason came in response to Vandenberg's apprehension that the administration's legislative proposal as written was too provocative. It was one thing to say such things, but it was quite another to put the same inflammatory language into an official document. On the spot, Acheson accommodated Vandenberg. No one wanted a prestige-engaging showdown with the Soviets, the kind Kennan in his long telegram had warned to avoid. Rewriting the proposed legislation, Acheson cleverly couched in arcane language the President's authority to send advisers to Greece and Turkey. His intention was to make the congressional authorization so abstruse that it would not force a Russian move in kind, which essentially was Vandenberg's worry. The alternative wording Acheson offered the Senate Foreign Relations Committee read: "The provisions of the Act of May 19, 1926, as amended, are hereby extended and made applicable to Turkey and Greece." For two decades the cited action had been the legal authority for Presidents' sending military advisers to nations in Central and South America. With this done, Truman's aid request was endorsed out of committee, approved by the Senate and the House, and on May 22, 1947, signed into law by Truman.

Congress's approving Truman's plan to aid Greece and Turkey would define for decades the Soviet Union's relationship with the United States; though not mentioned in this legislation, the USSR was now officially America's chief adversary. That essentially was what all the discussion had been about the previous year, from Kennan's long telegram on through the Clifford-Elsey memorandum. The decision to aid Greece and Turkey had settled the point. Politicians such as Wallace and Pepper who believed that the nature of the relationship was still an open question would later pay dearly at the polls for their miscalculation.

With this point established, the great follow-up question immediately emerged: How could the United States best battle its adversary? By springtime of 1947 this was being discussed all over Washington. Appropriately, given his prominent role in the question just settled, Kennan, because of Forrestal, would exert great influence on the answer. The sequence of events that caused this to happen started in December 1946, when the Navy Secretary sent Kennan for comment a study on Marxism and Soviet power done by a member of Forrestal's immediate staff. Kennan, who at the time was finishing up his fall term at the National War College, looked it over carefully and, though he deemed it well done, decided that producing his own treatise on the subject would be easier than making piecemeal comments on the one in hand. He asked Forrestal if he minded and was encouraged to set to work. The result was a submission tendered to the secretary on January 31, 1947. In Kennan's words, it focused on "Soviet power as a problem in policy for the United States." The paper proposed a plan for meeting the Soviet challenge. What Kennan suggested, essentially, was that the United States must contain the Soviet Union until it collapsed in and of its own weight or until its leadership mellowed. He believed that even in a country with a long history of cruel despots, Stalin's Russia was particularly cruel and authoritarian, and that the threat posed would diminish with his passing. Kennan later described what he envisioned:

> The purpose of "containment" as then conceived was not to perpetuate the status quo to which the military operations and political arrangements of World War II had led; it was to tide us over a difficult time and bring us to a point where we could discuss effectively with the Russians the drawbacks and dangers this status quo involved, and to arrange with them for its peaceful replacement by a better and sounder one.

Forrestal was impressed, as he had been with the long telegram. And whereas that earlier analysis had clarified for him the nature of the beast, Kennan's current effort explained how to tame it. Inadvertently, Kennan had placed the decision to aid Greece and Turkey into a scheme of action. With his Truman Doctrine, the President provided the policy context. Things were coming together. Responding to Kennan's recent work, Forrestal wrote him, "It is extremely well-done and I am going to suggest to the Secretary that he read it." He was referring to Marshall.

Kennan later was anguished when containment was perceived as a military strategy when in fact he had in mind mostly a political and economic policy to effect the same thing; but he should have anticipated this interpretation, since his recommendations were in response to an inquiry by a very high-ranking figure in the military establishment. In any event, the "doctrine of containment" became a grand military scheme to check Soviet expansionism. That the crisis in Greece and Turkey happened when it did, just as Kennan's latest ideas were making the rounds, also put them in a martial cast; in those instances, military aid and military advisers were the only means of addressing the problems in the short term. Furthermore, that during this crisis period Congress opened deliberations on the new military budget and re-opened deliberations on military reorganization encouraged the focus on military-type containment.

Kennan eventually got the opportunity to stress nonmilitary means of containing the Soviet Union. Marshall selected him to direct the State Department's newly created rough equivalent of the Department of War's Division of Operations and Plans. He was expected to start after he finished the National War College's first academic year. When Kennan did begin, Marshall placed him in the only office that had an adjoining door to his own and afforded him the privilege of entering his office by this direct route, without checking with the receptionist. Furthermore, Kennan's "Policy Planning Staff," as it came to be called, had the same sort of free-agency status. It operated outside of the State Department's bureaucracy and became the secretary's personal policy-planning staff. How Kennan came to get this job is uncertain, but there is a good possibility that it was the product of behind-the-scenes work by his patron, the Secretary of the Navy. The likelihood is that Marshall decided to make Kennan his policy-planning director only a matter of days after Forrestal showed him Kennan's January 31, 1947, treatise.

Given the landmark foreign-affairs and military-policy legislation that the Republican-controlled House and Senate passed during 1947 and 1948 while working with Truman, their reputation as the "Do-Nothing Eightieth Congress" has to be one of the most unfair ever attached to a group of politicians. Truman hung the moniker on them in 1948, during one of the most skillfully waged presidential campaigns in American history. The tag really pertained only to social legislation. In addition to affirming the Truman Doctrine by supporting aid for Greece and Turkey, the Eightieth reorganized the military, authorized the Marshall Plan to save Western Europe from economic collapse, sent a large appropriation to Nationalist China as part of the Marshall Plan, voted economic support for South Korea, supported the permanent deployment to the Mediterranean of a large Navy force that would be designated the Sixth Fleet, and laid the groundwork for NATO, the North Atlantic Treaty Organization, by passing the Vandenberg Resolution, which authorized military alliances during peacetime.

Public hearings on military reorganization convened a few days after the aid to Greece and Turkey was approved. By this time, all the major compromises had been worked out within the administration; it was a matter of keeping them together long enough for Congress to scrutinize them and pass them into law. The danger was that some key figures' testimony might unhinge the whole thing. This very nearly happened because of what Eisenhower had to say on March 25, 1947, and what Under Secretary of War Kenneth C. Royall said on April 15. Eisenhower told the Senate Armed Services Committee that he regretted that the bill did not establish the single Chief of Staff position as initially proposed, and that he hoped this would be legislated at some later date. And Royall's description of the powers he assumed the Secretary of Defense would have was entirely at odds with that to which Forrestal and Patterson had agreed. Royall said he thought the Defense Secretary would have very broad, virtually absolute, powers in assigning roles and missions. These comments riled the Navy establishment, of course. Implicit in Eisenhower's statements was that the Army viewed the legislation being considered as only a temporary measure, one that should be seriously modified as soon as possible. Royall's remarks conjured up all sorts of nightmares, such as a Secretary of Defense putting the new Air Force in charge of the Navy's aviation units and assigning the Marine Corps's major missions to the Army.

Reaction was immediate. Vandegrift complained publicly, which alerted the Corps's supporters to the danger, and also caused Clifford to complain to Forrestal about the Commandant's attitude. Forrestal was spurred to work Congress even harder to get his version of unification passed. He evidenced his exasperation in a diary entry one day after Royall testified. Recounting a dinner conversation with Senator Millard E. Tydings during which they discussed unification, he wrote that he had "to confess I was somewhat shaken by the recurring evidence of the Army's intransigence in regard to the chain-of-command concept (when, as a matter of fact, during [the] war they had not been able to issue a single order to MacArthur — and they couldn't now)." Tydings tried to reassure him, observing that he thought the bill would get through the Senate. The Maryland Democrat also believed that, if necessary, the Senate would approve protective clauses to assure the future of the Marine Corps and of Naval Aviation.

There were greater worries, which put everyone in a mood to do this. One was the US economy — inflation, in particular. Reduced spending was deemed the key for keeping it under control. Completing reorganization presumably would facilitate working out a coordinated military strategy that the Armed Services committees could consider. These and the Appropriations committees were having trouble knowing where to begin when it came to spending money on the military.

About two weeks after Royall's testimony, on April 28, 1947, Marshall finally returned from the foreign ministers' meeting in Moscow, and what he had to say about that state of affairs added more pressure. It made the current round of reorganization patter sound like quibbling. The Secretary of State thought that all Europe was on the verge of economic collapse. Furthermore, his weeks of negotiations with the Soviets and a startling personal meeting with Stalin had convinced him that they were not interested in any sort of collaborative aid effort. His conclusion was that in Europe the United States had to go it alone and had to act quickly. A measure of Marshall's renown was that a few hours after he arrived back in Washington, he delivered a radio address to the nation. "The patient is sinking while the doctors deliberate," he warned. He correctly surmised that Stalin wanted to stall development of a recovery plan for Europe because economic catastrophe and political turmoil there would serve the interests of local Communists and the Soviet Union.

The very next day, Marshall called Kennan in and told him that because of the emergency he would be unable to finish the year at the War College and instead must set up the Policy Planning Staff immediately. Marshall wanted them, under Kennan's management, to produce a plan for Europe's short-term and long-term economic recovery, and he wanted recommendations submitted to him within two weeks. The crisis was not Marshall's only reason for the short deadline. He wanted to get the State Department ahead of Congress and everyone else with ideas about what to do; he did not want to have to react defensively. This is why Truman had wanted him in the job. Probably no other man had the worldwide prestige to step in and be a strong Secretary of State from the first day. "The more I see and talk to him the more certain I am he's the great one of the age," the President had written as a notation on his appointment sheet of February 18, 1947. "I am surely lucky to have his friendship and support." Marshall has a free hand over there at the State Department, Truman told reporters.

Within several days of the meeting with Marshall, Kennan had formed his staff. They included academics, Foreign Service officers, and Colonel Charles Bonesteel, the Rhodes scholar who with Dean Rusk had divided Korea at the thirty-eighth parallel. (Rusk was at the present time temporarily assigned to State Department duty as a special assistant to the under secretary.) According to Kennan, all the planners were "intellectually hardheaded" people who were aware of "the awesome responsibility" Marshall had bestowed upon them. Kennan said that their meetings, which often went on late into the night, forced him "into an intellectual agony more intensive than anything I had ever previously experienced." Their debating was so untempered, and they became so exhausted, that one night Kennan had to excuse himself from the meeting, whereupon he walked around the building, weeping, as he regained his composure.

The Policy Planning Staff's recommendations were submitted to Marshall on May 23, about ten days after the initial deadline. Kennan had written the final draft. Copies were distributed to Acheson; William L. Clayton, the under secretary of state for economic affairs; Charles Bohlen, then serving as the special assistant to the secretary; and a few others. The next morning Marshall gathered these men in his office and, going around the room, one by one, had them comment.

The recommendations had been divided into short- and long-term categories, as requested, and reflected the only guidance Marshall had given Kennan, which was, quite simply, "Avoid trivia." For the short term, the staff recommended a crash program of mining and distributing coal to industry. That was basically it. The long-term plan was more subtle, but again, only the essentials were presented. The first major point was that Europeans themselves, working collectively, must develop a coordinated plan for their recovery, and that the United States should, generally speaking, limit its involvement to loaning them the funds needed. The funds might be used for individual national-recovery plans, but the staff thought the Europeans should work this out themselves. Otherwise, the United States would be faced with competing interests and would subject itself to charges of favoritism. The second major point was that the nations choosing to participate should request all the funds they needed to make themselves financially self-supporting. There would be no coming back for more funding. The third major point was that the primary objective of the US occupation of its zone in Germany should be its economic recovery. The thinking was that Germany's revival was fundamental to the revival of all Europe. The fourth major point was that all European nations should be invited to participate, including the Soviet Union and those nations of Eastern Europe it dominated. As Kennan later put it, the staff decided "that if anyone was to divide the European continent, it should be the Russians, with their response, not we with our offer."

The criticisms raised in the meeting with Marshall had to do with the inclusion of the Soviets and the belief that the participating nations could not get together to develop a recovery plan. After Kennan responded to these points, the secretary dismissed the group without comment, as was his custom. Kennan did not know what Marshall had decided until he read the text of the now-famous speech Marshall delivered on June 5, 1947, as part of Harvard University's commencement activities.

Just like Truman's speech to Congress in March, Marshall's speech to Harvard alumni focused the political establishment's attention on problems overseas. At the same time, both addresses highlighted just how parochial the military reorganization debate had become. The whole thing was overdone. About everyone involved was of the view that it was time to serve up what was there. A few days after Marshall's speech, the Senate Armed Services Committee approved a military reorganization bill and sent it to the floor. Hearings in the House on another version of it continued in the Committee on Executive Expenditures, chaired by Clare E. Hoffman, a Michigan Republican. Hoffman was looking for some sort of issue that might develop into something useful in the presidential campaign, now only a year away. But the proceedings were so superfluous that his Republican colleagues pressured him to cut them short. Even Admiral King was now prepared to endorse the reorganization bills being considered in the Senate and the House — a clear indication that these pieces of legislation represented Forrestal's views, not Truman's.

Fittingly, Kennan reentered the picture at this point in a dramatic way. It had been a remarkable eighteen months for him. Without going back to James Madison's several months at the Constitutional Convention in 1787, one would be hard put to find another American intellectual who had exerted as much influence on the affairs of state as Kennan had during this period. But his fame was the result of yet another paper — a version of the one he did for Forrestal back in January in which he talked about containment. While in the process of writing the analysis for Forrestal, Kennan delivered an informal presentation to the Council of Foreign Relations in New York. Afterward, editor Hamilton Fish Armstrong asked him whether he had something along the same lines that he might submit for publication in the organization's magazine, *Foreign Affairs*. Kennan thought of the paper he was about to submit to Forrestal, and after getting the latter's permission and the approval of the State Department's Committee on Unofficial Publication, he sent it to Armstrong, asking that he be given the secret byline "X." That Kennan actually believed his authorship could remain anonymous indicates that he was not very worldly about the prominence he was achieving for himself. Nor did he know when he submitted the article that during the period before publication Marshall would put him to work as his idea man. The article was published in late June, in the July issue of *Foreign Affairs*, under the title "The Sources of Soviet Conduct." The highly unusual byline served only to call attention to the piece. Arthur Krock of the *New York Times* remembered being shown the paper by Forrestal, and before long Kennan was publicly identified as the mystery author. Because of his access to Marshall, his directorship of the Policy Planning Staff, and his recent key work on the Marshall Plan, which had got around, great importance was accorded the essay in *Foreign Affairs*. In this way, during the summer of 1947, Kennan not only achieved fame but popularized the notion of containment; he thereby made a prime contribution toward creating the political consensus for the military alliances it would entail.

By the beginning of July, a reorganization bill was finally voted out of Hoffman's committee and sent to the floor of the House, which on the nineteenth passed its version. Not having been held up by the likes of Hoffman's dilatory work, the Senate had passed its version a couple of weeks before. A conference committee then went to work on a compromise. During these final stages, interest developed about whom Truman would appoint to the new position of Secretary of Defense. The conventional wisdom was that Patterson would get the job since he had consistently supported the President's positions and was more compatible with him than the other obvious candidate, James Forrestal. A dark-horse candidate was Symington. What few knew was that Patterson had already declined the job offer. Several years of public service had left him almost broke, and he wanted to return to the private practice of law in New York. Patterson ended speculation about his future when he resigned as Secretary of the Army, citing financial hardship.

About a week later, on July 24, the Senate adopted the conference report. The House followed the next day. The following morning, the *New York Times* reported what the legislation would do once Truman signed it into law. It all sounded so simple; making it work seemed so easy. According to the *Times,*

> The President would preside over meetings of a newly created National Security Council, consisting of the heads of the units making up an also new National Military Establishment. The council would assess and appraise the objectives, commitments and risks of the United States in relation to actual and potential military power, and make recommendations.
>
> Operating under the council would be a Central Intelligence Agency, which would assemble, correlate and evaluate intelligence relating to national security and give it appropriate dissemination. . . .
>
> Heading up the National Military Establishment would be the Secretary of Defense, who would have Cabinet rank, and who, according to highly informed quarters, would be James Forrestal, present Secretary of the Navy.
>
> While the Secretary of Defense would establish general policies and programs and exercise general direction, the service secretaries, without Cabinet rank, could report and recommend to the President on departmental matters.

The morning this account was published, Truman announced to Forrestal at a private meeting of the two in the Oval Office that, indeed, he was making him the first Secretary of Defense. The President candidly admitted that he had initially offered the job to Patterson.

Forrestal immediately accepted the appointment, and the two men chatted easily for about forty-five minutes. Truman no doubt was in a melancholy mood. Later in the day, after signing into law the National Security Act, which officials in Congress were preparing for his signature, he would be departing for Grandview, Missouri. His ninety-four-year-old mother, Martha, was in critical condition after a fall that broke her hip. Truman had visited her four times since the February accident, once for twelve days, and now her condition had taken a turn for the worse.

Among the topics that Truman and Forrestal touched on that morning were World War II and Adolf Hitler. Truman commented that Hitler had made two great mistakes: his decision to attack Poland and his failure to invade England after the fall of France. The chancy prospect of crossing the English Channel terrified Hitler, said Truman, observing that five years later Eisenhower showed it could be done.

The Navy Secretary was taken aback that the President believed that an Army officer had achieved the crossing that led to the successful Allied landings on the Normandy beaches. He countered that there was a vast difference between the two cases, it being that Hitler had the troops but lacked a navy powerful enough to get them across. In his diary Forrestal later wrote of the exchange: "I could not help but think at the time that it illustrated the work that we had to do to impress on him the fact that the crossing of a body of water is not a casual business." Indeed, the President was still a soldier, heart and soul.

When their meeting was finished, Truman was still awaiting the bill. He impatiently decided to travel to National Airport, which is across the Potomac River and downstream a few miles, where his aircraft, a DC-4 nicknamed the *Sacred Cow,* was being readied. He idled his time in the cabin until shortly after noon, when the bill was delivered; he quickly signed, making it law. Within minutes the plane was aloft, but the delay had kept him from seeing his mother one last time before she died. As his aircraft passed over Cincinnati, he was informed that she had expired. "Well, now she won't have to suffer anymore," he said.

Truman also signed two executive orders while on the ground at National Airport. One appointed Forrestal Secretary of Defense, and the other assigned roles and missions to the services. The latter directive had been the product of much haggling in recent months. Ultimately, Forrestal, Patterson, Clifford, and the President had reached an agreement. It would prove to be as beguilingly straightforward as the new reorganization law itself, because the tenor of its words was to authorize not limit. The services were bound to interpret their authority expansively, and this inevitably was going to cause conflict. Yet, the most that Forrestal as Secretary of Defense would be able to do was encourage coordination; he would not have the authority to order them into line. This restriction had been his idea, one that he himself had imposed on Truman, so he would have to learn to live with it. Still, he had an inkling of what was in store. "This office will probably be the greatest cemetery for dead cats in history," he wrote a friend.

CHAPTER 6

★ ★ ★ ★ ★ ★ ★ ★ ★ ★ ★ ★ ★ ★

PLAYING WITH FIRE

THE FEDERAL BUDGET is where a President imposes his policies. During Truman's presidency the process of planning one and getting it passed into law normally took about a year, which meant that the preliminary effort commenced during midsummer. First, the President worked with his director of the budget and his cabinet members to develop individual fiscal plans for programs and the departments. These he formally submitted to Congress in January in his budget message. The legislators then investigated, debated, modified, amended, and sometimes completely rewrote his proposals, finally passing the various appropriations bills before the start of the government's fiscal year, July 1. Truman got down to this business when he returned to Washington after his mother's funeral. Fiscal year 1948 having just begun, he set in motion planning for the next.

On August 1, 1947, Truman sent Forrestal a memorandum concerning the budget for fiscal year 1949 that established a cap of $11.025 billion for the National Military Establishment. James Webb's Bureau of the Budget had developed these figures with Truman's guidance; they were mostly a function of debt reduction goals, not defense needs. Since becoming President, Truman had managed budget surpluses each year. However, given the political instability throughout the world and Stalin's menacing ways, many planners were of Forrestal's view that the military needed more money. But to the populace, which wanted to reduce the national debt, lower inflation, and reduce taxes, the figure would seem quite high, their standard being the prewar years.

For personal and political reasons, Truman was disposed to accommodate the public all he could on the matter, and Forrestal decided not to oppose his wishes. On August 4, 1947, he wrote the President, saying, "I fully realize the difficulties with which you will be faced next year in bringing national income and expenditure figures into balance and assure you of my support in carrying out your instructions." Forrestal realized that he would have all he could handle getting the new National Military Establishment up and running. In fact, to minimize friction and simplify the budget-making process for the military this first time through, he planned to recommend to Truman that each of the three services get almost equal shares of the budget being planned. He surmised that this approach would temporarily mollify each of the services, and though it would not address defense needs precisely, he felt it was the best he could do under existing circumstances.

One of Forrestal's dictums, which he often repeated, was that "removing human frictions is ninety-nine percent of governing," so this is what he, as the first Secretary of Defense, set out to do initially with the service secretaries and the Joint Chiefs. The way the National Security Act was written, he could not order them to do anything; this made him dependent upon their goodwill and willingness to compromise.

The most difficult to deal with, by far, would be Air Force people, who from day one, following reorganization, emerged the dominant service. Their perception, which public opinion supported, was that they would win the next war, and that fleets and armies were obsolescent; that Air Force pilots had the mission to deliver the atomic bomb against the enemy's homeland during the next war was the basis for this perception. And they would demand a share of the defense budget commensurate with their perceived status. They thought that the lion's share was their due and that in the not-too-distant future they would get it. Politicians were so focused on airpower that both Truman and Congress had appointed blue-ribbon commissions to make air policy recommendations. Truman had recently formed the President's Air Policy Commission under the chairmanship of Thomas K. Finletter, a New York lawyer who first entered public service during World War II as a special assistant to Secretary of State Cordell Hull. And the Republicans who controlled Congress, not wanting to allow Truman to use his commission to form unopposed a consensus for his own policies, whatever they might become, created a panel of their own. Theirs they named the Congressional Aviation Policy Board. Its cochairmen were Senator R. Owen Brewster, a Republican from Maine, and Congressman Carl Hinshaw, a Republican from California. In the fall of 1947 and in early 1948, as both groups conducted widely publicized, separate hearings, they would become well known as the Finletter Commission and the Brewster-Hinshaw Board.

That Truman had made Stuart Symington the first Secretary of the Air Force had further complicated Forrestal's dealings with that service. Back in July when Forrestal was informed about his own appointment, the President had asked him about Symington's, and the Defense Secretary–designate's reaction betrayed his wariness. "I said one's friends were frequently more difficult as partners than strangers," Forrestal wrote in his diary. There was more to his concern than this, though.

Forrestal and Symington had known one another for years, the latter being the kind of businessman whom investment bankers contract to turn around ailing companies. It is work suited only for strong-willed, rugged managers with tough constitutions who are attracted to it as much by the challenge as the lucrative stock options. Several years before World War II, some bankers had put together such an incentive package and lured Symington to Saint Louis to invigorate the faltering Emerson Electric Company. He succeeded, as usual, and in the process met Truman, the senator, because of the Truman Committee's work; Emerson was by then manufacturing turrets and other military hardware. Both men were favorably impressed. Symington was taken by Truman's "incredible, quiet strength," and was pleasantly surprised that when the Truman Committee's investigators visited Emerson, they were, as Symington put it, "exactly the opposite of the hacks from the [Military Affairs] Committee. They were quiet, respectful of our employees, just wanted facts."

In 1945, within days of becoming President, Truman sent for Symington. "Stu," he said to him, "I want to drop a load of coal on you" — which was his folksy way of announcing that he wanted Symington to become chairman of the Surplus Property Board. After World War I, a scandal over criminal mismanagement of surplus war equipment had sent some budget officials to prison. Truman, who was trying to anticipate problems as he had with the Truman Committee, thought that Symington would be the strong hand to keep such things from happening again. Friends of Symington recommended that he not accept the job, but his father-in-law, James E. Wadsworth, Jr., a former Republican senator from New York who had chaired the Military Affairs Committee during the latter part of the Wilson presidency, offered some advice to convince him otherwise: "If the President of the United States asks you to help with his great job, you should be honored to accept." Symington did so and became a Truman favorite, a top troubleshooter. That Symington, a Yale man, played poker cemented their relationship on a very personal level; here was Truman's kind of businessman — someone as comfortable on Main Street as on Wall Street. During his seven years in the Truman administration, Symington at various times ran four different agencies or departments. So Symington, given his headstrong ways and his having the President's confidence and friendship, was potentially serious trouble for Forrestal.

As for the other two service secretaries, Forrestal reasonably anticipated relatively easy dealings with them. The new Navy Secretary was John L. Sullivan, a prominent lawyer from New Hampshire who had been assistant secretary of the Navy for air and the under secretary under Forrestal. The Army Secretary was Kenneth Royall, the Harvard-educated trial lawyer from North Carolina who had served as under secretary to Patterson for about a year and a half. Royall would be criticized by some Army partisans for being a weak advocate, but the Army's more basic problem was that through reorganization it had lost its air arm, which, since it was technologically driven, was in a stronger position to get appropriations during peacetime. At this point the Army was the weakest politically of the three services.

Great wartime figures composed the first post-reorganization Chiefs: Eisenhower, Nimitz, and Spaatz. Vandegrift of the Marine Corps was also a figure of renown, but in those days, as noted, the Commandant was not a member of the Joint Chiefs of Staff. He was not particularly annoyed by this, being pleased enough that the Corps had survived reorganization. Having done his part in saving it, he was making plans to retire; he did so on December 31, 1947, after four full years on the job. The attitude of his immediate superior was about the same; Nimitz felt he had done his part to thwart Army reorganization plans and Air Force designs on Navy aviation. He stepped down December 15, 1947, after two years as CNO. To a degree, Eisenhower and Spaatz also looked upon reorganization as a personal milestone. Eisenhower stepped down in February 1948, after twenty-seven months on the job, and Spaatz left the following April, after twenty-six months in his post.

Since these military personnel changes were imminent when Forrestal started work as Defense Secretary, they were among the first business he took up with Truman. Both men wanted new people they could work with easily. The candidates for Chief of Naval Operations were vice admirals D. C. Ramsey, William H. P. Blandy, and Louis Denfeld. The latter, who had become somewhat the Washington apparatchik, was campaigning for it by having people such as James Farley, the former Democratic National Committee chairman and postmaster general, tout his candidacy. Forrestal reacted negatively to this, but noted that "it is obvious" that Denfeld would be "the easiest of the lot to work with." He was the consummate bureaucrat, not a man of passion and strongly held views. Nor had the war stoked his fires; during most of it he had served in the capital as the Navy's top personnel officer. He got Truman's nod, much to the dismay of many Navy officers who thought the job should go to someone with combat experience. That he had not paid his dues in full was only part of the complaint; Arleigh Burke, a senior captain then, felt that because Denfeld lacked combat experience, he did not fully comprehend how airpower had changed naval warfare. Denfeld had come up in battleships.

As for who would take charge of the Army, Truman and Forrestal agreed that General Omar Bradley was the "obvious selection." During the latter stages of the war in Europe, he had been field commander of the largest American combat unit in history. While commander of the Twelfth Army Group, he led forty-three divisions comprising more than a million men locked in battle along a 640-mile front.

Eisenhower was eager to step down and relieve himself of the frustration of Washington work. "A commander in a theater of war has as his most difficult task the clarifying of his own convictions and conclusions," he wrote in his diary. "In Washington the job has not even started when self-conviction has been achieved." Now he had decided that the thing for him to do was accept an offer to become president of Columbia University. According to his biographer Stephen Ambrose, Eisenhower made the trustees stipulate that the job "included no involvement in purely academic matters, no responsibility for fund raising, no excessive entertaining, and no burdensome administrative details." Some thought he would use the position to make a run for the US presidency. Truman was amused to tell Forrestal that Eisenhower, after a recent trip to Tokyo, had warned him that Mac-Arthur would be a candidate for President in 1948; and that shortly thereafter another visitor back from Tokyo had warned him that Eisenhower would be a candidate in 1948.

The top Air Force job would pass from Spaatz to Hoyt Vandenberg. The difference in ages between the two men was almost eight years; the latter, only forty-nine, had leapfrogged past many more senior men on his way to the top. Wartime service had boosted his climb, but what helped him out most, when it came down to the final selection, was Senator Vandenberg's being his uncle. As Kennan observed in another context, "elaborate deference" was being paid the senator at the time of his nephew's appointment; it had to do with his pivotal role in getting Marshall Plan legislation through the Senate and the administration's needing his help to get through Congress some sort of long-term military compact with Western European nations.

Hoyt Vandenberg's youth was typical of Air Force leaders. That service had become a huge organization in just a few years. During the 1947 Christmas holidays, Forrestal visited Eglin Field, Florida, which was a major Air Force testing center, and Maxwell Field, Alabama, where the new Air University was located, and was struck by the immaturity of the senior officers there. Writing Sherman afterward, he observed, "One of the real difficulties is becoming more manifest every day: the gap in the Air Force of wise and experienced leadership in the upper ranks." However, he was confident the talent was there. "Ten or even five years from now they will be all right," he wrote.

Truman did not get worked up much about who would be the next Commandant. He handled it rather perfunctorily, as if keeping his distance. He had not forgiven Vandegrift for helping torpedo his first reorganization bill, and still had not developed a tolerance for the Marines' elitist attitude. He did not bother to interview the two lieutenant generals who were finalists — Clifton Cates, a veteran of Belleau Wood, and Lemuel Shepherd, Jr., a veteran of both Belleau Wood and Guadalcanal. After reviewing their records, he called them in and, addressing Shepherd, said, "It's all even practically. You're younger then he. Cates is senior to you on the seniority list. You'll have to take your chances later." Turning to Cates, he said, "You're going to be Commandant." Including the salutes, the meeting lasted about three minutes.

More than anything else, the Commandant, the Chiefs, the service secretaries, and the Secretary of Defense are planners, so while the latter settled into his job and tried to open up communications, the rest reexamined their roles, missions, capabilities, and demands. All understood that at some point down the line Forrestal would call everyone together to hammer out some agreement. The roles-and-missions statement that Truman signed along with the National Security Act had papered over difficulties. Furthermore, equal funding shares for the three services meant the allotments were not based on any defense plan or tied to the need for certain weapon systems, so there was an obvious unreality about the notion. Defense priorities were more complex than such disbursement implied.

The Navy, under Sullivan, decided to conduct a very formal reappraisal of its future. The ranking admirals had come to him presenting the Supercarrier as their top priority, and he ordered internal Navy Department hearings conducted. Starting during the late fall of 1947, these went on some weeks; the idea was that Secretary Sullivan had to be convinced of the ship's worth. This exercise was probably his way of saying that he, not Forrestal, was now in charge of the Navy. Having been a top Navy Department official for about four years, he had been in a position to resolve the question for himself long before. Predictably, he reaffirmed Forrestal's decision as Navy Secretary to make the Supercarrier top priority.

As for the Air Force reappraisal, Symington and Spaatz required no more than a conversation over a cup of coffee. Unlike the Army and the Navy, the new Air Force was enjoying the continuity of top civilian and military leadership, so Symington offered no pretense that his service's goals had changed.

Spaatz was a strong influence on Symington. Robert A. Lovett, who for some four years during World War II had served as assistant secretary of war for air, had highly commended the Air Force officer to him. Symington respected a man of conviction, which Spaatz was in spades; he had worked with most of the famed aviators of the past and, thus, carried some of their aura and most of their feelings. An example was Spaatz's hatred of the Navy. "There are two governments in Washington," he would say, "the government of the United States and the United States Navy." Symington identified with this irascible style, and for this combination of reasons Spaatz became for him "one of the great men of my life." At the time, Spaatz was fifty-six, and Symington, forty-six.

From the start of their working relationship, Symington had deferred to Spaatz's professional judgment. "There are two things I would like to do," he told the general. "One, give you all, if possible, the benefit of any business experience I've had." In particular, Symington wanted to correct the Army Air Forces' logistical problems and streamline its financial systems. The second thing Symington told Spaatz he planned to do was pursue those goals that Spaatz and the other Army Air Forces leaders set for him. His approach was just the opposite of what Sullivan's evidently was; Symington relied completely on the judgment of his officers in uniform. "You and your staff decide what we should have from the Congress in the way of an Air Force," Symington told him, "then I will try to sell that to Judge Patterson and the Bureau of the Budget and the President and the Congress." Eventually, Spaatz came back to Symington to say that Army Air Forces leaders wanted a seventy-group Air Force, which would include all sorts of strategic and tactical aircraft, mostly bombers, fighters, and transports. And so, during the next four years, Symington became a passionate advocate for that goal. For Air Force officers — proud of their new service yet insecure, confident yet defensive — it was a goal that stood for their service's finally attaining its rightful status. Consequently, in the fall of 1947, forces were lining up for a budgetary fight somewhere down the line. On one side was the Navy's Supercarrier, and on the other, the Air Force's seventy groups, which the B-36 would come to symbolize.

The Department of the Army's reappraisal under Royall projected serious manpower problems. The US Army had always been small during peacetime, but never had it had such extensive occupation and peacekeeping responsibilities. By pre–World War II standards, the Army of late 1947 was large, numbering about 550,000, but even this figure was short of authorized strength, because the Army could not entice enough young men to join.

The most acute Army manpower shortage was in Korea, where Lieutenant General John R. Hodge's thinly manned XXIV Corps was trying to maintain order amid very severe economic and political chaos. There were potential trouble-spots elsewhere, too, including Palestine, which after World War I had been mandated to Great Britain. The British were in the process of being forced out and would soon announce that May 14, 1948, would be their last day there. Members of the Zionist movement were fighting to partition the region for a Jewish homeland, so the situation was turbulent, even with the presence of the British; it could only get worse without them. What the United States should or could do had not been decided. Many were saying that more than a hundred thousand GIs would be needed in the Middle East. Greece was another place some people were saying the Army was going to have to send more soldiers. Things were not going well there either, even with American aid and advisers.

For the Army, therefore, the future boiled down to a long-term shortage of men. What additional manpower requirements Stalin himself might directly impose was something else altogether. As Marshall described the situation, the United States was playing with fire and had nothing with which to put it out. Given this mounting pressure, the Army latched on to universal military training as its funding goal for fiscal year 1949; this proposal was its equivalent to the Navy's Supercarrier program and the Air Force's seventy groups. And like the Air Force, the Army was already complaining to Forrestal that since the Navy had such a small future role, it should not get a one-third share of the budget.

Forrestal had been planning to leave public service when Truman unexpectedly appointed him Secretary of Defense. Seven years had passed since he went to work for Roosevelt as an administrative assistant. The whole time, he worked under conditions of war, hot and cold. He was an exacting administrator who, a subordinate recalled, wanted to know what he was signing, why, and why not something else. He attacked the challenge with the same vigor with which he had hit Wall Street as a young man — working late into the night; conducting business meetings of some sort during breakfast, lunch, and dinner; trying to make policy rather than react to it; reading widely and keeping a diary; and giving dinner speeches, which typically required late-afternoon travel and late-evening return, without disruption of the next workday. There were also a number of long inspection trips. He was on the beaches of Iwo Jima a few hours after the first assault waves landed, and thus was the first Navy Secretary to come under enemy fire during overseas action; theater crowds applauded his bravery as they watched Movietone film footage of the event. According to his friend Arthur Krock, Forrestal, by visiting the battle zone, was trying to assuage a burden of conscience, troubled as he was by the responsibility of ordering sailors and marines to risk their lives. He took his jobs as Navy under secretary and, later, secretary so seriously, and accepted their responsibilities so completely, that he felt the full weight of the associated pressure. Still, he always rose to the occasion — and so he was, as usual, stimulated by the challenge of succeeding as Secretary of Defense.

Forrestal's wartime experience prepared him well for the job in all respects except one: the partisan politics that followed the resumption of peace. The extraordinary bipartisanship that Roosevelt forged during the war with the appointments of Henry Stimson and Frank Knox, most notably, and that Truman was able to prolong with the support of Senator Vandenberg, did not survive the election year 1948. In fact, it started coming apart during the fall of 1947. The effect on Forrestal was that Democratic-party professionals, who had never thought of him as one of their own, began scrutinizing him more closely than Republicans did. Some of them wanted his job, which from the moment of its creation became a political plum of almost equal weight to that of the Secretary of State appointment.

Given his lack of experience in politics, Forrestal was woefully unconscious about protecting himself. Typical of how he worked and how nonpartisan he could be was his response upon hearing Republican senator Henry Cabot Lodge, Jr., discuss at a dinner party how the executive branch of the federal government should be reorganized. The morning after the affair, Forrestal called in one of his assistants, W. J. McNeil, whose views on the subject he listened to and approved. He then arranged to have him meet with Lodge. Later that very day, McNeil and Lodge met in the senator's office and drafted proposed legislation creating a commission to study reorganization of the executive branch. The Republican-controlled Congress reported the bill with felicity, voting approval of the Lodge-Brown Act. Truman signed it into law, though easily might have been angered that one of his cabinet members was the catalyst for legislation sponsored by the opposition party to study his branch of government. Fortunately for Forrestal, Truman was on record as favoring executive-branch reorganization reforms and he accepted the law with good grace. (At least publicly he did.) The President even appointed Herbert Hoover, a former Republican President, as the study commission's chairman. Still, the Defense Secretary's being so cozy with Republicans would eventually hurt him.

Forrestal's foremost problem arising out of partisan politics had to do with Palestine. He and the Joint Chiefs opposed creation of a homeland for Jews there. Their position was essentially the same as that of the British government, which held the view that support for the idea would cause Arab nations to cut off the supply of oil and access to the Suez Canal. Indeed, back in March 1945, Saudi Arabia, Egypt, Syria, and Lebanon had pledged in writing to take united action should the status quo of Arabs in Palestine and Transjordan be threatened. Additionally, Forrestal and the Chiefs worried that US support for the Zionist movement would cause Arab nations to invite in the Soviets.

Truman personally had overcome these trepidations. In 1946, he tried to help the Democratic candidate for governor of New York running against Dewey by announcing on Yom Kippur that "our government could give its support" for partition of Palestine; this was another way of saying that the United States conditionally backed carving a Jewish nation out of the British mandate. The issue had been a matter of active public discussion since World War I, but no President had ever gone further in support of a Jewish homeland than Truman did in this instance.

Pressed to the limits of their capability and tolerance, the British in mid-1947 referred the Palestine question to the United Nations, which took up the issue in September, just as Forrestal was beginning his new job. From the outset, he had opposed the President's position on Palestine as resolutely as he had his ideas on military reorganization. Meanwhile, during the period leading up to the UN vote on partition, the White House was being swamped with mail supporting the Zionist cause; Truman, by his own account, was being subjected to the most intensive lobbying effort of his presidency.

Forrestal's adamant and well-known opposition made implacable enemies of some very influential people. One of them was Postmaster General Robert Hannegan, a close friend of the President's who was chairman of the Democratic National Committee. During a cabinet luncheon Forrestal rebuked him for saying that large campaign contributions for the 1948 campaign were at stake. Forrestal kept at this into early 1948, several months after Truman announced his official position on Palestine and even after the United Nations voted for partition. By that time, he had firmly established himself as anti-Semitic, though this evidently was an erroneous impression. Jewish friends, such as Bernard Baruch, defended him. But nothing in all his days in Washington hurt him so much. Just when he needed all the influence he could muster to get the military services moving in one direction, he had isolated himself as no enemy could have.

Truman delivered his FY1949 budget message to Congress on January 12, 1948, and almost immediately events overseas began impinging on his plans to spend only $11.025 billion on the military. Back in December, a conference of foreign ministers of the Big Four powers had come apart. Molotov had been boorishly obdurate and no agreement was reached. Marshall was not surprised, given his personal meeting with Stalin in April 1946, but Britain's Ernest Bevin and France's Georges Bidault, representing very insecure governments needing relief of any sort, were devastated by the failure.

Given this disappointment, British leaders decided that Great Britain needed the collective help of other nations to defend itself. To this end, Bevin wrote Marshall on January 12, 1948, asking him what the reaction of the United States would be if his government contacted the leaders of France and the Benelux nations about such an agreement. His motives were subtly concealed though obvious; he was cleverly drawing the United States into the creation of this alliance, hoping it would eventually associate itself fully. He was acting on a new fundamental reality, which was that Great Britain's security was now ultimately tied to US economic, political, and military power. Very quickly, Marshall wrote Bevin back that the United States would respond positively to such an idea, leaving unclear how. The answer satisfied Bevin's needs. Bolstered by this general assurance, he proposed in Parliament on January 22 the formation of a "Western Union" of the aforementioned nations. They, in turn, reacted positively and, as a result, the five European nations involved committed themselves to sending emissaries to Brussels in early March to discuss a mutual-defense pact.

Next to affect Truman's plans for the US military was a series of events involving European nations bordering the Soviet Union. The first was a coup in Czechoslovakia staged by local Communists; it climaxed February 24. About a year earlier they had won most of the seats in parliamentary elections and had formed an uneasy coalition with other parties, but this arrangement came apart when the Communist interior minister started firing non-Communists on the police force. Eventually, the Communists intimidated the elderly president, Edvard Beneš, into appointing members of their party to all the ministerial vacancies save one; the lone non-Communist was the foreign minister, Jan G. Masaryk, who was the son of the republic's first president. What frightened Beneš was the Communists' arresting their opponents.

The general impression in the West was that the Russians were deeply involved in this seizure of power. Exactly how was unknown. Deputy Foreign Minister Valerian A. Zorin of the Soviet Union had arrived in Prague on the eve of Beneš's capitulation, ostensibly to supervise the distribution of Russian wheat. And Soviet troops massed on the border had obviously helped intimidate Beneš.

Though Czechoslovakia was one of the more remote European nations for Americans, what had happened there reverberated strongly in Washington. President Woodrow Wilson's efforts during post–World War I negotiations had led to the creation of the Czechoslovakian republic. It had been a stable democracy until the World War II interregnum, and US policymakers had hoped that its government, by being the only popularly elected one in Eastern Europe, could, by the example of its success, encourage other Eastern Europeans to demand the same for themselves. The coup was all the more unsettling because the conditions that led to it loosely matched those in a number of Western European nations, especially Italy and France: economic dislocation, political instability, and a large faction of Communists. Another aspect of it particularly troubling for Truman was that it strongly suggested that coalition governments with Communists did not work — that the Communists would take advantage of the situation to seize power. He had, of course, long been trying to force on Chiang a coalition with Mao's Communists. Truman had hardly had time to absorb these implications when Stalin began exerting pressure elsewhere. On February 27, word got out that the Soviet leader had offered Finland a mutual-defense pact, an unwelcome bear hug.

So official Washington was thus primed for a March 5, 1948, cable from General Lucius Clay, the US military governor in Germany, to Lieutenant General Stephen J. Chamberlin, director of intelligence for the Army General Staff. Chamberlin had asked Clay for information that might support the Army's request for additional funding, and this was the reply:

> For many months, based on logical analysis, I have felt and held that war was unlikely for at least ten years. Within the last few weeks, I have felt a subtle change in Soviet attitude which I cannot define but which now gives me a feeling that it may come with dramatic suddenness. I cannot support this change in my own thinking with any data or outward evidence in relationships other than to describe it as a feeling of a new tenseness in every Soviet individual with whom we have official relations. I am unable to submit any official report in the absence of supporting data but my feeling is real. You may advise the Chief of Staff of this for whatever it may be worth if you feel it advisable.

Bradley, who had succeeded Eisenhower only twenty-six days before, was informed immediately. Word then spread through official Washington like fire. A genuine war scare ensued.

Because Clay's telegram was a top-secret document, the stir it caused within the government was not duplicated throughout the population; however, this all changed six days later, on March 11, when the extraordinary news of Masaryk's purported suicide was headlined in newspapers across the country. According to the official Czech news agency, he had jumped to his death from a window of his apartment at the Foreign Ministry.

Had the Soviets tried, they could not have contrived a more personal way of arousing the emotions of Americans, who had become familiar with the man. Masaryk's ties to America and his affection for it were widely known. His mother had been born in the United States. When he was twenty years old, he arrived in the United States with eighty dollars in his pockets and lived the life of an immigrant for a few years. He worked as a laborer in an ironworks and as a pianist in a movie theater while attending Boston University part-time. He indicated later that he had wanted to get out from under his father's shadow and find himself. He did, and decided to follow in his father's footsteps. For his first diplomatic assignment, his father posted him to Washington as chargé d'affaires. During World War II, he served as foreign minister of the government in exile and deliberately kept a high profile in the United States. A bon vivant, Masaryk was widely liked and respected; *Time* once reported facetiously that he was "the best pianist among contemporary foreign ministers."

For many Americans, Jan Masaryk had come to define Czechoslovakia more than had geography, politics, or any other single factor. Now, in death, he shockingly symbolized for them what it meant for free people to be taken over by Communists. He was a most unlikely person to have taken his own life, and so Americans were horrified by the crude boldness with which the Communists must have killed him. It was easy to imagine KGB agents bursting into his residence, wrestling him to the ground to gain control of his arms and legs, and then jamming the frantic man through an open window.

Following Masaryk's death, attention quickly refocused on events in Germany. For some months the Soviets had occasionally delayed trains bound for Berlin from the three western sectors as they traveled through the sector of occupied Germany controlled by the USSR. This troubling situation dramatically worsened when Clay's counterpart, Marshal Vasily Sokolovsky, proclaimed that as of April 1 all Americans passing through the Soviet sector by rail and on highways would be forced to present identification papers.

Virtually everyone in Washington saw these events of early 1948 as part of a composite picture: one of Stalin challenging American resolve to defend non-Communist states in Europe. Bevin and Bidault also saw things that way. The presumption was that Stalin was taking advantage of the US military's strained capacity to react. His information on American forces was probably about as good as Truman's, and everyone knew it. Coincidentally, the President had had a full-scale status briefing on his armed forces six days before the Czech coup. The bad news was that the deployment of anything more than a division would necessitate a partial mobilization; otherwise, the force in reserve would be too small. By year's end the Army would be 165,000 short of its authorized strength. Major General Alfred M. Gruenther, the head of the Joint Staff, which is the body of officers and enlisted men and women from all the services who support the work of the Secretary of Defense, told the President this on February 18.

Therefore, Truman's basic reaction to the pressure from friend and foe alike was to address his manpower problem. Initially, he took the long-term approach. Pursuant to this, Marshall broached universal military training (UMT) as a possibility to members of the Senate Armed Services Committee on the morning of March 2, seven days after the coup in Czechoslovakia. What he stressed was the nation's need to convey to the world that there was "continuity, firmness and will" behind American foreign policy. The reaction he got — Republican senator Leverett Saltonstall of Massachusetts expressed it most forcefully — was that the committee would not support the idea unless the Secretary of State or the President himself could spark widespread public support for it by making some sort of dramatic statement or speech.

Somewhat suspiciously, Clay's cable warning of the possibility of imminent war was received at the Pentagon only three days later. There is no known evidence to suggest that Clay was coaxed into responding to Chamberlin's request the way he did; however, his words perfectly suited the administration's need.

The cable arrived on a Friday, and the following Monday Forrestal was scheduled to testify before the Senate Armed Services Committee about the FY1949 budget and how UMT fit into plans. Over the weekend all the committee's members were informed about Clay's warning, so how to react to the possibility of war became the main item on their agenda. Forrestal took the opportunity to press vigorously for UMT. The reaction was respectful but tepid, not much better than that Truman had elicited from the Central Park throng back in 1945 when the Navy celebrated victory. Clay's telegram had been dramatic enough news; the senators just felt there had to be a better way. However, a President's request under such conditions could not be denied without hearings, so members voted unanimously to conduct them on UMT. Forrestal was pleased. Afterward he told reporters that "events are making progress for us." Elaborating, he said: "The atmosphere I'd say is considerably improved, the improvement derived from other events that one can't take much pleasure in. I think the political aspect of it is much better."

Two days later reports of Masaryk's death were broadcast in the United States, and that afternoon Forrestal called a press conference to announce that the following day he would be convening at Key West Naval Base a prolonged meeting of the Joint Chiefs to work out a strategic war plan. It was to be the first serious attempt since unification to move beyond the simplistic planning that equal funding for the three services denoted. He hoped that the isolation of Key West would focus the minds of the participants and also give them a sense of urgency. He had already told the President that if the Chiefs did not produce some sort of roles-and-missions statement, he would do it for them; whether he had such authority was dubious — though he could only blame himself for the lack.

As they sat down together for another try, this time with the Secretary of Defense intensively involved, outside pressures again impinged. Marshall informed Forrestal about an aide-mémoire from Bevin that said that Norway, like Finland, was now fearful of a mutual-defense pact being forced on it by the Soviet Union. This presented the Chiefs with the possibility of the Russians' getting naval bases on the Atlantic. Bevin used this as an excuse to encourage US planners to build on the five-nation alliance then being negotiated in Brussels and to start thinking about Atlantic and Mediterranean security. However, for the officers gathered at Key West these recommendations remained in the background; they had more fundamental issues to work out.

Unfortunately, the resulting document did not have the finality that Forrestal intended it to have, mostly because it left too much unspecified. The Navy was evidently authorized to build a Supercarrier, but not to launch its planes as a strategic force — in other words, the carrier would only use its planes to protect the fleet, basically. This did not make much sense. Stirring emotions was a recurrence of Air Force feeling that the Navy was trying to elbow in on its strategic air mission because that is where new funding was likely to go. Only two days after the Key West meeting adjourned, Symington was complaining to Forrestal about there being two air forces. Recounting their conversation, Forrestal wrote, "I said what he really had in mind was a modification of [the National Security Act], and he agreed that was the case."

Unexpectedly, the biggest news to come out of the Key West conference was the Chiefs' recommending that the draft law be reenacted. Shortly before their lunch break on the last day of discussions, they had taken this up and quickly decided that UMT would not satisfy their short-term manpower needs. Word of their recommendation reached Truman within minutes, and sometime that afternoon, evidently, he decided that a revival of the draft law by Congress might be a dramatic enough move to convince Stalin of American resolve. Reenactment would give him the authority to conscript the manpower needed. And so, the next morning he announced to reporters that he would address a joint session of Congress on March 17. Forrestal, who did not participate in this decision, learned of it when he arrived back in Washington a couple of hours later. According to Budget Director Webb, "What Truman wanted to do in asking for the draft was to give the Soviets a signal that although we had cut down on military spending, we were ready to go back up again."

In his address on the seventeenth, Truman for the first time specifically named the Soviet Union as the cause for much of the political turmoil in the world. He had not made that reference even in his forthright speech about aid to Greece and Turkey. This time he did, saying it was the "one nation" bent on disrupting the peace and undermining the West. He called it "this growing menace," and described Soviet policy that had led him to this conclusion. "It is this ruthless course of action and the clear design to extend it to the remaining free nations of Europe," he said, "that have brought about the critical situation in Europe today. . . . I believe that we have reached a point at which the position of the United States should be made unmistakenly clear. . . . There are times in world history when it is far wiser to act than to hesitate."

Having presented this assessment of the situation, Truman then laid out what he as Commander in Chief wanted. On this afternoon, he listed only three things: quick enactment of the Marshall Plan, which was already moving through Congress; "temporary" reenactment of the draft "in order to maintain our Armed Forces at their authorized strength"; and adoption of UMT as "the only means by which the civilian components of our Armed Forces can be built up to the strength required."

Given less notice was his endorsing in this speech the so-called Brussels Union, a military alliance that negotiations by emissaries from Britain, France, Belgium, the Netherlands, and Luxembourg had produced within the last twenty-four hours. Truman said that "the United States will, by appropriate means, extend to the free nations the support which the situation requires. I am sure that the determination of the free countries of Europe to protect themselves will be matched by an equal determination on our part to help them protect themselves." He did not elaborate.

Congress had only begun to consider Truman's March 17 proposals when on April 1 the Soviets began stopping US troop trains headed for Berlin. Forewarned, Clay and decision-makers back in Washington had worked out a plan. Clay had wanted to use armed force to defend against boarding, saying, "Any weakness on our part will lose us prestige important now." He argued that doing anything less would only delay the inevitable. "If the Soviets mean war, we will only deter the next provocation a few days." But the mood in Washington was that of caution. "If our action now should provoke war," Bradley responded to Clay, "we must be sure that the fault is not ours." Truman approved ordering the trains to proceed, but insisted on nothing out of the ordinary in terms of the number of armed guards and the weapons they carried. Russian soldiers were not to be allowed aboard, and American GIs were not to fire unless fired upon.

The first of three trains got under way at midnight, April 1, and was stopped at the first Soviet checkpoint. Wilting under the pressure, its commandant allowed aboard the Russians, who permitted the train to proceed after an inspection. However, the commandants of the next two trains followed orders and refused the Russians permission to board, so passage for these was blocked. Clay, who was closely monitoring the situation, ordered them to back out. His alternative was to order an armed force in to capture the switching station. As a stopgap measure, he put into operation a small airlift, which was to grow in magnitude daily.

The next Soviet step was to try to intimidate Clay into stopping the airlift. Though not firing their weapons, Russian fighter pilots began harassing the transports of the Western allies. Most of the transports were American, but on April 5 a Soviet fighter collided in midair with a British transport, killing all fourteen passengers aboard, which included two Americans, and also the Soviet pilot. This accident sobered the Soviets somewhat. Sokolovsky apologized to Clay, whose countermove was to order fighter-plane escorts for the transports.

These goings-on made the congressional follow-up to Truman's March 17 speech all the more intense. The address had been interpreted as a call to arms, and the crisis in Germany reinforced this perception. Thus, congressional leaders anticipated the President's submitting to them a longer list of requests once his staff had time to develop them. To their surprise, he did not, as if hoping that his open cards on the table would bring Stalin up short. The result was that Congress took the lead in defining the arms buildup. Though they enacted draft and Marshall Plan legislation within a short time as requested, they rejected UMT as an alternative and opted for a buildup of airpower instead.

The question then arose about how to spend this new money tagged for airpower buildup. Air Force people wanted all of it, since a strategic air buildup was what was envisioned. The Navy's advocates argued that it should get a share, since its carrier-borne planes were a contingent strategic strike force. Reflecting the Air Force's growing political power, the House passed early in the debate a resolution that endorsed its getting seventy groups. This was in large measure the result of the efforts of Congressman Carl Vinson, who, though of the Democratic minority, was extraordinarily influential. Some colleagues called him the father of the modern Navy because of his thirty years of work on the House Naval Affairs Committee, beginning in 1917. Now he seemed to be vying for Air Force paternity honors. He realized that all the new base construction would be for the Air Force, and he wanted his district and the rest of Georgia to get more than their shares. He was not called "the Swamp Fox" for nothing. However, during this phase of the airpower debate, the Republican majorities in Congress more friendly to the Navy reasserted themselves, and Navy aviation received a reasonably large share of aviation procurement funding that became law via the fiscal year of 1949 supplemental bill — about a third of what the Air Force got. When these supplemental appropriations were added to the regular fiscal year 1949 appropriations, here is how the services fared: Army — $5.8 billion; Navy and Marine Corps — $4.42 billion; Air Force — $2.942 billion. The office of the Secretary of Defense was appropriated $7 million, so total military funding was $13.169 billion. But these figures don't tell the whole story. Approximately half of the Army's regular funding was really for the Air Force, "pending its complete separation from the Army," notes the OSD's official history. So, in terms of benefit received, the disposition of funds for fiscal year 1949 was actually something like this: Army — $3.47 billion; Navy and Marine Corps — $4.42 billion; Air Force — $5.27 billion.

Interestingly, Truman ended up wanting only a $1.5 billion supplemental appropriations package for fiscal year 1949, instead of the one for about $4 billion that Congress forced on him. There are several reasons why he wanted the smaller amount. Truman the liberal had at this point not reconciled himself to a buildup of the career military; this is why, as noted, he found the UMT alternative — all good citizens coming to the aid of their country — so attractive. His controlling motivation, though, was a desire to cap postwar inflation, which he was certain increased government spending would fuel. He might have been thinking about all the haberdashers whom another inflation-and-credit-crunch cycle would put out of business. He was definitely thinking about the voters. They wanted military spending kept low unless war was probable, and Truman agreed. Though the Republicans got their way as to the amount of the supplemental appropriations bill and where it was to be spent, the President's handling of this crisis period seems to have been another of those long-term political pluses that added up unnoticed and ultimately gave him a victory in the November elections. He projected himself to voters as a resolute Commander in Chief who was fiscally responsible.

The crisis over Berlin reached peak intensity when the Soviets blocked all highway, river, and rail access from the three western sectors of Germany. This blockade even included civilian traffic. To sustain the 2.5 million people living in the three western sectors of Berlin, Truman decided to develop Clay's stopgap airlift into a massive operation. During the meeting at which the President announced his decision, General Vandenberg demurred, saying that the assignment might strain Air Force capabilities beyond the breaking point. Truman brusquely replied that if the Air Force could not handle the airlift, it certainly was not ready for the alternative, which was full-scale war. In all, 2,343,015 sorties were eventually flown by transport pilots during a thirteen-month period. Navy planes and crews, and those of allies, supported what was basically a US Air Force operation.

To dissuade Stalin from further escalation, Truman deployed two squadrons of B-29s to the US sector of Germany and later two groups totaling sixty B-29s to Great Britain. The widely held presumption was that some of them carried atomic bombs; this was untrue, but it served Truman's purposes. His use of airpower during this first Berlin crisis was probably its most effective use during the postwar period. War was averted, and Stalin was eventually forced to lift the blockade because of worldwide condemnation of his actions.

Important is the fact that during the crisis Truman communicated his willingness to use atomic bombs. Word got around, and somehow this resolve was most certainly conveyed unofficially to Stalin. Forrestal, worried that the nation was relying on a weapon that the President might refuse to use, asked him about it on September 13. The Defense Secretary recounted in his diary that "the President said that he prayed that he would never have to make such a decision, but that if it became necessary, no one need have a misgiving but what he would do so."

This was consistent with the attitude of the American people to an overwhelming degree, as was confirmed informally by Forrestal the next evening when Philip Graham, the thirty-three-year-old publisher of the *Washington Post*, hosted him, Marshall, Bradley, and nineteen of the nation's most influential editors and publishers. The gathering in Graham's home was for the mutual benefit of the journalists and the administration, so, during the discussion that followed the officials' briefings, Forrestal asked the members of the fourth estate for their opinion on using the atomic bomb.

Summarizing their responses later, Forrestal noted their "unanimous agreement that in the event of war the American people would not only have no question as to propriety of the use of the atomic bomb, but would in fact expect it to be used." This widespread public endorsement translated into bipartisan consensus. John Foster Dulles, who was a sort of Republican Secretary-of-State-in-waiting, told Marshall subsequently that "the American people would execute you if you did not use the bomb."

It was with this mind-set — knowledge of the American people's almost universal approval for his using atomic bombs — that Truman was already laying plans for his FY1950 budget. Each day that the airlift continued without Soviet interruption, he became more confident that war was unlikely; the sense of things among top military officers was that if the Soviets refrained from shooting at US aircraft, they did not want war. Concurrently, he became more confident that he could resume paring down the military budget; however, the Chiefs did not see it this way. Though the President came to decide that they should get only $15 billion for fiscal year

1950, they initially asked for $30 billion. It was Forrestal's task to reconcile them to the much lower number.

What the military heads had their eyes on was the growing list of US military commitments around the world, the most notable being the one in Europe. Following up Truman's endorsement of the Brussels Union, Marshall and Under Secretary of State Robert Lovett had negotiated with Senator Vandenberg a bipartisan agreement as to how to proceed; the Senate endorsed the agreed-upon approach on June 11, 1948, by passing Resolution 329. The so-called Vandenberg Resolution affirmed that US policy sought to achieve international peace through the United Nations, but declared that it was in the country's interest to associate "by constitutional process, with such regional and other collective arrangements as are based on continuous and effective self-help and mutual aid, and as affect the national security." This amounted to advance notice that the Senate would ratify a treaty such as the one eventually signed with eleven other nations on April 4, 1949, that created the North Atlantic Treaty Organization. Following Senate ratification on July 21, 1949, and Truman's signing the instrument of ratification on July 25, the United States would be formally committed to defend Western Europe should the Soviets invade.

George Kennan criticized the fact that the administration's reaction to the events of early 1948, right from the start, was a military response. His conclusion was that it set an avoidable course that would lead to an unnecessary arms buildup on both sides. According to his assessment, a diplomatic reaction would have been sufficient, and the United States could have made Western Europe's future more secure by helping it focus on its economic recovery.

He was not present to argue his case, though, because two days after the coup in Czechoslovakia he departed Washington bound for the Far East, where he had an important meeting with MacArthur scheduled. He also made a comprehensive personal survey of the situation in Japan, Okinawa, and the Philippines, and upon returning to Washington was hospitalized at the National Naval Medical Center in Bethesda, Maryland, for duodenal ulcers. He did not return to his desk in the office adjoining Marshall's until April 19, by which time the administration had set a firm military course. Kennan, who had been a major figure in policy formulation since the day Forrestal read his long telegram, had no say at this juncture.

It so happened that Kennan's perception of events was entirely different from that of Clay, whose views had played a primary role in Truman's reaction. Kennan foresaw no war, and in fact believed that armed conflict was the last thing Stalin wanted with the United States. Kennan was being consistent about this. In his long telegram he had observed that "Soviet power . . . does not take unnecessary risks. . . . Thus, if the adversary has sufficient force and makes clear his readiness to use it, he rarely has to do so." He believed that US containment policy had already put Stalin on the defensive and that the moves the dictator was orchestrating were actually consolidations of power, not bold advances. He thought that the American position in Europe was improving and that when Marshall Plan legislation was enacted by Congress and the money started flowing into Western Europe, the improvement would be dramatic. Kennan felt that the Soviets had caused the Czech coup to happen but that this was something they could have done for months; in his view, they had delayed doing so only as long as Communist parties in Western Europe had a reasonable chance of coming to power. In such a situation, the Czech republic was useful as a reputed example of how Communists in a democratic society were willing to share power. What was extraordinary about this line of reasoning is that Kennan presented it to Marshall two and a half months before the actual event, in a paper dated November 6, 1947. In it he warned the Secretary of State to expect a "sweeping away of democratic institutions" in Czechoslovakia.

Kennan did not see Clay's cable until mid-March, when he arrived in the Philippines to assess the situation there. And when he read it, he was appalled. "I cannot help but believe," he wrote years later, "that a deeper background in Russian affairs would have saved him from the error of interpretation that this message reflected, and that the State Department, together with the rest of official Washington, would have done better in evaluating his message to rely on the judgment of some of us who knew something about Russia." He cabled his remonstrations, but to no apparent effect. He blamed this militarization of US policy-making on military people's dominating the process. In addition to the Secretaries of Defense, Army, Navy, and Air Force and the Chiefs of the services, key policymakers with military backgrounds included the Secretary of State (General Marshall), the director of the CIA (Lieutenant General Hoyt Vandenberg), and the ambassador to Moscow (General Walter Bedell Smith, Eisenhower's wartime chief of staff). Furthermore, Clay and MacArthur were virtual independent agents in Germany and Japan, the two epicenters of US foreign policy during the postwar years. Each man had a strong tendency to involve Washington only when he wanted to share responsibility for controversial decisions.

But Kennan's criticism ignored the fundamental reason Truman responded militarily. Indeed, Marshall, who embodied the Army in the public mind, warned the President that he might "pull the trigger" by calling for the draft in his March 17 speech, meaning that in the highly charged environment of the day he might spark war. Recounting Marshall's warning to his staff the day before addressing the joint session of Congress, Truman said he would rather run this risk than let the American people be caught off guard as they had been in 1941. So Pearl Harbor was the dominant reason that Truman, by fits and starts, resorted to rearming. The President and that generation of people advising him had been traumatized by the Japanese surprise attack six and a half years earlier.

The same day that Truman was commenting to his staff about this, Forrestal, who was not present, was recording identical personal feelings. "Our effort now is to try to make the Russians see the folly of continuing an aggression which will lead to war," he wrote, "or, if it is impossible to restore them to sanity, [to ensure] that we at least have a start which will enable us to prevent our being caught flat-footed as we were in 1941." This state of mind also explains the incredibly alarmist intelligence estimates of the period. No one in the bureaucracy wanted to be accused of having been caught off guard and of not having warned the President. On March 16 the CIA, coordinating with the Departments of State, Army, Navy, and Air Force, would only give him assurances that war was not probable during the next sixty days. Not surprisingly, Truman commented to his staff that the United States was "sunk" if Congress did not respond to his speech. Two weeks later, conditions were such that the Air Force refused to sign off on a two-week extension of this assurance.

Kennan was most troubled by Truman's having pledged US support for the Brussels Union, an action that led to the formal NATO association. Kennan perceived endless possibilities for military waste in the creation of a peacetime alliance with Western Europe from which the nation would have great difficulty extricating itself. And he felt that US participation in NATO would needlessly fuel Russian paranoia.

Under the circumstances, Kennan thought the best he could do was propose some sort of modified alliance plan. The idea he started advancing was the so-called dumbbell concept: the proposition that the United States and Canada should form a military alliance on their side of the Atlantic that would commit them to a "unilateral political and military guarantee" to come to the aid of the Brussels Union on the other side of the Atlantic. Without the peacetime physical presence of American forces in Europe, the Europeans would be forced to prepare more actively for their own defense and not complacently let the United States do it. There would be no institutionalization of US involvement in Europe, with American posts and bases having to be built and Americans becoming key players in the huge military bureaucracy that was sure to follow. The savings would be considerable, it would be less provocative, and yet it would assure friend and foe alike that the United States was determined to defend Western Europe; this was Kennan's analysis. The thinking was not entirely original and others in the State Department shared the same views. But none of them had Kennan's access.

This time his being one thin door away from the Secretary of State did not help, though. He was told that the dumbbell arrangement would violate Senator Vandenberg's principle of reciprocity — the idea that Western Europe had to agree to defend the United States. Kennan's personal reaction was that it was preposterous to think that the nation needed such protection. He also deemed it absurd that a rather provincial politician was accorded such influence over foreign policy, but he got nowhere arguing his case. The administration, as noted, did not want to risk alienating Vandenberg. Significantly, Kennan was never again a key player in policy-making. In his memoirs, he discussed his confusion as to why. "The greatest mystery of my own role in Washington in those years," he wrote,

> . . . was why so much attention was paid in certain instances . . . to what I had to say, and so little in others. The only answer could be that Washington's reactions were deeply subjective, influenced more by domestic-political moods and institutional interests than by any theoretical considerations of our international position. It was I who was naive — naive in the assumption that the mere statement on a single occasion of a sound analysis or appreciation, even if invited or noted or nominally accepted by one's immediate superiors, had an appreciable effect on the vast, turgid, self-centered, and highly emotional process by which the views and reactions of official Washington were finally evolved.

The Berlin airlift and associated talk of war was near peak intensity during the summer of 1948, so Forrestal had trouble putting military leaders in a compromising mood about their budget requests for fiscal year 1950. To facilitate doing so, he first appointed a board of three flag officers, or generals, chaired by General Joseph McNarney, to look for duplication and economies. They came back with a figure of $23.6 billion, still about 65 percent more than what Truman was insisting on. They probably entertained notions that the President would narrow the gap himself at this point, but, focused on reelection as he was, he did not budge a dollar. The pressure mounted on Forrestal. Already it had taken its toll, though this was not obvious to anyone but the most discerning.

One such person was the portrait artist Al Murray, who was having considerable difficulty completing Forrestal's official portrait, begun the previous fall. Twice Murray neared completion, only to find a distraught facial image emerge on the canvas. Murray did not notice this progression during the sittings, which were infrequent, short, and full of interruptions. Kay Foley, Forrestal's longtime secretary, was screening his calls, but he had insisted that some be put through to his private dining room, where the sittings took place; Murray noticed that Symington called frequently, more than others. Forrestal would get involved in business, and Murray would be left without a subject.

The artist finally decided that he had to get Forrestal out of his office environment if progress was to be made, so he set up shop in the Corcoran Gallery and convinced Arleigh Burke, a mutual acquaintance of the artist and the subject, to show up. The captain had since 1947 been assigned to the Navy's General Board, which planned deployment of forces and force requirements. His office was not far from the gallery, in one of the Navy buildings near the Mall. (Indicative of its continuing estrangement, the Navy still had not moved into the Pentagon.) Murray thought that Burke could get a conversation going with the secretary and get his mind off his problems briefly. Forrestal liked Burke and especially admired his combat record. He was deferential toward such men, as if trying too hard to be accepted, and even addressed them by their nicknames, which sometimes dated back to academy days and sounded awkward coming from a man such as he, not given to frivolity.

Forrestal was pleased by Burke's surprise appearance and the two of them chatted easily about a broad range of subjects. With the secretary seated in a chair on a platform and Burke about ten feet away, Murray worked feverishly to make the most of the session. Nonetheless, the distraught image of a disturbed man was what again emerged from the oils on his canvas, which in 1949 was put on permanent display in the office of the Secretary of Defense.

Forrestal was in an agonizing, impossible predicament because the President was doggedly determined to cap military spending at $15 billion for fiscal year 1950, a sum that had no iota of correlation to what he had committed the nation to do with its military forces. Forrestal was carefully linking costs to commitments and strategic planning, and no matter how hard he worked the numbers, they came up short. This marked the first time that someone planning the military budget was taking a methodical approach. Unfortunately for Forrestal, Truman refused to believe his accounting, even refused to discuss a number higher than his sacred $15 billion.

For Forrestal, at issue was what the nation would be prepared to do if war broke out in Europe. With the $15 billion, the Defense Secretary found, the military would have only enough money to be ready to launch retaliatory atomic-bomb strikes from air bases in Great Britain. With $18.5 billion, the military could also try to hold the Mediterranean in the early stages of conflict. With the help of Joint Staff director Arthur Gruenther, Forrestal also approached the problem from another direction, using manpower figures as the controlling factor. He decided that 1,964,000 men and 70 air groups would be the force composition required for an effective reaction immediately at the outset of war; but this would cost $20 billion. The President's $15 billion would allow for a force composition of only 1,625,000 men and a mere 51-group Air Force.

Assuming that Forrestal's computations were correct, it followed that more than $20 billion would be reasonable if one wanted to avoid an atomic war from the outset. Furthermore, exigencies were popping up, all part of the new worldwide responsibilities of the United States. For example, on October 21, 1948, the State Department matter-of-factly notified the Defense Department that 4,000 to 6,000 US soldiers would be needed as guard forces in Jerusalem to implement the Bernadotte Plan, which was named after the UN mediator who had worked out a compromise proposal about dividing Palestine between Arabs and Israelis. Truman was piling up these responsibilities as if there were no associated costs. Concurrently, Forrestal was trying anything to squeeze fat from the military's operating budget. For instance, when the McNarney Board suggested that the Army was issuing too many trousers to its soldiers, the topic came up for discussion at a meeting of the Joint Chiefs presided over by the Secretary of Defense. "On the question of your pants, Brad, the seven pairs per man . . . ," Forrestal said, opening this memorable discourse.

Bradley was most reasonable about the pants — "I think we can put it off," he told Forrestal. But on the larger issues, such as strategic force structure, he and the other Chiefs were as adamant as Truman was, though at odds. As they saw it, the President was asking them to sign off on the idea that $15 billion was sufficient to defend the nation and its interests, and they would not because they were certain it was not. Caught in between was Forrestal, toward whom the President's attitude was, in essence, "You work it out." This hard view was partly a function of the fact that Forrestal had blocked Truman's original reorganization plan, which would have given the Defense Secretary authority to impose budget discipline. As things turned out, Forrestal was making so little progress that Webb was prompted to observe to David Lilienthal, the chairman of the Atomic Energy Commission, "The President is his own Secretary of Defense now; he has to be because Forrestal won't take hold." Actually, this was true only to the extent that Truman was having to deal with people going over Forrestal's head — Symington, most notably. Another sure indication of dissension within the military establishment and a sign that Forrestal was losing control were the leaked stories that filled the newspapers.

Forrestal tried every management technique he could think of to compensate for his lack of authority. Encouraging compromise did not work; the service secretaries and the Chiefs ignored his plea that they divide the military budget into roughly equal parts for another year. Nor did a change of scenery work. On August 20, 1948, he convened another conference of the Joint Chiefs outside Washington, leading them to the Quonset Air Station near Newport, Rhode Island, this time. His approach was to focus again on roles and missions in hopes that duplications might be acknowledged and savings realized. What he did instead was inadvertently set the Air Force and the Navy upon one another once more. A "treaty" was signed at Newport, but it had conflicting provisions, most notably these:

• The service having the primary function must determine the requirements, but in determining these requirements must take into account the contributions which may be made by forces from other services.
• Subject to control by higher authority, each service, in the fields of its primary missions, must have exclusive responsibility for programming and planning, and the necessary authority.

What these provisions did was set up a situation in which the Navy could argue that the Air Force did not need all the bombers it wanted because the Navy's existing carrier-based planes could do the job; and the Air Force could ignore this argument since it had exclusive responsibility for the programming and planning of the strategic air mission.

Consequently, the Newport conference was a bust. The only thing it did was draw the battle lines more sharply. This time Army people were virtually on the sidelines, though they rooted for the Air Force in hopes that the infighting might lead to revisions in the National Security Act that advanced their organizational ideas. Such changes were in the realm of possibility. The Hoover Commission — which, in compliance with the Lodge-Brown Act, Truman had appointed to look into reorganization of the whole executive branch of government — had decided to study the National Military Establishment and had delegated the job to Ferdinand Eberstadt, Forrestal's friend who had developed the Navy's first merger plan. Though the largest organization in the executive branch, it initially had been excluded from the commission's purview, but given Forrestal's trouble making it work, even he thought the commission should take a look.

When Eberstadt conducted secret hearings during October 1948, the Army–Air Force alliance against the Navy became evident, as did the strategies that the Air Force and Navy would use against each other. Army Secretary Royall proposed that the Air Force absorb all Navy aviation. And Symington recommended to Eberstadt that his task force consider "consolidation" — the Army's organization plan — as the only way of imposing discipline on recalcitrant Navy officers. The Navy responded by challenging the B-36's ability to penetrate enemy airspace and fulfill its strategic bombing mission. Contrary to the custom during World War II, these bombers would be flying in unescorted by fighters, which did not have sufficient range. Testifying for the Navy at these hearings were John Nicholas Brown, the assistant secretary of the Navy for air, and Arthur W. Radford, the deputy chief of naval operations for air. The latter was emerging as the Navy's most effective advocate, a spokesperson much more aggressive and articulate than Louis Denfeld.

Reacting to these Navy officials' testimony, Symington wrote a memorandum to Eberstadt in which he decried their "unwarranted attack on the Air Force." He alleged that the Navy was attacking the B-36 because its officers wanted at least part of the Air Force's strategic air mission. To support this contention, he cited a memo written in January by Rear Admiral Daniel V. Gallery that had been leaked to the press. Gallery had written in part:

> For the past two years our defense of the Navy has been based mainly in old familiar arguments about exercising control of the seas. Much has been said about anti-submarine warfare, naval reconnaissance, protection of shipping, and amphibious operations. It has been assumed, at least implicitly, that the next war will not be much different from the last one. This assumption is basically wrong, and if we stick to it the Navy will soon be obsolete. The next war will be a lot different from any previous one. It seems obvious that the next time our Sunday Punch will be an Atom Bomb aimed at the enemy capital or industrial centers and that the outcome of the war will be determined by strategic bombing. . . . I think the time is right now for the Navy to start an aggressive campaign aimed at proving that the Navy can deliver the Atom Bomb more effectively than the Air Forces can.

Though Symington was successful in calling Navy officers' motives into question, their criticism of the B-36 was having the effect they intended. Forrestal, for one, was troubled by the Navy's allegations. "I understand bombers cannot operate without fighter escort," he commented to Symington one day.

"That's not true," answered the Air Force Secretary, before asking where Forrestal had gotten his information.

"Well, I got it on good authority," he said.

After Symington denied the charge a second time, Forrestal said, "Prove it to me. Come over to my house tomorrow night for dinner and bring somebody with you who can demonstrate it isn't true."

Symington checked around to see who best should accompany him and decided on Curtis LeMay, then a lieutenant general serving as the Air Force's deputy chief of staff for research and development. The next night the two traveled to Forrestal's home in Georgetown, where they were joined by two other guests, Secretary of the Navy John Sullivan and Rear Admiral William S. Parsons, who while flying aboard the *Enola Gay* during World War II had armed the atomic bomb dropped on Hiroshima.

Toward the end of dinner, Forrestal looked at Symington and said, "I've been told that bombers can't operate without fighters."

Symington again denied the charge and, turning to LeMay, said, "Here's somebody who knows a lot about it from practical experience."

"General, what are your thoughts on it?" asked Forrestal.

"Well," replied LeMay, "one day in England we got our weather signals switched about a shuttle raid over Germany. The escort fighters didn't come up, so when the bombers, B-17s, broke into the sun around twenty thousand feet, we had no fighter escort at all; and when we hit the Dutch coast, we ran into the whole German fighter air force without any fighters at all."

"What raid was that?" Forrestal asked.

"Schweinfurt," LeMay answered.

"You lost a lot of bombers, didn't you?" observed Forrestal.

"Yes, sir," said LeMay, "but we wiped the target off the face of the earth."

"How do you know that?" Forrestal asked.

With dramatic effect, LeMay put down the cigar he was chewing and replied, "I led the first group, sir."

Forrestal looked at him for a time, while everyone sat there in silence, and finally said, "That's good enough for me." Symington said the Defense Secretary never again formally voiced this particular criticism to him.

By this time, however, all of Forrestal's reservations about Symington's being appointed Secretary of the Air Force had been realized. He was relentless, having developed the fervor of a convert, and was more intolerant of Navy viewpoints than were some Air Force aviators who had fought the good fight many years longer. One day Symington happened to spot Air Force Lieutenant General E. R. ("Pete") Quesada in a bar at the Hilton Hotel talking with journalist Hanson Baldwin, whom Quesada had met during the war. Symington deemed the newsman a Navy partisan because he was an Annapolis graduate, so the next morning he called Quesada to his office.

"You don't pick your drinking companions very carefully, do you?" asked Symington.

"I pick my own friends," responded Quesada, who turned and walked out, not to be intimidated.

Forrestal was the principal object of Symington's intensity, though. Forrestal had installed a squawk box communications system on his and the service secretaries' desks. With it, all they had to do to communicate with him was push a button; they could avoid receptionists and secretaries. Forrestal was trying to foster harmony. Unfortunately, the squawk boxes caused him nothing but grief and were eventually removed. According to Forrestal's assistants, Symington abused the privilege and interrupted him about every thirty minutes with a question or some bit of information.

"Jim, I just got some new figures on that cost of the air wing aboard that carrier," he would say, according to one account. Symington knew what he was doing; he was keeping the pressure on, keeping Forrestal, who was still strongly associated with the Navy, off balance. And he did so with the confidence of someone who enjoyed a personal rapport with the President and who knew that the Congress, the President, and the American people were moving strongly in favor of making the Air Force the key element in the nation's defense.

Dealing with Symington was, of course, only one of many pressures weighing on Forrestal, and by election time their cumulative effect was becoming more obvious. He was making some stupid moves. For example, he let it be known that *when* Tom Dewey was elected, he would be willing to remain in the cabinet as either Secretary of Defense or Secretary of State. He went so far as to have unauthorized private meetings with the Republican candidate. Years later, Dewey said that Forrestal "came to see me at least two or three times during the latter half of 1948. He was disturbed about the condition of our defense and we discussed it at considerable length." Republicans were making known Forrestal's acceptability on the new cabinet. Congresswoman Margaret Chase Smith of Maine endorsed his being reappointed by inserting into the *Congressional Record* an editorial from the *Portland Press-Herald* that said: "When — it is hardly necessary to put in an 'if' — Governor Dewey is elected President next fall, he will have about 10 weeks in which to select a Cabinet . . . [and] there is one man in the Truman Cabinet who richly deserves to be retained. That is James Forrestal."

But worse for Forrestal than his widespread support among Republicans was the widespread enmity among Democrat politicos he was incurring unnecessarily. With less than three weeks left before the election, he was not on record as having contributed to Truman's campaign organization. This caused George E. Allen, one of the Democratic fund-raisers, to send him a letter that read like a collection notice. "I know that recently you have been asked many times to contribute to the Democratic Campaign," wrote Allen, "but this is, as far as I am concerned, the final request. . . . Would you join me in making a donation?"

In response, Forrestal, a wealthy man, had a Marine Corps sergeant deliver $100 in cash as his contribution to the National Truman-Barkley Club. This meager amount became a matter of intense discussion when reported in newspapers in January. A friend and attorney named Walter Dunnington came to Forrestal's defense, saying that a $2,500 contribution to the campaign credited to him was actually Forrestal's. Upon entering government service, Forrestal had established a fund for such expenditures, and Dunnington was supposed to administer it as directed by him. Few Truman partisans were placated by this explanation, though. The President's was a campaign that had been so short of funds that railroad officials stopped his campaign train in Oklahoma City and refused to allow it to proceed until past-due accounts were paid in full. Fortunately for Truman, some oilmen who had been invited into the *Ferdinand Magellan,* his private car, passed the hat among themselves to raise the funds and got him going again. This was just days before the election.

At the end, though, it was Dewey's campaign that was sidetracked. On November 2 Truman scored a decisive victory in the electoral count, 303 to 189. Henry Wallace and his Progressive Party of America, which was essentially the Democratic party's left wing broken away, was not a decisive factor, as anticipated. Nor was Strom Thurmond and his Dixicrat party, which was the right wing of the Democratic party broken away.

Truman's victory quickly ended the prevarication on military spending. Forrestal went to work to get the Chiefs to reduce it from the last agreed-to level, which was $23.6 billion. By December 1, the Chiefs had trimmed down their total budget requests to $16.9 billion. Forrestal held out hope that this would satisfy Truman; it was, after all, down from the original request by nearly half. But the President dismissed it on December 9, and restated his demand for a $15-billion limit. By the time of his budget message, he would lower it to $14.2 billion.

Even in what was by then a disturbed emotional state, Forrestal had to know that his days as Secretary of Defense were numbered. A sure sign was that in December his diary trailed off into nothing. But it was not within him to quit his position under conditions that smacked of failure. Close friends tried to get him to resign or, at least, to take a long rest, but he seems to have developed the feeling that he was indispensable. He had been a high-profile leader of the military establishment for about eight years. Maybe he had trouble imagining himself being anything else. Or anything less. Whatever the case, that the international situation was still dangerous reinforced his disposition to stay on the job. He had become too ill to help himself.

Unfortunately, his home life was no help; it was actually a destabilizing influence. Hanson Baldwin happened to see just how bad it was when he flew in for one of his monthly chats with military leaders. He called Mrs. Foley, who was under standing instructions to fit the military-affairs editor into Forrestal's schedule. On this occasion in December, Baldwin was invited to join the Defense Secretary at his home during cocktail hour. When he arrived at about five-thirty, two other guests were already there, a woman and an ambassador, and Forrestal was still at work. Before long the latter came in racing, his pace frenetic, like that of a person behind schedule and trying to catch up. Then the doorbell rang, and a foreign official demanding a private session presented himself. By the time Forrestal returned to his original party of three, it was half past six and he was even more fretful, knowing that his guests had been waiting for him. Baldwin tried to excuse himself, but Forrestal would not allow him to leave.

"Oh, no, don't go," said Forrestal. "Stay for dinner. We'll go up and have dinner with Josie."

Baldwin, who was married to Helen Bruce, of the prominent old-line family, was acquainted with Forrestal's wife, Josephine, socially. Over the years, Josephine had become an alcoholic and now was spending much of the day in bed. The situation was "very unpleasant," Baldwin recalled. "We went up and had dinner on our knees, sitting alongside the bed, and she talked. She made a little sense, not too much."

Sometime during this period, Forrestal called Clark Clifford — Clifford could not remember exactly when — to say that the National Security Act of 1947 was too weak and that, as a result, he could not administer the National Military Establishment. Significantly, the Hoover Commission task force led by Eberstadt had reached the same conclusion. The secretary had tried everything to get the Navy and Air Force to reach some common ground and had failed. He had made significant progress in some ways, as measured by his getting the Chiefs and the service secretaries to agree on a proposed FY1950 budget that was close to what the President wanted. But the gap was symbolic of the extra authority he needed, and he now recognized this fact. He discussed the matter at length with Clifford, who promptly arranged a meeting with the President and accompanied him into the Oval Office.

"President Truman," said Forrestal, "I have come over to confess to you that I've been terribly wrong. We have to have a stronger law." Such an admission is a rare thing, Clifford later observed. "It was very gratifying to President Truman," he said, adding that he sensed Truman knew all along this would happen. However, this won Forrestal no leeway when, on December 20, he made one last, desperate appeal to Truman to lift his budget cap. All he wanted was $700 million more for some long-range-bomber groups, but Truman turned him down flat — a good indication that he had already decided to get himself a new Secretary of Defense. It so happened that the man who wanted the job was a person to whom the President was very deeply indebted: Louis Johnson, the Washington attorney who had been Truman's chief fund-raiser during the election campaign.

On Christmas Eve of 1948, in the late afternoon hours, a contented Arleigh Burke sat in the cabin of his ship — the light cruiser *Huntington,* docked at the Philadelphia Navy Yard — contemplating with satisfaction the holidays to come and the successful cruise just completed. Shortly after the portrait session with Forrestal the previous summer, he had escaped the confining clutches of his Washington office job and returned to sea. At Taranto, Italy, Burke had taken command of his warship and, for a brief time, sailed her with the newly constituted Sixth Fleet in the Mediterranean. Then, quite unexpectedly, he was ordered to take it on a solo diplomatic cruise to certain designated ports in the Red Sea, the Indian Ocean, and the South Atlantic before docking at Philadelphia Navy Yard. The *Huntington* was a fine ship, but Burke was a better captain. That his ship was designated this duty was no accident. Burke was a battle commander of renown.

Ever the good Navy wife, Bobbie Burke had driven to Philadelphia from Washington, D.C., to greet her husband as the *Huntington* docked. Beforehand she had rented a local apartment, where they planned to stay for a month during the holiday season; after that, he would take the ship to Atlantic Fleet headquarters in Norfolk, work up new orders for his crew, and set sail on another voyage.

But most unexpectedly these plans were dashed. Burke's Christmas Eve repose was interrupted by a call on the shore phone. Rear Admiral Charles Wellborn, the deputy chief of naval operations for administration, was on the line with an emergency message. Denfeld had ordered an immediate change in Burke's duty station. Burke was to return to Washington.

Complying with these orders, he did so two days after Christmas, following a change-of-command ceremony. Bobbie did not watch it, that being taboo for women in those days, especially a woman by herself. She sat in their car during the whole thing.

One complication that morning was two hundred pounds of prime beef Burke had purchased in Argentina during the *Huntington*'s port call there. Filets selling for about ten cents a pound were too much of a bargain for a military man making about $500 per month to pass up. US Customs and meat inspectors had examined and approved this voyage souvenir by the time the change-of-command ceremony was finished. Luckily, two husky yeomen managed to fit it into the Plymouth's trunk. Burke then covered it with ice. He loaded the backseat of the car, too, filling it to the roof with his shipboard gear. By ten that morning, the Burkes were driving slowly down old US 1 toward the nation's capital, so overloaded they could not see out their rear window and the car's rear springs were flat. It was rather inglorious transport for a man on a mission to save the United States Navy. The second phase of the reorganization struggle was under way — the fight over how to modify the 1947 law. That it was all about strategy would be more evident to the public this time.

Burke had been appointed assistant chief of naval operations for operational research and policy, a new staff agency to be known in Navy parlance as Op. 23. His job would be to develop a coherent picture of Navy strategy in this age of jet propulsion and atomic weaponry, and to organize the Navy's presentation of it, which would also entail countering critics' claims and charges. Op. 23's forerunner units had been, first, the Secretary's Committee on Research and Organization, known by the acronym SECOR, and later, the Unification Committee, called UNICOM. SECOR was constituted to support those Navy officials who were arguing the Navy's case before enactment of the National Security Act of 1947. UNICOM was constituted after it became apparent that that legislation had not settled the unification fight. Radford had been directly involved in SECOR and acted as a sort of godfather for UNICOM, as he would for Burke's Op. 23. Association with all three units was risky. The head of UNICOM had been fired and the unit itself disbanded because of a press leak.

By the time Burke reported to Denfeld, the Navy was in dire straits. Clearly, the 151-year-old department had lost its position of pre–World War II preeminence to the 1½-year-old Department of the Air Force. Not only the politicians but also most of the media had turned against the Navy in favor of the Air Force. The month Burke arrived back in Washington, *Reader's Digest* published an article entitled "Navy, or an Air Force?" by William Bradford Huie, a writer who for years had been a confidant of senior Air Force officers. The magazine published three more articles by Huie on the subject in its January, March, and April 1949 issues. Each had the same pro–Air Force, anti-Navy slant. In those days before widespread television news viewing, *Reader's Digest,* with its circulation of six million, was especially powerful in influencing the tone of coverage by many news outlets, when it tried. In that regard, Huie's articles were also timed to have as great an impact as possible on the FY 1950 military-budget debates about to begin in earnest in Congress, following Truman's budget message.

Just how far the Navy had fallen and how much convincing Burke and his counterparts had to do was evidenced by a briefing he was ordered to give soon after his return to Washington. Truman had asked Eisenhower to take leave of his position at Columbia and return for "two or three months" as a consultant. He was to preside over meetings of the Chiefs as they prepared a war plan that could form the basis of the FY 1950 military budget, to be formulated using integrated-force concepts. Eisenhower agreed to help and began work on January 21, 1949. He immediately asked Denfeld for a Navy briefing, and Burke was assigned the task.

The scene was extraordinary: Eisenhower seated alone in a rather large auditorium, except for a few staff people on the fringes, listening intently to Burke, by himself on the stage. It was precisely the circumstance that Forrestal and the Navy had fought so hard to avoid before reorganization in 1947. Eisenhower was essentially acting as the dreaded Chief of Staff in charge of all the military. Sure, Forrestal was a Navy man, and that being so, Ike's involvement was a case of turnabout is fair play. But the Army and the Air Force were not paranoid like the Navy, for whom Burke standing up there onstage presenting the Navy case to the famous General of the Army was a nightmare come true. That Army and Air Force briefers had to do the same thing did not assuage Navy fears. The situation admirals had always agonized over was precisely this one — a Navy man trying to justify the Navy and its component parts to an Army man. To them, it meant that the Navy was losing control of its destiny. And they were right.

Earlier in January at the White House, Forrestal had assisted in preparing Truman's State of the Union address. During a pertinent meeting presided over by Truman, Clifford happened to select a chair next to the Defense Secretary. His line of sight was toward Forrestal, and he could not help but notice that the man was constantly scratching and rubbing a spot on his scalp that had become an open sore. Clifford found it "very disquieting," he recalled. On a couple of later occasions, he noticed that it was getting larger.

Later in the month Walter Winchell and Drew Pearson began attacking Forrestal during their Sunday-evening radio broadcasts and in their columns. Winchell dredged up his 1929 income tax problems; denounced the National Security Council — Forrestal's creation — as being designed "to throw the country into war without even notifying Congress"; and said that Truman would accept Forrestal's resignation when it was tendered. Such letters from cabinet members at the beginning of a new term are normally perfunctory and are not accepted, but the charges accompanying the prediction were so personal as to indicate that inside information had been issued suggesting Forrestal was on his way out. For instance, Winchell and Pearson accused Forrestal of cowardice, saying that in 1937, when a jewel thief robbed his wife, he ran. In fact, Forrestal was asleep inside their Manhattan residence when, at 2:10 AM, Josephine arrived out front in the limousine of a friend who had escorted her to a party at the Plaza Hotel. The robber jumped inside the car when it rolled to a halt.

This charge in particular riled Forrestal and no longer could he listen to any of the commentators, he told friends. He ordered his attorneys to prepare libel papers against Winchell, but never had them filed. Prominent publications such as *Time* and the *New York Times* discussed Pearson's charge and set the record straight, but the damage to Forrestal was more personal than public, his emotions being so fragile. Krock was so exercised about the matter that he wired Pearson, demanding corrections.

Like others having the occasion to work closely with Forrestal during this period, Eisenhower was stunned by the man's deteriorating mental health. One incident in particular struck him. It involved the B-36 question: should more of them be produced? For many hours Forrestal and Eisenhower sat side by side listening to the arguments, for and against. In the end, it was the presentations of scientists, not military men, that proved persuasive. Their advice was that the B-36 was the only weapon system the United States would have available during the next several years capable of delivering the atomic bomb onto targets deep in the Soviet Union. On that basis, the two leaders concurred that the obvious choice was to build more B-36s, but not as many as the Air Force wanted. (They had previously rejected the Navy's Supercarrier for near-term use, it being only an experimental idea; its keel had not even been laid.)

But a few minutes after leaving the meeting in which they reached this decision about the B-36, Forrestal turned to Eisenhower as they walked down a Pentagon hallway and said, "You know, Ike, I think we'll have to go into this B-36 matter a little bit more deeply."

"I was shocked," Eisenhower recalled, "and for the first time realized that either the man was losing his memory or was becoming so confused that he could not concentrate."

These stories got around, so very few people within the Washington milieu were surprised to learn that Forrestal's role was at an end. On March 1, 1949, Truman invited him to the White House and ordered him to prepare immediately his letter of resignation. In January, Forrestal had been told through intermediaries that Johnson would succeed him about May 1, but Forrestal refused to believe this was happening to him. He personally disliked the man and did not deem him worthy of the position. Consequently, Truman's order seemed to him abrupt and was shattering; Forrestal's nervous state, and probably, too, the feeling that he had failed, contributed to his reaction. However, he complied, and on March 28 graciously watched his successor sworn in.

Paranoia then overwhelmed Forrestal within a matter of days. He was convinced that Communists, Zionists, and White House officials were out to get him. "Bob, they're after me," he told Lovett after traveling to Hobe Sound, Florida, to meet Josephine and close friends at the under secretary of state's private compound there. He thought someone was bugging his phone and that the Communists were planning an imminent invasion. His normally tight lips were now so drawn they were barely visible as a line. At least one person stayed with him constantly after he attempted suicide while at the compound. How he tried to do it was kept secret by his friends, although it is known that knives, razor blades, belts, and other potential instruments of death were kept from him. He wondered aloud whether he was being punished for having been a "bad Catholic," not having practiced his faith since college and having married a divorced woman.

Dr. William Menninger, the famed psychiatrist from Topeka, Kansas, who was also a consultant to the surgeon general of the Army, flew in. His conclusion was that Forrestal was suffering from severe depression of the type seen during the war, caused by combat fatigue. Eberstadt, acting for the family, helped convince Forrestal that he should be admitted immediately to the Navy's hospital in Bethesda.

After seven weeks of treatment, he was thought to be improving. But at approximately 1:45 AM on Sunday, May 22, 1949, he interrupted his work of copying by hand Sophocles' *Chorus of Ajax* and, while an attendant was away briefly, jumped to his death through a window in his room on the hospital's sixteenth floor. He was fifty-seven years old, and as much a casualty of the cold war as a soldier shot through the heart would be.

He was buried several days later following services in Memorial Amphitheater at Arlington National Cemetery. The last such funeral had been for Pershing. Sixty-five hundred people were present, including Truman and Vice President Alben Barkley. So, too, was Senator Vandenberg, who recorded the event in his diary that night.

> It was a full military funeral. Of course Jimmy wasn't very big — but the casket looked *so small!* There were four of the most famous bands in the country. The Marine Band played "Nearer My God to Thee" with infinite pathos. The Navy Band played Handel's "Largo" — and of course that put me wholly out of commission. The Air Force Band played "Lead Kindly Light" — !!!
>
> And then as they slowly marched from the Amphitheater to the high hillside where Jimmy finds his peace at last, the big Army Band played "Onward Christian Soldiers" — and I thought I would expire. There was something about it all which was so intimately tragic and yet so spiritually exalted.

Carrying the infighting to the edge of his grave, his family named as pallbearers all the service secretaries except Symington.

*   *   *

Louis Johnson, Forrestal's successor, was a World War I veteran, a colonel in the Army Reserves, a former national commander of the American Legion, and a former assistant secretary of war whom Roosevelt had eased out as he formed his bipartisan coalition under Stimson and Knox before World War II. He could not wait to show the military he was in charge. Starting out, his views coincided with Truman's in all respects, so he could not have cared less that the latter's personal attitudes and policies had created a highly charged, polarized environment — these attitudes and policies being, in particular, the President's distrust of the career military, his distaste for the Navy, and especially the Marine Corps, and his disposition to keep decreasing already austere military budgets while dramatically increasing the roles of the US military services in world affairs. Like Truman, Johnson perceived that the public wanted small defense budgets, and since he himself wanted to be President, he always tried to do him one better by this measure. His personal staff talked openly about helping "the boss" look good so he could run for the presidency in 1952. He was not subtle about anything he did, so domestic political considerations overrode worries about what was going on in the rest of the world. His first objective was to become the dominant figure in the cabinet. This was possible because Marshall had stepped down as Secretary of State the day Truman was inaugurated for his second term. The general had had a kidney with a benign cyst removed. Acheson had succeeded him.

Johnson was a bald bear of a man, weighing two hundred pounds, with a disposition to match. He had none of the tentativeness associated with a deep thinker like Forrestal. His having achieved success very early in life had permanently reinforced his sense of the correctness of his judgment. At age twenty-six, during his first term in the West Virginia House of Delegates, the state's legislature, he was elected majority leader, an achievement that infused him with great ambition.

Johnson interrupted his political career to serve in World War I and, like Truman, effectively used that experience and the associations that evolved from it to promote his future. His being the American Legion's commander carried him into national politics and brought him to Washington. And in 1945 the capital became his permanent base of operations when he and his law partner, Philip Steptoe, opened up a branch office of their firm there. For years they had had well-established offices in Virginia and West Virginia.

Johnson understood the value that military men placed on symbols, so his first act as Defense Secretary was to order vacated the largest office he could find in the Pentagon. Then, making a show of it, he closed off the nearby River Entrance to the huge building while workmen refurbished the office for his occupancy. Normally, hundreds of workers passed through these doorways each day. And to make the office interior properly imposing, he had Pershing's desk found and made it a centerpiece.

Quickly, he made other symbolic moves. Nine days after being sworn in as Secretary of Defense, he ordered an end to annual service celebrations like the one in 1945 on the Hudson River that Truman had attended to help the Navy commemorate. In Johnson's view — and he was right on this point — they were blatant evidence of service rivalry. Indeed, the divisive celebrations were degenerating into massive publicity stunts. During Air Force Day festivities the previous fall, Symington and Chief of Staff Hoyt Vandenberg had ordered massed flights of B-29s over a number of major American cities and flyovers of smaller formations of B-36s in 103 others. Johnson even ended temporarily the Marine Corps's hallowed tradition of having a formal dining-in on its birthday.

His most shocking symbolic action had to do with the Navy, though. Twenty-one days after his swearing-in, that service had finally laid, with great fanfare, the keel for its Supercarrier. Years of relentless political effort had gotten the admirals to this point. On their own initiative and with congressional approval, they had forgone $364 million in funds already appropriated for building other ships and applied it to the building of this great ship. They conveyed how important the vessel was to them by calling it the *United States*. Yet, five days later Johnson, with the President's backing, ordered a halt to its construction and canceled the project. He did so without notifying Sullivan and Denfeld beforehand. Sullivan resigned in protest, and Truman appointed as his successor a fellow from Nebraska who admitted to the media that he had never been on a body of water larger than a lake. His name was Frank Matthews, and because of this remark he was thereafter referred to as "Rowboat Matthews" by Navy officers. He was a nationally prominent Catholic lay leader who had helped swing a divided Nebraska delegation to Truman at the 1948 Democratic National Convention.

Congressional leadership supported Johnson's cancellation of the Supercarrier; sentiment in Congress, as noted, was now running heavily in favor of the Air Force. That the Democrats had regained control of both legislative bodies several months earlier was very significant. During the two years of Republican majorities, the Navy had fared relatively well, its most notable achievement being the adoption of the Navy's reorganization plan in 1947.

A measure of the difficult days ahead for the Navy in dealing with Congress was the fact that its most effective advocate there was a minority-party junior member of Vinson's committee — Republican James Van Zandt of Pennsylvania. Aggressiveness was his long suit. A Navy Reservist who had served in both world wars, Van Zandt began making all sorts of allegations on the House floor. He charged that the Air Force was wildly exaggerating the capabilities of the B-36. And he accused Symington and Johnson of pushing the B-36 because they had a financial interest in the plane's primary contractor, Lockheed Aircraft Company. The media widely circulated both allegations, which gained a degree of currency because of an element of truth. The B-36 was propeller-driven; jet engines would be added to improve its speed and altitude capability, but as the combination indicates, this bomber was a transition aircraft. Intercontinental bombers that were fully jet-propelled would be introduced within the near future. Therefore, the question was whether pouring money into B-36 development was wasteful. Van Zandt thought so. As for the conflict-of-interest charges, Symington had made enough enemies who wanted to believe them that the stories took on a life of their own. Others deemed him suspect merely because he had been successful in big business and was involved in defense contracting before he entered government service. The charge against Johnson was plausible because he had been a member of the Lockheed board of directors.

These accusations came at the same time the Truman administration was fending off accusations of influence peddling and corruption. Colonel James Hunt, a close friend of Vaughan's who was in charge of letting some contracts for restoring the White House, got caught charging businessmen fees of 5 percent to get them. Incredibly, such practices were not illegal then, but there was an unmistakable odor about them. During the ensuing congressional and press investigations, Vaughan himself was tainted. In all his small-minded, bumbling glory, he had gotten a perfume manufacturer priority seating on a military aircraft flight to Europe in May 1945 and had abetted the giving of a Deepfreeze to Mrs. Truman from another businessman. She was unaware of the circumstances of its delivery and, in fact, had it carted off because it did not work. Nonetheless, Vaughan's indiscretions and "five-percenters" such as Hunt made Van Zandt's allegations believable and amplified the B-36 controversy.

Van Zandt so riled Air Force officials, who otherwise had everything going their way, that they ordered agents of the Air Force Office of Special Investigation to tail the congressman and various Navy officers believed to be feeding him information. Normally these operatives acted as the Air Force's detectives, investigating criminal cases on Air Force bases, be they burglaries or espionage. Major Joe Carroll was in charge of the special team of investigators looking into the leaks to Van Zandt. The propriety of their domestic spying was never questioned. They learned that one source of information for the Navy was Glenn Martin, whose company's smaller bombers were losing out to Lockheed's big ones and who had an old score to settle with the President dating back to the Truman Committee days.

Some of Van Zandt's material was also coming from Burke's Op. 23, which had produced a brochure called "The Bombing Myth." His unit was discreetly investigating and sometimes challenging Air Force and Army claims and proposals, while also trying to develop a coherent Navy position. This being a battle of ideas, Burke worked hard to assemble a staff of able thinkers who were good writers. He had a reputation for having an eye for talent. During World War II, for example, he appointed as his executive officer an all-American football player from the University of Colorado who had become a Rhodes scholar, Lieutenant (Junior Grade) Byron ("Whizzer") White. Having grown up on a farm not far from Boulder, Burke had followed the young man's outstanding college career. He ordered White to analyze and question everything about his battle plans. In practical terms, he thus made certain that an intelligent subordinate felt free to challenge his boss boldly. The result was better battle plans and, in White's case, a better Supreme Court justice later on, when President Kennedy appointed him to serve on the nation's highest court. While head of Op. 23, Burke tried to sign up as writing talent Lieutenant Commander Edward Beach, who declined because he had just been given command of a sub. Burke had read a cogent magazine article by him; this was years before Beach wrote *Run Silent, Run Deep* and became famous as a novelist and historian.

Greater opportunities elsewhere were only part of the reason Burke had trouble recruiting talented people. Navy and Marine officers knew that assignment to Op. 23 was a great career risk. The unit was working in active opposition to administration policy and the expressed personal wishes of the Secretary of Defense and the President.

Caution was certainly the byword. Burke warned his people that the Navy Intelligence Service and the Federal Bureau of Investigation would subject them all to rigorous background checks and that follow-up investigations would be conducted randomly during the life of the project. If anyone had something in his past that might subject him to blackmail, Burke said he wanted to know about it; he was evidently worried that enemies — namely, the US Air Force and the US Army, not the Russians — would use it to pry loose sensitive information.

Burke also warned his people about possible infiltration, a concern that seems to have been justified by events. Op. 23's support staff was almost entirely composed of Navy and Marine enlisted people (some of whom had marginal clerical skills), even though the trend throughout the services was to convert such job slots to civilian positions, given the shortage of people in uniform. The Navy's Bureau of Personnel persistently urged Burke to follow this trend, and at one point he relented by agreeing to interview a young woman who had applied for a secretarial job after responding to a notice of position availability. She passed the preliminary tests with ease, so Dorothy Jenson, Burke's personal secretary, brought the applicant in to meet him and take her final test — dictation from Burke. Using shorthand and without asking a single question or Burke's having to repeat himself or slow down, she transcribed a long letter. He requested it forthwith and she promptly typed it and delivered it to him. It was perfect; she even duplicated Burke's errors verbatim. She clearly deserved the job, but, as a matter of course, Burke told her that he would let her know later. He then called in Jensen.

"We'd better hire that girl," he said.

"No, sir," she replied. "You don't want that girl."

Burke was incredulous. "Why?" he asked.

"She's too good," said Jenson. "That girl is a court stenographer. She is really good. The pay, the job that she would take, are far below her capability. She can get a job anywhere in the government at a much higher salary than you can pay her. So there must be a reason for it."

Forthwith, Burke changed his mind; he didn't hire the woman. Later, it was determined that she was the wife of an Air Force major.

As matters developed in the nation's capital, Burke and his Op. 23 staff were making lots of enemies. The unit began issuing position papers attacking the old Army idea that centralization and consolidation would save millions. Johnson was traveling around the country giving speeches, telling audiences that he was going to deliver a stronger defense with fewer dollars. Behind Johnson's promise was Truman's determination to amend the National Security Act by strengthening the authority of the Defense Secretary and moving toward the more centralized organizational structure that the Army had always wanted. These goals had received a powerful boost when on February 28, 1949, the Hoover Commission, following up on the work of the Eberstadt Task Force, issued its formal report on the National Military Establishment. The commission concluded that the present setup was "perilously close to the weakest type of department" and recommended strengthening the hand of the Secretary of Defense over the separate departments and giving "the singleness of control" that is the "essence of efficiency." To achieve this, commission members would (1) make the Defense Secretary the sole person accountable to the President and Congress for the military; (2) reduce the Secretaries of the Army, Navy, and Air Force to under secretary rank and deny them the right to appeal over the head of the Defense Secretary; (3) create the position of Chairman of the Joint Chiefs of Staff, making this person the sole link between the Defense Secretary and his military advisers; and (4) grant the Defense Secretary "full power" over the preparation of the military budget and over expenditures authorized by Congress. According to the commission, the fact that the armed services once considered a budget of $30 billion for fiscal year 1950 reflected "a lack of realistic understanding by the three military departments of the economic and social factors of national security."

Eisenhower, in his consulting capacity, had some input into this proposal, but very little. He focused on helping the Chiefs develop a strategic plan for fiscal year 1950 that would not exceed Truman's $15-billion cap. He failed, but came close. He produced a $16-billion budget, which he thought would almost do what Forrestal's $18.5-billion budget would do — that is, provide for launching an atomic-bomb strike from Great Britain and holding some key bases in the Mediterranean region. Eisenhower proposed cutting the Navy back more. His view, which he confided to friend Everett Hazlett then, was that "our present Navy can scarcely be justified on the basis of the naval strength of any potential enemy." In his diary, Eisenhower termed the Supercarrier a "supertarget." He also told Hazlett that he wondered how the Navy could justify a large army of its own; that was his perception of the Marine Corps.

After Johnson succeeded Forrestal, Eisenhower continued presiding over meetings of the Joint Chiefs; in effect, he was an unofficial chairman of the Joint Chiefs. The President was hoping that Eisenhower could bring more discipline to the deliberations and get the Chiefs to accept his policies. This arrangement did not last long, though. Truman's and Johnson's insistence that the military keep on cutting back made Eisenhower think they were not interested in his advice and were only using him to make their policies more credible. A health problem (chronic ileitis) gave him the excuse to start distancing himself from the administration and by late summer he cut all ties. On June 4, 1949, he wrote in his diary this estimate of where Truman was leading the nation: "Of course the results [of an inadequate defense policy] will not show up until we get into serious trouble. We are repeating our history of decades, we just don't believe we ever will get into a real jam."

This was a serious charge and too important for military leaders such as Eisenhower to keep to themselves much longer. It was only a matter of time before somebody made headlines with it and set Truman up for a fall should the nation be caught unprepared.

Johnson's pitch to the American people was that he could save a billion dollars a year by consolidating functions. This being a contention that would impinge on the Navy, Burke and his group aggressively began undermining it in secret. Their presumption was that each of the services was so large that in most cases economies of scale had already been fully realized. And so they set about finding examples to challenge Johnson's contention that he could save money by consolidating. A mundane one they found involved undershirts. For years each service had purchased its own undershirts. The Navy had ordered white; the Marine Corps, green; and the Army, brown. The Air Force, upon becoming a separate service, began ordering white. Then Johnson's people decided that the Army was going to order everybody's undershirts. The contract let for bidding was enormous, far exceeding the capacity of any single manufacturer. The result was that every bidder was essentially a middleman or broker, who had to subcontract piecemeal with the same manufacturers who had been doing the work all along. The middleman's percentage actually increased the cost of the undershirts to the military. And a more expensive undershirt was only part of the problem. Thinking in terms of economy of scale, the Army had specified that all the undershirts be of brown cloth. The result was awful uniform color combinations when the undershirts were worn under Navy white or blue uniforms, Marine Corps green, and Air Force blue.

Huie's articles in *Reader's Digest* were also subjected to the scrutiny of Burke, who later said that Op. 23 compiled seven typewritten pages of falsehoods in them. Press partisanship was indeed prevalent, not confined to Huie or the likes of Spaatz, who, having retired from the Air Force about a year after reorganization, was writing a column for *Newsweek*. Thousands of newspeople had recently been in uniform during World War II and had a natural loyalty to the branch in which they served. The partisanship even extended to the comic strips. Focusing on Air Force people were "Terry and the Pirates" and "Steve Canyon." Promoting Navy people was "Buzz Sawyer." The Army, being out of the game, got "Beetle Bailey" and "Sergeant Bilko." But the clear winner, in terms of favorable press treatment, was the Air Force. The feeling that technology and nuclear weapons would dominate future wars and thus warranted exploitation overwhelmed the sentimental loyalties of a lot of servicemen-turned-journalists.

Reserve status was another affiliation that colored the judgment of various newspeople. One such Navy protagonist was David Lawrence of the *U.S. News & World Report*, whose nationally syndicated column became an outlet for anti–Air Force material that riled LeMay, especially. Lawrence's criticism focused on the B-36s of LeMay's Strategic Air Command, which he had taken over from George Kenney in the fall of 1948, shortly after his dinner at Forrestal's home. LeMay was outraged by what he later charged were "damn lies" in Lawrence's columns.

SAC headquarters had recently been moved from Andrews Air Force Base, Maryland, to Offutt AFB outside Omaha, Nebraska, and what totally discomfited LeMay was that the *Omaha World-Herald* printed what Lawrence wrote. In response, LeMay ordered his chief press officer to go through the paper's morgue files, looking for everything the columnist had said about B-36s and strategic bombing, and thereafter to monitor his columns. When errors were found, the press officer was instructed by LeMay to print up the column with its errors underlined in red on one side of a page and corrections to it on the other, and mail copies to the editor of every paper that carried Lawrence, accompanied by a cover letter, signed by LeMay, that roughly read, "Dear Editor: I understand your object is to print the truth. That being the case, why do you print this?"

Newspapers began canceling the column and, according to LeMay, Lawrence very quickly stopped writing about B-36s and strategic bombing. Lawrence wrote LeMay, asking him what he was up to, but the general tossed the correspondence into his wastebasket, unanswered. LeMay said Symington later told him that he had proof the Navy League was paying Lawrence to attack the Air Force. That charge was not made publicly or substantiated, but the Navy League and the newly formed Air Force Association were, indeed, very active. There was also a Marine Corps League and the Association of the US Army. All these organizations are still active; their typical members are people who either have served in the relevant service branch or live in a community near one of its installations and thus have an indirect economic interest. During the summer of 1949, the Navy League and the Air Force Association each appropriated $500,000 for promotion campaigns to support their favored service.

One point the Navy continued to press against B-36 adherents was the plane's vulnerability to enemy fighters. Van Zandt aggressively pushed this point in Congress, and eventually the pressure caused the House of Representatives to pass a nonbinding resolution that asked Johnson to order mock battles between Air Force B-36s and Navy Banshee fighters. It was the same sort of thing Congress had done during Billy Mitchell's heyday; in both instances, the proposals had been hard for any legislator to vote against. This time, though, it had no practical effect.

Johnson and Symington ignored the resolution; such was the Air Force's position of strength. In fact, the Air Force even refused to allow Navy pilots inside a B-36. And, in line with Air Force recommendations that the Navy's large carriers be mothballed, Johnson in July 1949 decreed that budgets for Navy and Marine aviation would be cut 50 percent from the previous year. This entailed reducing the number of large Essex-class carriers from 8 to 4; the smaller Saipan class from 10 to 8; the carrier air groups from 14 to 6; Marine Corps aviation squadrons from 23 to 12; and Navy patrol squadrons from 30 to 20.

The final devastating blow for the Navy came on August 10, 1949, when the President signed into law very significant revisions to the National Security Act of 1947. In effect, he was discarding the Navy organization plan Forrestal had gotten passed and replacing it with one in line with the Army's. Hoover, who had overseen the study of the executive branch in an admirably bipartisan way, had helped Truman gain broad support for his proposals; the House had on August 2 approved the bill by a vote of 356 to 7. Among the new law's provisions were these:

• The National Military Establishment was henceforth to be known as the Department of Defense, a title with connotations of the greater centralized control that was wrought.

• The position of Chairman of the Joint Chiefs of Staff was created. He was to preside over meetings of the Chiefs so as to bring order to their deliberations, though he would not have a vote. He was authorized to have direct access to the President, a factor that greatly enhanced his power.

• To facilitate the Defense Secretary's greater administrative control, the new office of Deputy Secretary of Defense was created, as were three new Assistant Secretary of Defense positions.

• The Secretaries of the Army, the Navy, and the Air Force were subordinated to the Secretary of Defense, removed from the National Security Council, and denied direct access to the President.

• The Vice President was made a member of the National Security Council.

• The Department of Defense and the three separate service departments were granted more flexible control of money appropriated them.

In summary, the loose National Military Establishment became the more structured Department of Defense because of the new law. The coordination concept was discarded in favor of one of control. And ever since, when Congress has infrequently modified the military's basic command structure, its legislation has strengthened control at the top and more nearly conformed to the original organization concept advanced by Marshall.

At this point, the Navy cause was dead in the water. Then, with considerable boldness, two Navy partisans, Congressman Van Zandt and Captain John Crommelin, acted as catalysts to spark public interest again in unification and strategy. This time top admirals would make the most of it. Heretofore, those advancing Navy interests had for the most part come across as self-serving advocates, upset because the Air Force was getting more money. This time, though, their criticism would have a more noble tone. They would argue that Truman was moving toward having atomic retaliation as his only military option should war break out. They would still use the B-36 as a target to make their case, but during this go-around would use it to symbolize the dramatic step of using atomic weaponry.

Van Zandt introduced a resolution in the House that called for the appointment of a select committee to investigate the capabilities of the B-36 and the decision to purchase more of them. It was the same sort of thing Truman had done shortly before World War II to start the Truman Committee. This put the Democratic House leadership in a quandary. Given the climate, Speaker Sam Rayburn could not quash Van Zandt's resolution without signaling a cover-up. House members would have the same problem in voting against it. Since House rules specified that the author of a bill establishing a select committee would be its chairman, Rayburn and Vinson were faced with the real possibility of having a Republican congressman in only his second consecutive term leading an investigation of two of the highest-ranking appointees of a Democratic President and the keystone decision of his defense program. Acting to avert this, Vinson announced that beginning in mid-August his House Armed Services Committee would investigate.

Vinson opened the hearings with discussion of a document called "History of B-36 Procurement," which the Air Force had commissioned one of its Reserve officers, H. Barton Leach of Harvard, to write. The committee was acting as if its role were to confirm what it knew all along. Expeditiously, a majority of members exonerated Johnson and Symington and affirmed the decision to buy B-36s, given the funding limits the President had demanded be put upon the military. With this done, Vinson adjourned the hearings temporarily. To retain control should something else surface or Van Zandt make another move, he left open the possibility of reconvening on the subject. By doing so, he was also hoping to placate Symington, who was pressing him to pinpoint Van Zandt's sources of information. Symington had ambitions to run for elected office and wanted those undermining his reputation publicly discredited. This, Vinson was reluctant to do. His astute perception was that if he pressed the committee to do so, he might cause a blowup within the Navy, whose people, because of its decline, were getting desperate. He realized that regular officers such as Burke were involved and that ruining their careers would only make the needed reconciliation of the services much more difficult.

When it became obvious that Symington would not be placated until he had someone's head, Cedric Worth, a special assistant to new Navy under secretary Dan Kimball, stepped forward to accept blame. Worth was a civilian, so he was the perfect fall guy. Kimball, who under Sullivan had been the assistant secretary of the Navy for air, had stayed on to become under secretary when the latter resigned to protest the Supercarrier's cancellation; and his office became a secret center within the Navy for fighting administration policies that favored the Air Force. Navy Secretary Matthews had no inkling of this. Worth, a former newsman and former Naval Reserve captain, was hired to channel pro-Navy and anti–Air Force material to reporters. Much of it was coming from Burke's Op. 23. Worth contacted Vinson to claim that he was the one who wrote a paper listing fifty-five allegations against the Air Force that were then used by Van Zandt to force the hearings.

Wanting no part of this, Vinson got Matthews to have the Navy conduct its own investigation. The trail led to Burke's deputy, Commander Thomas Davis, who claimed he did not know to what use Worth was putting the information he gave him. Only Worth was fired; since Matthews was sensitive to causing a strong reaction within the ranks, he left Kimball and everyone in Op. 23 alone.

Vinson's and Matthews's careful minding of Navy sensitivities went for naught, though, for on September 8, 1949, Johnson's Defense Management Committee announced that the FY1951 budget for the Navy would be cut another $353 million. The recent amendment to the National Security Act had given him, as Secretary of Defense, the power to impose this readily, so the Navy was again apoplectic. Two days after this announcement, Crommelin, borrowing a page from Mitchell's old script, invited court-martial by calling a press conference at his home to attack unification and claim that the Joint Chiefs and the Secretary of Defense were trying to eliminate the Navy. The forty-six-year-old was on the support staff of the Joint Chiefs; however, the reason he could attract reporters to his home and prompt the *New York Times* to print an Associated Press account of his charges on page one had more to do with his being a member of a prominent Navy family. He was one of five brothers who were Naval Academy graduates. Two had been killed during the war. He had been air officer and executive officer of the carrier *Enterprise* for fifteen months. After the war he had been the first captain of the new carrier *Saipan*.

Overnight, Crommelin became the toast of the Navy. Admiral Halsey, who was in retirement, told reporters that Crommelin had demonstrated "wonderful courage" and "deserved the help . . . of all naval officers." Almost immediately some rear admirals provided precisely that, speaking out publicly in his support.

Matthews and Denfeld were not pleased. They had an incipient rebellion on their hands. To quell it, Matthews, in a carefully worded letter, warned all senior Navy officers not to criticize publicly the administration's defense plans; such criticism should be put in writing and sent up through the chain of command for possible use in the hearings Vinson had tentatively scheduled to reconvene in October. Trying to minimize the growing discontent, he rather disingenuously suggested in his letter that statements by Crommelin and the others who had followed his example were "inspired largely by apprehensions concerning the future of naval aviation."

Such a notion galled Vice Admiral Gerald Bogan, USNA class of 1916, an old battleship man and nonaviator who was assigned to the Pacific Fleet. He was one of the recipients of Matthews's letter. His reply, which began with the salutation "My Dear Secretary," read as if written by a proctor to a pupil. He wrote that the suggestion that parochial interests, such as Navy aviation's future, were

> the genesis of Crommelin's release is the most superficial gloss and does not remotely touch the heart of the question. The basic reason behind all of it is a genuine fear in the Navy for the security of our country if the policies followed in the Department of Defense since the National Security Act became law are not dramatically changed, and soon. . . .
>
> The morale of the Navy is lower today than at any time since I entered the commissioned ranks in 1916. . . .
>
> . . . the country is being . . . sold a false bill of goods. . . .
>
> . . . at a time as potentially critical as ever existed during our history, the public has been lured into complacency by irresponsible speeches by advocates of [the strategic bombing] theory. The result could be a great national and world-wide catastrophe.

Bogan believed that the administration had made the public believe that strategic bombers (B-36s currently) with atomic bombs were a panacea. He thought the whole unification and strategy debate should be reopened and said so in his final paragraph.

Radford, the newly appointed commander of the Pacific Fleet and Bogan's immediate superior, gave what the latter had to say a positive endorsement in a cover letter. Surprisingly, so did Denfeld, though he hedged his support by quoting his esteemed wartime predecessor, Admiral King, to buttress his doing so. Crommelin's last fateful act was to release to the press these endorsements and Bogan's letter, which made news across the country.

The resonance of Bogan's allegation that the administration's military policies were leaving the United States vulnerable was magnified many times by the concurrence of two stunning international developments — the Soviets' detonating an atomic bomb for the first time, about five years sooner than expected, and Mao's proclaiming the People's Republic of China after sweeping Chiang's Nationalist forces from the field. Word about the first was leaked to reporters shortly after Truman was notified, and was confirmed by him in a statement issued a few days later, on September 23, 1949. Mao issued his proclamation October 1, 1949. Communism was powerfully resurgent, and Americans were frightened. Senator Vandenberg expressed their feelings best, perhaps. "This is now a different world," he said, referring to the Soviets' now having the bomb, too.

This was the national mood when Vinson announced plans to resume hearings beginning October 6, 1949, this time to reexamine the subject of "Unification and Strategy." It was during these hearings that the long-building Navy blowup occurred. Nothing quite like the "revolt of the admirals," as it came to be called, had happened before; nor has it since. Military officers of the highest rank, in a congressional setting where strict decorum usually rules, attacked one another with raw honesty. When Matthews, the first witness, testified that "the general morale of the Navy is good," Navy officers in the audience booed him loudly. Radford, who followed him, sarcastically referred to "bomber generals" as he discredited their theories and referred to their B-36 as a "billion-dollar blunder." A string of witnesses, whose testimony was coordinated by Burke, continued this game of hardball to the end, by which time the administration began hitting back. Via reporters, Matthews issued Denfeld a not-so-subtle threat before the latter took the stand. "Denfeld hasn't been disloyal — yet," he said.

He would be shortly, though. The CNO's second line of testimony was: "As the senior military spokesman for the Navy, I want to state forthwith that I fully support the broad conclusions presented to this committee by the Naval and Marine officers who have preceded me." Denfeld, who risked getting fired for saying this and risked ostracism if he did not, had come down on the side of Radford and other Navy loyalists who had foisted on him a simple choice — are you with us or not? — as if he were a captain deciding whether to abandon his crew. Thereafter in his testimony Denfeld challenged the decision-making procedures that led to cancellation of the Super-carrier and approval of B-36 procurement. He insinuated that Omar Bradley, now Chairman of the Joint Chiefs of Staff, the position newly created by the amendment to the National Security Act, had reneged on promises to support the Supercarrier. Bradley, when his turn came to testify, fired back, denying this and calling the admirals "fancy Dans."

Aside from the degree of rancor exhibited, what was unique about the hearings was Radford's questioning whether the President could use the nation's atomic bombs. The admiral touched upon two aspects of this. One was that a President might only be able to use these weapons during the most acute crises. The second was that a President might be forced to limit use of them to battlefield targets and exempt cities.

A year before, during the early stages of the Berlin crisis, Forrestal had asked Truman whether he was prepared to use atomic bombs and was told to have no doubt. And the endorsement of this option by the publishers gathered at Phil Graham's home had been a good indication of widespread public support for it. But the Berlin crisis had involved a vital US interest — Western Europe. What if an enemy threatened to attack a not-so-vital American interest, something other than Western Europe, Japan, or the United States itself? Radford did not develop his logic to this point, but he was on this track. His point was that the threat of atomic retaliation was not a credible deterrent in such cases because it was too severe a response for a President to order. He was presenting these ideas to support his contention that the United States needed a balanced force structure with a strong Navy, too, and should not rely so much on strategic airpower. This touched upon the critical point as to whether the United States could use atomic weaponry against population centers, as planned. "In my opinion," said Radford, "the American people, if they were well-informed on all factors involved, would consider such a war morally reprehensible." He did approve of the tactical use of atomic bombs against combatants, delivered with a high degree of accuracy by fighters and small bombers, but not the indiscriminate use of them on cities. He did not discuss whether a President might be constrained from using atomic bombs, even tactically, should the enemy be able to respond in kind. That possibility had only developed during the last few weeks, and perhaps he, like everybody else in the country, including Truman, was having difficulty coming to grips with it.

Six days after Vinson adjourned the hearings, the President opened his next scheduled press conference with a prepared statement. "I have received a request from the Secretary of the Navy," he said, "to transfer Admiral Denfeld to another post, and I have given him permission to do it." This was three months after Truman had in August reappointed him to another two-year term. The President was, in effect, firing him for speaking out. The CNO would opt for early retirement rather than accept this humiliation. He would not be the only victim. Crommelin was forced to retire, and when the Navy Selection Board unanimously selected Burke for promotion to rear admiral, Matthews ordered its members to reconvene and remove his name.

Burke was both distraught and disgusted when informed of what had happened. He also believed he was finished, like Crommelin was. Not since he was a Colorado farm boy, when he set his sites on Annapolis, had his professional life and goals seemed so out of reach. And when this discombobulation engendered fear, he left town. He took thirty days leave effective immediately and, after he and wife, Bobbie, had loaded up the old Plymouth again, headed south, his only objective to put distance between themselves and Washington.

If you were a military man, Navy or not, you had by this time gotten the message, which was this: you risked your career if you spoke against Truman administration policies, and telling Congress the truth as you saw it was no excuse. Consequently, for the first time in a long time, all was quiet in the ranks. Even the admirals fell in line. Theirs was not to reason why. Admiral Sherman, who succeeded Denfeld on November 2, 1949, made liquidating Op. 23 one of his first orders of business. All the military began following Truman obsequiously; but, come what may, the blame as well as the responsibility was now all his. This is what Truman had done to himself during his final round with the Navy.

News of the Soviet atomic-bomb explosion had spread fear across the country. That event and the fall of China to the Communists had made a deep and permanent impression. Truman, for his part, had kept the confident look on his face and proceeded with his plans to ask Congress in January for another small military budget — only $13.5 billion, which was about another billion below the figure that had driven Forrestal mad.

There were, though, a couple of early indications that he was becoming less intransigent about all this than he appeared and that he might even be having second thoughts. His reaction to the Soviets' having developed the atomic bomb was to have more of the devices produced faster for the United States; he took this action about the time Vinson was wrapping up his unification-and-strategy hearings in October. And his reaction to receiving the Navy's promotion list with Arleigh Burke's name excised therefrom was to restore it. The latter move was of lesser moment than the first, but significant. He seems to have been motivated by more than just fair play and public pressure, although Burke's restoration to the promotion list followed within hours of the *New York Times*'s and the *Washington Post*'s publishing articles in their Sunday papers about Burke's war record and how he had been victimized by the infighting over a national military strategy. Truman was becoming more amenable to advice about military affairs, which was an abrupt change; the intensity of the recent controversy seems to have shocked him. Nonetheless, he was still preoccupied with defending the nation and its interests on the cheap, with big bombs carried by big planes.

One person who got the President's ear during this period was, of all people, a retired Navy man — Rear Admiral Lewis L. Strauss, a member of the Atomic Energy Commission. He and a handful of other people, mostly scientists, were aware of the theoretical possibility of a weapon called the hydrogen bomb that was hundreds or even thousands of times more powerful than the atom bomb; and he had concluded that the United States should commence a crash program to develop it. Truman had never heard about this hydrogen bomb, and Strauss decided the President never would if commission chairman Lilienthal and a majority of the members had their way. The loss of life at Hiroshima and Nagasaki had so profoundly affected many scientists who worked on the Manhattan Project that they made it a point of honor to see that their creation was never again used and that nothing worse was made. Dr. Oppenheimer was one such scientist. So Strauss decided that to get word about the hydrogen bomb to the President, he would have to circumvent the commission by using back channels. The route he chose was through another senior Navy officer, Rear Admiral Sidney Souers, who was a consultant to the President on national security affairs. Strauss and Souers had become friends during the war. Almost immediately the latter sent back word to Strauss that the President wanted him to force the issue with the commission as soon as possible by getting them to vote on it.

Predictably, the special committee of scientists that advised the commission had voted unanimously against a hydrogen bomb program on moral and technical grounds. Dr. James Conant, Harvard's president, had written their statement, which said that a hydrogen bomb would be "in a totally different category from an atomic bomb. . . . Its use would involve a decision to slaughter a vast number of civilians. . . . Therefore, a superbomb might become a weapon of genocide."

This appraisal was no doubt correct in all respects; the problem was that the Soviets would build it anyway. Regardless, after considering the scientists' report, commission members voted three to two against the hydrogen bomb development program. Lilienthal voted with the majority; however, because of the grave implications for the nation's security, he composed a memorandum for Truman — "to lay the problem before you," as he put it. This had been done rather quickly and quietly, until November 1, 1949, when, through Congress, news of a hydrogen bomb was leaked to the media.

By November 19, two months after the Soviet test explosion, the President had had time to set up an advisory committee composed of Secretary of State Acheson, Secretary of Defense Johnson, and Atomic Energy Commission Chairman Lilienthal to assist him; they essentially constituted a special committee of the National Security Council. Their charge was to analyze the technical, military, and political aspects of hydrogen bomb development, which, by the time they submitted their report on January 31, 1950, had been a matter of widespread public discussion for several months. They recommended to Truman that he proceed by ordering scientists to investigate further the feasibility of this thermonuclear weapon and that concurrently Acheson and Johnson "undertake a reexamination of our strategic plans, in light of the probable fission [atomic] bomb capability and possible thermonuclear bomb capability of the Soviet Union."

Truman adopted both of these recommendations. He revealed the state of mind that shaped his thinking to a State Department atomic-energy-policy expert named Gordon Arneson. The latter was in the Oval Office as Truman waited for Acheson, Johnson, and Lilienthal to walk over from the Old Executive Office Building with their recommendations following their last meeting on the subject. During the few idle minutes, an introspective Truman was prompted to start talking, probably as much to make Arneson feel comfortable as for any other reason. Truman glanced at the famous placard on his desk — "The Buck Stops Here" — and his comments were in that vein. Arneson later recorded what he had to say: "He mused about how many 'bucks' he had stopped: the abrupt termination of Lend-Lease after the war: bad advice, a blooper; the Truman Doctrine re Greece and Turkey: good; the Berlin airlift: right again; and the Marshall Plan: a 'ten strike.' Overall, the batting average was pretty good, he thought."

Then Truman paused; something else was on his mind. According to Arneson, "he wondered . . . whether the decision to reduce drastically the defense budget might have been unwise. True, it had been enthusiastically welcomed by the public and the Congress. But, considering the unsettled state of world affairs and especially the uncooperativeness of the Russians, was it prudent? He sighed."

Predictably, Republicans were assessing Truman's record, too. And as they saw it, his military and foreign policies were emerging as disasters. Ever since that day back in November 1945 when Patrick Hurley, the Republican oilman from Tulsa, abruptly resigned as Truman's special envoy to China and charged that Communist sympathizers in the State Department were making policy, Republicans had distanced themselves from virtually everything Truman did there. Now their discretion was about to pay them enormous, long-term political dividends at home. That the outcome in China would almost certainly have been the same had their own proposals been followed made no difference.

To make matters worse for Truman and the Democrats, other events had started breaking against them in a most unfortunate way. Two had occurred earlier in January 1950, and two others followed in February. The first was a speech that Acheson delivered, to a National Press Club luncheon audience, in which he described the American "defense perimeter" in Asia. He described it as a line that passed far enough west to include the Philippines, continued north to the Ryukyu Archipelago and included all of Japan, and then passed back through the Aleutian Islands to Alaska. This was really nothing new; MacArthur had described publicly the same defense line ten months earlier; consequently, reporters made nothing much of what Acheson said. However, MacArthur's comments had come before the fall of China to the Communists; Acheson's had come after. Furthermore, events later in the year would put Acheson's remarks in a different context, and Republicans would use Acheson's comments to substantiate charges that Democrats were appeasers, for Acheson seemed to have ruled out US intervention on the Asian mainland, no matter what happened there. John M. Chang, the Republic of Korea's ambassador to the United States, anxiously called the State Department to inquire whether his country had been inadvertently left outside the perimeter. He was assured by W. Walton Butterworth, the assistant secretary of state for Far Eastern affairs, that the United States, by its commitment to the UN Charter, was committed to defend South Korea in concert with many other nations, and that this actually transcended the nation's self-interest as demarcated by the line. In his speech, Acheson had made a vague reference to what the United Nations would do if problems developed on the Asian continent, and the foregoing was Butterworth's interpretation of it.

The second event had occurred on January 22, 1950. A jury that day rendered a verdict of guilty against Alger Hiss on charges of perjury. Hiss was a personal friend of Acheson and as his protégé had risen to the position of assistant secretary of state for Far Eastern affairs before resigning from government in 1946. His conviction was for lying to a grand jury about having passed classified documents to a Communist agent. The finding of guilty said, in effect, that Hiss had committed espionage, though he had not been charged with that crime because of the statute of limitations. Some months before, Truman had referred to a related investigation of Hiss by the House Un-American Activities Committee as a "red herring," so now the words were served up to him to eat. More significant, Hiss's conviction made credible such Republican charges as Congressman Richard Nixon's statement that it confirmed a "definite, determined and deliberate" effort by the administration to cover up the Hiss "conspiracy." Acheson unwittingly reinforced this contention when on the twenty-fifth Hiss was sentenced to five years in prison. Acheson was conducting a press conference when the news reached the room, and he reacted by saying that "whatever the outcome of any appeal Mr. Hiss or his lawyers may take in this case, I do not intend to turn my back on Alger Hiss." He said this out of loyalty to a friend, but he had much higher responsibilities and his remark opened the State Department to charges that it "coddled" Communists.

The third event was the February 2 arrest in London of Dr. Klaus Fuchs, chief of the theoretical physics division of the British Atomic Energy Research Establishment, on charges of espionage. Since Fuchs had worked on the Manhattan Project, he was now presumed to have passed atomic-bomb secrets to the Russians. This shocking news completely undercut those in the United States who were arguing that some sort of arms-control agreement was possible. No one could say the Russians could be trusted and not be called a fool. Or worse.

The fourth event was a speech delivered nine days later in Wheeling, West Virginia, by Senator Joseph McCarthy, in which he said that he had obtained a long list of Communists who worked in the State Department. The following day he cabled the President about allegations of there being fifty-seven. He demanded that Truman make public their files, as well as those of others whom the Loyalty Review Board deemed security risks "because of . . . communistic connections." His warning to Truman was this: "Failure on your part will label the Democratic party of being the bedfellow of inter-national communism."

Truman did not answer McCarthy's telegram, but he and his advisers could not ignore the pressure — the hysteria — that was developing. Very quickly, he began abandoning his deeply held liberal convictions against a large professional military. Under the circumstances, his idea that UMT was the answer seemed as quaint as his spiritual idol Andy Jackson's shoulder brushes, which, in the old, old Army, designated high rank. On March 10, 1950, Truman approved an emergency program to develop a hydrogen bomb. And on April 7, pursuant to the recommendation rendered as part of the H-bomb study, Acheson submitted for his evaluation the reappraisal of the administration's military and foreign policies. It was to have been a joint project of the Secretaries of State and Defense, but ended up having as its exclusive author Acheson. Johnson was so certain of his preeminence in Truman's administration, and so set on establishing this as a fact, that he was refusing to share any responsibility with Acheson, whom he perceived as his only possible rival. He erred grievously, for Acheson had the talent and confidence to steal the show. Furthermore, at the time, Acheson had more reason than any top official to demonstrate that he was a staunch, vigilant anti-Communist. It served Acheson's need that Paul Nitze, a conservative protégé of Forrestal's who saw things the late Defense Secretary's way, had by this time become the new director of the Policy Planning Staff, replacing Kennan who had resigned in the fall of 1949. Recognizing that he had lost influence, he left the State Department altogether the following summer, to pursue independent research at Princeton's Institute for Advanced Study. The staff had done the basic work for NSC-68, as the report came to be called, and Nitze, unlike Kennan, had always emphasized the military aspects of the cold war. Not surprisingly, NSC-68 emphasized a dramatic rearmament program to meet the Soviet threat in particular and the Communist threat generally.

Truman assigned the paper to the National Security Council staff to develop the cost implications of this recommendation, and what they came back with was this: the military's budget for fiscal year 1951 was going to cost about $40 billion. The news must have hit Truman like a slap. This was $10 billion more than the Chiefs of Staff had originally wanted for the current year and almost three times what he had ended up asking Congress to appropriate. After all he had said and done in recent years, it was going to be hard to explain the need for this drastic policy change; however, he would end up having all the help he needed and more.

CHAPTER 7

★ ★ ★ ★ ★ ★ ★ ★ ★ ★ ★ ★ ★ ★

DRAWING THE LINE

SATURDAY AFTERNOON, June 24, 1950, warm and beautiful in most of the United States, was conducive to rest and peaceful thoughts. Truman was flying home to Independence to begin a vacation. Acheson was tending the garden of his country residence, Harewood Farm, in Maryland. At another place in that state called Scientist's Cliff, located on Chesapeake Bay, Army Chief of Staff J. Lawton Collins, who had succeeded Bradley when the latter became chairman, was settling into the cozy cottage that he used as a weekend escape.

On the other side of the world, on the Korean Peninsula, where the hands of the clock had already swept past midnight into Sunday, darkness and pouring rain were conducive to making war on those with peaceful thoughts — as was the middle-of-the-weekend timing. There, at four o'clock in the morning, at a half-dozen points along the thirty-eighth parallel, a thousand 122-millimeter howitzers aimed south flashed as one, hurling tons of steel whistling through the rain, signaling the start of another major war and the possibility of another world war only five years after the last. This deadly shower continued for two hours. Then, at six, at the sound of bugle calls, vanguard soldiers of a 90,000-man invasion force began trotting down five unpaved roads leading south behind phalanxes of heavy, Russian-made T-34 tanks. At one other attack point on the east coast of the peninsula, some of them conducted a crude though successful amphibious operation using junks and sampans, coming ashore behind the defenders' forward position. The army of the Democratic People's Republic of Korea was invading the Republic of Korea. It was also challenging the Truman administration's tightfisted military-spending policy and overreliance on strategic bombers, though this notion would have been the last to have occurred to the soldiers.

* * *

Since that day back in September 1945 when colonels Rusk and Bonesteel proposed the thirty-eighth parallel as the line to separate the Soviet and American occupation zones in the Korean Peninsula, the temporary division had taken on all aspects of a permanent border between two independent nations. What finally set in motion the processes that eventually divided the peninsula officially was a Truman-administration decision to withdraw American troops because of priority commitments elsewhere. The United States and the Soviet Union had each refused to negotiate reunification of the two halves on any terms other than their own, so in September 1947 the State Department, out of frustration, referred the matter of Korean independence to the United Nations. Subsequently, the UN General Assembly endorsed an American-sponsored resolution calling for member nations to conduct elections throughout the peninsula in which voters would select delegates to what amounted to a constitutional convention. This convocation, after due deliberation, was to determine a form of government for the Korean people.

From the start, the Soviets signaled trouble. Their UN delegate warned of "grave consequences" should the General Assembly support this American plan. Then, when members did anyway, the Ukraine refused to assign a representative to the UN Temporary Commission, which was to supervise the elections. The rest of the commission decided to proceed with its work, but on January 23, 1948, the Russian commander in the Soviet occupation zone denied them entry into the north to supervise elections there.

Shortly thereafter, events in Europe began affecting Korea. During the next couple of months, the Communists in Czechoslovakia staged their coup, Stalin tried to intimidate Finland into forming a mutual-defense pact, Clay composed his cable that warned of war, Masaryk died under mysterious circumstances, Truman endorsed the Brussels Union, Norway sought American reassurances, and the Russians started stopping American troop trains bound for Berlin through the Soviet sector. These mounting pressures convinced the administration that Truman had to act quickly to shift the 30,000-man Army occupation force in Korea to Europe. To this end, Ambassador-at-Large Philip C. Jessup raised again before the UN General Assembly the subject of elections in Korea. This time he proposed that the commission proceed with elections in the south. This initiative was endorsed and elections were conducted on May 1, 1948. In these, the staunchly anti-Communist party of seventy-three-year-old Syngman Rhee won a majority of the delegate seats, and this led to his election as president of the provisional government of the Republic of Korea.

All his adult life, Rhee had worked for a Korea independent of Japan, which had colonized the peninsula for thirty-five years. Forced into exile, he had lived outside Korea for forty-three years, intermittently in the United

States, where he earned a bachelor's degree from George Washington University in 1907, a master's from Harvard in 1908, and a doctorate from Princeton in 1910. He was a wily operator, but as late as mid-1945, Chiang's experts on Korean affairs did not give him or any of the other exiled Korean leaders whom they and the Americans supported much chance of success. The assessment by Dr. Hein-ming, the chief of the Russian Department of the Nationalists' Foreign Affairs office, was that these men had "no roots and no following in Korea." At the time, Chiang controlled most of China in his fight against Mao, so he had reason to worry about who controlled Korea, which shared a border with the Chinese province of Manchuria. Should the Soviets or a Communist surrogate control Korea, Mao would be strengthened. About two years later, it was Mao who was worrying about who controlled Korea. After October 1, 1949, when he took control of China, he began viewing the American presence, which Rhee had come to represent, as a threat to his security.

The reaction in northern Korea to the elections in the south was immediate. The People's Committee, which the Soviets had set up, proclaimed the Democratic People's Republic of Korea and named as premier thirty-six-year-old Kim Il Sung.

The American plan as to what to do next had been set forth in a National Security Council paper dated April 2, 1948, that Truman had approved. NSC-8, as it was designated, set as a goal having all American occupation forces out of South Korea by December 31, 1948. On the other hand, the paper enunciated the view that the United States should try to keep the Soviets from taking control of Korea since that situation would "enhance the political and strategic position of the Soviet Union with respect to both China and Japan and adversely affect the position of the U.S. in those areas and throughout the Far East." However, the writers of NSC-8, which included the Joint Chiefs, qualified this concern; the document said that "the U.S. should not become so irrevocably involved in the Korean situation that any action taken by a faction in Korea or by any other power in Korea could be considered a *casus belli* for the U.S." On moral grounds, mostly, Bradley had some second thoughts about this, since South Korea was an American creation. As a consequence, the JCS support staff studied the matter again, but they reaffirmed NSC-8. They found that Korea was of "little strategic value to the United States" and said that an American military commitment there would be "ill advised." Their analysis noted one possible way to save South Korea should it be invaded. UN members might agree to a "police action" by an "international force" to which the United States might contribute "units."

The US troop withdrawal commenced in September 1948. Concurrently, the Soviets began withdrawing their occupation units. At Rhee's request, US authorities agreed to keep in Korea one regimental combat team — a self-contained fighting force of one regiment of infantry, one battalion of artillery, a company of tanks, and other specialized smaller elements.

Each of the two Korean leaders during his inaugural speech had vowed to unify Korea under his leadership, and, in that regard, the Truman administration was more worried about Rhee's invading the north than Kim's invading the south. Major General John Hodge, the commander of the American occupation force, deemed Rhee emotionally unstable and devious, and found working with him "the worst job I ever had." To curtail Rhee's ambition, the decision was made in Washington to support only the creation of a 50,000-man constabulary force in the south. This would not be an army and would be incapable of thwarting an invasion; it would be strictly for internal security, and Truman realized this. The United States rejected Rhee's requests for tanks, motorized artillery, and aircraft, because he might use them to invade the north.

The Soviets took an entirely different approach. They vigorously supported Kim in developing a full-fledged army of ten divisions composed of 135,000 soldiers. One of these units was an armored division equipped with 150 T-34 tanks. The Russians also provided a full complement of heavy artillery weapons, including motorized 122-millimeter howitzers. They also trained and equipped a North Korean air force.

By early 1949 the disparity between the indigenous Korean forces had become obvious and alarming. The Joint Chiefs reassessed the situation, and on March 23 Truman approved their recommendation to train and equip an eight-division ROK army of 100,000 men. This was five days before Forrestal relinquished his position to Johnson. However, the President once more denied Rhee's request for tanks, mobile artillery, and aircraft, for the same reason as before.

The US regimental combat team was withdrawn. The decision to train an ROK army had altered plans. The Joint Chiefs decided that assigning 500 military instructors to South Korea would be a more effective use of manpower. The basic authority for sending such advisers overseas had been established in 1947 when Congress authorized aid to Greece and Turkey; Congress reaffirmed it in this instance by appropriating funds to support their work. Installed as commander of this training unit, which was designated the Korean Military Advisory Group (KMAG), was Brigadier General W. Lynn Roberts, an Army officer.

When Hodge's occupation force was in South Korea, the US Army was the executive agent for American policy there. The chain of command went from Hodge to MacArthur to Bradley to Royall and then to Truman. After the withdrawal, the State Department became the executive agent. The person on the scene in charge was no longer a military commander but rather the American ambassador to the Republic of Korea, fifty-year-old John J. Muccio, a highly competent Korea expert. Roberts reported to him. The new line of authority passed from Muccio to Acheson and on to Truman. This new arrangement pleased MacArthur because Korea was no longer his responsibility. He had worried about not having enough US troops to defend it, though at Rhee's inaugural, which he attended, he, in the presence of reporters, told the South Korean leader, "If Korea should ever be attacked by the Communists, I will defend it as I would California." This pledge notwithstanding, he had, as noted, on March 1, 1949, during an interview with a *New York Times* reporter, placed the Republic of Korea outside the defense perimeter of the United States, just as Acheson had in January 1950 at the National Press Club.

As these inconsistencies suggest, American ambivalence toward South Korea was bipartisan. Republican leadership in the House and the Senate helped defeat a Truman request for $60 million in economic aid for Rhee's government, and on January 19, 1950, Republicans in the House voted almost as a block to defeat an administration proposal to send 500 more Army advisers to South Korea. The proposition failed by a vote of 192 to 193.

Even so, Roberts touted making substantial progress with the men he had. In March 1950 he reported that the North Korean army was definitely "inferior" to the ROK army. As events would demonstrate, his judgment was skewed because he perceived progress in military preparedness in South Korea as a reflection on himself and because he was determined to sell the Republic of Korea as a viable nation, a perception he thought would bolster Korea-related legislation in Congress. He worked tirelessly to show that South Korea could defend itself. VIPs and reporters were warmly welcomed to see for themselves. In increasing numbers they came, and he wined, dined, and entertained them with parades and choreographed shows of military prowess. Frank Gibney of *Time* was only one of many reporters who was favorably impressed. In June 1950, only days before the invasion by Communist forces from the north, he wrote: "Most observers now rate the 100,000-man South Korean Army as the best of its size in Asia . . . and no one now believes that the Russian-trained North Korean Army could pull off a quick, successful invasion of the South without heavy reinforcements." Collins intended to fly to South Korea for a firsthand look, but did not find the time during his first ten months as Army Chief of Staff. Roberts's status reports might have made him complacent. On the other hand, American activities in South Korea, including Roberts's, were the State Department's responsibility. More than likely, Collins's not personally judging the status of things in South Korea was most indicative of the low priority that the Truman administration had assigned that nation, compared with what was happening in Europe. As for Roberts, God spares some the wages of their sins, and so it was with him. Totally by coincidence, he retired one week before the North Korean invasion.

An hour after the North Korean soldiers commenced their advance, five of the American advisers radioed superiors in Seoul that the Seventeenth ROK Regiment, to which they were attached, was being overrun. This was in the Ongjin Peninsula, a northern region along South Korea's western coastline. The five then fled by air transport, their flight a harbinger that an ROK retreat would soon become a rout.

Though three hours had passed since the first salvo from the howitzers, what was happening had not yet emerged clearly. During the last couple of years, even when American occupation forces were present, small North Korean units had occasionally probed ROK defensive positions, conducting brief forays across the border. They had always retreated quickly when met by force. This time was different, but it was only obvious immediately to soldiers up front. Senior South Korean and American officials in Seoul needed more time to recognize that the frantic reports coming in were not isolated and in fact applied across a broad front. Truman, the only man in the world in a position to marshal the power to stop the invasion, did not get word of it for another five hours. Muccio and his staff were cautious in confirming so important an event. This offensive by a Soviet proxy state was the first attempt by the Communist bloc to force its will by a military invasion, instead of by subversion.

MacArthur was the first high-ranking US official outside Korea informed of what was happening. His intelligence officer, Major General Charles Willoughby, had posted a small detachment to South Korea to keep abreast of things, even though MacArthur's only responsibilities there after occupation forces were withdrawn were logistical support for the embassy and KMAG and, if ever necessary, emergency evacuation of Americans living in South Korea. This detachment operated outside official channels, reporting directly to MacArthur's staff at the Dai Ichi, his headquarters; in this instance, this was done at about the time the five advisers reported that their position was being overrun. A duty officer, in turn, called MacArthur. "General," he said, "we have just received a dispatch from Seoul, advising that the North Koreans have struck in great strength south across the Thirty-Eighth Parallel at four o'clock this morning."

MacArthur was shocked. "It couldn't be," he told himself. To him, it was like December 1941, when he was in the Philippines, all over again.

"Not again!" he thought. "I must still be asleep and dreaming. Not again!" This is how he remembered his reaction about fourteen years later.

Dressed in his nightclothes and the gray, wool bathrobe issued him when a plebe at West Point in 1899, he began pacing back and forth in his bedroom, his fists deep in the side pockets of the old robe. His staff and his wife, Jean, had left him alone. Intrusions from the outside were minimal for a time, because the phone system between Seoul and Tokyo was still closed for the weekend. Communications were rudimentary then; the region had still not recovered from the devastation of the world war and the conditions in Korea were rather primitive. In Tokyo, only a few military people were aware of what was happening.

Kaesong, the first major city to fall, was captured an hour later. An hour and a half after that, Muccio and the embassy's Army attaché each cabled Washington for the first time. The latter's message was logged in at the Pentagon at 2125 hours — 9:25 PM, Saturday. Muccio's was logged in at the State Department at 9:26. Johnson and Bradley were in an airplane flying back from Tokyo and did not learn of the invasion until about midnight. Collins was informed the following morning, his staff having decided he would need all the rest he could get for the coming days and that the situation had not come into focus. It was left to the State Department, as executive agent in South Korea, and Acheson, in particular, to get things moving.

Like MacArthur, Acheson was shocked. His immediate reaction was that the United States should call for an emergency meeting of the UN Security Council and ask members to declare that North Korea had committed an act of aggression against South Korea. After mulling matters over for a half-hour, he phoned Truman, who had just completed a late meal and retired to his library with Bess and their daughter, Margaret. The women had delayed dinner by attending a wedding. "Mr. President, I have very serious news," said Acheson. "The North Koreans have invaded South Korea."

Though calm and controlled, Truman's natural impulse was to return to Washington immediately. Acheson suggested that he remain in Missouri overnight, until Muccio provided more details. The ambassador's alerting cable had described only "Korean army reports which [are] partly confirmed by KMAG field advisor." The cable continued: "Am conferring with KMAG advisors and Korean officials this morning re situation. It would appear from nature of attack and manner in which it was launched that it constitutes all out offensive against ROK."

Truman agreed that he would remain in Independence for the time being, and told Acheson to proceed with his plan to ask the Security Council to convene in emergency session. Acheson's expressed intent was to have news of this initiative in the morning papers alongside the first press accounts of the invasion. At the outset, he wanted to convey the impression that the administration was not going to sit by passively. Pressure from domestic politics was already impinging on the decision-making process. The two men were trying to stay ahead of news commentators and Republican critics. Rusk, the assistant secretary for Far Eastern affairs then, later recalled that the State Department accorded "utmost importance" to meeting press deadlines with this information.

Overnight, message centers at the State Department and the Pentagon started coming alive. At 2:05 AM, Sunday, Washington time, the State Department processed another cable from Muccio. He stated that KMAG had asked MacArthur to ship forthwith a ten-day supply of ammunition to the ROK army. This required Washington approval, and by midmorning MacArthur was asking for it, incorporating the request in his first Korean War status report. At this point, though, his only responsibility remained getting the Americans in South Korea out safely.

The news was bad. Willoughby's Korean detachment had determined that the enemy had captured all South Korean territory west of the Imjin River. This region in the far northwestern part of the country included the Ongjin Peninsula, Kaesong, and the village of Panmunjom.

At 6:46 AM, Sunday, Washington time, Muccio cabled with additional disturbing news. Four North Korean fighter planes had strafed Kimpo Airfield near Seoul, he said. During recent months, this able activist had without success been lobbying for US combat aircraft for South Korea. In this message, he tried again, saying that he hoped "some positive and speedy action can be taken at this late date to remedy this deficiency which is [an] exceedingly serious threat and handicap." Within hours Truman approved this request and ROK pilots were flown to Japan to fly the aircraft back. Sensing that planes alone would not be enough, Muccio warned that American pilots would also be needed. "Rhee and other Korean officials will look to US for air assistance above all else," he stated. "Future course of hostilities may depend largely on whether US will or will not give adequate air assistance."

By this time, Collins had been awakened. At about nine, from the Pentagon, he began his first teletype conference with Tokyo, communicating with Willoughby, who reported that North Korean tanks were so near the US embassy in Seoul that Muccio and MacArthur had agreed to evacuate all Americans except essential personnel. The operation was to begin at first light in Seoul, Tuesday morning, only about eight hours away. Their evacuation plan required Truman's approval because it called for US naval and air protection.

At 9:59 AM, Sunday, the State Department received a pertinent message from its embassy in Moscow. Walworth Barbour, the chargé d'affaires there, warned of the larger implications of the North Korean invasion. It represented, he said, a "clear-cut Soviet challenge which in our considered opinion US should answer firmly and swiftly as it constitutes direct threat [to] our leadership of free world against Soviet Communist imperialism. ROK is creation of US policy and [there could be] repercussions for US in Japan, SEA [Southeast Asia] and in other areas as well." He stated emphatically that the United States must immediately declare its readiness "to assist ROK maintain its independence by all means at our disposal, including military help."

By remarkable coincidence, given that he would become America's quintessential cold-warrior, John Foster Dulles was in Tokyo on official US business. Acheson had appointed him his special representative to negotiate the peace treaty with Japan. Dulles himself would have been Secretary of State had Dewey defeated Truman. His appointment as negotiator was part of the administration's continuing effort to broaden support for its foreign policy. Dulles's prestige was such that when he took a side trip to Seoul and the thirty-eighth parallel on June 17, seven days before the invasion, he was invited to speak before the South Korean National Assembly. The American people will be "faithful to the cause of human freedom and loyal to those everywhere who honorably support it," he told them. With the Communist invasion now under way, Dulles expressed these sentiments more specifically in a cable to Acheson. Composed jointly with John Allison, a State Department Far East expert, it said: "It is possible that South Koreans may themselves contain and repulse attack and, if so, this is best way. If, however, it appears they cannot do so then we believe that US force should be used even though this risks Russian counter moves. To sit by while Korea is overrun by unprovoked armed attack would start disastrous chain of events leading more probably to world war."

When Acheson called Truman back after initially notifying him, the time was about 11:30 AM in Independence. Truman had spent the morning inspecting conditions at the farm in Grandview, Missouri, whose ownership he shared with his brother and sister. The Secretary of State informed him that Muccio, with much more information at hand, had confirmed a full-scale invasion and that the Security Council would meet at 2:00 PM, New York time. Acheson said he thought members would approve a resolution that US Ambassador to the United Nations Warren Austin would propose condemning the aggression and endorsing a cease-fire. But judging from recent dealings with the North Koreans and their Communist allies, both Acheson and Truman surmised that Kim's government would ignore the international body and that Truman would be forced into making some important decisions immediately. To that end, the President told Acheson to meet with the service secretaries and the Chiefs of Staff to prepare collectively a list of recommendations that would be ready for him when he arrived back in Washington that evening. Truman apparently assumed that Johnson and Bradley would not be returning from Tokyo in time. In fact, they did, but made the dubious decision to keep a long-standing commitment to attend a military conference in Norfolk; this possibly was a convenient excuse for Johnson to avoid a meeting presided over by Acheson.

Before calling Truman this second time, Acheson no doubt reviewed all the relevant cables that had come into his department and Johnson's since the invasion, and he probably (judging by his memoirs) passed the information along to Truman, generally, at least. The two department heads' differences complicated working relationships, but so many military officers by this time despised Johnson for his autocratic and penurious ways that they would have ignored his wishes had he wanted to be uncooperative. In March, Symington — of all people — had resigned to protest insufficient funding for the Air Force; Thomas Finletter had succeeded him. Furthermore, some of Acheson's chief assistants had established close working relationships with counterparts in the Defense Department. Rusk and Army Secretary Frank Pace, Jr., a thirty-eight-year-old attorney from Little Rock, Arkansas, who was beginning only his third month on the job, were together socially when informed Saturday evening of the North Korean attack.

Truman, if confidants who were near him are to be believed, decided before departing Independence to go to war. Daughter Margaret, whom he put to work helping make preparations to leave, wrote in her diary for that day: "Northern or Communist Korea is marching in on Southern Korea and we are going to fight." While trotting across the tarmac to the plane, Brigadier General Wallace Graham, Truman's personal physician, told Anthony Leviero of the *New York Times* and Edwin Darby of *Time*, "The boss is going to hit those fellows hard." With the information Acheson had relayed to him, which he had pondered virtually alone out in Missouri, away from the Washington apparat that was beginning to hum, Truman evidently had established what he was willing to do, though he was still making guarded statements in public.

With the threat he faced now clearly in focus, Truman was eager to get things moving. This was typical of him. His departure from Kansas City Municipal Airport was so hasty he left two aides behind. He almost left without an aircraft navigator: Truman ordered the pilot to take off without Air Force Captain E. P. Christensen, who arrived as the plane was taxiing toward the runway. Commandeering a car and driver, Christensen raced up alongside. A hatch in the nose was opened and he climbed aboard using a rope ladder.

Immediately after his conversation with the President, Acheson called the interdepartmental meeting of State and Defense Department officials that Truman had ordered and within minutes convened it. The exchanges were brisk; the tension compressed thought processes, and each man in attendance had much to do. Acheson first reviewed the diplomatic plan of action to be set in motion at the United Nations within a couple of hours. The recommendations for Truman that the group developed were mostly reactions to requests that had come in overnight from Seoul and Tokyo. The consensus was that MacArthur should be allowed to ship military equipment to the ROK army, even if earmarked for other missions; that control of US military personnel and activities in South Korea should be shifted from Muccio to MacArthur; that MacArthur should be given authority to use air and naval forces to protect Kimpo Airfield; that if the UN Security Council asked members to intervene militarily, MacArthur should be put in charge of the forces available, including elements of the Seventh Fleet; and that he be ordered to stabilize the front and then restore the original boundary, if possible. The group's prevailing mood matched Truman's.

That afternoon, Collins cabled news of these tentative plans to Willoughby and Major General Edward Almond, MacArthur's chief of staff. They were elated, maybe even surprised. "Come over and join the fight," they answered. "We are delighted with your lines of action and this should turn the trick. Thank you." This flippancy was misplaced élan not justified by the facts, and was the last such display for some time (though it would later come to be typical of Almond). During this exchange, those in Tokyo also told Collins that MacArthur had decided to ship mortars and artillery to South Korea, along with the requested ammunition.

This done, Collins set about reviewing all the instructions and documents pertaining to South Korea that he had ordered his assistant chief of staff for operations, Major General Charles Bolte, to gather. Armies need more than ammunition to go to war; the paperwork has to be in order, too. Collins gave special attention to the existing mission statements and orders that governed MacArthur and KMAG. All these were going to have to be rewritten. At three, Sunday afternoon, he briefed the Secretaries of the Army, the Navy, and the Air Force on these matters.

En route to Washington, Truman radioed Acheson to tell him to arrange a second meeting that evening at Blair House, the President's residence at 1651 Pennsylvania Avenue while the White House was being renovated. He wanted to confer with some of his top State and Defense Department officials. In his memoirs, Truman referred to this group, with whom he continued to meet throughout the crisis, as the National Security Council; this was technically incorrect, since some attendees were not NSC members.

The gathering was not so institutionally directed, the NSC machinery being so new. At the time, Truman informally referred to those invited that evening as his War Cabinet. They tended to refer to themselves as the Blair House Group. Both casual descriptions indicate that those invited were tabbed by Acheson principally for their special expertise. All held high positions of responsibility, but the small distinction of why they were invited seems to have had the salutary effect of causing them to give more forth-rightly their individual counsel rather than a department's official viewpoint. As a result, the decisions over the coming days were remarkably crisp and controlled, as if the product of clearheaded individuals determined to meet the challenge, not tentative bureaucrats worried about exposing themselves and their departments.

Speeches at the United Nations preceding the crucial vote on the US-sponsored resolution lasted almost four hours. Shortly before six on Sunday evening, a few minutes before Truman arrived in Washington, the Security Council by a vote of nine to zero condemned the North Korean invasion as a "breach of the peace," called for a cease-fire, and asked members "to render every assistance to the United Nations in the execution of this resolution and to refrain from giving assistance to the North Korean authorities." The Yugoslav delegate who was present abstained. Jacob Malik, the Soviet delegate, did not attend, continuing a Soviet boycott that had begun about six months earlier. His country was protesting the Security Council's refusal to unseat the Nationalist Chinese delegate and accept the credentials of the one from the Communist-controlled mainland. The Soviet boycott this day was a crucial strategic mistake, because a no-vote by Malik would have vetoed the resolution, which legitimatized direct American involvement and encouraged worldwide sympathy for the South Koreans and condemnation of the North Koreans. Apparently, Truman and Acheson, in having the matter brought before the Security Council so quickly, surprised the Soviets. The bureaucracy at the Kremlin did not have time to consider the implications of having Malik boycott this meeting. Thus, the attack's coming on a weekend had worked against the Soviets, too, though they should have been prepared; it was inconceivable that Kim had not involved them in his planning. They had installed him and had equipped his military forces.

Waiting for Truman at the bottom of a ramp at National Airport were Acheson, Johnson, Bradley, and Webb, who in April 1949 had moved over from his budget-director post to become under secretary of state when Lovett resigned. For the fifteen-minute ride into Washington, the three civilians joined Truman in a limousine — Acheson next to him in the backseat, Johnson and Webb in front of them in jump seats. Acheson had in hand the proposals that, on Truman's order, the State-Defense working group had formulated that afternoon. "By God, I am going to let them have it," Truman asserted, prompting Johnson to reach back and shake his hand.

The meeting at Blair House was set for 7:30 PM, with dinner served beforehand. Present were Truman, Acheson, Johnson, Webb, and Bradley; Secretaries Pace, Matthews, and Finletter; Chiefs Collins, Sherman, and Vandenberg; Assistant Secretary of State for UN Affairs John Hickerson; and Ambassador-at-Large Jessup. Commandant Cates was not invited. While awaiting the arrival of one of the group, they sipped drinks and listened to Acheson recount his department's activities that day and what had happened at the United Nations. At one point, Johnson interrupted him, saying he would like to have Bradley read a memorandum about Formosa that MacArthur had prepared for them during their inspection trip to the Far East. Truman assented and Bradley read the whole thing aloud. In it, MacArthur asserted that the strategic interests of the United States would be "in serious jeopardy" if a hostile power took control of the island. He was referring to Communist China. "Unless the United States's political-military strategic position in the Far East is to be abandoned," MacArthur wrote, "it is obvious that the time must come in the foreseeable future when a line must be drawn beyond which Communist expansion will be stopped." MacArthur asked that he be permitted to conduct a survey of Taiwan to determine what was needed to defend it. When Bradley finished, Truman said that there would be no more discussion of Formosa until after dinner. Collins sensed that the President deemed the Formosa topic a diversion from the business at hand.

In any case, Truman had heard all he wanted to hear about the China issue, because for months now, Republican conservatives in Congress had been accusing his administration of losing China to the Communists. Now they would charge that its loss had led to the crisis in Korea. MacArthur's being a hero to these conservatives and his tendency to play up to them had to make the President uncomfortable. The United States had never really had China to lose, but the charge that he and the Democrats had lost it had a deep and enduring appeal. This was because Americans, on the basis of their country's World War II experience, still had an exaggerated sense of the possibilities of American military power.

After the servants cleared the dinner table, Acheson reopened the discussion by summarizing the cables Muccio had sent. Once again Johnson interrupted him, insisting that the group address the possibility of a Communist attack on Formosa before talking about the crisis in Korea. The two briefly but vigorously argued the point until Truman again vetoed the suggestion. Acheson then presented the working group's recommendations.

That done, Truman invited general discussion before asking each person to comment in turn. The Chiefs' view reflected their branch's respective biases. Vandenberg and Sherman thought that only US air and naval support might be necessary to stop the North Koreans. Collins said that would not be enough if the ROK army were badly hurt; American soldiers might be needed, he thought. To evaluate this possibility, he asked that MacArthur be allowed to send a survey team to South Korea. Each of the three Chiefs described the disposition of American forces in the Far East. Most of the Seventh Fleet was on a course for the Philippines. When Truman asked, Sherman said it would take about a day and a half for the warships to reverse course to reach the Korean Peninsula. The President also wanted to know if US forces could destroy Soviet air bases in the region. Vandenberg said yes, but that atomic bombs might be needed. Johnson warned against delegating too much responsibility to MacArthur. The Secretary of Defense was not much of a military man but was a keen politician and, in that regard, sensed potential trouble. He was also wary of committing American troops on the Asian continent. The worry, widely held within the American military, was that a Western power could not match the vast manpower resources of China, should it get involved. Pace and Bradley voiced the same reservation. On the other hand, Bradley, echoing MacArthur's view, said that the United States had to draw the line somewhere against Communist aggression and Korea had become the place.

It was amazing how the Communists' physical act of invading South Korea had cleared up everyone's head like a slap in the face. In theoretical discussion about what to do in such an event, Bradley and MacArthur both had said that South Korea was outside the nation's strategic interest and thus not worthy of intervention to save. But this had been a sterile military judgment, not touched by politics. In retrospect, at least, these officers' sudden change of heart is a reminder that going to war is a political act brought on by political considerations. These considerations were now over-whelming established military plans that were sterile of them.

Surprisingly, this conference was the first conducted by Truman that Collins attended. The Army Chief was impressed. He thought the President had a "rare talent for listening to his advisers in this field" and surmised that his special attention was motivated by his lack of foreign-affairs experience. According to Collins, Truman "was ever ready to hear both sides of a proposition and would balance them objectively and finally come up with a clear-cut, fearless decision. Once a decision was taken, he rarely deviated from it and always accepted full responsibility for the outcome, good or bad."

Forrestal would have been stunned by such behavior on Truman's part — particularly his listening to both sides of an argument. Unless Forrestal had seen him do so with his own eyes, he would have discounted Collins's assessment, it having come from an Army man. What had happened was this: Heretofore Truman had frequently allowed domestic political considerations to control his policy-making in foreign and military affairs. Domestic politics was where his chief interest lay; he also had a confident grasp of it. He was not so confident about foreign and military affairs, and this was why, with war pressing on him, he was giving advisers such as Collins the full focus of his attention.

At this point, Truman was not ready to commit himself, though. He seems to have backed off his earlier bold assertions made in the limousine and while back in Independence. Perhaps he saw the wisdom of bringing the American public along with him step by step. His advisers' thinking was tempering his opening moves, which were cautious and preliminary. He did agree with Bradley that the time had come to draw the line. This had been done in Europe. Now it had to be done in Asia. But during this evening, the only operational objective he set for MacArthur was the evacuation of noncombatant US citizens. The amount of military supplies and equipment MacArthur was authorized to ship the ROK army was limited to that the general deemed necessary to keep the Seoul-Kimpo-Inchon area secure while these Americans were evacuated.

The same thinking was to govern use of American air and naval units. Those that could reach the scene in time were to support the evacuation. MacArthur was not to allow bombing runs or support fire north of the thirty-eighth parallel. Rather, he was to send to South Korea immediately a survey team of US military officers and have them make a battlefront estimate of what was needed to stop the North Koreans. Meanwhile, Sherman was to have those US warships headed for the Philippines reverse course.

Truman also issued a couple of planning directives. The Air Force was to develop a plan to knock out the Soviet air bases in the region, and the State and Defense departments were to determine "the next probable place in which Soviet action might take place." To a man, those at Blair House that night were certain that the Russians were orchestrating the whole thing. The North Korean attack might be a diversion from some action in a more strategically important region, it was thought. Given his reaction to Johnson's entreaties, Truman was obviously not too worried about an attack on Formosa, probably because the Seventh Fleet could quickly interpose and block an amphibious invasion. There was also a sense that a recent lesson of history was that World War II might have been prevented if the Germans had been challenged earlier, and that therefore, for similar preventive reasons, the United States had to force the Soviets' proxy back across the border.

Truman's most telling move that evening was a decision he did not make. He kept Muccio and the State Department in charge in South Korea; he decided not to replace them with MacArthur and the Defense Department. No wartime chain of command was established. Other than evacuation, the military's mission, still subject to Muccio's direction, was not enlarged beyond KMAG's advisory work. Truman did ask the Chiefs to prepare the necessary orders for use in case combat units were needed. Holding out hope for some miracle, Truman was biding his time, though time was running out and everyone knew it.

Upon instruction, MacArthur set in motion evacuation plans and appointed Army Brigadier General John Church to head the on-scene survey group. Church would require about twenty-four hours to get his team together and organized.

Concurrently, President Rhee was composing a desperate plea for help. It was sent to Washington by telegraphic cable and delivered to Truman personally that day by the ROK ambassador, who was almost in tears. Rhee then boarded a train with his cabinet and fled the capital of Seoul for Taegu, 150 miles south. North Korean forces had captured Uijongbu, a city so situated that they could mount an attack on Seoul from it; both are north of the Han River. The only positive development was that two American Air Force fighter pilots covering the evacuation from Kimpo Airfield scored the first US air-to-air combat victory. They shot down a Soviet-made, propeller-driven, YAK fighter plane.

By the time daylight Monday broke in Washington, a batch of cables bearing this and other, overwhelmingly bad news had come into the State Department building and the Pentagon. One from Muccio reported "rapid deterioration and disintegration." MacArthur, still relying on Willoughby's intelligence detachment in South Korea for most of his information, cabled that "South Korean casualties as an index to fighting have not shown adequate resistance capabilities or the will to fight and our estimate is that a complete collapse is imminent." The detachment was relying on a network of agents that the Japanese had in Korea.

That morning Truman issued his first statement on the crisis to the media. "Those responsible for this act of aggression must realize how seriously the government of the United States views such threats to the peace of the world," he said. "Willful disregard of the obligation to keep the peace cannot be tolerated by nations that support the United Nations Charter." Referring to the UN resolution passed the evening before, he asserted that the United States "will vigorously support the effort of the Council to terminate this serious breach of the peace." In the worldwide scheme of things, Truman was beginning to see Korea as the "Greece of the Far East."

This was the phrase he used in describing the situation to George Elsey, who had become his administrative assistant. The similarity Truman saw was that Greece, in early 1947, had been the first major test in Europe of American will to stop communism; his thinking was that Korea would be the first test in Asia. (He had not seen China in these terms.) But he was presently in much more serious trouble in Korea than he had been in Greece, and the degree of US commitment about to ensue would reflect that.

At 7:29 PM, Monday, June 26, 1950, Acheson telephoned Truman to recommend that he immediately convene another meeting of the Blair House Group. The list of attendees was about the same each time; someone occasionally had to substitute. The meeting began at nine. Bradley first briefed them on the military situation. The Joint Chiefs followed. With his word of the YAK's having been shot down, Vandenberg had the only good news. Truman said he hoped more would meet that fate. Then Acheson took the floor. Like a military staff officer, he began making recommendations about tactics to the Commander in Chief. He proposed that the area of operation of American air and naval units be expanded. He thought Truman ought to authorize air strikes and support fire anywhere south of the thirty-eighth parallel. To confine them to the area around Seoul was to wait until it was too late to keep the evacuation points there open. This was in line with his wanting to save the whole country, not just protect the evacuation points. Acheson also recommended strengthening the Philippines and increasing aid to French Indochina; this indicated his worry that, through proxies, the Soviets would step up pressure elsewhere.

Bradley commented that airpower had not been very effective thus far, to which Acheson responded that it at least allowed the United States to do something. The Air Force's problems of practical application were legion at this point. There was no ground-to-air coordination for hitting targets. There was no air plan; it was a matter of hitting targets of opportunity. And because planes were operating from bases outside Korea, they were using up almost half their fuel before they reached target areas. Consequently, pilots were expending munitions quickly and rather carelessly so as to save fuel for the return trip.

At this point, no one had proposed ground forces, but Bradley reminded the President that if they were sent in, not enough troops would be left over to meet obligations elsewhere, unless the nation mobilized for war. Collins agreed that such a mobilization would be imperative. Reflexively, perhaps, Truman said, "I don't want to go to war." Everyone there knew that that was where he was headed, though. Abandoning Korea without a fight was not seriously considered, despite all that had been suggested to the contrary. Acheson explained later that doing so would have been "highly destructive of the power and prestige of the United States." By "prestige" he said he meant "the shadow cast by power, which is of great deterrent importance. Therefore," he concluded, "we could not accept the conquest of this important area by a Soviet puppet under the very guns of our defensive perimeter with no more resistance than words and gestures in the Security Council." Significant concentrations of US forces were only seven hundred miles away in Japan, so not fighting would make the United States seem cowardly.

Truman still had not consulted members of Congress. Some conservative Republicans were already denouncing Democrats in general and Acheson in particular, accusing them of being at fault for what was happening and, predictably, associating the situation with the collapse of China the previous year. On the floor of the Senate, George Malone of Nevada charged that "it is fairly clear what happened in China and what is now happening in Korea were brought about deliberately by the advisers of the President [Roosevelt] at Yalta and by the advisers of the State Department since then."

Acutely sensitive to such accusations, Acheson especially did not want to risk a Communist Chinese invasion of Formosa. On the other hand, Truman and his Blair House advisers did not want Chiang to start something. To handle both possibilities, Truman ordered elements of the Seventh Fleet into the Formosa Strait. During the planning discussions, these ships' dual mission was openly acknowledged. Finally, the President told Johnson to convey to MacArthur via scramble phone a new set of instructions. Truman was now going to expand the zone of operations for the air war to include all of South Korea.

About the time Truman adjourned this second Blair House meeting, Church and his survey team were landing at Suwon Airfield, about twenty miles south of Seoul. He had never seen the country before. He told Harold Noble, the Seoul embassy's First Secretary, who was traveling with him, that he would rather have "a hundred New York City policemen than the whole Korean army." Noble took umbrage at the remark; however, given the South Koreans' past training as a constabulary force, the remark was not entirely inappropriate. Furthermore, no sooner had Church set up a make-shift headquarters than he and his thirteen officers and two enlisted men were engulfed by tens of thousands of these ROK soldiers and their citizenry, a tide moving south. Some of the roads became almost impassable as a result, but he managed to get a team member to each ROK division.

Truman's most important business on Tuesday morning, June 27, was conducting his first meeting about the crisis with senior congressional leaders of both parties. Acheson and Johnson were with him. So were the Joint Chiefs and the service secretaries. The Secretary of State presented an overview and advocated bold American leadership in the crisis to bolster the will and confidence of South Korean leaders and of allied nations in Europe. As might be expected, the latter were in a state of near panic, fearful about how the US reaction to events in Asia might affect Stalin's attitude about what the Soviet Union could get away with in Europe. On the other hand, Acheson, in response to a question, observed that the European allies of the United States could offer little tangible help in South Korea.

Truman told the congressmen that there was no doubt that the Soviets were behind the North Korean aggression and that the United States had to react so as to keep the Communists from gobbling up Asia one piece at a time. He then read a planned statement that he said had been formulated pursuant to the UN Security Council's resolution passed on Sunday. "The attack upon Korea makes it plain beyond all doubt," he said, "that Communism has passed beyond the use of subversion to conquer independent nations and will now use armed invasion and war. It has defied the orders of the Security Council. . . . In these circumstances the occupation of Formosa by Communist forces would be a direct threat to the security of the Pacific area and to United States forces performing their lawful and necessary functions in that area." Truman was establishing justification for going in. Some of the congressmen suggested wording changes and asked questions. House majority leader John McCormack of Massachusetts asked whether the Navy would have to be enlarged. Before anyone could answer, Johnson interrupted to say that a study was already under way to determine the force composition needed if the United States went to war in South Korea and that a balanced program would be maintained. Senator Millard Tydings reported that the Senate Armed Services Committee, which he chaired, had already voted to extend the draft and give the President authority to call out the National Guard.

The lawmakers were thus supportive during the meeting, and that afternoon, when McCormack interrupted House proceedings to read Truman's statement as it was released, members stood and applauded. The scene was repeated moments later in the Senate, when Scott W. Lucas, an Illinois Democrat who happened to be presiding, read it. The applause was bipartisan, coming even from such Republican conservatives as California's William Knowland, a senator harshly critical of the administration because of what had happened in China; he had decided that Truman was firming his resolve against the Communists in Asia.

That afternoon, international support for Truman's position began building. Executing a plan developed by Acheson and his staff, approved by Truman, and informally reviewed by the congressional leaders, UN delegate Austin introduced his second resolution in three days. This one declared that "urgent military measures are required" in South Korea and proposed that member nations "furnish such assistance to the Republic of Korea as may be necessary to repel the armed attack" and restore "international peace and security in the area." It passed by a vote of seven to one, thus becoming the first such sanction in UN history. The Yugoslav delegate cast the negative vote and those from India and Egypt abstained. Malik of the Soviet Union was absent again. A legal basis for Truman's ordering US troops into South Korea and for the use of air and naval power on an ongoing basis had been established. With this done, Truman made the Defense Department the executive agent for US interests in South Korea and extended MacArthur's region of responsibility to that country.

The threat posed by UN sanction was of insufficient weight to save the day, however. Or the next, for that matter. On June 28, Wednesday, at about sunrise, the North Koreans broke through the last organized resistance around Seoul and began moving into its suburbs. Later in the day they captured the city. MacArthur, following Truman's orders limiting attacks to south of the thirty-eighth parallel, had ordered every available US plane within range to help in the attempt to stop them. They came out of bases in Japan and Guam — B-26s, B-29s, and F-80s — but this hastily thrown-together air campaign was ineffective in stopping the drive or slowing it much.

The ugly truth was now perfectly clear to those in the combat area. Extreme action by Truman was going to be necessary. Conventional air-power could not even engage the enemy's troops, much less stop them. The Air Force did not have enough planes to rain down a curtain of bombs, in effect, to block movement. And so, when an enemy tank was destroyed it was pushed off the road and others proceeded apace. There were so few aircraft as compared to the number of vehicles and troops relentlessly moving south that a North Korean soldier faced only minimal risk of being killed by bombs or bullets from a plane. To him, US airpower in Korean skies was not an intimidating presence. Therefore, in only several days of combat, the army of a backward country had made a mockery of the preceding years' heralded hearings and lengthy strategizing about airpower, sessions dominated by experts who had seemed so wise and prescient. Men such as Thomas Finletter, who had chaired the administration's airpower study group, had parlayed the prestige accorded him into positions of greater influence. Finletter's ultimate reward had been Truman's making him Symington's successor as Secretary of the Air Force two months before the North Koreans invaded the south. Anyone who had followed the reorganization travail of the services had to wonder now why there had been so much anguish about which of the services would control airpower.

As it happened, the administration had prepared for the wrong war; in particular, the administration had prepared for the wrong air war. Tactical fighters and bombers in great numbers were what was needed in Korea — smaller planes that could support troops in battle. (Also needed in great numbers were air transports to get troops into position, but that was not obvious yet. It would be soon.) The administration, buttressed by bomber generals, as Radford had called them, had spent available funds on long-range strategic bombers that could drop atomic bombs; the whole fleet of them was of little use in the current conflict unless Truman was prepared to escalate the war dramatically, into a completely different realm. Ironically, the Navy itself, by fighting so hard to get a share of the strategic bombing mission, had affirmed as correct the administration's decision to focus on it. Only during the admirals' revolt the previous fall had Navy officers such as Radford begun questioning this course effectively.

Truman was going to have to order American infantry units to South Korea if the Communists were to be stopped and then driven back across the border. This is precisely what Church radioed MacArthur this Wednesday as night descended on South Korea and all grew black.

The ominous news about the fall of Seoul was the foreboding start to Wednesday in the United States. Truman first got the news from aides bearing a fresh stack of cables. Millions of other Americans got it from the morning papers and radio announcers. The public was getting basic information just a few hours behind the President. The effect was electric. At midmorning, pedestrians applauded Truman as he strode from his limousine to a convention of the Reserve Officers Association. In spite of early Republican sniping, an overwhelming majority of Americans believed he had done everything right thus far. Acheson's idea to take the matter immediately before the United Nations was key. Furthermore, the invasion was such blatant aggression that even Truman's old adversary Henry Wallace, the Interior Secretary he had had to fire, was supporting him publicly.

Wednesday afternoon Truman held another meeting of the Blair House Group. Finletter proposed that General Vandenberg be sent to Tokyo to confer with MacArthur so that there would be a "mutual understanding between Washington and Tokyo." The suggestion was premature, though, because Truman was not yet set on his ultimate course of action. He told Finletter that for the time being all the Chiefs were needed in Washington. Bradley interrupted the proceedings, arriving late with news that the Senate had acted favorably on the recommendations of Tydings's committee. Members had voted to extend the draft and to authorize the President to call to active duty the National Guard and the Reserves. Finletter then wanted to talk about bombing Communist air bases north of the thirty-eighth parallel.

He and Vandenberg — the whole Air Force — were already frustrated by the ineffectiveness of the air campaign. The secretary pointed out the bases on a map. The North Koreans were hitting targets in the south and then racing back across the border that American pilots could not cross. Finletter wanted to bomb their bases so as to give the ROK army "the full value of our air support." Acheson was against it and so was Truman, for the time being. The President said he "didn't want to decide that now." The clear implication was that he might change his mind. In front of everyone, Johnson, talking to his Air Force Chief of Staff as if he were a cadet, assertively asked him whether he understood his orders. Vandenberg said yes, that his pilots could not bomb north of the thirty-eighth parallel.

Events were narrowing Truman's options by the hour. Acheson suggested that the military determine what forces were available if the President decided to order them in. Truman accepted the idea and that afternoon the Joint Chiefs of Staff ordered their Joint Strategic Survey Committee to see what Truman could do militarily if Air Force and Navy bombing and support fire failed to make a difference. Committee members were given a forty-eight-hour deadline to come up with something. The Chiefs also told them to determine whether air operations north of the thirty-eighth parallel might preclude Truman's having to order in US ground troops. Given the administration's investment in airpower, virtually everyone was having trouble believing that the Air Force effort was so ineffectual. The Chiefs' instructions also reflected how far decision-makers in Washington were from the scene, both literally and figuratively. Muccio would have told them that more than aerial bombardment was needed. During recent hours he had been driving around in a jeep looking for the South Korean government.

At about the same time that Wednesday evening in Korea, Church, who was still in Suwong, received a strange message from Tokyo. "A high-ranking officer" would be arriving the next morning for an inspection tour. Was Suwon Airfield still operational? Could the visitor's plane land there? Church replied that it could.

MacArthur had decided to investigate the situation personally now that he was in charge. He wanted to research the same basic question that the Joint Strategic Survey Committee was working on. Could the Air Force and the Navy and the nation's logistical apparatus sustain the Republic of Korea? Or were large infantry units needed? "In past wars there has been only one way for me to learn such things," MacArthur told four reporters he handpicked to accompany him. "There is only one way now. I have decided to go to Korea and see for myself."

Thursday morning in Tokyo, wind, rain, and fog made flying dangerous. The ceiling was zero, but MacArthur's pilot, Lieutenant Colonel Anthony Story, was ready to go. The left engine of MacArthur's plane, the *Bataan*, was revved up, the propeller wash whipping a fine mist down the ramp, when Air Force Lieutenant General George Stratemeyer, Far East Air Force commander and, as such, MacArthur's air chief, told Story the plane was grounded. A few minutes later MacArthur arrived, dressed in khakis that had been washed, starched, and pressed so many times they had faded to off-white. He had topped off his dress ensemble with a leather windbreaker and his trademark floppy campaign hat adorned with thick swirls of gold braid. A pair of binoculars hung from his neck and, in spite of the weather, he wore sunglasses. He carried himself with his usual jaunty, confident gait, as if no more preoccupied than an officer on his way to a parade. Informed of Stratemeyer's decision, he promptly reversed it. The latter protested vigorously, but MacArthur quickly silenced him with a question that hit the heart of the man's ego: "But you'd go yourself, wouldn't you? We go."

During the flight, he resumed the pacing he had started four days earlier, walking up and down the aisles of his forward compartment, this time with his hands, palms inward, stuffed into his back trouser pockets. As MacArthur walked his way across the Sea of Japan, enemy pilots were strafing Suwon Airfield, his destination. En route, Stratemeyer began pressuring him to authorize air strikes on the bases North Korean pilots were using to hit targets in the south. He was unaware that only a few hours earlier Truman had considered exactly the same request from Finletter and rejected it, for the time being.

"How can I bomb north of the Thirty-Eighth Parallel without Washington hanging me?" he asked Willoughby. His intelligence office did not know, so MacArthur began pondering his own question aloud. The JCS directive had not authorized bombing strikes north, he noted, but it had not specifically forbidden them either. Therefore, one might construe the directive as permissive rather than restrictive. This was the dubious line of reasoning he expressed, like a clever attorney trying to get his client out of a contract. The audacity of this sort of reasoning partially explains why Johnson was so direct and denigrating with Vandenberg. MacArthur decided that his discretionary powers as a field commander gave him the authority. He told Stratemeyer to go ahead. Forthwith the Air Force general ordered a message be sent his deputy, Major General Earle Partridge. "Take out North Korean airfields immediately. No publicity. MacArthur approves."

Four enemy fighter planes were still strafing Suwon Airfield when Story banked the *Bataan* for final approach. The pilot of one spotted the slow-moving passenger plane and headed for it. Stratemeyer had ordered a fighter escort of four P-51 Mustangs, and the pilot of one snapped his plane out of the tight formation, ready to hunt the hunter. MacArthur was the only passenger watching the drama. The others had hit the aisle floor when an aide screamed, "Mayday!" MacArthur went to the window instead.

"We've got him cold," he said firmly, pleased by what he saw. Story suddenly ended the general's viewing by taking evasive action. The attacking pilot escaped without firing a shot and his compatriots did not extend the brief encounter. Story brought the *Bataan* in sure-handedly on the pock-marked runway and taxied fast toward the operations tower, passing within twenty feet of a C-54 transport afire and billowing smoke. Church was waiting and, soon after MacArthur's arrival, Muccio and Noble appeared on the scene. Having succeeded in his search, Muccio had with him President Rhee, ROK chief of staff Chae Byong Duk, and other, lower-ranking US and South Korean officials. Church had not invited the Koreans, but Noble fortunately had gotten Muccio to intervene and avert the snub. MacArthur greeted Rhee warmly, putting both hands gently on the old man's shoulders as he looked him in the eyes. "We're in a hell of a fix," said Rhee, sounding as if he had spent some time in west Texas when living in the United States.

Within minutes, the entire group retired to an old schoolhouse, where Church commenced a briefing, using a large map. When he finished, MacArthur turned to the unfortunate Chae, an overweight general with the soft look of a couturier, and asked him what he proposed to do. Three-quarters of his army having already been either destroyed or dispersed, he replied that he planned to round up two million South Korean youths and lead them in sweeping the Communists and their tanks from the countryside. An uncomfortable silence followed as MacArthur took several long draws from his corncob pipe, puffing each one separately into the air while staring at the man. Before returning to Tokyo that evening, MacArthur told Rhee he needed to appoint a new chief of staff and within forty-eight hours he did.

MacArthur quickly tired of such discussion and the briefing. Slapping his hands on his knees as he rose to his feet, he said, "Let's go to the front for a look." Church tried to talk him out of it, the area being so insecure, but his mind was set. An old black Dodge was found for him and off he went in the company of his senior staff, a few guards, and a group of reporters — more of them now; a few based in South Korea had joined the four who flew in with MacArthur. They had been getting copy out since Sunday, not long after Truman got word of the invasion. Wire service reporters had produced the first bulletins. The entourage followed the Dodge in jeeps. There was not a single paved road in all rural South Korea, so in many places the route was a slurry of mud and the going was difficult. During the twenty-mile drive, they passed thousands of people trudging toward them.

In the Seoul area, the Han River was the battlefront. Communist forces had not crossed the river since capturing the city. Upon reaching the Han, the drivers pulled off the road and up to the edge of a palisade that afforded a good vantage to the northeast of the capital afire and its huge, slow-twisting tornado of smoke. Sounds of North Korean mortar rounds exploding and distant machine-gun and rifle fire punctuated the silence. After studying the scene a short time, MacArthur spotted what he thought was a better survey point on a hill closer to the river. "What do you say we push over there, Ned?" he asked rhetorically, almost, of Almond. Everyone reboarded his vehicle. The Dodge was quite conspicuous among the jeeps as they trundled closer. The vehicles could not travel the entire distance, so the party walked partway. For an hour, MacArthur stood on this perch, most of the time using his binoculars and not talking much while deep in thought. It was an impressive performance on his part, a display of the confidence and the purpose all great captains have.

He flew back to Tokyo that same Thursday evening and arrived just after eight. An added passenger for the return trip was Marguerite Higgins of the *New York Herald Tribune*. During an on-board interview, he told her: "The moment I reach Tokyo, I shall send President Truman my recommendation for the immediate dispatch of American divisions to Korea. But I have no idea whether he will accept my recommendations." He had written them longhand on a yellow legal pad, his reading glasses perched on his nose. He actually waited about eighteen hours before submitting them to Washington.

The first order of business on Thursday for Johnson, Collins, and the other Chiefs was the recommendations of the Joint Strategic Survey Committee. Members had completed their work. Typical of committee efforts, it was a compromise, a sort of averaging of the range of ideas between aggressively responding and doing nothing. Members hung US hopes for saving South Korea on air and naval power. They decided that MacArthur should be allowed to order strikes against enemy bases north of the border if he felt "serious risk of loss of Southern Korea might be obviated thereby." No one in Washington was aware that MacArthur had already ordered them.

Top Defense Department officials met during morning hours to weigh the recommendations. Most thought they did not go far enough. Collins thought the time had come for US ground troops. To the surprise of some, Johnson was the most hawkish. He was still nursing ambitions of becoming President and sensed that the public's mood was changing, so his was changing with it. He seemed intent on going to war with the entire Communist world, though the United States was woefully unprepared for even this limited one — a condition for which most of the officials in the room blamed him personally, along with Truman's austere military budgeting policies. After long discussion, it became obvious to everyone in attendance that they were not going to resolve anything and should move the meeting to the White House. Johnson contacted Truman, who agreed to let them.

Early afternoon, the Blair House Group was together again. Johnson took the lead; this was logical, since the Defense Department was now responsible. He read a directive that he proposed be sent MacArthur. It was rather open-ended and Truman rejected it outright, saying he did not want "the implication that we were planning to go to war against the Soviet Union." Recalling his reaction in his memoirs, Truman wrote, "I stated categorically that I did not wish to see even the slightest implication of such a plan." Kennan's eighteenth-century limited-warfare concepts were becoming Truman's mind-set. Though general warfare was the kind for which he had best prepared the military, he was determined to avoid it. He would keep his strategic bombers loaded with nuclear weapons out of Korea.

The President had decided to stick with air and naval power until he heard from MacArthur. It was a holding action and, as Acheson had pointed out during the first crisis meeting, it demonstrated that the United States was trying to do something. As for the employment of airpower, Acheson said he did not see why the Air Force should be "restricted in its task by a rigid application of the Thirty-Eighth Parallel as a restraining line," as long as US pilots did not fly across the Yalu River into Manchuria. According to Collins, who later summarized the directive that Truman approved for MacArthur, the general was authorized

> to (1) employ U.S. Army service troops to maintain communications and other essential services in South Korea, (2) employ U.S. Army combat troops to secure a port and air base in the Pusan-Chinhae area at the southern tip of Korea, (3) employ naval and air forces in North Korea well clear of the frontiers of Manchuria and the Soviet Union, (4) by naval and air action secure Formosa from invasion by Chinese Communists and likewise prevent any invasion of mainland China from Formosa, and (5) continue to send supplies and ammunition from Japan to the ROK Army and furnish an estimate of additional requirements.

With this directive, MacArthur would soon have authority to do what he had already done — that is, order air and naval strikes in the north. This was one of two threshold decisions by the President entailed in the directive. The other, and more significant, was the decision to send in US combat troops, even though only to rear areas.

At the meeting, Acheson introduced one other important consideration: the possibility of direct involvement by the Soviet Union and the People's Republic of China. The Soviets had just answered a State Department note that asked them to stop the North Koreans. In their letter they blamed South Korea and said they planned to adhere to the "principle of impermissibility of interference by foreign powers in the internal affairs of Korea." Acheson said his people interpreted this to mean that the Russians would not get directly involved in the fighting. "This means," Truman observed, "that the Soviets are going to let the Chinese and the North Koreans do the fighting for them." Acheson concurred that the Chinese "might" enter the war, but said that neither his department nor the CIA had intelligence information to suggest that. Truman decided to include a proviso to MacArthur's instructions explicitly stating that they did "not constitute a decision to engage in war with the Soviet Union if Soviet forces intervene in Korea," where proximity favored them tremendously. The President wanted to control decision-making at that next possible step of escalation, not delegate such authority to MacArthur. In that regard, he told Johnson to tell MacArthur he wanted a "full and complete report on the Far East each day," remarking that during World War II he almost had to place personal phone calls to him to get information.

Truman adjourned the meeting in the late afternoon, and not long thereafter Acheson returned with an important message from the nationalist Chinese ambassador. Chiang was offering to send 33,000 troops to South Korea if the United States would transport them. Truman, in line with his political objective of getting as many nations as possible involved under UN auspices, was inclined to accept the offer. Acheson was not, suggesting that it made little sense to move an army from a country that was a potential invasion target itself. He also sensed that putting Chiang's soldiers back on the Asian mainland would greatly expand the war and that this is what the Nationalist Chinese leader wanted, his thinking being that the American military would win the war and restore him to power on the mainland.

Truman's new orders for MacArthur were transmitted from the Pentagon on Thursday evening, Washington time. In Tokyo, it was already Friday morning. By early afternoon there, MacArthur's staff began transmitting his trip report, which included his recommendations for action. It took a while because it ran to some two thousand words.

Length may have been the primary reason MacArthur took so long after his return from South Korea to prepare the report, though he had told Higgins he would send it immediately. Or perhaps MacArthur, wise about the dynamics of decision-making in Washington, wanted to see what daylight Thursday there would produce. He knew that important meetings would be held, and might have wanted to learn in which direction sentiment was moving and what Truman's thinking was.

MacArthur had become very cautious at this point in dealings with Truman and the Joint Chiefs. During the next six hours, he continued to conduct himself more as a lawyer than a warrior. For example, MacArthur did not request that American combat units be sent to Korea until after Truman had already ordered them there. The President having been the first to have crossed this threshold, MacArthur was then much more at ease recommending that US combat units not only be ordered to the Pusan rear area but also to the battlefront. The final paragraphs of MacArthur's trip report said:

> The only assurance for the holding of the present line, and the ability to regain later the lost ground, is through the introduction of U.S. ground combat forces into the Korea battle area. . . .
>
> If authorized, it is my intention immediately to move a U.S. regimental combat team to the reinforcement of the vital area discussed and to provide for a possible build-up to a two division strength from the troops in Japan for an early counter-offense. . . .
>
> Unless provision is made for the full utilization of the Army-Navy-Air team in this shattered area, our mission will be needlessly costly to life, money and prestige. At worst it might even be doomed to failure.

By the time these words were received at the Pentagon, Friday was a few minutes old. Collins, who was upstairs sleeping on a cot in an anteroom to the Joint Chiefs' offices, was awakened by a duty officer. The general was not surprised that the moment of decision regarding the ultimate act of escalation — the ordering of US troops to the battlefront — had come. But he wanted to communicate directly with MacArthur before pressing the matter on up to Truman, who, as Commander in Chief, was the only person with authority to order such action. Collins directed that his staff, and MacArthur and his staff, be ready for a teleconference in several hours — at 3:00 AM in Washington and 4:00 PM in Tokyo, on Friday, June 30, in both cities.

The Washington group gathered in the Army's teleconference room several floors below ground level. With Collins were Arthur Gruenther, now a lieutenant general and the deputy chief of staff for plans; Matthew Ridgway, also a lieutenant general and the deputy chief of staff for operations and administration; a few other high-ranking Army staff officers; and two State Department representatives — Rusk and Neil Bond, the Korean Desk officer. With MacArthur were Almond and five of his principal staff officers. Gathering these people and getting the session under way took forty minutes longer than Collins had hoped.

Having initiated this memorable event, Collins had developed with his staff a series of questions for MacArthur. At 3:40 AM an enlisted man began typing the first of them into an electronic keyboard. All talking stopped. The only sound was a clicking noise as the man's fingers danced atop the keys. Room light was low so that the group could more clearly see a large viewing screen on which words appeared as the first message was typed. The darkness inside the room and outside the building, having a somewhat dramatic effect, contributed to the sense of uncertainty. The word characters crawled right to left, forming sentences much like a horizontal electronic stock-ticker does, except that when a line was filled with words, it froze on the screen and another began forming under it. Letters being transmitted appeared almost simultaneously on a duplicate screen at the Dai Ichi in Tokyo, where in a smaller communications center a stolid MacArthur and his senior staff also sat in rapt attention. Collins personally had designed this communications system. The first message this early morning was from him and was designated "DA-1," for Department of the Army No. 1.

> Authorization proposed in your C56942 will require Presidential decision which will take several hours for consideration. Meanwhile, you are authorized in accordance with Para. 2B, JCS 84631, to move one RCT [regimental combat team] immediately to Pusan base area. This will be amplified [later].

Seconds after the last letter of this message appeared on the screen, soldiers in both communications centers moved about quickly, distributing teletyped copies of it to each of the participants. "The air was fraught with tension," recalled Collins. This was serious business, nothing less than talk of war. Recollecting the memory years later, he said: "All the men present, though outwardly calm, realized the critical importance of the impending discussions between conferees on opposite sides of the world. We instinctively spoke with hushed voices as the questions, numbered serially, were flashed on the screen, and we pictured in our minds the gathering in Tokyo where answers were being framed that would vitally affect our participation in this strange new war."

Within several minutes, MacArthur's words began edging across the screen. Both groups focused forward again. One never quite grew accustomed to this communications system, with its characters that popped up out of nowhere. There was something mysterious about it, like sounds coming from a hulk at the bottom of the sea.

MacArthur's first message was designated FECOM-1, using the acronym for Far East command.

Your authorization, while establishing basic principle that U.S. ground combat troops may be used in Korea, does not give sufficient latitude for efficient operation in present situation. It does not satisfy the basic requirement contained in my message C56942. Time is of essence and a clear-cut decision without delay is imperative.

After another interval, Collins responded with DA-2.

I was present at White House conference late afternoon June 29 when decision was made to authorize action covered in JCS 84631. Tenor of decision clearly indicated to me that the President would wish carefully to consider with his top advisers authorizing introduction of American combat forces into battle area. Will not authorization given you in DA-1 permit initiation of movement? Prior to completion of this movement we should be able to obtain definite decision on your proposal. Does this meet your requirement for the present?

MacArthur did not respond. He was being extremely careful about not saying too much for the record. "We took this to mean that General MacArthur stood by his emphatic plea for a decision 'without delay,' " recalled Collins. MacArthur was putting pressure on the Army Chief.

The communications back and forth resumed, with the Collins group shifting the focus of discussion. But the Army Chief was really only creating time for himself to ponder his course of action regarding MacArthur's first message. By the time the Pentagon group had transmitted another six messages to Tokyo, he had decided what he was going to do.

DA-9 Ref FEC-1
I will proceed immediately through Secretary of the Army to request Presidential approval your proposal to move one RCT into forward combat area. Will advise you soon as possible, perhaps within half hour.

MacArthur did not respond to that message either.

Collins stepped from the room and called Pace, who was at home. Collins had alerted him beforehand about this early-morning telecon scheduled with MacArthur, but the Secretary of the Army chose to have the generals conduct it without him. Pace agreed to take the matter to the President immediately. Without first contacting Johnson, he called Truman. He previously had been his budget director, after Webb — at thirty-five, the youngest in history up to that point — so the two had a comfortable working relationship. The President himself picked up the receiver. He was in his bedroom on the second floor that looked down on Pennsylvania Avenue. Bess was still asleep in her room down the hall. Truman was alert and had already shaved. Getting up at about this time was a farm-boy habit.

Pace read to him part of MacArthur's trip report that had come in at midnight and FECOM-1; as he did so, the President responded at intervals with uh-huhs and hmmms. That done, Truman asked what the JCS thought. Pace told him that Collins had not had time to confer with them, but that he and his senior staff recommended approval.

Truman did not hesitate. Immediately, he delegated MacArthur authority to order the combat team to the front line of fighting in South Korea. He reserved judgment about ordering in the two divisions MacArthur wanted. He planned to confer with his top advisers first. The conversation ended and Pace called Collins, informing him that the President had approved sending in the combat team.

During the interim, Collins's staff had dealt with matters of less importance. These diversions stopped immediately when he returned with the news. Quickly, he composed word of it for transmittal to MacArthur. The keys started clicking again and the characters crawled across the screens.

DA-10
Your recommendation to move one Regimental Combat Team to combat area is approved. You will be advised later as to further build-up.

MacArthur seemed to jump. His response was immediate.

FEC Item 8 Reur DA-10
Acknowledge. Is there anything further now?

DA-11 ended the transmissions. Referring to MacArthur's battlefront inspection, Collins responded:

Everyone here delighted your prompt action in personally securing first-hand view of situation. Congratulations and best wishes. We have full confidence in you and your command.
Nothing further here. End DA-11.

The news then began rippling through the government.

By seven, Truman was in the Oval Office. A staff officer from the Pentagon was there to brief him on developments overnight in Korea. A few minutes after the hour, he placed separate phone calls to Johnson and Pace. He wanted them to consider MacArthur's request for the two divisions and Chiang's offer of what amounted to two more. They were to give him their judgments at an 8:30 meeting of the Blair House Group. Truman then began thinking aloud, letting off steam, fussing and fuming before he put on his official face. Elsey was there and tried to take note of all his comments. Truman rambled on about how the Russians were going to attack in the Black Sea or the Persian Gulf next. He said that they had coveted these prizes since Ivan the Terrible, who was a hero in Russia now like Stalin and Lenin.

At virtually the same time that Truman called Johnson and Pace, the phone rang in the quarters of Lieutenant Colonel Charles ("Brad") Smith, a US Army battalion commander posted in Japan on the island of Kyushu, where it was about nine o'clock on Saturday evening. His wife picked up the receiver. On the line was Colonel Richard Stephens, Smith's superior and his regimental commander. About two hours had passed since MacArthur and Collins's teleconference ended, and orders were now being passed down the chain of command. Smith had been up all the previous night because his battalion at Camp Wood had been put on alert, so he was in a deep sleep when his wife jostled him awake. He leapt for the phone. Stephens's message was short. "The lid has blown off," he said. "Get on your clothes and report to the CP [command post]." Within minutes, Smith had kissed his family goodbye. He would lead into combat the first US unit to fight the North Koreans.

Though only thirty-four, the 1939 West Point graduate already had a history of being where US wars began. On December 7, 1941, he was a lieutenant in charge of a company assigned to Schofield Barracks on the Hawaiian island of Oahu when the Japanese conducted their surprise attack. Schofield Barracks was one of their principal targets. Not long thereafter, Smith fought in the first major US Army battle of World War II, serving at Guadalcanal under Collins, who remembered him well. The Regular Army was like that — small, in a sense. Within minutes, Smith was contacting his officers, who began alerting the sergeants, who roused the men from slumber and into a night of darkness and driving rain.

In Washington, at 8:30 AM, Truman convened his meeting. It lasted only thirty minutes. He received the advice presented and saw no need for elaboration. He told the group he was inclined to accept Chiang's offer. Acheson remained adamantly against it. He thought it would prompt the Chinese Communists to enter the war. The Joint Chiefs wanted to reject it, too. Chiang's troops were no better trained than the South Koreans and would have to be completely reequipped. Reports were that even MacArthur was now against using the Nationalist Chinese, so Truman accepted the advice. Then, getting ahead of pressure of counsel, he announced his decision to authorize MacArthur to deploy to Korea all ground forces under his command. These totaled four divisions, two more than MacArthur requested. No objections or reservations were voiced. At this point, Sherman proposed that the Navy blockade North Korean ports. No one protested, Truman approved, and the meeting was adjourned. Before noon, the President was in another meeting, this one with congressmen.

At Camp Wood, Smith's men were packing and loading equipment. Most of them would carry an M-1 rifle, 120 rounds of .30-caliber ammunition, and two days' worth of C rations. Others would crew one of eight mortar units and ten recoilless rifles or bazookas, instead of carrying a rifle. Preparations took six hours. At three o'clock in the morning on Saturday, July 1, 1950, an Army truck convoy loaded with the soldiers and equipment of Task Force Smith, as this unit came to be called, pulled out of Camp Wood and began the seventy-five-mile drive to Itazuke Air Base. Rain was still pouring down. War was like that, Collins later observed; it was always raining at the start, or so it seemed. The task force numbered 540 officers and men — Smith's battalion, less two infantry companies, plus a detachment from the Fifty-second Field Artillery. Some of the infantry platoons were short, so cooks and clerks from headquarters company filled in. Smith would have liked to have had his whole battalion with him, but there was not room. The two companies were left behind because in all of MacArthur's Far East command, the Air Force could only come up with six C-54 transports to take Task Force Smith to Korea.

Smith and his men were part of the Twenty-fourth Infantry Division and their commander, Major General William Dean, was waiting for them on the tarmac at Itazuke. As they climbed out of the trucks, every man wet to the skin, and formed up before reloading onto the aircraft, Dean gave Smith his orders. They were vague, but as precise as Dean could make them.

"When you get to Pusan," he told Smith, "head for Taejon. We want to stop the North Koreans as far north as possible. Contact General Church. If you can't locate him, go to Taejon and beyond if you can. Sorry I can't give you more information. That's all I've got. Good luck to you, and God bless you and your men."

Three and a half more days of exhausting travel were in store, complicated by the problems that beset people in a hurry. The first two aircraft to arrive over the Pusan airstrip could not land because of fog. It lifted, but not before these planes returned to Japan, the men and equipment aboard lost to Smith. Once on the ground, the task force was delayed by exuberant crowds of cheering South Koreans waving American flags. It was difficult for the men not to smile even though they were going into battle.

The Americans boarded a train that took them partway to Taejon, a town south of the Kum River, some 139 miles from Seoul. ROK trucks, which they drove themselves, carried them the final leg of their journey. South Korean soldiers assigned as drivers fled upon learning the direction of travel was north. "You are stupid," one of them told Smith. "The war is that way."

Smith decided that the place to make a stand was an area several miles north of Osan, a village north of Taejon. There the road the North Koreans would follow passed through an irregular line of hills. The low ground was to the north, so he could easily observe the approaches. At his front, Smith deployed his men over a mile stretch of land along the forward slopes of the hills — too thinly, but the best he could do with the small number of soldiers he had. The far more numerous North Koreans were going to outflank him, no matter what. Smith had no reserves and faced the main invasion force, the same one MacArthur had seen in Seoul and that now was following a western route down the length of South Korea at about walking speed. The North Koreans were meeting no resistance now, but were being very deliberate about not getting too far ahead of their supply lines. Most of Smith's infantrymen were on high ground, partway up the forward slopes. Some bazooka teams were at road level, as were the howitzer crews, one of which had concealed its 105-millimeter howitzer roadside, close to the forward positions, where it could enfilade the passage. Four others were positioned back about two thousand yards. In front of everyone, including the infantrymen, were some artillery spotters. At three in the morning, July 5, Smith's small force was finally in place. Ten days had passed since Truman was first told about the North Korean invasion.

Not long after sunrise, at about seven, Smith spotted through his binoculars vanguard T-34 tanks in trail. They were followed by long columns of soldiers, and many more tanks, that stretched to the horizon. For an hour, Smith's men held their fire. Finally, at 8:16, as forward tanks were passing over a point in the road the artillery crews had already registered, Smith ordered in the first howitzer rounds. There were no direct hits, but the shells slammed in squarely among the tanks. Nonetheless, they caused no damage. The tanks continued to advance without any perceptible adverse effect. It was later determined that because of heavy armor, they were impervious to standard US artillery shells. The GIs were stunned. If they had not known it before, they did now: some of them were going to die this day, though most were not even twenty.

The only effective rounds against the T-34s proved to be high-explosive antitank ammunition known by the acronym HEAT. The Army had developed HEAT ammo after World War II, but only a limited inventory had been produced because of the austere postwar budgets. Most HEAT rounds were stored in Western Europe, positioned for use against a possible Soviet invasion there. MacArthur's Far East command had been allotted only a spare number of them. Smith's artillerymen had just eighteen HEAT rounds. The bazooka teams did not have any, so Second Lieutenant Ollie Conner and his men hid in a silt trench alongside the road until the first two tanks passed, thinking that they might destroy them from the rear, where they were more vulnerable. From as close as fifteen yards, he fired twenty-two bazooka rounds. He and his assistant loaded and fired at a ferocious pace. The noise was deafening, but the effect was nil. Each projectile was deflected or exploded harmlessly.

As the same two tanks crested a hill, a forward howitzer crew blasted them with HEAT rounds. Immediately they were stopped, one afire, but more tanks kept coming. Loading and firing to save their lives, the crew quickly expended its four remaining HEAT rounds and began firing standard howitzer rounds, riflelike. There was no arching trajectory; the shooting was point-blank.

The hits jolted the tanks, but did no harm; maybe crewmen inside were rattled around. Within a few minutes, one of them spotted the heroic little band and their smoking howitzer. A turret was turned, a cannon aimed and fired, and the Americans were left dead or dying.

Task Force Smith had fought valiantly. But by 10:15 AM about forty tanks had passed through. Flanked by North Korean infantry and almost surrounded, Smith ordered an immediate withdrawal. He could not wait for the cover of darkness. Worse, some of the wounded were going to have to be left behind. "Lieutenant, what is going to happen to us?" one of them asked an officer, himself wounded, dragging himself past. The man handed him a grenade. "This is the best I can do for you," he said. Abandoning the wounded is against US Army doctrine, but Smith's was a Hobson's choice. He decided to save those who could fight their way out rather than risk losing his entire unit. One hundred and fifty were killed.

For some time, matters did not improve for US forces. During the next week, the North Koreans swept through one newly deployed Twenty-fourth Division battalion after another. Some of the units fought well; some did not. Dean fired one of his regimental commanders, Colonel Jay Loveless, for ordering a premature withdrawal.

For the United States, these contests availed only a little more time. By the middle of July, Dean's Twenty-fourth had suffered so many casualties it was a division in name only. Each of his regiments had been reduced to battalion size. The North Koreans were advancing so inexorably against his men that on July 19 Dean himself was cut off. Before being betrayed by a couple of South Korean peasants, he evaded capture for thirty-six days, breaking his shoulder and losing sixty pounds in the process. Before the shooting war started, Truman's penurious military-spending policy had had a compelling appeal to most Americans, as if evidence of prudent management; however, the North Koreans had abruptly blown away the logic behind it by crossing the thirty-eighth parallel. Strategic bombers had not deterred these Communists. And so US soldiers were now paying for this mistake.

On July 13 MacArthur appointed Lieutenant General Walton Walker, USMA class of 1912, to be field commander of all US ground forces in South Korea, which were designated the Eighth Army. During World War II, Walker had served as a corps commander under General George Patton and was aggressive even by the latter's standards. "My toughest son of a bitch," Patton said of him. But in midsummer of 1950, American forces could not be bold and aggressive. Walker had no choice but to fight a delaying action. He held on while the US military machine tried to get itself going. Everything had to be built up and synchronized — supplies, equipment, troop strength, air and naval power. This takes time. Walker gradually withdrew toward Pusan and established a redoubt that kept contracting as all the different North Korean invasion forces converged. At one point, Walker was forced to deploy his units so thinly that two divisions positioned side by side were sixty-five miles apart. Normally, US divisions in defensive positions are no more than ten to twelve miles apart. However, he worked very effectively his advantage of interior lines, moving units around inside the perimeter to concentrate them at enemy attack points. Occasionally, he even ordered US forces on the offensive for short bursts to keep the enemy off balance. Collins thought he was doing a masterful job.

Nonetheless, by late summer, Walker's leading the heroic "defense of the Pusan Perimeter," as the American media called the fight, sounded to Americans back home vaguely like "Custer's Last Stand." And they had read all they could stomach about American-made shells bouncing off Russian-made tanks and American prisoners being shot by soldiers of an enemy with whom they were only vaguely familiar. They began wondering what had happened to the vaunted force that so recently had vanquished two formidable foes. They started asking questions.

The answers were not going to be happy ones for Truman and his administration. It would be impossible to explain why North Korea, a third-rate nation that was only two years old, had fourteen divisions, while the United States, with its commitments far-flung the world over, had only thirteen — twelve Army, one Marine Corps. To a growing number of Americans, it made no difference that they themselves had supported Truman's austere military-spending policies. Truman, Johnson, the Joint Chiefs: to varying degrees, the people were going to blame them. Except for some brief upticks, Truman's popularity would decline the rest of his presidency and for some years thereafter.

That the Communists had dared such bald aggression and that the United

States was so incapable of deterring it or stopping it shocked Truman, too. Publicly, he was his old self — confident, determined, sorry about nothing. But privately he admitted to making the military cuts too deep, and that, for the sake of saving money, he had relied too much on strategic bombers and atomic weapons.

What he had done was consistent with historical precedent. The nation had always cut back after a war, as he did after World War II. In comparison to previous Presidents, he actually kept in being a relatively formidable force. Furthermore, his liberal's inclination to give social needs priority was admirable. It was also hard to fault his distrust of the military as an institution. What he had not counted on was how different and how much more dangerous the world had become after World War II than it had been before. Atomic weaponry was only part of the reason. The fundamental cause was the titanic ideological struggle that had developed between communist and capitalist societies, a historical anomaly as unusual in duration as the Wars of the Roses or even the Hundred Years War, comparatively speaking.

But good excuses won't make things right when you've been wrong, so Truman, ever the pragmatic politician, moved quickly to cut his losses. In that regard, he made firing his Secretary of Defense his first order of business. That Johnson, in zealously following Truman's military-budget strictures, had been more Catholic than the pope, to use Truman biographer Robert Donovan's description, would not save him. When voters thought of Truman's military-spending policy, the image that came to mind was Johnson knocking generals' heads together and lopping budget requests for things such as HEAT rounds, so Johnson had to go. Congressional elections were fast approaching. Overnight, the North Koreans had turned Johnson's rather popular public image into a very negative one.

The new trend in this conservative direction had, as noted, begun the previous year with news of the Russian atomic bomb and the Communist takeover in China. It accelerated dramatically when young American soldiers started arriving home in coffins. Shock waves from the first two events focused on Washington, whereas those caused by the casualties of this new war were reaching all the little places.

Furthermore, Johnson had begun to annoy Truman. Without compunction he made critical comments to him about the White House staff. In dealing with Acheson, his behavior was pathological at times, so possessed was he with being the President's most important man. An extraordinary example of his typical behavior had occurred earlier in the year, when the two men were supposed to be working together on what would become NSC-68. Acheson convened a meeting to discuss a State-Defense policy review group's recommendations for changing national security policy. Johnson showed up, but had decided that Acheson had deliberately not given him enough time to prepare. A fairly large number of people were present, some seated at a center table, the others in chairs along the walls. After an initial protest, and after declining Acheson's offer to recess so that he could take time to read pertinent documents, Johnson startled everyone, especially Acheson. As a way of showing his displeasure, the Defense Secretary had been gazing at the ceiling while leaning so far back in his chair that its front legs were off the ground. "Suddenly," Acheson recalled, "he lunged forward with a crash of chair legs on the floor and fists on the table, scaring me out of my shoes. No one, he shouted, was going to make arrangements for him to meet with another Cabinet officer and a roomful of people and be told what he was going to report to the President." The session was quickly adjourned, having lasted only fourteen minutes.

Perhaps it was inevitable that Johnson eventually started challenging Truman more directly. Nurturing his ambition to become President, he had in 1949 begun currying the goodwill of conservative columnists and politicians, Truman's natural enemies. Columnist Marquis Childs reported that Johnson made a deal with Republican conservatives to leak them information damaging to Acheson if they would not pillory him, Johnson, when attacking the Truman administration. He became so audacious that, using Republican contacts in his home state, he floated the notion that he would be willing to accept the GOP nomination and run on that ticket as a conservative.

Johnson was so arrogant and ambitious that he became reckless. Early in July, for instance, he stayed on the phone with Senator Robert Taft after Averell Harriman, a presidential adviser on the White House staff then, arrived for an appointment, and made some very inflammatory statements in his presence. Johnson complimented the Republican leader for a recent speech in which he had attacked Truman for not involving Congress early enough in decisions on South Korea and had called for Acheson's resignation. The speech was "something that needed to be said," Johnson observed. After getting off the phone, Johnson proceeded to tell Harriman that if they "could get Acheson out," he would see to it that Harriman was appointed Secretary of State. Enraged, Harriman reported the exchange to Truman, who was not surprised. The President was aware of Johnson's disloyalty and already had a replacement in mind.

Seven days after the North Koreans invaded the South, Truman had climbed into a limousine with his daughter, Margaret, for a Sunday drive to Leesburg to visit Marshall. Since stepping down as Secretary of State, the general had had a kidney removed and had not fully recovered his vitality, but had nonetheless been a very active president of the American Red Cross while in semiretirement. Truman explained his problem and asked him unofficially whether he would accept appointment to the position of Secretary of Defense. Marshall was almost seventy, past his prime, and happy with what he was doing, but told Truman he was a good soldier and, once again, would serve if asked to do so by his Commander in Chief. The one stipulation he had was Lovett's agreeing to become deputy secretary of defense.

What ultimately caused Truman to overcome final reservations about firing Johnson was an incident in late August 1950 involving MacArthur. The Veterans of Foreign Wars had wanted the latter to prepare some sort of message for delivery at their national convention in Chicago. MacArthur complied, and about a week before the scheduled event his staff sent copies to various conservative publications. One of them, *U.S. News & World Report*, decided to reprint the whole text. The Associated Press then obtained a copy of the magazine and put MacArthur's comments on the wire. Administration officials saw them for the first time at this point.

"In view of misconceptions currently being voiced concerning the relationship of Formosa to our strategic potential in the Pacific," MacArthur had written, "I believe it in the public interest to avail myself of this opportunity to state my views thereon." Among his views were these:

• From islands off the coast of Asia the United States "can dominate with air power every Asiatic port from Vladivostok to Singapore and prevent any hostile movement into the Pacific."

• "Nothing could be more fallacious than the threadbare argument by those who advocate appeasement and defeatism in the Pacific that if we defend Formosa we alienate continental Asia."

• Orientals respect "aggressive, resolute and dynamic leadership" but not that "characterized by timidity or vacillation."

These observations had explosive implications. One was that the United States was going to spread the fighting in Korea beyond the peninsula. This was the last thing Truman wanted American adversaries to think; he wanted to limit the war. Another implication was that top administration officials were still arguing about whether or not to protect Formosa; MacArthur knew this was not the case. The President had already assigned him operational control of Seventh Fleet ships to defend it.

The unnamed object of MacArthur's VFW statement was Acheson, the target of choice for Republican conservatives. Well-informed people, especially the President, also judged MacArthur's statement in the context of his political ambitions.

Truman grew visibly upset when reading it and, as the matter developed, ended up shifting his ire to Johnson. His immediate reaction was that he would force MacArthur to withdraw it. That it had already been published was a minor point to him, he was so angry. The man he instructed to convey these orders was Johnson, who accepted the assignment but then could not bring himself to do it. Most likely he was fearful of offending his newfound conservative Republican friends and compromising his political future. He feverishly placed phone calls to Acheson and others, pleading his point that a statement already made public could not be withdrawn. When Truman learned about Johnson's dalliance, he telephoned him and dictated the message he wanted sent to MacArthur: "The President of the United States directs that you withdraw your message . . . because various features with respect to Formosa are in conflict with the policy of the United States and its position in the United Nations."

Incredibly, Johnson still did not carry out Truman's instructions. He made more phone calls, questioning whether Truman really knew what he was doing. Only after Harriman emphatically assured him that the President did, did Johnson finally send the directive. MacArthur, in turn, told VFW officials that "I regret to inform you that I have been directed to withdraw my message." In his memoirs, MacArthur said he was "astonished" by Truman's reaction.

Following this episode, Truman called Marshall, who was in Michigan on a fishing vacation, to ask that he stop by the White House on his return to Virginia. During their meeting a few days later, Truman told the general that though he felt guilty about bringing him out of retirement, he needed him to serve as Defense Secretary during this Korean crisis. Marshall said he would do whatever was necessary but knew he would be haunted by various conservative publishers who deemed him a Communist-appeaser. They did not think he had done enough to save Chiang while serving as Truman's special emissary to China and, later, his Secretary of State. And they deemed the idea of forcing a Communist coalition on Chiang an outrage; Marshall had had something to do with this US policy objective. These critics included, by Truman's estimate, "Hearst and Scripps Howard, McCormick and all the rest of the traitorous and sabotage press."

The act of firing Johnson, who Truman said was "the most ego maniac I've ever come in contact with — and I've seen a lot," was something he dreaded and postponed twice. Finally, on September 11, the press forced the issue. Someone leaked news of Truman's intentions to Ernest Vaccaro, the White House correspondent for the Associated Press, and that morning's paper carried his report. Johnson, believing himself indispensable and too powerful to be dismissed, called Truman directly to check its accuracy.

Come by at four o'clock this afternoon, the President said.

"Well he came," Truman wrote in his diary, "and I opened the conversation by telling him he'd have to quit. He was unable to talk. I've never felt quite so uncomfortable. But he finally said he'd like a couple of days to think about it. I said all right."

As with the MacArthur-VFW flap, Johnson was finding it impossible to come to grips with what was happening to him. The next morning, he showed up at the White House with Finletter, whose presence made it impossible for Truman to bring up the subject of Johnson's resignation. Afterward, the latter got away quickly, as if the whole matter would pass if he could hold on for a time.

Truman ended up having to act for Johnson. He called Stephen Early, the deputy secretary of defense, and told him that Johnson should write a letter of resignation stating that the secretary felt the pressure the President was under and that he had decided he should quit and recommend Marshall as his successor. The letter was to be delivered to him by Johnson that afternoon at the cabinet meeting at four.

As the result of Early's efforts, Johnson showed up, letter in hand. Truman recollected that "he looked like he'd been beaten. He followed me into my office after the Cabinet adjourned and begged me not to fire him. Then he handed me the [soon-to-be] published letter — unsigned. I said 'Louis you haven't signed this — sign it.' He wept and said he didn't think I'd make him do it."

Truman, his mind always alert to some sort of historical twist, noted in his diary a couple of days later that he had finally forced Johnson out and made Marshall's appointment on Pershing's birthday. He recalled that the first time he and Marshall had served the nation together on a Pershing birthday was in 1918, when both were in Pershing's army in France. The President did not note the irony of Johnson's having to use Pershing's birthday to clean out Pershing's desk. Johnson did not reemerge politically. Years later, he underwent surgery for a brain tumor (which generous friends said was the cause of his insufferable behavior) and died of its complications.

Whereas the outbreak of the Korean War caused a profound change in Truman's military policies by forcing him to endorse the unprecedented buildup of a huge, permanent military establishment that for years he doggedly had tried to avoid, his firing of Johnson marked the beginning of a personal accommodation with the professional military. The new war, which would entail a much lengthier wartime stint as Commander in Chief for him than the previous war had, would force him to work closely with his top generals and admirals for an extended period. During peacetime he had tried to avoid them altogether; Collins had to wait a year before seeing the President conduct a meeting. Given Truman's political outlook and personal style, he had not felt comfortable around high-ranking officers or even trusted them, though he found excuses to make exceptions of people such as Marshall and Leahy. Now, gradually, he would come to the realization that most successful military men of his day — Bradley, Collins, Sherman, Vandenberg, Cates, and Burke, for instance, as well as Leahy and Marshall — had backgrounds very similar to his own. The Chairman of the Joint Chiefs was from Clark, Missouri. The Chief of Naval Operations, from Melrose, Massachusetts. The Air Force Chief of Staff, Lowell, Massachusetts. The Marine Corps Commandant, Tiptonville, Tennessee. Burke, the future CNO, whose career Truman had restored, had grown up on a farm near Boulder, Colorado. Leahy was from Hampton, Iowa; Marshall, Uniontown, Pennsylvania. Collins was from the Deep South, though a larger city, New Orleans. None of these men had a father who was a career military man. Each of them shared the same small-town values that had shaped Truman's outlook on life. West Point and Annapolis had not changed these attitudes. In large part, their individual decisions to attend the nation's military academies, their motivation to see it through to graduate, and their determination to climb to the top were fueled by the idealism of Truman's rural America. Later, Truman commented to Bradley, in all seriousness, "I wish I'd known you better, earlier. I'd have made you President." He meant that he would have groomed him to be the Democratic nominee in 1952. For a liberal like Truman, the accommodation with military men was fortunate, for they would be around in growing numbers for many years to come.

CHAPTER 8

★ ★ ★ ★ ★ ★ ★ ★ ★ ★ ★ ★ ★

THROWING CAUTION TO THE WIND

I N ALL WAYS, starting with the overall objective he had assigned MacArthur, Truman was determined to limit the war in Korea. He had no aim but driving the Communist invaders back across the border that divided the two Koreas. He had not thought about following that up with an invasion of North Korea and unifying the peninsula under Syngman Rhee's non-Communist rule, an approach that would have been more consistent with the traditional American way of waging war. In this regard, he forbade movements of US ground units beyond the thirty-eighth parallel.

Truman was intent on executing his containment policy in the Far East, as he had in Europe. But like Kennan, the man whose thinking had inspired containment, he had decided that atomic weapons made total war unthinkable. Accordingly, their nonuse was another limitation he planned to impose. He made no move to put them in place to save the Eighth Army, if necessary. So, as of the outset of this war, he evidently was determined to use them only as a deterrent, to keep the Soviet Union from attacking the United States, Western Europe, or Japan.

He probably should have conveyed this information beforehand to his senior military officers, though. Since World War II, people such as Lieutenant General James Gavin had been formulating plans based on the assumption that atomic bombs would be used as if they were just like any other weapon, though more powerful. They were going to be surprised to learn otherwise, and some of them were going to be very disappointed. The American people were going to be surprised, too, because the President, along with Stuart Symington, Thomas Finletter, Carl Spaatz, and others, had done a good job of selling them on the merits of atomic bombs. So, in addition to having to explain why his soldiers did not have all the weapons they needed, Truman was going to have to explain why they could not use the most important weapon they had.

Other limitations he planned to impose would cause him domestic political problems that were even more acute. To localize the fighting to the Korean Peninsula, he planned to restrict Air Force and Navy targeting of conventional weapons. He was determined to hold fast to orders already issued that US aircraft and ships stay clear of those northern regions where North Korea bordered the Soviet Union and Manchuria, which is a province of the People's Republic of China. This would completely discomfit pilots when they saw supplies pouring in from staging areas beyond their limits. According to Air Force doctrine, the main air campaign should be focused on such depots. The worst alternative, which Truman in effect was ordering, was to hold off trying to destroy enemy supplies until they had been loaded into trucks and sent on their way. Interdiction, as this effort is called, is much less effective. Furthermore, fighter planes are best for interdiction, because their smaller size allows them to sweep down low over moving targets, such as trucks, and attack them with bombs and bullets much more accurately than bombers can from much higher altitudes; but the Air Force, consistent with administration policy and its own institutional bias, had put almost all its money into bombers. There would not be enough fighter planes to go around. And interdiction represented only half the need for this kind of aircraft. The Air Force was also obliged to render close air support for Army units locked in combat. The clear picture that thus emerged right from the start of this war — Bradley had noted as much during the Blair House Group's first meeting — was that Air Force pilots were going to have trouble winning it, though beforehand they and the American public had, to a great degree, bet the future on their doing so.

Given these limitations and the woeful unfitness for combat of MacArthur's soldiers, who had grown accustomed to the easy life of occupation duties, Truman's modest war objective seemed, at most, a remote possibility during the summer of 1950. Walker was totally preoccupied with the thought of the North Koreans driving the Eighth Army off the peninsula, not the Eighth Army driving the North Koreans back across the thirty-eighth parallel. On July 26 he had requested MacArthur's permission to order another retreat — to better defensive positions on the opposite bank of the Naktong River, with his headquarters and those of Rhee's government relocated from Taegu to Pusan. He conveyed this request to MacArthur through Almond, who was appalled by the thought of giving the enemy another inch. MacArthur's reaction was about the same, though Almond, who was a very volatile man, amplified it to some degree. Subordinates had come to expect this of MacArthur's chief of staff, who was incredibly zealous about pleasing his boss. They sensed Almond's feeling he had missed his great chance for leadership during World War II and that MacArthur had given him his due, finally. As for Walker's request, Almond's recommendation to MacArthur was that they fly to Taegu for a set-to with Walker, which is what they did the next morning.

MacArthur did not like Walker. Already he had prepared a list of possible replacements in case he decided to fire him, Matthew Ridgway's name being at the top. Irrespective of justification, Walker was the focus of MacArthur's disappointment in the war's direction thus far. And on a more personal level, MacArthur, a one-of-a-kind character, probably found it hard to respect Walker because he so obviously aped the style of Patton, his patron. On his head Walker wore a highly polished helmet, just as Patton had, and though he did not carry pearl-handled .45s, his equivalent affectation was to stuff an upholstered pistol inside his belt like a barroom dandy. Squat and pugnacious-looking, he otherwise was devoid of any touch of elegance, the kind of thing that MacArthur admired so much and had cultivated personally over the years. Nor would MacArthur have admired the lack of subtlety Walker displayed by driving around in a jeep equipped with a siren, a blinking red light, and a grab bar. Only jeeps used in ceremonial festivities normally have the latter, which a reviewing officer holds on to while standing. With siren wailing, red light blinking, and him standing up as his driver raced from unit to unit, Walker looked like a military policeman in search of a parade.

At Taegu MacArthur told Walker that he had to hang on. "Walker," he said, ". . . there will be no Dunkirk in this command. To retire to Pusan will be unacceptable." Help is on the way, he said; reinforcements will be pouring in. MacArthur also told him that he was developing a plan that would end the war. He said he was going to land a force behind the enemy's lines and trap him, and to get this done, Walker had to buy time by holding on. And so, Walker, thus fortified, walked a short distance to where he had assembled his staff and in the presence of MacArthur and Almond issued what was to become a famous order. "This army fights where it stands," he said. Almond would always recall with delight the very surprised looks on the faces of the men who listened.

MacArthur's plan involved using Marines, of all people, as his spearhead force. Cates had set this in motion as a possibility only four days after the North Koreans invaded the South. It was another instance of an aggressive Commandant forcing the issue. The result would be a victory as compelling as Belleau Wood or Guadalcanal.

Like George Barnett during World War I, Cates wanted his Marines to fight so they could prove the Corps's worth. And like Barnett, he had trouble getting the attention of the powers that be. Even the Secretary of the Navy would not give him an appointment until June 30, which was six days after the invasion began. Cates had not presented his case directly to the Joint Chiefs of Staff because he was not a member, and the current state of war had not changed this working relationship. He finally got a meeting with Forrest Sherman by intercepting him in a Pentagon corridor on June 29. During that brief encounter, he told the CNO that the Corps had a regimental combat team of 6,500 men supported by an air group ready to go.

All things being equal, Sherman's next step, since he endorsed sending them, would have been to notify J. Lawton Collins. But he and Cates associated the Army Chief of Staff with Army efforts to eliminate the Corps. Therefore, Sherman decided instead to use back channels and to notify Vice Admiral C. Turner Joy, who was on MacArthur's staff. The idea was to apprise MacArthur informally of the Marine regiment's availability so that he would be the one to initiate official discussion about using Marines in this land war on the Korean Peninsula. A theater commander with MacArthur's problems would be difficult to turn down. As expected, he jumped at the opportunity to get the Marines and cabled Collins his formal request. All this transpired in a matter of hours.

It so happened that the very next day, Cates finally met with Navy Secretary Frank Matthews, who said he had not heard anyone mention the possibility of Marines fighting in Korea; but all this was changing at the time he said it. That very afternoon, David Lawrence, in his nationally syndicated *New York Herald Tribune* column, once again inserted himself into interservice politics by making public Cates's offer. This time his writing had an immediate impact. "The United States Marines are at San Diego, all packed and ready to sail," he wrote, "and will be invaluable as reinforcements for MacArthur's troops." He noted that approval to send them was uncertain. He had been tipped off, obviously, probably by a Marine. The matter's becoming known added pressure on Collins to send the regiment; not sending them would be virtually impossible to justify, since Walker was having such trouble.

On July 3 the Chiefs met to discuss MacArthur's request for the Marines, and this time Cates was invited, as was customary when Marine matters were discussed. Somewhat surprisingly, opposition came from the Air Force, not the Army. Vandenberg opposed sending the Marine air group. Essentially, he was raising the Air Force's contention that the Marine Corps, as well as the Navy, should not have any aircraft of its own. But these were desperate hours and MacArthur needed all the firepower he could get. Furthermore, Cates vehemently made the point that Marine ground and air units were so closely integrated that leaving the latter home was inconceivable. All things considered, the Chiefs cut short fighting among themselves and asked the President to approve the immediate deployment of the regiment, as well as the air group, and he did so forthwith; however, he was not pleased about being crowded by Cates and his Corps, and he took note. So did Bradley, who, in spite of the merits of Cates's initiative, thought the leak to Lawrence was another example of the Navy–Marine Corps claque putting its interests ahead of everyone else's.

Bradley realized that the door was now open for sending more Marines to Korea. Indeed, to that end, Lemuel Shepherd, who after losing out to Cates for the commandancy had become the highest-ranking Marine in the Pacific, serving on Radford's staff in Honolulu, wasted no time flying to Tokyo for a meeting with MacArthur. Officially, he went to make arrangements for deploying the regiment, which by then had been designated the First Provisional Marine Brigade. Unofficially, he arrived at the Dai Ichi to offer MacArthur the services of more Marines.

Shepherd's timing was perfect. MacArthur was distressed because the day before — for lack of manpower, primarily — he had been forced to cancel Operation Bluehearts, his first plan to use Navy ships to land American units behind enemy lines. As anticipated, MacArthur remarked, "I wish I had the entire 1st Marine Division under my command again, as I have a job for them to do." During World War II, the First had served under Mac-Arthur; and the brigade now being deployed from Camp Pendleton, California, was of the First. Shepherd's reaction was immediate.

"Why don't you ask for it, general?" he said, prompting MacArthur to pop forward in his huge chair.

"That's the kind of talk I like to hear," he said. "Do you think I can get it?"

Shepherd told him he thought he could and assured MacArthur that the division, minus the men already on their way, could be ready by September 1. There were many more Army soldiers than Marines, but a smaller number of them were available for deployment to Asia because the Army had the mission to defend Europe. The Marines' potential impact in Korea was enormous. A Marine division, which in wartime included more than 22,000 men, was about twice the size of an Army division. Shepherd assured MacArthur that it would not be necessary to coordinate this offer with Cates.

MacArthur acted posthaste. "You sit down and write me a dispatch to the JCS," he told Shepherd, who did so in Almond's office after excusing himself. The decorated veteran of two wars later recalled that the thought of composing the message while MacArthur watched him from a few feet away had intimidated him. Alone, Shepherd completed this paperwork in good order, and so it was that the cable from MacArthur requesting more Marines that was in Collins's hands a few hours later had, unknown to him, been written by a Marine.

Collins's reflexive response was to reject the proposal. He did not want more Marines in Korea. He was aware of the First Marine Division's being thinly manned. And beyond unspoken parochial considerations, he, as well as Truman, Bradley, and the other Chiefs, was wary of overcommitting to Korea, leaving the nation vulnerable to Soviet moves elsewhere. The Chiefs had already decided that American forces should be withdrawn from South Korea if the Soviets started something in a region of more strategic importance to the United States. This decision had been made a couple of weeks before Walker's staff, for other reasons, started thinking of withdrawal.

Collins decided to answer MacArthur's request personally instead of by cable. He was about to make his first inspection trip to the war zone, anyway; during his journey, he would stop over in Tokyo.

On July 13, he met with MacArthur. "General," he said, addressing the man who was sixteen years his senior and wore five stars, one more than his four, "you are going to have to win the war out here with the troops available to you in Japan and Korea."

MacArthur just looked at him and smiled. "Joe," he said, "you are going to have to change your mind."

The Blair House Group met on July 19. By that time, Dean's division had been decimated, and the next day the commander himself would be reported missing. The dire situation that evening prompted Truman to nod approval for calling up the Marine Corps Reserve to fill the ranks of the First Marine Division; however, the President made one concession to those opposing a greater Marine presence in Korea. Siding with Vandenberg, he refused to call up the Marine Air Reserve, even though MacArthur would need the extra airpower.

As before, word of what was happening began appearing in newspapers — initially in the columns of those friendly to the Navy and the Marine Corps, and then in standard news reports. Lawrence again got the story ahead of the pack. He wrote that MacArthur was not getting these Marine Air Reserve reinforcements because of the "sensitive feeling here at the Pentagon that the Marines should not have their own aviation." In reaction, Bradley sarcastically asked Cates if he "couldn't do something to stop Lawrence's critical articles," since as Commandant he "was the only one that could do it." Cates, aware that he was not the first practitioner of the game being played, "thanked him for the compliment."

With the matter having been made public, members of Congress got involved. The most notable was Carl Vinson, who commenced to make short work of his opposition. Pressure from him caused the Chiefs to change their minds, and then Truman relented by calling to active duty the Marine Reserve aviators and their support people. This was the third time in about four years that Congress in general and Vinson in particular had given voice to Marine opposition to administration policy.

Truman could not have imagined that his decision to give MacArthur the entire, fully manned First Marine Division would be one of the pivotal decisions of the war; once in position they would constitute no more than about 15 percent of the UN ground forces under MacArthur's command in Korea. Nevertheless, given the chain of events that were set in motion, this was one of the most significant military-affairs decisions of his presidency. MacArthur's getting the extra Marines allowed him to plan with confidence an amphibious strike behind enemy lines at Inchon. Its success would lay to rest any notions that the United States did not need a Navy or a Marine Corps, and would test in the most extraordinary ways Truman's determination to wage limited war.

MacArthur called his Inchon plan Operation Chromite. How it took shape reflected his aloof management style and Almond's importance to him. As MacArthur's chief of staff, Almond was his fulcrum. Except for Brigadier General Courtney Whitney, an old friend and lawyer who was chief of the general headquarters (GHQ) section that oversaw Japan's governmental reform, MacArthur insisted that all officers work through Almond. This made functionaries — to use Almond's word for them — out of the generals in charge of the individual sections; they were not collaborators. Staff initiatives were not encouraged, so ideas rarely percolated up to MacArthur. Years later Almond, as devoted to MacArthur as ever, offered as justification the latter's "high intelligence" and being "way ahead" of his staff. According to Almond, MacArthur was "willing to listen to sound proposals, [but] he was quick to detect fallacious or shallow reasoning"; he was "very attentive as a listener up to the point that he decided that the discussion was bogging down in minor points." In other words, MacArthur intimidated his staff. This would cause problems as events unfolded. So would another of Almond's roles, that of acting as MacArthur's shield once he made a decision. At that point, Almond would be crudely intolerant of anyone urging anything else.

MacArthur's office was on the top floor of the six-story Dai Ichi Building. Before World War II, the Dai Ichi had been the headquarters of an insurance company of that name, which in Japanese means "Number One." The space was large and imposing. As was his wont, even on airplanes, MacArthur often paced there while thinking or talking, but usually he worked seated in a throne-sized chair behind an enormous desk. He kept it absolutely clean, stripped of any evidence of records and communications, unless he was working on a project, which he normally dealt with one at a time. When he finished the one at hand, he would clean his working area completely in preparation for the next. He had no telephone, though one of his aides in an outer office did. He might have picked up this wont from President Hoover, who had appointed him Army Chief of Staff in 1930. Hoover had not had a phone in his office either.

Almond's office was also on the sixth floor, separated from MacArthur's by a paneled conference room filled with maps. These rooms were interconnected, and the general sometimes strolled in to discuss business with Almond, though he was not given to small talk, except about West Point football scores.

Office arrangements and working procedures were not the only ways MacArthur kept himself extremely aloof from his staff; his working hours were very unusual. Following a habit developed back in 1919 when he became superintendent of the US Military Academy, he arrived for work at ten-thirty each morning, usually seven days per week. This first segment of his workday lasted until he finished all tasks that needed to be acted on that day. Then, between two and two-thirty in the afternoon, he would return to his embassy residence for lunch, after which he took a short nap. At four-thirty or five, he would have himself driven back to his office, where he worked into the evening hours, staying sometimes as late as midnight. Until the North Korean invasion, occupation duties had filled his workday, and under his direction the occupation powers had worked to reorganize Japan's social, political, and economic structures, while implementing such massive reforms as land redistribution. He had virtually no evening social life, even of an official nature. When important visitors came to town, he hosted them only for lunch, after receiving them initially in his office. He and his wife, Jean, then consigned hosting duties to Almond and his wife, Margaret.

Given all his responsibilities, Almond had a very demanding job, but he attacked it with zeal; his dominant trait was his incredible energy. He was also abrasive and very smart, though not to the degree that his self-confidence assured him. Without someone else's constraining influence, his ideas, though imaginative, had a touch of wildness about them. Almond came to work about an hour and a half before MacArthur did and, unless he was hosting a visitor, he stayed until MacArthur departed. He pushed the Dai Ichi staff hard, acknowledging himself to be very impatient, a natural tendency that was exaggerated by his determination to satisfy MacArthur, who wanted things done in "minimum reasonable time."

Almond recalled MacArthur's mentioning Inchon as the proposed point of attack in Operation Chromite on or about July 20, which would have been the same day, Tokyo time, that Truman approved calling up the Marine Reserves and giving MacArthur the Marine division. According to biographer William Manchester, MacArthur conceived the Inchon operation while standing on that high bluff overlooking the Han River and Seoul. From the outset, MacArthur insisted that it be carried out in mid-September. To strike at Inchon and do it as soon as possible were MacArthur's "earliest and most important decisions," observed Vice Admiral Arthur D. Struble, the commander of the Seventh Fleet, whose crews would conduct the landings. MacArthur's first planning step was to meet with Almond alone. The latter then called in Brigadier General Edwin Wright, MacArthur's operations officer, and ordered him to develop the plans comprehensively, involving at that point no other section but Willoughby's intelligence people. Wright's was a joint staff of Army, Navy, and Air Force officers complemented by one Marine lieutenant colonel. When this group reached certain critical junctures in the planning process, they formulated alternatives, listing the advantages and the disadvantages of each, and presented them to Almond, who alone consulted MacArthur, ordinarily in the conference room, with maps at hand. MacArthur then decided what he wanted done and Almond would inform Wright, who with his section proceeded to the next juncture.

By mid-August, planning had progressed to the point that the different services' preparatory activities had to be coordinated. The most significant recent development had been MacArthur's gaining approval to land a second division at Inchon, the Army's Seventh Infantry, which was based in Japan. It had been thinly manned, but was being brought up to full strength by whole battalions and individual fillers from the States and also 8,600 ROK soldiers. How this hybrid force would perform was potentially problematic; but using the South Koreans was the only way to man the division fully, and it was hoped that their going into combat next to Americans would bolster their performance. MacArthur planned to rely primarily on the Marines; the addition of the Seventh would allow him to exploit much more effectively a successful landing at Inchon. Altogether he would have a landing force of about 40,000 soldiers, supported by more than 230 ships.

On August 15, 1950, MacArthur appointed Major General Clark Ruffner project officer and ordered him to start bringing all the elements of Operation Chromite together. Immediately, Joy and Stratemeyer, MacArthur's Navy and Air Force deputies, were involved. Like Almond and Shepherd, Ruffner was a Virginia Military Institute graduate (though it was MacArthur himself who selected him for this important task). The Inchon landings would be proud days for that venerable institution. By the time they occurred, Marshall, another VMI graduate, would be nominated Secretary of Defense. And those who knew would take note that a former VMI superintendent, Major General John Lejeune, was most responsible for the Marine Corps's having developed the amphibious doctrine that had been so important in the Pacific theater during World War II and that would be executed again with such precision at Inchon.

Ruffner was assigned five officers and twelve enlisted men; designated "Group X," they began their work the day after his appointment, in an old airplane hangar at the motor pool in downtown Tokyo. Engineers quickly built them a large, rubber relief map of the Inchon-Seoul region and it became their primary focus of attention. Some of the supporting data had been developed by Major General John Hodge's occupation troops during their three years in South Korea. Current aerial reconnaissance was also very useful. Researchers gleaned a great deal of information about topography, currents, tides, and water depths from Japanese repositories that had been built up during their long colonization of the peninsula. Sometimes these information sources were at odds; an American agent sent in to investigate some of the discrepancies discovered that the Japanese figures were "on the money." The South Koreans themselves, having been preoccupied with more pressing problems of nation building, had not developed information of much use. Nor did they seem to have the expertise to apply their general knowledge, on issues such as whether a causeway from the mainland to Wolmi Do, an island in Inchon harbor, could support the weight of tanks. A frantic search through military personnel files led to Army Warrant Officer W. R. Miller, who had lived on Wolmi Do during occupation days, running recreation boats. Forthwith, he was assigned to work with Ruffner's people. Wolmi Do was to be the mandatory first tactical objective of Operation Chromite. Troops could not be brought onto the mainland safely with active enemy forces supported by artillery behind them.

Gradually, the clear impression emerged that landing at Inchon presented so many formidable natural problems that if the Navy and the Marine Corps could execute this phase of the operation successfully, retaking Seoul would be inevitable after hard fighting. The thinking was that Inchon would be the last place the North Koreans would expect an attack, given the inherent challenges it presented. "We drew up a list of every natural and geographic handicap — and Inchon had 'em all," said Lieutenant Commander Arlie Capps, one of the Navy planners.

Inchon's widely fluctuating tides were the most obvious natural problem. The difference between high and low tidewater levels was about thirty-two feet — one of the highest ranges in the world. At low tide, the water receded completely from two of the three proposed landing points in the harbor, exposing about a thousand yards of vast, stinking mud flats in front of one and about forty-five hundred yards in front of the other. Passage across these quagmires was impossible. Furthermore, even at high tide, there were insurmountable problems most days of the month for landing craft bringing ashore the soldiers and their jeeps, trucks, and tanks. Twenty-nine feet was the minimum water depth needed to bring them ashore, and this occurred only once per month for a period of three to four days.

The approaches to the harbor from the Yellow Sea were also hazardous. There were two, which merged not very far from the harbor itself. Relative to the other, one was straight and free of salt pans and other obstacles, but it was more parallel to the mainland. This presented a serious problem, for the long line of ships would surely then be spotted and fired upon. The alternative was the much more circuitous and narrow Flying Fish Channel, nine miles long and so constructed at points that a single ship would block passage. This geography and the size of the tide combined to create another problem — a very swift current. As Captain Norman Sears, the man who would lead the vanguard ships, observed afterward, "Flying Fish Channel was well named. A fish almost had to fly to beat the current, and check his navigation past the mudbanks, islands, and curves in the channel." Currents in it ran as fast as seven to eight knots, almost the top speed for some of the landing craft. Nonetheless, this was the invasion route chosen because it was less exposed to the mainland.

MacArthur was determined to risk these difficulties because Seoul would no doubt fall quickly; it was only twenty-five miles from Inchon. The psychological impact on the enemy and for the UN cause worldwide would be enormous, he believed. Furthermore, Seoul was the nexus of the roads and rails that the North Koreans were using to supply their units fighting Walker's Eighth Army. Within days of losing Seoul, the Communists would have to break away from the Pusan-perimeter battlefront.

From the outset, key figures opposed Inchon as the landing site. One was Rear Admiral James Doyle, who would be in charge of the actual landing operation. He was the Navy's most experienced amphibious-operations officer still on active duty, and was convinced that from the Navy's standpoint it was too risky and that MacArthur, given his insistence, was not fully aware of the difficulties. On or about August 21, Doyle stopped by Almond's office to make this point.

"The general is not interested in details," Almond told him.

"He *must* be made aware of the details," Doyle asserted.

But Almond brushed them aside as "mechanical problems." MacArthur probably had told Almond to keep doubters away, and Doyle might well have suspected this. Still, he was shocked by Almond's comment, much as Forrestal had been by Truman's assertion that it was Eisenhower who proved to Hitler that an army could cross the English Channel. Both statements reflected a gross underestimation of the Navy's role and the complexities of what it did.

Doyle's calling on Almond was also a matter of professional courtesy to MacArthur. The Joint Chiefs were flying to Tokyo to "find out exactly what the plan was," as Collins put it, and pass judgment, and Doyle wanted him to know that during the meeting with them he was going to oppose Inchon as the landing site. Doyle had the clear impression that the CNO had the same negative opinion.

On August 23 Wright convened the all-important meeting in Mac-Arthur's conference room. Joining MacArthur were Collins, Sherman, and Lieutenant General Idwal Edwards, whom Vandenberg had made his representative. Also present were admirals Radford, Joy, and Doyle, and major generals Doyle G. Hickey and Ruffner. Hickey was MacArthur's deputy chief of staff. Almond, who was responsible for making the arrangements, had not invited any Marine generals, though Shepherd and Major General Oliver P. Smith were in Tokyo, hoping to get a call. At Inchon, Smith would command the Marine division. Almond might have been alerted to the fact that Smith and especially Shepherd also opposed Inchon as the landing site.

Most of the briefers were Navy officers whom Wright introduced. Mac-Arthur listened stoically to their remarks, puffing on his pipe, knowing that Sherman's response was key. Collins, as the Chiefs' executive agent for running the war, had the authority to void the Inchon selection but was prudent enough to defer to Sherman as to the landing's feasibility. What MacArthur did not know was that Sherman had already decided to support the landing there, though he had been conveying just the opposite impression. Like Doyle, Collins thought Sherman was against it; and Shepherd, who kept a journal, was even more certain of it. His August 21 entry read that the Chief of Naval Operations was "unquestionably opposed to the proposed plan."

Sherman was a very complex, capable individual. Perhaps he had wanted to avoid becoming an advocate by announcing in advance his support for the plan. Whatever the reason, by the time of the meeting he endorsed the Inchon operation because of a burning parochial motive. He wanted to use it to mute talk by influential people such as Bradley and Spaatz that the United States no longer needed a surface Navy. Only a year had passed since Denfeld, his predecessor, had lost the confidence of virtually the entire Navy for not defending its interests (before making a comeback at the hearings, which got him fired), and Sherman was determined to make that nightmarish episode a dim memory by dramatically showing at Inchon the value of the fleet.

The day before, he had first revealed his intent during a secret meeting with Admiral Struble, the Seventh Fleet commander, aboard the latter's flagship, the *Rochester*, which had just returned to the Japanese port of Sasebo following missions off the South Korean coast. "Rip," he said, using Struble's nickname, which dated back to Annapolis days,

> I'm going to back the Inchon operation completely. I think it's sound. If it is approved, it will be held very soon, and you will recognize the importance of the Navy's doing everything possible for its success. . . . You are to command the operation and I want you to get up to Tokyo as soon as you can, with a staff, and get the best possible plan prepared. You'll find many problems up there, but you'll be able to handle it.

When the last briefer finished, Doyle rose and, addressing MacArthur, said somewhat disingenuously, "General, I have not been asked nor have I volunteered my opinion about this landing. If I were asked, however, the best I can say is that Inchon is not impossible."

MacArthur's temperate response was that if the fleet could not make it, it would be withdrawn.

"No, general, we don't know how to do that," answered Doyle. "Once we start ashore we'll keep going."

Collins then asked about alternatives. How about someplace farther south? Kunsan, perhaps? Or Posung-Myong? Landings there would be easy. Collins was drawing out MacArthur and testing his reasoning. MacArthur's men, Almond especially, revealed later that they resented the evident doubt of the Army Chief, which prompted Collins to write that he questioned MacArthur's thinking "not in a contentious way, as has sometimes been pictured." Doyle continued raising questions, too. He pointed out that enemy shore batteries could command both waterways, at which point in the discussion Sherman suddenly decided to show his colors. He rebuked Doyle personally. "*I* wouldn't hesitate to take a ship up there," he said.

The statement exhilarated MacArthur, who grasped immediately that he had won his way. "Spoken like a Farragut!" he roared.

Thus inspired, he rose to speak a few minutes later. The briefers having finished, it was time for his say. He put his pipe down, which he managed to do to dramatic effect, and his audience fell silent. The briefing had lasted about one hour and twenty minutes and he would talk another forty-five.

"Seoul is the target," he began.

There followed as impressive a performance as any writer or actor could contrive. He was eloquent, yet passionate. His delivery was so fluid that everyone thought he was speaking extemporaneously, though it was not his nature to leave such important matters entirely to chance. On such occasions in the past, he had carefully written passages beforehand and memorized them. He might have this time. Genius is usually a function of such hard work and preparation.

The purpose of MacArthur's plan was to achieve a strategic masterstroke, not a mere tactical victory or reinforcement of the Eighth Army; this he tried to convey at the outset of his presentation. He believed fervently that a successful landing at Inchon would end the war quickly. Of the landing force, he said, "It will be the anvil upon which Walker will smash the Reds."

Point by point, he then addressed the worries and countered the alternatives. He did not minimize the dangers, but argued that they were worth risking. He said that thousands of casualties could be avoided if the operation rendered unnecessary a frontal drive back up the peninsula.

To stir his listeners' imagination, he drew from eighteenth-century history a legendary precedent. He recalled that in the year 1759, also in mid-September, the British general James Wolfe sailed from England to take Quebec by putting a flanking force ashore at the base of a steep cliff, the last place the French had expected a landing. It was called "a mad scheme" until Wolfe took the city easily, he said.

MacArthur finished with a flourish. He observed that an amphibious landing is a powerful military device. "I have used it ten times before, but never with such a large force as is available now." Assuring the admirals and appealing to their pride, he said, "The Navy has never let me down in the past, and it will not let me down this time." He was looking straight into Sherman's eyes. Then, drawing upon an old Navy tradition, he said that if the unforeseen occurred, he would accept full responsibility. But he was confident of grand success, not utter failure. "I realize," he continued, "that Inchon is a five thousand to one gamble, but I am used to taking such odds." Finally, lowering his voice to a whisper, he said, "We shall land at Inchon and I shall crush them!"

Almond remembered Sherman standing up and applauding. The Navy Chief later told Shepherd that MacArthur's performance was "spellbinding." Everyone concurred, apparently. According to the obstreperous Doyle, "If MacArthur had gone on the stage, you never would have heard of John Barrymore."

Regardless, approval was not immediate. The visitors had to discuss the matter with Bradley in Washington. In the meantime, MacArthur lobbied the Marines. He had Shepherd come to his office the next morning. The senior Marine was allowed to advance his case for choosing an alternate site, while MacArthur listened carefully. He then responded with a thirty-minute analysis. As he had the evening before, he emphasized the strategic importance of Seoul. "For a five dollar ante," he said, "I have an opportunity to win $50,000, and I have decided that is what I'm going to do." Approval came four days later by cable from Collins.

By this time, MacArthur had decided that the two-division invasion force would be called the X Corps. Naming its commander was a delicate proposition, which is probably why MacArthur did not reveal his choice before the Chiefs approved the operation; he did not want the selection to become an issue. Sherman suggested Shepherd to him as X Corps commander. As a lieutenant general, Shepherd was of the customary rank for a corps commander; furthermore, the First Marine Division would be the main component; and, most important, Shepherd had a permanent staff already in place that was trained for amphibious operations. Wright and Hickey supported this rationale. In a memorandum to Almond, Wright wrote: "[X Corps] headquarters must be one that can operate in the field as a going concern with such things as situation reports, operations reports, communications, etc. happening automatically. A provisional command group selected from GHQ officers will not be a going concern . . . no matter how efficient the individuals are." To this, Hickey added his endorsement. He then forwarded this paperwork to Almond, who forthwith sent it back with the notation "Return without action." Soon it became clear why: Almond had not wanted to eliminate himself from consideration. This was prudent, for MacArthur did, in fact, appoint him X Corps commander. At last he would have his day in the sun.

That would have ended discussion about the matter, save some temporary mutterings by disappointed Marines, had MacArthur not announced concurrently that he was retaining Almond as his chief of staff. This was very unconventional and created a potential conflict of interest. Being GHQ chief of staff was at cross-purposes with being a subordinate commander. A chief of staff traditionally helps a senior commander control his subordinate commanders. Thus, for example, given his working relationship with MacArthur, Almond, as his chief of staff, would be able to approve many of his own requests made as X Corps commander; he could give his unit's supply requests priority over Walker's, and would. Indeed, the whole Almond-Walker relationship was skewed to make the former much more powerful, even though he was a lower-ranking officer in charge of a smaller organization.

The dual authority made Almond powerful in additional, more subtle ways. At fifty-one, he was much more vigorous than MacArthur at seventy. Collins, who was fifty-four, later noted that he, though stationed back in Washington, visited the battle zone in Korea much more frequently than MacArthur did. Because of his renowned vigor, Almond had become an unusually important communications conduit for problems and ideas, though it may not have been evident to disappointed callers such as Doyle. Keeping MacArthur informed had probably been the most important part of his job. He could not do that once he was leading a corps in combat. So MacArthur would become even more isolated, given his strong tendency toward being aloof and the position he held. As a sort of proconsul of a conquered people with a centuries-old religious tradition for leader worship, MacArthur had been installed in their temple next to the sun god's emissary, the emperor himself — a place that, as it turned out, perfectly suited MacArthur's ever-growing estimation of himself. As eager as Almond was to do MacArthur's bidding, he still exposed him to unrarefied air from outside the temple. Though Hickey would help Almond with his duties back in Tokyo and try to deal with MacArthur personally, he did not have Almond's standing with him and would not have the time to develop a close working relationship; their offices were not even on the same floor. In summary, Almond's dual roles were potentially a very serious problem that a crisis situation would quickly expose; they might even contribute to causing this crisis.

Nevertheless, Collins and the Chiefs did not intervene. Instead, the Army Chief worked to help Almond manage. When Almond, whom he did not like personally, gave Collins a list of men he wanted for the X Corps staff, he almost had "heart failure," Almond recalled, and objected at first; "These men are in important jobs," he said. But he did not argue the point that the war in Korea had first priority, and within a brief time had about half of them in Japan ready for combat.

Washington allowed Almond's two appointments to stand for a couple of reasons. One was the strong precedent, dating back most notably to Abraham Lincoln's presidency, that commanders should be left to lead their armies and fight as they saw fit, as long as they followed certain broad guidelines and achieved the objectives assigned them. In this instance, however, the primary reason the top brass did not object to this command arrangement was as much personal as historical. Even collectively, they were no match for MacArthur. Truman tried unsuccessfully to balance things out by promoting Bradley, with congressional approval, to five-star rank in mid-September, but that did not make much difference. Nor did it make any difference that all the Chiefs were confident men whose individual self-esteem was bolstered by brave performance in combat, a lifetime of extraordinary success, and the prestige of the institutions they led; or that Collins and Sherman were particularly bright. What mattered was that they did not match MacArthur's prestige within military circles and with the public at large.

*   *   *

Concerns about Almond's appointment notwithstanding, the stage was set, the curtain about to rise. Then, suddenly, Truman, like an errant producer, riled the cast in a most foolish way. Reacting to a proposal by Republican congressman Gordon McDonough of California that the Commandant be made a permanent member of the Joint Chiefs of Staff, he composed one of the most ill timed and imprudent letters ever written by a President. In the process of telling McDonough his idea was awful, Truman wrote that the Marine Corps was nothing more than "the Navy's police force" and that it would be nothing more as long as he was President, in spite of its having "a propaganda machine that is almost equal to Stalin's." He wrote these words two days after Collins informed MacArthur he could execute a strike at Inchon led by thousands of Marines.

McDonough released Truman's letter to the news media on September 5, and overnight the public swamped the White House with angry telegrams, many of them from parents who had lost their sons at such places as Guadalcanal, Tarawa, and Iwo Jima. The reaction from radio commentators and newspaper editors could not have been much more vehemently negative had they known about Inchon, which was still a secret. Cates later observed that Truman's letter, coming when it did, was one of the best things that ever happened to the Marine Corps. Within twenty-four hours of its being made public, the President sued for peace, calling Cates to his office to apologize personally and to give him a second letter to that effect. Then he asked the Commandant to accompany him to the convention of the Marine Corps League, which by remarkable coincidence was having its annual meeting in Washington. To them he repeated his apologies.

In retrospect, it seems clear that Truman's angry reaction to McDonough's proposal betrayed worries about issues more profound than the possibility of zealous Marines undermining the delicate compromises that had formally unified the services. This was the explanation Truman offered for his behavior, though the real reason for his agitated state was more likely his having committed the nation to war on his own. Since he had not established a formal consensus for war by asking Congress to declare it, Republicans were positioning their party to take advantage of issues as they developed. McDonough's proposing that the Commandant be made a member of the Joint Chiefs was an early example of this and a relatively minor one, compared to what would happen later.

Traditionally, American political parties had closed ranks during wartime, but it would not be so this time. The Republican party, whose foreign policy had come to be dominated by the young conservatives who made opposition to communism a crusade, would eventually line up against all the limitations that Truman planned to impose to cap the Korean War. Senator

Vandenberg might have been a compromising influence had he not been dying of cancer. In that same unlucky vein, Truman had MacArthur as his general running the war, a man whom Republican conservatives championed and would support vigorously should he and Truman have a falling out. Fortunately for Truman, Marshall had agreed to serve as his Secretary of Defense; news of this was made public three days before the Inchon landings. Marshall was the only military man still in government service whose stature with the public and within the military was equal to Mac-Arthur's. Eisenhower was a more popular national figure, but he was out of uniform, and in terms of longevity, and military roles played, even he was no match for these two. They had no equal. Without Marshall by his side, Truman's presidency might not have survived the coming months.

It was perhaps by fate ordained that Marshall would stand with Truman and MacArthur against him, eventually. Marshall's father had been a civilian, active in local Democratic-party politics, whereas MacArthur's had been a very-high-ranking career Army officer. This, to a large extent, explains why they were such different men. It was not that living on Army posts while growing up had shaped MacArthur's attitudes a certain way; it was that his father's being the Army's only three-star general during his day and one of the nation's most famous war heroes had boosted his son's career in so many extraordinary ways. The father, Arthur MacArthur, had won the Congressional Medal of Honor at Missionary Ridge during the Civil War and, as commander of the US force that invaded the Philippines during the Spanish-American War, had forced the surrender of the Spanish captain-general at Manila. As a consequence, MacArthur the son had been the consummate insider throughout his career, as he shot up through the ranks. His mother, Mary, a shrewd woman who was well known for having contributed mightily to her husband's success, had even helped her son get promoted to brigadier general and major general by writing none other than General Pershing, whom she had known as one of her husband's junior officers. MacArthur's first and second stars had closely followed her efforts. One of her letters included this passage: "I am presuming on a long and loyal friendship for you — to open my heart in this appeal for my Boy — and ask if you can't find it convenient to give him his promotion during your regime as Chief of Staff. . . . *You* have never failed me yet. . . . Won't you be real good and sweet — The 'Dear Old Jack' of long ago?"

As late as his becoming Chief of Staff, MacArthur was benefiting from his father's reputation; the Army's top ranks were still loaded with men who had served under him, given how the son had shot up far ahead of his age group. It was no wonder, then, that years before the war in Korea,

MacArthur's many contacts, coupled with his manifold talents, had made ignoring the rules that applied to everyone else second nature to him. "It's the orders you disobey that make you famous," he had told a friend during World War I, while explaining his bizarre nonregulation combat ensembles, which sometimes included a plum-colored satin necktie. He had become more subtle about this sort of thing by the time he was the five-star general in Tokyo in charge of the Far East, but his dress still hinted at his rebellious nature; he now refused to wear a tie at all, as specified in the regulations, and he donned his Class A hat, the kind with a bill, without its required grommet, the result being a floppy look. Truman, who had the eye of a sergeant in such matters, grumbled to his staff about these indiscretions when, in October, he met MacArthur at Wake Island.

Marshall, in sharp contrast to MacArthur, had always been an outsider, mostly because he did not go to West Point. In 1901, when he became an officer, the Military Academy produced nearly all the small Army's second lieutenants, whose commissions, unlike Marshall's, were conferred automatically. Thereafter, Marshall conducted himself as an outsider, even after winning the respect of such West Point graduates as Pershing during World War I, when he planned the Saint-Mihiel offensive and played a key role in the Meuse-Argonne attack. Subsequently, during the five years he served as Pershing's aide, Marshall and Pershing became close, but he still did not avail himself of the influence of the old American Expeditionary Force commander, who in 1939 wanted to write a letter for him as Roosevelt was pondering whom to name his Army Chief of Staff. Marshall explained his rationale to an Atlanta newspaperman, whose offer of help he also declined. "My strength within the Army," he said, "has rested on the well-known fact that I attended strictly to business and enlisted no influence of any sort at any time."

Upon becoming a lieutenant, Marshall quickly developed into the type of officer who finds security in the system and is bolstered by its assurances that if you work by the rules and perform ably, you will be rewarded in due time. He became the classic "good soldier," as he had labeled himself before Truman when he agreed to become his Secretary of Defense. He was no constitutional scholar, but he learned very early on that the President, as Commander in Chief, was supposed to control the American military and was ultimately responsible for running the nation's wars. At the same juncture, MacArthur came to see himself as a Napoleonic genius who could win any battle. This is partly why he was boldly daring Inchon's dangers.

Truman was fortunate that Marshall not only acceded to his authority but also greed with him about how to fight the cold war. MacArthur, the man apt to challenge his authority, did not. In Korea, administration policy, as noted, meant limiting US objectives and power. MacArthur had not explicitly stated that he would challenge these limitations if the course of the war forced his hand, but Truman had picked up strong signals that he would. These signals usually involved Chiang; MacArthur seemed preoccupied with the defense of Formosa. Knowing that it did not warrant the worry, because the Navy was in the Formosa Strait, Truman realized that MacArthur must be fretting about how to ensure Chiang's return to power on the mainland. This explained Truman's consternation with MacArthur's VFW speech and, earlier, with MacArthur's highly publicized trip to Formosa on July 31 to visit Chiang. As the general responsible for the island's defense, MacArthur had the standing to make the trip, but the implications troubled Truman. As Acheson put it, the visit implied a "tie-up" with Chiang and suggested that the United States was thinking about expanding the Korean conflict into a general war against communism throughout Asia. MacArthur had made clear that he, at least, was thinking about it when on August 6 he received Harriman, whom Truman had sent to Tokyo to reiterate his position. Traveling with this visitor were generals Norstad and Ridgway. Harriman, who by then was serving the President as his special counsel, had known MacArthur since he was the Military Academy's superintendent, when they hunted ducks together. MacArthur told his old acquaintance that the United States must never recognize Mao's government in China, as Britain and France already had. "We should fight the Communists every place," he said, "fight them like hell!"

That Marshall and MacArthur had such different views of the cold war was rooted in World War II. Marshall's view had evolved from his having been a principal coauthor of the so-called Europe-first war plan that the United States implemented during that conflict. It called for defeating Germany first, and afterward focusing on Japan. MacArthur's view evolved from his having been a leader in the second-priority conflict against the Japanese. That there was a correlation between which World War II theater a man was associated with and how he viewed the cold war was later determined by sociologist Morris Janowitz in his classic study of American military officers. With extensive interviewing, he established rather conclusively that those strongly associated with the war in Europe against Germany, as Marshall was, were content with Truman's cold-war policy of containment and the limited-warfare concepts it entailed, and that those strongly associated with the war in the Far East, as MacArthur was, favored using whatever force was necessary to fight communism — they wanted it rolled back. These correlations were "so powerful," wrote Janowitz, that Army officers such as General Albert Wedemeyer, who had served in the

Far East, "emerged as advocates of massive and strategic air power at the expense of reliance on ground forces." In marked contrast to European officers, he found that Far Eastern officers were "not inclined to acknowledge any limitations in the pursuit of total victory."

The root cause of this sharp difference of opinion, Janowitz found, had to do with the vast expansion of Communist-controlled regions, especially in China, that World War II had wrought. Far Eastern officers placed much blame for this on the Europe-first plan. Their contention was that they would have saved China, while in the process of defeating Japan more quickly, had they and their Nationalist Chinese allies been given a greater share of the resources that were sent to Europe. They were particularly upset that those serving in Europe had gotten such a disproportionate share of available aircraft and crews. Virtually all Far Eastern officers also faulted the Truman administration's postwar China policy, which, as noted, had been to push Chiang into working out a coalition with the Communists, instead of building up his forces and somehow bolstering his government. According to Janowitz, they pointed to a number of reasons why this alternative policy was not implemented, and in doing so, they accused China emissary Marshall of "blocking a military aid policy."

Officers who had mostly been involved with the war in Europe had little of this preoccupation with China. They regretted the Communists' having taken over there and in Eastern Europe, but they did not see this as the outgrowth of the Europe-first war plan, which they believed had been prosecuted reasonably well and was a limited success even in terms of the cold war that followed. They attributed Chiang's demise mostly to rampant corruption in his government and army. Like Marshall, whose views on China were a function of his friend General Stilwell's troubles with the Nationalist leader, they thought that Chiang's only chance at staying in power on the mainland had been some sort of reconciliation with the Communists, such as a coalition government. And exhibiting the same sort of pragmatism, they supported Truman's containment and limited-war policies.

Janowitz's research also produced another important finding, one that revealed something Truman had known intuitively and needed no study to tell him. The sociologist determined that most career officers supported Truman's cold-war policies not only because they were influenced by having served in Europe, but also because Marshall endorsed them. In other words, their personal loyalty to Marshall was reason enough for them not to rebel against the limitations Truman was imposing in Korea, even when disaster seemed imminent.

There were a number of reasons for them to side personally with Marshall instead of MacArthur. Marshall's career, unlike MacArthur's, was one they could relate to and not resent. For example, as a lieutenant, Marshall had been ordered to survey on horseback hundreds of square miles of southwest-Texas desert during July and August, when temperatures some-times reached 130 degrees Fahrenheit; MacArthur's equivalent experience when of the same rank had been a nine-month journey throughout Asia with his father, whom he accompanied as aide, during which they were hosted by generals and admirals, rajas and royalty.

Furthermore, the senior officer corps on active duty at the time of the Korean War had gotten to known Marshall personally, whereas they had been denied that opportunity with MacArthur, primarily because he attained high rank early in his career. As outstanding as Marshall had been, Mac-Arthur, who was commissioned an officer sixteen months after him, was made a general eighteen years before he was. For a number of years, Mac-Arthur's peer group were men about twenty years older than him. At the time MacArthur was promoted to brigadier general in 1918, Bradley was a captain with two months' time in grade, Collins and Sherman were lieuten-ants who had been officers about a year, and Hoyt Vandenberg was begin-ning his senior year in high school.

By contrast, rank had not put Marshall in a different realm from those officers who would be key during the Korean War. When he and Ridgway served together in Tientsin, he was a lieutenant colonel and Ridgway a captain. And later, as the Infantry School's assistant commandant, Marshall was still a lieutenant colonel when Bradley, Collins, and Ridgway served under him as captains. He personally appointed Bradley chief of the school's weapons section, and made Collins and Ridgway tactics instructors. It was during this assignment that Marshall first earned the personal respect and loyalty of hundreds of mostly Army officers who passed through the school as captains and majors. (Two Marines in attendance had been O. P. Smith and Lewis B. ["Chesty"] Puller, who at the present stages of their careers were about to lead the Marines ashore at Inchon; Colonel Puller was one of Smith's regimental commanders.) Many of the former Army students at the Infantry School came to refer to themselves as "Marshall men," because he had so revitalized the school and, in the process, invigorated their careers. Later, during World War II, Marshall personally made dozens of them generals.

By the time of the Korean War, Bradley, Collins, and Ridgway — whose combined support would be crucial for Truman — felt a deep degree of loyalty to Marshall. Various little stories connected them to him. Marshall was Ridgway's houseguest in April 1939 when Roosevelt telephoned with news that he was appointing Marshall Army Chief of Staff. A month later, when Marshall traveled to Brazil to negotiate American use of airfields in the Natal bulge as the starting point for flights across the South Atlantic to North Africa, he took Ridgway with him; their transport was the cruiser *Nashville*, and during long hours alone together, as they sat on the deck of the ship in front of the forward turret, staring out to sea, Marshall used Ridgway as a sounding board as he detailed his plan to fight the coming war.

As for Collins, when, shortly after Pearl Harbor, his wife thought he had died in a California plane crash along with some other generals, he found upon landing a short time afterward that Marshall had reserved an open telephone line for the Collinses' use; this was at a time when the war effort made such personal calls virtually impossible.

And as for Bradley, his undying loyalty to Marshall was cemented in December 1944. During the Battle of the Bulge, Field Marshal Bernard L. Montgomery of Great Britain, supported by the Fleet Street press, tried to have Bradley fired and himself named "Land Force Commander" in Europe, a prospect that Marshall shut down completely with this cable to Eisenhower: "Under no circumstances make any concessions of any kind whatsoever. You not only have our complete confidence but there would be terrific resentment in this country following such action. . . . You are doing a fine job and go on and give them hell." German successes had shaken the confidence of both Eisenhower and Bradley, but Marshall's reassurance restored both men and very nearly prompted Eisenhower to fire Montgomery.

The personal loyalty to Marshall felt by the other two chiefs was much more indirect in origin and, in Sherman's case, not very consequential; during World War II, Marshall had affably agreed to the admiral's request that he see that his horse was properly cared for at Army stables near Washington. Vandenberg's loyalty to Marshall was a function of Hap Arnold's; the latter had been gratified by Marshall's strong support for the Army Air Forces. Vandenberg also had an extra measure of loyalty to Truman himself, because the President had previously granted him a quasi-political appointment as chief of the Central Intelligence Group and because he had reached down so far in the ranks to make him the Air Force Chief of Staff.

MacArthur was capable of evoking the same degree of personal loyalty that Marshall was; no one was more loyal to Marshall that Edward Almond and Courtney Whitney were to MacArthur. However, there was something exclusionary about the loyalty MacArthur engendered. Whereas Marshall's was expansive and encouraged the same, one officer to another, down through the ranks, the kind that MacArthur demanded raised barriers. Those closest to him were there to keep others away, and they, in turn, were more inclined than they might otherwise have been to do the same for themselves. The reason was MacArthur's extreme egocentrism. For instance, on the eve of World War II, MacArthur was only interested in keeping Eisenhower on his staff as a valuable assistant, not in opening up greater opportunities for him elsewhere, though he easily could have done so. Eisenhower, who had labored hard for him as his personal assistant for six and a half years, finally had to engineer his own reassignment. In sharp contrast, Marshall, who ordered Eisenhower to Washington five days after Pearl Harbor, quickly moved him up through the War Plans Division to its top job, and within another six months appointed him commander of the European theater of operations. A few months after this giant boost toward fame, Eisenhower confided to an assistant his relative assessment of the two men. "I wouldn't trade one Marshall for fifty MacArthurs," he said.

And so it was that on September 15, 1950 — as Marine landing craft, some of them painted with the lettering "Truman's Police Force" by their occupants, plowed through the dark waters of Inchon harbor toward Wolmi Do and the Korean mainland itself — the American military was on the verge of a deep political split within its ranks such as not seen since the Civil War. The dispute would be about the Truman-imposed limitations, which Inchon would bring to the fore, making them a big issue back home. Whether the operation succeeded or failed, Truman was going to be pressed hard to lift some of them. If it succeeded, the American public, per all US war-making precedent, would expect him to invade North Korea, destroy the remnants of its army there, and unite the peninsula under Rhee's non-Communist leadership. Such punishment seemed due the enemy. If Inchon failed, the American public would expect him to do whatever necessary to save the Eighth Army. A Dunkirk-type withdrawal would be politically impossible for Truman, even if it became strategically prudent. And among Far Eastern officers, such a move would resound as a most humiliating affirmation that Europe-first thinking now controlled cold-war policy. Ordering use of atomic bombs would be a much more politically palatable step. Collins was confident that Walker's lines could hold and that such drastic measures would not be necessary, but the American public would probably not tolerate a prolonged stalemate along the Pusan perimeter; one alternative Truman would be pressed to accept instead of calling up more Americans was Chiang's troop offer. In terms of domestic political stakes at risk, Truman had put himself and the Democrats in a no-win situation, if he remained adamant about his imposed limitations. They made victory in the conventional American sense impossible. So the Republicans could hardly lose, no matter what happened.

Mindful of this, Truman knew the grave danger to himself that Mac-Arthur posed. Given his great stature and the fact that he had a constituency both inside and outside the military — a very rare situation for an American military officer — MacArthur could exploit a rift of his own creation. He potentially could wrest control of the war from Truman and put his presidency at risk — and he had already demonstrated some leanings toward doing this.

Truman would not be too surprised when events led him to a confrontation with MacArthur. For years, Democratic politicians had not trusted the general. Fixed foremost in the minds of those of Truman's generation was the way MacArthur, as Chief of Staff, had in 1932 crushed the so-called Bonus Marchers, a legion of destitute World War I veterans who were demonstrating in the capital for early payment of money promised them by law for their wartime service. MacArthur was certain they were Communist-led, but there was no connection. Settling in for a long-term demonstration, about eleven hundred of the twenty thousand marchers established quarters in some empty Treasury Department buildings on Pennsylvania Avenue, and when trouble erupted as police tried to evict them, Secretary of War Patrick Hurley told MacArthur to "surround the affected area and clear it without delay." This MacArthur did with abandon, controlling events personally at the scene. In the late afternoon of July 27, 1932, he used tear gas and soldiers on horseback with drawn sabers to remove them. Then, that night, he had his units drive the rest of the marchers and their families from a large makeshift encampment along the Anacostia River. Hoover had sent orders to him not to pursue them to this point, but MacArthur evidently ignored these instructions, explaining later that he was "too busy" to hear them. Among the casualties that day were two babies who were asphyxiated by tear gas and a seven-year-old boy who was bayoneted through the leg as he tried to retrieve his pet rabbit.

Newspapers reflected that most Americans felt excessive force was used. Many veterans — Truman among them, no doubt — could not believe MacArthur had turned on his former doughboys so harshly. Whitney offered one excuse many years later (and at the same time inadvertently demonstrated the sort of reinforcement MacArthur was getting from some of his close associates during the Korean War). According to him, a secret plan was discovered that connected the Bonus Marchers to Communists — a plan that called for "the public trial and hanging in front of the Capitol of high government officials." Whitney wrote that MacArthur's name was at the top of the list.

The episode prompted Roosevelt to observe to Rexford Tugwell, an adviser, that MacArthur, along with Huey Long, was one of the two most dangerous men in America. Nonetheless, as President, he held MacArthur in high esteem as a professional soldier. "Douglas," he told him face-to-face, "I think you are our best general, but I believe you would be our worst politician." For older Democratic leaders such as Truman, this was Mac-Arthur's legacy. As William Manchester stated it, one of Roosevelt's most challenging tasks as President was "to exploit MacArthur's military genius while hamstringing him politically." And so it would be for Truman, who would try to reconcile MacArthur to the limits of American power as he had him fight a war.

CHAPTER 9

★ ★ ★ ★ ★ ★ ★ ★ ★ ★ ★ ★ ★ ★

TESTING THE LIMITS

INCHON ACCOMPLISHED almost everything MacArthur had promised it would, although he betrayed anxiety about it by throwing up when he went ashore. Within a couple of hours of the first waves of landing craft reaching shore at 6:33 AM on September 15, 1950, the Marines had captured Wolmi Do, and within another twenty-two, had achieved all their landing objectives and established their beachheads. On September 17 they captured Kimpo Airfield on the outskirts of Seoul, and on September 25, when a regiment of the Seventh Infantry Division captured South Mountain, a height that dominates the capital, MacArthur deemed Seoul a liberated city; he issued a communiqué the next day saying so. Four days later he flew in from Tokyo with his wife to conduct a ceremony marking Rhee's restoration to power.

Not everything had gone as planned, though. The Marines had been poised to retake Seoul and had earned the honor of doing so, but in a dispute over the pace of their advance Almond ordered them to one side and ordered elements of the Seventh to enter the city first. Interservice rivalry seems to have been a partial motivation, but the principal reason was O. P. Smith's refusal to promise Almond that his Marines would capture Seoul by September 25, which was exactly three months after the Communist invasion began. MacArthur had told Almond that retaking the city on this date would have certain dramatic value for the United Nations. Smith had refused to cooperate because he thought the idea was a publicity stunt that would needlessly increase casualties. As it turned out, when Almond informed MacArthur that the X Corps controlled Seoul, the Marines were still engaged in dangerous fighting in city streets, where the North Korean commander had decided to make his stand. They were unable to force an end to this until September 28.

There had also been problems farther south. The Eighth Army only succeeded in breaking out of the Pusan perimeter once word spread among North Korean soldiers about what was happening behind them at Seoul and resistance began disintegrating on about the twenty-fifth. Then the enemy retreated more rapidly than expected and the X Corps moved more slowly than expected in blocking their escape route. As a result, an estimated 40,000 Communist soldiers made it back across the thirty-eighth parallel.

These disappointments notwithstanding, the war was over at this point, in terms of Truman's stated limited-war objective of driving the invaders out of South Korea. However, given how grim all prospects had been before Inchon, Truman had not counted on a broad cross-section of American public-opinion leaders immediately afterward pressing him hard to order MacArthur to invade North Korea, destroy the remnants of its army, and reunite the peninsula politically under Rhee's non-Communist leadership. What specifically sparked this intense discussion was a casual comment by Walker to reporters that he would stop at the border to await UN approval to pursue. Congressman Hugh D. Scott, Jr., of Pennsylvania, a former chairman of the Republican National Committee, accused the State Department staff, whom he referred to as the "Hiss Survivors Association," of planning "to subvert our military victory by calling a halt at the 38th parallel. The scheme is to cringe behind this line." To this type hue and cry, loyal Democrats added their voices, also urging Truman on. Senator Joseph C. O'Mahoney of Wyoming wrote him to say, "Let us occupy every military air field in North Korea and every military stronghold." Even the *New York Times*, a leading voice of the eastern establishment, joined more ideologically driven papers, such as McCormick's *Chicago Tribune*, in endorsing a UN invasion of North Korea.

What had happened was that MacArthur's extraordinarily successful Inchon operation, which commentators were already comparing to some of the classic victories of such legendary captains as Hannibal, had emboldened everyone, including Truman. And he, like most, was also outraged to learn that during the North Koreans' headlong retreat, they had executed noncombatants and POWs. At Taejon, the bodies of more than five thousand South Korean civilians and forty American soldiers, bound together by wire, had been found buried in shallow graves. Finally, and, ironically, because of MacArthur, this Democratic President had a chance to silence his right-wing critics. If he could see to it that the Communist government in North Korea was vanquished, Republicans would have trouble accusing Democrats of being soft on communism.

There would be risks in his ordering UN forces to invade North Korea, the most serious being that the People's Republic of China might enter the war; but direct involvement by the Soviet Union was now considered much less likely. According to Acheson, Truman accepted the CIA's estimate that though Chinese intervention was a "continuing possibility," it was an improbability. However, the Chinese Communists were warning that they would fight if US forces crossed the thirty-eighth parallel. On September 27, in Delhi, India, Foreign Minister Girja Bajpai informed Ambassador Loy Henderson of the United States that he had reason to believe that China would do so if UN forces invaded North Korea. Then the Chinese Foreign Office began releasing statements warning that China would stand with its neighbor North Korea. And in a series of meetings, Premier Chou En-lai personally conveyed the impression to India's ambassador to China, K. M. Panikkar, that China would not sit by idly. Word of this was relayed to the State Department by British emissaries.

For various reasons, those in a position to affect US policy did not trust Panikkar, who, by Truman's later estimate, "had in the past played the game of the Chinese Communists fairly regularly, so that his statement could not be taken as that of an impartial observer." Harriman recalled that "it was not considered very solid information at the time." Truman also thought that the Chinese were trying to use the Indians to upset UN unanimity. Another possibility was that they were reacting to two US fighter planes' having strayed across the Chinese border and strafed an airfield in Manchuria. Acheson later testified that "among the reasons for believing that [the Chinese] would not come in were the amount of well trained troops which they would have to commit, the possible weakening of the government of China itself, [and] the lack of real advantage to China itself in coming in." This was the British position; they could not see how it was in China's interest to fight. Implicit in this was knowledge of how much Communist China wanted to be seated in the United Nations and thereby legitimize in the West its new government.

MacArthur's intelligence staff, looking at it from a military standpoint, deemed it illogical that the Chinese would take up the war at this late date because the UN armies were now very strong. The Chinese would have entered, if at all, when the UN presence was weak; that was the thinking. No one at GHQ was reading the intercepted Chinese messages that were piling up because no one understood the Mandarin dialect, which the Chinese government used.

Some lower-ranking officials did take the Chinese threats seriously. One was Edmund Clubb, director of the State Department's Chinese-affairs office. About the time British diplomats were relaying the first of Chou's messages, Clubb by memorandum informed Rusk, the assistant secretary of state for Far Eastern affairs, that reports were "indicating that important elements of Lin Piao's 4th Field Army had moved into Manchuria." The

Fourth, comprised of about 450,000 men, was the main Communist force that had defeated Chiang's Nationalists. Lin Piao personally was a man of great acclaim; he had been on the Long March with Mao and was deemed the best Chinese strategist and commander. Confusing matters for American intelligence officers was that "home" for the Fourth Field Army was Manchuria; however, this fact did not put Clubb at ease. "That those Chinese troops will participate in the Korean fighting is the most interesting possible explanation of their movement," he warned Rusk.

Truman decided to accept the risk of direct Chinese intervention and, more remotely, Soviet intervention. His order to MacArthur to invade North Korea coincided with the first of the warnings from China. He issued it September 27, 1950, informing MacArthur that he was to develop a plan whose objective was "the destruction of the North Korean Armed Forces." Generally, MacArthur had Truman's permission to operate anywhere in the north; however, the President did lay down some restrictions. Under no circumstances was MacArthur to hit targets in China or the Soviet Union, which were contiguous to North Korea's upper regions. In fact, Truman and his Washington advisers deemed this northern area so sensitive that he ordered MacArthur to use only ROK units to advance into it when the offensive entered its final phase. This limitation was intended to show that UN forces had no aggressive intentions beyond the Yalu River, the natural feature that constituted most of North Korea's northern border. A huge army composed of many Occidentals advancing toward China's border had all sorts of explosive implications for Orientals, given how Western powers had in the past conquered and colonized much of China. Still, Truman seems not to have been sensitive enough to this Chinese fear.

There were other reasons why Truman would come to regret his September 27 directive. Wanting to call off the offensive if the Soviets or the Chinese intervened, he concurrently delegated to MacArthur the authority to decide whether they had. It was a very dubious move. Though reports of battle contact with Chinese or Russians would reach MacArthur before they reached officials in Washington, the latter controlled various worldwide intelligence networks whose information MacArthur was not in a position to correlate. Furthermore, this determination was of such fundamental political importance that Truman should have retained for himself exclusive authority for making it. MacArthur's input should merely have been another estimate of the situation, especially since his behavior had forewarned Truman that he might allow his personal political opinions to control his judgment. Truman was aware of MacArthur's conviction that the United States somehow had to end Communist control of China. It was not inconceivable that MacArthur wanted to start a war with China.

Another problem with Truman's September 27 directive was that it was not clear enough. The President did not admit to this even in his memoirs six years later. He wrote then that MacArthur "was authorized to conduct military operations north of the 38th parallel in Korea, provided that at the time of such operation there had been no entry into North Korea by major Soviet or Chinese Communist forces, no announcement of intended entry, or no threat by Russian or Chinese Communists to counter our operations militarily in North Korea." Superficially, these guidelines may have seemed precise, but in view of the great decision involved, they were woefully vague. These instructions left many questions unsettled. What constituted "major Soviet or Chinese Communist forces"? One division? Three divisions? Twenty divisions? Another unsettled question was, How many Chinese "volunteers" constituted a major force? As later interpreted by the administration, not even tens of thousands, as long as they came in as individual replacements for North Koreans and not as organized Chinese opposition. As for Truman's telling MacArthur to halt his forces if there was a "threat by Russian or Chinese Communists to counter our operations militarily," that instruction was by the boards before the operation got under way.

When some ROK units crossed the thirty-eighth parallel on September 30 and established a command post eight miles north of the line, Chou publicly declared that the Chinese people "absolutely will not tolerate foreign aggression [in North Korea] nor will they supinely tolerate seeing their neighbors being savagely invaded by imperialists." Threats by nations normally do not get much more specific, but no one in Washington was too concerned about this one, for Acheson's enumerated reasons and also because Truman and everyone else in a position to influence policy had become so optimistic as to be careless. Chou's threat did not cause Truman to modify his instructions to MacArthur. During the September 29 cabinet meeting, White House staffer Matthew Connelly recorded one manifestation of this optimism. He summarized some comments by Acheson as follows: "Plans are being developed to set up a commission to get into Korea and start rehabilitation. The 38th Parallel will be ignored. Korea will be used as a stage to prove what Western Democracy can do to help the underprivileged countries of the world." A short time later, on September 30 in Korea, MacArthur, acting on Truman's instructions, issued his first surrender ultimatum to Kim Il Sung.

MacArthur believed that the offensive Truman authorized him to make would be the final one of the war, and everyone back in Washington was eager to help make it so, including Marshall. With Truman's approval, he sent MacArthur this accommodating message: "We want you to feel un-hampered tactically and strategically to proceed north of the 38th parallel." Walker's comment to reporters about having to regroup his units at the border, pending instructions, had prompted Marshall to send it. Marshall was referring only to the border crossing itself, not the overall operation, and was telling MacArthur that Walker was wrong, that he should proceed across following a plan that best suited tactical and strategic considerations. Marshall did *not* intend to give MacArthur free rein in the whole of North Korea.

However, Marshall knew better than to be less than precise with Mac-Arthur. During World War II, the "architect of victory" had masterfully controlled field commanders from his Washington office. But Marshall was not in good health; his world-weary eyes were evidence of that. Worst of all, he had been on the job as Secretary of Defense only nine days when he cabled his message to MacArthur. From a walking start, he had stepped into a fast-paced flow of events and decision-making and had not brought himself up to speed. The same did not apply to MacArthur, though he too was past his prime. Seizing the moment, he shot back by cable, "Unless and until the enemy capitulates, I regard all of Korea open for our military operations." Marshall and the Joint Chiefs did not reply.

By October 2, 1950, MacArthur had formulated his basic plan to finish off his adversary. To set it in motion, he issued formal orders to Walker and Almond that day. Incredible logistics problems would ensue and, for that reason, he left it to his two senior field commanders to name the dates his multipronged assault would commence. The Eighth Army and the X Corps would not have to step off at the same time. The First Marine Division was to return to Inchon, where its men were to remount all its equipment on the ships that brought them ashore, and then reboard themselves. The Navy would then transport them down and around the tip of the Korean Peninsula and up the coast, bringing them ashore as the spearhead unit, far north of the thirty-eighth parallel. How the rest of the X Corps would redeploy was more complicated. These units would initially travel southeasterly by motor transport from Seoul to Pusan, where they too would load their equipment onto Navy ships and board for the leapfrog advance north. The Eighth Army, which had been bottled up near Pusan, would actually meet these X Corps units while moving in the opposite direction on the same roads, from the southeast to the northwest. The Seoul area was the planned jumping-off point for the Eighth's attack north. The unsurfaced roads would be filled bumper-to-bumper in both directions by trains of trucks, tanks, artillery, jeeps, and troops. Complicating the Eighth Army's problems was that all its ammunition and supplies had to come through the port at Inchon, which could not be used for this purpose until the Marines had shipped out. An airlift was not feasible because of the enormous tonnage involved.

On a map, representation of all these and later movements brought a viewer's breath up short. Had anyone but MacArthur conceived it, it would have been dismissed out of hand. But no one, not even the Joint Chiefs, was going to question the cogitation of the master so recently after Inchon. Somewhere amid the swoops and swirls, genius was to be found, it was thought. There was some concern that MacArthur was splitting his armies, putting the Eighth Army and the X Corps on opposite coastlines of North Korea, but he had so recently made a mockery of conventional wisdom that no one was about to object strenuously at this point.

While Walker and Almond set MacArthur's plan in motion, rumblings from China continued. On October 3, Julius Holmes, the chargé d'affaires at the US embassy in London, cabled the State Department that on that day "Foreign Minister Chou En-lai called in Panikkar and informed him that if UN Armed Forces crossed the 38th parallel China would send troops across frontier [to] participate in defense North Korea. He said this action would not take place if only South Koreans crossed parallel." This cable was coded urgent, so Acheson was notified immediately. His perception was that Chou's comments were not an authoritative statement of Chinese policy, but he forwarded it to Truman, who agreed with Acheson's assessment. Nonetheless, these persistent threats were troubling; the President ordered the new CIA director, Bedell Smith, who recently had relinquished his Moscow ambassadorial post, to have the situation assessed. Truman's breathing was getting a little shorter, his chest a little tighter, as the post-Inchon exhilaration wore off. The danger of a general war was increasing the closer he got to winning this limited war. And he knew it. The sooner he got it over with, the better.

Lieutenant General Frank Milburn, commander of the Eighth Army's I Corps, agreed. His three divisions and one brigade would spearhead Walker's attack north. The longer he waited to get going, the more time he gave the North Koreans to dig in and resist. Soldiers from MacArthur on down expected fanatical resistance. Already the enemy was filling with mines much of the road that connected Seoul with Pyongyang, the North Korean capital. To minimize the I Corps's difficulty, Milburn beat the timetable MacArthur envisioned by about a week. On October 5 he began assembling his divisions near Kaesong, just south of the border. On the seventh, he ordered patrols to cross. These were the first Americans to enter North Korea.

Later that same calendar day in New York, the UN General Assembly passed by a vote of forty-seven to five a British-sponsored resolution authorizing the invasion. Within hours, early morning October 9 in Korea and Japan, MacArthur, following instructions from Truman, delivered a second surrender ultimatum to Kim Il Sung. As he spoke, the engines of hundreds of American tanks were already idling, their operators poised to bolt for points north. At 9:00 AM they did. Major General Hobart Gay's First Cavalry Division led the way. An almost endless line of other units and vehicles followed.

On the opposite side of the peninsula, the ROK divisions that had begun crossing the border September 30 were still plowing through disorganized resistance like ships through flotsam. For organizational purposes, they had since been assigned to the X Corps and Almond's control. Their speed of advance was startling. They were already 110 miles into North Korea, on the outskirts of Wonsan, the first major objective, as the First Cavalry rolled across the border.

In the meantime, signals of Chinese intervention kept popping up. One was word passed by Willoughby's agents that thousands of Chinese soldiers were moving through Manchuria toward the North Korean border. This was essentially the same news Clubb had reported a week or so earlier. MacArthur immediately cabled Willoughby's report to the Chiefs.

Their reply was just one of a torrent of messages flooding communications lines on the ninth. With each passing day, the Chiefs were more inclined to ignore Chinese protestation. Believing that Mao had waited too long to act, they notified MacArthur that even if his armies encountered major Chinese units, he should continue pressing the attack as long as there was a reasonable chance of success.

The next day, October 10, the Chinese Ministry of Foreign Affairs issued another statement, which included the following: "The American war of invasion in Korea has been a serious menace to the security of China from its very start." However, two days later, the CIA assessment that Truman had asked Bedell Smith to generate supported the Chiefs' optimistic outlook.

The next day, October 13 in Washington, Truman boarded the *Independence*, bound for Wake Island. "Have to talk to God's righthand man tomorrow," he wrote his cousin, Nellie Noland, while airborne. He was referring to MacArthur. The two men were going to meet for the first time.

Truman's administrative assistant George Elsey was the prime mover behind this rendezvous. Because of Inchon's success, politics was the principal motivation. MacArthur had become a national hero again, and it might help Democrats in the off-year elections if he were seen conferring with the Democratic Commander in Chief. Truman deserved to collect some political dividends since he was the one who had risked the political capital. Truman and MacArthur's coming together was also meant to convey an impression of a President in charge. To ensure as much as possible this spin on the story, Truman permitted only White House–based reporters to cover the event. Those in Tokyo who covered MacArthur on a daily basis and who thus might have a greater sense of loyalty to him were barred.

Acheson and Marshall were against the meeting. The Secretary of State was as stiff about political campaigning as a member of the House of Lords; from first mention of it, he deemed the idea of the meeting "distasteful." The Secretary of Defense did not think that MacArthur should be out of position, since he was supposed to be controlling a huge offensive then. The septuagenarian general would be crossing three time zones to reach Wake. Sixty-six-year-old Truman would travel even farther, having selected Wake as the meeting place to allay Marshall's concern about the strain on MacArthur. The President would travel across seven time zones. There was also some worry that the highly publicized one-day conference might make the Soviets and the Chinese think that something very big was afoot, such as an attack on China.

When on the fifteenth, shortly after sunrise, Truman stepped from his plane at Wake Island, MacArthur was waiting at the bottom of the ramp to greet him. During a brief photo session, both men struck natural, confident poses. A photo that the United Press distributed throughout the world was a classic depiction of the decorum associated with each man: Truman with heels together, legs straight, chest forward, shoulders back, hands behind him as if in a military parade-rest position, and his large, wide-open eyes locked straight-ahead on the camera lens; MacArthur with feet a few inches apart and one slightly in front of the other, one knee bent and his weight favoring one side so that his body had a casual cant, hands on his hips, and his eyes, barely visible through narrow openings, locked on an imaginary point above and beyond; Truman, as if in doughboy uniform with leggings, posing for the hometown paper; MacArthur, as if wearing a bicorne and cape, posing for a painting. The two were not of the same century, much less of like mind.

Initially, Truman and MacArthur met alone in a Quonset hut for thirty minutes. No official account of what was said was made, though, according to Truman, MacArthur apologized for his VFW speech and said he regretted being made "a chump" — MacArthur's word, as quoted by Truman — by Republicans during the last election.

Shortly after this meeting, a conference was convened in a one-story concrete-and-frame building. Joining the two principals were Bradley, Pace, Harriman, Rusk, Ambassador-at-Large Philip Jessup, Special Counsel Charles Murphy, and Press Secretary Charles Ross, all of whom accompanied Truman; and Muccio, Administrative Assistant Laurence Bunker, Whitney, and Radford, who had arrived with MacArthur. Vernice Anderson, Jessup's clerical assistant, was in a small side-room using shorthand to record verbatim most of what was said. MacArthur noted her with surprise when she stepped from her cubbyhole as the meeting adjourned. He had been under the impression that the exchanges were off-the-record, except for the notes some participants took. In a few months, how and why she was stationed where she was would become points of partisan debate. Her being within earshot would arouse suspicions that MacArthur had been set up. Officially, she was on Wake to type the official communiqué. She said she had set up her typewriter in the small room to type that announcement and that when the meeting convened, she stepped inside and closed the latticed door. Some in the larger room could see her, though MacArthur could not. She explained that she started recording the discussion because she had nothing else to do. Her innocent explanation strained credibility, such matters not normally being so casual at such a high level. But no one has ever come forward with knowledge or proof of a contrary explanation.

What is additionally suspicious, and something that MacArthur biographer D. Clayton James found "astonishing," was the Truman-MacArthur exchange on the possibility of Chinese intervention. "One question by Truman," James wrote, "a single response by MacArthur, and absolutely no follow-up questions, challenges, or further mention." Conceivably, Truman's real purpose for the conference was to get MacArthur to tell him, face-to-face, his estimates. Then Truman could more convincingly assert that he had relied on MacArthur's assurances, should the Chinese surprise everyone by fighting. When things went bad later, Anderson's notes served to document MacArthur's confidence in his final offensive and highlighted his erroneous judgment about the Chinese. But there was ample other documentation to establish these points. Indeed, there was documentation that virtually everyone of importance in the US government thought the same about the Chinese entering the war. Concerning this possibility, MacArthur told Truman, "I should say in my opinion there is very little. Had either country [China or the Soviet Union] intervened at the start, their intervention would have been decisive. I do not believe at this time they will endeavor to throw good money after bad." Elaborating, MacArthur continued: "In the case of the Chinese Communists, they have in Manchuria scattered around three hundred thousand troops. Of these probably not more than a hundred thousand or a hundred and twenty-five thousand are distributed along the Yalu River. Of those, they would have the greatest difficulty getting more than fifty thousand or sixty thousand across the river into North Korea. They have no air."

In his memoirs, MacArthur maintained that when referring to airpower in this instance, he was telegraphing his presumption that Truman would authorize him to bomb bridges, bases, troops, supplies, roads, railways, and whatever else necessary in Manchuria, in order to halt a Chinese offensive. Radford, in his memoirs, said he interpreted MacArthur's remark the same way. Use of airpower would more and more be one of the major issues that defined the opposing views of Truman and MacArthur. Because Truman remained silent now, a profound misunderstanding with enormous implications was in the making.

This meeting, which had convened at 7:30 AM, lasted about an hour and a half. Shortly after it adjourned, the parties boarded their planes for long flights in opposite directions. In the meantime, Chinese soldiers were doing some international traveling of their own. A large number of them assigned to Lin Piao's Fourth Field Army were crossing Yalu River bridges into North Korea at night afoot. Truman's having forbade reconnaissance flights over Manchuria was helping them go undetected, by and large. Once across the border, they were hiding in the vast, uncharted Taebaek Mountains, a natural barrier that divides much of the length of North Korea. By the end of the month, their numbers were as big as the surprise they promised — 180,000, organized into eighteen divisions. But the Taebaeks easily hid them. In these northern reaches, the range is about fifty miles wide. Roads crossing the mountains were few and primitive. Given the extremely rugged terrain, detection was difficult even from aircraft.

These Chinese in hiding were known for their ability to live on a bag of rice per day and still fight. But, in fact, most of the Eighth Army was doing about as well. By mid-October, a typical meal for anyone in Gay's vanguard division was "a slice of Spam and half canteen of grapefruit juice once a day," remembered one private. This was one American army not traveling on its stomach. Unchecked, relentless success since Inchon had put offensive forces far ahead of logistical support, and MacArthur had exacerbated the problem by the speed and complexity of his moves. Food stores were only one of many supply items held up; everything was.

Some facets of MacArthur's plan were ahead of schedule in mid-October. In the east, the ROKs captured Wonsan on October 10. In the west, the Eighth Army captured Pyongyang on October 19. Rather than hold ground and risk annihilation, Kim had led a retreat of his remaining divisions from Pyongyang, Wonsan, and, farther up the western coast, Iwon, and was establishing a defense perimeter of his own in the far northern reaches of his country.

Even at this stage, MacArthur hoped to trap them before they made good their escape and at the same time free about 2,500 American POWs they had with them. This plan went awry because the North Koreans were withdrawing too quickly and because the Marines could not get ashore. Motivated no doubt by what had happened to them at Inchon, the North Koreans had seeded Wonsan harbor with an estimated 2,000 to 4,000 contact mines. Removing them was time-consuming, especially since the Navy had precious few minesweepers. As a consequence, the ships with the Marines aboard had to steam back and forth off Wonsan for seven days. An outbreak of dysentery made this unproductive exercise even more demoralizing. Had the Marines gotten ashore on schedule, MacArthur envisioned having them charge west across the peninsula to converge on Pyongyang with the Eighth Army. Theoretically, they would have blocked the North Koreans' escape as the Eighth pushed them back. When it became evident that the Communists would have removed themselves far to the north by the time the Marines got off the ships, MacArthur tried one stopgap effort to cut off his enemy's retreat. On October 20 he had the 187th Airborne Regiment dropped behind enemy lines; but this was done too late, and they were of insufficient strength to close the enemy's escape route up the western corridor.

Because the bulk of the North Korean force had avoided entrapment a second time at Pyongyang, Truman faced a decision about how to finish them off. He had forbidden deployment of American units into the upper border regions of North Korea. Since so many enemy soldiers had escaped, doubt now arose that the South Koreans could do the job alone, as planned. Before Pyongyang was captured, MacArthur had recommended, and the Joint Chiefs, with Truman's concurrence, had approved, a line connecting the North Korean cities of Chongju, Yongwon, and Hamhung as the imaginary boundary that American units would not cross. This MacArthur abrogated unilaterally, without consultation. On the twenty-fourth, he instructed Walker and Almond "to use any and all ground forces . . . as necessary to secure all of North Korea." They were to "drive forward with all speed." The tens of thousands of Chinese soldiers hidden in the mountains ahead were still undetected.

Truman had the opportunity to remand MacArthur's order. Within hours of its issue, the Joint Chiefs learned of it through back channels and cabled MacArthur. His orders to Walker and Almond were "not in consonance" with earlier instructions, they said. They wanted to know what he was doing.

In response, MacArthur explained that the South Koreans "were not strong enough to secure North Korea by themselves." He had issued his order to send Americans up to the Chinese and Soviet borders because of "military necessity." He viewed the Chongju-Yongwon-Hamhung line more as an initial objective than a prohibitive boundary, he said. He advanced the argument that Marshall's having told him to "feel unhampered tactically and strategically to proceed north of the 38th parallel" freed him of constraints. He said that "this entire subject was covered in my conference at Wake Island."

In Washington there was a pause and, concurrently, the kind of audible silence that dominates as cardplayers first see the hands dealt them. Truman liked what he saw. Remnants of the North Korean army were still on the run and running out of room. And a few days earlier, the CIA had essentially reaffirmed to him earlier estimates that China would not enter the war, though the assessment noted that Chinese troops might advance into North Korea far enough to protect some electrical generating plants and pumping stations. Still, Truman risked much by pressing his luck. Nevertheless, he decided not to countermand MacArthur's order. He accepted the risk. He and the CIA seem to have focused too much on information that buttressed what they wanted to believe and diminished the rest.

Domestic politics was a big factor, and was becoming more important by the day. Driving the Communists out of power in Korea would help the President and his party. In the US Senate race in California, Republican congressman Richard Nixon was telling civic clubs that his opponent, Democratic congresswoman Helen Gahagan Douglas, was "pink right down to her underwear." In the US Senate race in Maryland, Senator McCarthy, while campaigning for his party's candidate, used this same theme to attack the incumbent there, Millard E. Tydings, and two other powerful Senate Democrats, Scott Lucas of Illinois and James O. McMahon of Connecticut. According to McCarthy, "Lucas provided the whitewash when I charged there were communists in high places in government; McMahon brought the bucket; Tydings, the brush. This trio, in my opinion, have done more than any others in this nation to shield traitors, protect the disloyal and confuse Americans in their desperate fight to clear out the communists."

In spite of Truman's ordering American intervention in Korea to turn back Communist forces, Republicans were making stick the charge that Democrats were soft on communism. And somewhat surprisingly, MacArthur's battle-field victories were not bolstering the popularity of Truman's party. The President knew, therefore, that Democrats would be hurt all the more if he reined in MacArthur now. Election Day was less than two weeks away.

What was not understood in Washington was the effect of all this campaign rhetoric on the Chinese, whose leaders had become paranoid, terrorized, almost, by the thought of a US-led invasion. They were as much in awe of what MacArthur had done at Inchon as anyone else and had seen how that victory emboldened Truman, who upon achieving his publicly stated objective of restoring the thirty-eighth parallel as the border, decided to invade North Korea. They also knew what Republican candidates were saying and worried about what Truman would be pressured to do.

Truman had erred by allowing MacArthur's order to stand, and his mistake began to become apparent the day after he made it. On October 25, 1950, strong resistance on the battlefront materialized out of nowhere. In the Eighth Army's western corridor, a brigade of British Commonwealth soldiers was suddenly locked in battle with a fresh North Korean unit bolstered by at least two dozen T-34 tanks, as well as self-propelled guns and other heavy weapons; the ROK First Division was almost surrounded by what was a much larger force; and two of three regiments of the ROK Sixth Division, traveling up separate roads, were attacked by forces of overwhelming size. In the X Corps's eastern corridor, a regiment of the ROK Third Division, trying to cross the mountains by way of the Chosin Reservoir, was also repulsed by a very large force.

American commanders tended to doubt this report because it came from South Koreans; however, word started spreading that Chinese "volunteers" were now involved in the fighting. Even so, concern was temperate since this was anticipated. The strong resistance was easily explained by the fact that the UN armies were on the offensive. One of the regiments of the ROK Sixth actually reached the Yalu, having by chance followed a road the enemy was not deployed to cover. Some of its soldiers filled a bottle with the river's water to give to Rhee and then celebrated by urinating in the stream. Soon thereafter they were discovered by an enemy force and driven back.

After several days of fighting, a clearer picture emerged as to what had happened to these South Korean units — a picture that was much more upsetting to UN commanders than initial reports. The ROK First had been stopped cold and had ceased to exist. Each of its regiments and one from another division had been attacked separately and almost cut off. Casualties had been very heavy and South Korean soldiers who could flee had done so individually. The import of these reversals was that the Eighth Army's right flank was now exposed.

Receiving the brunt of the increased pressure was the British Commonwealth's brigade, which kept fighting, though its commander, Charles Green, was killed. His soldiers fought hard for a week, until given reprieve by an American regiment of the Twenty-fourth Infantry Division. The lead battalion of this regiment was commanded by none other than Brad Smith, who had led into combat the first American unit to fight in Korea. To his right flank, advancing on another road, was another of the Twenty-fourth's regiments, this one led by Colonel John Throckmorton. On October 29, Throckmorton's men were hit hard by one of the fresh North Korean units steeled with tanks and self-propelled guns. But supported by Air Force fighter planes, his unit pushed them back and took eighty-nine prisoners. Two of them were Chinese; Throckmorton's interrogators were certain of it. "But nobody back at division, or higher echelons, believed they were Chinese," remembered Throckmorton. These two, thought to be either deserters or stragglers, became the first Chinese POWs taken by Americans in this war.

The next day, on the east side of the Taebaeks, the ROK regiment that had been hurled back from the approaches to the Chosin Reservoir also took some prisoners. Alarmed by this stiff resistance and disturbed by reports that the ROKs' prisoners were Chinese, Almond, accompanied by First Lieutenant Alexander Haig, one of his aides, flew out to assess the situation firsthand. Through an interpreter, Almond interrogated the prisoners himself. Interviewed separately, they corroborated one another's stories. They said they were assigned to the 124th Division of the Chinese Communist forces and that another division was nearby.

Almond returned to Wonsan and immediately sent a personal radio message to MacArthur informing him that organized Chinese forces were now fighting in North Korea. In the meantime, Smith and Throckmorton resumed their advances following their separate routes. On October 31, Throckmorton's regiment was hit a second time, but his men broke through again. Unmolested, the battalion under Smith advanced farther this day. But on November 1, after he and Throckmorton were ordered by Major General John Church to halt, he was hit hard once more. Smith's reconnaissance patrols had gotten as close as eighteen miles from the Yalu and, hence, China; Throckmorton's about thirty. The two men were farther from home than any American ground commanders in combat would likely ever be again, and the Chinese prisoners and the stiff resistance had aroused their suspicions. They were becoming very concerned. The cold, snowy weather was a reminder of just how exposed they were. "By that time," Throckmorton recalled, "I could feel the hair raising on the back of my neck." Smith, for his part, had to wonder whether his luck had finally run out. He had survived the suicide mission undertaken by his task force back on July 5. This time he should have been nowhere near the dangerous situation in which he found himself. Orders for him to return immediately stateside had come in before this operation, but his commander had extended his duty so that he would have the honor of leading his unit all the way to the Yalu.

In Washington a few hours later, Truman, as his November 1 workday began, probably had the same sense of foreboding that Smith and Throckmorton had. In his morning report, Bedell Smith rendered the CIA's revised estimate of the situation. He reported that "fresh, newly equipped North Korean troops have appeared in the North Korean fighting, and it has been clearly established that Chinese Communist troops are also opposing UN forces." The CIA's new assessment was that the Chinese "probably genuinely fear an invasion of Manchuria despite the clear-cut definition of UN objectives." The agency was reacting to hard evidence this time — well-equipped enemy soldiers already encountered in the fight.

This ominous report was a hint of the kind of month Truman was going to have. So, too, was the attempt by a pair of Puerto Rican nationalists to kill him that afternoon. Their crude understanding of the current state of American politics led them to believe that murdering Truman would cause a revolution in the United States and that during the ensuing turmoil Puerto Rico would win independence. Their estimate, though farfetched, nevertheless indicates how fighting communism had polarized Democrats and Republicans and charged the political climate.

Back in Korea and Japan, intelligence officers' perceptions of what the Chinese army was up to were still overly influenced by what MacArthur wanted them to see. He did not want exaggerated fears engendering timidity and robbing him of the victory at hand. Military history is replete with examples of fear overtaking a victorious army on the march and bringing it to a halt long before a routed enemy has the capacity to turn and stop it. Accordingly, MacArthur's subordinates were minimizing the significance of the presence of Chinese soldiers. Almond had taken Willoughby to see the POWs below Chosin, and neither the latter nor Almond's own intelligence officer, Lieutenant Colonel William W. Quinn, was alarmed. They concluded that the CCF did not pose a danger because these Chinese were volunteers, so Almond ordered the X Corps to proceed according to plan.

Perhaps the most creative example of this sort of conforming of facts to prevailing assumptions was an intelligence estimate by Lieutenant Colonel James Tarkenton, who was Walker's intelligence officer. His career was on the rise because of Willoughby's patronage; however, his fortunes would soon decline very quickly. The Chinese prisoners taken in the west belonged to a multiplicity of battalions, and this led Tarkenton to the conclusion that Chinese leaders were forming regiments from battalions of many different divisions; it was a dubious way to minimize the enemy's numbers. He could not bring himself to consider that the reason the prisoners were from many different battalions was because there were many Chinese divisions in Korea. No one was going to accuse Tarkenton of being an alarmist — a serious charge in MacArthur's army.

Walker already had a reputation back at the Dai Ichi for not being aggressive enough; it dated back to those weeks of fighting in the Pusan perimeter. Consequently, Walker kept his apprehensions to himself, though he was now reluctant to press the offensive. The trouble his units had encountered during the past few days worried him. Through his chain of command, he ordered commanders such as Throckmorton and Brad Smith to withdraw their men to more defensible positions on the south bank of the Chongchon River. Personally, he wanted to link up with the X Corps at the "waist" of the peninsula, even farther south — roughly at a line connecting the cities of Sinanju and Hamhung on either coast — but he was reluctant to propose that to MacArthur. Instead, he formulated a stratagem to buy himself some time. He explained to MacArthur that the Eighth Army's offensive had been brought to a halt because of logistics problems.

MacArthur could not deny the supply problems his armies were contending with, given how rapidly they had advanced. Also obvious was that their offensives had stalled, especially that of the Eighth Army. He therefore decided to accede to Walker's wishes and allow both the Eighth Army and the X Corps to replenish and reorganize for a final thrust. MacArthur decided that in the meantime he would use airpower to "isolate the battlefield" and destroy the enemy by hitting "every means of communications and every installation, factory, city, [and] village" in it. Twelve bridges crossed the Yalu from Manchuria and he wanted destroyed that portion of each on the North Korean side.

To accomplish these orders, Stratemeyer was to fly his crews "to exhaustion if necessary." MacArthur seems not to have considered the use of atomic bombs, a move only Truman had the authority to order. The situation was not deemed that grave, it seems. Still unknown to the general was the extent of the Chinese intrusion; a quarter million of its soldiers were now marshaling in two northern regions of North Korea. MacArthur thought their number was about 35,000; this was the estimate he gave Ambassador Muccio.

There was one critical limitation that MacArthur imposed on Stratemeyer. His crews could not violate Chinese airspace. The Air Force general thought this restriction made the missions virtually impossible, but was willing to try. The border between North Korea and China ran down the middle of the Yalu, which followed a tortuous course through the mountains.

One of the idiosyncrasies of a unified command structure, which MacArthur's was, is that a senior officer may simultaneously be holding down more than one position — in parlance, he may be wearing more than one hat. In Stratemeyer's case, he was the ranking Air Force staff officer working for MacArthur and also commander of USAF's Far Eastern Air Force. The chain of command for the first responsibility passed through MacArthur and then to Collins and the Joint Chiefs; that for the latter passed through the Pacific Air Force (PACAF) commander in Hawaii and then to Vandenberg. After MacArthur ordered the air campaign, Stratemeyer passed word of it to PACAF. This news quickly got to Washington and shocked everybody — the Chiefs, Marshall, Acheson, Truman. MacArthur, for his part, had not notified anyone. The bombing of the bridges was a direct violation of the President's instructions of September 27. Complicating matters further was a US proposal being weighed by the UN Security Council. Acheson wanted the council to condemn Chinese troop movements into North Korea; American bombs falling on the Chinese side of the border would void this diplomatic initiative, which was deemed important. The allies, especially the British, would be highly agitated.

The bombers were practically on takeoff roll when Truman was notified. MacArthur was essentially forcing on Truman another fundamental policy change. Truman was flying home to Missouri again to cast his vote in the off-year congressional elections the next day when Acheson reached him by phone. They talked the matter over and were of like mind. Truman decided not to authorize the attacks on the bridges unless "there was an immediate and serious threat to the security of our troops." It was the first time Truman had countermanded a MacArthur field order. He wanted him to justify bombing the bridges. The same day, November 6 in Washington, the Chiefs cabled MacArthur that "until further orders, postpone all bombing of targets within five miles of Manchurian border" and provide reasons for bombing the bridges.

This was the most dramatic affirmation yet of Truman's intent to limit the air war. This was a new thing; before Korea, nations' airplanes attacked any targets that would directly or indirectly support the ground campaign. Being an old soldier and an all-out fighter himself, Truman probably disliked the idea about as much as MacArthur did, but he felt he had to keep the war from spreading. That night in his diary he commented generally on his job: "It's hell to be President of the Greatest Most Powerful Nation on Earth. I'd rather be 'first in the Iberian Village.' " Truman had always recognized the heavy burdens of responsibility his job entailed. However, it was not until this war in Korea that he came to realize just how much atomic weaponry had complicated the exercise of power and thus added to his burdens. Counting on using atomic bombs, he had reorganized the whole military and cut way back on its spending. But instead of fighting the Soviets in Europe, as anticipated, the United States had ended up fighting the Chinese in Asia. This wild turn of events was forcing him to change his thinking and upsetting many of his plans — for use of airpower, in particular — before they were ever implemented.

By contrast, MacArthur, being true to his World War II/Asian theater orientation, accepted no substitutes for total victory. Truman's limiting his actions "astonished" him, he later wrote. He actually drafted a cable — Hickey saw it — in which he requested his own "immediate relief." Korean War historian Clay Blair, Jr., saw this act as a clever ruse; he suggested that MacArthur knew that Hickey would immediately pass word upward through back channels, thus producing his desired effect. In his memoirs, MacArthur wrote that Hickey convinced him that he could not abandon his men at this point.

Whatever the reason, MacArthur did not resign and instead, within hours, shot off a cable even more startling than his orders to Stratemeyer. In it he described a situation almost antithetical to the reassuring perception he had related two days earlier to Muccio. He informed the Chiefs that

> men and material in large force are pouring across all bridges over the Yalu from Manchuria. This movement not only jeopardizes but threatens the ultimate destruction of the forces under my command. . . . The only way to stop this reinforcement . . . is the destruction of these bridges. . . . Every hour that this is postponed will be paid for dearly in American and United Nations blood. . . . Under the gravest protest that I can make, I am suspending this strike and carrying out your instructions.

He ended his message with this denigrating fillip: "I trust that the matter will be immediately brought to the attention of the President as I believe your instructions may well result in a calamity of major proportions for which I cannot accept the responsibility without his personal and direct understanding of the situation."

Bradley, who was taken aback by this vitriol, immediately called Truman in Independence. It was still November 6, election eve in the United States. Faced with the possibility that his top field commander would resign in protest, charging that the Commander in Chief was refusing to take steps to protect American soldiers in combat, Truman capitulated. He authorized MacArthur to have the Sinuiju bridges bombed. News of MacArthur's resignation would have broken as voters were preparing to go to the polls, a prospect Truman could not abide. As it was, Democrats lost twenty-eight seats in the House of Representatives and five in the Senate, Tydings and Lucas among them. The Democrats did manage to retain control of both bodies. But their control now seemed tenuous, as did their party's hold on the White House.

Bombing the Sinuiju bridges had no significant impact on what was going on in North Korea. But MacArthur's forcing Truman to change his mind about it showed the lengths to which the general was willing to go to impose his views. Only superficially was their estrangement a clash of personalities. They had come to have fundamentally different views about the use of power and what was possible in warfare during this new era of atomic weaponry. MacArthur was drawing on the past for his object lessons, whereas Truman, the first President to have to contend with the horrific dangers that weapons of mass destruction posed, had struck out on a new course.

MacArthur's behavior was going to result in a blowup with Truman unless the war ended first. For example, when MacArthur made the claim that Chinese were "pouring across" the bridges, he had no idea he was accurate. That he did not is made clear by the first of a number of communiqués he issued during the next couple of weeks — "posterity papers," as his detractors viewed them. This first one, issued November 6 from the Dai Ichi, read in part:

> The present situation is this. While the North Korean forces with which we were initially engaged have been destroyed or rendered impotent for military action, a new and fresh army faces us, backed up by a possibility of large alien reserves and adequate supplies within reach of the enemy but beyond the limits of our present sphere of military action. Whether and to what extent these reserves will be moved forward remains to be seen and is a matter of gravest international significance.

From this statement, it is obvious that MacArthur thought that Lin Piao's Fourth Field Army, which he described as "alien reserves," were still on the north side of the Yalu in Manchuria, "beyond the limits of our present sphere of military action." He also believed that, along with the North Koreans, the Chinese elements that had recently fought the Eighth Army and the X Corps had been rendered impotent.

This important piece of intelligence no doubt pleased the Chinese commander, who reinforced MacArthur's perception of the situation by having his units generally break contact with US and South Korean troops. Without MacArthur realizing it, Lin Piao had completed his battle plan's first phase, which was a cautious testing of his own troops and his foe. He would use the next few weeks planning, organizing, and getting supplies across the Yalu at night, while he awaited a propitious time to launch a major offensive. MacArthur would use this lull period the same way. Reinforcements were coming not only from the continental United States but also from other UN member states, whose leaders now eagerly wanted to have a role in the victory.

MacArthur expected to set his plan in motion on November 24. It called for Walker's Eighth to resume the offensive in the west this day and to push forward to the Yalu as quickly as possible. Three days later, Almond's X Corps in the east was to strike north — ROK divisions would sweep up the coastal plain and into the northeast panhandle; the First Marine Division, supported by the Seventh Infantry Division and other American units, would drive northwest over forty miles of mountains to the important crossroad town of Mupyong-ni in the Taebaeks, and there cut the line of communications of Communist units fighting the Eighth Army to the south. Worried that MacArthur had so split his forces that they could not support one another, the Chiefs had wanted this planned conjunction sooner, but had been reluctant to force it on him. His planning staff under Wright was responsible for his making this change, which Almond also encouraged.

MacArthur's finally agreeing to bring his forces together was one of the few concessions to anyone from the general, who now believed he belonged to the ages. His new manner of meeting important visitors reflected this demeanor. According to William J. Sebald, the ranking US diplomat in Tokyo, who with his wife, Edith, frequently escorted VIPs to MacArthur's residence, Jean MacArthur would greet them at the door and host them for cocktails, and then, with near-perfect timing, when the tedium of small talk had heightened anticipation of him, a curtain would be drawn suddenly and the man himself would stride through to greet his guests with his usual effusion.

So MacArthur was confident his final offensive would work, and he conveyed his certainty when he visited Eighth Army units on its eve. According to *Time*, this is what he told John Church (who since his advisory days had picked up a second star and command of a division): "I have already promised wives and mothers that the boys of the 24th Division will be back by Christmas. Don't make me a liar." A wire service reporter gave a similar account. Consistent with this reporting, some correspondents dubbed this offensive the "Home-for-Christmas Drive." Others called it the "End-the-War Offensive."

The Marines' jump-off point was the Chosin Reservoir, which is where they were on the twenty-fourth. This man-made body of water about twelve miles long is on a plateau forty-five hundred feet up. Vegetation around the reservoir is fairly sparse, mostly brush and scrub trees, so erosion cuts countless deep arroyos into the water's edge. The result is a very irregular shoreline with inlets as jagged as broken glass — which is what, in fact, the reservoir's surface now resembled. Beneath a surface glaze was more than a foot of ice. In these mountains, winter had set in. Temperatures at night were dropping to minus twenty-seven degrees Fahrenheit. And the wind seemed to blow incessantly, sometimes up to thirty-five miles per hour.

Getting to the reservoir had not been easy for the Marines. Almond had ordered them up that way pell-mell as soon as they got off the ships at Wonsan on October 26. The last leg of the route in particular was nothing more than a one-lane trail that made a winding, steep, 2,500-foot climb in just eight miles, and edged along cliffs. This route — Funchilin Pass, as it is called — brought them out on the plateau. The road then passed north through the village of Koto-ri, two miles in, and then, eleven miles farther, through Hangaru-ri, which is only one and a half miles of marshland from the southern tip of the reservoir.

Complicating this trek for the Marines were Chinese soldiers who began shooting at them when they started the climb. O. P. Smith had worried about this possibility, but it was Almond's notion that "there was nobody out there," Smith recalled, for that is what Almond told him when he protested. About six thousand Chinese were in the attack force. Though unable to concentrate his much larger unit on them, Smith's men drove them away. Their subsequent reports about captured Chinese were ignored, as other such reports had been. Because of Almond, who mirrored MacArthur's every mood, an "end-of-war atmosphere" pervaded in all X Corps units except the First Marines, who, because of Smith, were wary. MacArthur had already told Almond that he would be senior occupation officer for North Korea.

What had worried Smith most since arriving alongside the reservoir was the possibility of getting trapped up there in the mountains. Funchilin Pass was the only way out south. He complained without success to Almond about this, too. Lieutenant Colonel William J. McCaffrey, Almond's deputy chief of staff, saw Smith's point. "We were all trying to get General Almond to exercise some caution in attacking over the mountains . . . ," McCaffrey said later, "but General Almond was not about to protest an order from General MacArthur."

Actually, Almond was inclined to move with abandon anyway, even without MacArthur's pushing him. Smith, who deemed him "brilliant," also thought he was so "egotistical" that he was blinded by his own arrogance. When the two first met back at the Dai Ichi, Almond had kept calling Smith "son," though both were major generals and Smith was older and had an earlier date of rank. But Smith's disdain for Almond was rooted in professional considerations, not personal ones, beginning with the disagreement they had had over the pace of the post-Inchon Marine advance on Seoul. Smith himself was being a little reckless in confiding his feelings to newsmen — though one, at least, concurred. This reporter had covered Almond's division in Italy during the previous war and said he could not understand "why they gave him a Corps." According to Smith, the reporter said Almond had maneuvered his World War II division so much that he was defeated by a single German battalion.

Another officer who, as of November 24, 1950, started having misgivings about Almond's impetuous style was Lieutenant Colonel Donald Faith, a battalion commander in the Seventh Infantry Division. During World War II, he had served as Ridgway's aide for more than three years. The son of a brigadier general, Faith enlisted in his home state of Virginia before Pearl Harbor and earned his commission through Officer Candidate School at Fort Benning, Georgia. A dental problem had barred admission to West Point. Faith's postwar assignments included service as a member of the joint military advisory group in China during the civil war between the Nationalists and the Communists. He had not yet led a unit in combat, except for a limited role in the Inchon landings, but clearly this thirty-two-year-old was a young man with a bright future in the Army.

With MacArthur's concurrence, Almond had decided that he wanted a regiment-size force from the Seventh to join the Marines at Chosin. When the Marines turned west to pass over the mountains, the regiment would protect their flank by first taking up positions on the east side of the reservoir. From there, it would also spearhead the Seventh's charge north toward the Yalu.

Almond had been unable to alert Seventh Division units that new orders were imminent until the evening of November 24. Earlier in the day, Walker had gotten the Eighth Army back on the offensive, but Almond was still playing catch-up because of problems with sea mines. On November 25 he at last issued his subordinate commanders their formal instructions for MacArthur's final offensive. They were to be at various specified jump-off points at noon on the twenty-sixth, which was less than twenty-four hours away. On the twenty-seventh, the X Corps was to attack.

From the outset, it was almost impossible for Faith and the other commanders in the Army regiment ordered up to the reservoir to execute these orders. His battalion at the time was traveling up the coastal plain, positioning itself to join the advance toward the Yalu. This was the easy avenue. For the outfits ahead of them, mostly ROK units, the going had been a breeze because the North Koreans had abandoned these flatlands for the security of the mountains. In tactical situations, airpower had become an overwhelming force since the disjointed effort of the early weeks of the war. To avoid destruction from the air, the enemy now traveled almost exclusively at night and in the mountains. This was where Faith's men headed, upon receipt of their new orders.

Moving by convoy toward Chosin, they got as far as the foot of Funchilin

Pass that evening. Few of them slept well subsequently because of the unremitting din coming from the roadway. Two-and-a-half-ton trucks whined and screamed around the clock, their drivers transporting up to the plateau the incredibly large piles of stocks and ammunition needed to sustain about 25,000 soldiers on the offensive. In some places, engineers had gouged out another lane along the edge of some of the cliffs to facilitate movement in both directions. Military police made some order out of this chaos, blowing whistles and bellowing at drivers to keep traffic moving where less than a month earlier the wind was the dominant sound. Even stalled vehicles did not stop traffic for long; they were pushed off the precipice posthaste and the frenetic shuttling resumed quickly.

Faith's battalion wound its way to the top the next morning, November 25. There, road signs pointed this way and that to different units like signposts in the New England countryside. At Hangaru-ri, the convoy made a right turn and followed the markers pointing to the Fifth Marine Regiment's positions, a route that took them along the reservoir, which was to their left. Faith's men and the rest of an Army regimental combat team were to relieve the Fifth so that it could rejoin its division, that under Smith's command, on the other side for the offensive.

By midafternoon they had reached an assembly point called Hudong-ni, a former village, about halfway up the reservoir. There Lieutenant Colonel Raymond L. Murray, the Fifth's commander, briefed Faith on the disposition of his Marines and enemy activity. He told him that earlier that day a platoon-size reconnaissance patrol supported by two tanks had advanced almost to the northern tip of the reservoir, near the dam, and had fought some brief skirmishes with a few scattered groups of Chinese soldiers. They had killed five, captured one, and destroyed an abandoned 75-millimeter gun. They had searched for signs of activity by large-scale units but had found none. One of Murray's battalion commanders had reconnoitered by helicopter an area even farther north, and also found nothing.

Murray's report basically reinforced the appraisal that Faith's men had immediately formed, which was that up on this plateau the elements were more worrisome than the enemy and, in fact, were one and the same. The long nights made it seem even worse; sunset these days was at about four-thirty and sunrise, seven forty-five. During this long interval, all a soldier wanted to do was burrow into a relatively warm hole and sleep. To do this, he had to scrape away snow and break through a layer of rocky tundra.

In spite of these conditions, Faith's men slept well their first night on the plateau. Too well, thought Second Lieutenant James Mortrude, a Reserve Officers' Training Corps graduate from the University of Washington. At two in the morning, during a snowfall, he crawled from his bedroll to check his platoon's perimeter defense and found only one of his guards awake. Checking adjacent platoons, he discovered the same alarming complacency. Only two or three guards were awake along his company's front. The next morning he punished the malingerers in his platoon, making them dig latrines, but the other platoon leaders resented his intrusion into their areas. Only the company commander's intercession prevented a fistfight.

Even by this time, the Army's supply problems had not been resolved. None of Faith's men had winter liners for their coats and most did not have long underwear. Some did not even have winter gloves. Many of them tried to get liners from Marines, who informed them that they had only the ones they wore. The Marines viewed them with a sense of superiority and pity, as professionals might amateurs who did not know what they were up against.

What his battalion was up against is precisely what Faith was determined to learn from Brigadier General Henry Hodes, the Seventh's assistant division commander, who drove up to the reservoir the first morning. Unfortunately, he did not know either. How well the Eighth Army was doing on the other side of the mountains would have been some indication, but it was too early to tell. On the other hand, nothing had yet changed anyone's positive estimate, and that included Faith's. He wanted to go on the offensive as soon as some tanks arrived, but Hodes denied him permission.

After the general departed, Faith decided to develop some intelligence of his own. He took his company commanders and platoon leaders six miles up the road to the forward Marine positions for a firsthand look. They learned that Marine patrols sent out that day had not noted significant enemy activity. However, back in the area of Faith's command post, his intelligence officer, who was interviewing North Korean refugees, was developing a different picture. The refugees were saying they had seen Chinese soldiers who claimed they were going to retake the plateau within the next few days. The caution this encouraged was reinforced by Murray when he informed Faith that his regiment of Marines would be pulling out for the opposite side of the reservoir early the next day.

Faith's immediate superior arrived on the scene later that day. This was Colonel Allan D. MacLean, who would command the battalions forming up east of Chosin, a force that would be designated the Thirty-second Infantry Regiment. MacLean was a forty-three-year-old West Point graduate with a reputation for being aggressive and ambitious. He was respected for his practice of staying up with his lead units, where the fighting was. Predictably, he approved Faith's request to move his battalion into the Marines' abandoned forward positions the next morning. At the time MacLean made this decision, he thought that his other two infantry battalions would be arriving on the heels of Faith's men and would reinforce them. One would; the other would never make it.

In addition to his three infantry battalions, MacLean's regimental combat team included an intelligence-and-reconnaissance (I&R) platoon, a medical company, a communications detachment, a tank company composed of twenty-two tanks, and an artillery battalion that was short one artillery battery but supplemented by a battery of M-19s and M-16s. Each of the latter was a deadly combination of guns mounted on a weapons carrier, a tanklike vehicle. The four M-19s had dual 40-millimeter Bofor antiaircraft guns; the four M-16s, four .50-caliber machine guns. Deployed as anti-personnel weapons, as they were in this case, they were incredible killing machines. The M-19s could fire, on a three-mile flat trajectory, shells that exploded like a grenade. On automatic for a minute, an M-19's destructive power was equivalent to that of 240 fragmentation grenades. The quad-fifties on the M-16s fired altogether at a rate of eighteen hundred rounds per minute.

On the twenty-seventh, Faith moved his battalion forward, as planned. Within a couple of hours, Lieutenant Colonel William Reilly's infantry battalion and another lieutenant colonel's artillery battalion began arriving. MacLean had them take up a position on the south side of an inlet that was about four road miles behind Faith's men.

The I&R platoon made a timely arrival that day, too, and MacLean immediately put them to work. He ordered them to check out a report that three hundred Chinese soldiers were in a village to the east that was located up a road to another lake, called Fusin Reservoir, at an even higher altitude. Within minutes they set out up a narrow road in jeeps equipped with mounted machine guns. After the last of them crested a hill, they were never seen again.

The Chinese division that swallowed this tiny force began attacking MacLean's undersized regiment shortly before midnight on November 27/28. Several hours earlier, on the other side of the reservoir, three Chinese divisions had begun attacking Smith's Marines, who that afternoon had begun an offensive of their own. Among the first in MacLean's regiment to die was Captain Edward Scullion, commander of Faith's A Company. He had bolted from his partially submerged command post when he heard rifle fire. Before getting shot, he had only had time to yell in wonderment about what was happening. Scullion's yelling woke Captain Edward Stamford, a Marine forward air controller assigned to the battalion. The first thing Stamford saw was the fur-rimmed face of a Chinese soldier staring at him through the entrance of his bunker. Stamford was still in his sleeping bag and before he could react, the man tossed a grenade. It exploded between Stamford's legs, but, remarkably, no fragments struck him. Some did hit two of his men, but the three escaped through a slit trench. Many others were not so lucky. They were killed where they lay, still in their sleeping bags. The Chinese had reconnoitered the regiment's forward positions well. They overran Scullion's command post and his mortar platoon from the rear before there was any alarm.

The noise alerted Faith, but he and his staff decided that South Koreans attached to Scullion's company were blasting shadows. They often would wake up shooting, beset by a perpetual state of nerves. They had had very little military training before being issued a uniform and a rifle and being sent off to help save their country. Two of Faith's staff officers confidently strode up to investigate. They got to the base of the hill on which Scullion had his command post before being challenged by someone. They did not understand what he said, but, thinking he was an ROK, they responded with the code word. The man who challenged them had been prone and facing away, but abruptly turned. This was the only notice the Americans had that he was an enemy soldier. Each dived for cover, but Captain Robert Haynes was too slow. A bullet hit him in the stomach. Captain Edward Bigger heard him exhale, as if someone had slugged him.

The Chinese were flowing into the low areas, surrounding the Americans and the ROKs up on an array of hills, and then attacking, which they did carefully. There were no suicide assaults by "hordes" of them, which is how American reporters fairly accurately described the reckless charges North Korean officers ordered. The Chinese hallmark was unremitting pressure. Against MacLean's unit, mortars were the heaviest supporting fire they had except for one North Korean tank and a self-propelled gun. And these were knocked out by a single GI, Corporal James Godfrey, a young man who because of being ordered to fight this strange war had discovered that shooting a 75-millimeter recoilless rifle was one of the things in life he did best. With his last round, he stopped about a hundred Chinese who were coming at him. Instantaneously, they seemed to vanish.

Godfrey was one of Faith's heroes this first night. Another was Stamford, the Marine. With Scullion dead, he took charge of A Company. As Marine air liaison, he was out of the chain of command, but a young company mortar officer asked him to do something. Stamford had fought as a ground soldier during World War II, before becoming a pilot. He got people firing back, and before long, the attackers, as frightened as the defenders, had backed off. A Company then held its high ground tenuously throughout the night.

Faith's battalion was not the only one on the east side hit this night. The other two down by the inlet had it even worse. In Reilly's battalion, the company that fought best was filled with replacements right out of an Army stockade. Inspired by their example, the South Koreans with them did well, too. Most of Reilly's other companies broke and ran. Captain Robert Kitz, K Company commander, was heard screaming that he would shoot anyone who did, but he made no difference. Before long, the ground outside Reilly's command post resembled an assembly area. Americans and Koreans alike convened there, looking for relative security. The scene was chaotic, a babble of voices. Reilly could not tell exactly when the Chinese came shooting their way into this scene. In every direction, guns had been firing; and with an American's tin ear for languages, the enemy's chatter sounded to him like his ally's. When they started machine-gunning his command post, he knew they were there. Then they started tossing grenades, which was their standard tactic. They always used lots of grenades. Eventually they started climbing through the command post's windows. By that time, those trapped inside had divided up which windows to guard. Reilly had decided to take them on sitting down. Seated in front of his window, he killed with his pistol the first three who tried to get through. During a lull that followed, he ran around the room trying to help shore up defenses. A Lieutenant Anderson, his assistant operations officer, whose right arm had been blown off, was having trouble getting his weapon unsheathed and, in shock, could not comprehend why. Reilly unsheathed it for him and put it in his remaining hand. This was the last thing Reilly remembered. Another grenade knocked him unconscious. The Chinese thought he was dead when they stripped him of anything of value, such as ammunition. No wonder; everyone else, including Anderson, was dead, and Reilly had four wounds — one in the right leg from a .50-caliber bullet, one above his right eye from a grenade concussion, a bullet hole through his right foot, and mortar fragments in his hands and upper legs.

The Chinese were coming from the east, down from the mountains where the reconnaissance platoon had disappeared. Reaching the reservoir, they started blocking the road and moving against MacLean's battalions from all directions. Two artillery batteries were overrun. A rear assault on inlet positions was abruptly stopped by Captain James R. McClymont, commander of the battery of M-16s and M-19s. Like Reilly, McClymont had not heard the fighting north of him. What alerted him were mortar rounds, which had begun falling around his command post at about dawn. With light-enhancing binoculars, he spotted an enemy column coming up the road. He was certain they were Chinese, dressed as they were in flapped caps, quilted coats, and tennis shoes, so he ordered his commander of the M-19s to open up. Tracer rounds leaped out and then the high-explosive shells began bursting amid the Chinese. Within seconds, McClymont observed no movement. About eighty of the enemy had died in an instant.

Actually, both sides did a lot of dying this night. The medical company met a fate similar to that of the reconnaissance platoon. Caught in traffic back in Funchilin Pass, its little convoy of vehicles did not arrive up on the plateau until late this first evening of battle. The company's commander ordered his men to stop at Hudong-ni — where MacLean had set up his rear command post — while he decided what to do next. For his decision, they would suffer; so would he. MacLean, up front with Faith, had left no instructions. Captain Robert E. Drake, commander of the tank company, urged his counterpart to keep his unit at Hudong-ni and follow his tanks up the next morning. He had been forward earlier in the day himself. Unable to find MacLean, Drake had followed Faith's recommendation to return to Hudong-ni for the night.

For some reason, the medical company's commander decided that he should move forward. His mind was probably on the offensive scheduled to begin the next day. Neither he nor anyone else there at Hudong-ni that night was aware of the fighting as close as a couple of miles forward. Communication between units was almost nonexistent. In some places, lines had been cut. In other situations, they had not been laid; units had anticipated attacking, not being attacked. And two-way radios were ineffective because of distance and terrain.

The medical company pulled out shortly after midnight and quickly disappeared into darkness. They got as far as a roadblock the Chinese had set up near a hairpin turn around the base of a hill designated 1221. At that point they were ambushed. Only four or five escaped; the rest were killed or captured and their vehicles destroyed. The company first sergeant, almost hysterical, made it back to Hudong-ni to tell Drake what had happened.

Daylight belonged to the Americans, who began asserting themselves on both sides of the reservoir as the Chinese withdrew from open areas. Airpower, as noted, was the major reason US forces and their allies were stronger when the sun was shining. They were highly mechanized and highly mobile in other respects, too — and this also made them more effective during daylight hours. Moreover, the daylight suited the psychology of the American soldier better than the dark of night; stealth has never been his hallmark.

Stamford reverted to being an air controller when Marine aircraft from the carrier *Leyte* appeared overhead at first light, bringing to bear their firepower on the Chinese attacking Faith's men. Reilly's were not so lucky; a First Lieutenant Johnson, their Fifth Air Force forward air controller, had been killed the night before. Close air-support strikes for Reilly's battalion were not nearly as accurate. Stamford worked with dramatic effect. All day the planes came and most of them carried canisters of napalm, a gasoline in jellied form. On impact, it floods into holes and trenches where soldiers hide, ignites with a scorching scream, and becomes a roiling orange-black inferno. This day such flames burned to death hundreds of Chinese. Many more, who in terror took flight and escaped the flames, died when they sucked superhot air into their lungs. Others who fled were machine-gunned by Faith's men. Whatever way a man was killed this day, within twenty-four hours he was frozen stiff like everyone else who died fighting up on this purgatory of fire and ice.

The pace had now quickened for the American side; the arrival of general officers was a sure sign. Smith helicoptered up to establish his command post at Hangaru-ri. Later that morning Almond flew in from Hamhung aboard a little L-17 to confer with him. Accompanying Almond was young Haig, who would go home a highly decorated officer as a result of his having served in proximity to Almond. The latter carried Silver Star medals in his pockets to award on the spot to whomever he deemed worthy of them, or whenever awarding them served his purposes. The Silver Star is the nation's third-highest combat award. Almond had picked up this habit from the French during World War I; he deemed American award procedures too bureaucratic. He ended up awarding Haig two Silver Stars. Up to this point in the war, no general was up front near the fighting more than Almond was, and when he and Haig got themselves into and out of a particularly dangerous situation, he was inclined to reward his protégé.

Another general on the plateau that morning was Hodes, the Seventh's assistant division commander. He had spent the night in a schoolhouse in Hudong-ni. Early this morning he decided that Drake should lead three of his tank platoons forward to check out what had happened to the medical company; Hodes would go along. He, Drake, and the first sergeant who had survived the ambush of the medical company rode in an open jeep behind Drake's command tank, followed by fifteen other tanks. This formidable force had traveled about two miles up the road when the first sergeant told them they were approaching the scene, which was hidden around a bend in the road on the opposite side of Hill 1221. Drake halted the column, and he and his two passengers got out of the jeep to match their map with the landscape. The first sergeant was motioning when a rifle shot cracked and he fell dead, a bullet wound in his head. A Chinese marksman had killed him instantly. Hodes scrambled for cover and Drake leapt into his command tank. Thus drawn into battle, the twenty-seven-year-old ordered it to begin. He told one platoon of five tanks to attack directly down the road; another platoon to do so to the right and into a low area, to protect that flank; and the third to advance to the left, directly up and over Hill 1221. There was no supporting infantry.

Soon it was evident to Hodes that the assault was an exercise in frustration with much larger implications for all of MacLean's men on the east side of the reservoir. When the tanks on the road neared the burned-out medical convoy, enemy weapon teams manning American-made 3.5-inch rocket launchers knocked out the first two. Their crews escaped to other tanks with covering fire, though some were wounded. Meanwhile, the tanks down below to the right became mired in a bog, after breaking through a frozen crust. Crews ended up having to machine-gun one another's vehicles clean of Chinese infantrymen, who swarmed down the slopes and climbed aboard to try pulling open the hatches. The tanks proceeding up Hill 1221 had a much different problem: they could not get traction on the frozen slope because the ascent was too steep. One of them slid back down out of control. Another threw a track.

Hodes decided help was needed; infantry, at least, and possibly air. Though he seems to have remained intent on prosecuting the offensive east of the reservoir, the thought surely occurred to him that most of MacLean's regiment, which was north of the roadblock, might be trapped, should they have to retreat. He returned to Hudong-ni for help, while Drake and his men kept at it until afternoon, when they also withdrew. As the day wore on, Drake observed hundreds of enemy soldiers in the mountains above to the east, moving south in long lines on what turned out to be Mongolian ponies. Though this mode of transportation was primitive, Drake found the composite scene ominous, given their numbers and that the Chinese above him were making progress south while his unit, trying to move in the opposite direction, was stopped cold. These Chinese were moving to his rear.

The same thought occurred to Faith, MacLean, and Hodes, who also saw them. Hodes had some other bad news to assimilate as well. While at Hudong-ni, he was informed that the infantry battalion MacLean was awaiting was stuck down at the bottom of Funchilin Pass; once more, the Chinese had blocked the traffic flow. Temporarily, it was assumed. They had done so from time to time. Presently it was too great a leap in logic to contemplate that Smith's huge Marine division, Inchon's heroes, and everybody else up on the plateau, might be trapped. Hodes decided to continue on south to Hangaru-ri to ask Smith for help and to find Almond, maybe. Subordinates easily encouraged him to travel by tank, instead of jeep.

The trouble of the trip did not serve his purposes. Smith told him he had no infantry to spare. And since Hodes arrived in the afternoon, he missed connecting with Almond, who, that morning, after taking a helicopter north from Hangaru-ri to MacLean and Faith's command post and back, had driven down off the plateau by jeep to get a close look at problems in the pass. As matters developed, his vehicle was one of the last to get through before the Chinese blocked the way.

Almond's visit with MacLean and Faith was memorable. He had wanted to buck them up and spur them on — though MacLean did not need encouragement. He told Almond that he thought his men could hold on until his remaining infantry battalion arrived on the scene, and that he could then go on the offensive. MacLean might have been parroting what he thought Almond wanted to hear. Whatever the case, Almond would have ignored any naysaying by him, as he had done with Smith. Negative reaction to Almond came from Faith, not MacLean.

Faith was already in a brooding mood when Almond arrived. Normally, when a junior officer gets the attention of a general, he is pleased, but the sight of Almond alighting did not lift Faith's impending sense of doom. A number of considerations influenced him. The Chinese attack had been very strong and taken him completely by surprise. But for the heroics of a few, they might have rolled up one of his flanks and done untold harm. And they still held the highest hill in Faith's defense perimeter, which they had captured the night before. His men had been trying all morning to dislodge them and could not, even with air support. Faith also had to be troubled that he could not communicate with the battalions behind him. Furthermore, for a lieutenant colonel, Faith had an unusually developed sense for the way large operations felt when they were going well; this he had learned from being at Ridgway's side so long. Everything felt wrong about this one.

So he was upset, and now Almond would make him bitter, by playing him to be the fool. According to US Army historian Martin Blumenson, this is what Almond told Faith: "The enemy who is delaying you for the moment is nothing more than remnants of Chinese divisions fleeing north. . . . We're still attacking and we're going all the way to the Yalu. Don't let a bunch of Chinese laundrymen stop you." Almond ordered Faith to resume the offensive. MacLean, who was present, did not object. The discussion was not prolonged.

When they finished, Almond said he wanted to award some Silver Stars. He said he had three and wanted to give one to Faith. Visibly annoyed with the idea, Faith protested, suggesting that others were more deserving; but Almond would not be denied and told him to round up two others. Coincidentally, Lieutenant Everett F. Smalley, a platoon leader who had been wounded the night before, was sitting nearby, and Sergeant George A. Stanley, who worked in the headquarters mess and had fought well, was walking by. Faith ordered them over, and while Haig dutifully wrote down in his notebook their full names, Almond pinned Silver Stars on their uniforms during a brief ceremony. Smalley had labored in the vineyards long enough to know that getting this medal was a very special honor. Afterward, he could not control his emotions. He burst forth with the good news. "Hey, guys," he was heard screaming, "I won the Silver Star, but I don't know what the hell for!" Faith reacted as emotionally, but much differently. After Almond lifted off, a number of witnesses saw him rip the medal from his uniform and sling it into the snow. Lieutenant Hugh R. May was close enough to hear him say of Almond, "What a damned [something]!" The last word he could not discern.

Faith surely had intensified his anger by unconsciously comparing Almond with Ridgway. Unlike Almond, Ridgway traveled to the front lines not just to be seen but to listen, observe, and react. Had Almond been the type to double-check assumptions that supported his thinking, he might have stopped to investigate at Reilly's command post, where he would have found that battalion commander seriously wounded and his staff dead. That discovery would have forced a sensible man into some rethinking; however, Almond was not doing his own thinking. MacArthur, back at the Dai Ichi, more than five hundred miles away, was doing it for him.

It so happened that MacArthur was changing both their minds about the time Almond left Faith's forward position. By early afternoon, November 28, 1950, the fog had lifted for MacArthur. Though still underestimating the enemy's numbers, he finally saw what had been there for weeks — huge, organized Chinese forces in North Korea. Communist China had entered the war, robbed him of victory, and was now trying to destroy his armies. That this might happen was a real possibility. Faith's precarious situation was indicative of the whole.

In the west, the Chinese offensive had begun during the early evening hours of November 25, though this was not fully realized by UN commanders until a few days later. By the morning of November 26, the ROK II Corps, which composed Walker's right flank, had ceased to exist as a coherent fighting force.

Throckmorton, Brad Smith, and their units were luckier than these ROK divisions. The opening Chinese drive missed them completely. But by November 28, when MacArthur had come to grips with his desperate situation, Throckmorton and Smith were withdrawing as quickly as they could, though in good order, to support what Walker called "fighting withdrawals." Like the fighting, the going was difficult. Conditions were not conducive to travel; this day thousands of UN vehicles were edging southerly once again, headlights on, through a blinding snowstorm. Conceivably the ROK II Corps's demise could lead to the entrapment of them all.

By late afternoon on the twenty-eighth, MacArthur's assessment had crystallized to the point that he could describe it in writing. He sent off a long radio message to the Joint Chiefs and followed that up with a press release, Communiqué No. 14.

Truman got word of MacArthur's transformed appraisal at 6:15 AM, Washington time, on the twenty-eighth. Bradley reached him at Blair House by phone, remarking that the Chinese had "come in with both feet." Mac-Arthur's message, which Bradley read to the President, stated that

> all hope of localization of the Korean conflict to enemy forces composed of NK troops with alien token elements can now be completely abandoned. . . . No pretext of minor support [by the People's Republic of China] under the guise of volunteerism or other subterfuge now has the slightest validity. We face an entirely new war. . . . It [is] quite evident that our present strength of force is not sufficient to meet this undeclared war by the Chinese with the inherent advantages which accrue thereby to them. . . . This command has done everything humanly possible within its capabilities but is now faced with conditions beyond its control and its strength.

MacArthur was saying that Truman was going to have to lay aside well-intentioned thoughts of limited warfare.

The pressure on the President was enormous. He had led the nation right up to the brink of another world war. He had tried to outflank the Republican right by ordering MacArthur to unify the two Koreas by force. Mac-Arthur's failure to do so now made Truman and his party even more vulnerable to charges that Democrats were soft on communism. As earlier, his determination to limit the conflict would be complicated by his theater commander, who shared the views of his political opponents and was their hero. What made Truman's predicament the worst possible political scenario was that the foe was the hated Chinese Communists; Republicans had for months been accusing Democrats of selling out Chiang's Nationalists to them. The Republican right wing had sought to make Marshall symbolic of this alleged deceit; McCarthy called him "a living lie" during a speech on the Senate floor. Now these same accusers would relentlessly press Truman to enlarge the war and end the "China problem" once and for all. This confluence of forces made some sort of upheaval inevitable.

Truman convened his daily staff meeting several hours after Bradley relayed MacArthur's shocking news. A keen observer present was author John Hersey, who was working on a profile of the President for the *New Yorker*. Before the dramatic turn of events in Korea, Hersey had been granted approval to attend. According to the author, Truman opened the meeting without mention of the crisis. Routine matters were addressed in what seemed to be customary fashion. These done, Truman fell silent, as did the others in the room.

"For a few moments," Hersey wrote,

> he shifted papers back and forth and straightened a pair of scissors and two paper cutters. . . . He had suddenly drooped a little; it appeared that something he would have liked to forget was back in his mind, close behind his hugely magnified eyes.
>
> "We've got a terrific situation on our hands," Truman said in a very quiet, solemn voice. "General Bradley called me at six-fifteen this morning. He told me a terrible message had come from General MacArthur."

He then summarized the message and things to be done in response in Washington.

"In outlining his concrete plans and acts," Hersey wrote,

> the President had hidden, as indeed he had all through the staff meeting up to this point, his feelings about this new development, with which he had lived for only about four hours. Now he paused for a few seconds, and suddenly all his driven-down emotions seemed to pour into his face. His mouth drew tight, his cheeks flushed. For a moment, it almost seemed as if he would sob. Then, in a voice that was of absolute personal courage — he said, "This is the worst situation we have had yet. We'll have to meet it as we've met all the rest. I've talked already this morning with Bradley, Marshall, Acheson, Harriman, and [Secretary of the Treasury John] Snyder, and they all agree with me that we're capable of meeting this thing. I know you fellows will work with us on it, and that we'll meet it."

About thirty minutes later in Tokyo, MacArthur convened a memorable meeting of his own. There it was late, 9:50 PM. MacArthur had taken the extraordinary step of ordering Walker and Almond to leave the front and in secret travel to Japan. He wanted to deliberate what to do next with them and his senior staff — Joy, Stratemeyer, Hickey, Willoughby, Whitney, and Wright. The site for the meeting was MacArthur's embassy residence. It started late because of Almond, who had been driving down off the reservoir when MacArthur decided he wanted him and Walker in Tokyo as soon as possible.

MacArthur asked his two senior field commanders lots of questions and, as was typical, delivered long monologues, analyzing the situation aloud. Judging from the cable that had nearly overwhelmed Truman, MacArthur had already decided to call off the offensive and go onto the defensive. By contrast, Walker and especially Almond were optimistic. As usual, both must have been anticipating what MacArthur wanted to hear, and were no doubt exhilarated that for once they were more confident than he. Walker thought that his forces could establish a defense line north and east of Pyongyang and hold that capital city. Almond believed that the First Marine Division and the Seventh Infantry Division, of which MacLean's regiment was a part, would resume the offensive soon.

For a time, the men discussed the possibility of forming the Eighth Army and the X Corps into a defense line across the waist of the Korean Peninsula. But this was dismissed quickly as implausible because each UN division would have been forced to defend a twenty-mile front. The discussions eventually focused on how best to help the Eighth Army, which seemed more hard-pressed. Picking up on Almond's confidence, Wright proposed ordering across the peninsula Almond's freshest unit, the Third Infantry Division. Eleven days earlier it had arrived from the States and was taking up positions down below Funchilin Pass to protect the Marines' left flank. Wright argued that it could be diverted from that mission.

MacArthur was unsettled about what to do when at one-thirty in the morning he ended deliberations so all could sleep. He had Walker and Almond stay over; before noon he would have orders for them. His thinking at this point was that Walker would be fortunate to hold Pyongyang as he said he could, and that Almond was wrong in thinking he could get the offensive going again up at the reservoir. Until the last couple of days, MacArthur had thought that the only enemy he faced up there were remnants of three divisions. Given the scale of Chinese intervention, intelligence estimates had doubled that to six full divisions. Actually, there were twelve.

Back in Korea, on all fronts, fighting intensified as MacArthur conducted his council of war. It was the second night of it for those east of the reservoir. The Chinese were attacking and regrouping, adding reserves about every thirty minutes. American mortar crews worked without letup, hoping to hit assembly areas. During the night some gun barrels split like wood; they were so hot and the air was so cold, the stress on the metal was too much. Once, at least, a mortar crew did hit an assembly area. It was an accidental strike. Mortrude, the platoon leader, had called for mortar fire along a ridge from which snipers were hitting his men. The first ranging round was long and hit behind it, but the explosion brought loud cries of pain. Immediately, Mortrude ordered fire for effect at repeat range, and blood-curdling screams accompanied these hits. He and his men were elated, this being war.

These hits brought only temporary relief in one sector. For Faith and those with him in his command post, the sounds of battle got closer and closer. His men were being forced to give ground. At one in the morning, his time, about thirty minutes after MacArthur had adjourned his meeting,

Faith ordered most of those in his command post to get outside and defend it. The situation had begun to deteriorate rapidly. The Chinese had turned A Company's left flank. At two, MacLean decided that Faith should lead his battalion in retreat to Reilly's positions south of the inlet, four miles down the road.

Getting the message out was not easy. Runners had to be sent to some platoons. However, at four-thirty that morning, the first of about sixty vehicles started edging south. Columns of soldiers on foot preceded them. Faith had ordered all cargoes in trucks unloaded and the wounded placed on board. No wounded were knowingly left behind. A Company's First Platoon was abandoned, however. Positioned as they were on the far left flank, these soldiers had been cut off and surrounded. Another platoon had tried to save them but was finally ordered to save itself and depart. The retreat caught the enemy by surprise. Pursuit was slow. Some speculated that the Chinese were attracted to the large stores of food left behind.

MacLean remained steadfastly optimistic even as a passenger in Faith's wretched baggage train. He still held to the belief that he could resume the offensive when his missing infantry battalion joined his other two. Relaying MacLean's instructions, no doubt, Faith told May, who was his motor officer, not to destroy any vehicles left behind that would not start because of the cold; just disable them. According to May, "it was the intent to reoccupy these positions within 24 hours."

Shortly after dawn, MacLean found reason to justify his optimism. Riding in his command jeep with his driver, his radioman, and another officer, he had just arrived at the north side of the inlet when warned to stop. This word came down from some of his soldiers who were trekking south on parallel high ground, serving as lookouts. They could see some enemy soldiers attacking Reilly's men and the artillery battalion. Artillery and rifle fire could be heard, so a firefight was obviously in progress. While surveying this scene on the opposite side of the inlet, MacLean suddenly spotted a column of soldiers coming from the south. "Those are my boys!" he exclaimed. Lieutenant Colonel Richard R. Reidy's long-overdue Second Battalion was finally arriving, he thought.

Almost immediately these men were fired upon and a fight erupted. MacLean thought his men were firing at one another — Reilly's versus Reidy's — and that he had to intervene quickly. The inlet was frozen over, so impulsively he began striding across the several hundred yards or so of ice, unescorted.

The realization that the troop column was shooting at him came too late. He was observed falling on the ice three or four times and was hit at least once. Since he kept going forward, MacLean appeared not to have comprehended that the soldiers he was approaching were Chinese until some of them ran out on the ice and took him captive. What happened to him would remain a mystery until after the war. Another American soldier would tell how he and MacLean, in early December, were among a group of prisoners marched north to a prison camp. POWs on this journey cared for him as best they could, but he died of gunshot wounds on the fourth day.

In MacLean's absence, Faith, being the senior officer, assumed command of what was left of the regiment. His battalion broke through resistance to join Reilly's, which during the night also had come close to being over-whelmed. McClymont's M-16s and M-19s had made the difference for Reilly's unit. Hundreds of Chinese lay dead inside the battalion's perimeter. There were also many American and South Korean casualties. Destroyed equipment was strewn about. It was an unsettling scene of devastation, but most seemed too tired, busy, and cold to dwell on it. Stamford sat down on the corpse of a Chinese soldier that was conveniently frozen as rigid as a park bench and quickly downed a can of rations. The act reflected his cheap estimate of life after two nights and a day of fighting; he would not have given much for his own chances.

About noon in Tokyo this day, November 29, MacArthur issued Walker and Almond their orders. It was a dose of reality for both, ending their delusions of a quick return to the offensive. He told Walker to try to hold Pyongyang but to abandon it if necessary to keep the Chinese from moving around his right flank. He told Almond to get the Marines and the Seventh Infantry Division's regiment down off the plateau, and to withdraw all the X Corps to the Hamhung-Hungnam coastal area, where they were to defend an enclave. He had a sea evacuation in mind, to join them up with the Eighth Army, but did not mention it this day.

Within twenty-four hours, the desperate plight of those up on the plateau was known to everyone. By then the Chinese had blocked all roads inter-connecting X Corps units. Once more Drake's tank company failed to break through to the inlet where Faith and the remnants of MacLean's regiment were.

A similar situation came to light later in the day. Recognizing that Hangaru-ri, the hub of UN activity on the plateau, was very vulnerable, Smith ordered Colonel Lewis Puller, whose regiment held Koto-ri, to send reinforcements forward "at all costs." Smith had to hold Hangaru-ri; oth-erwise his two Marine regiments north and west of the reservoir would most certainly be trapped. Their escape route was through Hangaru-ri. On Smith's orders, the regiments were just now beginning to fight their way south, incurring very heavy casualties. Though Puller was under attack and hard-pressed to hold his position, he marshaled some disparate X Corps units that had fought their way up Funchilin Pass and gotten no farther. Reinforcing them with thirty tanks, he sent them off toward Smith's bastion. This composite force totaled about 900 men, the most prominent of them being 250 British Royal Marines led by Lieutenant Colonel Douglas Drysdale, a commando, whom Puller put in charge. They became known as Task Force Drysdale. Only about a third of them reached Hangaru-ri. Chinese soldiers who were dug into high ground dominating the eleven-mile road came close to killing or capturing them all. This gauntlet aptly became known as "Hell's Fire Valley."

While the Chinese were systematically destroying Drysdale's task force — eventually hand-to-hand — the Joint Chiefs convened another of many emergency meetings they had during this period. They started deliberating in the morning on the twenty-ninth, Washington time. By early afternoon, they had not done much except voice their diminishing confidence in MacArthur. He had his units "scattered from hell to breakfast," as Collins later put it, betraying annoyance with himself for having allowed it to happen. Sherman wanted the Chiefs to start giving MacArthur orders, but the others shied away from the idea. They did approve MacArthur's plan to go on the defensive, however. Their principal worry was about what was going on up at Chosin. They thought that the Marines and everybody else up on the plateau might be trapped. A cable they sent MacArthur at 2:30 PM, their time, showed their concern. "What are your plans re the coordination of operations of 8th Army and X Corps and the positioning of X Corps, the units of which appear to us to be exposed?" they asked.

By this time, not even Almond had to be told how vulnerable his troops had become. What particularly alarmed him was a staff report rendered him at his Hamhung headquarters the morning of November 30; he was told about how the Chinese were blocking all the roads up to and on the reservoir plain. Those most exposed were Faith's men. For this situation, Almond blamed Major General David G. Barr, commander of the Seventh Infantry Division, not himself. MacLean's regiment, now led by Faith, was part of the Seventh. When Barr showed up for a nine o'clock meeting that morning, Almond heaped scorn on him for not getting all of MacLean's battalions deployed together on a timely basis. Almond put Smith in charge of getting everybody down from the plateau, but Barr helicoptered up to Hangaru-ri, anyway, to confer with Smith about supporting the MacLean regiment's withdrawal in particular.

Smith could spare him nothing except air support. In fact, that afternoon Smith ordered Drake's tank company to quit trying to reach the inlet and to redeploy immediately to Hangaru-ri to bolster defenses there. It would prove to be a timely order, for Drake's unit was instrumental that night in staving off an all-out attempt to overrun this critical strongpoint. But Barr thus had no encouraging news to deliver to Faith and his men when he reboarded his helicopter to fly from Hangaru-ri to the inlet.

By chance, Faith had ordered Mortrude's platoon to clear an area for helicopters to land. He had anticipated their flying up to evacuate the wounded. The troops were generally feeling better about their situation. The prevailing sentiment was that the worst was past, even though stragglers who made it back inside American lines reported that the area was "crawling with Chinese." The worst tale of the night had to do with the elements; one man froze to death in his foxhole in a sitting position.

Not long after a landing area had been cleared, Barr's helicopter landed. Mortrude was surprised and pleased when his division commander, not a medic, stepped out. But Barr immediately stifled an enthusiastic welcome by brusquely striding off to Faith's command post. His reaction was understandable, though inappropriate. He could not face these men squarely. Until he met with Faith, he was unaware that MacLean was missing. The two talked privately for about thirty minutes. The most disturbing news was that Task Force Faith, as it came to be called, was going to have to carry out its own wounded on trucks. There would be no medical evacuation by air. Helicopters were unavailable. There were too many casualties elsewhere. Already, Faith had more than five hundred wounded. Moving them by truck meant that the road would have to be used in a breakout to Hangaru-ri; there would be no cutting across the terrain or the frozen surface of the lake. Barr told Faith to expect air support only.

Truman was generally aware of what was going on, up to the minute. Bradley was showing him JCS messages to MacArthur just before they were sent. He knew that those up on the plateau might be trapped. So when the President conducted a news conference later that day, he had had at least a night of sleeping with the nightmare of Smith's Marines — a description that came to refer to all Americans caught up there — being killed down to the last man, and with the horrific vision of them being marched off to China as prisoners, their hands on their heads. The political ramifications of such a calamity were almost imponderable. Less than three months earlier, this huge Marine division had been the focus of a blizzard of publicity. Reporters such as Marguerite Higgins of the *New York Herald Tribune,* whom at Inchon Smith allowed to accompany the Marines ashore against Almond's orders, had made them national heroes, much as Gibbons had the Belleau Wood Marines. (For her coverage, Higgins later won the Pulitzer Prize.) If Truman, the man whose democratic administration had "lost" China, did not now do everything in his power to save the Marines, he was conceivably risking his presidency. Grousing opponents were already talking publicly about impeachment proceedings. Subconsciously, this thinking might have prompted his railing against lawmakers this day in his diary. Among other things, he wrote: "I suppose that Presidents in the past have had hostile Congresses — but they were frankly of the opposition. This one — the 81st — happens to be of my own party on the surface. But the majority is made up of Republicans and recalcitrant Southern 'Democrats' — who are not Democrats. So I get the responsibility and the blame."

The crisis situation in Korea was well understood on its political and personal levels by the White House press corps gathered to hear Truman's opening remarks and ask him questions at the news conference. The American public was acutely aware of the situation, too. Colleagues of these reporters were up near Chosin and also with the Eighth Army. Not surprisingly, the sense of desperation on the ground was leading to talk that the time had come for the Air Force to deliver the nation and MacArthur's armies from evil. Airpower and atomic weaponry had, after all, been described as a panacea by witnesses testifying at the previous fall's "Unification and Strategy" hearings conducted by Vinson's committee.

Truman opened his press conference by announcing that, because of escalation by the Communist bloc in Korea, he was asking Congress for an additional $18 billion to support the military. "The request will include a substantial amount for the Atomic Energy Commission, in addition to large amounts for the Army, the Navy, and the Air Force," he said.

When their time to ask questions came, reporters quickly focused on the more immediate initiatives he was going to take and whether some enemy targets that had been off-limits might now be bombed. In this regard, someone asked Truman whether a decision to attack Manchuria was the United Nation's, not his.

"Yes," the President replied.

"In other words," said the reporter, following up, "if the United Nations resolution should authorize General MacArthur to go further than he has, he will —"

Interrupting him, Truman said, "We will take whatever steps are necessary to meet the military situation, just as we always have."

"Will that include the atomic bomb?" asked Jack Doherty of the *New York Daily News*.

"That includes every weapon we have," Truman answered.

"Does that mean that there is active consideration for the use of the atomic bomb?" asked Paul Leach of the *Chicago Daily News*.

"There has always been consideration of its use," said Truman. "I don't want to see it used. It is a terrible weapon, and it should not be used on innocent men, women and children who have nothing whatever to do with this military aggression. That happens when it is used."

This was very big news. Reporters wanted to burst from the room to file word that Truman was actively considering dropping atomic bombs on North Koreans and Chinese. But dutifully they followed protocol, raising questions about other issues, while waiting for the United Press's Merriman Smith, the senior wire service reporter, to stand and thank the President, thus signaling the end to the press conference. However, when Smith rose this time, he chose to keep the conference going. Given the import of Truman's earlier comments, Smith wanted to give him the opportunity to reiterate them or retract them.

"Did we understand you clearly that the use of the atomic bomb is under active consideration?" he said.

"Always has been," Truman responded. "It is one of our weapons."

During more follow-up questioning, Truman went on to say that he would leave targeting of the atomic bomb to the military and that if he decided to authorize its employment, "the military commander in the field will have charge of the use of the weapons, as he always has."

The press conference ended shortly thereafter and within minutes bulletins were alerting newsrooms throughout the world. The United Press's read: "President Truman said today that the United States has under consideration use of the atomic bomb in connection with the war in Korea."

Outside the United States, the reaction was mostly negative. A Saudi Arabian diplomat told Eleanor Roosevelt, a member of the US delegation to the United Nations, that "the people of the whole Asiatic continent would . . . never forget that the atomic bomb was first used against the Japanese and later against the Chinese, but never against any white peoples. This fact would have a disastrous effect upon the relations of the United States with the rest of the world for years to come." The Americans' closest allies, the British, were appalled, too. Attlee requested an immediate meeting with the President and got it, departing London posthaste.

Attlee and leaders of other allied nations whose troops were fighting in Korea were alarmed that Truman might already have delegated to MacArthur the decision to use the atomic bomb. All these officials had already deduced that the general would involve them in a wider war in China if he could. To allay their concerns, White House Press Secretary Ross issued a clarification, which stated that the President had not authorized the use of atomic weapons. But Ross did not deny that Truman was considering using them.

Indeed, the day before his press conference, the military's Joint Strategic

Survey Committee issued a report saying that the situation in Korea might deteriorate to the point that dropping atomic bombs on Chinese forces might be the only way to prevent them from overrunning United Nations units. Collins had ordered the committee to study the idea further.

Using atomic bombs to good effect in North Korea was another matter, however. The Communists had no airfield there. And because the Chinese army was one afoot, and not mechanized, that type of target did not exist. That left targeting Chinese troop concentrations, a task that would be difficult. The Chinese had already demonstrated how hard it was to find their armies. More important, the situation was so fluid in North Korea at this point that Chinese troop concentrations did not remain targets long. By the time the Air Force responded by getting a bomber with an atomic weapon overhead, the troops might well have moved elsewhere. Another complication in targeting Chinese troops in North Korea was that concentrations of them were pressing closely against UN troops. In such situations, an A-bomb explosion would kill as many Americans and South Koreans as Chinese. Bombing enemy troop concentrations in China itself was more feasible, but that was another matter altogether. These considerations, quite apparent now that fighting was under way, were more evidence of peacetime planning not matching up with wartime exigencies, or, put another way, of theory having no practical relevance.

Irrespective of these implications, though, the President was going to have trouble making the American people accept this logic if the Chinese overran the Marines, or some such disaster befell the Eighth Army, and he did not use every weapon at his disposal to prevent it.

While Truman was conducting his news conference, the American soldiers up on the plateau near the inlet were fending off another all-out assault. The previous night had been tranquil by comparison. The Chinese commander now seemed to be under orders to finish off Task Force Faith before dawn; the struggle had been going on for three nights and three days. Everyone within the perimeter was bone-tired; getting shot at was about the only thing that kept a healthy man awake and his mind off the cold temporarily. This did not apply to the wounded, whose pain kept them acutely alert and conscious. Their cries could be heard throughout the night, sometimes over the sounds of battle. During these hours of darkness, about as many seemed to die of exposure as from their wounds. However, this particular night an enemy mortar round landed in the middle of their concentration at the center of the perimeter, and a number died quickly that way. But even with the intrusion of death's hand, the number of wounded increased during the night. By daylight, Dr. Vincent Navarre, the chief surgeon, and his corpsmen were completely out of medical supplies, and because of the elements, they could not even comfort their patients. On Faith's orders, details collected the dead and carried them out of the battle area down to the edge of the inlet, where they would be protected by an embankment. Most of the bodies were frozen as rigid as logs, and were carried and stacked as such. Several rows four feet high accumulated.

On the morning of December 1, low-hanging clouds and snow flurries reinforced a feeling of doom. By around nine o'clock, when a Marine Corsair pilot radioed Stamford that he was overhead, Faith had already decided to order a breakout attempt this day. Stamford so informed the pilot, and together they coordinated a plan. Meteorologists on the *Leyte* had forecast clearing skies over the reservoir at about noon, and the pilot promised to be there leading a flight of Corsairs. The breakout would begin with close air support. Preparations began immediately, but were complicated by so many officers and sergeants having been lost; the chain of command had become a tenuous strand.

From high ground, Chinese commanders easily judged what was happening and intensified their attacks. A prolonged mortar barrage made walking about dangerous. One round detonated near Faith's command post. He had just ended a meeting and a clutch of five officers who paused outside to talk was ripped with shrapnel. Both of Captain Jack Thompson's legs were broken — mortal injuries, given the conditions; he died later in the day. Bigger was hit in the legs, back, and face with shrapnel, a piece of which tore out one of his eyes. A corpsman pushed it back into the empty socket and covered it with a patch. Bigger hobbled off on his own power, using two poles as canes.

Faith's plan was simple. Only trucks and McClymont's M-16s and M-19s would be driven out. Artillery pieces would be abandoned. Supplies on trucks were also to be unloaded and left behind to make room for the wounded. This would not amount to much. Stores of equipment and ammunition were so low that soldiers had resorted to scavenging socks and bullets from the stacks of dead. Most of the wounded were laid directly onto the vacated truck floorboards, although hammocks were improvised for some. An average load was about twenty-five wounded men. But the loading was not orderly, given the chaotic situation; one truck started off with about fifty crammed aboard. A full-track M-19, whose tread system resembled a tank's, was to lead the way, followed by an infantry battalion, the convoy of trucks, and, finally, the other infantry battalion. Other M-19s and M-16s were to be interspersed. An M-19 would also bring up the rear. As the column stepped off, the artillery battalion and the heavy-mortar company were to bombard points along the road of march until they had expended all their shells. After destroying their field pieces, they were to join the column as infantrymen, helping to guard the wounded in the trucks.

The Chinese also had plans. Many now swarmed down to positions near the road, some very close. Faith's men could see this happening. The task force was going to have to run a gauntlet of fire about ten miles long.

It got about fifty yards before the enemy opened up with furious machine-gun fire from positions at multiple elevations on both sides. Fortunately for the Americans, the weather forecasters had been accurate; the sun shone through broken clouds, so the Corsairs circling overhead could operate. Most were loaded with napalm.

The first two planes made dummy runs. There were so many Chinese in the surrounding hills, a pilot could see their heads move down and then up as the planes swept past. One of them told Stamford that it was the first time in the war he could see the enemy he was targeting.

The initial strike was a napalm run. Mortrude happened to be in the turret of the lead M-19, which had stalled when the first horrendous burst of machine-gun fire erupted, startling the driver, whose action evidently caused the engine to quit. Whatever the cause, he could not restart the engine. Mortrude was glancing back when the napalm canisters started tumbling short of their intended target into the column behind him. He had just enough time to duck into the turret before the napalm ignited and a sheet of flame flashed overhead. The heat soared but quickly dissipated where he was. Infantrymen marching nearby were not so lucky. A fair number were set afire and cried horrible screams, while gasping for help to die. They ran around frantically, tearing off their clothing. One exception was Second Lieutenant George Foster, who only five months earlier had been graduated from West Point; he and many of his classmates were then sent directly to Korea, without Fort Benning infantry training, because of the emergency. After the ball of flames rolled forward, Mortrude piled out of the M-19 and suddenly found himself face-to-face with Foster, whose clothing was partially burned off, exposing his blackened and charred skin. He was a horrible sight, but what struck Mortrude and many others was how incredibly calm Foster was; he was in shock, probably. Foster walked over to a soldier, asked him for a cigarette, and then strolled away, never to be seen again. One witness remembers four or five being burned to death; about ten who survived were loaded onto the lead trucks with other wounded men.

Most of the fireball that burned these Americans enveloped Chinese positions. The Corsair was flying very fast, and the momentum of the canister it dropped propelled the napalm jelly up the side of a hill from which hundreds of enemy soldiers were firing on the convoy. Many of them were set afire, too.

Chaos ensued on both sides as the flames subsided; Faith's men were as eager to bolt to the rear as the Chinese were to escape the smoking hillside. According to Stamford, it was Faith's personal intervention that kept them from running. The young lieutenant colonel raced to the front with pistol drawn, yelling threats as well as encouragement. One by one, his men turned to face the front. In this fashion Faith seized the opportunity before the Chinese commander did, and the convoy began to move. The Corsairs were everywhere now, rocketing and strafing, and many of the American soldiers experienced a surge of confidence. Major Hugh Robbins, who was among the wounded in one of the trucks, noticed the grins on their young faces; the men even encouraged the wounded, telling them they were all going to make it out now. There was a sense that the Chinese were giving way.

The macabre scene belied their confidence. The machine-gun fire had caused many casualties. According to Robbins, dead and dying Americans and Chinese were scattered in clumps all along the roadside, their fresh blood "forming pools from which steam rose into the freezing air." And more Americans and South Koreans started falling as enemy fire intensified again.

A person could walk faster than the convoy was traveling, but even its slow speed was too fast to allow for loading all the wounded into trucks. Some were left behind; it was one indication that discipline was breaking down. There were a number of others. Many men whom Faith ordered to stay on the high ground above the road began coming down the slopes, as the convoy began moving steadily. And in the rear, Reilly's battalion, which because of casualties had been reconstituted as K Company, began setting off on its own over the reservoir, led by its senior officer, Captain Kitz. They did not get very far before some of them fell through the ice and drowned in the frigid water.

As for the wounded, few were as cognizant as Robbins. For the Chinese, landing a bullet among them was as easy as hitting a load of melons. Robbins noted "the continual smack of slugs slapping the truck." Private Edward Bilyou, who drove a truck most of the day, would later recall that one wounded soldier in his vehicle got hit three more times by rifle fire. But drivers were the primary targets; the job was deemed "a form of suicide," said Bilyou, who was a replacement himself.

All the same, progress was steady for another mile, until the lead vehicles came upon a blown bridge. It was a complete surprise; none of the pilots had told Stamford about it, and no one on the ground had thought to ask about the possibility. The stream was small, but given the steep banks at the bridge crossing, the trucks had to leave the road at a point about 150 yards back to find a reasonably flat bypass; it was a frozen swamp with hummocks topped with tall grass. Getting across it was a very rough ride. The wounded were violently tossed about; Robbins said he was almost knocked unconscious. A Captain Swenty, who watched and listened to the agonizing yells of the wounded, was certain that some of them with broken bones died of shock during the transit. Some of the trucks broke through the frozen ground and got stuck and had to be pulled out by an M-19. Getting the whole convoy across took an interminable two hours.

Small-arms fire was unremitting. From the rear now, even. The M-19 assigned to the rear had not even departed the inlet. Faith, who was racing up and down the column in his jeep, siren wailing, was stunned to learn this. At one point, the M-19's driver had shut off its engine to save fuel and could not restart it. That K Company soldiers were not where they were supposed to be also allowed the Chinese to approach; having failed in their first attempt to take a shortcut across reservoir ice, Kitz and the others now walked up the road past the trucks, ignoring those left behind. They were no longer a military unit, but rather a free-lance pack, officers and NCOs prominent among them. May, who had taken upon himself to supervise the stream crossing, tried unsuccessfully to make them stop.

The convoy re-formed on the opposite side before proceeding. The vehicles were soon brought to a halt again at Hill 1221, the one whose opposite slope and the Chinese on it had twice thwarted Drake's tank company. At the hairpin turn around its base, the Chinese had piled logs across the road and positioned machine-gun crews on both sides.

Most of the convoy was arrayed bumper-to-bumper along the base of Hill 1221 when halted. From steep heights directly above, enemy soldiers pumped bullets into the trucks. Some wounded started climbing out of them as best they could. Robbins was one who did, certain that his surviving depended on it. The road cut into the side of Hill 1221, so the ditch between the slope and the trucks afforded the best protection. Wounded and able alike stacked up there, refusing to move.

Faith was moving about, trying to put together an attack up the slope, but organized effort was becoming difficult. Units were now mostly intermixed and without leadership. With his .45-caliber pistol, Faith shot dead two ROK soldiers who refused to untie themselves from the axles of two trucks. They either thought it was the safest way out or were trying to hide. By this time, the Chinese were attacking hand-to-hand at the rear of the convoy. They bayoneted one South Korean and captured some Americans before being driven off the first time.

Captain Bigger was one officer who led an attack up the hill. That he did so was a wonder, given his eye and leg injuries. He formed a unit by appealing to the men he knew personally and rousing others by hitting them with the poles he was using for crutches. What started out tentatively built up momentum. Mortrude was among the attackers and later recalled how one GI, mad with fatigue and frustration, had jumped into an enemy foxhole and choked to death its occupant.

The Americans were well up the hill when Corsairs mistakenly began strafing and rocketing them. They suffered casualties and panicked. Dispirited, they abandoned the assault and began streaming off the hillside toward the reservoir, with designs on making a break across the ice to Hangaru-ri. Bigger joined them. "It was a case of leading where they were headed," he recalled.

Other groups took up the sporadic attacks, and after two hours the Chinese were driven from the face of Hill 1221. By then it was dark and the last of the fighter-bombers was returning to the *Leyte*. What was left of Task Force Faith was on its own.

To get it moving again, the roadblock positions still had to be overwhelmed. Part of the reason for attacking the heights was to outflank them; this maneuver was achieved by a group of soldiers led by Captain Earle Jordan. Two other groups, each composed of about seventy-five men, hit the Chinese machine gunners head-on. Faith led one of these; Major Robert Jones led the other. They proceeded on opposite sides of the road, some distance from it. They had very nearly cleared the way for the convoy when a lone Chinese popped up from his hiding place and tossed a grenade, which exploded near Faith. Heavy fragments pierced his chest and lodged above his heart. The men converged around him; he was not dead, but he was dying. They wrapped him in a blanket and shortly thereafter carried him down to the road and put him into the cab of a truck. The convoy then resumed movement. But it was just about finished. "When LTC Faith was hit, the Task Force ceased to exist," Captain Jordan later reported.

Major Jones's official report was that "many hundreds" of wounded were left behind near Hill 1221; former US Army historian Roy E. Appleman, who deserves credit for resurrecting what happened to the Americans east of Chosin, surmised that there was not room on the trucks. More trucks had been knocked out of action at this spot, so the operable ones became overloaded.

For many in the disintegrating task force, if not most, it was now every man for himself. That was certainly true of virtually all those who were proceeding in gaggles across the ice toward Hangaru-ri. A large group of them came upon four severely wounded Americans whose blood-soaked clothing had frozen them to the ice, but they ignored their pleas for assistance and left them behind to die. (The injured men were rescued later, however, and recalled their excruciating ordeal. At close range, the Chinese had deliberately broken their legs with machine-gun fire.) Some of the groups taking the shorter, safer route over ice were composed of as many as two hundred men. Marines came out to lead them through the mine fields that were part of Hangaru-ri's perimeter defenses.

Back on the road, the convoy proceeded in fits and starts like a dying animal. On the south side of Hill 1221, the Chinese had blocked the road with the burned-out hulks of two of Drake's tanks and the medical company's vehicles. With herculean effort, the men pushed some of the latter off the road to open up a wide enough avenue. The Chinese did not offer much resistance here.

A couple of hundred yards down the road, the convoy was stopped by a second blown bridge. Stamford, the Marine, who in others' absence was becoming ad hoc leader, though only a captain, and a few others reconnoitered the situation and found that the trucks could cross on a railroad trestle nearby. This they did, laboriously, one by one, shuddering violently on the ties.

After the trestle crossing, about fifteen trucks were all that were left of the convoy; about thirty had started out originally. The M-19s and M-16s had been knocked out, too, so the convoy was almost totally without protection. Infantrymen walking alongside had dwindled to a handful. As the last of the trucks joined the others in a line, all was dark and quiet, except for the moonlight and the sound of the idling engines, a rumble that carried a considerable distance in the cold air. The survivors, especially those in the cabs, had one final horror-filled ride ahead of them. All knew that the Chinese would hit them again; the only uncertainty was when and where. Stamford, to his own discomfiture, would find out first: it was a few minutes later, another two hundred yards down the road. When scouting ahead, he and several other men were hit at that point. He survived, but was taken prisoner. Within a short time, he managed to escape during some confusion, and later that night walked the ice to Hangaru-ri.

Faith was in the lead truck. At some point north of the trestle he had been shot as he sat in the cab, and he now had two serious wounds. His truck was being driven by Private Russell Barney, whose quick jump ahead of the rest of the convoy on this last leg apparently surprised the Chinese. He passed this ambush without getting hit. The next truck also made it through, but seventy-five yards beyond was hit head-on by a rocket. The cab of the third was blasted with concentrated volleys of small-arms fire; the Chinese were now on the mark. The driver was surely hit, for the truck veered off the road into a draw, tossing most of the wounded out onto the frozen ground. These last remnants of the convoy never went beyond this stretch of the road, which ran near the edge of the reservoir. The driver of the next truck in line evidently abandoned his vehicle to escape and those behind him could not pass. One driver attempted to nudge aside the truck that blocked them, but he caused it to roll into the draw and overturn, pinning the wounded under it. They pleaded for help that would not come. Nor could anyone save a fellow trapped inside the cap, who kicked it frantically.

Chinese soldiers were now detonating grenades at the rear end of the short line. Those who could walk or crawl were attempting to escape. Major Crosby P. Miller, who had three machine-gun slugs in his legs, two fingers blown off, and his other hand frozen around a stick he was using as a cane, stopped long enough to help a Lieutenant Mazzulla, whose bleeding wounds had frozen him fast to his truck seat. Because of his own injuries, Miller could not get into the cab, but he did manage to hand Mazzulla his pocketknife. The young officer could not cut himself free with it, though, so he handed it back to its owner, thanked him, and leaned back to await his fate. Miller was luckier and made it back to Hangaru-ri.

Miller was one of approximately 1,900 survivors of what had been MacLean's regiment. Only 385 of these men were still fit for combat; the rest were wounded or had frozen limbs. Five nights earlier the unit had been composed of about 3,300 able-bodied men. More than 1,400 were killed or captured.

Another 319 would have died had it not been for Lieutenant Colonel Olin Beall, a Marine who was commander of Smith's motor transport battalion, which was responsible for the sector through which the survivors passed. When they started coming through his lines, he drove out on the ice in a jeep to pick up the most seriously wounded. One trip led to another, and each time he traveled farther out. Eventually, he worked his way to the convoy's last resting place, miles beyond his perimeter. Chinese soldiers were still in the area; he saw them. He approached this ghost train anyway, certain that he would find some Americans still alive. With disgust, he had noted the complete breakdown of unit discipline the stragglers evidenced and knew they must have abandoned their wounded to die. For twelve hours he picked through the bodies on the trucks and scoured the area, rescuing some. The Chinese could easily have shot and killed him, but did not.

Much to Smith's annoyance, Almond was flying up to Hangaru-ri every day to offer advice. But his was a chastened style of leadership now; he did not interfere with the Marine general's decision-making. The most important thing Smith decided to do was fly out the wounded. There were many and the number was mounting each passing hour. Smith knew that if his division had to carry them down in trucks, it would have to assume a much more defensive posture and would be much more vulnerable. Conversely, if helicopters flew in to get the wounded of Task Force Faith, as Faith supposed would happen, Smith's unit would very likely survive in reasonably good form.

Smith decided he needed a landing strip. The small helicopters of the period could carry only a few passengers, so fixed-wing transport was necessary. Since the Air Force would be assigned the mission, Smith had to involve Almond, who would coordinate with higher authority. Almond's response to Smith's call for help was, "What casualties?"

"That's the kind of thing we were up against," Smith recalled years later. He suspected that Almond had a "blind spot" for casualties, a psychological defense mechanism that he had developed to protect himself from the realization that young men were getting themselves killed trying to carry out his orders. The origin of Almond's problem seems self-evident. During World War II, his only son and his only son-in-law were both killed in combat.

Survivors from what initially had been MacLean's regimental combat team who walked into Hangaru-ri the afternoon of December 1, or who were carted in by Beall, were stunned to hear the sounds of aircraft landing and taking off. That afternoon the first plane, an Air Force C-47, bounced to a rough stop on the uncompleted field, the only place up on the plateau where a fixed-wing aircraft could land. After a quick turnaround, the pilot took off with twenty-four critically wounded passengers. During the next four days, Air Force planes of this type and some Marine transports carted out a total of 4,081.

Much to Smith's consternation, some of these were able-bodied survivors of MacLean's regiment who feigned injuries by wrapping themselves in blankets. This practice was abruptly ended with closer inspections. Air Force officers had thought that Marine officers were doing the inspecting, and the latter had thought that the former were. The malingerers were emotionally exhausted, but their real reason for boarding was their certainty that the Marine division would meet their regiment's fate. They did not want to be with them when that occurred. It so happened that their sense of impending doom was supported by events elsewhere. The collapse of the Eighth Army's right flank had widened the gap between it and Almond's X Corps. As the Chiefs supposed, the latter was more exposed and vulnerable than ever.

The ongoing dialogue among Truman's top advisers about what to do picked up December 1 at the Pentagon. Acheson, Marshall, Lovett, Bedell Smith, Bradley, and Collins were the main figures present at a meeting convened to discuss the situation. MacLean's regiment had been crushed hours before. The two Marine regiments west of the reservoir, commanded by Murray and Homer L. Litzenberg, Jr., still had miles of fighting ahead of them before they reached Hangaru-ri. Their future was problematic. If they made it, they still had to fight down through Funchilin Pass with the rest of the First Marine Division. The situation in the west part of the peninsula was also very grim but did not seem quite as perilous. At least the entire UN force there was not on the verge of destruction, as in the east part.

Bad news about what had happened to the Second Infantry Division, which was on the Eighth's right flank with the ROKs, had just come in, though. It had been forced to run a six-mile gauntlet through a mountain pass. A head count taken earlier in the day revealed that the division had suffered 4,940 casualties during the last month, about a third of its men. Most of these losses had occurred during the last few days. Major General Laurence Keiser, who believed himself to be the "goat for MacArthur's blunder," had been relieved of command. His replacement was Major General Robert McClure, fifty-four, a Collins favorite. The two had met in 1938 while instructors at the Army War College. Collins had helped foster McClure's career progression since that time. When Collins commanded the Twenty-fifth Infantry Division at Guadalcanal, McClure had been one of his regimental commanders. During much of World War II, McClure had been involved in heavy combat. On Bougainville, he led the American division against the Japanese.

What no one had realized was how these experiences had drained Mc-Clure of energy and confidence. He was not up to meeting the challenge foisted on him in Korea at this stage. (Because of the events of the last week or so, a number of other division commanders were not much better off; Church, for one, was handicapped by poor physical health.) McClure was so overwhelmed that upon taking charge on December 1, he withdrew from reality and kept himself drunk and in his trailer. This remarkable situation was documented by none other than S. L. A. Marshall, who, since that day in 1925 when he interviewed Billy Mitchell for the *El Paso Herald,* had become a renowned military-affairs columnist and author and a colonel in the Army Reserve. Marshall was in Korea on temporary active duty to prepare a study on tactics and weapons. He happened to be with the Second Infantry Division when McClure was put in charge. McClure called him in for a chat, the substance of which Marshall later recounted in his memoir.

According to Marshall, McClure "said right out that the new orders were a terrible shock to his nervous system, that he had never expected to lead troops in battle again, and that for the first time he was not up to it. He went on, 'I can only brace myself by hitting the bottle.' " McClure told Marshall to "program" him, so that it would look like he was in charge. Fortunately for the division, eight of the Second's nine battalion commanders were seasoned combat veterans who needed no prodding and little direction. The enemy was pretty much dictating what to do, anyway. McClure "stayed in his van day after day and did not get out to the troops," reported Marshall. His only contact with them was during dinner, when subordinate commanders or outstanding enlisted men were invited to dine with him. "A few hours before the formation I would go to McClure and tell him it was time for a brace," recalled Marshall. "He would shower and take a few pills. Usually when he appeared he would be shining, with no sign of wooziness." McClure was one of the worst examples, certainly, of how far MacArthur's proud army had fallen in the few days since the Chinese had entered the war, but he was indicative of the whole.

Given the overall situation, the VIPs who convened December 1 at the Pentagon and discussed various grim scenarios could not do much more than hope MacArthur's forces could pull themselves together. That a rout was possible was evident from field reports. Acheson hoped that they could regroup and establish a defense line across the Korean Peninsula. Secretary of Defense Marshall thought that establishing defense enclaves on both coasts was more feasible. However, such concentrations would make UN forces vulnerable to air attacks by either Chinese or Russian planes, a chilling possibility. Collins observed that if that should happen, the President's "only chance" of saving them would be ordering the atomic bomb dropped or perhaps threatening to use it. He did not think these alternatives would necessarily lead to another world war; however, most others did. If the Soviet Union entered the war directly, the Chiefs' plan was "Europe first" — to withdraw US forces from Korea immediately and stop the enemy in Europe, where the nation's interests were deemed primary by the administration and US forces were better prepared to fight. The conditions in Korea were thought to favor the Communists too much. Bedell Smith, at this meeting, recommended that the United States get out of Korea immediately and not wait for matters to get worse. He thought that the Soviets, at minimum cost to themselves, were beginning to hamper the nation's ability to rearm Western Europe and help defend it. Lovett was dubious about Bedell Smith's proposition and suggested that the loss of Korea might jeopardize Japan.

During the next twenty-four hours, the situation continued to deteriorate. So as not to panic the public, Truman tried to adhere to some semblance of a normal schedule. On the afternoon of December 2, he attended the Army-Navy football game in Philadelphia. But at the Pentagon, this Saturday was a workday for many. Lovett, who was on the job, got a phone call from Bernard Baruch, Forrestal's old friend who had been an unofficial adviser to a succession of Presidents. Baruch thought that the time had come for the President to use the atomic bomb. Lovett relayed the message to Marshall and Acheson. "What would it be dropped on?" the Defense Secretary asked curtly. He was referring to the problem of targets. He was also affirming Truman's determination to limit the war. He doubted that atomic bombs would be decisive at this point. An ancillary concern was that if they were used in Korea and were ineffective, their deterrent value would be diminished. Still, given the circumstances, such talk would have sounded to the public like the quibbling of men afraid to use them. The moment of reckoning was coming. When Truman got back to Washington after the football game, Acheson called and requested that he, Marshall, and Bradley meet with him that evening.

They did so in the Oval Office at the White House. Bradley apprised Truman that the worsening situation would reach a "crash state" within the next forty-eight to seventy-two hours; the crisis situation up near Chosin Reservoir was uppermost in his mind. Within that time frame, Litzenberg's and Murray's regiments of Marines would have fought their way south to Hangaru-ri and joined up with the rest of O. P. Smith's division there, or the Chinese would have proved they would fail. Before bedtime, Truman inscribed this in his diary: "The conference was the most solemn one I've had since the Atomic Bomb conference in Berlin. . . . *It looks very bad.*" The emphasis on the last sentence was his. The Berlin conference to which he was referring was that which he had conducted with his advisers before deciding to drop the atomic bomb on Hiroshima.

As Bradley was making his dire prediction, MacArthur was articulating an even worse estimate in a cable he was preparing. It arrived in Washington the next day, December 3. He said that all his troops except the Marines were "mentally fatigued and physically battered" and that the ROKs were of "negligible" value against an enemy that was "fresh, completely organized and apparently in peak condition." His forces would have to abandon Pyongyang and withdraw to the Seoul area, he said. He seemed on the verge of despair; he certainly was trying to effect a change of policy. He wrote that "unless ground reinforcements of greatest magnitude are promptly supplied, [this command] will be either forced into successive withdrawals with diminished power or resistance after each such move, or will be forced to take up beachhead bastion positions, which, while insuring a degree of prolonged resistance, would afford little hope of anything beyond defense." His previous directives were outmoded, he said, given massive Chinese intervention. "This calls for political decisions and strategic plans . . . adequate fully to meet the realities involved," he wrote. After he dispatched this cable, he told William Sebald that "the evacuation of all or part of the Americans in Japan might become necessary."

Pressure on Truman to lift his limitations and enlarge the war was concurrently coming from Republican politicians such as McCarthy, who was saying that Truman should be impeached if he did not accept Chiang's offer of Nationalist Chinese troops. MacArthur now wanted them, after initially saying no. And a number of other Republican members of Congress had resumed demands that Acheson be fired. These were Truman's worst moments as President, concluded Robert J. Donovan, his biographer.

On December 3, virtually every important US foreign-policy and military figure in Washington, except the President himself, met at the Pentagon to forge recommendations to him about what to do next in the war and to consider how to respond to MacArthur. Attendance had become more formal and institutionally directed since the early days of the war and the Blair House Group. The consensus was that there was a "probability" of war with the Soviet Union and that it was almost inevitable that Korea would have to be abandoned. Like MacArthur, the Joint Chiefs, all of whom were in attendance, had concluded that there were too few UN soldiers and no natural defense lines across the peninsula, such as a river, that made a stand possible within the near future. They were coming to the view that the best course of action was to establish one or two defensive enclaves, as Marshall had talked about earlier, and try to hold on. They had not decided what to do beyond that. One enclave would be far south, around Pusan, as before. The other would be the Hamhung-Hungnam area, which was in the far northeast. The Eighth Army would defend the former; the X Corps, the latter. That the two forces could reach these enclaves intact was an open question. This was especially true of Almond's, they believed.

Remarkably, the group's discussion got hung up on whether MacArthur should be dictated to as to the course of action. As during other war management discussions, Marshall said that MacArthur, as theater commander, must not be told what tactics to use and that he should be given as much latitude as possible. This attitude irked Ridgway, who as deputy chief of staff for operations and administration had delivered the opening status briefing. MacArthur himself would have been contemptuous of the dickering. He occasionally quoted his father as saying, "Doug, councils of war breed timidity." Marshall did have one trenchant observation, though. Alluding to Arthur MacArthur's son, he said: "When soldiers have morale problems, it's the commanding officer's fault. But when a general has morale problems, it's the general's fault."

Ridgway, who quickly tired of the discussion's tedious direction, believed that the Chiefs and the others should ignore protocol and tell MacArthur precisely what he was supposed to do. The war was at another juncture; tactical decisions were going to determine whether the war would be kept limited or not. Underlying Ridgway's sentiments was his appraisal that MacArthur had made many mistakes and put his forces in the precarious position they found themselves in; among these mistakes were MacArthur's retaining control of the X Corps through Almond instead of delegating it to Walker; the "reckless" dispersal of his forces; and his ignoring as insignificant the Chinese soldiers taken prisoner from many units prior to the Chinese offensive. After listening to the other participants drone on, off-point, Ridgway could not hold his tongue. Here is his account of what happened next:

> Having secured permission to speak, I blurted out — perhaps too bluntly but with deep feeling — that I felt we had already spent too damn much time on debate and that immediate action was needed. We owed it, I insisted, to the men in the field and to the God to whom we must answer for those men's lives to stop talking and to act. My only answer from the twenty men who sat around the wide table, and the twenty others who sat around the walls in the rear, was complete silence. . . .
>
> The meeting broke up with no decision taken. The Secretaries of State and Defense left the room and the Joint Chiefs lingered to talk among themselves for a few moments. I approached Hoyt Vandenberg, whom I had known since he was a cadet and I an instructor at West Point. With Van I had no need for double talk.
>
> "Why," I asked him, "don't the Joint Chiefs send orders to MacArthur and *tell* him what to do?" Van shook his head. "What good would that do? He wouldn't obey the orders. What *can* we do?"
>
> At this I exploded. "You can relieve any commander who won't obey his orders, can't you?" I exclaimed. The look on Van's face was one I shall never forget. His lips parted and he looked at me with an expression both puzzled and amazed. He walked away without saying a word.

Compared to MacArthur, Ridgway was evidently more naturally disposed to handle what an American field commander was going to have to put up with during the nuclear age at hand. To a degree, Presidents had always controlled from Washington US armies locked in combat, but not nearly to the extent that now seemed necessary. General warfare had become so inconceivably dangerous a prospect that Presidents would want to start controlling all sorts of operational decisions that might escalate a conflict. Ridgway understood that limited warfare involved restraint, which by implication meant control from Washington.

What to do next in Korea would await Collins's return from a trip to the war zone; when the group adjourned, he departed. On behalf of Truman and the others, he would see what was going on. No one any longer trusted what MacArthur was saying. The general was sent this curt instruction: "We consider that the preservation of your forces is now the primary consideration. Consolidation of forces into beachheads is concurred in."

But MacArthur was not the only man in a spot. So were Bradley and Collins. The Army Chief, especially, could end up like Admiral Denfeld, abandoned by the senior officers under him. Gavin was one of many top officers wondering why more was not being done to save the fighting men. During the summer, when "the prospects of the defeat of the 8th Army were real and compelling," as he put it, he and Major General Kenneth Nichols, who had been deputy to General Groves during the Manhattan Project, had called on Ridgway "and urged that he recommend to the Chief of Staff that he in turn recommend to the President that we use nuclear weapons against the North Korean forces." Nothing came of their recommendation, and Gavin expressed contempt because the United States did not have "the moral courage to make the decision to use them" for tactical purposes. Reflecting this mood, the Joint Chiefs' Joint Strategic Survey Committee proposed on December 3 that atomic bombs be used against targets of opportunity to avert disaster should an evacuation from Korea be necessary. MacArthur, however, never formally asked Truman or the Chiefs to use atomic weapons in Korea, though he did provide the Chiefs a list of recommended atomic bomb targets when asked to do so.

Rusk viewed this talk of withdrawal and atomic bombs as defeatism, and on December 4 he vented his emotions like a commander fresh from battle. During a meeting with top State Department people, he berated them for their attitude, saying that the United States should not give the Chinese a victory without their paying a high price on the battlefield. To give the fighting forces backbone, he recommended that MacArthur be relieved and replaced by Collins. His sense of things was that MacArthur had lost his nerve. Collins himself would later say that MacArthur's messages had become "pretty frantic."

After this State Department meeting, Acheson was moved to call Marshall to tell him that "what we needed was dogged determination to find a place to hold and fight the Chinese to a standstill. This was a far better stance for the United States than to talk about withdrawing from Korea or going off on a policy of our own of bombing and blockading China." Recounting the conversation in his memoirs, Acheson said that Marshall agreed, but on two conditions: that the X Corps be evacuated safely, which entailed the Marines getting down off the plateau and out of the mountains first; and that "we . . . not dig ourselves into a hole without an exit."

At this point, Acheson loaded Rusk into a limousine with him, and they were driven over to see the President. Acheson liked and respected Rusk for volunteering to be Hiss's successor as assistant secretary of state for Far

Eastern affairs. It was a position lower in rank to the one Rusk had had at the time; furthermore, Hiss's conviction had tainted it, and Truman administration policies in China and Korea had been so controversial that it was a political hot seat. At the White House, Acheson asked Rusk to repeat his impassioned remarks. This time Rusk cited every historical precedent he could think of in arguing that UN forces, against the odds, could hold on and must. He cited British resolve during the Battle of Britain; American resolve during the dark days after Pearl Harbor; and even Russian resolve during the Battle of Stalingrad. "Mr. President, we just can't let them do this to the United States," Rusk implored.

Rusk's reference to British history was apt, for later in the day Attlee arrived in Washington and was immediately received by Truman. The British prime minister was determined to remain in the capital while the critical decisions were being made and until the crisis passed. Attlee was most worried about the possibility of a dramatic escalation in the war. For two reasons, the British were opposed to this happening: they had at risk vast commercial interests on the China mainland, and they were worried that the United States could not defend Western Europe if it were fighting China in a full-fledged war. This situation might arise in a couple of ways, Attlee believed. The surest would be for Truman to order the atomic bomb dropped or for him to have MacArthur take either the air war or the land war into China proper. The trigger for both acts would be public opinion. Attlee thought that Americans would demand that Truman do something dramatic should a major part of MacArthur's forces get trapped or pinned down, suffering heavy losses indefinitely. To avert these possibilities, Attlee sought a written commitment from Truman that he would not use the atomic bomb unless he gained British concurrence beforehand; his fallback objective was Truman's agreeing in writing to consult at least with British leaders beforehand; and he wanted Truman to accept the idea of a cease-fire, which he proposed enticing Mao's China to accept in return for a seat in the United Nations.

Truman rejected Attlee's propositions, but he admitted that public pressure on him to do something drastic was mounting. The minutes of their first meeting reported that "the President said that demands are now being made. He hoped that the line could be held in Korea until the situation was better for negotiation. All of his military advisers tell him there is no chance to do this, but he still wanted to try." Public pressure made it impossible for Truman to trade a seat in the United Nations for a cease-fire, even if he wanted to do so. Republicans, especially, were citing Communist China's war on UN forces as the ultimate reason it should be kept out of the organization; most Americans would have concurred. As for dropping the atomic bomb, Truman would say only that he would consult with the British government beforehand; he agreed to this verbally, before Attlee departed Washington, but not in writing.

Uppermost in Truman's mind when dealing with Attlee was assuring him that the United States was not going to renege on its commitment to defend Western Europe. The President told him that America's European responsibilities were primary. "We are not going to run out on our obligations," he said. And that included obligations to South Korea. According to the minutes, the President

> thought that if we abandoned Korea the South Koreans would all be murdered and that we could not face that in view of the fact that they have fought bravely on our side and we have put in so much to help them. We may be subjected to bombing from Manchuria by the Russians and Chinese Communists which might destroy everything we have. He was worried about the situation. He did not like to go into a situation such as this and then to admit that we were licked. He would rather fight to a finish. That was the way he had felt from the beginning. . . . He wanted to make it perfectly plain here that we do not desert our friends when the going is rough.

These sentiments expressed by Truman reflect not only the influence of Rusk and Acheson but also the President's combative disposition.

Truman's bracing convictions notwithstanding, his British ally was positive that the President and his advisers had not settled on a course of action. A cease-fire without condition was one idea floating around. Another was economic and political pressure on China; according to British cabinet minutes, the Truman administration "had been considering the idea of limited war against China by way of an economic blockade and stirring up internal trouble in China." Truman, Acheson, and Marshall were now of a single mind on one point, though; if the Communists were going to force US troops out of Korea, they were going to have to drive them down to and off the beaches, as had happened at Dunkirk. South Korea would not be abandoned without a fight.

Collins was in Korea by the time Truman first met with Attlee. During a brief Tokyo stopover, he had listened to MacArthur's complaints about limitations and had been briefed by some of the latter's staff. Collins deemed these men panderers who in their misplaced loyalty had been telling MacArthur what he wanted to hear. Now they were telling MacArthur how bad things were, and he was trying to use the information to pressure Truman into changing his war policies.

Coincidentally, during Collins's first day in Korea, there was a surge of

confidence among UN forces up on the plateau. What caused it was Litzenberg's and Murray's regiments breaking through to Hangaru-ri. They had
had to fight all the way from Yudam-ni, located about twelve miles northwest, and had suffered terrible casualties; but the division was forming up
as one again. Smith now had about 10,000 men together at Hangaru-ri. The
Chinese would not be able to overwhelm his division piecemeal, as had been
a possibility. Smith's plan now was to attack south, battling eleven miles
through Hell's Fire Valley to Koto-ri, where he would absorb his other
regiment, the one led by Puller. Puller had under his command 4,200
Marines and 1,500 army troops, some of them South Korean. From Koto-
ri, the whole division and its complement would burst forth down the
mountain through Funchilin Pass. Smith planned to conduct the operation
as he would an offensive and was positive this force would make it down
intact. He dismissed as foolhardy a proposal of the USAF's Far Eastern Air
Force that he destroy all his heavy weaponry and have his men flown out.

No one was more grateful for the deliverance of Litzenberg's and Murray's regiments than Almond was. On December 5, with only a day to spare,
these Marines had saved him from having to face Collins without being able
to offer much more than intangible assurances that he could save his corps.
Collins was visiting Walker that day and was expecting to see Almond at
Hamhung on the sixth. Almond was so relieved he was crying when he
showed up on the plateau at Hangaru-ri with awards to bestow. For some
reason he had only one medal, but nonetheless he was determined to honor
Smith, Litzenberg, Murray, and Beall. Smith suggested that Beall get this
particular medal. As Almond pinned it on, he wept. "I don't know what he
was weeping about, whether from the cold or emotion, or what," Smith
recalled contemptuously, but, in truth, he knew.

While Collins was in Korea assessing the situation, MacArthur continued
doing what he could to influence the orders he would be given. To pressure
the Democratic administration, he caused two news stories to be published.
The first appeared on December 1 and the second on December 5. The
former grew out of questions asked by the editors of *U.S. News & World
Report;* the latter, from a statement he gave Hugh Baillie, president of
United Press. In them he described the nation's European allies as being
"selfish" and "shortsighted" for not wanting to take strong action against the
Chinese. Asked by the editors whether the prohibition of military strikes
into Manchuria was a hindrance, he replied, "An enormous handicap, without precedent in military history." In chastising the European allies, he said:
"Any breach of freedom in the East carries with it a sinister threat to
freedom in the West. . . . If the fight is not waged . . . here, it will indeed
be fought, and possibly lost on the battlefields of Europe."

Truman was not swayed by either story, and certainly was not amused, especially since he was hosting Attlee when the second one broke. In response, that very day the President issued instructions stating that any government official who intended to make speeches or public statements on foreign policy must have them approved beforehand by senior departmental officials in Washington. Truman left no doubt that he was addressing MacArthur specifically; these orders applied to "officials in the field as well as to those in Washington," he said. For good measure, everyone was warned to exercise "extreme caution in public statements." These instructions were immediately cabled to Tokyo, marked to MacArthur's attention. In effect, Truman was giving him legal notice to hold his tongue.

From the perspective of those in Washington, the status of forces in Korea had not changed much December 5. The strain was still awful, as was indicated to some extent by the fact that Truman's talks with Attlee this second day ran into late afternoon. To these men, immediate prospects for a better situation hinged on Smith's getting his division off the plateau and out of the mountains. The first stage of this dramatic effort was scheduled to begin within a few hours, at 7:00 AM, December 6, Korea time, when the Marines would try to break out of Hangaru-ri.

Amid this tension of war, Truman had on his evening schedule a civil occasion of filial joy. His daughter, Margaret, a professionally trained soprano, would be performing in concert at Constitution Hall, which was to be filled with a friendly audience. The Trumans would escort Attlee. But such was the temper of the times for Truman that even this occasion was marred for him by two intruding events — one very sad and one very annoying. Earlier that day, Charlie Ross, Truman's press secretary and a Pulitzer Prize–winning journalist, suddenly slumped sideways in his chair, unable to speak, while preparing for a television interview. Within minutes he was dead of a stroke. Ross was one of the First Family's closest friends and was to have had dinner with them that evening. He, the President, and Bess Truman had been graduated together from Independence High School back in 1901.

Truman was called at Blair House. According to Margaret, "Dad was shattered by the news." She herself was not told of Ross's death until after her performance, which Truman managed to enjoy anyway. The next morning he still had a father's glow. Then he picked up the *Washington Post* to read the review by music critic Paul Hume. Miss Truman "is flat a good deal of the time," Hume said, noting that "she cannot sing with anything approaching professional finish." Put succinctly, he went on, she "cannot sing very well."

Truman blew his top. He was uptight anyway; at that very instant,

Smith's Marines were battling thousands of Chinese in Hell's Fire Valley, so the old doughboy was in no mood to tolerate a man who seemed to relish picking on young women back home; that is probably how he saw it. He took pen in hand and scribbled a note.

> Mr. Hume: I've just read your lousy review of Margaret's concert. I've come to the conclusion that you are an eight ulcer man on four ulcer pay.
>
> It seems to me that you are a frustrated old man who wishes he could have been successful. When you write such poppycock as was in the back section of the paper you work for it shows conclusively that you're off the beam and at least four of your ulcers are at work.
>
> Some day I hope to meet you. When that happens you'll need a new nose, a lot of beefsteak for black eyes, and perhaps a supporter below!
>
> Pegler [Westbrook Pegler, a columnist with whom Truman had an ongoing feud], a gutter snipe, is a gentleman along side you. I hope you'll accept this statement as a worse insult than a reflection on your ancestry.

To get this hot missive through his staff's protective shield, Truman called in Samuel Mitchell, a White House attendant, and asked him to go to the nearest public mailbox on the street and drop it in.

By this time, Collins was finishing a full day with Almond, part of it in the field. The past two days had been encouraging. Both Walker and Almond now thought that their armies could retire to coastal enclaves in good order. Collins agreed. A British correspondent who called the Marines' part in this plan a "retreat" was admonished by Smith. It could not be a retreat, he said, because there was no "rear"; his division was completely surrounded. "We're not retreating. We are just advancing in a different direction," he said.

The Marines' getting out of the mountains had become a major media event reported in progress throughout the world. Journalists had flown up to Hangaru-ri to join them. Among the press corps were Higgins of the *Herald Tribune* and *Life* photographer David Douglas Duncan.

Almond told Collins he thought he could hold out through the winter, defending an enclave in the Hamhung-Hungnam area, but Walker had told him he thought the Eighth Army and the X Corps should finally be combined and together defend a common defense line, the old Pusan perimeter. Collins agreed; he thought Almond was being too optimistic.

Collins stopped in Tokyo again during his return trip to Washington. By this time, he recalled, "I was firmly convinced we were not going to be driven off the peninsula." He told MacArthur this and ever so delicately convinced him that the Eighth Army and the X Corps had to be combined under Walker's command. Somewhat reluctantly, MacArthur agreed, though he held to his negative forecast. He said that if the Chinese army continued its offensive beyond the thirty-eighth parallel, UN forces would have to be evacuated, unless he was reinforced with 200,000 more troops and unless some limitations were removed — most notably, the prohibitions against bombing or blockading of China. That the enemy enjoyed sanctuary within its borders galled both him and, especially, Air Force officers to no end.

Collins departed Tokyo for Washington on December 7. Shortly before, MacArthur issued orders to Almond to withdraw from North Korea by ship through Hungnam and redeploy to the Pusan area. "At such time, X Corps will pass command to the Eighth Army," he informed him.

For some reason, Collins did not convey to Washington his positive assessment of the turn of events until he arrived there. Perhaps he did not want MacArthur to know precisely what he would be telling the President. Whatever the reason was, his personal delivery of the good news to Truman, Attlee, and their top advisers at the White House, on December 8, was particularly dramatic. The news "was like a ray of sunshine" suddenly cast across the room, Bradley recalled. Though the situation "remained serious," Collins cautioned them, it was "no longer critical" and UN forces could defend a sizable Pusan perimeter indefinitely. Truman and everyone else in the room were tremendously relieved. So too, in turn, were members of Congress; this news had a great impact on the Hill, Collins recounted. To stave off disaster, Truman was not going to have to take the war to China itself, as MacArthur and the vocal Republican right were pressing him to do. Nor was he going to be forced by overwhelming enemy pressure to drop atomic bombs. Relieved of this worry, Attlee departed Washington the next day. That Truman, even when in desperate need of relief for his beleaguered forces, had not used these weapons and, in fact, had not even set in motion preliminary activity for doing so, established a very strong precedent not only for future Presidents but also for future Soviet leaders for many years to come. Intent on limiting the war, Truman overturned all previous posturing and planning, including his own.

The Marines found that getting down through Funchilin Pass was easier than the struggle to regroup at Hangaru-ri and force an avenue through Hell's Fire Valley. As MacLean, Faith, and Drysdale had learned too late, the Chinese more easily massed for attack up on the plateau; they had difficulty doing so in the pass. This last leg had its high drama, though. A blown-out bridge raised apprehension at home that the Marines' escape was blocked. But while under fire, engineers replaced it with a temporary span, forcing Chinese POWs to do the heavy work. Reporters burnished their accounts of this story by calling the structure "The Bridge at Koto-ri," which gave it a certain luster of legend.

Support for the fight down through Funchilin Pass was well coordinated and effective. It included close air support and artillery fire, some of which was produced by US units down below. A battalion also fought its way up the pass as far as possible. The Marines in Litzenberg's and Murray's regiments, when they reached the bottom, had fought almost every step of forty miles. Finally, once at the bottom, they were carted by truck and train through a protected corridor to Hungnam, where twenty-eight Navy ships awaited them. They boarded from December 11 to December 14, and on the fifteenth they sailed for Pusan, where the division went into reserve status for an extended period while it recouped its losses, which were considerable. The 25,000-man division suffered 10,500 casualties during its three months in North Korea; more than 1,500 died of their wounds. Most of the corpses were tagged and buried in mass graves at Yudam-ni and Koto-ri.

The performance of Smith's men at Inchon and Chosin restored the Marines to a prominent place in the nation's pantheon of heroes, but rave reviews and Smith's protest that his unit was not in retreat notwithstanding, this was no way to win a war; the Marines and the rest of the UN forces were indeed in headlong retreat. In fourteen days, ending on December 24, the Navy, in a remarkable logistical feat, had shipped out 105,000 US and Korean soldiers, 91,000 refugees, 17,500 vehicles, and 350,000 tons of bulk cargo.

Turning things around, which would be at least as much of a psychological problem as a physical one, was not going to be easy. As quickly as possible, Walker needed to get his now-unified forces to some physical barrier they could defend, turn them around to face the enemy, and restore their confidence. On December 23, 1950, he was trying to facilitate this three-step process as he sped north in his jeep, against the flow of the bumper-to-bumper traffic of the Eighth Army, which was still in North Korea but moving south. The dirt road was frozen. As was customary for him, he was standing up, holding on to the grab bar, as his siren wailed and his red light blinked. With him were an aide, a bodyguard, and a driver. Suddenly, without warning, a weapons carrier popped out of line and directly into their path, moving toward them. Its civilian South Korean driver, annoyed by the slow pace, was trying to pass. A collision was unavoidable, and all four in the jeep were thrown violently into a ditch. Each was seriously injured, but Walker was the only one to die. At a nearby MASH unit, he was pronounced dead on arrival. For many of his men, news of what happened must have come as further confirmation that they were doomed.

Within minutes of the incident, MacArthur was notified of Walker's death. He immediately telephoned Collins in Washington, who, in turn, contacted Pace, Marshall, and Truman. All these men, including

MacArthur, reaffirmed their contingency plan to name Matthew Ridgway as commander of the Eighth Army. At that moment Ridgway was having dinner with his wife, Penny, at the home of Army friends. Collins checked the duty desk, got the number where he could be reached, called him to the phone, and gave him the stunning news.

At the other end of the line, Ridgway evidenced no visible reaction. He returned to the group and finished his after-dinner drink without commenting on the phone call or his new appointment. He did not even tell his wife that evening. Deciding that she would need the sleep, he held off and told her the next morning while they were having coffee. They had been married only three years and had spent almost every one of those days together, so their parting would not be easy. She was thirty-two, he fifty-four; they had a son twenty-two months old. This was Ridgway's third marriage (and the one that would last). Such marital instability would have caused serious problems for an ambitious Army officer with less formidable a reputation. It had also helped him that he was a Marshall protégé, like Collins and Bradley. Fueling talk about his third marriage was his wife's having been married to an Air Force enlisted man. Some generals' wives were said to have resented her instant promotion.

Two cables were on Ridgway's Pentagon desk that morning, both from MacArthur. One was addressed to Collins: "Thanks and deepest appreciation, Joe, to you and the Secretary [Pace] for letting me have Ridgway." The other was to Ridgway himself: "I look forward with keenest anticipation to your joining this command. Your welcome by all ranks will be of the heartiest. . . ."

Telegrams began arriving from subordinates who had served with Ridgway during World War II. Others called or dropped by personally. Almost all wanted him to order them to Korea. A number of them he eventually did, including some he appointed division commanders.

Ridgway agreed with Marshall and Collins that he should depart immediately for Korea, via Japan, where he would confer with MacArthur. Arrangements were made forthwith and a four-engine Air Force Constellation was readied at Andrews Air Force Base. He returned home for dinner and to pack. His luggage included a .45-caliber pistol, an M-1 rifle, the parachute harness he had worn during World War II, and six wool socks that Gavin had given him during the Battle of the Bulge. He then kissed his wife and toddler good-bye. At ten that night he was airborne. Already it was Christmas Eve in the Far East.

CHAPTER 10

★ ★ ★ ★ ★ ★ ★ ★ ★ ★ ★ ★ ★ ★

LIMITING THE LOSSES

MATTHEW RIDGWAY would become the model American soldier of the new age. This was partly because he was a Marshall man and had reconciled himself to the limits of American power in a modern era whose dominant feature militarily was nuclear weaponry; but even more important, it was because he succeeded grandly despite these limits.

Both Ridgway and his father, Thomas, were West Point graduates (the classes of 1917 and 1883, respectively); however, Matthew Ridgway's renowned self-discipline was born not of the martial arts taught at that institution but of the fine arts taught at home. His discipline was basically that of a highly refined person. Apparently, most of his urbanity came from his mother, Ruth, whom he described years later as "very cultured" and "beautiful." On the keyboard, she was as proficient as a concert pianist, he recalled; and he also remembered fondly the "beautiful things" she kept in the home. He reflected her influence when, as a teenager, on the first occasion he hosted his father to some entertainment, he escorted him to a performance of the Boston Opera Company.

His father's cultural influence on him was of the literary kind; the articulate gentleman loved the written and spoken word and fostered his son's appreciation of the importance of both in one's development. As a result, Matthew Ridgway developed a passion for biography and history. Thomas Ridgway had developed his own keen interest in reading during the years he was assigned to remote Army posts. In this regard, he was much like MacArthur's erudite father, and, though some would criticize their sons for having stilted speech with personalities to match, most recognized that they were boosted immeasurably by their command of the language.

Surprisingly, Ridgway's father did not encourage his son's interest in a military career. What really turned Matthew Ridgway's head was President Theodore Roosevelt's marshaling the Great White Fleet in 1907 and ordering it off on a cruise around the world. Thomas Ridgway was serving at Fort Monroe, Virginia, when these ships rendezvoused off Hampton Roads and was still there with his family when they returned two years later. Matthew had watched them from the front porch of their home. The voyage "stimulated my interest very much," he recalled, "and I thought it fascinating to go around the world." He then began thinking seriously about trying for an appointment to the Naval Academy. The allure of the sea gradually waned for him, but not the attraction of an academy education. When the time came, he won one of the presidential appointments, which were reserved for the children of career military people.

Ridgway's home life was quite comfortable and many of his relatives were professional people of considerable means. So it is noteworthy that what especially pleased him about the academy was that wealth and family background were "of no consequence at all; everybody stood on his own merits." In such an environment, he thrived. Intelligent and already self-disciplined, he found that effort was rewarded in full measure. This reinforcement caused him to take on more and more responsibilities, and thus inculcated in him a lifetime behavior pattern characterized by prodigious energy. He took on as many jobs as he could handle, he said, both the glamorous and the mundane; during his senior year he was not only brigade adjutant, the number-five-ranking cadet in the chain of command, but also football manager.

Given his parents' interest in the fine arts, it was natural that from the outset of his military career, he viewed leadership not as a science but as an art form. He described leadership as "art of the first order with infinite forms of expression." He held firm to this conviction throughout his career. Leadership is not the same as management, he believed. The latter, he would say, is overemphasized and diminishes the "human element," which is the "total thing."

He began practicing the art of leadership while a cadet, as had MacArthur. In this regard, the German textbooks then used by the West Point faculty in military-training classes greatly impressed Ridgway. These compilations of essays had straightforward titles such as *Letters on Artillery*, *Letters on Cavalry*, and *Letters on Infantry*. The latter, which was written by the Prussian Prinz zu Hohenlohe-Ingelfingen, insightfully discussed the ramifications of the mass military mobilization of a nation's population. A class-based society being his reference point, Hohenlohe-Ingelfingen observed that a commander should learn as much as he could about his soldiers' backgrounds — whether a man was poor, what problems he had, and how his father earned a living, for example.

Determined to apply immediately some aspect of this personal approach,

Ridgway set about trying to learn the first names of all upperclassmen so that he could identify them on sight; there were more than four hundred, but he eventually succeeded. The exercise taught him a valuable lesson. "Calling people by name has a powerful effect," he later observed. During his professional career, he developed this skill to a very high degree and was celebrated — true or not — for having immediate recall of the names of thousands of soldiers of all ranks.

Ridgway missed combat during World War I, though he volunteered for it. He was scheduled to depart for the war zone with the Third Division when the war ended. That his senior-year West Point roommate was killed in the fighting heightened his sense that he had failed to be where he should have been. Nonetheless, he learned many lessons from World War I, drawing upon the experiences of others by reading their accounts and talking to them. When in 1918, much to his consternation, he was assigned to West Point to teach French, which he did not know, he helped form a small discussion group composed mostly of men who had fought in France. One of the men was Courtney Hodges, who like Ridgway would become a highly successful corps commander during World War II. The group met twice weekly to discuss tactics and share any bits of professional information they had learned from personal experience or reading. Long after retirement, Ridgway still remembered these meetings and their "priceless" value. He kept copious notes, a practice he extended to all sorts of career development activities. Anything he thought might help him in the future, he put to writing or pecked out on his typewriter.

Many officers contributed to Ridgway's notes, usually without knowing it. One was Major General Harold B. Fiske, under whom he served in Panama. The latter was of the Old Army. "There is no excuse that would explain; there is no excuse that will excuse," Fiske used to say. There was more than a little of this Old Army philosophy in Ridgway. He had no tolerance for those who said they did not have enough time. "Stretch out your day," he would tell them, meaning, burn the midnight oil. Fiske also reinforced for Ridgway Hohenlohe-Ingelfingen's lesson about the need to accentuate in a soldier's mind his singular importance in the scheme of things, because doing so boosted his morale and gave him assurance that he was more than cannon fodder. Rapport with the lowly soldier was to become a Ridgway hallmark.

Another was physical fitness. It was while he was West Point's athletic director under MacArthur that he discerned the correlation between athletics and leadership. "In my opinion," he later observed, "there is only one excuse for being in our Army, and that is to be ready to fight at any time, to be in top-flight physical conditioning, and to be at a high training level." The intensity with which he pursued these goals was widely known. As a young officer on maneuvers in the field, he would return to his tent after a long day of arduous activity, only to don sneakers and shorts in which to run a couple of miles. He felt that if, alternatively, he played a game of "violent tennis," it broke up his mental pattern and caused him to relax. As a thirty-two-year-old, he was invited to train with the US military-pentathlon team that was scheduled to compete in the 1928 Olympics; military pentathlon had equestrian, swimming, running, and shooting events. Ridgway had a solid chance of making the team but declined the invitation because it entailed forgoing normal military duty for a year. When he was commander of the Eighty-second Airborne Division, none of his field officers could beat him on the obstacle course, and only a few of his men could.

Ironically, after World War II, Truman tried to convince Ridgway to quit the Army and become ambassador to Argentina. During the immediate postwar years, American generals were held in high esteem at home and abroad, and the President nominated for ambassadorships some of them with excellent war records. Fortunately for Truman, Ridgway declined and, as a result, was still in uniform and in a position to take command of the Eighth Army on December 26, 1950. Ridgway declined the ambassadorship because he "couldn't visualize myself going to cocktail parties." He sought out Marshall's assurance that he was not disobeying any order by not accepting. "You have a completely free choice, Ridgway," Marshall told him, and instead, he was appointed commanding general of the Mediterranean theater of operations.

When Eisenhower became Army Chief of Staff, he made Ridgway a member of the Military Committee of the United Nations. During this period, Ridgway was much involved in the Forrestal-directed survey of what Soviet intentions were. In a study dated February 3, 1947 — which was about a year after Kennan transmitted his long telegram, and thirty-seven days before Truman asked Congress for aid for Greece and Turkey — Ridgway concluded that the Soviet aim was global hegemony and the proliferation of Communist governments throughout the world. During a casual meeting, Acheson complimented him on his effort and said that it was having an impact in high places.

Otherwise, Ridgway found UN diplomacy as contrary to his nature as he had anticipated ambassadorial work would be — a self-appraisal with which his American colleagues would have agreed. Members reportedly were embarrassed by Ridgway's refusal to shake hands with Soviet UN ambassador Andrei Y. Vishinsky, because he had called the United States a warmonger.

Ridgway was returned to his element when he was again assigned to Panama, this time as the senior military officer. Then, in September of

1949, he was named deputy chief of staff for operations and administration, the position he held when selected to lead the Eighth Army and a "situation which perfectly suited his personality, his drive, his initiative, and everything perfectly well," Collins later observed.

The Constellation that transported Ridgway to Korea made refueling stops at Takoma, Washington, and Adak, Alaska, where he got a haircut, before touching down at 11:30 PM, December 25, 1950, in Tokyo, his intermediate stop. During this leg of his journey he composed a letter to Walker's widow. Doyle Hickey, a good friend, met him at the airport and escorted him to MacArthur's guest quarters at the embassy. In the middle of the night, before retiring, Ridgway composed a eulogy for Walker, which he had Hickey transmit to the Eighth Army.

The next morning, he met with MacArthur, whose staff briefed him. Given the position he had held back in Washington, none of them could tell him much more than he already knew. Some of the information presented was so woefully vague as to be useless. On the status map, the Chinese army was depicted as a large "goose egg" with the number "174,000" written in its center. There was little sense about where individual enemy divisions were because UN forces had broken contact with them in early December. Furthermore, the correct number of Chinese soldiers in Korea by this time was closer to 300,000.

MacArthur was his gracious self, and so their meeting went well. It might have been awkward, otherwise; MacArthur wanted Ridgway to succeed, but he wished Truman would see things his way; these emotions were at cross-purposes somewhat. As for Ridgway's deportment, though he would not countenance an officer's thinking he was above following orders, he was by nature as aggressive as MacArthur, so he readily identified with the emotions that were causing MacArthur to give Washington heartburn.

MacArthur at the moment was actually eager to give Ridgway free rein and fade from public view temporarily. He was pleased to have someone else primarily associated with what was going on in Korea. "He didn't come to see me in Korea until things were turned around and going the other way," recalled Ridgway. "The Eighth Army is yours, Matt," MacArthur told him. "Do what you think best."

Later in the day, Ridgway donned his combat uniform and departed for South Korea. While his plane was tossed about in a storm, he composed his second message to the Eighth Army. "I have, with little advance notice, assumed heavy responsibilities before in battle," he wrote, "but never with greater opportunities for service to our loved ones and our nation in beating back a world menace which free peoples cannot tolerate. It is an honored privilege to share this service with you and with our comrades of the Navy and the Air Force. You will have my utmost. I shall expect yours." He was getting down to business, and the tone of his remarks evidenced no doubt he could do the job.

He landed at Taegu shortly before dark. His first impression was how cold it was. Dispensing with all ceremony, he traveled straight from the airstrip to the main Eighth Army headquarters, located nearby; old friends had gathered there to welcome him, and he talked with them into the night. At sunrise, he was airborne in his command plane, a converted B-17 Flying Fortress, which he already had christened *Hi Penny!* Ridgway sat in the bombardier's seat in the plane's Plexiglas nose, carefully examining the terrain, while the pilot followed at three thousand feet the route the general had plotted for him. For six months Ridgway had been poring over maps of Korea; now he was fixing in his mind the actual images to associate with them. For a commander of a mechanized army, it was not a pretty picture: many high mountains and no modern roads.

Nonetheless, these conditions were not half his problem. His chief difficulty, which touched all others, was transforming the psychology of his army. "It was . . . a defeated army . . . a disintegrating army," recalled Colonel Harold K. Johnson, commander of the First Cavalry Division's Eighth Cavalry Regiment and a future Chief of Staff. "It was an army not in retreat but in flight," he recalled. "It was something bordering on disgrace."

After his reconnaissance in the B-17, Ridgway began making his personal presence felt. He started by meeting individually with his corps commanders: I Corps's Milburn, IX Corps's John Coulter, and X Corps's Almond. Until recently, Almond had reported directly to MacArthur, whereas Milburn and Coulter had reported to Walker, who, in turn, reported to MacArthur. Now all three were under the immediate command of Ridgway, who was the only one who reported to MacArthur.

Of his three corps commanders, Ridgway knew well only his old friend Milburn. For the time being, the new field commander decided to retain all three men as his senior officers, but he issued each a stern warning that he would not tolerate their present conduct, which by his estimate amounted to a lack of leadership. He admonished them for ignoring the fundamentals, such as reconnaissance. Almond especially seemed affected by the lecture. His also included a warning against free-lancing through Tokyo, even though he was still MacArthur's chief of staff. Ridgway informed him in no uncertain terms that he, Ridgway, not MacArthur, was now his immediate superior. "Almond came out of that meeting a very sober guy," recalled Major General William McCaffrey, who back then was a colonel serving as deputy chief of staff for the IX Corps.

Rhee was next on Ridgway's agenda during his first full day in Korea. "He greeted me rather impassively," Ridgway later recounted, "but I extended my hand at once and said, right from the heart, for I had no time to sort over ceremonial phrases: 'I'm glad to see you, Mr. President, glad to be here, and I mean to stay.' That was the one word the old gentleman seemed to have been awaiting. His face broke into a smile as warm as the Eastern Sun, his eyes grew moist, and he took my extended hand in both of his."

Rhee wanted to do anything he could to help and so Ridgway, who was accustomed to thinking big, told him he needed thirty thousand of his good citizens digging revetments north of Seoul. They were there the next morning. Ridgway, who exuded confidence and determination, had given Rhee cause for hope.

On December 29, the Chiefs, with Truman's approval, delineated to MacArthur a cautious plan to save South Korea, while at the same time conceding "from all estimates available that the Chinese Communists possess the capability of forcing UN forces out of Korea if they choose to exercise it." The plan did not involve a greater commitment by the United States or other UN member nations and, thus, tried to minimize the risk of escalating the conflict into a general war. What it amounted to, essentially, was a reversion to Truman's limited-warfare policies, those with which they had started. They did not specifically reset an objective, primarily because Chinese intervention had left UN forces too discombobulated to determine what was possible. The plan called for raising as many more ROK divisions as possible by conscripting more South Koreans, and for devising tactics that would inflict casualties so heavy on the Chinese that their leadership would decide that taking South Korea was not worth it. MacArthur was also told to prepare for the worst; he was to attempt to hold a series of defense lines he himself had proposed, but not risk a Dunkirk-style evacuation. There had been some rethinking on this point. The Chiefs went so far as to set a fallback point that, if retreated to, was to trigger MacArthur to "commence a withdrawal to Japan."

This cable made MacArthur apoplectic, almost. To his staff he ranted about Washington losing its "will to win," and on December 30, after working into the late evening hours, he prepared with them a reply that again recommended expanding the war. On his mind was a New Year's offensive by the Chinese that Ridgway was forecasting. His specific recommendations essentially matched earlier ones he had made, the most significant one being that airpower be used against China proper. He ended his cable by saying that he would have the Eighth Army fight until driven off the beaches near Pusan before ordering a withdrawal. Earlier, in an agitated state, Marshall had said the same thing, but had thought better of it. Such procrastination was a good way to lose all of the Eighth Army, but MacArthur was determined not to be the one to order such an ignominious end to the war as withdrawal.

As field commander, Ridgway had more immediate concerns, though he supported MacArthur's recommendations, calling them "brilliant." With his own reputation now on the line, he already seemed to be seeing things more like MacArthur was. Understandably, he wanted all the help he could get, and this was probably the reason why at this juncture he suddenly endorsed a plan to expand the war. He would not do so again. The pressure on him was enormous, for he sensed that the enemy was about to redouble its efforts. "I felt it in my bones that the Chinese would launch a major offensive on New Year's Eve," he recalled. Acting on that intuition, he proceeded earlier that day to his forward command post, where he was when, in fact, they did.

ROK units broke first, their soldiers fleeing in trucks that almost ran over Ridgway as he personally tried to block their passage. "I'd never had such an experience before," he later wrote,

> and I pray to God I never witness such a spectacle again. They were coming down the road in trucks, the men standing, packed so close together in those big carriers another small boy could not have found space among them. They had abandoned their heavy artillery, their machine guns — all their crew-served weapons. Only a few had kept their rifles. Their only thought was to get away, to put miles between them and the fearful enemy that was at their heels. . . . I might as well have tried to stop the flow of the Han.

He was even more discomfited when he spotted six truckloads of Americans in this helter-skelter convoy. They were from Church's Twenty-fourth Infantry Division. Unlike the situation with the Koreans, Ridgway could speak their language on a number of levels, so he got them stopped and turned around. But the effort was to no avail, for within hours he was forced to issue orders for a general withdrawal.

The brunt of the renewed Chinese offensive was directed at Seoul, so Ridgway ordered the Eighth Army units north of the city to withdraw to the defense line that the South Koreans were digging. However, this proved of little use, there being no natural barriers there behind which to rally his army. Consequently, two days later, on January 3, 1951, he ordered the South Korean capital abandoned to the enemy. He wanted to put the Han River between them and most of his men. The Han flows to the west into the Yellow Sea, but as a line on a map traces easterly from the coastline across about a third of the breadth of the Korean Peninsula before trailing off sharply south-southeast. Therefore, not all of the Eighth Army could seek refuge behind the Han. Along the Eighth Army's easterly flank, Almond's X Corps would have to use other barriers or create its own, which is why Lin Piao, the Chinese commander, would soon shift his point of attack to there.

The evening of January 3, Ridgway was down at river's edge when a major part of his army started across the Han at Seoul. Permanent bridges there had been destroyed since that day in June when MacArthur, from a vantage on a hill on the opposite bank, had watched the city being captured for the first time in this war. The scene was even more dramatic this time. The temperature was zero and the Han was frozen over. Whether shifting ice would break three pontoon bridges Ridgway planned to use to get his army across was an open question. He was there to see whether it would and to bolster confidence. Each one of these temporary structures surged and swayed as the forward vehicles in the bumper-to-bumper traffic lines started across. Fortunately for the withdrawing forces, the bridges did hold and the traffic flowed without significant interruption throughout the night.

Just as with MacArthur earlier, the memory of civilian refugees left an indelible impression on Ridgway. "Off to the right and left of the bridges," he later wrote,

> was being enacted one of the great human tragedies of our time. Hundreds of thousands of Koreans were running, stumbling, falling, as they fled across the ice. Women with tiny babies in their arms, men bearing their old, sick, crippled fathers and mothers on their backs, others bent under great bundles of household gear flowed down the northern bank and across the ice toward the frozen plain on the southern shore. Some pushed little two-wheeled carts piled high with goods and little children. Others prodded burdened oxen. . . . There was no weeping, no crying. Without a sound, except the dry whisper of their slippers on the snow, and the deep pant of their hard-driven breath, they moved in utter silence.

For a time, even the Han did not slow the Chinese and North Koreans much. They crossed the river, too, close behind. Then Lin Piao thought better of it, slowed his advance in the west, and secretly began shifting forces to the east. Nonetheless, by January 6, Ridgway, since arriving in the war zone, had lost sixty miles of ground to his Chinese counterpart. His only offense was a token of his defiance. He personally nailed an old pajama bottom with a slit in the seat to the wall of his Seoul headquarters below a sign that said:

TO THE COMMANDING GENERAL CCF:
WITH THE COMPLIMENTS OF THE
COMMANDING GENERAL EIGHTH ARMY

Ridgway deemed the Eighth Army's performance shameful. He convened his three corps commanders and gave them unremitting hell again. They and their men were being consumed by self-pity, he said.

Ridgway was in the field most of the day; he departed in the morning and returned in late afternoon. Reports of his visits emanated from virtually every point along the front. One alert photographer caught him kneeling down to tie the shoe of a soldier who was using both hands to steady a mortar he was carrying on his shoulders.

Ridgway's first offensive had an almost imperceptible beginning. It started with his calling on Colonel John Michaelis, a regimental commander, who would forever after remember vividly the scene. "He came to my CP in a jeep," recalled Michaelis,

> grenades hung on his shoulder harness, brisk-walking, battle-eyed, looking right at you. He said, "Michaelis, what are tanks for?" I said, "To kill." He said, "Take your tanks north." I said, "Fine, sir. It's easy to take them there. It's getting back that's going to be most difficult. They always cut the road behind you." He said, "Who said anything about coming back? If you can stay up there twenty-four hours, I'll send the division up. If the division can stay up there twenty-four hours, I'll send the corps up."

As Michaelis saw it, "That was the magic that was Ridgway."

"We're not going back anymore," Ridgway told Lieutenant Colonel Thomas Dolvin, whose tank battalion was made part of Task Force Michaelis; "we're going to advance." And at nightfall on January 7 they did. Being a fairly large force, they took the whole night to move out. Ridgway had ordered Michaelis to go as far as Osan, if he could, and he managed to do so. The unit's only problem was the mass of refugees moving in the opposite direction, clogging the road. However, this short advance developed invaluable intelligence. It revealed that the Chinese were not pursuing in the western sector, that they had stopped at Osan.

Word that at least some UN soldiers were advancing spread quickly throughout the Eighth Army. The news was not exactly exhilarating, but was at least heartening. The operation caused a marked change in the mindset of those involved and began restoring their confidence. This positive influence touched others more directly when Ridgway, true to his word, ordered the Twenty-fifth Infantry Division and then all the I Corps forward in stages.

Michaelis's advance represented the first time since November 25 that any UN unit had gone forward, but this change in direction was too small for the Joint Chiefs back in Washington to take notice, especially since they were still focused on MacArthur's very negative reporting and his pleas to expand the war. About twenty-four hours after Michaelis's advance, they responded to MacArthur's December 30 cable, informing him that there was "little possibility" that his proposed policy changes would be adopted and no possibility that Chiang's offer of ground forces would be accepted. They did say that should the situation be "stabilized," two National Guard divisions could be deployed to Japan. Should the worst come to pass, the Chiefs informed MacArthur, he had the authority to order a withdrawal from Korea. They were delegating that to him.

It was this latter subject in particular that MacArthur addressed the next day in his reply. The most recent JCS message had strengthened his conviction that he was being set up as the fall guy should an evacuation become necessary, and this caused him to be more graphic about his intentions than he had been in his December 30 cable. In his January 10 reply, he told them that if he could not wage war on China proper, he would rather hold on in South Korea to the last man. He said: "Under the extraordinary limitations and conditions imposed upon the command in Korea its military position is untenable, but it can hold for any length of time up to its complete destruction, if overriding political considerations so dictate." In the same message, MacArthur not too subtly blamed morale problems in his ranks on policy equivocation by the administration, prompting Marshall to remark to Rusk, "When a general complains of the morale of his troops, the time has come to look into his own." It was the second time in recent days the Defense Secretary had made such a remark.

Marshall was not denying that the situation was grim. On January 10 Lin Piao renewed the Communist offensive by ordering North Korean units to bolt out of Wonju, South Korea, into Almond's X Corps positions on the UN eastern flank. Massive Chinese units were being deployed behind the North Koreans, and if the enemy broke through, Ridgway's escape route to Pusan would be threatened and he might be forced to seek MacArthur's permission to begin the much-discussed and dreaded evacuation. The night before the battle was joined south of Wonju, Ridgway wrote in his diary: "This may be the first crisis of World War III. The issues that are really at stake are the power and prestige of our great nation." The situation had not been as tense since the Marines were trapped in the mountains up near the Chosin Reservoir.

In such situations, even confident men equivocate. Within a matter of hours, Ridgway changed his mind three times about using the First Marine Division to bolster Almond. He had promised Smith that his men would not have to serve under Almond ever again; however, given the looming crisis, Ridgway decided he had to renege and assign the First Marines to the

X Corps on an emergency basis. Then, quickly, he remanded that order, deciding that he somehow would deploy them under his direct control. Finally, in short order, he canceled that command; the Marines were to stay in reserve. The reason for the last instruction was Almond's corps's being able to hold back the enemy onslaught without Marine help.

That battle was fought in horribly inclement weather. Temperatures dipped down to around zero degrees Fahrenheit and the snow was knee-deep. The key unit on the UN side in this critical struggle was the Second Infantry Division, and its key weapon was artillery, which inflicted "staggering" casualties on the North Koreans.

During the second day of this carnage, Ridgway was encouraged enough to compose a personal, unofficial letter to his friend General Wade H. Haislip, the Army vice chief of staff. Such back-channel communication is a time-honored Army practice, not done idly in such situations. Dated January 11, the letter was carried by courier and read, in part:

> All goes well here. There are several major problems, solutions to which lie behind the days ahead. Yet we discern their outline. We think we see inside. We believe we shall lick them all.
>
> The power is here. The strength and the means we have — short perhaps of Soviet military intervention. My one over-riding problem, dominating all others, is to achieve the spiritual awakening of the latent capabilities of this command. If God permits me to do that, we shall achieve more, far more, than our people think possible — and perhaps inflict a bloody defeat on the Chinese which even China will long remember, wanton as she is in the sacrifice of lives.

Haislip must have excitedly raced into Collins's office with the letter in hand. Ridgway was not prone to prattle and everyone knew it. What was so astonishing about this forecast was how much at variance it was with Mac-Arthur's doomsday estimates, which had influenced the Chiefs to order a staff study about what to do if the situation deteriorated further. By coincidence, Ridgway's letter to Haislip arrived in Washington only a few hours before the Joint Chiefs met on January 12 to formulate another message to MacArthur and to decide whether to approve the staff study. The good news notwithstanding, the Chiefs moved cautiously, sending this message to Mac-Arthur at noon:

> Based on all the factors known to us, including particularly those presented in your recent messages, we are forced to the conclusion that it is infeasible under existing conditions, including sustained major effort by Communist China, to hold for a protracted period a position in Korea.
>
> However, it would be to our national interest, also to the interest of the

UN, to gain some further time for essentially diplomatic and military consultations with UN countries participating in Korean effort before you issue firm instructions for initiative of evacuation of troops from Korea.

It is important also to United States prestige worldwide . . . that Korea not be evacuated unless actually forced by military considerations, and that maximum practicable punishment be inflicted on communist aggressors.

The staff study that the Chiefs passed judgment on during their January 12 meeting had reappraised the "soft" policies toward Communist China, given that forced evacuation seemed inevitable. Sherman, the man who had come to MacArthur's rescue with his timely support for the Inchon plan, was the principal mover in this reappraisal. Unmistakably, he was again moving toward MacArthur's view and, given his powers of persuasion, bringing the Chiefs with him. At his behest, they "tentatively agreed" to his view that "all appropriate means" should be taken to prevent the "further spread by force of Communism on the mainland of Asia," and endorsed three specific staff study recommendations: that "restrictions" imposed on Chiang's forces be removed; that the US should provide "logistical support" for anti-Communist guerrillas operating on the China mainland; and that aerial reconnaissance of Manchuria and the coast of Communist China be authorized. The only main recommendation they did not approve was MacArthur's wanting a naval blockade of China imposed, whether other UN members wanted to go along or not. Instead, the Chiefs recommended that the United States "prepare" to "place it in effect" as soon as "our position in Korea is stabilized or when we have evacuated Korea, and depending upon circumstances then obtaining." The Chiefs submitted these tentative recommendations in a paper to Marshall, who, without revealing his judgment of them, passed them along for "information" to the National Security Council. Pressed by events in the war zone as they perceived them, the Chiefs were moving into MacArthur's camp, with only Marshall potentially blocking the way. This situation seems to be what Marshall was referring to when he later observed, "We were at our lowest point."

The Chiefs' changing view showed how difficult these men were finding it to keep the war limited and fight with only a fraction of the power at their disposal. No doubt they were thinking about the trouble in store for them should the war be lost. Their wavering reaffirmed for Truman Marshall's importance to him. Recalling these difficult days, Acheson was to observe that, in all the nation's history, Marshall was the only individual who would have been capable of holding together at Valley Forge the Continental Army as Washington did.

The reason the Chiefs approved the staff study recommendations only "tentatively" must have been the confusion caused by Ridgway's letter to

Haislip. And so, upon Marshall's recommendation, the Chiefs decided to send Collins to Korea, once more, via Tokyo, to ascertain what was going on and whose status reports were correct — MacArthur's or Ridgway's. Hoyt Vandenberg accompanied him, and the two departed Andrews Air Force Base a few hours after the Chiefs adjourned their meeting. They carried with them, unadvisedly, it seems, a copy of the staff study that had just been submitted to Marshall. Whether the latter knew this is not known.

A paper they did not carry was one Acheson had wanted them to review with MacArthur that would provide him current "political guidance." Bradley successfully opposed the suggestion on the grounds that they should focus on purely military matters. As a result, Truman was persuaded to take the highly unusual step of composing a letter to this effect for MacArthur. The basic thrust of it matched that of the Joint Chiefs' latest message. In a very accommodating tone, which Acheson later described as "imaginative, kind and thoughtful," the President told MacArthur that UN forces must resist in Korea as long as possible and gave ten reasons why this was so. However, he conceded that an evacuation might become necessary because the "limited forces" available to the general might make "resistance" impossible "militarily." In this event, Truman said he wanted it "clear to the world" that evacuation was "forced upon us by military necessity." He even talked about continuing the fight on certain offshore islands. He summed up his appraisal this way: "We shall not accept the result [evacuation] politically or militarily until the aggression has been rectified." This statement conveyed more than he intended, implying the same yearning to become reciprocally more aggressive that was developing among the Chiefs.

Truman's personal letter was sent to MacArthur via JCS channels and arrived in Tokyo at about the same time Collins and Vandenberg did on January 15. Informants had probably already told MacArthur about Sherman's aggressive influence and the Chiefs' having tentatively approved a contingency paper that adopted a number of the main ideas he had been advocating. According to Korean War historian Clay Blair, Jr., "that, plus Truman's warlike vow to *rectify* Peking's aggression . . . may have led MacArthur to believe that he had won the policy battle after all, that his programs for all-out war with Red China now had a very good probability of being approved — provided, of course, that Eighth Army was forced to evacuate."

To awaken the spirit of the Eighth Army, Ridgway had already decided he needed many new commanders to replace old ones who were beyond redemption or would take too long to save. Because he personally spent so much time in the field, he quickly developed his own appraisals of what was going on. He discovered, among other things, that misleading and false reports had been filed, as some commanders contrived to create the impression that their units were withdrawing under pressure, when, in fact there was none; they were withdrawing only to get better terrain. He also discerned woeful underuse of artillery. Commanders had been pleading for fire support but had not been using that which they controlled themselves. To end this practice, he made it virtually a capital crime to abandon artillery pieces. Faith had done this up at Chosin, but he had no choice; for him, it was a matter of making room to carry out all his wounded. During the Eighth Army's long retreat down the Korean Peninsula, its units had abandoned the equivalent of thirteen regular artillery battalions' worth of artillery pieces.

Ridgway eventually removed five of the six US Army division commanders, including Major General McClure and Major General David Barr, whose regiment under MacLean and Faith had been destroyed. Commanders and staff officers "who were manifestly not of the aggressive mind," as he put it, lost their jobs. He wanted them to "get off their hunkers and visit troops in the field." He informed Collins during his visit that he could not execute his plans unless his commanders were aggressive and for that reason "above all else, we had to learn to be ruthless with our general officers," he recalled. Other, less senior officers — assistant division commanders, commanders of regiments and battalions — were sent packing, too. In particular, he pressed the Pentagon for "younger brigadier generals," men whose energy still matched their ambitions. He wanted these type people leading in combat. One senior staff officer brought his promising career to a close when, in early January, he made the mistake of briefing Ridgway on Eighth Army withdrawal plans after only taking into account predicted weather conditions. The man had not even considered whether the enemy was forcing the retreat or not. "I was shocked," Ridgway commented later. Believing that a staff officer's job was in many ways more difficult than that of a commander — the former had to lead more subtly, since he did not have actual command authority — Ridgway had already started bringing in many "tried and true" World War II staff officers.

Ridgway's insistence on ruthlessness notwithstanding, firings were being handled as discreetly as possible. Public humiliation causes bitterness and controversy, and he did not have the time for such distractions. A brutal firing also makes the replacement too tentative, something Ridgway did not want. An overall examination of the Eighth Army's command structure and the changes he wrought during his first thirty days evidences a housecleaning, but he gave most men he dismissed an alibi to take home with them. After retirement, Ridgway explained his reason for this in personal terms:

you can "ruin a man for life . . . if you take too drastic action. But if you . . . can be patient with him, give him a little chance to get on his feet spiritually now, not so much physically, . . . his spirit might equal the challenge and you can save him for life."

Ridgway acknowledged a special duty not to shame older officers with long, admirable career records, which invariably included World War II combat. His handling of his three corps commanders, once he determined that Coulter and Milburn were too timid and Almond too reckless, shows how artfully he could cope with personnel problems.

He removed Coulter by promoting him to lieutenant general and making him his deputy commander responsible for liaison with the ROK army and Rhee; this was a meaningless job that would get Coulter out of the chain of command. To help mask his true purpose, he even gave Coulter a medal. Virtually all fired senior officers got them. With Milburn, his loyal, old friend, Ridgway could not bring himself to employ even these machinations, so he literally moved in with the I Corps, making it his home base, imposing his attitude as well as his presence.

As for Almond, Ridgway kept him on a short leash. He observed that "Almond was one of the few commanders I've had that, instead of ever having to push at all, I would have to keep an eye on, else he, maybe in his boldness, would have jeopardized his command or executed a very risky operation." This is consistent with what O. P. Smith remembered about him. "I'll say this for Almond," he observed, "he was never beaten."

On January 15, Ridgway, as noted, kept his promise to John Michaelis and began moving the I Corps up behind his regiment in stages. He called the operation Wolfhound. This time the ROK army had cleared the main road of refugees. Michaelis's vanguard, backed up by the powerful force behind it, plowed through resistance at Osan before being halted north of that city at almost the same spot where, on July 5, Brad Smith's task force made the first unsuccessful attempt at stopping the Communists. From the opposite side, the Chinese were taking advantage of the same defensive terrain features that Smith had tried to use. And as the enemy had earlier, the Americans broke through, fighting their way to the outskirts of Suwon. There, very large Chinese forces were gathering, and this readily became apparent. Anticipating a strong counterattack, Ridgway withdrew the four regiments involved in Wolfhound and arrayed them in interlocking defensive positions near Osan, hoping the Chinese would pursue. But they did not, leaving the impression that they were unwilling to fight. As a consequence, the GIs involved became more confident and, to them, the enemy became less formidable.

Collins and Vandenberg had arrived in the war zone the day Operation Wolfhound commenced, and the Army Chief could feel the "improved spirit Ridgway had already imparted to his men." What he and Vandenberg saw during three days there confirmed this initial impression, and on January 17 Collins cabled the following estimate to Bradley back in Washington: "Eighth Army in good shape and improving daily under Ridgway's leadership. Morale very satisfactory considering conditions. . . . On the whole Eighth Army now in position and prepared to punish severely any mass attack."

Bradley notified Marshall, who called Truman. According to Bradley, "As the word spread through the upper levels of government that day, you could almost hear the sighs of relief." There had been rays of hope before, but now, for the first time since Chosin, the sun did indeed shine. Ridgway's generalship might well have saved Truman's presidency. There were other implications; had Ridgway not reversed the Eighth Army's fortunes, Truman might well have tried to redeem himself by expanding the war when faced with the alternative, a humiliating withdrawal from Korea and the harsh retribution of an embittered American public. Furthermore, without Ridgway's having accomplished what he did — it was one of the most remarkable feats in US military history — the impact of Marshall's standing behind Truman, a critical element throughout this crisis, might have waned, to dire, divisive effect.

Collins's message had two very important concrete results. The first was almost immediate. When the National Security Council met that afternoon, its members rejected the Chiefs' January 12 paper, thus dismissing contingency plans to expand the war. The second was that the administration and the Joint Chiefs, including Sherman, transferred all their faith from MacArthur to Ridgway. Overnight, Ridgway became the man to whom they turned. MacArthur had used up virtually the entire store of trust and confidence that his career and his Inchon victory had earned him. He was found to be fundamentally wrong — again — and this time about the status of his own men, whom he was saying the Communists were about to drive into the sea. MacArthur had dealt himself out of a strategic-planning role. "Perhaps this was the real end of that overshadowing career," observed military historian Walter Millis. What would make MacArthur's demotion doubly shocking to him was that he had seemed so close to winning the policy battle only three days earlier, when Collins, en route to Korea, had stopped to confer with him in Tokyo.

He would not quit, though. Ever the fighter, in policy debates as well as war, MacArthur was desperate to create a new dynamic. And so, two days later, on January 20, the day after the X Corps recaptured Wonju, he flew to Korea, landing at Taegu. He did not leave the airfield and stayed only one and a half hours, during which time he consulted with Ridgway and held a news conference. Evidently, he had two primary purposes for his visit: he wanted to associate himself with Ridgway's success and he wanted to show that he shared the American public's exasperation with a seemingly aimless war that was then generating thirteen hundred casualties per week. Maybe subconsciously he also wanted to remind his soldiers that he was in charge of the war effort, not Ridgway; the latter's performance was making it easy for them to forget. In his comments to reporters, MacArthur sang a new tune of confident control; he belittled any notion of withdrawal and said, "This command intends to maintain a military position in Korea just as long as the statesmen of the UN decide we should do so." Despite this reference to the United Nations, his statement was actually a backhanded slap at the administration and what its critics were calling Truman's "no-win" policies.

Intended or not, and it most likely was, MacArthur was signaling a new tack and another step toward the political arena, a step that Democrats had long suspected he would one day take. He was in effect asking Republican conservatives for their invitation, and in the near future would be even less subtle about soliciting it. Already some of their number were touting him as a vice presidential candidate to run in the 1952 elections with Senator Taft, the GOP front-runner.

Had ambition alone caused MacArthur to set himself against Truman and his Democratic administration, his attacks on existing policy would have resonated with a hollow tone. But MacArthur sincerely believed that American soldiers were dying for no real purpose and, as fundamentally, he thought Truman, Acheson, and Marshall had the nation's international priorities reversed. His views on those had not changed since those months long before when he traveled through Asia as his father's aide. As part of his preparation for that journey, he had read Senator Albert J. Beveridge's famous 1910 oration, and what he had seen since then had confirmed for him all the Indiana Republican had had to say, including his statement that "the power that rules the Pacific . . . is the power that rules the world."

Caught in the middle of this policy struggle was Ridgway, who was disturbed by MacArthur's Taegu press conference. He worried that his superior officer had demeaned the mission of the Eighth Army and adversely affected his soldiers' fragile confidence. That evening he reacted by retiring to his tent to compose an extraordinary message that he had read to all his soldiers the next day. His finished product was proof that even in a soldier's hands the pen is mightier than the sword. Very cleverly, he changed the meaning of what MacArthur intended to convey.

In his letter, Ridgway proposed to answer two questions for his men: "Why are we here?" and "What are we fighting for?" He began by transforming the negative connotation of MacArthur's comments. "The answer to the first question," he wrote,

is simple and conclusive. We are here because of the decisions of the properly constituted authorities of our respective governments. As the Commander in Chief, United Nations Command, General of the Army Douglas MacArthur has said: "This command intends to maintain a military position in Korea just as long as the statesmen of the United Nations decide we should so do." The answer is simple because further comment is unnecessary. It is conclusive because the loyalty we give, and expect, precludes any slightest questioning of these orders.

The second question is of much greater significance, and every member of this command is entitled to a full and reasoned answer. Mine follows.

To me the issues are clear. It is not a question of this or that Korean town or village. Real estate is, here, incidental. It is not restricted to the issue of freedom for our South Korean Allies, . . . though that freedom is a symbol of the wider issues and included among them. The real issues are whether the power of Western civilization, as God has permitted it to flower in our own beloved lands, shall defy and defeat Communism; whether the rule of men who shoot their prisoners, enslave their citizens, and deride the dignity of man shall displace the rule of those to whom the individual and his individual rights are sacred; whether we are to survive with God's hand to guide and lead us, or to perish in the dead existence of a Godless world.

If these be true, and to me they are, beyond any possibility of challenge, then this has long ceased to be a fight for freedom for our Korean Allies alone and for their national survival. It has become, and continues to be, a fight for our own freedom, for our own survival, in an honorable, independent national existence. . . .

In the final analysis, the issue now joined right here in Korea is whether Communism or individual freedom shall prevail; whether the flight of fear-driven people we have witnessed here shall be checked, or shall at some future time, however distant, engulf our own loved ones in all its misery and despair.

These are the things for which we fight. Never have members of any military command had a greater challenge than we, or a finer opportunity to show ourselves and our people at their best — and thus do honor to the profession of arms, and to those brave men who bred us.

Four regiments had these words read to them the next day before dawn when they jumped off on another reconnaissance in force, like the one Task Force Michaelis had executed the week before. The earlier one had been a I Corps operation; this time both the I Corps and the IX Corps were involved.

Ridgway had assigned one regiment from each of four different US Army divisions to the operation, spreading the risk as well as the potential for positively influencing many more soldiers. Harold K. Johnson's Eighth Cavalry led it and got as far as the Inchon area. Nowhere did they encounter significant opposition. The other three regiments met light resistance, too. As planned, all four withdrew after the maneuvers, which exhilarated all involved. Their confidence soared. They had advanced; the feared enemy had not beaten them back. In fact, his presence had hardly been felt.

Immediately, Ridgway decided to act on this intelligence. He ordered all the I Corps and the IX Corps to begin an advance two days hence; it was code-named Operation Thunderbolt. He wanted them to reach the south bank of the Han. Kimpo Airfield and Inchon were to be two major objectives along the way.

Evidently, Lin Piao had withdrawn his forces to the other side of the river, but Ridgway was wary of a trap. The day before the operation was to begin, he climbed aboard his small plane and for two hours flew over the "lonely, empty land" in front of his troops, "skimming the ridge tops, ducking into valleys, circling over the dead villages." Lieutenant General Earle Partridge, the Fifth Air Force commander, had insisted on being his pilot. November's surprise disaster was on Ridgway's mind, but he saw nothing and convinced himself that he "would not be sending Eighth Army into a trap in which it could be destroyed."

The next morning, the thousands of soldiers of the two corps began cautiously moving forward, with Ridgway carefully controlling their movements. Units did not advance beyond certain phase lines until all nearby had reached them. Artillery barrages preceded their march, which also had strong support from Air Force, Navy, and Marine aircraft. Navy warships supported I Corps units along the western coastal waters. The Chinese had abandoned Suwon, except for some guerrilla fighters left behind to harass. Some Chinese soldiers encountered were armed only with hand grenades, which indicated that the enemy was having supply problems.

An important battle, albeit small, occurred the second day of Thunderbolt. It involved a Turkish brigade operating as part of the I Corps. The Turks used bayonets to overwhelm Chinese entrenched on a hillside. Everyone was tense and eager for any kind of news, so word of this dramatic episode shot through the ranks. The Turks had killed four hundred that way, it was said. Actually, the number was much smaller; a more careful examination determined that most of the 152 dead had been killed by artillery fire. But Ridgway, to suite his purposes, did not publicize a correction; the central fact was that the Turks had sought out the enemy for hand-to-hand combat.

An officer who had not kept notes on leadership for twenty years might not have made the most of the situation. In the tradition of wise old General Fisk, Ridgway immediately grasped the event's potential as a symbol for his rejuvenated army. It was tangible and graphic — something to make a soldier believe that others like him were willing to risk their lives to attack the enemy with zeal.

Forthwith, Ridgway ordered every man in the Eighth Army to fix bayonets. "The job is to kill Chinese," he told them melodramatically. It was like a scene from an old war movie, when the actors charge up a ridge and a battle hymn is played.

The Eighth Army surged forward. By early February, all three corps were locked in combat. In the X Corps's zone, a Chinese division that counterattacked was obliterated by Marine close-air support. And on February 7, as if to confirm the Eighth Army's renewed fighting spirit, a US Army company in the I Corps staged what S. L. A. Marshall later described as the "greatest bayonet attack by U.S. soldiers since Cold Harbor in the Civil War." Three days later, Kimpo Airfield was retaken.

Success seemed to have materialized as an act of will. The change in the course of the war was so total that even under Almond's rash leadership, tragedy turned into triumph. Absorbed with a complicated double envelopment of North Korean units in an area north of Wonju, he had ignored the threat of Chinese forces in the area, though Ridgway and his staff had warned him about them. The Chinese counterattacked when Almond's corps was most vulnerable. An ROK division was surrounded immediately and destroyed; some 7,500 men were killed or captured. This rout endangered the whole corps. The Chinese pushed aside two other ROK divisions and trapped a number of smaller units, including a Dutch battalion that lost 1,537. This turned out to be Lin Piao's second attempt to break through at Wonju, so the whole UN position was again at risk. Ridgway was prepared to call off his offensive in the west and rush reinforcements to the southeast to protect Pusan, his principal supply point and escape route.

Fortunately for the UN cause, Almond put Brigadier General George Stewart, the Second Infantry Division's assistant commander, in charge of making a stand with the disparate X Corps units that the enemy was pushing into Wonju. Steward insisted that Colonel Loyal Haynes, his artillery commander, bracket the approach routes with engineering precision. With intense effort, Haynes's artillery crews derived the exact coordinates for laying a shell down on any point along a road that would be the enemy's main line of attack.

Incredibly, in broad daylight, four Chinese divisions marched into this setup, paradelike, even more foolishly than the North Koreans had in the first assault on Wonju. Their casualties were horrendous, but those still standing kept marching. The scene defied comprehension. According to an Army historian, "pilots reported the river running red with the blood of the massacred troops."

Haynes finally told Stewart he was running low of ammunition and had to stop. "Keep firing until the last shell has been used," Stewart told him. Later, Haynes called back to say that his weapons were overheating. "Keep firing until the gun barrels melt," Stewart ordered.

The surviving Chinese eventually broke and ran, and many of those that did fell victim to air attacks. More than five thousand dead Chinese soldiers were counted along the road. The number injured was many times that. This massacre on Valentine's Day, 1951, which became known as the "Wonju shoot," virtually ended the possibility of the Chinese offensive succeeding. Four days later, on February 18, Ridgway was notified that Communist forces were withdrawing from some positions in front of the IX Corps.

On a roll now, Ridgway called his senior commanders and staff together, and ordered a huge offensive to begin only sixty hours hence. He wanted to drive all Communist forces north across the Han before they could reorganize. For this he brought the big, replenished, 25,000-man Marine division out of reserve and assigned it to the IX Corps to spearhead the assault. Seven other divisions were also involved — more than 100,000 soldiers altogether. Both sides now fielded huge armies, about 500,000 each; Chinese reinforcements were pouring in from Manchuria, and Rhee had rapidly enlarged his army.

Ridgway aptly called his offensive plan Operation Killer — perhaps the last honest name an American military operation has had. Rusk, vocal and assertive as usual, was put off by the code name and complained to Collins "that to many people Korea now means only killing, a process of killing Americans, Chinese, and Koreans." Ridgway's reaction, essentially, was that anyone in the war zone could confirm that the conflict was precisely that. He was, in his own words, "by nature opposed to any effort to 'sell' war to people as an only mildly unpleasant business that requires very little in the way of blood." But Rusk's objection caused subsequent operations to be given inane titles.

During Killer, which was launched on February 21, Ridgway wanted to push as far north as possible before the Chinese counterattacked. He was astute politically and recognized that a stalemate in the general region of the thirty-eighth parallel, the original border, would be an acceptable end to this war. In a few days, MacArthur's behavior would incite him to say outright that his mission was to "stop" communism, not drive it back.

These days, MacArthur was finding Korea a much more salubrious clime and was visiting frequently, showing up shortly before operations began. Thinking MacArthur was inadvertently tipping off the enemy, Ridgway would eventually ask him, ever so deferentially, to arrive after operations began, and he would assent. During these visits he usually made a point of publicly preaching policy, in violation of Truman's instructions of December 6, 1950.

Gradually MacArthur's criticism became less subtle, more openly at odds with administration policy. Upon landing at Suwon on January 28, shortly after the city was recaptured, he said, "This is exactly where I came in seven months ago to start this crusade. The stake we fight for now, however, is more than Korea — it is to free Asia." During a February 13 trip, he kept his feelings in check, but during another, on March 7, he read a statement that was classic legerdemain: "[With] a continuation of the existing limitations upon our freedom of counter-offensive action, and no major additions to our organizational strength, the battle lines cannot fail in time to reach a point of theoretical military stalemate. . . . Vital decisions have yet to be made — decisions far beyond the scope of the authority vested in me as the military commander."

MacArthur was relentless. He was not going to fade away. This one became known as his "die for tie" statement, and it so upset Ridgway that he again challenged MacArthur, without saying so directly, with a statement of his own. He was worried that MacArthur's words might convince American soldiers they were risking their lives for nothing. On March 12, Ridgway told reporters that it would be a "tremendous victory" if the Eighth Army reached the thirty-eighth parallel.

"We didn't set out to conquer China," he said.

> We set out to stop Communism. We have demonstrated the superiority on the battlefield of our men. If China fails to throw us into the sea, that is a defeat of incalculable proportions. If China fails to drive us from Korea, she will have failed monumentally. . . .
>
> The things for which we are fighting here are of such overwhelming importance I can't conceive of any member of our fighting forces feeling that there lies ahead any field of indefinite or indeterminate action.

No one in a position of high authority was now going to defer to MacArthur's judgment, as they had in the past, so his only options were either to use enemy activity or verified intelligence about prospective enemy activity to appeal directly to the American public, which still held him in high esteem.

It so happened that early in March the intelligence picture had begun

developing to suit his purposes. Indications were that Communist commanders were assembling in Manchuria another huge ground force and also a
large air force. In addition, there were worrisome signals that the Russians
were concentrating a large submarine force in the region. If the Soviet
Union were to get involved in the fighting, Truman's determination to limit
the war was by the boards.

While intelligence officers were riveted to these goings-on, the attention
of Americans back home who were following the war was focused on the
resurgence of UN forces, particularly the Eighth Army's drive toward the
thirty-eighth parallel. Consequently, the debate in Washington refocused on
what the war aim should be now that worries about UN forces being driven
off the peninsula had receded. The present, official war aim was the reunification of the two Koreas under non-Communist leadership — the one that
Truman had adopted when success at Inchon and the ensuing political pressure prompted him to order American troops and their UN allies to invade
North Korea. MacArthur, of course, wanted at the very least to retain this
goal.

The Republican party's wing of New Right conservatives — composed
mostly of younger GOP members of Congress whose dominant tenet was
anticommunism — held the same view. This pitted MacArthur and them
against key policymakers within the administration, who were developing a
much different consensus. Most of the latter were for reverting to the
original war aim of only driving the Communists out of South Korea.
MacArthur and his political allies might have guessed as much, and even if
they did not, John Foster Dulles's brother Allen, who was one of Bedell
Smith's deputies at the CIA, was keeping them informed about what thinking was evolving, according to historian Michael Schaller. To thwart the
prospect of a reduced war aim, MacArthur had already begun to intensify
his public appeals, using reporters. This was the context for his "die for tie"
statement of March 7. In it he warned of a "savage slaughter" of Americans
should UN forces engage in a war of attrition, which is what he anticipated
would result if the United Nations tried to negotiate an end to the war
instead of trying to win it.

House majority leader Martin, MacArthur's old friend, also had been
trying to make this point. The very next day, March 8, he sent the general
a recent speech of his own in which he advocated using thousands of Chiang's
Nationalist troops to open up "a second front in Asia" and proclaimed, "If
we are not in Korea to win, then this Truman administration should be
indicted for the murder of thousands of American boys." Martin's accompanying letter read in part:

In the current discussions of foreign policy and overall strategy many of us have been distressed that, although the European aspects have been heavily emphasized, we have been without the views of yourself as Commander in Chief of the Far Eastern Command.

I think it is imperative to the security of our Nation and for the safety of the world that policies of the United States embrace the broadest possible strategy and that in our earnest desire to protect Europe we not weaken our position in Asia.

He went on to ask MacArthur for his views — "on a confidential basis or otherwise." In the years since, no evidence has surfaced to indicate that MacArthur contrived to have Martin send him this letter, but its timing was perfect for him. He had gotten an invitation to convey his policy arguments directly to the central forum for such national deliberation, the Congress.

While this missive was still en route, MacArthur put the intelligence estimate of a new Chinese buildup and of Russian naval activity to work to shake up thinking in Washington. He used the information to support a request that atomic bombs be made available to him "on a call basis," which meant he would have control of them so that he could use them immediately on "D day" should the Russians launch an invasion of Japan. Two weeks would pass before he got any sort of answer. The long silence was an indication of how much the thinking in Washington and his own were diverging and how little interest there was in his views. This was March 10, and five days later the Eighth Army recaptured Seoul. The retaking of the capital was a sure sign to MacArthur that he had precious little time left to influence Truman's conclusions about how to fight the war.

By the fifteenth, MacArthur had received Martin's letter. The tone of a public statement he made that day, together with the melancholia that gripped him during a visit to the war zone on the seventeenth, indicated that he had decided to answer it in such a way that Truman would have no choice but to relieve him. "As I have on several occasions pointed out," he said,

the conditions under which we are conducting military operations in Korea do not favor engaging in positional warfare on any line across the peninsula. Specifically with reference with the 38th Parallel, there are no natural defense features anywhere near its immediate proximity. The terrain is such that to establish a conventional defense system in reasonable depth would require such a sizeable force that if we had it, and could logistically maintain it, we would be able to drive the Chinese Communists back across the Yalu, hold that river as our future main line of defense, and proceed to the accomplishment of our mission in the unification of Korea.

During the trip to Korea, he talked about "fundamental decisions" that were going to have to be made to avoid a "heavy cost in Allied blood." Then he climbed into a jeep with Ridgway and O. P. Smith and had the driver take them many miles up toward the front. During the next hours he said hardly anything, alone with his thoughts, as if in a trance. His only words were spoken to tell the generals with him to keep going forward whenever they asked; for miles, GIs taking photographs to send home lined the road.

Three days later, on March 20, MacArthur answered Martin's letter by telegram, without requesting confidentiality. His response included these passages:

> My views and recommendations with respect to the situation created by Red China's entry into the war against us in Korea have been submitted to Washington in most complete detail. Generally, these views are well known and clearly understood, as they follow the conventional pattern of meeting force with maximum counterforce, as we have never failed to do in the past. Your view with respect to the utilization of the Chinese forces on Formosa is in conflict with neither logic nor this tradition.
>
> It seems strangely difficult for some to realize that here in Asia is where the Communist conspirators have elected to make their play for global conquest and that we have joined the issue they raised on the battlefield; that here we fight Europe's war with arms while the diplomats there still fight it with words; that if we lose the war to Communism in Asia the fall of Europe is inevitable, win and Europe most probably would avoid war and yet preserve freedom. As you pointed out, we must win. There is no substitute for victory.

The recapture of Seoul on the fifteenth imposed the same tight decision deadlines on those in Washington as it did on MacArthur. Up to that point, the State and Defense departments were still unable to reconstitute an overall policy plan for the war in light of China's entry. The diplomats insisted on a clear delineation of military capabilities before deciding on political objectives, and the generals insisted on a resolution of political objectives in Korea before delineating military courses of action. However, by March 19, when top officials from both departments met together, they had settled on Truman's initial war aim of driving the Communists out of South Korea and, pursuant to that, had decided that a truce offer should be made to the enemy before UN forces reached the thirty-eighth parallel. A major consideration during their deliberations was pressure from UN allies, all of whom seemed to be beseeching the administration to negotiate an end to the war. NATO, which was based on the concept of collective security, was in the throes of its formative development, so what the allies wanted done influenced Truman far beyond what their actual contribution to the war effort would indicate. Furthermore, Truman was convinced that the Soviets were trying to draw the United States into a prolonged war in Asia in order to undermine America's commitment to NATO. As a longtime Europe-first advocate, Truman was determined not to allow this.

The principals present at the March 19 meeting were Marshall, Acheson, and the Joint Chiefs, and their focus that day was on the draft of a statement that State Department staffers had written for Truman to make. After being reworked in this meeting and somewhat more within the next twenty-four hours, it ultimately included these passages:

> The Unified Command is prepared to enter into arrangements which would conclude the fighting and ensure against its resumption. Such arrangements would open the way for a broader settlement in Korea, including the withdrawal of foreign forces from Korea. . . .
>
> A prompt settlement of the Korean problem would greatly reduce international tension in the Far East and would open the way for the consideration of other problems in that area by the processes of peaceful settlement envisaged in the Charter of the United Nations.

This proposed presidential issuance still had not been put before Truman when those in attendance decided to ask MacArthur, perfunctorily, for his input. Truman, who was ending a short vacation in Key West, Florida, said later that he would have approved the statement written for him. In his memoirs, he approvingly recounted the group's reasoning, which was that "since we had been able to inflict heavy casualties on the Chinese and were pushing them back to and beyond the 38th Parallel, it would now be in their interest at least as much as ours to halt the fighting."

The language of the statement was well intended, but to Asia-firsters who believed passionately that Truman and his administration had lost China to the Communists by undermining Chiang, it had the trappings of a sellout. To them, the statement that the proposed arrangements would "open the way for the consideration of other problems in that area" meant that Chiang was about to be sold out again, in that the United States would acquiesce to Communist China's claim to Formosa and seat Mao's representative at the United Nations. William Sebald, the ranking US diplomat in Tokyo, recorded in his diary that MacArthur told him Truman and his advisers were plotting to "hand over . . . Formosa to Red China." The possibility of such a transfer later prompted Courtney Whitney to assess the administration's peace plan as "one of the most disgraceful plots in U.S. history." This view was probably an accurate reflection of MacArthur's.

Whether MacArthur had been tipped off through back channels about these goings-on is unknown. When inviting his input on March 20 by cable, the Joint Chiefs informed him of them superficially. The JCS message read:

State planning presidential announcement shortly that, with clearing of bulk of South Korean aggressors, United Nations now prepared to discuss conditions of settlement in Korea. Strong UN feeling persists that further diplomatic effort towards settlement should be made before any advance with major forces north of 38th parallel. Time will be required to determine diplomatic reactions and permit new negotiations that may develop. Recognizing that parallel has no military significance, State has asked JCS what authority you should have to permit sufficient freedom of action for next few weeks to provide security for UN forces and maintain contact with enemy. Your recommendation desired.

MacArthur rifled back his input within a few hours, and did not even refer to the peace initiative. In a message dated March 21, he said:

Recommend that no further military restrictions be imposed on the United Nations Command in Korea. The inhibitions which already exist should not be increased. The military disadvantages arising from restrictions on the scope of our Air and Naval operations coupled with the disparity between the size of our command and the enemy ground potential renders it completely impracticable to attempt to clear North Korea or to make any appreciable effort to that end.

He quickly followed up that cable with one requesting permission to move the Seventh Fleet closer to the mainland China coast "to make a show of force" and "obtain area familiarization" for American pilots and ship captains. Admiral Joy, his Navy chief, had put him up to this; however, since MacArthur had approved the idea, Bradley later speculated that the Chiefs' message about a peace offer had "snapped his brilliant but brittle mind" because it made MacArthur realize that "there would be no all-out war with China directed from Tokyo." The Chairman of the Joint Chiefs of Staff came to the conclusion that it was either this state of mind or an ambition to catapult himself into a run for the presidency in 1952 that prompted MacArthur to take immediate steps to sabotage the administration's peace initiative.

He took the first step on March 23. Without consulting or even informing the Joint Chiefs beforehand, as ordered, he unilaterally authorized Ridgway to cross the thirty-eighth parallel. As noted, the Eighth Army commander wanted to keep the enemy forces off balance in order to impede their ability to mass for an attack. He had in mind destroying their supply depots in North Korea and seizing positions that his own forces could defend more easily than those along the border, but he had no intention of driving all the way through North Korea to the Yalu and beyond, as MacArthur wanted to do.

The following day, MacArthur took the second step by issuing a communiqué that would, if anything, spur the Chinese to fight. Truman saw it as an "ultimatum" to the Chinese, and they probably did also. In it, MacArthur said that "round-the-clock massive air and naval bombardment" had left enemy units in forward areas incapable of sustained operations; that "Red China, of such exaggerated and vaunted military power, lacks the industrial capacity" for modern war; and that UN superiority in firepower and airpower was such that "it cannot be overcome by bravery, however fanatical, or the most gross indifference to human loss."

Threatening to expand the war, he warned that if the United Nations were to end "its tolerant effort to contain the war to the area of Korea" and begin conducting military operations against Chinese "coastal areas and interior bases," it would "doom Red China to the risk of military collapse."

Having laid all this out, MacArthur announced: "Within the area of my authority as military commander . . . I stand ready at any time to confer in the field with the Commander-in-Chief of the enemy forces in an earnest effort to find any military means whereby the realization of the political objectives of the United Nations in Korea, to which no nation may justifiably take exceptions, might be accomplished without further bloodshed."

According to Bradley, the statement's "defiant, mocking tone seemed calculated to sabotage any chance for a settlement"; he observed, too, that "it directly and forcibly challenged the United States policy of limited war in Korea." That these were MacArthur's purposes, there is little doubt, though in his memoirs he wrote that at the time he deemed it a "routine communiqué."

In Washington, it was still March 23 when reporters' first accounts of MacArthur's communiqué started coming across the wire and were broadcast on radio. And though it was late on a Friday evening, within an hour Lovett, Rusk, and a few others gathered at Acheson's Georgetown home to assess the damage done. More than anything, those in attendance used the occasion to vent their anger. Acheson called MacArthur's action "a major act of sabotage of a Government operation" and "insubordination of the grossest sort." His observation of Lovett was that the deputy defense secretary, who was "usually imperturbable and given to ironic humor under pressure, was angrier than I have ever seen him." However, Lovett conceded that what MacArthur said was "probably the most popular public statement anyone has ever made." The American public's dissatisfaction with the war was rising sharply, as Truman's popularity, which was mostly a function of war sentiment, was plummeting. Lovett told Acheson that "if the President challenged" MacArthur's statement, "he would be in the position at once of being on the side of sin." By issuing his communiqué, MacArthur had established himself in the public's perception as the one for peace, as well as victory. Even so, Lovett believed that MacArthur "must be removed and removed at once." They concluded such rumination at about one o'clock in the morning.

Truman was furious, too. He wanted to kick MacArthur into the North China Sea, he told his daughter, Margaret. "I was never so put out in my life," she heard him say. "It's the lousiest trick a Commander-in-Chief can have done to him by an underling." He said MacArthur had made it impossible for him to announce a settlement proposal, and had "prevented a cease-fire proposition right there."

The next morning, Acheson, Lovett, and Rusk met with the Joint Chiefs. According to Marshall, the group decided that "whatever chance there may have been at that time to negotiate a settlement of the Korean conflict" was gone. The group also developed three recommendations: that MacArthur should again be ordered, in very specific terms, not to make statements on foreign policy without prior clearance; that the State Department should release its own communiqué saying that the "political issues" MacArthur had discussed were being addressed by officials in Washington and at the United Nations; and that Rusk should meet with the ambassadors of the thirteen nations who had people serving in MacArthur's UN command to tell them that the general's statements were "unauthorized and unexpected." US emissaries had nearly completed clearing Truman's proposed statement with representatives of these governments when MacArthur issued his communiqué.

At noon Truman met with Acheson, Lovett, Rusk, and Collins at the White House and accepted these recommendations. According to Acheson, the President was "perfectly calm" but "appeared to be in a state of mind that combined disbelief with controlled fury." Truman later wrote that Mac-Arthur had now "left me no choice — I could no longer tolerate his insubordination." But he would follow a very deliberate course, reining in a temperament that no doubt inclined him to fire MacArthur immediately. He proceeded slowly for several reasons. First, there was a slight chance the Chinese might accept MacArthur's offer to meet. Second, the public, not knowing that MacArthur had preemptively ended the administration's peace initiative, would think he was being punished for trying to make peace if he was abruptly dismissed. And third, and most important, Truman had to make certain that the leaders of the military establishment were behind him.

The latter consideration may have been one of the reasons MacArthur's request for ready access to atomic bombs was suddenly given careful attention. On March 23, only hours before MacArthur issued his communiqué, the Chiefs had finally responded to his request of March 10, saying only that they would "consider" it. Then, suddenly, the idea got serious attention. Evidently, the more the Chiefs thought about Truman's firing MacArthur, the more they worried about accusations that they were not fully supporting the men in the field. Bradley's excuse for the change of heart was "alarming intelligence information (from a classified source) that the Soviet Union was preparing for a major military move." In early April high officials informed Dean, the chairman of the Atomic Energy Commission, that Truman might soon order him to transfer control of some atomic bombs to the Air Force.

Events dramatically accelerated on Thursday, April 5, when on the House floor Martin stood to be recognized and then proceeded to read MacArthur's March 20 telegram to him. His explanation for waiting so long was that he had not known exactly what to do with it.

Roger Tubby, the President's assistant press secretary, was the first person in the White House to learn what had happened. Bulletins crossed the wire and bells started ringing. "House Republican Leader Martin of Massachusetts told the House today that General MacArthur favors use of Chinese Nationalist troops in Korean fighting," the Associated Press lead read. Tubby took copies of the dispatch forthwith to Truman, whose immediate response was to call Marshall. The latter was "revolted" that MacArthur would use a leader of the opposition to argue his case.

This time MacArthur had gone too far; Truman would get him now. His problems with MacArthur had become intensely personal, and thus had reached the point at which he usually started acting petty and vindictive. On his calendar Truman scribbled this notation:

> The situation with regard to the Far Eastern General has become a political one.
> MacArthur has made himself a center of controversy, publicly and privately. He has always been a controversial figure.
> He has had two wives — one a social light [*sic*] he married at 42, the other a Tennessee girl he married in his middle fifties after No. 1 had divorced him.

That night Truman recorded some further thoughts in his diary, the contents of which he confided in no one, except perhaps Bess. "This looks like the last straw," he wrote.

> Rank insubordination. . . .
> I call in Gen. Marshall, Dean Acheson, Mr. Harriman and Gen. Bradley before Cabinet to discuss situation. I've come to the conclusion that our Big General in the Far East must be recalled. I don't express any opinion or make known my decision.

Direct the four to meet again Friday afternoon and go over all the situation.

All the advisers when they met on April 6, 1951, urged caution. "If you relieve MacArthur," Acheson said, "you will have the biggest fight of your administration." Later he wrote that he felt at the time that Truman had to have the unanimous support of his top civilian and military advisers, especially Marshall and the Joint Chiefs. Marshall evidently had reached the same conclusion and, given his subsequent conduct, had decided it was important that the Chiefs reach their consensus free of pressure from him. He asked for more time to reflect, though he did observe that relieving MacArthur would undermine attempts to get the military-appropriations bill through Congress. This was not as shallow an objection as in retrospect it might seem. Since early January 1951, isolationists led by Senator Taft, who since the previous fall's elections had emerged as the likely GOP presidential nominee in 1952, had launched a strong attack against the administration's support of NATO, which was the cornerstone commitment of the administration's foreign and military policies. "The Great Debate," as Taft was calling the ongoing policy struggle, had focused on Truman's authority to order more troops to Europe and on funding for them. Firing MacArthur would supercharge the political environment and make it nearly impossible for any Republican lawmakers to support Truman in the policy debate.

Bradley voiced the Chiefs' wariness of firing MacArthur. He did not want to proceed until Collins, who was on an inspection trip in the South, returned to town. Nagging him was the "considerable doubt in my mind that MacArthur had committed a clear-cut case of insubordination as defined in Army Regulations." Before adjourning the meeting after about an hour, Truman instructed Bradley to convene the Chiefs when Collins returned and asked Marshall to review all the key communications between the Chiefs and MacArthur during the last two years.

That same day, in the afternoon, the same group reconvened, without the President, in Marshall's office. According to Bradley, Marshall did not want to fire MacArthur outright, and suggested that he be called home for consultations. Acheson's immediate response was that bringing MacArthur home "in the full panoply of his commands" would be the "road to disaster." He noted the alliance between MacArthur and Republican conservatives — "primitives," he called them — which, he predicted, would become more overt, and he said he was certain that this alliance would impair Truman's ability to act. Marshall immediately recognized the wisdom of this line of reasoning and withdrew his proposal.

Not all matters taken up this day were deferred, though. Later, after briefing Truman about the alarming intelligence reports of Chinese and Soviet buildups in the Far East, Bradley recommended that MacArthur be granted contingent authority to order air and naval strikes, using conventional weaponry, against the China mainland; he also recommended that some atomic bombs be transferred to military control for shipment to Air Force bases in Guam and Okinawa. Reports now were saying that the Russians had gathered seventy submarines in the seas near Vladivostok and Sakhalin. The military's main fears, which Bradley conveyed, were twofold: that huge numbers of Chinese troops were again gathering in Manchuria, and that the submarines were going to sink supply ships bound for Korea and Japan, as prelude to an invasion of the latter. According to historian Schaller, no one seemed to think of these enemy buildups as defensive in nature — forces to be employed should Truman lift his limitations and order the ground war expanded into China, for example.

Truman approved both of Bradley's recommendations. MacArthur would be permitted to order conventional strikes against air bases in Manchuria and the Shantung Peninsula of China if he determined that "major" assaults against UN forces were coming from them. And later in the day the President called in Dean to explain the situation and order him to transfer nine atomic bombs to military control. That Truman would reverse himself and give MacArthur more authority at this tense stage is indicative of how politically vulnerable the President and his party were. Should the enemy's renewed military buildup be prelude to another huge offensive that forced another allied reversal, Republican conservatives would cite it as being another tragic example of Truman and his fellow Democrats' having hamstrung the military, with the usual dreadful consequences.

Dean complied, though not before voicing reservations. A few days earlier he had written in his diary how worried he was about turning over control of these powerful weapons to field commanders "who had little knowledge concerning effects." He was especially leery of MacArthur. Truman allayed these concerns by assuring Dean that operational control of the weapons was to be confined to the Strategic Air Command, whose chain of command did not run through MacArthur. Dean signed the order and four days later, on April 10, the Air Force began transporting the nine atomic bombs across the Pacific.

It might have surprised Dean to know that Bradley was as worried about MacArthur as he was. The Chairman of the Joint Chiefs decided not to tell MacArthur that Truman had authorized contingent air strikes on China. "I was now so wary of MacArthur," he said, "that I deliberately withheld the message and all knowledge of its existence from him, fearing that he might,

as I wrote at the time, 'make a premature decision in carrying it out.' "
During the next several days, Bradley's precaution was formalized. Truman
decided that, if time permitted, he would tell Bradley when to give Mac-
Arthur authority to bomb the bases in China; and that if an emergency
situation precluded taking the time necessary, the Joint Chiefs would be
authorized to inform MacArthur of his authority. As when the Marines
were trapped up at Chosin and Walker's forces were reeling from the
Chinese assault on the other side of the peninsula, the British government
asked for assurances that it would be consulted in advance of air attacks on
China, but was not given them.

On Saturday, April 7, at 8:50 AM, Truman convened another meeting
with Marshall, Acheson, Harriman, and Bradley. The President's recollection of what transpired was that Marshall reported he had read all of the
important messages between the Chiefs and MacArthur and that "Mac-
Arthur should have been fired two years ago." However, Bradley later
reported that this account was erroneous, and that no such recommendation
was made by anyone. Given Marshall's subsequent conduct, Bradley's account of the proceedings is probably the more accurate of the two. After
about an hour and ten minutes, the group adjourned, apparently having
achieved nothing more by their comings and goings in limousines than
arousing the curiosity of White House reporters, who, according to Robert
Donovan of the *New York Times*, were finding that their usual sources of
information were dry. That a story was developing was obvious. That it
concerned MacArthur was only one of the possibilities, given a war going
on, the enemy buildup, and the Great Debate. However, Hanson Baldwin
had focused on the MacArthur story in a recent column.

Truman ended the meeting after asking his advisers to ponder the matter
over the weekend. He told them that they would meet again on Monday and
that he would not announce his decision before then.

That same day, remarkably, another MacArthur interview was published, as if to remind these men pondering the general's fate that they were
not dealing with an isolated act of indiscretion. A report had circulated that
ROK draftees were being released from active duty because the United
States would not supply them weapons, and the editor of the *Freeman,* an
ultraconservative publication, had written MacArthur to ask why. His reply, which was published on the seventh, was that the matter "involves basic
political decisions beyond my authority." In effect, he blamed Truman and
his policymakers, though earlier in the year he, too, had recommended that
no more ROK conscripts be armed because they were proving themselves to
be inept.

Marshall and Bradley continued their deliberations in Marshall's office after leaving the White House. Their perception was that Truman was going to fire MacArthur for insubordination. "God forbid! — a Billy Mitchell–type court martial," Bradley exclaimed later, with a shudder. To avert this, the two men tried their hands at writing MacArthur another letter telling him to shut up, but soon gave up the effort. Each agonized about having to end his own long career by ending MacArthur's. That, in and of itself, was terrible, and the abuse that conservative politicians and possibly the public at large would heap upon them was another awful dimension. Marshall had agreed to be Secretary of Defense for only one year, which would be finished in September; for some months, given health problems and his determination to step down permanently this time, he had been grooming Lovett to be his successor. Bradley's two-year term as Chairman of the Joint Chiefs would be up in August. Another discomfiting thought was that since MacArthur's challenging Truman's limitations on the war was so intrinsically political, the Chiefs were going to be charged with becoming politicized if they recommended that he be fired.

Nonetheless, the upshot of the Marshall-Bradley meeting was that the Defense Secretary confronted reality and decided to make preparations for relieving MacArthur. In formulating this plan, Marshall was sensitive to accusations that he was jealous of MacArthur and had a score to settle. On another level, he felt that MacArthur, given his long and distinguished career, deserved the courtesy of personal and private notice before any public announcement from the White House. Army Secretary Pace was traveling in the Far East and had recently been cordially received by MacArthur, so Marshall decided that the thirty-eight-year-old official should deliver the news. The thought of Pace, a mere acolyte compared to the two figures between whom he would find himself, confronting MacArthur, who had been a general almost as long as Pace was old, would be sadly amusing to a lot of people.

Communicating with Pace presented a problem for Marshall. Messages sent through Tokyo would be intercepted by MacArthur people who would notify him immediately. Therefore, Marshall decided to order Pace to travel to Korea, so that he could communicate with him through State Department channels, via Muccio's office. To set up this situation, Marshall sent Pace this baffling message through Tokyo: "This is explicit. Repeat this is explicit. You will proceed to Korea and remain there until you hear from me."

It was but a short time later that MacArthur revealed to Almond that he knew Truman might relieve him. At 5:45 PM, Sunday, April 8, Tokyo time, Almond, who had been taking a few days' leave from the war zone, called on MacArthur to say good-bye. According to Almond, "He looked rather disconsolate and said to me: 'I may not see you anymore, so good-bye,

Ned.' I said: 'I don't understand what you mean.' He said: 'I have become politically involved and may be relieved by the president.' "

In Washington a few hours later — at 2:00 PM on Sunday, there — the Joint Chiefs finally convened to discuss the matter, Collins having returned from his trip. Their charge, in Marshall's words, was to give their opinions "from a strictly military viewpoint." Their deliberations followed the pattern of Marshall and Bradley's conversation the day before. Initially, they tried avoiding the inevitable and talked of keeping MacArthur in charge of the occupation in Japan but terminating his control over Ridgway and the Eighth Army. But eventually they reconciled themselves to the fact that MacArthur's views were incompatible with Truman's war aims and that he could not stay on. A consensus developed that basically matched the conclusion Bradley had come to the night before, as he tossed and turned in bed. "It was not a question of who was right or wrong," he had decided. "As the ultimate in civilian control over the military, Commander in Chief Truman had every right to replace a general who defied his policy and in whom he had lost confidence." Wanting to minimize the controversy that would ensue, the Chiefs eschewed mention of "insubordination," given the legal ramifications. "In point of fact," Bradley later wrote, "MacArthur had stretched but had not legally violated any JCS directives. He had violated the President's December 6 [1950] directive, relayed to him by the JCS, but this did not constitute violation of a direct JCS order." As a cadet, Bradley probably would have deemed this distinction he was drawing quibbling.

Bradley summarized the recommendations of the Chiefs in a memorandum that he prepared about a month later, and the participants affirmed that it was an accurate accounting for the record.

> 1. By his public statements and by his official communications to us, he [MacArthur] had indicated that he was not in sympathy with the decision to try to limit the conflict in Korea. This would make it difficult for him to carry out Joint Chiefs of Staff directives. Since we had decided to try to confine the conflict to Korea and avoid a third world war, it was necessary to have a commander more responsive to control from Washington.
>
> 2. General MacArthur had failed to comply with the Presidential directive to clear statements on policy before making such statements public. He had also taken independent action in proposing to negotiate directly with the enemy field commander for an armistice and had made that statement public, despite the fact that he knew the President had such a proposal under consideration from a governmental level.
>
> 3. The Joint Chiefs of Staff have felt, and feel now, that the military must be controlled by civilian authority in this country. (The Congress itself was very careful to emphasize this point in the National Security Act of 1947 and in its amendment in 1949.) They have always adhered to this principle and

they felt that General MacArthur's actions were continuing to jeopardize the civilian control over the military authorities.

The April 8 JCS meeting adjourned at four, after two hours, and the participants took five minutes to walk down to Marshall's office to present their recommendations. Marshall first asked all four men to tell him individually what they thought and then he asked for their collective view, which Bradley conveyed. Marshall listened intently but did not express his own opinion; later he would testify that he had concurred. He instructed Bradley to repeat the Chiefs' judgment the next morning during their meeting with the President, who also had spent part of Sunday conferring about what to do. Speaker Rayburn and Chief Justice Fred Vinson, an old friend whom Truman was encouraging to run for President, met with him at Blair House, and he talked by telephone to Vice President Barkley, who was hospitalized for tests. They focused mostly on the political and constitutional ramifications of dismissing MacArthur, but Truman did not reveal his plans to them. Barkley was in the uncomfortable position of having a daughter married to a nephew of MacArthur.

Truman also spent part of Sunday seeking guidance from his history books, as he had done so often on other matters. He found accounts of a familiar-sounding, near-parallel situation and reread them closely. They told of Lincoln's problems with the politically ambitious commander of the Army of the Potomac, Major General George B. McClellan. One distinction was that McClellan was afraid to fight, whereas MacArthur wanted to take on the whole Communist world; however, both generals consorted with their Commander in Chief's political opposition in Congress. Lincoln eventually relieved McClellan of his command for making political statements to Congress and the press, as much as for his reticence on the battlefield. Truman also noted that McClellan thereafter ran for President against Lincoln in 1864.

The next day, Monday, April 9, the President began informing privately selected key figures what he planned to do. First, he met with Democratic congressional leaders. Marshall no doubt had told him the day before what the Joint Chiefs were going to recommend, because he announced his decision to these political leaders before meeting soon thereafter with Marshall, Acheson, Harriman, and Bradley; he had assured Bradley that he would await the Chiefs' recommendation before announcing his. During this second meeting, Bradley formally conveyed the JCS recommendation, and the other three advisers concurred with it. Truman then told them to prepare the necessary paperwork, intending to implement Marshall's plan and have Pace notify MacArthur in person before he as President announced the news to

White House reporters at his regularly scheduled weekly news conference on Thursday, three days hence.

Truman himself probably thwarted these plans. At a meeting the next morning, he told his staff: "So you won't need to read about it in the papers, I fired MacArthur yesterday from all his jobs." Having resigned himself to this difficult decision, he was in a relaxed mood and seemed to enjoy their shocked reaction as he elaborated. "He's going to be regarded as a worse double-crosser than McClellan," Truman told them. "He did just what McClellan did. . . . He worked with the minority to undercut the administration when there was a war on. . . . Everybody seems to think I don't have courage enough to do it. We'll let 'em think so, then we'll announce it."

By late afternoon, as Pace's instructions were being sent to him via coded messages through Muccio's office in Pusan, the administration got its first media inquiry. Acting on a tip from one of his editors, the *Chicago Tribune*'s Pentagon correspondent, Lloyd Norman, called Bradley's aide and speechwriter, Colonel Chester V. Clifton, asking him to comment on the rumor that an important resignation in Tokyo was imminent. The *Tribune*, Robert McCormick's paper, was an archfoe of Truman and Democrats generally; editorially, the paper supported using Chiang's soldiers to help fight the Korean War and also advocated widening the war into Communist China. It thus appeared that MacArthur had somehow learned he was going to be relieved, that he had decided to resign beforehand, and that one of his people had passed this information to the *Tribune*. Norman told Clifton that his paper was making arrangements to open a phone line to Tokyo to handle the story.

Clifton requested some time to investigate and said he would call back. He then called Bradley, who was in the Cabinet Room at the White House with Harriman, Rusk, Elsey, staff adviser Matthew Connelly, Press Secretary Joseph Short, and Short's assistant, Roger Tubby, working on documents that would be released at the time of Truman's announcement. Norman's inquiry shocked these men, and intense discussion ensued about what to do. Events were to prove that their reaction was poor. Long frustrated with MacArthur, some of them wanted too much to punish him. Harriman, Special Counsel Charles Murphy, Connelly, and Tubby were adamant about not letting him resign, their thinking being that he would thereby put the administration on the defensive. The opposite proved true. Rusk was the one most insistent about proceeding as planned — in an "orderly way," as he put it. Acheson agreed. Tubby's reaction to that idea, which he recorded in his journal, was "Why should we spare the Genl's feelings when he has behaved so outrageously toward President? In unethical, insubordinate, insolent way?" This missed the point; the group's primary concern should have been the American public's reaction, not that of MacArthur, whom they were about to make a martyr. Tubby's vindictive reaction won the argument; given his secondary position, Tubby was unusually confident among these men because he had been the State Department's chief press officer and, thus, had come to know Acheson and Rusk well.

Marshall, who had taken his wife to a movie being shown at the Fort Myer theater, was not interrupted in his entertainment, although he, along with Truman and MacArthur, would be most affected by the general's relief and how it was handled.

At ten o'clock that evening, Bradley, Harriman, Rusk, Connelly, and Short walked across Pennsylvania Avenue to Blair House to confer with Truman. Tubby and Elsey stayed behind to continue working on papers that would be released to reporters. Within thirty minutes, Truman had approved the group's recommendation that he proceed with the firing as planned, and Short telephoned Tubby, telling him to send to the mimeograph room the supporting documents they had prepared and also the presidential order appointing Ridgway as MacArthur's successor. Spurred by another inquiry — this one from the Mutual Broadcasting System — and a warning from Norman that the *Tribune* was preparing to go with a story the next morning, Truman approved the announcement's being made at 1:00 AM, Washington time, 2:00 PM, Tokyo time, April 11 in both cities. White House switchboard operators had already been alerted to report for work, and they were ordered to start calling immediately all reporters accredited to cover the White House beat, informing them that Short would be releasing an important statement and taking questions at 1:00 AM. Given the early-morning hour chosen for the announcement, mentioning its importance was hardly necessary.

All this was in motion by the time Marshall returned to his quarters at Fort Myer. Reacting quickly, he sent Pace a third message, this one canceling previous instructions that called for the Army Secretary's involvement. It so happened that because of "mechanical problems," Pace had not received those earlier orders, so Marshall's follow-up confused him. The Army Secretary was now told to "disregard" his instructions and to "advise General Matthew B. Ridgway that he is now the Supreme Commander in the Pacific; General MacArthur relieved. You will proceed to Tokyo where you will assist General Ridgway in assuming . . . his command."

A more important cable was the one sent to MacArthur by Bradley at midnight, only an hour before the press conference, which read:

> I have been directed to relay the following message to you from President Truman:
> I deeply regret that it becomes my duty as President and Commander in

Chief of the United States military forces to replace you as Supreme Commander, Allied Powers; Commander in Chief, United Nations Command; Commander in Chief, Far East; and Commanding General, U.S. Army, Far East. You will turn over your commands effective at once to Lieutenant General Matthew B. Ridgway. You are authorized to have issued such orders as are necessary to complete desired travel to such places as you may select. My reasons for your replacement will be made concurrently with the delivery to you of the foregoing order, and are contained in the next following message.

[Signed] Harry S. Truman

The "next following message" read:

With deep regret I have concluded that General of the Army Douglas MacArthur is unable to give his wholehearted support to the policies of the United States government and of the United Nations in matters pertaining to his official duties. In view of the specific responsibilities imposed upon me by the Constitution of the United States and the added responsibility which has been entrusted to me by the United Nations, I have decided that I must make a change of command in the Far East. I have, therefore, relieved General MacArthur of his command and have designated Lieutenant General Matthew B. Ridgway as his successor.

Full and vigorous debate on matters of national policy is a vital element in the constitutional system of our free democracy. It is fundamental, however, that military commanders must be governed by the policies and directives issued to them in the manner provided by our laws and Constitution. In time of crisis, this consideration is particularly compelling.

General MacArthur's place in history as one of our greatest commanders is fully established. The Nation owes him a debt of gratitude for the distinguished and exceptional service which he has rendered his country in posts of great responsibility. For that reason I repeat my regret at the necessity for the action I feel compelled to take in this case.

[Signed] Harry S. Truman

By dismissing MacArthur, Truman dramatically reaffirmed the primacy of civilian authority over the military as set forth in the Constitution and established a precedent that will probably dominate US military governance for as long as Lincoln's did, if not longer.

MacArthur was hosting a luncheon at the embassy for Senator Warren G. Magnuson, a Democrat from Washington State, when he got word that he had been fired. The news had stopped presses and interrupted regular programming throughout the world, and word was immediately relayed to him via his wife after aide Sidney L. Huff heard a radio bulletin. "Jeannie," MacArthur responded, "we're going home at last." He was the picture of composure. He did not excuse himself or hurry the meal. Bradley's cable arrived afterward, as he was about to return to his Dai Ichi office.

Ridgway also first got word of the firing from the radio via an intermediary. He was escorting Pace on an inspection trip when a reporter who had heard a bulletin asked him "whether I was not due congratulations." According to Ridgway, "I just stared back at the correspondent and told him quite honestly that I did not know what he was talking about." As in Tokyo, official word was slower to arrive, delayed in part by Pace and Ridgway's being up in a plane. They actually flew over Chinese-held positions for an extended period, inadvertently demonstrating how dominant UN/US airpower was. When they reached their destination, Throckmorton's command post, Pace had a message to call Major Leven C. Allen, the Eighth Army's chief of staff. The Army Secretary got through to him at about 4:45 PM and was read Marshall's cable. Pace, who is fondly remembered for his sense of humor, was stunned, and responded by saying, "Read that to me once more, Lev — I don't want to relieve General MacArthur on one reading."

Pace then proceeded to carry out his instructions, which were to inform Ridgway of his promotion and to support him any way he could. A hailstorm was under way at the time and, recalled Pace,

> I took General Ridgway out in the hail. General Ridgway used to wear those live grenades, and I thought if that hailstorm hits one of those live grenades, they're going to need a new supreme commander *and* a new [Army] secretary. . . . I said, "General Ridgway, it's my duty to advise you that you're now the supreme commander of the Pacific; General MacArthur [is] relieved." He said, "I can't believe it, Mr. Secretary." I said, "I can't either, so I'll repeat it. You're now the supreme commander of the . . . Pacific. . . . General MacArthur [is] relieved."

That evening, the two of them flew back to Ridgway's command post at Yoju. There the new commander of all UN forces made his first order of business composing a short note to Marshall, which he dispatched through back channels. "Earnestly hope," he wrote, "that great responsibilities entrusted me may be discharged in a manner to meet your approbation. Faithfully, Ridgway."

CHAPTER 11

★ ★ ★ ★ ★ ★ ★ ★ ★ ★ ★ ★ ★ ★ ★

HOLDING THE LINE

ABOUT FOUR MONTHS before Truman relieved MacArthur, the shock of Chinese intervention in Korea had intensified the political debate in the United State about how deeply involved the nation should become in protecting Western Europe. Critics such as Senator Taft saw no end to this business of fighting other people's wars.

Disaster in Korea highlighted the potential for another disaster in Europe. Five US divisions and their allies were reeling from the advances of the Chinese army, and yet, in Europe, the United States had only two divisions to stop the larger and much better equipped Soviet army. This obvious deficiency, which the success of the Chinese had underscored, forced policymakers on both sides of the Atlantic to do some precise calculations about the force structure needed to make NATO more than a paper alliance.

Taft did not share Truman's sense that it was in the nation's interest to pledge to defend Western Europe. A fervent isolationist, he had been one of thirteen senators who in 1949 had voted against ratification of the NATO Treaty. Unlike his friend Arthur Vandenberg, World War II and events afterward had not converted him to an expansive view of the world. Consequently, he was poised to challenge the numbers Truman and his advisers submitted about what was needed to help defend Western Europe.

Taft was widely admired in the Senate for his honesty and convictions, but, as noted, since World War II he had focused most of his influence and energy on domestic affairs. Increasingly, his conservative colleagues had made the same transition Vandenberg had. However, by late 1950 Taft's influence on foreign-affairs policy was on the rise again. With China having entered the war in Korea, the public, too, began to fear that the fighting could go on forever. Suddenly less popular was the idea of defending the so-called free world; Taft's conviction that Truman's overseas military obligations were not worth the cost seemed much more prudent.

Taft's influence was also magnified by the fact that, as noted previously, he had emerged from the 1950 congressional elections as the favorite to win the Republican party's presidential nomination two years hence. Dewey was still the titular head of the GOP, but the general feeling among party activists was that he had squandered his opportunity with his humiliating defeat in 1948 and that Taft now deserved his chance. He had tried but failed to win the nomination in 1940 and 1948. There was also a feeling that the GOP had strayed from its basic tenets by supporting Dewey, a moderate who espoused internationalism and an active federal government.

The prospects or, at least, the possibilities, then, for the Republican party, from the perspective of late 1950, were these:

• *Near term:* Taft and the old guard reopening the debate about Truman's foreign and military policies and the commitments they entailed.

• *Intermediate term:* Taft winning the GOP nomination and defeating Truman, whose popularity among voters was falling even faster than their support for the war in Korea.

• *Long term:* President Taft ordering US troops home from Korea and eviscerating the nation's NATO commitment by refusing to back it up with US military power.

European leaders had cause for alarm, which is why the Council of Ministers of NATO, when it convened on December 18, 1950, voted to recommend to Truman that he appoint Eisenhower supreme commander of the military force that the council members wanted formed with urgency. Politics, at least as much as military considerations, motivated their choice. Eisenhower, who was universally popular with the American people, be they Republican or Democrat, was uniquely capable of winning support for NATO.

Behind the scenes, the Truman administration had been involved in the ministers' request. Indeed, the President had consulted Eisenhower before their vote. The general had agreed to accept the appointment on the condition that Truman "order" him do so. He said he would not respond to a mere request. Eisenhower's reason was his sensitivity to being thought ambitious — a concern that was relevant since important people of both parties were calling on him to run for President; he did not want to encourage them. This unusual situation was the product not only of his extreme popularity but also of no one's knowing for sure which political party he belonged to; he would not say.

News of Eisenhower's appointment as Supreme Allied Commander, Europe, on December 19, 1950, prompted the invigorated old guard to intensify the Great Debate over the direction of US foreign policy and the military commitments fundamental to it. The very next day, Hoover accused the Truman administration of involving the United States too deeply in Europe and Asia. He proposed that American forces withdraw from both continents and that the nation use its formidable naval and air forces, together with the natural protection of the Atlantic and the Pacific, to make the United States the "Gibraltar of Western civilization." The concept he presented was a modification of the old "fortress America" thinking of pre–World War II days. Hoover's concession to all the change wrought since then and to activist New Right conservatives was his allowing that the United States should help defend Japan, Formosa, the Philippines, and the British Isles. Fundamental to what he proposed was the belief that the nation should keep its ground forces out of any fighting in either Asia or Europe. The former President said Truman was "inviting another Korea" by assigning US troops to Europe.

When the first session of the Eighty-second Congress convened on January 3, 1951 — as the Eighth Army, under Ridgway, continued its chaotic retreat — the Great Debate was formalized quickly. On the first day of that session, Senator Kenneth S. Wherry of Nebraska and Congressman Frederic R. Coudert, Jr., of New York, both old-guard Republican allies of Taft, introduced resolutions that would put Congress on record as being against a President's ability to dispatch US military units throughout the world without first getting Congress's approval. This is what Truman had done in Korea of his own volition, and this, clearly, was how he planned to handle matters in Europe. Wherry, Coudert, Hoover, and Taft were calling such action a usurpation of power by the President.

Truman responded to the resolutions the day after they were introduced. During a January 4, 1951, press conference, reporters queried him about them. Did he think he needed congressional authority to send troops overseas, he was asked. "No, I do not," he replied.

The next day, on the Senate floor, Taft picked up the dialogue during a speech that was a comprehensive presentation of his thinking. "The president has no power to agree to send American troops to fight in Europe a war between members of the Atlantic pact and the Soviet Union," he said. He charged that the administration was beginning a dangerous trend of resorting to international agreements instead of the more formal treaties that under the Constitution required Senate ratification.

Three days later, Truman delivered his State of the Union address. A lot was on his mind. On the home front, there was more scandal in his administration — this time in the Reconstruction Finance Corporation — in addition to hyperinflation fears and calls for wage and price controls, plus a serious, first-of-its-kind dispute with Federal Reserve Board members who wanted to raise interest rates. On the overseas front, there was, most notably, the rout in Korea and a possible evacuation, as well as the prospect of a Soviet invasion of Western Europe — a possibility that some were saying was presaged by China's entering the Korean conflict. Thus pressured, Truman was not in a compromising mood. "We are preparing for a full wartime mobilization," he said, hinting that Taft and others like him who were trying to restrict his authority were appeasers.

This mean allusion was indicative of how strongly Truman felt about the issue of controlling troop disposition. So was his reaction to a remark made on January 9 by Senator Tom Connally, a Texas Democrat who was chairman of the Foreign Relations Committee. In a conciliatory way, Connally said that he was certain the administration would consult Congress on troop commitments. Truman's brusque retort was, "I don't ask their permission, I just consult them."

The Great Debate became more focused when on January 22 Wherry called for hearings on the troop question — that is, how many more divisions Truman planned to send to Europe. The fact that the Senate Foreign Relations and Armed Services committees voted to conduct joint hearings demonstrated the seriousness of the Taft-led attack on Truman's activist foreign-affairs and military policies. It was also indicative of how worried Democrats in Congress were about this issue that the old guard had seized. The Democrats had majorities in both bodies of Congress; those in the Senate could have blocked such high-profile hearings, but they were afraid to do so. They could sense the public's changing mood. Those of them up for reelection in less than two years did not want to shut off debate and by doing so lock themselves on to Truman, come what may. This was the Washington backdrop that was emboldening MacArthur from afar, and the scene into which Eisenhower, another Marshall man, stepped when he agreed to become commander of NATO's military forces.

Eisenhower's first move was to ready himself for important consultations with European leaders. Truman needed their assurances that their nations were willing to raise armies in peacetime to support their common defense. He also wanted to know whether they would support a rearmed German state being a full NATO partner. Eisenhower was instructed to get these assurances to his satisfaction during a whirlwind eleven-nation journey. He was to leave as soon as possible, and this he did after three days of briefings. Only hours after witnessing interment ceremonies for General Walker at Arlington National Cemetery on January 2, 1951, he departed.

Europe that January was beset by another harsh winter, almost as bad as that of 1945/46. At Oslo, Eisenhower's pilot brought his plane down through a blinding snowstorm so severe that the crew of a trailing press plane decided not to risk it and landed elsewhere.

Eisenhower brought back with him good news despite the bad weather. He was assured "more or less" that each nation was prepared "to do its part." This assessment on his part, given his credibility, was very important news. Taft and other critics were saying that the Europeans wanted a large, permanent US military force assigned to protect them. This actually was true, but Eisenhower felt that he had forced them to reconcile themselves to getting, in his own words, "reinforcement, but only on a temporary, emergency basis. . . . This meant in my mind, and I so told them, that the thickly populated areas of Western Europe should be able to provide the vast bulk of the land and conventional forces needed, even if we had to provide a few divisions to give them confidence as each country achieved a respectable strength of its own."

Eisenhower was such an independent agent — his standing was a function of his popularity, not his presidential appointment — that upon returning to the United States, he did not go directly to Washington to report to Truman personally. Instead, his plane landed at Stewart Field, New York, so that he could find repose in the friendly environs of the Thayer Hotel at West Point, while he carefully wrote two important speeches — the first to be delivered to what essentially would be a joint session of Congress, and the other live, on radio and television, to the American people. Only after four days of preparation did he pack up his speeches, summon his wife, Mamie, who had joined him there, and depart with her for the nation's capital. Truman demonstrated how important Eisenhower was to him and the NATO cause by meeting him at National Airport — and the honor of that courtesy was magnified by the fact that to get there, the President traveled on roads encrusted with snow and ice. These conditions and the resulting traffic snarl delayed Truman's arrival at the airport and kept Eisenhower's plane circling overhead all the while.

Upon their reaching the Oval Office, Eisenhower lifted Truman's spirits considerably. The general later recalled that there, for the first time, he reported "that NATO was a feasible military alliance, that if we could unify the forces of the various countries and establish them under a single command we could build an effective defense. . . . [The caveat was] that our nation, for a time, would have to keep in Europe something like six divisions."

The next morning, February 1, 1951, Eisenhower delivered the first of his important speeches. He appeared before virtually all the members of the House and the Senate in an informal and highly unusual meeting held in a Library of Congress auditorium named for, of all people, old-guard isolationist Calvin Coolidge. The import of Eisenhower's message was the same as that he had rendered the President the day before, but this time he was an advocate. No time was allotted for questions; the size of the audience made this somewhat impractical, and the chairmen of several key committees jealously reserved this prerogative for themselves and their members.

Later that day, Eisenhower testified in private for two hours before the Senate Foreign Relations Committee, and the day after, before a joint meeting of the House Foreign Affairs and Armed Services committees. It was during his committee testimony that he first gained a full appreciation of the vehemence and strength of the opposition that Taft and his allies were mounting against Truman's cold-war policies. He "was questioned almost to the point of cross-examination," he recalled.

Eisenhower gave his speech to the nation on February 1, 1951. It was a well-honed piece of work that he rendered naturally and with feeling. To facilitate delivery and eye contact with the camera and his audience beyond, he had had the entire thirty-minute presentation printed on large cue cards, which were held up on either side of the camera.

At this juncture Eisenhower had done all on the home front that Truman had thought to ask of him. The President was now eager for him to return to Europe and take on the job of organizing NATO's defense; however, Eisenhower, out of personal conviction, conceived of another initiative. He decided to meet one-on-one with Taft to try to convince him that Truman's planned military commitment to NATO was crucial and that Truman had the authority to order US military units to Europe to make good this commitment.

The invitation was tendered, and Taft accepted. Eisenhower was encouraged that the senator suggested a discreet meeting at the Pentagon, instead of one up on Capitol Hill, where it would be highly publicized. This implied to him that Taft's position on the question was somewhat flexible. Not long after Eisenhower's speech to the nation, evidently (the general did not record precisely when), Taft was driven to one of the more obscure entrances and disappeared into the huge structure without being seen by reporters. Thus began one of the most important meetings in American political history.

Eisenhower was fully satisfied with his lot in life, as well he should have been. Military success had been his beyond anyone's wildest dreams, except perhaps MacArthur's dreams, and yet it had not motivated him to seek the presidency. Politics, particularly American politics, did not suit him. He observed once that he preferred the British system, in which candidates stand for office rather than run for them. Although he was capable of great warmth, a career in the military and his having become a general had made him aloof frequently, not unlike Marshall was. However, the nation's future and Europe's were overriding concerns for him. He was willing to do whatever was necessary to save Western Europe from Soviet domination, chiefly because he bore in mind American economic and security interests, which were so inextricably tied to Europe's. Furthermore, since he had so recently led Allied forces in liberating Europe from Nazi tyranny, he had a personal interest in keeping it free.

Given these considerations, Eisenhower had decided before meeting with Taft that if he could get him to "agree that collective security should be adopted as a definite feature of our foreign policy" and thus change his stand against a US military commitment to NATO, he himself would irrevocably renounce running for the presidency. This meant disclaiming any ambition for the office so strongly that a subsequent about-face would be practically impossible. Pursuant to doing this, he had called several staff assistants into his office shortly before Taft's arrival and together they composed such a statement. As best as Eisenhower was able to recall later, it read: "Having been called back to military duty, I want to announce that my name may not be used by anyone as a candidate for President — and if any do I will repudiate such efforts." This he had put into one of his pockets. Of course, Taft knew nothing of it as he sat down with Eisenhower. Nor did Eisenhower tell him directly, though he alluded to his intentions. Eisenhower's test of a true change of heart by Taft was the latter's willingness to change his mind without Eisenhower's giving him explicit assurances that he would not run against him.

In his published account of the meeting, Eisenhower recalled what happened.

> My sole question was, "Would you, and your associates in the Congress, agree that collective security is necessary for us in Western Europe — and will you support this idea as a bi-partisan policy?"
>
> I explained that if the principle were accepted wholeheartedly, if he could answer "yes," I would be completely happy in the new job and would spend my next years attempting to fulfill the great responsibility given me. But if this was going to be a matter of deep and serious division within the Congress, between the Congress and the President, then NATO would be set back, and I would probably be back in the United States.

Taft — an honest man of great conviction who, if anything, was invigorated by resisting pressure — was, as Eisenhower perceived him, "suspicious of my motives." Taft refused to commit himself, saying only, several times, "I do not know whether I shall vote for four divisions or six divisions or two divisions." Eisenhower assured him that he wanted no commitment in such detail, but only one of principle. This Taft would not give and their long meeting ended cordially, at which time Eisenhower beckoned his staff assistants to return to his office. In front of them he retrieved the slip of paper from his pocket and tore it up, instructing them "to forget about it completely."

Eisenhower had influenced Taft, however. Publicly, the senator would soon waver, saying that he "would not object to a few more divisions, simply to show the Europeans that we are interested and will participate." Earlier, Taft had keyed his defeating administration plans for NATO on constitutional grounds — Truman's not having the authority to order additional troops to Europe without first getting congressional approval. His new tactic was more specific to the situation. He seemed to be thinking of a commitment cap and a time limit for it. Unfortunately for him, he had not correctly considered what this tactical move on his part would do to his chances of winning the Great Debate.

Marshall exploited Taft's error when he testified February 15, 1951, before a joint meeting of the Senate Foreign Relations and Armed Services committees. How many was "a few more," the Defense Secretary asked. As Acheson later wrote, "Taft was neatly caught. 'A few' was more than two, three anyway, which reduced the great strategic issue . . . to an argument over one division to Europe" when, with Truman's permission, Marshall revealed that the administration proposed sending only four more presently. Neither Marshall nor Bradley would offer assurances that more would not be needed, but Taft's dissent suddenly seemed petty. He tried to reorient his attack on constitutional grounds, but never regained the momentum he had had at the outset of the Great Debate. Acheson, in his testimony that followed, developed a picture of Taft's objections as dilatory. "Our allies are building their forces *now*," he said. "The time for our own contribution is *now*. If each should wait to appraise its partners' efforts before determining its own, the result would be as disastrous as it would be obvious."

Those on either side of the Great Debate did not line up purely by party affiliation. For example, Republican senators Henry Cabot Lodge of Massachusetts and William Knowland of California supported Truman's NATO troop commitment, and Democratic senator Paul Douglas of Illinois opposed it. Lodge was a moderate; Knowland, a New Right conservative; and Douglas, a constitutional scholar.

At first, Taft's cause was aided by the disastrous course of events in Korea. On January 3, 1951, when Ridgway ordered Seoul abandoned and then led a retreat across the ice-clogged Han River, the reaction of some Senate and House members was panic, and impulsively they wanted to reduce US commitments worldwide, not increase them. In like but opposite manner,

Ridgway's subsequent success made nervous members more comfortable with the NATO commitment.

The debate lasted until April. Taft forces managed only to pass a face-saving, watered-down version of the resolution that had no force of law. It endorsed Eisenhower's appointment and also sending no more than four divisions "without further Congressional approval." Truman's reaction, since the resolution's negative provision did not bind him, was to acclaim it as "further evidence that the country stands firm in its support of the North Atlantic Treaty."

Had Taft been more deliberate about winning the active support of Knowland and other New Right Republicans who criticized Truman's Asian policies as not being aggressive enough, he would have been more successful in challenging Truman's support for NATO. The Eighth Army's miraculous turnaround behind Ridgway notwithstanding, public frustration was mounting because the limitations that Truman was imposing were giving the war an inconclusive quality. Minority leader Martin's letter to MacArthur, which the Great Debate prompted, and the public's emotional support of MacArthur during ensuing developments, were signals to Taft of the potential support he could tap into if somehow he could reconcile his isolationist views with an aggressive Asian policy. He would not ignore these signals for long; as Bradley observed, "In time, his views would very nearly coincide with MacArthur's."

No sooner had Truman, with the pivotal help of Eisenhower and Marshall, capped the Great Debate, than his firing MacArthur reopened it with an explosion. This time the debate jeopardized not just his policies of containment, limited warfare, and Europe-first, but his very presidency. Americans were angry. Within forty-eight hours of the middle-of-the-night announcement, 125,000 of them sent telegrams to the White House through Western Union, which had to force many of them to address Truman as something other than a moron. Only a small number commended the President on his action.

Republicans took this outpouring to mean that their time had finally come. With the confidence of winners, they swiftly moved to capitalize on the situation, focusing their efforts on the next presidential election, which was only nineteen months away.

Once again, Hoover was Taft's point man. The seventy-seven-year-old had been awakened to receive the news, and after conferring quickly with Taft and a few other Republican leaders, had placed a phone call to Mac-Arthur. It was still daytime there in Tokyo, where the general was to be found at his embassy residence in his West Point bathrobe, instead of at the

Dai Ichi as usual. He had been receiving individually some of his aides, who appeared more upset than he. Sebald had arrived in tears. All his senior staff would decide to leave with him, and it was this subject — where he would go — that Hoover called to discuss. MacArthur had been thinking about a leisurely tour of the Philippines, Oceania, and Australia until Hoover warned him to come "straight home as quickly as possible, before Truman and Marshall and their crowd of propagandists can smear you."

MacArthur readily assented to this advice, and the next morning at nine-thirty in Washington, some Republican legislators convened in Martin's office to plan for his return. With Taft presiding, they decided to invite MacArthur to address a joint session of Congress. Taft beforehand had talked with the Senate majority leader, Ernest W. McFarland of Arizona, and Rayburn about this and, given the public's overwhelmingly negative reaction, which was already obvious, the two Democratic leaders had had no choice but to assent. As a colleague who also was from a conservative part of the country observed, "The people in my section are almost hysterical." At the meeting of Republican legislators Taft delivered an impassioned speech in which he asked his colleagues to work for Truman's impeachment. Some in attendance soon acted on this advice. During a speech on the Senate floor later in the day, William Jenner of Indiana said, "This country is in the hands of a secret inner coterie which is directed by agents of the Soviet Union. . . . Our only choice is to impeach President Truman." McCarthy's recitation of this theme was more visceral. "The son of a bitch ought to be impeached," he told reporters. He accused Truman of having been drunk on "bourbon and Benedictine" when he ordered MacArthur removed.

MacArthur departed Tokyo five days later, on April 16, 1951. He left the embassy for the airport at about six-thirty in the morning, but despite the early hour, a quarter million Japanese lined his route. But the numbers of people who greeted him upon his return to the United States, which he had not visited in fourteen years, were even more impressive. His reception during a Honolulu stopover was a harbinger. An estimated 100,000 people were at Hickam Field and lined a twenty-mile route to the University of Hawaii, where the school's president, Gregg Sinclair, conferred upon him a doctorate of civil law, telling the audience, "General MacArthur is one of the great Americans of this age, and in the opinion of many in this group, one of the greatest Americans of all times." Clearly, MacArthur was not returning in disgrace.

His plane landed at San Francisco at 8:29 PM on April 18, and when he stepped out onto the ramp, bathed in the beams of massed spotlights, ten thousand people surged through police lines to get a closer look. Pushed aside and lost in the crowd was California governor Earl Warren. An estimated half million people lined the streets leading to MacArthur's suite at the Saint Francis Hotel. The next morning, the same number of people gave him a parade.

All this adulation had serious political implications, which a reporter probed with a question as MacArthur stood resplendent on the steps of City Hall. "I was just asked if I intend to enter politics," he said. "My reply was no. I have no political aspirations whatsoever. I do not intend to run for political office, and I hope that my name will never be used in a political way. The only politics I have is contained in a single phrase known well to all of you — 'God Bless America!' "

Later that day, MacArthur and his entourage departed for Washington. When they arrived shortly after midnight on April 19, twelve thousand people were at National Airport waiting. The official reception committee included Marshall, all the Joint Chiefs, the congressional leadership of both parties, and Harry Vaughan, who was there as Truman's personal representative. Their dutiful presence is evidence of the empowerment of personal popularity in American society. To mollify the public, they were showing as much respect as possible, which is why a determined Marshall was the first to shake MacArthur's hand. The crowd was surging forward by the time MacArthur stepped from the ramp, and Martin's younger brother later admitted that in the melee he tried to block Marshall's approach so as to favor the House minority leader, but the Secretary of Defense would not be denied. Alerted by what had happened in San Francisco, some photographers and reporters on the scene wore football helmets, which suited the action. The Chiefs' presenting the MacArthurs a silver tea set amid all this did not.

MacArthur's speech to Congress was the next day. Ceremonial procedures are a prelude to this great honor and on this occasion, they had a decidedly dramatic effect. They heightened the anticipation. A general had been invited to attack a President for how he was running a war. And, of course, MacArthur was not just any general. Furthermore, he was very much a curiosity; few had seen him in the flesh for years, because he had been out of the country so long, and as the oldest American in uniform, he hearkened better, less complicated times.

The House of Representatives convened at noon, with the gallery already filled, save for a few seats reserved, as is customary, for the special guests of the person addressing the lawmakers. At 12:13 Jean MacArthur was escorted to one of these and everyone in the chamber stood to applaud. Three minutes later some of the general staff officers escorted thirteen-year-old Arthur MacArthur to the well of the House, where he was seated a few feet from the spot where his father would stand during his speech. It was a clever, softening touch by the latter. Conversation noise rose a few decibels as people noted the young man's presence. Two minutes later floodlights were turned on to illuminate the lectern for television coverage. Then all ninety-six senators strode in together and took their places in temporary seating in the aisles. Conspicuous absentees were Marshall and the Joint Chiefs, all of whom normally would have sat down front. A few more pregnant moments passed before the sergeant at arms, at 12:31, shouted from the back of the hall, "Mr. Speaker, General of the Army Douglas MacArthur!" Immediately, all jumped to their feet, applauding and, in many cases, shouting.

MacArthur had begun work on his speech while still in Tokyo. By the time he arrived in Washington, it had gone through three drafts. The night before, following his post-midnight arrival, he had applied finishing touches. "Mr. President, Mr. Speaker, distinguished Members of Congress," he began, "I stand on this rostrum with a sense of deep humility and great pride in the reflection that this forum of legislative debate represents human liberty in the purest form yet devised. . . . I address you with neither rancor nor bitterness in the fading twilight of life with but one purpose in mind: to serve my country." With this he sparked his first ovation. Twenty-nine more would follow this one. He wasted few words before launching his attack on Truman's limited-warfare policies. At last, it was completely open and direct, no longer confined to secret cables or rambling communiqués.

He chose to focus his remarks on "the general areas of Asia," concerning which he presented his historical perspective on Chinese Communist aggression for his audience, which included thirty million people tuned in on radio and television. That nation's imperialistic aims were evident "not only in Korea, but also in Indochina and Tibet, and pointing potentially toward the south." The leaders of China had started a new war in Korea, he said, just as he and his armies were about to win the one the North Koreans had started. To him, how to respond was clear. "Once war is forced upon us," he said, "there is no alternative than to apply every available means to bring it to a swift end. War's very object is victory — not prolonged indecision." He accused Truman's administration of not reacting to the enlarged war that Chinese entry had caused, and called for "new decisions in the diplomatic sphere to permit the realistic adjustment of military strategy." They have "not been forthcoming," he said. Invading Manchuria was not his plan, he observed, though "the new situation did urgently demand a drastic revision of strategic planning if our political aim was to defeat this new enemy as we had defeated the old." He then presented five specific recommendations about how to do this. He wanted to end the policy of giving sanctuary to enemy forces north of the Yalu, intensify the economic blockade of China, institute a naval blockade of it, begin aerial reconnaissance of its coastal regions and Manchuria, and start using Chiang's Nationalist soldiers as raiding forces on the Chinese mainland. These were toned-down modifications of his December 30 proposals to the Chiefs in which he advocated using airpower to destroy China's "industrial capacity to wage war" and using Chiang's forces as reinforcements directly involved in the fighting in Korea. He reported to his listeners that it was his "understanding that from a military standpoint the above views have been fully shared in the past by practically every military leader concerned with the Korean strategy, including our own Joint Chiefs of Staff." He was alluding to the Chiefs' January 12, 1951, contingency recommendations that proposed being much more aggressive in combating Chinese Communist aggression. In effect, he was inviting military leaders to join him in challenging Truman's policy.

MacArthur ended his speech dramatically. On the verge of losing emotional control, and using the refrain of an old English army song, he affirmed in whisperlike tones the future Truman had imposed on him, which he said was to "just fade away." He might have meant it, but probably did not. Whatever the case, conservatives would not let him.

Truman's relationship with his former Asian-theater commander having deteriorated to this low point, he and the Chiefs worked to build on the already firm relationship with the new one. To begin with, Ridgway was given the option of retaining command of the Eighth Army concurrently with his new position. He declined, thinking that he could run the war as effectively by closely monitoring the efforts of an able subordinate commander. He had anticipated being able to make this appointment himself, but the Joint Chiefs informed him that Lieutenant General James Van Fleet would be his successor. Collins, who had long touted Van Fleet's talents, was the person behind this appointment. He had been responsible for his coming to Marshall's attention during World War II. Collins probably selected Van Fleet for the Eighth Army command slot because the latter was extraordinarily talented in organizing and training units. Collins had noted these strengths when Van Fleet was a colonel in charge of a regiment in Europe. This had led to Van Fleet's being appointed commander of the Military Advisory Group in Greece when, in 1947, Congress had authorized and funded Truman's proposal to aid Greece and Turkey. The idea here in Korea was that the new leader of the Eighth Army was going to have to help the ROK army to grow and develop so that it could take over more of the fight. Van Fleet seemed particularly suited to this task, and was also an able combat commander.

The true measure of the trust and confidence that Truman, Marshall, and the Chiefs had in Ridgway was not to be seen in the naming of his successor; rather, it was shown by the degree to which they delegated him authority that they had denied MacArthur. On April 22, 1951, the Chinese launched their long-anticipated spring offensive, involving an estimated 337,000 soldiers. This land offensive, in and of itself, was worrisome enough. Even more daunting was the thought that it was part of a larger scheme. Consequently, Collins informed Ridgway that for the purposes of contingency planning, the President had authorized air strikes on Chinese air bases in Manchuria and the Shantung Peninsula should a "major air attack" be launched from them; however, Collins emphasized that the Chiefs were retaining for themselves the decision to order these strikes, and that Ridgway would have to seek their final approval.

Sensitive to the possibility that this might be too restrictive, they asked Ridgway whether the arrangement afforded him the flexibility to respond quickly enough. His answer was an unaccommodating no, which caused the Chiefs to meet with Truman and persuade him that the decision should be delegated to Ridgway, who was informed of his new authority on April 28. They even permitted him to order immediate air reconnaissance of the enemy air bases in Manchuria and the Shantung Peninsula, "made at high altitudes and as surreptitiously as possible."

Very soon it became clear that the air strikes north were not going to be necessary. Chinese and Soviet leaders were following Truman's lead in deciding to limit the war. Chinese MiGs confined their flights to the northwestern region of the Korean Peninsula and nothing came of the threatening moves by the Soviet submarines. Nor did the Chinese enter the fighting in French Indochina, where an independence movement led mostly by Communists was trying to drive out the French. The fighting in Korea did not spread. The huge armies on either side of what was roughly the thirty-eighth parallel, by pounding against one another, were gradually forging by fire stable battle lines. The Eighth Army had held up well against the current pounding. Though an ROK division in the center had collapsed, allowing a Chinese force to break through, Van Fleet redeployed his units, pulling back those in the east by about thirty-five miles. Advancing forces were eventually stopped only five miles north of Seoul. Still, the capital city did not fall this time, and would not again.

To American military leaders, the enemy's lack of success in its recent offensive confirmed that short of some sort of major escalation, it did not have the power to win the Korean War. Chinese casualties had been horrendous because UN forces had almost total air superiority and overwhelming numbers of artillery pieces working. The Chinese were lightly armed, so their huge expenditure of manpower could not counterbalance these US advantages.

The stalemate that MacArthur had predicted and Truman and the Chiefs had recently hoped for was at hand. As a result, the National Security Council met May 1, 1951, to discuss the options. The meeting initiated studies that during the next month would lead to Truman's formally approving a new government policy to try to settle the war politically. MacArthur and Republican conservatives would decry it, but MacArthur would no longer be able to say that "political decisions" needed to be made about what the nation wanted by fighting in Korea. Truman was ready to settle on a non-Communist South Korea, letting North Korea be. During his administration, there would be no more attempts to roll back communism. Containing it was enough, and was all he could do.

The NSC meeting of May 1, 1951, was timely, for two days later members of the Senate Foreign Relations and Armed Services committees convened what came to be called the MacArthur hearings, to study the "Military Situation in the Far East." Senator Richard Russell, who was chairman of Armed Services, was selected by his colleagues to preside.

The stakes were very high, so both political parties carefully planned their strategies. Republicans planned to shift quickly from MacArthur's firing to a general examination of US policy in Asia, especially China. Democrats wanted to dampen the public zeal that MacArthur had aroused for himself and thereby deflect another conservative thrust at Truman's foreign policy. According to George Reedy, Democrats feared that a misstep could "build up MacArthur to the point where *anything* is his for the asking." Reedy worked for Senator Lyndon Johnson and was made a MacArthur-committee staffer temporarily. Johnson, who was on the Foreign Relations Committee, was a key figure in formulating the Democrats' strategy.

Republicans wanted open hearings, complete with live radio and television coverage, but the Democratic majority would have none of it. Citing national security concerns, they voted for hearings closed to reporters and spectators and agreed only to release at the end of each hearing day an edited transcript of what was said. The enemy of their immediate concern was MacArthur, and by blocking his direct access to the public through the media, they ensured that the hearings would become a tedious bore. Stacks of transcripts did not have the high-impact quotient of live media coverage.

Given these procedures, the greatest potential danger for Truman lay not in the charges being advanced by his political enemies, but in the inevitably newsworthy answers rendered by the Joint Chiefs — particularly since Mac-

Arthur, during his speech before Congress, had said they agreed with him about how to fight the war. Preceding the Chiefs were MacArthur, who testified first and for three days, and Marshall, who testified for six days. Then it was Bradley, Collins, Vandenberg, and Sherman, in that order. Bradley testified for six days; the others, two days each. And much to Truman's relief — though he had no evident doubt — all stood behind him solidly. Each denied MacArthur's assertion that they "fully shared" his views about widening the war with Communist China. Bradley stated that view this way: "Frankly, in the opinion of the Joint Chiefs of Staff, this strategy would involve us in the wrong war, at the wrong place, at the wrong time, and with the wrong enemy." They said that MacArthur had misunderstood the nature of their staff-study recommendations of January 12, 1951; they insisted that these were contingent upon a much worse state of affairs in Korea than had then existed. One by one, they reaffirmed Truman's limited-warfare policies in Korea as the best military course of action. This "sanctuary business," said Vandenberg, "is operating on both sides."

Asked how he thought the war could be concluded, Bradley did say that the Chiefs might recommend some sort of escalation, rather than let it drag on indefinitely. However, he noted that Chinese forces were losing so many soldiers on the battlefield that he thought their leadership might decide it was in China's best interest to negotiate an end. Concurrently, the Chinese launched a second, huge, spring offensive the second day of Bradley's testimony. The enemy's plan was to mass five armies in a drive to split the IX and X Corps, but it proved another disaster for the attackers. Artillery, tanks, and airpower again stopped them. Van Fleet ordered a counterattack that enveloped thousands of Chinese. Ten thousand of them were captured.

With UN strength thus brutally established, the negotiated settlement of which Bradley and Marshall had spoken during their testimony now seemed a definite possibility. As noted, and not coincidentally, during these days Truman approved that objective as official policy. On June 1, 1951, UN Secretary General Trygve Lie announced that a cease-fire roughly along the thirty-eighth parallel would satisfy the objectives that UN member nations had been fighting for, if peace and security followed.

Concurrently, plans were being drawn up by Ridgway for establishing positions from which UN forces would inflict maximum casualties on Chinese troops. Pursuant to this, the Chiefs, Acheson, and Marshall were all involved in discussions about how much flexibility Ridgway should be given with regard to crossing the thirty-eighth parallel. On June 5, 1951, Marshall departed the capital, bound for Korea, ostensibly to find out.

In all probability, though, his motivation for going was as much personal as official and had a lot to do with his being scheduled to retire, after a delay for the MacArthur hearings, on the last day of the month. This is the most reasonable explanation for this sudden decision to visit the war zone. Perhaps he was beset by the same type of melancholy that had overtaken MacArthur shortly before his dismissal. Each man was upset about stepping down when a war was on and his soldiers were still in the field fighting. Just how that would play on the mind of a general who had been in uniform for about fifty years, only those two could say.

Marshall wanted to be taken to the front, and this is what Ridgway, who was escorting him, proposed to do when they visited the I Corps's area of operation. They were to travel there by small observation plane so that Marshall could view the terrain. However, at this juncture, a very intense storm overtook them, and Ridgway suggested they cancel the plane ride and return to base by jeep. But Marshall would have none of it. He asked Ridgway whether he would go if alone, and when he answered yes, Marshall said, "Let's go!" The scene was a reenactment of MacArthur's decision to fly into a storm when he made his first trip to Korea after the North Korean invasion. According to Colonel James T. Quirk, who was accompanying Marshall as his press officer, "The pilots shuddered, as did we, and off we went into squalls, rain, and wind. . . . It was so dangerous it was silly." That Marshall was able to see much terrain, given the conditions, is doubtful. The experience did seem to increase his frustration and anger about the war. He told Ridgway that combat conditions in Korea were much worse than he or anyone else back in the United States realized, which was an extraordinary admission. He also told him that he knew Chou En-lai rather well and, alluding to what the Chinese premier would respond to, said he was going to recommend to the President that the United States threaten "to give them a taste of the atom" unless the fighting stopped. Whether he did is unknown.

Then, on June 23, 1951, eleven days after Marshall arrived back in Washington, Jacob Malik, the Soviet ambassador to the United Nations, observed during an interview that he thought the war could be settled. Because of this development, Truman asked Marshall to delay his retirement once again, and he did.

Malik's signal also alerted the administration to take the next step. Ridgway, following instructions, broadcast a message to the commander of Chinese forces, saying that he was willing to send a representative to a cease-fire conference. Two days later, the North Korean chief of staff, General Nam Il, answering for his army and the Chinese "volunteers," announced his willingness to do the same. Ridgway's chief representative was Vice Admiral C. Turner Joy, and on July 10, 1951, he met his counterpart, General Nam, at Kaesong for the first time. Later they moved their meeting place to Panmunjom.

Belying this hopeful development, the war was far from finished; however, in this spring of 1951 Truman had withstood the best his enemies could muster to force a change in his cold-war policies. MacArthur hadn't made him expand the war (the "MacArthur hearings" had calmed frustrated Americans, not enflamed them), and the Chinese hadn't made him quit it. For this he could thank Marshall, steadfast and strong. His standing with Truman had given each of the Chiefs the courage to stand with him, too. Conservative Republicans would accuse them of playing politics, but because of Marshall this charge would never gain credence among military men. Any one of them (and Ridgway, too) could have ruined Truman's presidency, but to a man they followed Marshall, thus allowing Truman to make new rules for fighting America's wars.

This policy victory notwithstanding, Truman would not find peace of any kind the rest of his days as president; indeed, by the time the killing stopped, the Soviet Union and the United States both would have new leaders. As Ridgway later observed, "the negotiations were just an extension of the battlefield. Whatever was eventually agreed on would necessarily reflect the military realities, and it was the bitter task of the soldier to impress the enemy with our ability to resist all his efforts." And so it would be for the duration of the cold war.

In spite of Eisenhower's professed lack of interest in becoming President, some of his many friends and admirers worked to keep his options open for the 1952 race. General Clay, who on May 26, 1949, had retired and become chairman of the board of Continental Can Corporation, headquartered in New York, wrote him soon after MacArthur's firing to pass on "an earnest request: that you let no one maneuver you into any . . . comment on the MacArthur incident." Clay said he had inside information that Taft supporters were going to try to maneuver him into saying something detrimental, "thus aligning you with the President and indirectly with his party and its inept conduct of government."

Thus alerted, Eisenhower wrote back, saying, "I assure you that I am going to maintain silence in every language known to man." He had happened to be with reporters when news of MacArthur's dismissal reached him, but had responded only with a look of surprise and the observation that an American in uniform has to accept certain limitations. With Clay's admonition in mind, he astutely wrote MacArthur to try to minimize their personal differences. In the letter he denounced "sensation-seeking columnists" who were trying to "promote the falsehood that you and I are mortal enemies."

Dewey was also working diligently for Eisenhower. The MacArthur flap worried him, too. He believed that Taft people were successfully exploiting the public's reaction and seizing the opportunity presented them to build common ground with the New Right conservatives who were such ardent MacArthur admirers. He worried that an alliance between the New Right and the old guard would guarantee Taft the 1952 Republican presidential nomination before Eisenhower even committed himself to run. So in May 1951 he sent an emissary to Eisenhower's headquarters in Paris to discuss the situation gingerly with the general. Dewey's controlling assumption seemed to be that if he pressed Eisenhower too hard, he would not run, but that if he kept him informed and demonstrated support, he would do the right thing. The go-between, Winthrop Aldrich, a banker with Chase Manhattan, told Eisenhower that he and Dewey agreed that he should presently "keep still" about a possible candidacy; however, he warned him of their profound worry that Taft's winning the nomination would be the GOP's death knell. Eisenhower agreed this was "a disastrous possibility." Aldrich got no commitment to run from Eisenhower — only what was to be an oft-repeated refrain that "I shall have to be *very clear* that I know it to be duty."

Throughout the rest of 1951, Eisenhower kept the hopes of Republican moderates alive by occasionally receiving some of them to talk politics. In early September he met with Senator Lodge, the Massachusetts Republican who had managed Senator Vandenberg's 1948 presidential campaign. Lodge explicitly stated Dewey's worry that unless Eisenhower soon presented himself as an alternative, Taft would have the nomination locked up. He beseeched Eisenhower to start building a political organization run by professionals. He did not think that the loosely organized, nonpartisan "Eisenhower for President" clubs that were springing up around the country with the encouragement of people such as Clay were enough. What subsequently transpired was also part of a pattern that developed. After listening to Eisenhower drone on about duty — his duty to fulfill his present responsibilities as NATO commander until people convinced him that running for president was an overriding one — Lodge returned to the States to begin doing, without Eisenhower's approval, what he had unsuccessfully proposed to the general.

In the meantime, MacArthur had begun speaking throughout the country. Funding most of this effort were archconservative, multimillionaire oilmen H. L. Hunt and Clint Murchison of Texas. In his speeches MacArthur attacked taxes and everything else a conservative politician would, and thus sounded more and more like a candidate himself, though he wore his uniform during each appearance. This stumping offended many veterans, and also other people who had somehow convinced themselves (or believed MacArthur's claims) that he was above getting involved in politics. Unlike Eisenhower, MacArthur made no attempt to husband his prestige. Although his presentations enhanced his position with Taft supporters and others who were strongly partisan, they diminished his popular appeal. By taking stands on various issues, he unavoidably alienated some people who believed Truman had mistreated him. Furthermore, what he had to say on the stump frequently sounded bizarre, as he applied his thinking to domestic politics. During a speech in Jackson, Mississippi, he said that the policies of the Democratic administration were "leading toward a Communist state with as dreadful certainty as though the leaders of the Kremlin were charting the course."

In sharp contrast, Eisenhower's remaining above the fray and apolitical made him all the more popular. Indeed, Truman met with him on November 5, 1951, at Blair House to assure him that his 1948 offer of support for the presidency was still good. Truman said he could "guarantee" him the Democratic nomination in 1952. Eisenhower demurred, saying that he had too many differences with the Democratic party's domestic policies.

In the November 7, 1951, edition of the *New York Times*, Arthur Krock broke the story of this meeting. The revelation may have been one reason why, on November 10, Clay met in New York with Dewey and some of the top operatives of the latter's 1948 campaign, including Herbert Brownell, Jr., the lawyer who had managed it. Clay had become Eisenhower's personal representative and was spending more time on his friend's unofficial campaign than he was working for Continental Can. He was keeping Eisenhower informed of behind-the-scenes developments by corresponding in code. The upshot of this meeting in New York was that these GOP kingpins, all of whom were of the party's moderate wing, selected Lodge to be the Eisenhower campaign's manager.

By early December, Lodge had become exasperated with Eisenhower's aloofness; he warned him that unless he resigned his NATO command and returned to campaign "the whole effort is hopeless." Flashing his temper, the general told him to disband the campaign. Clay wrote Eisenhower to imply that he was reneging on his agreement to run if his backers stirred up enough support to convince him it was his duty to run. In reply, Eisenhower reminded Clay of Army Regulation 600-10: "Members of the Regular Army, while on active duty, may accept nomination for public office, provided such nomination is tendered without direct or indirect activity or solicitation on their part."

Later in the month, with pressure on him continuing to mount, Eisenhower provided a more specific explanation for his reticence. Displaying an acute political sensitivity, he explained to Cliff Roberts and Bill Robinson, two professionals who had joined the Eisenhower for President organization, that his successfully establishing NATO's military organization was a prerequisite for his successful candidacy. Second, he observed that "the seeker is never so popular as the sought. People want what they think they can't get." Third, he said that if he returned to campaign now he would be forced to take stands on controversial issues that would cost him more than would be gained. Fourth, he said that his position as the top military commander in Europe insulated him from political attack, and in the long run would not only protect his popularity but also prevent the rift in the Republican party that would potentially develop if he were to get in a long-running debate with Taft.

Eisenhower's logic was sound, and the timing he suggested would, as it turned out, be honored, though Lodge did impose one significant modification: without Eisenhower's permission, he entered his name in the New Hampshire Republican primary and the ones thereafter. This miffed Eisenhower, but Lodge probably saved his candidacy by doing so. Ironically, even though Eisenhower's act was wearing thin with supporters, it continued to be well received by the population as a whole, while MacArthur's aggressive campaigning was pleasing party pros but losing him popularity, if dwindling crowds at his speeches were an indication.

By the time he wrote his official NATO report, Eisenhower was able to claim success. "Patterns of development have been devised, security plans prepared, organizations set up, logistic and support measures initiated, first candid reexaminations made and, from now on, progress will . . . follow the lines . . . already marked out," he wrote. Though this statement served Eisenhower's political purposes, it accurately reflected the growing acceptance of the concept and implementation of collective security among the leaders of Western European nations. The French, especially, had been as fearful of rearmed Germans as of the Russians. A breakthrough was French premier René Pleven's idea that German units be limited to division size and that they be integrated into the larger multinational scheme under Eisenhower's command. Eisenhower actively encouraged this sort of European army, and an affirmation of leaders' confidence that such a thing would work was their signing, on May 27, 1952, not long before Eisenhower's departure, the treaty that created the European Defense Community.

Eisenhower, ready to campaign finally, departed Europe for the States on June 1, 1952, and three days later in Abilene, Kansas, delivered his first nationally televised political speech. At that moment he and Taft each had about 450 committed GOP delegates; MacArthur lagged far behind; 604 were necessary to win the nomination. In his Abilene speech, Eisenhower exploited several kinds of issues. Some were the kind that any Republican candidate would have used. For example, he excoriated the Democrats for corruption in government, inflation, and high taxation. Another was the kind that a Republican moderate, as well as a Truman Democrat, would use against an old-guard conservative such as Taft; accordingly, he decried "the utter futility of any policy of isolation." The third kind of issue he exploited was that which he and Taft both would use to woo New Right conservatives. These Republicans had become the pivotal swing group, whose support was necessary for either Eisenhower or Taft to win the GOP's nomination. To appeal to them, Eisenhower lambasted Yalta secrecy and the loss of China to the Communists.

The Taft campaign, given the importance of these New Right conservatives, turned to MacArthur, who appeared to be the ideal running mate to help foil Eisenhower. He was not only a five-star general and national hero, too, but also the embodiment of Asia-first thinking, which New Right conservatives espoused. He would stand in stark contrast to Eisenhower, who embodied Truman's Europe-first foreign policy. Exactly how Taft and MacArthur planned to work together to block Eisenhower's candidacy is uncertain. What is certain is that about a month before the Republican convention, MacArthur hosted Taft for breakfast in his Waldorf Astoria suite to work things out. Courtney Whitney, who was there, said that MacArthur pledged to support Taft's candidacy fully and that Taft, in turn, said he would make MacArthur his running mate and, if elected, appoint him overall commander of the armed forces. Louis Sullivan, a New York City policeman assigned as his bodyguard, who also attended the breakfast, remembers it differently. According to his recollection, in comments made later to William Manchester, "the agreement was that Taft would try on the first ballot. If he felt he was picking up support, he would go on. If he felt he was going to lose he would go to the rostrum, withdraw, and ask his delegates to vote for MacArthur."

A third version comes from the hand of Taft himself. After his death, a holograph was found in his desk drawer in which he delineated the agreement as he understood it: "If Senator Taft receives the Republican nomination, in the course of his acceptance he will announce his intention to appeal to General MacArthur's patriotism to permit his name to be presented to the convention as his [Taft's] choice of running mate"; and furthermore, Taft would announce that, if elected, MacArthur would share with him responsibility for "the formulation of all foreign policy bearing on national security."

Whatever the plan, it was set in motion June 10, 1952, when Republican officialdom controlled by Taft announced that MacArthur would be the keynote speaker at the national convention in Chicago; Taft's hope was that

MacArthur would electrify the audience and thereby enhance the prospects of both of them. There was some indication that Taft's plan would not work. During convention preliminaries, John Foster Dulles got the GOP's platform committee to approve a plank that affirmed all of the Truman administration's commitments to Europe. Taft, MacArthur, and Hoover had publicly opposed the measure, so its passage was a victory for the moderates who backed Eisenhower. Then there was the problem of MacArthur's speech, so important for him and Taft, yet so bad that it was out of character, much like the civilian suit he wore while delivering it. Until he strode through the lobby of the Waldorf six hours earlier, on his way to catch a United Airlines flight to Chicago, he had not since his return to the United States worn civilian clothes in public.

MacArthur's disappointing performance was not what ended Taft's candidacy, though. Rather, it was a shrewd decision by Lodge to mention to fellow senator Richard Nixon that Eisenhower was thinking about making him his running mate, should he win the nomination. The California delegation's votes were crucial in a credentials battle between the Taft and the Eisenhower organizations about the seating of delegations from Texas and Georgia. Each candidate's organization claimed to have a slate of delegates that had legitimately won representation, so the convention as a whole was forced to decide which to seat. Governor Warren, who had been Dewey's running mate in 1948 and was presently California's favorite-son candidate for the nomination, was his delegation's leader, and he worked to keep it neutral in this credentials battle because he had in mind becoming a compromise presidential nominee. Nixon, however, ended his hopes. By threats and cajolery, he wrested leadership from Warren. California then sided with the Eisenhower organization. Had the Taft people won this vote, their man would likely have won the nomination. Eisenhower's victory was that narrow. And so narrowly achieved, too, was the thwarting of this threat to Truman's whole slate of cold-war and military policies. Taft had pledged to change them, and no one doubted he would, if elected.

Lodge had been right about the nomination: winning it was the hard part. Eisenhower easily defeated Adlai Stevenson, the Democratic nominee, who was governor of Illinois. Truman had announced much earlier that he would not seek reelection. Legally, he could have run again pursuant to the exemption provided for him in the recently ratified Twenty-second Amendment, which limited presidential terms. But he decided not to, citing historical precedent and also personal reasons. "In my opinion eight years as President is enough and sometimes too much for any man to serve in that capacity," he had written in a secret memorandum for the record. And he had decided, which he recounted in his memoirs, that it was "better for me, the party, and for the country to have a change of leadership."

Stevenson, who was the grandson of Grover Cleveland's vice president, had at first seemed reticent about running, but this in part was a deliberate strategy. Wanting to distance himself from the unpopular Truman, he adopted a coy attitude in response to the latter's entreaties to run and promises of support. During the campaign, he and Eisenhower both promised to "clean up the mess in Washington."

Stevenson's criticism stung Truman, but, all things considered, he was ready to do battle for any Democratic nominee. He even tried to replicate his effective whistle-stop campaign of 1948; however, this time there was no dramatic revival of the Democratic party's fortunes. Voters appeared set on getting real change by installing a Republican in the White House. Even Taft probably could have won, though Eisenhower's being the GOP nominee made their choice easy. Republican majorities were also voted into the Senate and the House of Representatives.

During the campaign, Eisenhower appeared to modify some of his foreign-policy views, which had been widely known. He essentially endorsed William Jenner's reelection, even though the old-guard Indiana Republican opposed nearly everything about the nation's foreign policy and had called Marshall a "front man for traitors." Appearing on the same platform with Jenner, who kept grasping Ike's hand and raising it into the air, Eisenhower said that "fear-mongers" were in charge in Washington, thus implying that all overseas commitments were too much ado. A few days later, amid great fanfare, he met with Taft to elicit his support and approved a statement Taft had prepared that said their foreign-policy views differed only in "degree." About this Stevenson observed that "Taft lost the nomination but won the nominee." Concurrently, Nixon, as Eisenhower's running mate, was accusing Stevenson of being a graduate of Acheson's "Cowardly College of Communist Containment." Consequently, there arose some uncertainty about whether these were aberrant views of the sort that campaigning encourages as candidates tailor their remarks to a certain audience or region of the country, or whether they were new compromise positions for Eisenhower.

On October 3, 1952, in Green Bay, Wisconsin, he got caught up in expedient politics and caused himself no end of embarrassment. Shortly before delivering a speech there, he deleted from the text a kind reference to Marshall, his benefactor. The passage lauded him "as a man and as a soldier, . . . dedicated with singular selflessness and the profoundest patriotism to the service of America." Governor Walter Kohler of Wisconsin convinced Eisenhower to remove the comment, on the grounds that it was an insult to McCarthy in his home state. To reporters, what had happened was obvious. They had been given advance transcripts of the planned speech and cited the discrepancy.

Truman in response lashed out at Eisenhower for his ingratitude and lack of resolution. He said that the latter "knew — and he knows today — that General Marshall's patriotism is above question. . . . Now, in his bid for votes, Eisenhower has endorsed Joe McCarthy for re-election — and humbly thanks him for riding on his train. . . . I had never thought the man who is now the Republican candidate would stoop so low." Marshall himself refused to be drawn into the controversy; he had no comment. However, some who claimed to know said that on subsequent evenings the old man tuned in to the news broadcasts to find out whether Eisenhower had somehow made amends. Marshall had at last been relieved of his public responsibilities on September 1, 1951. This time his retirement was final. An added reason for his wanting to quit as Secretary of Defense was his wife's health.

The biggest news of the campaign did not involve personal loyalties, though. Instead, it had to do with the issue that bothered Americans most: the war in Korea. On October 24, 1952, during a speech in Detroit, Eisenhower said that if elected he would "forego the diversions of politics and concentrate on the job of ending the Korean War. . . . That job requires a personal trip to Korea. I shall make that trip. Only in that way could I learn how best to serve the American people in the cause of peace. I shall go to Korea." Truman, in his diary, described this as a "demagogic statement," but most assuredly he recognized its devastating effectiveness as a political ploy. For Eisenhower, it brought to the fore his qualifications for handling the complicated international climate and especially the war, and highlighted Stevenson's relative lack of experience. In Detroit that day, Eisenhower ended any chance Stevenson had.

Like so much of what Eisenhower as President would say, what he meant in Detroit was difficult to read. Implicit in what he proposed to do was a willingness to make a dramatic policy change in order to end the war. Conservatives read it that way. MacArthur read it that way. So did Lieutenant General Mark Clark, who had succeeded Ridgway, by then Army vice chief of staff. The ramifications could be far-reaching. How the Korean War was being fought was fundamental to the Truman administration's containment scheme and Europe-first emphasis. Eisenhower's views were metamorphosing on the campaign trail, or so it seemed, and possibly becoming a threat to these policies — a threat of equal measure, perhaps, to the one that Taft's defeat had averted.

*   *   *

Eisenhower departed for Korea twenty-five days after the election. He did so in secret while his staff issued press releases that conveyed the impression he was hard at work within the confines of his home, which at the time was the official residence for Columbia University presidents. That school's board of trustees had declined to accept his letter of resignation when he returned to Europe to become NATO's Supreme Commander, so officially he was still Columbia's president.

Already Eisenhower had announced his nominees for many top positions in his upcoming administration, the first being John Foster Dulles as Secretary of State. He brought two of the appointees along with him to Korea: Secretary of Defense designate Charles E. Wilson, president of General Motors, and Attorney General designate Herbert Brownell. Bradley, who had eleven more months to serve on his second two-year term as Chairman of the Joint Chiefs, was the third high-ranking person joining Eisenhower. At a stopover at Iwo Jima, he picked up another: Admiral Arthur Radford, one of the men Bradley had called a fancy Dan back in 1949 during the unification struggle. No one was certain of what implications Radford's inclusion in Eisenhower's party had; he was known to be an Asia-first advocate, as Navy officers tended to be.

By the time Eisenhower reached Korea, though, Clark and Rhee were certain that he intended to widen the war. Clark and his staff had worked up a plan to drive the Chinese back across the Yalu and unite the two Koreas as a single nation, using Chiang's army as reinforcements. The plan also included sea and air operations against targets in China. Rhee, on his own initiative, had developed the same sort of scheme; he wanted "victory." Both men were eager to present their proposals to Eisenhower. What surprised them was that the President-elect denied them the chance. He in fact minimized his contact with Rhee, spending a total of only about an hour with him during two meetings and declining to review a parade and speak to the South Korean National Assembly. Instead, Eisenhower kept his own counsel and traveled the front lines for three days as any other competent senior commander would. Dressed in arctic-style clothing, he talked to troops and commanders, watched artillery duels along the nearly stationary front, and carefully examined the terrain, sometimes by light plane.

Like Ridgway a year earlier, he did not care for what he saw, but for different reasons. "In view of the strength of the positions the enemy had developed, it was obvious that any frontal attack would present great difficulties," he wrote in his memoirs. "My conclusion as I left Korea was that we could not stand forever on a static front and continue to accept casualties without any visible results. Small attacks on small hills would not end this war."

MacArthur was, of course, prepared to tell him how to end the war. In fact, on December 5, 1952, the day Eisenhower started his return trip, MacArthur told a meeting of the National Association of Manufacturers that he had "a clear and definite solution" to the Korean conflict, one that involved no "increased danger of provoking universal conflict." Asked by reporters what it was, he said he would tell only Eisenhower.

Most of the President-elect's advisers wanted him to avoid such a meeting, or at least to meet with MacArthur secretly. Having worked for Mac-Arthur for about ten years, Eisenhower understood the situation better than they and rejected their advice; to do either would actually arouse suspicion and interest and create the dramatic effect that MacArthur was masterful at playing into usually. Eisenhower instead announced publicly that he was "looking forward" to getting "the full benefit of [MacArthur's] thinking and experience." Truman interjected his own announcement, saying that MacArthur ought to speak up if he had an idea for ending the war.

In the meantime, Eisenhower took a slow boat home, partway. Actually, it was a cruiser, the USS *Helena*, which he and his party transferred to at Guam from their aircraft. This change of transportation evidenced his considerable experience and also his penchant for organization. In very personal ways, Eisenhower knew how to move and control large organizations.

Aboard the *Helena*, Eisenhower sealed himself off from the outside world, his mind fully focused on the greatest challenge of his life. He created for himself a situation very much like the one Marshall had when he traveled to South America on the *Nashville* with Ridgway, and Truman had en route to the Potsdam Conference. When the *Helena* reached Wake Island, Eisenhower brought aboard more people who would be top officials and advisers in his administration. Added to the ship manifest were Dulles, Gordon Humphrey, Douglas McKay, Joseph Dodge, Emmet Hughes, and Clay. Humphrey, the president of Mark A. Hanna Company, a large conglomerate headquartered in Cleveland, was the designated Secretary of the Treasury. McKay, the outgoing Oregon governor and a highly successful automobile dealer, would be Secretary of the Interior. Dodge, a Detroit bank president and formerly the director of fiscal affairs for the occupation of Germany, was the incoming director of the Bureau of the Budget. Hughes, a Time Inc. editor, was to become a presidential assistant who, among other things, would write speeches. Clay had been instrumental in the appointment of most of the aforementioned. Eisenhower had asked him and Brownell to survey prospective talent and recommend cabinet-level appointees.

The voyage from Wake to Pearl Harbor lasted three days. Eisenhower conducted conferences the whole time, interspersed with periods of relax-ation and reflection. Topics discussed ranged from the domestic situation to foreign affairs. Underlying everything was the Korean War. All aspects of government were tied to the prolonged combat in this far-off land. A fiscal as well as emotional drain, it had virtually paralyzed Truman-administration policymakers, who anticipated a $10-billion deficit in the budget being planned, that for fiscal year 1954. Consequently, virtually all planning discussions aboard the *Helena*, whether about foreign or domestic affairs, invariably returned to the topic of the war.

Money was the common denominator of all these policy formulations Eisenhower was addressing, and the military was getting the biggest share. Influenced by childhood memories of a financial catastrophe his father had endured and his own difficulties getting a start in life before winning an appointment to West Point, Eisenhower was every bit the hard-money man Truman was. For that reason, it should not have been surprising that Eisenhower was gravitating toward a post–Korean War military strategy very similar to that which Truman at one point had tried to make work. He was strongly inclined to emphasize airpower and nuclear weapons at the expense of conventional forces. In fact, the Joint Chiefs were laying the groundwork for a return to this philosophy of "massive retaliation." Eisenhower's decrying Truman's wild fluctuations in defense spending, which his changing policies and appointments had engendered, is what would distinguish his overall military concept. He wanted enough funds to pay for a deterrent force that he deemed reasonable in size, and no more; "no feast or famine" was the expression he often used to describe his attitude about defense appropriations, adviser Bryce Harlow recalled.

Unlike the situation in the early years of Truman's presidency, during Eisenhower's administration the imbalance of favoring nuclear forces over conventional ones would be a reasonable response to the military challenges the United States faced; this is how Eisenhower assessed it. First, he would not cut conventional forces back nearly so much as Truman had after World War II; and second, he reasoned that prospects for a stable world order were much better in 1952 than they had been in 1946, when the postwar Communist threat became obvious. A principal reason, Eisenhower believed, for the new stability was Truman's having intervened in Korea to make good his pledge to contain communism. The President-elect was convinced that the United States would have a long breathing spell before any Communist nation dared such overt aggression again. Truman had proved a point and had obviated the need for Eisenhower to maintain a big Army and a big Navy. The latter concluded that a nuclear strike force superior to that the Soviets had would now be sufficient to stabilize US relations with that superpower. Furthermore, he had dealt with the Russians enough to realize that his having been a general would have a heavy impact on the thinking of Russian and Chinese leaders. He did not think they would gamble against the odds of his using military power, as they had a number of times with Truman. Indeed, his reputation was worldwide; no man was ever so internationally prominent before becoming President as Eisenhower was. The Soviets and Chinese especially would respect his past.

Eisenhower believed that controlling defense budgets in the manner he planned would save enough to allow him to balance the federal budget within four years. This, in turn, would permit him to stimulate the economy by cutting taxes. Eisenhower, the former general, believed fervently that national power was more a function of economic strength than military might. He would make a succinct statement of his attitude during his first State of the Union message: "To amass military power without regard to our economic capacity would be to defend ourselves against one kind of disaster by inviting another." All these considerations were part of what he called the "great equation" — the factors that determined how much the United States could and should spend on defense. That barely a month after his election Eisenhower had most of his key advisers aboard a ship delving into the solution to this equation is testimony to his understanding of the problem.

By the time Eisenhower and his crew of hearties reached port, they had already worked out generally what his administration meant to do during his first term: the war in Korea would be brought to an end as quickly as possible, somehow; Communist aggression would be deterred primarily by the Air Force, whose bombers would be ready at all times to hit any country that was the source of aggression (this was to avoid stationing large US ground units throughout the world); conventional-forces expenditures for the Army, the Navy, and the Air Force would be cut deeply; domestic spending would remain about the same, with New Deal programs being kept in place; and, with savings realized by reduced expenditures on defense, the budget would be balanced by the time Eisenhower campaigned for a second term so that tax cuts could be proposed to Congress.

During these shipboard discussions, Dulles was the adviser who vigorously advanced the nuclear-deterrent idea, a concept Eisenhower embraced since it conformed with his own thinking. Asia-first advocates on board were Wilson and Radford, but they were unable to influence his thinking; Eisenhower was certain of the proposition that world peace and the best interests of the United States were better served by the nation's primarily focusing its power on preventing Soviet aggression in Europe. He was not influenced by the fact that the 1952 Republican-party platform included some Asia-first ideas: unification of the two Koreas and taking the steps necessary to end Communist control of China.

Step one of Eisenhower's plan was finding a way to end the fighting in Korea. He began this process immediately after the *Helena* docked at Pearl Harbor on December 14, 1952. A brief statement he read to reporters concerned the war. "We face an enemy," he said, "whom we cannot hope to impress by words, however eloquent, but only by deeds — executed under circumstances of our own choosing." Eyes widened. His listeners took notice of the words "deeds . . . of our own choosing," which Eisenhower would use a number of times during the coming weeks. They conveyed two important impressions: that he would not allow the enemy to continue dictating the course of the war, and that he was thinking about using nuclear weapons. As it turned out, his promised meeting with MacArthur reinforced these impressions.

Three days after he returned to New York, the two men sat down together. MacArthur had prepared for him a memorandum entitled "On Ending the Korean War." His ideas therein were fantastic. Eisenhower should call for a tête-à-tête with Stalin, MacArthur wrote, during which the President would inform the Soviet leader that the United States would act "to clear North Korea of enemy forces . . . through the atomic bombing of enemy military concentrations in North Korea and the sowing of fields of suitable radioactive materials . . . to close major lines of enemy supply and communication leading south from the Yalu"; and that the United States would employ an aerial bombing campaign "to neutralize Red China's capability to wage modern war" — all of this unless the following demands were met: Korea and Germany be permitted to choose their own governments; Korea, Japan, Germany, and Austria be allowed to be neutral nations whose status was guaranteed by the United States and the Soviet Union; and the United States and the Soviet Union incorporate into their respective constitutions provisions that would outlaw war.

MacArthur's proposing to threaten use of nuclear weapons did not startle Eisenhower; he had the same thing in mind — but not in conjunction with such extraordinary demands. Nor did the incoming President intend to be so confrontational about it. He wanted to avoid using the bomb if at all possible, and it seemed to him that MacArthur's plan to end the war would virtually guarantee that he would have to use it. Eisenhower believed that Stalin would reject the demands out-of-hand and accept the consequences. This assessment had a historical foundation. In the days immediately after the United States dropped the atomic bombs on Hiroshima and Nagasaki, Stalin's minions negotiating postwar agreements with American representatives actually increased their demands, as if to show that the Soviet Union would not be intimidated by the bomb. At the time, Stalin reportedly remarked that "atomic bombs are meant to frighten those with weak nerves."

Eisenhower did not have to ponder MacArthur's memo to conclude that it was outlandish, but he disguised his feelings. "General," he said, "this is something of a new thing. I'll have to look at the understanding between ourselves and our allies, on the prosecution of this war because if we're going to bomb bases on the other side of the Yalu, if we're going to extend the war, we have to make sure we're not offending the whole world."

MacArthur initially thought Eisenhower "agreed that I was right," but he was to be disappointed. He later told some close friends, "The trouble with Eisenhower is that he doesn't have the guts to make a policy decision. He never did and he never will."

Eisenhower evidently had MacArthur and the New Right conservatives in mind as he prepared his first State of the Union address, delivered February 2, 1953. Knowing that they wanted a clear-cut victory in Korea, he cleverly organized the speech so as to convey the mistaken impression that he was pursuing a radical departure from Truman's foreign policy. Up front, he repudiated the Yalta agreement and also announced, "I am issuing instructions that the Seventh Fleet no longer be employed to shield Communist China." These references were to such highly charged political topics that reporters focused on them, and legislators of both parties were eager to respond. Democrats interviewed afterward affirmed their support for the Yalta agreement, which Franklin Roosevelt had negotiated, while many Republicans, on the other hand, blamed it for Eastern Europe's being Communist and controlled by the Soviets. And New Right conservatives, especially, praised the "unleashing of Chiang Kai-shek" on Communist China. The impression created was that Eisenhower was encouraging an invasion of the Chinese mainland by Nationalist forces. Actually, Chiang's forces were still woefully unprepared to take this step, and Eisenhower was unwilling to prepare them, but the misbegotten message served his purpose. Reporters developed the theme of how the new President was going to be tougher on communism than his predecessor had been. They were not aware that months earlier Truman had ordered the Seventh Fleet commander to encourage coastal raids of the Chinese mainland by Chiang's soldiers.

Whereas MacArthur disdained Eisenhower's restrained approach, Eisenhower himself worried that he was being reckless. The morning of the speech, he wrote in his diary that he wished he had more time for "study, exploration and analysis." But he sensed that he did not, that he had to get ahead of events and political pressure. He had to act while enemy uncertainty about a new President worked in his favor and before the Korean War became his own. Of his speech, he wrote: "I hope, and pray, that it does not contain blunders that we will later regret."

The media's focus on his comments about Yalta and his orders for the

Seventh Fleet resonated around the world. That the nation's allies, especially British and French leaders, were upset and publicly voiced worries of a wider war, actually bode well. The Communist adversaries must have derived the same impression of Eisenhower's aggressive intentions. Eisenhower had to have Dulles personally reassure Prime Minister Churchill and Anthony Eden, his foreign minister, that US policy had not changed, that Eisenhower supported limiting the Korean War. Churchill, whose Conservative party had been voted back into power, was as ready as ever to fight Communists, but, like Attlee before him, was alarmed that the United States might end up compromising its European defense commitments.

One potential misunderstanding among the United States and its allies was brewing, though — over whether using nuclear weapons amounted to an escalation of the war. Truman and his key advisers had decided that it did, absolutely, which is why they by all accounts only considered using them when UN forces were about to be overrun. For application in Korea, Truman seemed to view them as weapons of last resort, a last-ditch measure to prevent a debacle. Eisenhower had a different view. He discussed this very point with members of his National Security Council on February 11, 1953, nine days after his State of the Union address. A request by Clark for permission to attack an enormous Chinese troop concentration in the area of Kaesong made the topic an issue. Bradley said Clark believed that the Chinese were about to launch an offensive and wanted to beat them to it. Eisenhower inquired about using an atomic bomb on this concentration of troops and supplies; "it provides a good target for this type of weapon," he observed. He said he did not welcome having to use it, but "we cannot go on the way we are indefinitely." Bradley did not think dropping the atomic bomb was a good idea. He questioned its effectiveness in this war, was worried about the allies' reaction, and thought UN forces presented the same kind of target; the Soviets had atomic weapons, too. Then Dulles made a pivotal point. After noting the moral implications and associated inhibitions, he observed that it was Soviet strategy to set "atomic weapons apart from all other weapons as being in a special category." Now is the time "we should try to break down this false distinction," he said. Soviet concerns were not altruistic; Stalin knew that he had a small nuclear inventory compared to that of the United States and very limited ability for delivering over long distances the bombs he had. The American atomic-bomb total had climbed to about sixteen hundred, and one more device was being produced every day.

Reacting to Bradley's concerns, Eisenhower added an infantry officer's perspective to the decision about whether to use the bomb or not. He said that since Britain and France were against using it in Korea, "we might well ask them to supply the three or more divisions needed to drive the

Communists back." The meeting concluded with the President's denying Clark approval to attack Kaesong.

That evening, Eisenhower must have continued thinking about nuclear weapons. During his cabinet meeting the next day, he proposed a way to use them to bring pressure to bear indirectly. Armistice negotiations had broken off over the issue of repatriation — the Communist side insisting that it be mandatory, the United Nations side insisting that it be voluntary. Eisenhower told Dulles to pass the word "discreetly" that unless armistice negotiations resumed and progressed satisfactorily, the United States would "move decisively without inhibition in our use of weapons. . . . We would not be limited by any world-wide gentleman's agreement."

Ironically, within a month, the course of the negotiations was dramatically affected by a natural event that had nothing to do with diplomatic power plays or the actual fighting. On March 5, 1953, Stalin died. Ten days after that, his successor, Georgy Malenkov, announced that the superpowers had no disputes that "cannot be decided by peaceful means, on the basis of mutual understanding."

Later that month, Eisenhower seized the opportunity for peace that Stalin's death afforded. He called in Hughes to discuss his writing a speech for him. "Both their government and ours now have new men in them," Eisenhower said during a long discussion that was mostly him thinking aloud. "The slate is clean. Now let us begin talking to each other."

It so happened that Hughes had recently talked to Dulles about what the United States should do if the Soviets sought an armistice for the Communist side, so he passed along what the Secretary of State had said. Dulles had told Hughes, "I don't think we can get much out of a Korean settlement until we have shown — before all Aisa — our clear superiority by giving the Chinese one hell of a licking." During a cabinet meeting earlier in the month, Dulles had urged giving the French all possible help to battle communism; "we can clear up Indochina by an eighteen-month all-out effort," he said. In that same meeting, he told the President that he did not see how the defense budget could be cut anytime soon, given the enormous demands on it, especially in Europe. Eisenhower immediately disagreed, reiterating his position that the nation's security was more a function of a sound economy, which he thought was largely a function of a balanced budget.

By the time Hughes met with Eisenhower to discuss a speech, the President had heard all he wanted about continuing to prosecute a war the American people did not want. Reacting to Dulles's comment about giving the Chinese a licking, Eisenhower stared at Hughes — as if to say, "Convey this to Dulles," — and said: "All right, then. If Mr. Dulles and all his sophisticated advisors really mean that they can not talk peace seriously, then I am in the wrong pew. For if it's war we should be talking about, I know the people to give me advice on that — and they're not in the State Department. Now either we cut out all this fooling around and make a serious bid for peace — or we forget the whole thing."

The next two weeks, Hughes worked hard on the speech with C. D. Jackson, the President's administrative assistant for psychological-warfare activities (a strange title that only a President who had been an Army officer would have been comfortable with). As was his custom, Eisenhower personally edited many of their drafts. On April 15, 1953, he delivered the finished product to the convention of the Society of Newspaper Editors at the Statler Hotel in Washington. He entitled it "The Chance for Peace," and its tone unmistakably was that of a man who wanted peace. He warned of the folly of an arms race. "The worst to be feared and the best to be expected can be simply stated," he said. "The worst is atomic war. The best would be this: a life of perpetual fear and tension; a burden of arms draining the wealth and the labor of all peoples."

His invitation to the Soviets to respond came in the form of a list of demands; by complying, they could show their good faith. Eisenhower realized that some of the items were unrealistic: "full independence of the East European nations" was one; reunification of Germany was another. Dulles had insisted on these, and Eisenhower included them as a sop to the conservatives. He himself hoped only for a return of POWs and "an honorable armistice," two of the other demands.

World reaction to the speech was more positive than to any delivered by an American since Marshall's European Recovery Program speech at Harvard. Indirectly, the Soviets reacted quickly. Almost immediately Communist representatives announced their willingness to resume talks at Panmunjom with their UN counterparts. And only five days after Eisenhower's speech, the first exchange of prisoners began.

The war seemed to be rapidly heading for a settlement, but not everyone was pleased. Dulles, supported by Defense Secretary Wilson, opposed any peace plan that did not lead to unification of Korea. The Secretary of State recommended going back to war unless a political settlement — reunification of Korea — was linked to a military armistice. Eisenhower rejected this advice out-of-hand, reminding Dulles that the American people would never allow it.

Another who opposed an armistice unless the peninsula was unified was Rhee. He informed Eisenhower that if the United States agreed to anything short of that he would ask American forces to leave his country. On April 23, 1953, Eisenhower warned him by letter that "any such action by your government could only result in disaster for your country, obliterating all that has been gained at such sacrifice by our peoples." At that point, American casualties had almost reached the ultimate totals for the war, which would be 54,246 killed and 103,284 wounded. (Another 5,178 Americans were captured or listed as missing in action.)

Prime Minister Jawaharlal Nehru of India served as a go-between for the United States and China. He even proposed a peace plan, which he gradually changed to conform almost exactly to the US proposal. Dulles met with him in Karachi, Pakistan, at which time the Indian leader tried to get a reading of American intentions should this peace initiative fail. Dulles did not threaten use of the atomic bomb, but the possibility was on Nehru's mind. Dulles sent Eisenhower this account of the meeting:

> Nehru brought up Korean armistice, referring particularly to my statement of preceding day, that if no (repeat no) armistice occurred hostilities might become more intense. He said if this happened it would be difficult to know what end might be. He urged withdrawal our armistice proposals as inconsistent with the Indian resolutions. He made no (repeat no) alternate proposal. He brought up again my reference to intensified operations, but I made no (repeat no) comment and allowed the topic to drop.

The hang-up in negotiations was repatriation of POWs; many Chinese prisoners in UN hands did not want to be repatriated. It was a problem of face-saving for their government, which was insisting on mandatory repatriation; however, on June 4, 1953, Chinese representatives presented a POW plan very similar to the current UN offer.

Conservative Republican senators were upset. What galled them, too, was that European leaders were talking about how a Korean armistice would clear the way for seating the Chinese Communists in the United Nations, in place of Chiang's Nationalists. To reassert themselves, they managed to attach to a bill reported out of the Senate Appropriations Committee a rider that barred US government contributions to the United Nations if Communist China were seated. Republican senators unanimously voted for it and their Democratic counterparts were fearful of voting against it.

Supremely confident about foreign policy, Eisenhower reacted forthrightly. He invited Republican leaders in Congress to the White House. "I am distressed that this rider might become law," he told them. "I oppose it because I believe that the United States cannot properly serve notice on the United Nations in such a manner, and more fundamentally, that the United States cannot live alone." He argued that this response to events was too rigid. Dealing with nations required flexibility. He reminded his listeners that Germany had until recently been a bitter enemy but was now a close ally.

He suggested that someday the same might be true of China. The legislators backed down, albeit reluctantly. They agreed to support a substitute motion by Senator William Knowland, a resolution that expressed the sentiment of the Senate against seating Communist China at the United Nations, but had no effect in law.

On June 8, 1953, Communist negotiators at Panmunjom agreed to voluntary repatriation. Under the watchful eyes of representatives of all sides, prisoners would be free to choose whether to return home or not. Peace was at hand, but Rhee and the Republican right were still against it unless the two Koreas were unified under non-Communist leadership. On June 19, Rhee tried to sabotage the pending cease-fire by unilaterally releasing 25,000 Chinese and North Korean prisoners, a blatant violation of the armistice agreements. It was a reckless, irresponsible action; he was risking loss of US support, which Eisenhower largely controlled and the Republic of Korea needed to survive. But denunciations of this peace initiative by prominent members of the President's own party had given Rhee the confidence to do what he did.

Eisenhower was conducting a cabinet meeting when told about Rhee's action. He was the first to mention the possibility of a coup. He would ignore Rhee "if there were some hope — like a palace revolt." He said, "We've got to figure out our next step. We can't sit in a state of suspended animation." Focusing on Dulles, he asked, "What about Allen?" He was referring to Dulles's brother, the CIA director. Talk of Rhee's overthrow had caused Eisenhower to think about agency work.

Before the Secretary of State could answer, Henry Cabot Lodge interrupted. Having lost his Senate seat to Democratic congressman John F. Kennedy during the recent election, Lodge was now serving as US ambassador to the United Nations. He reported that earlier in the day MacArthur had predicted to him that within two weeks Rhee would be killed. (Lodge and MacArthur had happened to be on the same airplane flight that morning.) "What's his basis for saying that?" Eisenhower asked. Lodge replied that, according to MacArthur, South Koreans who wanted peace would kill him.

Eisenhower decided to send Walter Robertson, an assistant secretary of state, to Korea to talk sense with Rhee. (Robertson was the homesick economic-affairs counselor who had been so helpful to Marshall during his mission to China in late 1945.) Rhee was to be reminded that he had granted the United Nations control of all ROK military forces during this war and that release of the POWs had violated this agreement. Eisenhower instructed Robertson to explain that the United States would withdraw its troops, cut off supplies to the ROK army, and forgo planned economic assistance if Rhee disrupted the peace process again.

As matters developed, Eisenhower more easily silenced Rhee than he would conservatives of his own party. During the June 19 cabinet meeting, Dulles intoned that "this situation [that is, fundamental disagreements with the ally the US was trying to help] is inherent in the type of policy we're trying to pursue" — as if to argue, tactfully, that US policy vis-à-vis the Communists should be less ambiguous; that the United States, with or without UN support, should fight on until Korea was unified. In the Senate, McCarthy said that "freedom-loving" people should commend Rhee for his act of defiance, and Knowland, the acting majority leader, said Eisenhower was to blame for the "breach" with Rhee. In the House, another Republican even went so far as to introduce a resolution commending Rhee for releasing the prisoners. Nonetheless, Rhee, persuaded by Eisenhower's threats, announced on July 8, 1953, that he would henceforth be cooperative.

Now only a short, tension-filled period remained before peace. On July 12, Communist forces launched a large offensive using three corps comprising fifteen divisions. It became obvious that the attack was directed only at ROK units; when American reinforcements appeared on the line, the Chinese broke contact, only to pick up the fight the next day against ROK positions. The reinforcing units that first night happened to be the Third Infantry Division, in which Eisenhower's son John served. Evidently, Communist leaders' objectives were to occupy as much land as possible before a cease-fire, and perhaps show Rhee how vulnerable he was without American support. The Eighth Army, under Lieutenant General Maxwell Taylor, who had succeeded Van Fleet on February 11, 1953, halted the Chinese after a six-mile advance. However, ROK casualties were very heavy. One ROK division was crushed.

This final offensive incited an angry Eisenhower into sending a scolding memorandum to Wilson. Earlier the President had suggested that the Defense Secretary and the Joint Chiefs consider sending two more divisions to Korea to bolster defenses. Nothing came of the recommendation because the Chiefs did not think the extra troops were needed. That Eisenhower had correctly forecast the need for reinforcements and their correct size must have exacerbated the Defense Secretary's incipient case of insecurity. Six months into his new job, this businessman-engineer was learning just how deficient his counsel was to the soldier he served.

At 10:00 AM on July 27, 1953, at Panmunjom, senior delegates of both sides met to sign unceremoniously nine copies of an armistice agreement. There were no speeches. This was not a peace treaty or political settlement of any kind. The Koreans seated on opposite sides of the table with their respective allies would remain enemies. They were only agreeing to stop killing one another and to the mechanics of putting that into effect. At 10:00

PM they were to hold their fire and not advance from the positions they held. The war had lasted thirty-one days longer than three years. Casualties had been horrendous. On the UN side, 996,937 had been killed, wounded, or were missing; on the Communist side, the total was 1,420,000.

The signing lasted only a matter of minutes. Eisenhower was on radio and television informing the American people of it exactly one hour after proceedings commenced at Panmunjom — at 10:00 PM, July 26, 1953, Washington time. He told the millions listening that "we have won an armistice on a single battleground — not peace in the world. We may not now relax our guard nor cease our quest."

Any hope Truman had of ending the Korean War during his administration ended October 8, 1952, when, less than a month before the election, Truman "on moral grounds" rejected Communist demands for mandatory repatriation of all their soldiers held captive by UN forces. Mostly these were former Nationalist soldiers and South Koreans whom the Communists had captured and pressed into service. Forced repatriation of these prisoners would have been expedient for Truman. Voters would have turned a blind eye to his doing so had that ended the war. As it happened, the fighting intensified when the talks broke down.

The same sort of issue had come up after World War II. Among the POWs held by US forces at the end of the war were many Soviets who had fought for Germany. Desperately, they resisted return, fearful of the consequences, but Truman ignored their pleas and sent them back. He personally regretted that decision, which was one reason why he was so insistent about not forcing repatriation on the Chinese and Korean captives.

Truman was like that. He usually learned from his mistakes and acted on what he learned, which sounds simple enough to do but never is, especially if you are a politician and the opposition makes capital of what you do wrong. Truman seemed not to concern himself about this when a matter of principle was at stake, though he was as partisan as any man who's been President. These considerations help explain how Truman, a man who abhorred the idea of his country's having a large professional military establishment, ended up creating the first one in the nation's history. Events forced him to change his mind, but a more dogmatic President, or one whose views were largely a function of public sentiment, would not have been up to the task of reacting so quickly to the incessant challenges thrown at him. Arguably, he overreacted in some instances; maybe he placed too much emphasis on military means to meet the Soviet threat and stop the spread of communism; however, the Marshall Plan is evidence of his having brought to bear all elements of American power.

What is striking about the response his administration formulated is how durable it proved to be. For almost forty years, eight Presidents, of both parties, followed the Truman administration's battle plan as if it were etched in stone. A series of his successors took it upon themselves to wage war in Vietnam in a futile attempt to duplicate his limited success in Korea; and to this day, following his example, Presidents go to war on their own authority, without seeking formal declarations from Congress. Furthermore, they have supported the United Nations and the idea of collective security, most notably as represented by NATO, which even now is maintained as the nation's key military alliance, seemingly beyond its time.

Within the US military, Truman's influence also endures. His successors have not only perpetuated his organizational ideas but also strengthened them, by helping to enact laws that have centralized even more control at the top under civilian and uniformed leaders who report to the President. And if the Republic lasts another two-hundred-plus years, ambitious American generals will no doubt be chastened by what Truman did to MacArthur.

Not all is good that came of Truman's example as Commander in Chief. Vietnam was a disaster, and the arms races he helped start soon spun out of control. The inventories of nuclear weapons built up by the superpowers are incomprehensibly dangerous.

Still, the world is a safer place for Truman having been Commander in Chief. Another leader might have been more likely to use atomic bombs to save the Eighth Army back during that terrible winter of 1950. Truman did not and thereby established the most important precedent of the cold-war era. Perhaps he did not because he had used them before and had had time and occasion to think about the matter more deeply than anybody else possibly could. Or perhaps it was simply a matter of his being the kind of person who while President of the United States carried on by hand an active correspondence with his mother, sister, brother, aunts, uncles, and cousins, and thus of his being someone who did all he could to confine the casualties of war to the battlefronts where soldiers die.

NOTES

CHAPTER 1

P.3 "This is the happiest": *New York Times*, Oct. 28, 1945.

3 forty-seven warships: Ibid.

3 1,166 large warships: *Annual Report of Department of the Navy*. This figure reflects forces as of August 31, 1945. The Navy's grand total of vessels, including landing craft and others of small size, was 68,936 as of this date.

4 largest air armada: *New York Times*, Oct. 28, 1945.

5 not all was right: Gaddis, *Long Peace*, pp. 29–32.

5 survey by E. C. Hooper: *New York Times*, Oct. 28, 1945.

6 "We shall not relent": Ibid.

6 "We are not going": Robert J. Donovan, *Conflict and Crisis*, p. 222.

6 Truman's basic idea: *New York Times*, Oct. 28, 1945.

6 10,400,000 men and women: DOD Selected Manpower *Stabilization:* FY 1986. "Principal Wars in Which United States Participated," p. 120.

7 Marshall had proposed: Collins, *Lightning Joe*, p. 334.

7 At Midway: Prange, Goldstein, and Dillon, *Miracle at Midway*.

8 Collins, up to Capitol Hill: US Senate Committee on Military Affairs, *Hearings on S. 84 and S. 1482;* Collins, *Lightning Joe*, pp. 334–339.

8 on his desk: Katherine Marshall, *Together*, p. 259.

8 time for General Eisenhower: Ambrose, *Eisenhower* 1:430, 432.

8 Marshalls plotted: Marshall, *Together*, p. 259.

9 "In a war unparalleled": Pogue, *George C. Marshall* 4:1–2.

9 picked up hitchhikers: Marshall, *Together*, p. 279.

9 "Hallelujah!": Ibid., p. 282.

9 "That phone call": Ibid.

9 "a considerable section": US Dept. of State, *Relations with China*, pp. 581–584 (from his letter of Nov. 26, 1945, to President Truman, transmitted through the Secretary of State). "We started the war in the Far East furnishing lend-lease supplies," Hurley went on, "and using all our reputation to undermine democracy and bolster imperialism and Communism" (p. 581).

9 wildly flamboyant: White, *In Search of History*, pp. 198–206; Barrett, *Dixie Mission*.

10 Hurley started: Bulhite, *Hurley*, chap. 11.

10 "When I saw": Pogue, *George C. Marshall* 4:29–30.

11 "And he looked": Ibid., p. 76.

11 In Berlin and Seoul: Manchester, *Glory and the Dream*, pp. 405–410.

11 brandy to drink: Ibid., p. 435.

11 found an excuse: Truman, *Memoirs* 1:570–571. As instructed by Truman, Marshall wrote MacArthur on Sept. 17, 1945, and on Oct. 19, 1945, suggesting that he return to the United States to be honored as Eisenhower and other top officers had been.

11 "the delicate and difficult": Ibid., p. 572.

11 "If I returned": Manchester, *American Caesar*, p. 568.

12 "never say a word": Stimson, *Stimson Papers*, Oct. 29, 1942, entry.

12 "Douglas, I think": MacArthur, *Reminiscences*, p. 96.

12 surreptitiously encouraging: Schaller, *Douglas MacArthur*, pp. 67–88, 135–157.

12 "I can see": Ibid., pp. 79–80.

12 "vice-president . . .": Ibid., p. 82.

12 "MacArthur for President Clubs": Vandenberg, *Private Papers*, pp. 82–83.

13 "left wingers and": Schaller, *Douglas MacArthur*, p. 83.

13 MacArthur's chances: Ibid., p. 118.

13 mythic proportions: Ibid., p. 119.

13 intervening when: Ibid., pp. 74–77.

13 "martyr out of him": Ickes.

13 "MacArthur would probably": Truman, *Off the Record*, p. 61.

13 "the last election": Gayn, *Japan Diary*, p. 346.

13 He would rule: Schaller, *American Occupation of Japan*, p. 20.

14 "spiritual vacuum": Schaller, *Douglas MacArthur*, p. 127.

14 "an opportunity": Ibid.

14 "learning how": Ibid.

14 conservative Republicans: Rae, *Liberal Republicans*, pp. 22–24.

14 "Missionaries, war relief": Hanson Baldwin, "Too Much Wishful Thinking about China," *Reader's Digest*, Aug. 1943, pp. 63–67.

14 "cement China": White, *In Search of History*, p. 207.

14 powerful political force: Ibid.

14 cut off aid to Chiang: Acheson, *Present at the Creation* p. 122.

15 "very clever ruse": Schaller, *Douglas MacArthur*, p. 136.

15 "shift onto": Ibid.

15 "pillor[y] him": Ibid.

15 "drastic cut": Ibid., p. 135.

15 "rapidly as ships": Ibid.

15 "to all the guys": *New York Times*, Jan. 13, 1946.

15 Maxwell Taylor . . . followed: Gavin hadn't liked Taylor since West Point days, when the former was a cadet and the latter an instructor. Gavin thought Taylor was too self-centered. They had become rivals, even fighting over whose unit should lead the parade. (James Gavin, interview with author, May 1986.)

15 "The All American Soldier": *New York Times*, Jan. 13, 1946.

16 "The war's over": Ibid.

CHAPTER 2

19 in a new direction: In his World War II history, Churchill called the period a time of imminent tragedy — thus, his title for his last work, *Triumph and Tragedy*.

20 in a diary: The original documents are stored in the Princeton University Library Archives. His diary entries encompass the dates Mar. 1944 through Mar. 1949; his papers, the years 1940 through 1949.

21 "I am more impressed": Forrestal, *Forrestal Diaries*, p. 61.

21 coherent rationale: Ibid., p. 117.

21 five thousand prints: Stewart and Pollard, "FDR, Collector."

21 had to walk: Symington, oral history, p. 32.

21 after Roosevelt died: Forrestal, *Forrestal Diaries*, p. 46.

22 Morrow Board Report: Davis, *Billy Mitchell Affair*, p. 226.

22 an article: "Our Armed Forces Must Be Unified."

22 in the Army: Anderson, *Presidents' Men*, p. 111.

22 Annapolis and West Point graduates: Forrestal, *Forrestal Diaries*, p. 88.

22 "During the Roosevelt Administration": Albion and Connery, *Forrestal and the Navy*, p. 261.

22 "Cherchez le Vaughan": Truman, *Off the Record*, p. 11.

22 actually attacking the President: Vaughan, oral history by Morrissey, pp. 104–106.

23 $21,000: Truman, *Memoirs* 1:185.

24 "said he was unshakably": Forrestal, *Forrestal Diaries*, p. 60.

24 "At considerable length": Ibid.

24 "Navy could not concur": Ibid.

24 "the Navy Department": Ibid., p. 61.

25 Potsdam: Mee, *Meeting at Potsdam*, p. 13. This trip was Truman's first abroad since World War I.

26 "guard" his office: Clifford, oral history, p. 3.

26 an informal duty: Rogow, *James Forrestal*, p. 273.

26 started out in life: Ibid., p. 51.

27 Roosevelt's campaign: Ibid., p. 57.

27 headstrong nature: Ibid., p. 66.

28 "passion for anonymity": Ibid., p. 99.

28 Forrestal told Hopkins: Ibid., p. 89.

28 avoid paying taxes: Ibid., pp. 84–88.

29 "very much like": Stimson, *On Active Service*, p. 291.

29 41,272 aircraft: US Department of the Navy, *Annual Report*. This is the number as of August 31, 1945.

29 "He thought he": Rogow, *James Forrestal*, p. 69.

29 during lunch hour: Ibid., p. 71.

30 when Vardaman had: Krock, *Memoirs*, p. 235. Vardaman told people he was promoted out of the White House because he didn't drink or smoke.

31 "a socialistic streak": Rogow, *James Forrestal*, pp. 69–70.

31 "he was being": Forrestal, *Forrestal Diaries*, p. 78.

31 thirty miles: Truman, *Memoirs* 1:432.

32 "much impressed": Forrestal, *Forrestal Diaries*, p. 81.

32 for breakfast there: Ibid., p. 28.

32 James Doolittle: "Service to Cast Off Caste," *Newsweek*, June 3, 1946, p. 26; "New Philosophy: Doolittle Investigation Board Report," *Time*, June 3, 1946; Gavin, *War and Peace*, p. 106.

32 "is in favor": Forrestal, *Forrestal Diaries*, p. 88.

33 "complete agreement": Ibid., p. 89.

33 "It was clear": Ibid.

33 West Point or Annapolis: Truman, *Memoirs* 1:142.

34 first big risk: Ibid., pp. 147–148.

34 "No man can be": Ibid., p. 149.

35 "paired": Margaret Truman, *Harry S. Truman*, p. 62.

35 "like partridges": Ibid., p. 150.

35 almost getting killed: Ibid.

35 pince-nez: Ibid., p. 151. He wore a pince-nez because the hooks on regular glasses rendered a gas mask ineffective (Vaughan, oral history by Morrissey, pp. 9–10).

35 good as any man: Anderson, *Presidents'
    Men*, p. 111.

35 "after a couple": Vaughan, oral history
    by Morrissey, p. 6.

36 "in the interest": Truman, *Memoirs*
    1:159.

36 Reserve Officers Association: Carlton
    and Slinkman, *The ROA Story*, p. 10.

36 reading history: Truman, *Memoirs*
    1:153–157.

36 "wringing-out process": Ibid., p. 154.

36 notes at a public sale: Ibid.

37 "whose men didn't": Ibid., p. 157.

37 self-proclaimed Jeffersonian: Ibid., p.
    22.

37 Jackson first defined: Huntington, *Sol-
    dier and the State*, p. 155.

37 Jacobson specifically remembered: Tru-
    man, *Memoirs* 2:189.

37 "My debt to history": Ibid. 1:138.

38 "I learned of": Ibid., p. 140.

38 seven years on active duty: Huntington,
    Soldier and the State, p. 158.

38 Jackson believed: Ibid., pp. 151–158.

38 "aristocratic caste": Ibid., p. 156.

39 Sylvanus Thayer: Ibid., p. 205.

39 appointed to only four: Ibid., p. 206.

39 standard means: Ibid., pp. 205–206.

40 "If they're wasting": Vaughan, oral his-
    tory by Morrissey, p. 16.

40 "Let's keep them": Ibid.

40 "I explained that": Truman, *Memoirs*
    1:188.

40 seventy hearings: Ibid., p. 197.

40 $15 billion: Ibid., p. 210.

40 committee's work: Ibid., pp. 207–209.

41 "Well, if that's": Ibid., p. 209.

41 atomic bomb: Rhodes, *Making of the
    Atomic Bomb*, p. 617.

41 Leahy, the Chief: Leahy, *I Was There*,
    p. 245.

42 "more than any": Truman, *Memoirs*
    1:461.

42 "For a brief period": Donovan, *Conflict
    and Crisis*, p. 73.

42 Stimson, who had preceded: Henry
    Lewis Stimson, "Decision to Use the
    A-Bomb," *Harper's Weekly*, Feb.
    1947, pp. 97–107.

42 for another eight days: Manchester,
    Glory and the Dream, p. 313.

42 Klaus Emil Fuchs: Mee, *Meeting at
    Potsdam*, p. 78; Truman, *Memoirs*
    1:458.

42 500,000 American lives: Ibid., p. 460.

42 would not shock: Truman, *Memoirs*
    1:462. The President's advisory panel
    of scientists and other prominent civil-
    ians reported, "We can propose no tech-
    nical demonstration likely to bring an
    end to the war; we see no acceptable
    alternative to direct military use."

43 "good use of it": Ibid., p. 458.

43 Hurley, Truman's special envoy: Tuch-
    man, *Stilwell*, p. 520.

43 "unworthy of consideration": Truman,
    Memoirs 1:438.

43 "Big bomb": Ibid., p. 464.

43 "This is the greatest": Ibid., p. 465.

44 "The Japanese government": Ibid., p.
    471.

CHAPTER 3

45 SWNCC: Schoenbaum, *Waging Peace
    and War*, pp. 116–117.

45 A stipulation: "The Secretary of War
    [Stimson] to the Acting Secretary of
    State," May 21, 1945, reprinted in
    *Foreign Relations of the United States,
    1945* 7:876 (hereafter cited as *FRUS*).

45 most military planners: Schoenbaum,
    Waging Peace and War, pp. 123–129.

45 By contrast, Manchuria: "Memoran-
    dum by Mr. DeWitt Poole of the Of-
    fice of Strategic Services," May 20,
    1945, reprinted in *FRUS, 1945* 7:871.
    "The two main Chinese worries are
    Manchuria and Korea," wrote Poole.

"Manchuria is definitely more important than Korea."

46 Strategic Policy Section: Schoenbaum, *Waging Peace and War*, p. 117.

46 arranged by Marshall: Ibid., p. 113.

46 deemed it a probability: Tuchman, *Stilwell*, p. 522.

46 Charles Bonesteel: Schoenbaum, *Waging Peace and War*, p. 118. Bonesteel's wife, Alice, bet Rusk a case of champagne that Rusk would one day be either President or Secretary of State.

47 American commanders: Truman, *Memoirs* 1:485.

47 "Sherman was wrong!": Donovan, *Conflict and Crisis*, p. 125.

48 "Berry's dispatches": Forrestal, *Forrestal Diaries*, p. 98.

48 "going back to bed": Ibid., p. 100.

48 "Tommy Atkins": Ibid.

48 "This is my second": Ibid.

48 one-third: Ibid., p. 162.

49 "Mr. President": Donovan, *Conflict and Crisis*, p. 97.

50 Within the US government: Janowitz, *Professional Soldier*, p. 313.

50 civil war had raged: Snow, *Red Star over China*, p. 35.

50 sure loser: Tuchman, *Stilwell*, p. 527.

50 Claire Chennault: Ibid., p. 360.

51 "complete authority": Ibid., p. 357.

51 enticed by airpower: Pogue, *George C. Marshall* 4:36.

52 "nothing can be done": Tuchman, *Stilwell*, p. 510.

53 "duality of policy": Acheson, *Present at the Creation*, pp. 139–140.

53 Acheson was acting secretary of state 350 of 562 days as under secretary of state, Byrnes and Marshall having to travel to postwar conferences so much.

53 "fellow traveler": Gaddis Smith, *Acheson*, p. 31.

53 "coexistence": *Life*, Nov. 20, 1950.

53 "the unification of China": Acheson, *Present at the Creation*, p. 147.

CHAPTER 4

55 Two days before: Forrestal, *Forrestal Diaries*, p. 119.

55 "a highly prejudiced": Simmons, "The Marines," p. 5.

55 did not plan to muzzle: Forrestal, *Forrestal Diaries*, p. 119.

55 "As I tried": Vandegrift, *Once a Marine*, p. 307 (letter of Nov. 30, 1945).

56 Japanese fleet surprised: Ibid., p. 122.

56 bright flashes: Ibid., pp. 130–132.

57 Richard M. Nixon: Nixon, *Memoirs*, p. 34.

57 Collins told the group: Simmons, "The Marines," pp. iii–iv, 2–3.

57 "Marine Corps Board": Ibid., p. 3.

58 "of naval warfare": Beach, *United States Navy*, p. 464.

59 largely responsible: Other reasons included a "huge cadre-conscript army thoroughly organized for war before war began [and] the prearranged employment of railroad nets for . . . rapid mobilization and deployment" (according to Weigley, *United States Army*, p. 273); also, wrought-iron artillery barrels, breach loaded (Manchester, *Arms of Krupp*, p. 131).

59 West Point cadets: Manchester, *American Caesar*, p. 149.

59 "simply perfect": Huntington, *Soldier and the State*, p. 235.

59 Sherman: Ibid., pp. 230, 231, 235, 239, 240.

60 Root's major contribution: Ibid., pp. 240–247; Weigley, *United States Army*, pp. 313–332. Root was a New York lawyer without previous military experience.

60 The old system: Weigley, *United States Army*, pp. 251–257.

61 semisocial organization: Beach, *United*

States Navy, pp. 247, 393. Navy officers assigned to the Navy Department were expected to make social calls to the White House.

61 he enticed: Ibid., p. 328.

61 At the time: Huntington, *Soldier and the State,* p. 276.

62 "It is not": Beach, *United States Navy,* p. 330.

62 Panama Canal: McCullough, *Path between the Seas,* p. 250.

62 battleship *Oregon:* Leahy, *I Was There,* p. 395.

62 "Great White Fleet": O'Connor, *Pacific Destiny,* pp. 344–348.

62 a genius of sorts: Beach, *United States Navy,* p. 407.

63 Martin Van Buren: Huntington, *Soldier and the State,* p. 248.

63 "calculated policy": Ibid., p. 258.

64 "responsible for": Ibid., p. 250.

64 "shall, under the": Ibid., pp. 250–251.

64 Army-style centralized control: Burke, oral history, p. 417.

65 Giulio Douhet: Davis, *Billy Mitchell Affair,* p. 197.

66 reformist political traditions: Ibid., p. 146.

66 Douglas MacArthur: Ibid.; Manchester, *American Caesar,* p. 60. MacArthur wrote a love sonnet to Mitchell's sister Harriet.

66 widowed mother: Davis, *Billy Mitchell Affair,* p. 146.

67 "They look with": Ibid., pp. 67–68.

67 "Declares America Helpless": Ibid.

68 to mislead them: Ibid., pp. 68–74.

68 "The entire experiment": Ibid., p. 74.

69 William Sims: Morison, *Admiral Sims,* pp. 504–505.

70 Service on battleships: Beach, *United States Navy,* p. 422.

70 "modern navy": Davis, *Billy Mitchell Affair,* p. 73.

70 announced plans: Ibid., p. 77.

71 had introduced bills: One was introduced by Congressman Charles F. Curry, Jr., a California Republican, who during World War I had served in the aviation section of the Signal Corps.

71 compelling need: Davis, *Billy Mitchell Affair,* p. 85.

71 John Weeks: Beach, *United States Navy,* p. 213. One of Weeks's roommates at Annapolis was George Barnett, who served as Commandant of the Marine Corps from 1914 to 1920 (*Proceedings of the United States Naval Institute,* Nov. 1986, p. 70).

71 "Bolshevik bug": Davis, *Billy Mitchell Affair,* p. 253.

71 Mason Patrick: Ibid., p. 119.

72 "air power doesn't": Coffey, *Hap,* p. 204.

72 Iowa State Fair: Davis, *Billy Mitchell Affair,* p. 216.

72 *Shenandoah:* Ibid., p. 234.

72 "These accidents": Ibid., pp. 218–221.

72 Dwight Morrow: Ibid., pp. 225–231. The panel included Congressman Carl Vinson and Major General James Harbord, an Army officer who had become famous leading a regiment of Marines at Belleau Wood during World War I.

73 The trial: James, *Years of MacArthur* 1:306–308.

73 Arnold had been caught: Coffey, *Hap,* pp. 5–6.

73 "the worst facility": Ibid., p. 6.

73 "Not a one": Davis, *Billy Mitchell Affair,* p. 207.

74 "We obeyed": Ibid.

74 *Utah:* LeMay and Kantor, *Mission with LeMay,* p. 152.

75 Andrews's offense: Ibid., p. 141.

76 "That man": Coffey, *Hap,* p. 80.

76 "The Navy raised": Ibid., p. 152.

76 "When it comes down": Curtis E.

LeMay, interview with author, May 22, 1986.

76 Army–Marine Corps rivalry: Even George Washington has been accused of having been an anti-Marine Army officer. (See Simmons, "The Marines," p. 1.)

76 142-year history: Heinl, *Soldiers of the Sea*, p. 203.

77 "First in the Fight": Ibid., p. 192; S. L. A. Marshall, *World War I*, p. 270.

77 first troop convoy: Heinl, *Soldiers of the Sea*, p. 195.

77 impressed Pershing: Simmons, "The Marines," p. viii. "While Marines are splendid troops, their use as a separate division is inadvisable," he told the Secretary of the Army. Later, he changed his mind.

77 pressing events: Marshall, *World War I*, p. 270.

78 Ludendorff's offensive: Ibid., pp. 278–279.

78 James Harbord: This marked the beginning of his rise to national prominence. Upon his retirement from active duty, David Sarnoff had him appointed chairman of the board of the Radio Corporation of America.

78 Vietnamese soldiers: Marshall, *World War I*, p. 277.

78 kaiser's son: Ibid., p. 281.

79 "Come on": Heinl, *Soldiers of the Sea*, p. 201.

79 1,497 casualties: Ibid., p. 210.

79 "Woods now U.S.": Marshall, *World War I*, p. 282.

79 Floyd Gibbons: Knightly, *First Casualty*, pp. 124–126.

80 "I am up front": Heinl, *Soldiers of the Sea*, p. 203.

80 was a friend: Marshall, *World War I*, p. 282.

80 *Tribune:* The paper's headline read, "Germans Stopped at Château Thierry

with Help of God and a Few Marines."

80 "saved Paris": Heinl, *Soldiers of the Sea*, p. 202.

81 front of the White House: Simmons, "The Marines," p. 119. "The whole nation has reason to be proud of them," said Wilson.

81 "foxholes": Heinl, *Soldiers of the Sea*, p. 195.

81 the first fights: Marshall, *World War I*, p. 277. "No tide or change came of them," Marshall noted.

81 665,000: Ibid., pp. 331–334.

82 Cates often observed: Edwin H. Simmons, interview with author.

82 "Nimitz does not know": Donovan, *Conflict and Crisis*, p. 172.

82 "the Army would not": Burke, oral history, p. 486.

82 "We could have won": LeMay, interview with author, May 22, 1986.

83 "The United States": Vandegrift and Asprey, *Once a Marine*, pp. 312–313.

83 "once Marine units": Simmons, "The Marines," p. 5.

84 "call a halt": Forrestal, *Forrestal Diaries*, p. 151.

84 "I don't know": Ibid.

84 Thomas bill: *New York Times*, Apr. 10, 1946.

85 "gave warning": Ibid.

85 "the Army proposal": Forrestal, *Forrestal Diaries*, p. 159. He testified May 1, 1946.

86 "For some time": *New York Times*, May 7, 1946.

87 "In placing its case": Ibid.

88 "Widespread publicity": Vandegrift and Asprey, *Once a Marine*, p. 316.

CHAPTER 5

89 "Molotov, conducting": Kennan, *Memoirs* 1:287.

90 "do business with": Forrestal, *Forrestal Diaries*, p. 78.

90 "any eventuality": Ibid., pp. 134–135.

90 "the declaration of": Ibid., p. 134.

90 that of a liberal: Truman, *Off the Record*, p. 53.

91 "I had experienced": Kennan, *Memoirs* 1:290; *FRUS, 1946* 7:698.

91 "anguished cry": Kennan, *Memoirs* 1:293.

92 "the basic features": *FRUS, 1946* 7:697–698.

92 "At the bottom": Ibid., pp. 696–709.

93 distributed hundreds: Ibid., p. 295; Manchester, *Glory and the Dream*, p. 436.

93 bier befitting: Rogow, *James Forrestal*, p. 179.

94 so positive: Forrestal, *Forrestal Diaries*, p. 171.

94 "that a gesture": Ibid., pp. 144–145.

94 played a key role: Vaughan, oral history by Morrissey, pp. 136–141.

94 "This is a": Ibid., pp. 138–139.

94 "marked applause": Donovan, *Conflict and Crisis*, p. 191.

95 "From Stettin": *New York Times*, Mar. 5, 1946.

95 " 'What is Russia' ": *New York Times*, Feb. 28, 1946.

95 Douhet had predicted: Gavin, *War and Peace*, p. 97.

95 in the midfifties: Ibid., p. 102.

96 naval warfare: By the summer of 1947, the Army was also thinking of the tactical use of atomic weaponry; however, all fissionable material was being allotted to strategic use — that is, bombs for bombers (ibid., p. 114).

97 "the most significant": Ibid., pp. 98–99.

97 "throw the books": Ibid., pp. 92, 112.

97 need for mobility: Ibid., pp. 107–112.

98 "the last great war": Ibid., p. 94.

98 long-term Navy project: Blair, *Atomic Submarine*, p. 15.

98 institutionalized the personal relationship: Bruce L. R. Smith, *Rand Corporation*, pp. 36–37.

98 Project RAND: Ibid., pp. 38, 66.

98 "the achievement": Ibid., p. 50.

99 "fear psychosis": Hanson Baldwin, "Rocket Program Splits Services; Army Air Forces Seeking Control," *New York Times*, May 12, 1946.

100 "Had enough?": Donovan, *Conflict and Crisis*, p. 229.

101 "more strictly political": Kennan, *Memoirs* 1:306.

101 "officers of Cabinet rank": Ibid., p. 306.

101 "It was a mark": Ibid., p. 308.

102 "But it was obvious": Ibid., pp. 308–309.

102 Two fundamental conclusions: Ibid., pp. 309–310, 311.

103 Kennan: Ibid., pp. 304, 310, 311, 312.

104 960,000 workers: Donovan, *Conflict and Crisis*, p. 121.

104 "I have seen": Ibid., pp. 216–217

104 May 13, 1946: Forrestal, *Forrestal Diaries*, p. 160.

105 "went out of its way": *New York Times*, May 18, 1946.

105 Forrestal: Forrestal, *Forrestal Diaries*, pp. 159, 161, 162, 163, 164, 165–166.

108 "political dynamite": *New York Times*, June 16, 1946.

109 "the Navy felt": Forrestal, *Forrestal Diaries*, p. 170.

110 Soviet agreement violations: Donovan, *Conflict and Crisis*, p. 221.

110 "American Relations": Krock, *Memoirs*, pp. 370–380. (The entire document is reprinted.)

111 "The Russians themselves": Acheson, *Present at the Creation*, p. 197.

111 "with special knowledge": Clifford, oral history, pp. 370–380.

111 "These gentlemen": Ibid.

112 Elsey wrote: Donovan, *Conflict and Crisis*, p. 221.

112 "I think the general": Ibid., p. 222.

112 "The Soviet Union": Memorandum, Clifford to Truman, Sept. 1946. Russian no. 2 folder. HST Library.

113 "How many copies": Clifford, oral history, pp. 375–377.

113 Wallace: Donovan, *Conflict and Crisis*, pp. 223–228.

114 "We can only": Ibid., p. 225.

114 "I must ask": Vandenberg, *Private Papers*, pp. 300–302.

115 "What do you": Donovan, *Conflict and Crisis*, p. 225.

115 "I am not": Hillman, *Mr. President*, p. 128.

115 Communist spies: Manchester, *Glory and the Dream*, p. 473.

117 "New Nationalists": Rae, *Liberàl Republicans*, pp. 36, 39.

117 "easy assumptions": Forrestal, *Forrestal Diaries*, p. 228.

118 "unmistakably to the continuance": Ibid., p. 222.

118 "Mr. Symington explained": Ibid.

118 December 4 luncheon: Ibid., pp. 227–228.

119 allies in Congress: Ibid., p. 227.

120 Katō: Ibid., p. 228.

120 "must have the attitude": Ibid., p. 229.

120 "The whole conversation": Ibid.

120 January 16, 1947: Ibid.

120 "way of enlisting": Ibid., p. 230.

121 politics was in transition: Donovan, *Conflict and Crisis*, p. 257.

121 Clement Attlee: Ibid., p. 277.

121 250 years: Morris, *Farewell the Trumpets*, p. 488.

121 "a blue piece of paper": Donovan, *Conflict and Crisis*, p. 277.

122 "His Majesty's Government": *FRUS*, *1947* 5:32–35, 35–37.

122 $6-billion cut: Acheson, *Present at the Creation*, p. 222.

123 "we should take": *FRUS*, *1947* 5:58.

123 "we mean business": Donovan, *Conflict and Crisis*, p. 279.

123 "Soviet domination": Ibid., p. 280; Pogue, *George C. Marshall* 4:165.

123 remarkable speech: Vandenberg, *Private Papers*, pp. 126–145.

124 fifty copies to Yalta: Donovan, *Conflict and Crisis*, p. 258.

124 "Mr. President": Acheson, *Present at the Creation*, p. 219.

124 "There has been": Clifford, *Counsel to the President*, p. 133

125 "you could hear": Donovan, *Conflict and Crisis*, p. 268.

125 "the opening gun": Ibid., p. 282.

125 "It must be": Acheson, *Present at the Creation*, p. 222.

125 remarkably expansive commitment: Jones, *Fifteen Weeks*, p. 155.

125 "amazement since": Ibid., p. 156.

126 "the people of America": Goulden, *The Best Years*, p. 269.

126 "My America": Ibid., p. 270.

126 "It scares me": Ibid., p. 268.

126 "Communist infiltration": Ibid., p. 270.

127 "The provisions": Ibid., pp. 268–269.

127 "Soviet power": Kennan, *Memoirs* 1:354–357.

128 "The purpose": Ibid., p. 365.

128 "It is extremely": Ibid., p. 355.

129 "doctrine of containment": Cray, *General of the Army*, pp. 607–610.

129 "Do-Nothing Eightieth": Donovan, *Conflict and Crisis*, pp. 257–265.

129 Eisenhower had to say: *New York Times*, Mar. 26, 1947.

130 "to confess I was": Forrestal, *Forrestal Diaries*, p. 258.

130 startling personal meeting: Pogue, *George C. Marshall* 4:210.

130 "The patient is sinking": *New York Times*, Apr. 29, 1947.

131 "The more I see": Truman, *Off the Record*, p. 109.

131 "intellectually hard-headed": Kennan, *Memoirs* 1:328.

131 Staff's recommendations: *FRUS, 1947* 3:223.

131 "Avoid trivia": Pogue, *George C. Marshall* 4:223.

132 "that if anyone": Kennan, *Memoirs* 1:343.

132 what Marshall had decided: Ibid. ("Almost total acceptance," wrote Kennan); Pogue, *George C. Marshall* 4:207.

132 Hoffman was looking: Forrestal, *Forrestal Diaries*, p. 292.

133 The article: X [George Kennan], "The Sources of Soviet Conduct," *Foreign Affairs*, July 1947, pp. 566–582.

133 Arthur Krock: Kennan, *Memoirs* 1:356.

135 "I could not help": Forrestal, *Forrestal Diaries*, p. 296.

135 "Well, now she": *New York Times*, July 27, 1947.

135 "This office": Forrestal, *Forrestal Diaries*, p. 299 (letter to Robert Sherwood, Aug. 27, 1947).

CHAPTER 6

136 $11.025 billion: Forrestal, *Forrestal Diaries*, pp. 351, 353.

136 "I fully realize": Ibid., p. 351.

137 "removing human frictions": Ibid., p. 465.

137 Finletter Commission and the Brewster-Hinshaw Board: Ibid., p. 389.

138 "I said one's friends": Ibid., p. 295.

138 "incredible, quiet strength": Symington, oral history, pp. 8, 10.

138 "Stu": Ibid., p. 15.

138 "If the President": Ibid., p. 16.

139 "it is obvious": Forrestal, *Forrestal Diaries*, p. 325.

139 he did not fully comprehend: Arleigh Burke, interview with author, Apr. 1986.

140 "obvious selection": Forrestal, *Forrestal Diaries*, p. 325.

140 "A commander": Dwight Eisenhower, *Eisenhower Diaries*, p. 138.

140 "included no": Ambrose, *Eisenhower* 1:471.

140 Truman was amused: Forrestal, *Forrestal Diaries*, p. 325.

140 "elaborate deference": Kennan, *Memoirs* 1:406.

140 "One of the real": Forrestal, *Forrestal Diaries*, p. 355.

141 "It's all even": Cates, oral history, pp. 206–208.

142 "There are two governments": Symington, oral history, p. 29.

142 "one of the great men": Ibid., p. 26.

142 "There are two things": Ibid.

142 550,000: Forrestal, *Forrestal Diaries*, p. 375.

142 John R. Hodge's: Blair, *Forgotten War*, p. 39.

143 playing with fire: Forrestal, *Forrestal Diaries*, p. 373.

143 subordinate recalled: Rogow, *James Forrestal*, p. 235.

143 assuage a burden: Ibid., p. 242.

144 Henry Cabot Lodge: Forrestal, *Forestal Diaries*, p. 324.

144 March 1945: Donovan, *Conflict and Crisis*, p. 313.

145 "our government": Ibid., p. 320.

145 Forrestal rebuked him: Ibid., p. 325.

145 after the United Nations: Ibid., p. 365.

145 FY1949 budget: Hammond, *Super Carriers and B-36 Bombers*, p. 5.

145 $11.025 billion: Ibid.

146 Bevin wrote Marshall: Pogue, *George C. Marshall* 4:316.

146 "Western Union": *FRUS, 1948* 3:1–12.

146 climaxed February 24: Forrestal, *Forrestal Diaries*, p. 382.

147 March 5, 1948, cable: Jean Smith, *Clay* 2:568–594.

148 "the best pianist": *Time*, Oct. 6, 1947.

148 Alfred M. Gruenther: Forrestal, *Forrestal Diaries*, p. 376.

149 seven days: 1948 was a leap year.

149 "continuity, firmness": Forrestal, *Forrestal Diaries*, p. 384.

149 "events are making": *New York Times*, Mar. 9, 1948.

150 do it for them: Ibid.

150 "I said what he": Ibid., p. 396.

150 "What Truman wanted": Truman, *Memoirs* 2:278–279.

150 "one nation": *New York Times*, Mar. 18, 1947.

150 "Any weakness": Smith, *Clay* 2:599–608.

153 $1.5 billion: Hammond, *Super Carriers and B-36 Bombers*, pp. 12, 13. This amounted to expansion just short of mobilization.

153 2.5 million: Manchester, *Glory and the Dream*, p. 441.

153 Truman brusquely: Truman, *Memoirs* 2:151.

153 sorties: Manchester, *Glory and the Dream*, p. 443.

154 two squadrons of B-29s: Robert J. Donovan, *Tumultuous Years*, pp. 367–378; Forrestal, *Forrestal Diaries*, pp. 455–457.

154 "the President said": Forrestal, *Forrestal Diaries*, p. 487.

154 Philip Graham: Ibid., pp. 487–488.

154 "unanimous agreement": Ibid., p. 488.

154 "the American people": Ibid.

154 only $15 billion: Hammond, *Super Carriers and B-36 Bombers*, p. 18.

155 "by constitutional process": Kennan, *Memoirs* 1:406.

155 July 21, 1949: Donovan, *Tumultuous Years*, p. 50. The vote was 82 to 13 in favor.

155 his assessment: Kennan, *Memoirs* 1:382. He thought that the United States would have been better off fighting on its own terms — economic and political.

155 long telegram: Kennan, *Memoirs* 1:547–559.

155 "Soviet power": Ibid., p. 557.

156 "sweeping away": Ibid., p. 378.

156 "I cannot help": Ibid., p. 400.

156 "pull the trigger": Pogue, *George C. Marshall* 4:299.

157 "Our effort now": Forrestal, *Forrestal Diaries*, p. 395.

157 March 16: Ibid., p. 409.

157 "sunk": Donovan, *Tumultuous Years*, p. 360.

157 refused to sign off: Ibid., p. 409.

157 "unilateral political and": Kennan, *Memoirs* 1:407.

158 principle of reciprocity: Ibid.

158 "The greatest mystery": Ibid., p. 403.

158 $23.6 billion: Rogow, *James Forrestal*, p. 302.

158 Al Murray: Burke, oral history, pp. 161–162, 590–591.

160 "On the question": Forrestal, *Forrestal Diaries*, p. 503.

160 "The President is": Lilienthal, *Atomic Energy Years*, p. 386.

161 Newport: Forrestal, *Forrestal Diaries*, pp. 475–479.

161 The service having: Ibid.

161 "consolidation": Hammond, *Super Carriers and B-36 Bombers*, p. 22.

162 "unwarranted attack": Ibid.

162 "For the past": *Philadelphia Inquirer*, Apr. 10, 1948.

162 "I understand bombers": Symington, oral history, pp. 48–53.

162 "Prove it to me": Symington, oral history, pp. 48–52.

163 "You don't pick": Baldwin, oral history, p. 460.

163 squawk box: Ibid., pp. 460–462.

164 *when* Tom Dewey was elected: Rogow, *James Forrestal*, p. 276.

164 "came to see me": Ibid.

164 "When — it is": Ibid.

164 "I know that": Ibid., p. 279.

165 $2,500 contribution: Ibid., p. 278.

165 Oklahoma City: Donovan, *Tumultuous Years*, p. 419; Redding, *Inside the Democratic Party*, p. 273.

166 "Oh, no, don't": Baldwin, oral history, pp. 461–464.

166 "President Truman": Clifford, oral history, p. 116.

166 "It was very gratifying": Ibid.

167 contented Arleigh Burke: Burke, oral history, p. 7.

168 parlance as Op. 23: Hammond, *Super Carriers and B-36 Bombers*, p. 23.

168 Had been a confidant: Ibid., p. 93 n. 100.

168 "two or three months": Ambrose, *Eisenhower* 1:486.

169 "very disquieting": Clifford, oral history, pp. 135–137.

169 "to throw the country": Rogow, *James Forrestal*, p. 27.

169 jewel thief: Ibid., p. 28.

170 Eisenhower was stunned: Eisenhower, *Eisenhower Diaries*, p. 152; Dwight D. Eisenhower, *At Ease*, pp. 330–331.

170 "You know, Ike": Ibid., p. 330.

170 "Bob, they're after me": Rogow, *James Forrestal*, p. 5.

171 "bad Catholic": Ibid., p. 9.

171 *Chorus of Ajax:* Ibid., pp. 17–18; Forrestal, *Forrestal Diaries*, p. 555.

171 "It was a full": Vandenberg, *Private Papers*, pp. 486–487.

171 except Symington: Baldwin, oral history, p. 467.

172 "the boss": Donovan, *Tumultuous Years*, p. 62.

172 Philip Steptoe: Philip Pride, interview with author.

173 ordered an end: Hammond, *Super Carriers and B-36 Bombers*, p. 27.

173 forgone $364 million: Ibid., p. 28.

173 James Van Zandt: Ibid., pp. 30–31.

174 billion dollar blunder: Ibid., p. 30.

174 influence peddling: Donovan, *Tumultuous Years*, p. 114.

174 agents of the Air Force: Hammond, *Super Carriers and B-36 Bombers*, pp. 33, 38.

175 *The Bombing Myth:* Ibid., p. 64.

175 Edward Beach: Burke, oral history, p. 530.

176 "We'd better hire": Ibid., pp. 536–38.

176 "perilously close": Rogow, *James Forrestal*, p. 317.

177 "our present Navy": Ambrose, *Eisenhower* 2:486.

177 perception of the Marine Corps: Ibid.

177 "Of course the": Eisenhower, *Eisenhower Diaries*, p. 159.

178 involved undershirts: Burke, oral history, pp. 571–573.

178 seven typewritten pages: Ibid., no. 12, p. 112.

178 "damn lies": LeMay, interview with author, May 22, 1986.

179 $500,000 for promotion: Hammond, *Super Carriers and B-36 Bombers*, p. 39.

179 refused to allow: Ibid.

180 National Security Act: *New York Times*, Aug. 11, 1949.

180 *New York Herald Tribune:* Donovan, *Tumultuous Years*, pp. 114–115.

180 Deepfreeze: Ibid., pp. 116–117.

181 "History of B-36 Procurement": Hammond, *Super Carriers and B-36 Bombers*, p. 32.

182 another $353 million: Ibid., p. 42.

182 page from Mitchell's: Ibid., p. 50.

182 "wonderful courage": Ibid., p. 42.

183 "inspired largely by": Ibid., p. 42; *New York Times*, Sept. 17, 1949.

183 Gerald Bogan: Hammond, *Super Carriers and B-36 Bombers*, p. 42.

183 "My Dear Secretary": Ibid., pp. 43–44.

184 "This is now": Vandenberg, *Private Papers*, p. 518.

184 "Unification and Strategy" hearings: Hammond, *Super Carriers and B-36 Bombers*, pp. 48–71.

184 "the general morale": Ibid., p. 49.

184 "bomber generals": Ibid., p. 51.

184 "billion-dollar blunder": Ibid.

184 "Denfield hasn't been": *Time*, Oct. 24, 1949, p. 27.

184 "As the senior": Hammond, *Super Carriers and B-36 Bombers*, p. 62.

184 "fancy Dans": Ibid., p. 67.

185 "In my opinion": Ibid., pp. 50–51.

185 "I have received": Harry S. Truman, *Public Papers* 1949:531.

185 Burke was both distraught: Potter, *Admiral Arleigh Burke*, pp. 328–329.

186 Arleigh Burke's name: Ibid., pp. 329–330.

186 Lewis L. Strauss: Donovan, *Tumultuous Years*, p. 148.

187 "in a totally different": Ibid., p. 151.

187 "to lay the problem": Ibid., p. 153.

187 "undertake a reexamination": Ibid., p. 155.

188 "He mused about": *Foreign Service Journal*, May/June 1961.

188 "defense perimeter": US Department of State, *American Foreign Policy, Basic Documents, 1950–1955*, p. 38.

189 John M. Chang: Donovan, *Tumultuous Years*, pp. 137–138.

189 "definite, determined and deliberate": Ibid., p. 134.

189 "whatever the outcome": Acheson, *Present at the Creation*, p. 360.

190 list of Communists: Donovan, *Tumultuous Years*, p. 162.

CHAPTER 7

193 "grave consequences": Truman, *Memoirs* 2:389.

193 adult life, Rhee: Blair, *Forgotten War*, p. 43.

194 "no roots": *FRUS, 1949* 7(pt. 2):873.

194 Kim Il Sung: Blair, *Forgotten War*, p. 43.

194 NSC-8: *FRUS, 1949* 7(pt. 2): 969–978.

194 "little strategic value": Ibid., 1056–1057.

195 "the worst job": Blair, *Forgotten War*, p. 44.

195 entirely different approach: Ibid., pp. 44–45.

195 500 military instructors: Ibid., p. 45.

196 "If Korea should": James, *Years of MacArthur* 3:395.

196 192 to 193: Manchester, *American Caesar*, p. 641.

196 "inferior": Blair, *Forgotten War*, p. 56.

196 "Most observers": *Time*, June 5, 1950, pp. 26–27.

196 Collins intended: Collins, *War in Peacetime*, p. 42.

197 MacArthur was the first: Manchester, *American Caesar*, p. 651.

197 logistical support: Collins, *War in Peacetime*, p. 12.

197 "General,": Manchester, *American Caesar*, p. 650.

197 "It couldn't be": Ibid.

198 Pentagon at 2125: Collins, *War in Peacetime*, p. 9.

198 State Department at 9:26: Truman, *Memoirs* 2:379.

198 Johnson and Bradley: Ibid., p. 378.

198 midnight: Collins, *War in Peacetime*, p. 11.

198 "Mr. President,": Truman, *Memoirs* 2:377–378; Acheson, *Present at the Creation*, p. 404.

198 "Korean army reports": Truman, *Memoirs* 2:379–380.

199 "utmost importance": Schoenbaum, *Waging Peace and War*, pp. 211–212.

199 "some positive and speedy": *FRUS, 1950* 7(pt. 1):132–133.

200 "clear-cut Soviet": Ibid., pp. 139–40.

200 "faithful to the cause": Manchester, *American Caesar*, p. 643.

200 John Allison: *FRUS, 1950* 7:140.

200 Acheson said he thought: Acheson, *Present at the Creation*, pp. 402–440.

201 differences complicated working: Ibid., p. 404.

201 "Northern or Communist": Margaret Truman, *Souvenir*, p. 275.

201 "The boss": *New York Times*, July 2, 1950.

202 "Come over and": Donovan, *Tumultuous Years*, p. 195.

203 "breach of the peace": *FRUS, 1950*, 7:155–156.

203 strategic mistake: Acheson, *Present at the Creation*, p. 408.

204 "By God": Donovan, *Tumultuous Years*, p. 197.

204 "in serious jeopardy": *FRUS, 1950* 7:161–165.

204 topic a diversion: Collins, *War in Peacetime*, p. 13.

204 again Johnson interrupted: Ibid.

205 "rare talent for": Ibid., p. 14.

206 At this point: Ibid., p. 15.

206 "the next probable": Schnabel and Watson, *Joint Chiefs*, pp. 81–82.

206 recent lesson: Truman later observed that there was "almost unspoken acceptance on the part of everyone that whatever had to be done to meet this aggression had to be done" (Truman, *Memoirs* 2:381).

207 almost in tears: Ibid., p. 383.

207 "rapid deterioration": *FRUS, 1950* 7:170.

207 "South Korean casualties": *New York Times*, June 27, 1950.

207 "Those responsible": Truman, *Public Papers*, 1950: 491–492.

207 "Greece of the": Truman, *Harry S. Truman*, p. 502.

208 June 26: Truman, *Memoirs* 2:383–384; Acheson, *Present at the Creation*, pp. 407–410.

208 "I don't want": Donovan, *Tumultuous Years*, p. 208.

208 "highly destructive": Acheson, *Present at the Creation*, p. 405.

209 "it is fairly clear": *Congressional Record*, Vol. 96, Part 7, p. 9154.

209 scramble phone: Truman, *Memoirs* 2:384.

209 "a hundred": Goulden, *Korea*, p. 93.

209 June 27: Truman, *Memoirs* 2:384–385; Acheson, *Present at the Creation*, pp. 409–410.

210 "The attack upon": Truman, *Public Papers*, 1950: 492.

210 National Guard: Truman, *Memoirs* 2:385.

210 "urgent military measures": *FRUS, 1950* 7:211.

212 "mutual understanding": Truman, *Memoirs* 2:387.

213 "the full value": Goulden, *Korea*, p. 91.

213 "didn't want to": Ibid., p. 92.

213 in a jeep looking: Ibid., p. 88.

213 "A high-ranking": Ibid., p. 89.

213 "In past wars": Manchester, *American Caesar*, p. 657.

214 "But you'd go": Ibid.; Sebald, *With MacArthur in Japan*, pp. 102–104.

214 "How can I": Goulden, *Korea*, p. 91.

214 "Take out": Appleman, *South to the Naktong*, p. 44; Goulden, *Korea*, p. 91; James, *Years of MacArthur* 3:428.

215 "Mayday!": Manchester, *American Caesar*, p. 658; *Life*, Apr. 23, 1951.

215 "We're in a": Goulden, *Korea*, p. 93.

215 "Let's go to": Ibid.

215 "What do you say": Manchester, *American Caesar*, p. 658.

215 "The moment I": Marguerite Higgins, *War in Korea*, pp. 30–34.

216 "serious risk of": Goulden, *Korea*, p. 99.

217 "the implication": Truman, *Memoirs* 2:388.

217 "I stated": Ibid.

217 "restricted in": Acheson, *Present at the Creation*, pp. 411–412.

217 "to (1) employ": Collins, *War in Peacetime*, p. 19.

218 "principle of impermissibility": *FRUS, 1950* 7:229.

218 "This means": Goulden, *Korea*, pp. 99–100.

218 "full and complete": Truman, *Memoirs* 2:389.

218 personal phone calls: Donovan, *Tumultuous Years*, p. 215.

218 two thousand words: *FRUS, 1950* 7:248–250.

219 "The only assurance": Schnabel, *Policy and Direction*, pp. 77–78.

219 group gathered: Collins, *War in Peacetime*, p. 21.

220 "Authorization proposed": *FRUS, 1950* 7:250.

220 "The air was": Collins, *War in Peacetime*, p. 21.

221 "Your authorization": *FRUS, 1950* 7:251.

221 "I was present": Ibid., p. 250.

221 "We took this": Collins, *War in Peacetime*, p. 22.

221 "DA-9": *FRUS, 1950* 7:251.

222 "DA-10": Ibid., p. 252.

222 "FEC Item 8": Ibid., p. 253.

223 Ivan the Terrible: Donovan, *Tumultuous Years*, p. 216.

223 "The lid has": Goulden, *Korea*, p. 109.

224 "When you get": Collins, *War in Peacetime*, p. 46.

224 "You are stupid": Goulden, *Korea*, p. 117.

226 "Lieutenant, what is": Ibid., p. 123.

226 Dean himself: Dean, *General Dean's Story*, p. 59.

227 "My toughest son": Goulden, *Korea*, p. 111.

228 "more Catholic": Donovan, *Tumultuous Years*, p. 266.

229 "Suddenly,": Acheson, *Present at the Creation*, p. 373.

229 Marquis Childs: Donovan, *Tumultuous Years*, p. 266.

229 became reckless: Truman, *Off the Record*, pp. 189–190.

229 "something that needed": Goulden, *Korea*, p. 159.

229 climbed into a limousine: Pogue, *George C. Marshall* 4:420.

230 "In view of": Goulden, *Korea*, p. 160.

230 grew visibly upset: Ibid., pp. 160–161; Acheson, *Present at the Creation*, pp. 423–424.

231 "The President": Truman, *Memoirs* 2:406.

231 "I regret to": MacArthur, *Reminiscences*, p. 341.

231 "Hearst and Scripps Howard": Truman, *Off the Record*, p. 192.

231 "most ego maniac": Ibid., p. 193.

232 "Well he came": Ibid.

232 "he looked": Ibid.

233 "I wish I'd": Bradley and Blair, *General's Life*, p. 656.

CHAPTER 8

234 James Gavin: Gavin, *War and Peace*, p. 92.

235 who was appalled: Appleman, *South to the Naktong*, pp. 175–176.

236 given him his due: Collins described Almond as "MacArthur's fair-haired

boy" (Collins, oral history, p. 334).

236 "Walker,": James, *Years of MacArthur* 3:446.

236 Walker, thus fortified; Appleman, *South to the Naktong*, pp. 205–209. Walker's speech became known as his "stand or die speech" (Blair, *Forgotten War*, p. 168).

236 "This army fights": Almond, oral history, p. 22.

236 Cates had set: Heinl, *Victory at High Tide*, p. 15.

237 on June 29: Ibid.

237 "The United States": *New York Herald Tribune*, July 3, 1950.

238 Shepherd's timing: Almond later recalled telling Shepherd beforehand that MacArthur's staff had made repeated requests for Marines but "we were told that there were none available" (Almond, oral history, p. 25).

238 "I wish I": Heinl, *Victory at High Tide*, p. 19.

239 Collins's reflexive response: Collins, *War in Peacetime*, p. 116.

239 "General,": Heinl, *Victory at High Tide*, p. 20.

239 "sensitive feeling here": *New York Herald Tribune*, July 7, 1950.

239 "couldn't do something": Heinl, *Victory at High Tide*, p. 22.

239 "thanked him": Ibid.

240 fully manned First: The total number of Marines would be 22,343 (ibid., p. 35).

240 "high intelligence": Almond, oral history, p. 61.

241 "minimum reasonable time": Ibid., p. 69.

241 July 20: Ibid., p. 22.

242 William Manchester: Manchester, *American Caesar*, p. 554.

242 "earliest and most": Heinl, *Victory at High Tide*, p. 33.

243 "on the money": Ibid., p. 34.

243 "We drew up": Karig, *War in Korea*, p. 161.

243 thirty-two feet: Almond, oral history, p. 32.

244 forty-five hundred yards: Heinl, *Victory at High Tide*, p. 27.

244 "Flying Fish Channel": Karig, *War in Korea*, p. 193.

244 "The general is": Heinl, *Victory at High Tide*, p. 32.

245 "find out exactly": Collins, oral history, p. 276.

245 "unquestionably opposed": Heinl, *Victory at High Tide*, p. 39.

246 "Rip": Ibid.

246 "General, I have": James, *Years of MacArthur* 3:468.

246 "not in a contentious": Collins, *War in Peacetime*, p. 123; Collins, oral history, p. 332.

246 "Spoken like a": Radford, *From Pearl Harbor to Vietnam*, pp. 230–237.

247 "It will be": Manchester, *American Caesar*, p. 576.

247 "a mad scheme": Heinl, *Victory at High Tide*, p. 41.

247 "I realize": James, *Years of MacArthur* 3:470.

247 "spellbinding": Heinl, *Victory at High Tide*, p. 42.

247 "If MacArthur": Ibid., p. 41.

248 "For a five dollar": Ibid., p. 43.

248 cable from Collins: Collins, *War in Peacetime*, p. 129.

248 called the X Corps: He got that from the "Group X" task force. MacArthur said: "The X Corps fought in the Pacific campaign and I will approve that" (Almond, oral history, p. 29).

248 "headquarters must be": Heinl, *Victory at High Tide*, pp. 53–54.

248 very unconventional: "But I can't execute two jobs," Almond recalled saying when MacArthur notified him of his new appointment. MacArthur replied,

"Well, we'll be home by Christmas and, therefore, it is only a short operation . . . Eighth Army will become the controlling factor as soon as we capture the ports of entry" (Almond, oral history, p. 29). The reaction in military circles was that it was a bizarre arrangement (Baldwin, oral history no. 5, p. 498).

249 "heart failure": Almond, oral history, p. 43.

250 "the Navy's police force": Heinl, *Victory at High Tide*, p. 71.

250 apologize personally: Ibid., p. 71.

251 His mother: Manchester, *American Caesar*, pp. 147–148 (see also pp. 106–107).

252 "It's the orders": Ibid., p. 88.

252 he planned: Pogue, *George C. Marshall* 1:172–179.

252 Pershing's aide: With Pershing he had "a kind of personal chief of staff relationship" (ibid., p. 196). Pershing's offer of this job to Marshall was conveyed by Colonel James Collins, the older brother of J. Lawton Collins.

252 "My strength within": Ibid., p. 327.

252 "good soldier": Ibid., 4:422.

253 "tie-up": Donovan, *Tumultuous Years*, p. 260.

253 "We should fight": Ibid., p. 262.

253 "so powerful": Janowitz, *Professional Soldier*, p. 290.

254 "not inclined": Ibid., pp. 288–289.

254 The root cause: Ibid., p. 290.

254 "blocking a military": Ibid., p. 289.

254 Marshall endorsed them: Ibid., pp. 297–299.

255 survey on horseback: Pogue, *George C. Marshall* 1:89.

255 in Tientsin: Ibid., p. 228.

255 served under him: Bradley taught use of weapons and developed weapons doctrine. Marshall recalled that Bradley had conducted "the best demonstration

I ever saw" (ibid., p. 258). Collins and Ridgway taught tactics in the section run by Joseph Stilwell. During this period, Collins formulated a new drill system for the Army (ibid., p. 268).

255 Smith and Puller: Oliver P. Smith, oral history, p. 44.

255 "Marshall men": Pogue, *George C. Marshall* 1:247.

255 Ridgway's houseguest: Ridgway, oral history, p. 43.

256 traveled to Brazil: Ibid.

256 California plane crash: Collins, oral history, p. 72.

256 "Land Force Commander": Bradley and Blair, *General's Life*, p. 377.

256 "Under no circumstances: Ibid., p. 376.

256 something exclusionary: Courtney Whitney and Charles Willoughby had been with MacArthur since Pearl Harbor, and were key figures around him that came to be known as the "Bataan crowd." MacArthur had known Whitney, a Manila lawyer, since the 1920s (Janowitz, *Professional Soldier*, p. 295).

257 "I wouldn't trade": Ambrose, *Eisenhower*, 1:135.

258 Bonus Marchers: Manchester, *American Caesar*, pp. 164–166, 173.

259 "Douglas": Ibid., p. 166.

259 "to exploit MacArthur's": Ibid.

CHAPTER 9

260 throwing up: Manchester, *American Caesar*, p. 691.

260 dispute over the pace: Smith, oral history, p. 232. Smith said Almond was imbued, to a dangerous degree, with the concepts of maneuver of fellow Virginia Military Institute graduate Stonewall Jackson. Later, Almond personally paid for the costs of restoring the Jackson Memorial Arch at VMI (ibid., p. 215).

260 Smith's refusal: Ibid., p. 203.

260 dramatic value: Heinl, *Victory at High Tide*, pp. 210–211.

260 still engaged: Smith, oral history, p. 203.

261 40,000: Blair, *Forgotten War*, p. 319.

261 comment by Walker: Pogue, *George C. Marshall* 4:457.

261 "Hiss Survivors": Donovan, *Tumultuous Years*, p. 277.

261 "Let us occupy": Ibid.

261 At Taejon, the bodies: Blair, *Forgotten War*, p. 312.

262 "continuing possibility": Donovan, *Tumultuous Years*, p. 285.

262 Bajpai informed: Ibid., p. 277.

262 Chou En-lai: Ibid., p. 279.

262 "had in the past": Truman, *Memoirs* 2:413.

262 "it was not": Donovan, *Tumultuous Years*, p. 279.

262 "among the reasons": US Senate, 82d Cong., vol. 116, p. 1921.

262 MacArthur's intelligence staff: James, *Years of MacArthur* 3:519.

262 Mandarin dialect: Blair, *Forgotten War*, p. 376.

262 "indicating that": Donovan, *Tumultuous Years*, p. 278.

263 "That those Chinese": Blair, *Forgotten War*, p. 337.

263 "the destruction of": *FRUS, 1950* 7:793, 781.

263 use only ROK units: Ibid., p. 781.

263 concurrently delegated: Ibid., pp. 781–782.

264 "was authorized to": Truman, *Memoirs* 2:411.

264 "absolutely will not": Schnabel, *Policy and Direction*, p. 197.

264 "Plans are being" *FRUS, 1950* 7:836.

265 "We want you": Ibid., p. 826.

265 "Unless and until": Ibid., p. 608.

265 his basic plan: Appleman, *South to the Naktong*, p. 613.

266 "Foreign Minister Chou": *FRUS, 1950* 7:839.

266 Frank Milburn: Blair, *Forgotten War*, p. 339.

267 if his armies encountered: Pogue, *George C. Marshall* 4:457.

267 "The American war": Donovan, *Tumultuous Years*, p. 280.

267 CIA assessment: Blair, *Forgotten War*, p. 338.

267 "Have to talk": Truman, *Off the Record*, pp. 195–196.

267 Elsey was the prime mover: Donovan, *Tumultuous Years*, p. 284.

268 Truman permitted only: MacArthur, *Reminiscences*, p. 410.

268 "distasteful": Acheson, *Present at the Creation*, p. 456.

268 Secretary of Defense: Blair, *Forgotten War*, p. 347.

268 something very big was afoot: Acheson, *Present at the Creation*, p. 456.

268 "a chump": Truman, *Memoirs* 2:416.

269 "astonishing": James, *Years of MacArthur* 3:349.

269 "I should say": *FRUS, 1950* 7:953.

270 Radford, in his memoirs: Radford, *From Pearl Harbor to Vietnam*, p. 244.

270 Fourth Field Army: Blair, *Forgotten War*, p. 337.

270 "a slice of Spam": Ibid., p. 342.

271 American POWs: Ibid., p. 362.

271 ships with the Marines: Ibid., pp. 365–366.

271 MacArthur had recommended: Ibid., pp. 351–352.

271 "to use any and all": Schnabel and Watson, *Joint Chiefs* 3:274–276.

271 "not in consonance": *FRUS, 1950* 7:995–996; Appleman, *South to the Naktong*, pp. 670–671.

272 "this entire subject": Ibid.

272 electrical generating plants: Truman, *Memoirs* 2:424.

272 "pink right down": Donovan, *Tumultuous Years*, p. 296.

272 "Lucas provided": Ibid.

273 October 25, 1950: Blair, *Forgotten War*, p. 369.

273 Chinese "volunteers": Donovan, *Tumultuous Years*, p. 290.

273 Charles Green: Ibid., p. 369.

274 "But nobody": Ibid., p. 370.

274 assess the situation: Blair, *Forgotten War*, pp. 372, 377; Roger Morris, *Haig*, p. 32.

274 Throckmorton's about thirty: Blair, *Forgotten War*, p. 370.

274 "By that time": Ibid., p. 371.

275 "fresh, newly equipped": Donovan, *Tumultuous Years*, p. 292.

275 MacArthur's subordinates: Appleman, *South to the Naktong*, pp. 757–765.

275 James Tarkenton: Blair, *Forgotten War*, pp. 377–378.

276 Walker kept his apprehensions: Ibid., p. 392.

276 halt because of: Schnabel, *Policy and Direction*, p. 235.

276 "isolate the battlefield": *FRUS, 1950* 7:973; Futrell, *Air Force in Korea*, pp. 209–210.

276 quarter million: Blair, *Forgotten War*, p. 394.

276 35,000: Ibid.

276 missions virtually impossible: Futrell, *Air Force in Korea*, p. 207.

277 Stratemeyer passed word: Ibid.; Acheson, *Present at the Creation*, pp. 463–464.

277 Acheson wanted: Blair, *Forgotten War*, pp. 393–394.

277 "there was an": *FRUS, 1950* 7:1055–1057.

277 "until further orders": Ibid., p. 1057.

277 "It's hell to be": Truman, *Off the Record*, p. 198.

278 "astonished": MacArthur, *Reminiscences*, pp. 420–421.

278 historian Clay Blair, Jr.: Blair, *Forgotten War*, p. 395.

278 "men and material": *FRUS, 1950* 7:1058.

278 "I trust that": Ibid.

278 Truman capitulated: Truman, *Memoirs* 2:433–437.

279 "posterity papers": Leckie, *Conflict*, p. 181.

279 "The present situation": Ibid.

280 Chiefs were responsible: Bradley and Blair, *General's Life*, p. 606; Collins, *War in Peacetime*, pp. 227, 234.

280 William J. Sebald: Baldwin, oral history, p. 499.

280 "I have already": Manchester, *American Caesar*, p. 724.

280 "Home-for-Christmas Drive": Ibid.

280 "End-the-War": Ibid.

281 "there was nobody": Smith, oral history, p. 216.

281 "end-of-war atmosphere": Ibid., p. 215.

281 possibility of getting trapped: Ibid., p. 216.

281 "We were all": Appleman, *East of Chosin*, p. 11.

281 deemed him "brilliant,": Smith, oral history, pp. 199–200. He also deemed him "arrogant" and "reckless" (ibid.).

281 calling Smith, "son,": Ibid., p. 200.

281 "why they gave": Ibid., p. 232.

282 Donald Faith: Blumenson, "Chosin Reservoir," p. 62; Appleman, *East of Chosin*, p. 20.

282 airpower had become: Futrell, *Air Force in Korea*, p. 475.

283 He told him: Appleman, *East of Chosin*, pp. 24–26; Blumenson, "Chosin Reservoir," p. 64.

283 James Mortrude: Appleman, *East of Chosin*, pp. 24–26.

284 winter liners: Ibid., p. 28; Blumenson, "Chosin Reservoir," p. 62.

284 Marines viewed them: Smith, oral history, p. 219.

284 Hodes denied him permission: Appleman, *East of Chosin*, p. 30; Blumenson, "Chosin Reservoir," pp. 63–64.

285 arriving on the heels: Appleman, *East of Chosin*, pp. 31–32; Blumenson, "Chosin Reservoir," pp. 63–64.

285 check out a report: Appleman, *East of Chosin*, p. 36.

285 Edward Scullion: Ibid., pp. 67, 70, 73, 83–84, 85, 86–87, 90.

289 carried Silver Star medals: Smith, oral history, p. 217.

289 he and Haig got: Morris, *Haig*, p. 37.

289 rifle shot cracked: Appleman, *East of Chosin*, p. 112.

290 Hodes decided: Ibid., pp. 114–115.

290 Mongolian ponies: Ibid., p. 118.

290 Smith told him: Smith, oral history, p. 215.

291 "The enemy who is": Blumenson, "Chosin Reservoir," pp. 69–70.

292 "Hey, guys": Gugeler, *Combat Actions*, p. 61.

292 "What a damned": Appleman, *East of Chosin*, p. 108.

292 "fighting withdrawals": Blair, *Forgotten War*, p. 452.

293 "come in with": Bradley and Blair, *General's Life*, p. 598.

293 "all hope of": *FRUS, 1950* 7:1237–1238.

293 another world war: Senator A. Willis Roberts was quoted at the time as saying, "I think the next three days will determine whether we are to be at war with China and Soviet Russia" (Donovan, *Tumultuous Years*, p. 307).

293 "a living lie": Hersey, "Profiles," p. 52.

294 memorable meeting: Whitney, *MacArthur*, pp. 423–424; Appleman, *East of Chosin*, pp. 168–171. Whitney erroneously reports the date of this Nov. 28 meeting as being Dec. 1, 1950.

294 Walker and especially Almond: Schnabel, *Policy and Direction*, pp. 278–279.

295 His thinking: MacArthur, *Reminiscences*, p. 371.

295 assembly areas: Appleman, *East of Chosin*, p. 129.

296 battalion in retreat: Ibid., p. 135; Blumenson, "Chosin Reservoir," pp. 70–71.

296 "it was the intent": Appleman, *East of Chosin*, p. 132.

296 "Those are my": Ibid., p. 146; Blumenson, "Chosin Reservoir," p. 72.

297 Stamford sat down: Appleman, *East of Chosin*, p. 148.

297 "at all costs": Montross and Canzona, *The Chosin Campaign*, p. 279.

298 Task Force Drysdale: Hastings, *Korean War*, p. 150.

298 "dispersed from hell": Collins, oral history, p. 336.

298 "What are your": US Senate, vol. 116, p. 972.

298 Almond heaped scorn: Smith, oral history, p. 218.

299 "crawling with Chinese": Appleman, *East of Chosin*, p. 174.

300 "I suppose that": Truman, *Off the Record*, p. 201.

300 press conference: Truman, *Public Papers* 1950:724–728.

301 "the people of": Donovan, *Tumultuous Years*, p. 310.

301–302 Strategic Survey Committee: Ibid., p. 308.

303 rigid as logs: Appleman, *East of Chosin*, p. 194.

303 order a breakout: Blumenson, "Chosin Reservoir," p. 77; Appleman, *East of Chosin*, p. 195.

303 Thompson's legs: Appleman, *East of Chosin*, p. 203.

304 One of them told: Ibid., p. 211; Blumenson, "Chosin Reservoir," p. 78.

304 George Foster: Appleman, *East of Chosin*, p. 210.

305 "forming pools from": Ibid., p. 217.

305 fell through the ice: Ibid., p. 222.

305 "the continual smack": Ibid., p. 229; Blumenson, "Chosin Reservoir," pp. 80–81.

305 "a form of suicide": Appleman, *East of Chosin*, p. 220.

306 Captain Swenty: Ibid., p. 226.

306 Faith shot dead: Ibid., p. 240.

307 "It was a case": Ibid., p. 243.

307 "When LTC Faith": Ibid., p. 251; Blumenson, "Chosin Reservoir," p. 81.

307 "many hundreds": Appleman, *East of Chosin*, p. 259.

308 broken their legs: Ibid., p. 290.

309 Lieutenant Mazzulla: Appleman, *East of Chosin*, p. 273.

309 to Smith's annoyance: Smith, oral history, p. 220.

310 "What casualties?": Ibid., p. 226.

310 "That's the kind": Ibid.

310 feigned injuries: Ibid., p. 227.

311 "goat for MacArthur's": Blair, *Forgotten War*, p. 497.

311 "said right out": S. L. A. Marshall, *Bringing Up the Rear*, pp. 188–189.

312 "only chance": *FRUS, 1950* 7:1280.

313 "What would it": Gaddis, *The Long Peace*, p. 116.

313 "crash state": *FRUS, 1950* 7:1310–1313.

313 "The conference was": Truman, *Off the Record*, pp. 201–202.

313 "mentally fatigued": *FRUS, 1950* 7:1320–1322.

314 "probability": Blair, *Forgotten War*, p. 529.

314 "Doug, councils of war": Manchester, *American Caesar*, p. 685.

314 "When soldiers have": Schoenbaum, *Waging Peace and War*, p. 220.

315 "reckless" dispersal: Blair, *Forgotten War*, p. 529.

315 "Having secured": Ridgway, *Korean War*, pp. 61–62.

315–316 "We consider that": Blair, *Forgotten War*, p. 529.

316 "the prospects of": Gavin, *War and Peace*, p. 116.

316 "the moral courage": Ibid.

316 Rusk viewed: Schoenbaum, *Waging Peace and War*, p. 219.

316 "pretty frantic": Collins, oral history, p. 340.

316 "what we needed": Schoenbaum, *Waging Peace and War*, p. 219.

316 "we . . . not dig": Acheson, *Present at the Creation*, p. 477.

317 "Mr. President": Schoenbaum, *Waging Peace and War*, p. 219.

317 Attlee arrived: Donovan, *Tumultuous Years*, pp. 316–319.

317 "the President said": *FRUS, 1950* 7:1368.

318 not in writing: Donovan, *Tumultuous Years*, p. 318.

318 "We are not": *FRUS, 1950* 7:1364.

318 "thought that if": Ibid., p. 1395.

318 "had been considering": Donovan, *Tumultuous Years*, p. 318.

318 panderers: They gave MacArthur "distorted advice," he said (Collins, oral history, p. 338). Baldwin said MacArthur's staff was divided into "satrapies" (Baldwin, oral history, p. 496).

319 dismissed as foolhardy: Smith, oral history, p. 240.

319 "I don't know": Ibid., p. 233.

319 "selfish": James, *Years of MacArthur* 3:541.

319 "An enormous handicap": Ibid.

320 "officials in the field": Bradley and Blair, *General's Life*, p. 662; James, *Years of MacArthur* 3:542.

320 "Dad was shattered": Truman, *Harry S. Truman*, p. 499.

320 "is flat": Donovan, *Tumultuous Years*, pp. 311–312.

321 "Mr. Hume": Ibid.

321 "We're not retreating": Montross and Canzona, *U.S. Marine Operations in Korea* 3:288–293.

321 "I was firmly": Collins, oral history, pp. 340–341.

322 "At such time,": Schnabel, *Policy and Direction*, p. 283.

322 "was like a ray": Bradley and Blair, *General's Life*, p. 607.

322 "remained serious": Collins, oral history, pp. 340–341.

323 10,500: Blair, *Forgotten War*, p. 542.

323 remarkable logistical feat: Cagle, *Sea War in Korea*, p. 165.

323 collision was unavoidable: Blair, *Forgotten War*, p. 553.

324 "Thanks and": Ibid., p. 564.

324 "I look forward": Ibid.

CHAPTER 10

325 "very cultured": Ridgway, oral history, p. 6.

325 literary kind: Ibid., p. 39.

326 "stimulated my interest": Ibid., p. 5.

326 "of no consequence": Ibid., p. 9.

326 "art of the": Ibid., p. 106.

326 "human element": Ibid., p. 32.

327 "Calling people by": Ibid., p. 23.

327 small discussion group: Ibid., pp. 47–48.

327 "priceless": Ibid., p. 48.

327 "There is no": Ibid., p. 52.

327 "Stretch out": Ibid., p. 24.

327 "In my opinion": Ibid., p. 7.

328 "violent tennis": Ibid., p. 24.

328 military-pentathlon team: Ibid., p. 9.

328 obstacle course: Ibid., p. 31.

328 "couldn't visualize": Ibid., p. 3.

328 "You have": Ibid.

328 Acheson complimented: Ibid., p. 16.

329 "situation which": Collins, oral history, p. 335.

329 "goose egg": Ridgway, *Soldier*, p. 205.

329 "He didn't come": Ridgway, oral history, p. 78.

329 "The Eighth Army": Blair, *Forgotten War*, p. 567.

329 "I have, with": Ibid., p. 569.

330 "It was . . .": Johnson, oral history, p. 53.

330 "Almond came out": Blair, *Forgotten War*, p. 573.

331 "He greeted me": Ridgway, *Korean War*, p. 84.

331 "from all estimates": *FRUS, 1950* 7:1625.

331 "commence a withdrawal": Ibid., p. 1626.

331 "will to win": MacArthur, *Reminiscences*, pp. 430–431.

332 "brilliant": Ridgway, *Soldier*, p. 208.

332 "I felt it": Ridgway, oral history, p. 109.

332 "I'd never had": Ibid., p. 210.

333 "Off to the": Ibid., p. 213.

333 "TO THE": Ibid., p. 214.

334 "He came to my": Blair, *Forgotten War*, p. 605.

334 "We're not going": Ibid.

335 "little possibility": *FRUS, 1951* 7(pt. 1):42.

335 "Under the extraordinary": Ibid., p. 56.

335 "When a general": Acheson, *Present at the Creation*, p. 515.

335 second time: See Chapter 9, p. 314.

335 "This may be": Blair, *Forgotten War*, p. 620.

336 "staggering": Ibid., p. 618.

336 "All goes well": Ibid., p. 627.

336 "Based on all": *FRUS, 1951* 7(pt. 1):69n.

337 "tentatively agreed": Ibid., p. 71.

337 "prepare": Ibid.

337 "information": Ibid., p. 70.

337 "We were at": Bradley and Blair, *General's Life*, p. 620.

338 "political guidance": *FRUS, 1951* 7(pt. 1):61.

338 Truman was persuaded: Truman, *Memoirs* 2:493–499.

338 "imaginative, kind and": Acheson, *Present at the Creation*, p. 516.

338 "that, plus Truman's": Blair, *Forgotten War*, p. 630.

339 commanders contrived: Ridgway, oral history, p. 54.

339 "who were manifestly": Ibid., p. 55.

339 "above all else,": Ridgway, *Korean War*, p. 90.

339 "young brigadier generals": Blair, *Forgotten War*, p. 1044, n. 49.

339 "I was shocked": Ridgway, oral history, p. 68

340 "ruin a man": Ibid., p. 119.

340 "Almond was one": Ibid., p. 75.

340 "I'll say this": Ibid., p. 76.

341 "improved spirit": Collins, *War in Peacetime*, p. 253.

341 "Eighth Army": *FRUS, 1951* 7(pt. 1):102–105; Collins, *War in Peacetime*, p. 253.

341 "As the word": Bradley and Blair, *General's Life*, p. 623.

341 "Perhaps this was": Millis, *Arms and the State*, p. 314.

342 "This command intends": Whitney, *MacArthur*, p. 459.

342 Beveridge's famous 1910 oration: Manchester, *American Caesar*, p. 79.

343 "Why are we here?": Ridgway, *Soldier*, pp. 207–208; idem, *Korean War*, pp. 204–205.

344 "lonely, empty land": Ridgway, *Soldier*, p. 216.

344 Turks used bayonets: Blair, *Forgotten War*, p. 657.

345 "The job is": Ibid.

345 "greatest bayonet attack": Ibid., p. 675.

346 "pilots reported the": Ibid., pp. 694–695.

346 "Wonju shoot": Ibid., p. 695.

346 "that to many": *FRUS, 1951* 7(pt. 1):229.

346 "by nature opposed": Ridgway, *Korean War*, pp. 110–111.

347 "This is exactly": Blair, *Forgotten War*, p. 659.

347 "die for tie": Ibid., p. 744.; Leckie, *Conflict*, pp. 265–266.

347 "tremendous victory": *FRUS, 1951* 7(pt. 1):229, 244.

347 "We didn't": Ibid.

348 brother Allen: Schaller, *Douglas MacArthur*, p. 224.

348 "savage slaughter": Leckie, *Conflict*, p. 265.

348 "a second front": Manchester, *American Caesar*, p. 763.

349 "In the current": Ibid.

349 "on a call basis": Schaller, *Douglas MacArthur*, p. 231.

349 "As I have said": *FRUS, 1951* 7(pt. 1):297.

350 "fundamental decisions": James, *Years of MacArthur*, 3:582.

350 jeep with Ridgway: Smith, oral history, pp. 235–236.

350 "My views and": *FRUS, 1951* 7(pt. 1):299.

351 "The Unified Command": Ibid., p. 301.

351 "since we had": Truman, *Memoirs* 2:497.

351 "hand over . . .": Schaller, *Douglas MacArthur*, p. 233.

351 "one of the": Whitney, *MacArthur*, p. 467.

352 "State planning presidential": *FRUS, 1951* 7(pt. 1):251.

352 "Recommend that no": Ibid., p. 255.

352 unilaterally authorized: Blair, *Forgotten War*, p. 763.

353 "ultimatum": Truman, *Memoirs* 2:501.

353 "round-the-clock": *FRUS, 1951* 7(pt. 1):265–266.

353 "its tolerant effort": Ibid.

353 "Within the area": MacArthur, *Reminiscences*, p. 387.

353 "defiant, mocking tone": Bradley and Blair, *General's Life*, p. 627.

353 "routine communiqué": MacArthur, *Reminiscences*, p. 387.

353 "a major act": Acheson, *Present at the Creation*, pp. 518–519.

353 "probably the most": Ibid.

354 "I was never": Truman, *Harry S. Truman*, p. 559.

354 "whatever chance": Collins, *War in Peacetime*, p. 270; *FRUS, 1951* 7(pt. 1): 266–267.

354 "political issues": Ibid., p. 267.

354 "perfectly calm": Acheson, *Present at the Creation*, p. 519.

354 "left me no choice.": Ibid.

355 "alarming intelligence": Bradley and Blair, *General's Life*, p. 629.

355 high officials: Schaller, *Douglas MacArthur*, p. 234: See also Dean, *Forging the Atomic Shield*, pp. 127–141.

355 "revolted": Donovan, *Tumultuous Years*, p. 352.

355 "The situation with": Ibid.

355 "This looks like": Truman, *Off the Record*, p. 210.

356 "If you relieve": Truman, *Memoirs* 2:507.

356 "The Great Debate": Acheson, *Present at the Creation*, p. 521; Donovan, *Conflict and Crisis*, pp. 352–353.

356 "considerable doubt": Bradley and Blair, *General's Life*, pp. 632–633.

356 "in the full panoply": James, *Years of MacArthur*, p. 592.

357 seventy submarines: Schaller, *Douglas MacArthur*, p. 235.

357 "major": Ibid.

357 "who had little": Ibid., p. 234.

357 nine atomic bombs: Ibid., p. 236.

357 "I was now": Bradley and Blair, *General's Life*, p. 630.

358 "MacArthur should have": Truman, *Memoirs* 2:448.

358 Bradley later reported: Bradley and Blair, *General's Life*, p. 633.

358 "involves basic political": Manchester, *American Caesar*, p. 763.

359 "God forbid!": Bradley and Blair, *General's Life*, p. 633.

359 Marshall-Bradley meeting: Ibid., p. 633.

359 "This is explicit": Blair, *Forgotten War*, p. 788.

359 "He looked rather": Ibid.

360 "from a strictly": Collins, *War in Peacetime*, p. 283; Bradley and Blair, *General's Life*, p. 634.

360 "It was not": Bradley and Blair, *General's Life*, p. 634.

360 "In point of fact": Ibid.

360 "1. By his public": Ibid., pp. 634–635.

362 "So you won't": Donovan, *Tumultuous Years*, p. 355.

362 *Chicago Tribune's*: Ibid., pp. 355–357; Bradley and Blair, *General's Life*, p. 636.

362 "orderly way": Donovan, *Tumultuous Years*, p. 356.

362 "Why should we": Ibid.

363 "mechanical problems": Blair, *Forgotten War*, p. 795.

363 "disregard": Ibid., p. 799.

363 "I have been": Ibid., p. 796.

364 "With deep regret": Truman, *Memoirs* 2:509.

364 "Jeannie,": Manchester, *American Caesar*, p. 772.

365 "whether I was": Ridgway, *Korean War*, pp. 157–158.

365 "Read that to": Pace, oral history, p. 37.

365 "I took General": Ibid., p. 38.

365 "Earnestly hope": Blair, *Forgotten War*, p. 800.

CHAPTER 11

367 "order" him: Eisenhower, *Eisenhower Diaries*, pp. 178–179.

368 "Gibralter of": Ambrose, *Eisenhower* 1:498.

368 "fortress America": Eisenhower's reaction to Hoover's views was that "he's getting senile" (Eisenhower, *Eisenhower Diaries*, p. 189).

368 "inviting another Korea": *New York Times*, Dec. 21, 1950, for text of Hoover's speech.

368 "No, I do not": Donovan, public papers, May 10, 1951, p. 4.

368 "The president has": Ibid.; *Congressional Record* 97 (pt. 1):59.

369 "We are preparing": Truman, *Public Papers*, 1951:6.

369 "I don't ask": Ibid., p. 20.

369 Great Debate: Donovan, *Tumultuous Years*, pp. 321–324.

370 "more or less": Eisenhower, *White House Years*, pp. 12–13; Bradley and Blair, *General's Life*, p. 642; Eisenhower, *At Ease*, pp. 366–367.

370 Thayer Hotel: Ambrose, *Eisenhower* 1:503.

370 snow and ice: Eisenhower, *At Ease*, p. 368.

370 "that NATO was": Ibid., p. 369.

371 testified in private: Ambrose, *Eisenhower* 1:504.

371 full appreciation: Bradley, *General's Life*, p. 645.

371 "was questioned almost": Eisenhower, *At Ease*, p. 369.

371 one-on-one with Taft: Ibid., pp. 368–369; Eisenhower, *White House Years*,

p. 14; idem, *Eisenhower Diaries*, p. 373.

372 "agree that collective": Eisenhower, *At Ease*, p. 371.

372 "Having been": Ibid., p. 372.

372 "My sole question": Ibid.

372 "suspicious of my motives": Ibid., p. 371.

373 "would not object": Acheson, *Present at the Creation*, p. 495.

373 "a few more": Ibid., p. 495.

373 "Our allies are": Ibid.

374 "without further Congressional": Ibid., p. 496.

374 "In time": Bradley, *General's Life*, p. 647.

375 "straight home": Ibid.

375 "The people in": Donovan, *Tumultuous Years*, p. 359.

375 "This country is": Ibid.

375 "The son of a": Ibid.

375 "General MacArthur": Manchester, *American Caesar*, p. 785.

376 half million people: Ibid.

376 "I was just": Ibid., p. 786.

376 football helmets: Ibid.

377 "Mr. President": *New York Times*, Mar. 20, 1951; Millis, *Arms and the State*, p. 321.

378 relationship with the new one: Truman, *Memoirs* 2:512–516.

378 Van Fleet's talents: Collins, oral history, p. 152.

379 "major air attack": Blair, *Forgotten War*, p. 817.

379 "made at high": *FRUS, 1951* 7(pt. 1):386.

380 MacArthur hearings: US Senate Committee on Armed Services, *Hearings on the "Military Situation in the Far East."*

380 "build up MacArthur": Schaller, *Douglas MacArthur*, p. 246.

381 "Frankly": Bradley and Blair, *General's Life*, p. 640.

381 "sanctuary business": Schaller, *Douglas MacArthur*, p. 248.

382 "Let's go!": Pogue, *George C. Marshall* 4:488.

382 "The pilots shuddered": Ibid.

382 "to give them": Ibid.

383 "an earnest request": Ambrose, *Eisenhower* 1:511.

383 "I assure you": Ibid.

383 "sensation-seeking columnists": Ibid., pp. 511–512.

384 "keep still": Ibid., p. 516.

384 "a disastrous possibility": Ibid.

385 "leading toward a": Manchester, *American Caesar*, p. 818.

385 "guarantee": Krock, *Memoirs*, pp. 267–269.

385 "the whole effort": Ambrose, *Eisenhower* 1:520.

385 "Members of the": Ibid.

386 "the seeker is": Ibid., pp. 520–521.

386 "Patterns of development": Ibid., p. 526.

386 Pleven's idea: Ibid., p. 508.

387 "the utter futility": Eisenhower, *White House Years*, p. 33.

387 Taft for breakfast: Manchester, *American Caesar*, p. 820.

387 MacArthur pledged: Whitney, *MacArthur*, pp. 521–524.

387 "If Senator Taft": Manchester, *American Caesar*, p. 820.

389 "clean up the mess": Truman, *Off the Record*, p. 272; Donovan, *Tumultuous Years*, p. 399.

389 "front man for": Ambrose, *Eisenhower* 1:552.

389 "fear-mongers": Ibid.

389 "degree": *New York Times*, Sept. 13, 1952.

389 "Taft lost": Ambrose, *Eisenhower* 1:553.

389 "Cowardly College": Ambrose, *Eisenhower* 1:553.

389 "as a man": Donovan, *Tumultuous Years*, p. 400; Truman, *Memoirs* 2:566.

390 "knew — and he": Truman, *Public Papers*, 1952–1953:784–785.

390 "forego the diversions": Ambrose, *Eisenhower* 1:569.

390 "demagogic statement": Truman, *Off the Record*, p. 280.

391 Clark and Rhee: Ambrose, *Eisenhower* 2:30–31.

391 "victory": Ibid.

391 "In view of": Eisenhower, *White House Years*, p. 95.

392 "a clear and": *New York Times*, Dec. 6, 1952.

392 "looking forward": Ambrose, *Eisenhower* 2:32.

393 $10-billion deficit: Ibid., p. 33.

393 "massive retaliation": Gaddis, *Long Peace*, p. 105.

393 "no feast or famine": Bryce Harlow, interview with author.

394 "To amass military": Ambrose, *Eisenhower* 2:47.

394 "great equation": Ibid., p. 33.

394 Asia-first advocates: Ibid.

395 "We face an enemy": *New York Times*, Dec. 15, 1952.

395 "On Ending the Korean War": MacArthur, *Reminiscences*, p. 412; Manchester, *American Caesar*, p. 822; Ambrose, *Eisenhower* 2:34.

395 "atomic bombs are": Gaddis, *Long Peace*, p. 109.

396 "General,": Ambrose, *Eisenhower* 2:35.

396 "agreed that I": James, *Years of MacArthur* 3:654.

396 "The trouble with": Lyon, *Eisenhower*, p. 472.

396 "I am issuing": Ambrose, *Eisenhower* 2:47.

396 "unleashing of Chiang": Ibid., 2:49.

396 "study, exploration": Eisenhower, *Eisenhower Diaries*, p. 226.

397 "it provides a": Ambrose, *Eisenhower* 2:51.

397 "atomic weapons apart": Gaddis, *Long Peace*, pp. 124–125.

397 "we might well": Ambrose, *Eisenhower* 2:51.

398 "discreetly": Ibid., p. 52.

398 "cannot be decided": Ibid., p. 91.

398 "Both their government": Ibid., p. 92.

398 "I don't think": Ibid., pp. 92–93.

398 "we can clear": Ibid., p. 71.

398 "All right": Ibid., pp. 92–93.

399 "The Chance for Peace": Ibid., pp. 94–95.

399 recommended going back: Ibid., p. 97.

399 "any such action": Ibid.

400 totals for the war: Bradley and Blair, *General's Life*, p. 661; Blair, *Forgotten War*, p. 975.

400 "Nehru brought up": Ambrose, *Eisenhower* 2:98.

400 "I am distressed": Ibid., p. 100.

401 "if there were": Ibid., p. 102.

401 "What's his basis": Ibid.

402 "this situation": Ibid., pp. 102–103.

402 "freedom loving": Ibid., p. 104.

402 "breach": Ibid.

402 July 12: Blair, *Forgotten War*, p. 976.

402 Panmunjom: Ibid., p. 975.

403 Casualties: Ibid.

403 "we have won": Ambrose, *Eisenhower* 2:106.

403 "on moral grounds": Truman, *Memoirs* 2:521.

BIBLIOGRAPHY

ACHESON, DEAN. *Fragments of My Fleece*. New York: Norton, 1971.

———. *Present at the Creation: My Years in the State Department*. New York: Norton, 1969.

ALBION, ROBERT GREENHAGH, AND ROBERT HOWE CONNERY. *Forrestal and the Navy*. New York: Columbia University Press, 1962.

ALMOND, EDWARD M. Oral history interview by Captain Thomas G. Fergusson. US Army Military History Institute, Carlisle Barracks, PA. Transcript 1975.

AMBROSE, STEPHEN E. *Eisenhower*. Vol. 1, *Soldier, General of the Army, President-elect, 1890–1952*. Vol. 2, *The President*. New York: Touchstone, 1983–1985.

AMBROSE, STEPHEN E., AND JAMES ALDEN, EDS. *The Military and American Society: Essays and Readings*. New York: Free Press, 1972.

ANDERSON, PATRICK. *The Presidents' Men: White House Assistants of Franklin D. Roosevelt, Harry S. Truman, Dwight D. Eisenhower, John F. Kennedy and Lyndon B. Johnson*. Garden City, NY: Doubleday, 1968.

Annual Report of the Secretary of the Navy to the President of the United States, FY1945. Washington, DC: US Government Printing Office, 1945.

APPLEMAN, ROY E. *Disaster in Korea: The Chinese Confront MacArthur*. College Station: Texas A&M University Press, 1989.

———. *East of Chosin: Entrapment and Breakout in Korea, 1950*. College Station: Texas A&M University Press, 1987.

———. *Escaping the Trap: The US Army X Corps in Northeast Korea, 1950*. College Station: Texas A&M University Press, 1990.

———. *Ridgway Duels for Korea*. College Station: Texas A&M University Press, 1990.

———. *South to the Naktong, North to the Yalu: June–November 1950, U.S. Army in the Korean War*. Washington, DC: US Government Printing Office, 1960.

AYERS, EBEN A. *Truman in the White House: The Diary of Eben A. Ayers*. Edited by Robert H. Ferrell. Columbia: University of Missouri Press, 1991.

BALDWIN, HANSON. Oral history interviews by John T. Mason, Jr. US Naval Institute, Annapolis, MD. Transcript 1975.

BARRETT, DAVID D. *Dixie Mission: The United States Army Observer Group in Yenan, 1944*. Berkeley: Center for Chinese Studies, University of California, 1970.

BEACH, EDWARD L. *The United States Navy: 200 Years*. New York: Henry Holt, 1986.

BIGGS, BRADLEY. *Gavin*. Hamden, CT: Archon Books, 1980.

BLAIR, CLAY, JR. *The Atomic Submarine and Admiral Rickover*. New York: Henry Holt, 1954.

————. *The Forgotten War: America in Korea, 1950–1953.* New York: Times Books, 1987.

BLUM, ROBERT M. *Drawing the Line: The Origins of the American Containment Policy in East Asia.* New York: Norton, 1982.

BLUMENSON, MARTIN. "Chosin Reservoir." Chapter 7 in Gugeler, *Combat Actions in Korea.*

BORTON, HUGH. *American Presurrender Planning for Postwar Japan.* New York: East Asian Institute, Columbia University, 1967.

BRADLEY, OMAR N. *A Soldier's Story.* New York: Simon and Schuster, 1983.

BRADLEY, OMAR N., AND CLAY BLAIR, JR. *A General's Life.* New York: Simon and Schuster, 1983.

BRINES, RUSSELL. *MacArthur's Japan.* Philadelphia: J. B. Lippincott, 1948.

BRODIE, BERNARD. *The Anatomy of Deterrence.* Santa Monica, CA: RAND, 1958.

————. *The Atomic Bomb and American Security.* New Haven: Yale Institute of International Studies, 1945.

————, ED. *The Absolute Weapon: Atomic Power and World Order.* New Haven: Yale Institute of International Studies, 1946.

BUCHAN, JOHN. *A History of the Great War.* Introduction by James Harbord. Annapolis: Nautical and Aviation Publishing Company of America, 1980.

BULHITE, RUSSELL D. *Patrick J. Hurley and American Foreign Policy.* Ithaca: Cornell University Press, 1973.

————. *Soviet-American Relations, 1945–50.* Norman: University of Oklahoma Press, 1981.

BURKE, ARLEIGH A. Oral history interviews by John T. Mason, Jr. US Naval Institute, Annapolis, MD. Transcript 1981.

CAGLE, MALCOLM W. *The Sea War in Korea.* Annapolis: US Naval Institute Press, 1957.

CARLTON, JOHN T., AND JOHN SLINKMAN. *The ROA Story.* Washington, DC: US Reserve Officers Association of the United States, 1982.

CHENNAULT, CLAIRE LEE. *Way of a Fighter.* New York: Putnam, 1949.

CHURCHILL, WINSTON S. *Triumph and Tragedy.* Boston: Houghton Mifflin, 1953.

CLARK, MARK W. *From the Danube to the Yalu.* New York: Harper and Brothers, 1954.

CLAUSEWITZ, KARL VON. *On War.* New York: Barnes and Nobel, 1956.

CLAY, LUCIUS D. *Decision in Germany.* Westport, CT: Greenwood Press, 1979.

————. Oral history interview by Jean Edward Smith. Columbia University, New York. Transcript 1970.

————. *The Papers of General Lucius D. Clay: Germany, 1945–1949.* Vols. 1 and 2. Edited by Jean Edward Smith. Bloomington: Institute of German Studies, 1974.

CLIFFORD, CLARK M. *Counsel to the President: A Memoir.* New York: Random House, 1991.

————. Oral history interviews by Jerry N. Hess. Harry S. Truman Library, Independence, MO. Transcript 1971.

COFFEY, THOMAS M. *Hap: The Story of the U.S. Air Force and the Man Who Built It.* New York: Viking Press, 1982.

COLETTA, PAOLO E. *The Bibliography of American Naval History.* Annapolis: US Naval Institute Press, 1981.

COLLINS, JAMES LAWTON. *Lightning Joe.* Baton Rouge: Louisiana State University Press, 1979.

————. Oral history interview by Lieutenant Colonel Charles C. Speron, US Army Military History Institute, Carlisle Barracks, PA. Transcript 1972.

————. *War in Peacetime: The History and Lessons of Korea.* Boston: Houghton Mifflin, 1969.

COPP, DEWITT S. *A Few Good Captains: The Men and Events That Shaped the Development of U.S. Air Power.* Garden City, NY: Doubleday, 1980.

CRAY, ED. *General of the Army: George C. Marshall, Soldier and Statesman.* New York: Touchstone, 1990.

DALLEK, ROBERT. *Franklin D. Roosevelt and American Foreign Policy, 1932–1945.* New York: Oxford University Press, 1978.

DAVIES, JOHN PATON, JR. *Dragon by the Tail: American, British, Japanese and Russian Encounters with China and One Another.* New York: Norton, 1972.

DAVIS, BURKE. *The Billy Mitchell Affair.* New York: Random House, 1967.

DEAN, GORDON E. *Forging the Atomic Shield: Excerpts from the Office Diary of Gordon E. Dean.* Edited by Roger M. Anders. Chapel Hill: University of North Carolina Press, 1987.

DEAN, WILLIAM F. *General Dean's Story.* New York: Viking Press, 1954.

DIVINE, ROBERT A. *Eisenhower and the Cold War.* New York: Oxford University Press, 1981.

DOENECKE, JUSTUS D. *Anti-intervention: A Bibliographical Introduction to Isolationism and Pacifism from World War I to the Early Cold War.* New York: Garland, 1987.

————. *Not to the Swift: The Old Isolationists in the Cold War Era.* Lewisburg, PA: Bucknell University Press, 1970.

DONOVAN, HEDLEY. *Roosevelt to Reagan: A Reporter's Encounters with Nine Presidents.* New York: Harper and Row, 1986.

DONOVAN, ROBERT J. *Conflict and Crisis: The Presidency of Harry S Truman, 1945–1948.* New York: Norton, 1977.

————. *Tumultuous Years: The Presidency of Harry S Truman, 1949–1953.* New York: Norton, 1982.

DOUHET, GIULIO. *The Command of the Air.* Translated by Dino Ferrari. Washington, DC: Office of Air Force History, 1983.

DUNCAN, DAVID DOUGLAS. *This Is War: A Photo Narrative of the Korean War.* New York: Harper and Brothers, 1951.

EISENHOWER, DAVID. *Eisenhower: At War, 1943–1945.* New York: Random House, 1986.

EISENHOWER, DWIGHT D. *At Ease: Stories I Tell My Friends.* Garden City, NY: Doubleday, 1967.

————. *The Eisenhower Diaries.* Edited by Robert H. Ferrell. New York: Norton, 1981.

————. "A Tank Discussion." *Infantry Journal,* Nov. 1950.

————. *The White House Years: Mandate for Change.* Garden City, NY: Doubleday, 1963.

FALK, STANLEY L. "The National Security Council Under Truman, Eisenhower, and Kennedy." *Political Science Quarterly,* Sept. 1964.

FARR, FINIS, *Rickenbacker's Luck.* Boston: Houghton Mifflin, 1979.

FERRELL, ROBERT E. *George C. Marshall as Secretary of State, 1947–1949.* New York: Cooper Square Publishers, 1966.

FINLETTER, THOMAS K. *Power and Policy: U.S. Foreign Policy and Military Power in the Hydrogen Age.* New York: Harcourt Brace, 1954.

Foreign Relations of the United States [FRUS]: 1945, The Conference at Malta and Yalta. Washington, DC: US Government Printing Office, 1955.

———. *Diplomatic Papers: The Conference at Berlin.* Vols. 1 and 2. Washington, DC: US Government Printing Office, 1972.

———. *1949, The Far East and Australia.* Vol. 7, 2 pts. Washington, DC: US Government Printing Office, 1975–1976.

———. *1949, The Far East: China.* Vol. 8. Washington, DC: US Government Printing Office, 1978.

———. *1949, The Far East: China.* Vol. 9. Washington, DC: US Government Printing Office, 1974.

———. *1950, Korea.* Vol. 7. Washington, DC: US Government Printing Office, 1976.

———. *1951, Korea and China.* Vol. 7, 2 pts. Washington, DC: US Government Printing Office, 1983.

FORRESTAL, JAMES. *The Forrestal Diaries.* Edited by Walter Millis. New York: Viking Press, 1951.

FUTRELL, ROBERT F. *Ideas, Concepts, Doctrine: A History of Basic Thinking in the United States Air Force.* Maxwell AFB, AL: Air University, 1974.

———. *The United States Air Force in Korea, 1950–1953.* Washington, DC: Office of Air Force History, 1983.

GADDIS, JOHN L. *The Long Peace: Inquiries into the History of the Cold War.* New York: Oxford University Press, 1987.

———. *Strategies of Containment.* New York: Oxford University Press, 1982.

GAVIN, JAMES. *War and Peace in the Space Age.* New York: Harper and Brothers, 1958.

GAYN, MARK. *Japan Diary.* Rutland, VT: Tuttle, 1981.

GEORGE, ALEXANDER L., AND RICHARD L. SMOKE. *Deterrence in American Foreign Policy: Theory and Practice.* New York: Columbia University Press, 1974.

GIOVANNETTI, LEN, AND FRED FREED. *The Decision to Drop the Bomb.* New York: Coward-McCann, 1965.

GOLDBERG, ALFRED. *A History of the United States Air Force, 1907–1957.* Princeton: D. Van Nostrand, 1957.

GOODPASTER, ANDREW. Oral history interview by Maclyn P. Burg. Dwight D. Eisenhower Library, Abilene, KS. Transcript 1976.

GOTTFRIED, PAUL, AND THOMAS FLEMING. *The Conservative Movement.* Boston: Twayne Publishers, 1988.

GOULDEN, JOSEPH C. *Korea: The Untold Story.* New York: Times Books, 1982.

GREENSTEIN, FRED I. *The Hidden-Hand Presidency: Eisenhower as Leader.* New York: Basic Books, 1982.

GUGELER, RUSSELL A. *Combat Actions in Korea: Infantry, Artillery, Armor.* Washington, DC: Combat Forces Press, 1954.

GUNTHER, JOHN. *The Riddle of MacArthur.* New York: Harper, 1951.

HAMMOND, PAUL Y. *Super Carriers and B-36 Bombers: Appropriations, Strategy, and Politics.* Indianapolis: Bobbs-Merrill, 1960.

HARBORD, JAMES G. *The American Army in France, 1917–1919.* Boston: Little, Brown, 1936.

HASTINGS, MAX. *The Korean War.* New York: Simon and Schuster, 1987.

HAYNES, RICHARD F. *The Awesome Power: Harry S. Truman as Commander in Chief.* Baton Rouge: Louisiana State University, 1973.

HEINL, ROBERT D. "The Right to Fight." *Proceedings of the United States Naval Institute*, Sept. 1961.

———. *Soldiers of the Sea: The United States Marine Corps, 1775–1962*. Annapolis: US Naval Institute Press, 1962.

———. *Victory at High Tide: The Inchon-Seoul Campaign*. New York: Lippincott, 1968.

HERKEN, GREGG. *The Winning Weapon: The Atomic Bomb and the Cold War, 1945–1950*. Princeton: Princeton University, 1982.

HERSEY, JOHN. "Profiles." *The New Yorker*, Apr. 14, 1951.

HEWES, JAMES E. *From Root to McNamara: Department of the Navy Organization, 1900–1963*. Washington, DC: US Government Printing Office, 1975.

HIGGINS, MARGUERITE. *War in Korea: The Report of a Woman Combat Correspondent*. Garden City, NY: Doubleday, 1951.

HIGGINS, TRUMBILL. *Korea and the Fall of MacArthur: A Précis in Limited War*. New York: Oxford University Press, 1960.

HUNT, FRAZIER. *The Untold Story of General MacArthur*. New York: Devin-Adair, 1954.

HUNTINGTON, SAMUEL P. *The Soldier and the State*. Cambridge: Belknap Press of Harvard, 1957.

ICKES, HAROLD L. *The Autobiography of a Curmudgeon*. Westport, CT: Greenwood Press, 1985.

———. *The Secret Diary of Harold Ickes*. 3 vols. New York: Simon and Schuster, 1953–1954.

ISAACSON, WALTER, AND EVAN THOMAS. *The Wise Men: Six Friends and the World They Made*. New York: Simon and Schuster, 1986.

JAMES, D. CLAYTON. *The Years of MacArthur*. 3 vols. Boston: Houghton Mifflin, 1970–1985.

JANOWITZ, MORRIS. *The Professional Soldier: A Social and Philosophical Portrait*. New York: Free Press, 1971.

JONES, JOSEPH MARION. *The Fifteen Weeks: February 21–June 5, 1947*. New York: Viking Press, 1955.

KARP, WALTER. "Truman vs. MacArthur." *American Heritage*, Apr./May 1984.

KEMPTON, MURRAY. "The Underestimation of Dwight D. Eisenhower." *Esquire*, Sept. 1967.

KENNAN, GEORGE F. *American Diplomacy, 1900–1950*. Chicago: University of Chicago Press: 1984.

———. *Memoirs*. Vol. 1, *1925–1950*. Vol. 2, *1950–1963*. New York, Pantheon Books, 1967–1972.

KENNEY, GEORGE. *General Kenney Reports*. New York: Duell, Sloan and Pearce, 1949.

KERNELL, SAMUEL, AND SAMUEL L. POPKIN. *Chief of Staff: Twenty-five Years of Managing the Presidency*. Berkeley: University of California Press, 1986.

KINNARD, DOUGLAS. "President Eisenhower and the Defense Budget." *Journal of Politics*, Aug./Nov. 1977.

KISSINGER, HENRY. *Bureaucracy, Politics, and Strategy*. Los Angeles: University of California, 1968.

———. *Nuclear Weapons and Foreign Policy*. Boulder, CO: Westview Press, 1984.

KNIGHTLY, PHILIP. *The First Casualty*. New York: Harcourt Brace Jovanovich, 1975.

KOEN, ROSS Y. *The China Lobby in American Politics*. New York: Octagon Books, 1974.

KORB, LAWRENCE J. *The Joint Chiefs of Staff: The First Twenty-five Years*. Bloomington: Indiana University Press, 1976.

KROCK, ARTHUR. *Memoirs: Sixty Years on the Firing Line*. New York: Funk and Wagnalls, 1968.

LARRABEE, ERIC. *Commander in Chief*. New York: Harper and Row, 1987.

LEAHY, WILLIAM D. *I Was There: The Personal Story of the Chief of Staff and Presidents Roosevelt and Truman Based on His Notes and Diaries Made at the Time*. New York: Whittlesey House, 1950.

LECKIE, ROBERT, *Conflict: The History of the Korean War*. New York: Putnam, 1962.

———. *The March to Glory: The Marine Breakout from Chosin*. New York: World Publishing, 1950.

LEMAY, CURTIS E., WITH MACKINLAY KANTOR. *Mission with LeMay*. New York: Doubleday, 1965.

LEUCHTENBURG, WILLIAM E. *In the Shadow of FDR: From Harry Truman to Ronald Reagan*. Ithaca: Cornell University Press, 1985.

LEVINE, STEVEN I. *The Anvil of Victory*. New York: Columbia University Press, 1987.

LIBBY, RUTHVEN. Oral history interviews by Etta-Belle Kitchen. US Naval Institute, Annapolis, MD. Transcript 1970.

LIE, TRYGVE. *In the Cause of Peace*. New York: Macmillan, 1954.

LONG, GAVIN. *MacArthur as Military Commander*. Princeton: Van Nostrand, 1969.

LOUIS, WILLIAM ROGER. *Imperialism at Bay*. New York: Oxford University Press, 1986.

LOVETT, ROBERT A. Oral history interviews by Richard D. McKinzie and Theodore A. Wilson. Harry S. Truman Library, Independence, MO. Transcript 1971.

LOWITT, RICHARD. *The Truman-MacArthur Controversy*. Chicago: Rand McNally, 1967.

MACARTHUR, DOUGLAS. *Reminiscences*. New York: McGraw-Hill, 1964.

MAHAN, ALFRED THAYER. *The Influence of Sea Power upon History, 1660–1783*. Boston: Little, Brown, 1894.

MANCHESTER, WILLIAM. *American Caesar: Douglas MacArthur, 1880–1964*. Boston: Little, Brown, 1978.

———. *The Arms of Krupp*. Boston: Little, Brown, 1970.

———. *The Glory and the Dream: A Narrative History of America, 1932–1972*. Boston: Little, Brown, 1974.

MARSHALL, KATHERINE TUPPER. *Together*. New York: Tupper and Love, 1946.

MARSHALL, S. L. A. *The American Heritage History of World War I*. New York: American Heritage, 1982.

———. *Bringing Up the Rear*. San Rafael, CA: Presidio Press, 1979.

———. *The River and the Gauntlet: Defeat of the Eighth Army by the Chinese Communist Forces, November 1950, in the Battle of the Chongchon River, Korea*. Alexandria, VA: Time-Life Books, 1982.

MCCULLOUGH, DAVID. *The Path Between the Seas: The Creation of the Panama Canal, 1870–1914*. New York: Simon and Schuster, 1977.

MEE, CHARLES L., JR. *Meeting at Potsdam*. New York: M. Evans, 1975.

MILLET, ALLAN R., AND PETER MASLOWSKI. *For the Common Defense*. New York: Free Press, 1984.

MILLIS, WALTER. *Arms and the State*. New York: Twentieth Century Fund, 1958.

MONTROSS, LYNN. *U.S. Marine Operations in Korea, 1950–1953.* Vol. 1, *The Pusan Perimeter*, by Montross and N. A. Canzona. Vol. 2, *The Inchon-Seoul Operation*, by Montross and Canzona. Vol. 3, *The Chosin Reservoir Campaign*, by Montross and Canzona. Vol. 4, *The East-Central Front*, by Montross, H. D. Kuokka, and N. W. Hicks.

MORISON, ELTING. *Admiral Sims and the Modern American Navy.* New York: Russell and Russell, 1968.

MORRIS, JAMES. *Farewell the Trumpets: An Imperial Retreat.* New York: Harcourt Brace Jovanovich, 1978.

MOSLEY, LEONARD. *Dulles: A Biography of Eleanor, Allen and John Foster Dulles and Their Family Network.* New York: Dial Press, 1978.

MOSSMAN, BILLY C. *U.S. Army in the Korean War: Ebb and Flow, November 1950–July 1951.* Washington, DC: Center for Military History, US Army, 1990.

NAGAI, YONOSUKE, AND AKIRA IRIYE. *The Origins of the Cold War in Asia.* New York: Columbia University Press, 1977.

NEWHOUSE, JOHN. *War and Peace in the Nuclear Age.* New York: Knopf, 1989.

NIXON, RICHARD M. *Memoirs.* New York: Simon and Schuster, 1990.

O'CONNOR, RICHARD. *Pacific Destiny: An Informal History of the U.S. in the Far East, 1776–1968.* Boston: Little, Brown, 1969.

OSHINSKY, DAVID M. *A Conspiracy So Immense: The World of Joe McCarthy.* New York: Free Press, 1983.

PARET, PETER, ED. *Makers of Modern Strategy: From Machiavelli to the Nuclear Age.* Princeton: Princeton University Press, 1986.

PARRISH, THOMAS. *Roosevelt and Marshall: Partners in Politics and War.* New York: William Morrow, 1990.

PFAFF, WILLIAM. *Barbarian Sentiments: How the American Century Ends.* New York: Hill and Wang, 1989.

POGUE, FORREST C. *George C. Marshall.* Vol. 1, *Education of a General.* Vol. 2, *Ordeal and Hope.* Vol. 3, *Organizer of Victory.* Vol. 4, *Statesman, 1945–1959.* New York: Viking Press, 1963–1987.

―――. *George C. Marshall and Reminiscences: Transcripts and Notes, 1956–57.* Edited by Larry L. Bland. Lexington, VA: George C. Marshall Research Foundation, 1986.

POLMAR, NORMAN, AND THOMAS B. ALLEN. *Rickover.* New York: Simon and Schuster, 1982.

POOLE, WALTER S. *The History of the Joint Chiefs of Staff: The Joint Chiefs and National Policy, 1950–52.* 4 vols. Reprinted as 5 vols. Wilmington, DE: 1979.

POTTER, E.B. *Admiral Arleigh Burke.* New York: Random House, 1990.

PRANGE, GORDON, DONALD GOLDSTEIN, AND KATHERINE DILLON. *Miracle at Midway.* New York: McGraw-Hill, 1982.

PURYEAR, EDGAR F., JR. *George S. Brown, General, U.S. Air Force: Destined for Stars.* Novato, CA: Presidio, 1983.

RADFORD, ARTHUR W. *From Pearl Harbor to Vietnam.* Stanford: Hoover Institute Press, 1980.

RAE, NICOL C. *The Decline and Fall of Liberal Republicans.* New York: Oxford University Press, 1989.

REARDON, STEVEN L. *History of the Office of the Secretary of Defense.* Vol. 1, *The Formative Years, 1947–1950.* Washington, DC: Historical Office of the Secretary of Defense, 1984.

REDDING, JOHN M. *Inside the Democratic Party.* Indianapolis: Bobbs-Merrill, 1958.

REEVES, THOMAS C. *The Life and Times of Joe McCarthy*. New York: Stein and Day, 1982.

RHODES, RICHARD. *The Making of the Atomic Bomb*. New York: Simon and Schuster, 1986.

RIDGWAY, MATTHEW B. *The Korean War*. Garden City, NY: Doubleday, 1967.

————. Oral history interviews by Colonel John M. Blair. US Army Military History Institute, Carlisle Barracks, PA. Transcript 1972.

————. *Soldier*. New York: Harper, 1956.

ROGOW, ARNOLD A. *James Forrestal: A Study of Personality, Politics, and Policy*. New York: Macmillan, 1963.

ROVERE, RICHARD, AND ARTHUR SCHLESINGER, JR. *The MacArthur Controversy and American Foreign Policy*. New York: Farrar, Straus and Giroux, 1965.

SCHALLER, MICHAEL. *The American Occupation of Japan: The Origins of the Cold War in Asia*. New York: Oxford University Press, 1985.

————. *Douglas MacArthur: The Far Eastern General*. New York: Oxford University Press, 1989.

————. *The United States and China in the Twentieth Century*. New York: Oxford University Press, 1990.

SCHNABEL, JAMES F. *United States Army in the Korean War: Policy and Direction: The First Year*. Washington, DC: Office of the Chief of Military History, US Army, 1972.

SCHNABEL, JAMES F., AND ROBERT J. WATSON. *The History of the Joint Chiefs of Staff: The Joint Chiefs of Staff and National Policy*. Vol. 3, *The Korean War*. Pt. 1. Washington, DC: Historical Division, Joint Secretariat, Joint Chiefs of Staff, 1986.

SCHOENBAUM, THOMAS J. *Waging Peace and War: Dean Rusk in the Truman, Kennedy, and Johnson Years*. New York: Simon and Schuster, 1988.

SEBALD, WILLIAM. *With MacArthur in Japan*. New York: Norton, 1965.

SHERRY, MICHAEL. *The Rise of American Airpower*. New Haven: Yale University Press, 1987.

SIMMONS, EDWIN H. "The Marines: Survival and Accommodation." Paper prepared for the George C. Marshall Foundation Conference on Evolution of the National Military Establishment Since World War II. US Marine Corps Historical Center, Washington, DC, 1977.

SMITH, BRUCE L.R. *The Rand Corporation*. Cambridge: Harvard University Press, 1966.

SMITH, GADDIS. *Dean Acheson*. New York: Cooper Square, 1972.

SMITH, OLIVER P. Oral history interview by Benis M. Frank. Historical Division, Headquarters, US Marine Corps, Washington, DC. Transcript 1973.

SMITH, RICHARD NORTON. *Thomas E. Dewey and His Times*. New York: Simon and Schuster, 1982.

SNOW, EDGAR. *Red Star over China*. New York: Modern Library, 1944.

SPECTOR, RONALD. *Eagle against the Sun: The American War with Japan*. New York: Free Press, 1985.

STEEL, RONALD. *Walter Lippmann and the American Century*. Boston: Little, Brown, 1980.

STIMSON, HENRY LEWIS, AND MCGEORGE BUNDY. *On Active Service in Peace and War*. New York: Harper and Brothers, 1948.

STOLER, MARK A. "The 'Pacific-First' Alternative in American World War II Strategy." *International History Review*, 1980.

STONE, I. F. *The Hidden History of the Korean War*. New York: Monthly Review Press, 1952.

STUECK, WILLIAM. *The Wedemeyer Mission*. Athens: University of Georgia Press, 1984.

SULLIVAN, JOHN L. Oral history interview by Jerry N. Hess. Harry S. Truman Library, Independence, MO. Transcript 1974.

SYMINGTON, STUART. Oral history interview by James R. Fuchs. Harry S. Truman Library, Independence, MO. Transcript 1983.

TAYLOR, MAXWELL D. *Swords and Plowshares*. New York: Norton, 1972.

————. *The Uncertain Trumpet*. New York: Harper and Brothers, 1960.

TRUMAN, HARRY S. *Letters Home*. Edited by Monte M. Poen. New York: Putnam, 1984.

————. *Memoirs*. Vol. 1, *Year of Decision*. Vol. 2, *Years of Trial and Hope, 1946–1952*. New York: Signet, 1965.

————. *Off the Record*. Edited by Robert H. Ferrell. New York: Harper and Row, 1980.

————. *The Public Papers of the Presidents of the United States: Harry S. Truman, 1945–1953*. 8 vols. Washington, DC: US Government Printing Office, 1957–1961.

TRUMAN, MARGARET. *Harry S. Truman*. New York: Morrow, 1973.

————. *Souvenir*. New York: McGraw-Hill, 1956.

TUCHMAN, BARBARA. *Stilwell and the American Experience in China, 1911–1945*. New York: Bantam, 1972.

US DEPARTMENT OF STATE. *American Foreign Policy; Basic Documents, 1950–1955*. New York: Arno Press, 1971.

————. *United States Relations with China, 1944–49*. Far Eastern Series. Washington, DC: US Government Printing Office, 1949.

US SENATE. Committee on Armed Services. *Hearings on the "Military Situation in the Far East."* 82d Cong., 1st sess., 1951.

————. Committee on Armed Services. *Hearings on "Universal Military Training."* 80th Cong., 2d sess., 1948.

————. Committee on Military Affairs. *Hearings on S. 84 and S. 1482*. 79th Cong., 1st sess., 1945.

United States Strategic Bombing Survey: Summary Report, European War. New York: Garland Publishing, 1976.

VANDEGRIFT, A. A., AS TOLD TO ROBERT B. ASPREY. *Once a Marine: The Memoirs of General A. A. Vandegrift*. New York: Norton, 1964.

VANDENBERG, ARTHUR H. *The Private Papers of Senator Vandenberg*. Edited by Arthur H. Vandenberg, Jr. Boston: Houghton Mifflin, 1952.

VAUGHAN, HARRY H. Oral history interviews by Charles T. Morrissey, Jan. 14 and Jan. 16, 1963, and Jerald L. Hill and William D. Stilley, Mar. 20, 1976. Harry S. Truman Library, Independence, MO. Transcripts 1963 and 1976.

WARD, GEOFFREY C. *Before the Trumpet: Young Franklin Roosevelt, 1882–1905*. New York: Harper and Row, 1985.

WATSON, ROBERT J. *The Joint Chiefs of Staff and National Policy, 1953–1954*. Washington, DC: Historical Division, Joint Chiefs of Staff, US Government Printing Office, 1986.

WEDEMEYER, ALBERT C. *Wedemeyer Reports!* New York: Henry Holt, 1958.

WEIGLEY, RUSSELL F. *The American Way of War: A History of United States Military Strategy and Policy*. Bloomington: Indiana University Press, 1973.

————. *The History of the United States Army*. New York: Macmillan, 1967.

WELLBORN, CHARLES, JR. Oral history interview by John T. Mason, Jr. US Naval Institute, Annapolis, MD. Transcript 1972.

WHITE, THEODORE H. *In Search of History*. New York: Warner Books, 1979.

WHITNEY, COURTNEY. *MacArthur: His Rendevous with History*. Westport CT: Greenwood Press, 1977.

WOHSTETTER, A. J., F. S. HOFFMAN, R. J. LUTZ, AND H. S. ROWEN. *Selection and Use of Strategic Air Bases*. Santa Monica, CA: RAND, 1954.

YARMOLINSKY, ADAM. *The Military Establishment: Its Impacts on American Society*. New York: Harper and Row, 1971.

YERGIN, DANIEL. *Shattered Peace: The Origins of the Cold War and the National Security State*. Boston: Houghton Mifflin, 1977.

INDEX

★ ★ ★ ★ ★ ★ ★ ★ ★ ★ ★ ★ ★ ★ ★